Dear reader,

thank you for your trust and for buying this book. I'm always greatly moved when I see someone with a desire to get closer to God, to accept Him as their Lord and Saviour and invite Him into their everyday life, to each and every part of it.

By studying His Word systematically, each and every day is a day we live with Him, we let Him illuminate the path of our lives.

I am glad that together we can walk this wonderful path. I ask each of you to pray for me, and I, for my part, promise to remember each and every one of you in my prayers.

Before every encounter with the Lord in His Word, let us pray to the Holy Spirit, may He guide us, for He is the true author of this Word and, at the same time, He knows us better than anyone else, better even than we know ourselves. May He speak directly to our hearts, our minds. May He enter with His Word into our lives, into all our affairs - the pleasant ones as well as the difficult ones

After praying to the Holy Spirit, let us read a given passage of the Scripture. Let's do this slowly, we may even repeat it several times. The Lord will speak to us sometimes through a whole passage, sometimes through a single sentence or word. Sometimes He speaks immediately, sometimes He speaks subtly, after a long time.

Let's write down what the Lord wants to say through the given passage. His Word will sustain us as we remember it throughout the day, act and live with it, with HIM.

May The Lord in Heaven bless you, dear reader. Amen.

CONTENTS

Principal celebrations of the liturgical year 2025, Cycles — lectionary for mass 3
January 4-52
February 52-100
March 101-155
April 155-228
May 228-276
June 276-325
July 325-378
August 378-431
September 431-476
October 477-524
November 524-575
December 575-629

PRINCIPAL CELEBRATIONS OF THE LITURGICAL YEAR 2025

First Sunday of Advent	December 1, 2024
Ash Wednesday	March 5, 2025
Easter Sunday	April 20, 2025
The Ascension of the Lord [Thursday]	May 29, 2025
Pentecost Sunday	June 8, 2025
The Most Holy Body and Blood of Christ	June 22, 2025
First Sunday of Advent	November 30, 2025

CYCLES — LECTIONARY FOR MASS

Sunday Cycle	YEAR C	December 1, 2024 to November 23, 2025
Weekday Cycle	CYCLE I	January 13 to March 4, 2025 June 9 to November 29, 2025
Sunday Cycle	YEAR A	November 30, 2025 to November 22, 2026

Wednesday, January 1, 2025
SOLEMNITY OF MARY, THE HOLY MOTHER OF GOD

First Reading: Numbers 6: 22-27

22 Yahweh spoke to Moses, saying, 23 "Speak to Aaron and to his sons, saying, 'This is how you shall bless the children of Israel.' You shall tell them, 24 'Yahweh bless you, and keep you. 25 Yahweh make his face to shine on you, and be gracious to you. 26 Yahweh lift up his face toward you, and give you peace.' 27 "So they shall put my name on the children of Israel; and I will bless them."

Responsorial Psalm: Psalms 67: 2-3, 5, 6, 8

2 That your way may be known on earth,
and your salvation among all nations,
3 let the peoples praise you, God.
Let all the peoples praise you.
5 Let the peoples praise you, God.
Let all the peoples praise you.
6 The earth has yielded its increase.
God, even our own God, will bless us.
8 God will bless us.
All the ends of the earth shall fear him.

Second Reading: Galatians 4: 4-7

4 But when the fullness of the time came, God sent out his Son, born to a woman, born under the law, 5 that he might redeem those who were under the law, that we might receive the adoption as children. 6 And because you are children, God sent out the Spirit of his Son into your hearts, crying, "Abba,† Father!" 7 So you are no longer a bondservant, but a son; and if a son, then an heir of God through Christ.

Gospel: Luke 2: 16-21

16 They came with haste and found both Mary and Joseph, and the baby was lying in the feeding trough. 17 When they saw it, they publicized widely the saying which was spoken to them about this child. 18 All who heard it wondered at the things which were spoken to them by the shepherds. 19 But Mary kept all these sayings, pondering them in her heart. 20 The shepherds returned, glorifying and praising God for all the things that they had heard and seen, just as it was told them. 21 When eight days were fulfilled for the

circumcision of the child, his name was called Jesus, which was given by the angel before he was conceived in the womb.

1. Invite the Holy Spirit into this reading, asking the Author of Scripture to speak to you through His Word
2. Read today's passage as many times as you need, take your time
3. Write down (below) what the Lord is saying to you today
4. Live with this Word in your heart through the day

_____

_____

Thuesday, January 2, 2025
Saints Basil the Great and Gregory Nazianzen, Bishops and Doctors of the Church

First Reading: First John 2:22-28

22 Who is the liar but he who denies that Jesus is the Christ? This is the Antichrist, he who denies the Father and the Son. 23 Whoever denies the Son doesn't have the Father. He who confesses the Son has the Father also. 24 Therefore, as for you, let that remain in you which you heard from the beginning. If that which you heard from the beginning remains in you, you also will remain in the Son, and in the Father. 25 This is the promise which he promised us, the eternal life.
26 These things I have written to you concerning those who would lead you astray. 27 As for you, the anointing which you received from him remains in you, and you don't need for anyone to teach you. But as his anointing teaches you concerning all things, and is true, and is no lie, and even as it taught you, you will remain in him.
28 Now, little children, remain in him, that when he appears, we may have boldness and not be ashamed before him at his coming.

Responsorial Psalm: Psalms 98: 1-4

1 Sing to Yahweh a new song,
for he has done marvelous things!
His right hand and his holy arm have worked salvation for him.
2 Yahweh has made known his salvation.
He has openly shown his righteousness in the sight of the nations.

3 He has remembered his loving kindness and his faithfulness toward the house of Israel. All the ends of the earth have seen the salvation of our God.
4 Make a joyful noise to Yahweh, all the earth!
Burst out and sing for joy, yes, sing praises!

Gospel: John 1: 19-28

19 This is John's testimony, when the Jews sent priests and Levites from Jerusalem to ask him, "Who are you?"
20 He declared, and didn't deny, but he declared, "I am not the Christ."
21 They asked him, "What then? Are you Elijah?" He said, "I am not." "Are you the prophet?" He answered, "No."
22 They said therefore to him, "Who are you? Give us an answer to take back to those who sent us. What do you say about yourself?"
23 He said, "I am the voice of one crying in the wilderness, 'Make straight the way of the Lord,'* as Isaiah the prophet said."
24 The ones who had been sent were from the Pharisees. 25 They asked him, "Why then do you baptize if you are not the Christ, nor Elijah, nor the prophet?"
26 John answered them, "I baptize in water, but among you stands one whom you don't know. 27 He is the one who comes after me, who is preferred before me, whose sandal strap I'm not worthy to loosen." 28 These things were done in Bethany beyond the Jordan, where John was baptizing.

1. Invite the Holy Spirit into this reading, asking the Author of Scripture to speak to you through His Word
2. Read today's passage as many times as you need, take your time
3. Write down (below) what the Lord is saying to you today
4. Live with this Word in your heart through the day

Friday, January 3, 2025
Christmas Weekday/ Holy Name of Jesus

First Reading: First John 2: 29 – 3: 6

29 If you know that he is righteous, you know that everyone who practices righteousness has been born of him.

1 See how great a love the Father has given to us, that we should be called children of God! For this cause the world doesn't know us, because it didn't know him. 2 Beloved, now we are children of God. It is not yet revealed what we will be; but we know that when he is revealed, we will be like him, for we will see him just as he is. 3 Everyone who has this hope set on him purifies himself, even as he is pure.
4 Everyone who sins also commits lawlessness. Sin is lawlessness. 5 You know that he was revealed to take away our sins, and no sin is in him. 6 Whoever remains in him doesn't sin. Whoever sins hasn't seen him and doesn't know him.

Responsorial Psalm: Psalms 98: 1, 3-6

1 Sing to Yahweh a new song,
for he has done marvelous things!
His right hand and his holy arm have worked salvation for him.
3 He has remembered his loving kindness and his faithfulness toward the house of Israel.
All the ends of the earth have seen the salvation of our God.
4 Make a joyful noise to Yahweh, all the earth!
Burst out and sing for joy, yes, sing praises!
5 Sing praises to Yahweh with the harp,
with the harp and the voice of melody.
6 With trumpets and sound of the ram's horn,
make a joyful noise before the King, Yahweh.

Gospel: John 1: 29-34

29 The next day, he saw Jesus coming to him, and said, "Behold,§ the Lamb of God, who takes away the sin of the world! 30 This is he of whom I said, 'After me comes a man who is preferred before me, for he was before me.' 31 I didn't know him, but for this reason I came baptizing in water, that he would be revealed to Israel." 32 John testified, saying, "I have seen the Spirit descending like a dove out of heaven, and it remained on him. 33 I didn't recognize him, but he who sent me to baptize in water said to me, 'On whomever you will see the Spirit descending and remaining on him is he who baptizes in the Holy Spirit.' 34 I have seen and have testified that this is the Son of God."

1. Invite the Holy Spirit into this reading, asking the Author of Scripture to speak to you through His Word
2. Read today's passage as many times as you need, take your time
3. Write down (below) what the Lord is saying to you today
4. Live with this Word in your heart through the day

Saturday, January 4, 2025
Elizabeth Ann Seton, Religious Obligatory Memorial

First Reading: First John 3: 7-10

7 Little children, let no one lead you astray. He who does righteousness is righteous, even as he is righteous. 8 He who sins is of the devil, for the devil has been sinning from the beginning. To this end the Son of God was revealed: that he might destroy the works of the devil. 9 Whoever is born of God doesn't commit sin, because his seed remains in him, and he can't sin, because he is born of God. 10 In this the children of God are revealed, and the children of the devil. Whoever doesn't do righteousness is not of God, neither is he who doesn't love his brother.

Responsorial Psalm: Psalms 98: 1, 7-8, 9

1 Sing to Yahweh a new song,
for he has done marvelous things!
His right hand and his holy arm have worked salvation for him.
7 Let the sea roar with its fullness;
the world, and those who dwell therein.
8 Let the rivers clap their hands.
Let the mountains sing for joy together.
9 Let them sing before Yahweh,
for he comes to judge the earth.
He will judge the world with righteousness,
and the peoples with equity.

Gospel: John 1: 35-42

35 Again, the next day, John was standing with two of his disciples, 36 and he looked at Jesus as he walked, and said, "Behold, the Lamb of God!" 37 The two disciples heard him speak, and they followed Jesus. 38 Jesus turned and saw them following, and said to them, "What are you looking for?"
They said to him, "Rabbi" (which is to say, being interpreted, Teacher), "where are you staying?"

39 He said to them, "Come and see."
They came and saw where he was staying, and they stayed with him that day. It was about the tenth hour.† 40 One of the two who heard John and followed him was Andrew, Simon Peter's brother. 41 He first found his own brother, Simon, and said to him, "We have found the Messiah!" (which is, being interpreted, Christ‡). 42 He brought him to Jesus. Jesus looked at him and said, "You are Simon the son of Jonah. You shall be called Cephas" (which is by interpretation, Peter).

1. Invite the Holy Spirit into this reading, asking the Author of Scripture to speak to you through His Word
2. Read today's passage as many times as you need, take your time
3. Write down (below) what the Lord is saying to you today
4. Live with this Word in your heart through the day

Sunday, January 5, 2025
THE EPIPHANY OF THE LORD

First Reading: Isaiah 60: 1-6

¹ "Arise, shine; for your light has come,
and Yahweh's glory has risen on you!
² For behold, darkness will cover the earth,
and thick darkness the peoples;
but Yahweh will arise on you,
and his glory shall be seen on you.
³ Nations will come to your light,
and kings to the brightness of your rising.

⁴ "Lift up your eyes all around, and see:
they all gather themselves together.
They come to you.
Your sons will come from far away,
and your daughters will be carried in arms.
⁵ Then you shall see and be radiant,
and your heart will thrill and be enlarged;

because the abundance of the sea will be turned to you.
The wealth of the nations will come to you.
⁶ A multitude of camels will cover you,
the dromedaries of Midian and Ephah.
All from Sheba will come.
They will bring gold and frankincense,
and will proclaim the praises of Yahweh.

Responsorial Psalm: Psalms 72: 1-2, 7-8, 10-13

¹ God, give the king your justice;
your righteousness to the royal son.
² He will judge your people with righteousness,
and your poor with justice.
⁷ In his days, the righteous shall flourish,
and abundance of peace, until the moon is no more.
⁸ He shall have dominion also from sea to sea,
from the River to the ends of the earth.
¹⁰ The kings of Tarshish and of the islands will bring tribute.
The kings of Sheba and Seba shall offer gifts.
¹¹ Yes, all kings shall fall down before him.
All nations shall serve him.
¹² For he will deliver the needy when he cries;
the poor, who has no helper.
¹³ He will have pity on the poor and needy.
He will save the souls of the needy.

Second Reading: Ephesians 3: 2-3a, 5-6

2 if it is so that you have heard of the administration of that grace of God which was given me toward you, 3 how that by revelation the mystery was made known to me, 5 which in other generations was not made known to the children of men, as it has now been revealed to his holy apostles and prophets in the Spirit, 6 that the Gentiles are fellow heirs and fellow members of the body, and fellow partakers of his promise in Christ Jesus through the Good News

Gospel: Matthew 2: 1-12

1 Now when Jesus was born in Bethlehem of Judea in the days of King Herod, behold, wise men† from the east came to Jerusalem, saying, 2 "Where is he who is born King of the

Jews? For we saw his star in the east, and have come to worship him." 3 When King Herod heard it, he was troubled, and all Jerusalem with him. 4 Gathering together all the chief priests and scribes of the people, he asked them where the Christ would be born. 5 They said to him, "In Bethlehem of Judea, for this is written through the prophet,

6 'You Bethlehem, land of Judah,
are in no way least among the princes of Judah;
for out of you shall come a governor
who shall shepherd my people, Israel.' "*

7 Then Herod secretly called the wise men, and learned from them exactly what time the star appeared. 8 He sent them to Bethlehem, and said, "Go and search diligently for the young child. When you have found him, bring me word, so that I also may come and worship him."

9 They, having heard the king, went their way; and behold, the star, which they saw in the east, went before them until it came and stood over where the young child was. 10 When they saw the star, they rejoiced with exceedingly great joy. 11 They came into the house and saw the young child with Mary, his mother, and they fell down and worshiped him. Opening their treasures, they offered to him gifts: gold, frankincense, and myrrh. 12 Being warned in a dream not to return to Herod, they went back to their own country another way.

1. Invite the Holy Spirit into this reading, asking the Author of Scripture to speak to you through His Word
2. Read today's passage as many times as you need, take your time
3. Write down (below) what the Lord is saying to you today
4. Live with this Word in your heart through the day

_____

_____

Monday, January 6, 2025
Saint André Bessette, Religious

First Reading: First John 3: 22 – 4: 6

22 so whatever we ask, we receive from him, because we keep his commandments and do the things that are pleasing in his sight. 23 This is his commandment, that we should believe in the name of his Son, Jesus Christ, and love one another, even as he commanded. 24 He

who keeps his commandments remains in him, and he in him. By this we know that he remains in us, by the Spirit which he gave us.

¹ Beloved, don't believe every spirit, but test the spirits, whether they are of God, because many false prophets have gone out into the world. ² By this you know the Spirit of God: every spirit who confesses that Jesus Christ has come in the flesh is of God, ³ and every spirit who doesn't confess that Jesus Christ has come in the flesh is not of God; and this is the spirit of the Antichrist, of whom you have heard that it comes. Now it is in the world already. ⁴ You are of God, little children, and have overcome them, because greater is he who is in you than he who is in the world. ⁵ They are of the world. Therefore they speak of the world, and the world hears them. ⁶ We are of God. He who knows God listens to us. He who is not of God doesn't listen to us. By this we know the spirit of truth, and the spirit of error.

Responsorial Psalm: Psalms 2: 7bc-8, 10-11

⁷b Yahweh said to me, "You are my son.
Today I have become your father.
⁸ Ask of me, and I will give the nations for your inheritance,
the uttermost parts of the earth for your possession.
¹⁰ Now therefore be wise, you kings.
Be instructed, you judges of the earth.
¹¹ Serve Yahweh with fear,
and rejoice with trembling.

Gospel: Matthew 4: 12-17, 23-25

¹² Now when Jesus heard that John was delivered up, he withdrew into Galilee. ¹³ Leaving Nazareth, he came and lived in Capernaum, which is by the sea, in the region of Zebulun and Naphtali, ¹⁴ that it might be fulfilled which was spoken through Isaiah the prophet, saying,
¹⁵ "The land of Zebulun and the land of Naphtali,
toward the sea, beyond the Jordan,
Galilee of the Gentiles,
¹⁶ the people who sat in darkness saw a great light;
to those who sat in the region and shadow of death,
to them light has dawned."*
¹⁷ From that time, Jesus began to preach, and to say, "Repent! For the Kingdom of Heaven is at hand."
²³ Jesus went about in all Galilee, teaching in their synagogues, preaching the Good News of the Kingdom, and healing every disease and every sickness among the people. ²⁴ The

report about him went out into all Syria. They brought to him all who were sick, afflicted with various diseases and torments, possessed with demons, epileptics, and paralytics; and he healed them. 25 Great multitudes from Galilee, Decapolis, Jerusalem, Judea, and from beyond the Jordan followed him.

1. Invite the Holy Spirit into this reading, asking the Author of Scripture to speak to you through His Word
2. Read today's passage as many times as you need, take your time
3. Write down (below) what the Lord is saying to you today
4. Live with this Word in your heart through the day

_____

_____

Tuesday, January 7, 2025
Saint Raymond of Penyafort, Priest

First Reading: First John 4: 7-10

7 Beloved, let's love one another, for love is of God; and everyone who loves has been born of God and knows God. 8 He who doesn't love doesn't know God, for God is love. 9 By this God's love was revealed in us, that God has sent his only born‡ Son into the world that we might live through him. 10 In this is love, not that we loved God, but that he loved us, and sent his Son as the atoning sacrifice‡ for our sins.

Responsorial Psalm: Psalms 72: 1-2, 3-4, 7-8

1 God, give the king your justice;
your righteousness to the royal son.
2 He will judge your people with righteousness,
and your poor with justice.
3 The mountains shall bring prosperity to the people.
The hills bring the fruit of righteousness.
4 He will judge the poor of the people.
He will save the children of the needy,
and will break the oppressor in pieces.
7 In his days, the righteous shall flourish,
and abundance of peace, until the moon is no more.

⁸ He shall have dominion also from sea to sea,
from the River to the ends of the earth.

Gospel: Mark 6: 34-44

³⁴ Jesus came out, saw a great multitude, and he had compassion on them because they were like sheep without a shepherd; and he began to teach them many things. ³⁵ When it was late in the day, his disciples came to him and said, "This place is deserted, and it is late in the day. ³⁶ Send them away, that they may go into the surrounding country and villages and buy themselves bread, for they have nothing to eat."
³⁷ But he answered them, "You give them something to eat."
They asked him, "Shall we go and buy two hundred denarii‡ worth of bread and give them something to eat?"
³⁸ He said to them, "How many loaves do you have? Go see."
When they knew, they said, "Five, and two fish."
³⁹ He commanded them that everyone should sit down in groups on the green grass. ⁴⁰ They sat down in ranks, by hundreds and by fifties. ⁴¹ He took the five loaves and the two fish; and looking up to heaven, he blessed and broke the loaves, and he gave to his disciples to set before them, and he divided the two fish among them all. ⁴² They all ate and were filled. ⁴³ They took up twelve baskets full of broken pieces and also of the fish. ⁴⁴ Those who ate the loaves were§ five thousand men.

1. Invite the Holy Spirit into this reading, asking the Author of Scripture to speak to you through His Word
2. Read today's passage as many times as you need, take your time
3. Write down (below) what the Lord is saying to you today
4. Live with this Word in your heart through the day

_____

_____

Wednesday, January 8, 2025

First Reading: First John 4: 11-18

¹¹ Beloved, if God loved us in this way, we also ought to love one another. ¹² No one has seen God at any time. If we love one another, God remains in us, and his love has been perfected in us.

13 By this we know that we remain in him and he in us, because he has given us of his Spirit. 14 We have seen and testify that the Father has sent the Son as the Savior of the world. 15 Whoever confesses that Jesus is the Son of God, God remains in him, and he in God. 16 We know and have believed the love which God has for us. God is love, and he who remains in love remains in God, and God remains in him. 17 In this, love has been made perfect among us, that we may have boldness in the day of judgment, because as he is, even so we are in this world. 18 There is no fear in love; but perfect love casts out fear, because fear has punishment. He who fears is not made perfect in love.

Responsorial Psalm: Psalms 72: 1-2, 10, 12-13

1 God, give the king your justice;
your righteousness to the royal son.
2 He will judge your people with righteousness,
and your poor with justice.
10 The kings of Tarshish and of the islands will bring tribute.
The kings of Sheba and Seba shall offer gifts.
12 For he will deliver the needy when he cries;
the poor, who has no helper.
13 He will have pity on the poor and needy.
He will save the souls of the needy.

Gospel: Mark 6: 45-52

45 Immediately he made his disciples get into the boat and go ahead to the other side, to Bethsaida, while he himself sent the multitude away. 46 After he had taken leave of them, he went up the mountain to pray.
47 When evening had come, the boat was in the middle of the sea, and he was alone on the land. 48 Seeing them distressed in rowing, for the wind was contrary to them, about the fourth watch of the night he came to them, walking on the sea; and he would have passed by them, 49 but they, when they saw him walking on the sea, supposed that it was a ghost, and cried out; 50 for they all saw him and were troubled. But he immediately spoke with them and said to them, "Cheer up! It is I! Don't be afraid." 51 He got into the boat with them; and the wind ceased, and they were very amazed among themselves, and marveled; 52 for they hadn't understood about the loaves, but their hearts were hardened.

1. Invite the Holy Spirit into this reading, asking the Author of Scripture to speak to you through His Word
2. Read today's passage as many times as you need, take your time
3. Write down (below) what the Lord is saying to you today

4. Live with this Word in your heart through the day

_____

_____

Thursday, January 9, 2025

First Reading: First John 4: 19 – 5: 4

¹⁹ We love him,§ because he first loved us. ²⁰ If a man says, "I love God," and hates his brother, he is a liar; for he who doesn't love his brother whom he has seen, how can he love God whom he has not seen? ²¹ This commandment we have from him, that he who loves God should also love his brother.
¹ Whoever believes that Jesus is the Christ has been born of God. Whoever loves the Father also loves the child who is born of him. ² By this we know that we love the children of God, when we love God and keep his commandments. ³ For this is loving God, that we keep his commandments. His commandments are not grievous. ⁴ For whatever is born of God overcomes the world. This is the victory that has overcome the world: your faith.

Responsorial Psalm: Psalms 72: 1-2, 14 and 15bc, 17

¹ God, give the king your justice;
your righteousness to the royal son.
² He will judge your people with righteousness,
and your poor with justice.
¹⁴ He will redeem their soul from oppression and violence.
Their blood will be precious in his sight.
¹⁵ᵇ Men will pray for him continually.
They will bless him all day long.
¹⁷ His name endures forever.
His name continues as long as the sun.
Men shall be blessed by him.
All nations will call him blessed.

Gospel: Luke 4: 14-22

¹⁴ Jesus returned in the power of the Spirit into Galilee, and news about him spread through all the surrounding area. ¹⁵ He taught in their synagogues, being glorified by all.

¹⁶ He came to Nazareth, where he had been brought up. He entered, as was his custom, into the synagogue on the Sabbath day, and stood up to read. ¹⁷ The book of the prophet Isaiah was handed to him. He opened the book, and found the place where it was written,
¹⁸ "The Spirit of the Lord is on me,
because he has anointed me to preach good news to the poor.
He has sent me to heal the broken hearted,‡
to proclaim release to the captives,
recovering of sight to the blind,
to deliver those who are crushed,
¹⁹ and to proclaim the acceptable year of the Lord."‡
²⁰ He closed the book, gave it back to the attendant, and sat down. The eyes of all in the synagogue were fastened on him. ²¹ He began to tell them, "Today, this Scripture has been fulfilled in your hearing."
²² All testified about him and wondered at the gracious words which proceeded out of his mouth; and they said, "Isn't this Joseph's son?"

1. Invite the Holy Spirit into this reading, asking the Author of Scripture to speak to you through His Word
2. Read today's passage as many times as you need, take your time
3. Write down (below) what the Lord is saying to you today
4. Live with this Word in your heart through the day

_____

_____

Friday, January 10, 2025

First Reading: First John 5: 5-13

⁵ Who is he who overcomes the world, but he who believes that Jesus is the Son of God?
⁶ This is he who came by water and blood, Jesus Christ; not with the water only, but with the water and the blood. It is the Spirit who testifies, because the Spirit is the truth. ⁷ For there are three who testify:‡ ⁸ the Spirit, the water, and the blood; and the three agree as one. ⁹ If we receive the witness of men, the witness of God is greater; for this is God's testimony which he has testified concerning his Son. ¹⁰ He who believes in the Son of God has the testimony in himself. He who doesn't believe God has made him a liar, because he has not believed in the testimony that God has given concerning his Son. ¹¹ The testimony

is this: that God gave to us eternal life, and this life is in his Son. ¹² He who has the Son has the life. He who doesn't have God's Son doesn't have the life.

¹³ These things I have written to you who believe in the name of the Son of God, that you may know that you have eternal life, and that you may continue to believe in the name of the Son of God.

Responsorial Psalm: Psalms 147: 12-13, 14-15, 19-20

¹² Praise Yahweh, Jerusalem!
Praise your God, Zion!
¹³ For he has strengthened the bars of your gates.
He has blessed your children within you.
¹⁴ He makes peace in your borders.
He fills you with the finest of the wheat.
¹⁵ He sends out his commandment to the earth.
His word runs very swiftly.
¹⁹ He shows his word to Jacob,
his statutes and his ordinances to Israel.
²⁰ He has not done this for just any nation.
They don't know his ordinances.
Praise Yah!

Gospel: Luke 5: 12-16

¹² While he was in one of the cities, behold, there was a man full of leprosy. When he saw Jesus, he fell on his face and begged him, saying, "Lord, if you want to, you can make me clean."
¹³ He stretched out his hand and touched him, saying, "I want to. Be made clean."
Immediately the leprosy left him. ¹⁴ He commanded him to tell no one, "But go your way and show yourself to the priest, and offer for your cleansing according to what Moses commanded, for a testimony to them."
¹⁵ But the report concerning him spread much more, and great multitudes came together to hear and to be healed by him of their infirmities. ¹⁶ But he withdrew himself into the desert and prayed.

1. Invite the Holy Spirit into this reading, asking the Author of Scripture to speak to you through His Word
2. Read today's passage as many times as you need, take your time
3. Write down (below) what the Lord is saying to you today
4. Live with this Word in your heart through the day

Saturday, January 11, 2025

First Reading: First John 5: 14-21

¹⁴ This is the boldness which we have toward him, that if we ask anything according to his will, he listens to us. ¹⁵ And if we know that he listens to us, whatever we ask, we know that we have the petitions which we have asked of him.
¹⁶ If anyone sees his brother sinning a sin not leading to death, he shall ask, and God will give him life for those who sin not leading to death. There is sin leading to death. I don't say that he should make a request concerning this. ¹⁷ All unrighteousness is sin, and there is sin not leading to death.
¹⁸ We know that whoever is born of God doesn't sin, but he who was born of God keeps himself, and the evil one doesn't touch him. ¹⁹ We know that we are of God, and the whole world lies in the power of the evil one. ²⁰ We know that the Son of God has come and has given us an understanding, that we know him who is true; and we are in him who is true, in his Son Jesus Christ. This is the true God and eternal life.
²¹ Little children, keep yourselves from idols.

Responsorial Psalm: Psalms 149: 1-6a, 9b

¹ Praise Yahweh!
Sing to Yahweh a new song,
his praise in the assembly of the saints.
² Let Israel rejoice in him who made them.
Let the children of Zion be joyful in their King.
³ Let them praise his name in the dance!
Let them sing praises to him with tambourine and harp!
⁴ For Yahweh takes pleasure in his people.
He crowns the humble with salvation.
⁵ Let the saints rejoice in honor.
Let them sing for joy on their beds.
⁶ May the high praises of God be in their mouths,
⁹ to execute on them the written judgment.
All his saints have this honor.

Praise Yah!

Gospel: John 3: 22-30

²² After these things, Jesus came with his disciples into the land of Judea. He stayed there with them and baptized. ²³ John also was baptizing in Enon near Salim, because there was much water there. They came and were baptized; ²⁴ for John was not yet thrown into prison. ²⁵ Therefore a dispute arose on the part of John's disciples with some Jews about purification. ²⁶ They came to John and said to him, "Rabbi, he who was with you beyond the Jordan, to whom you have testified, behold, he baptizes, and everyone is coming to him."
²⁷ John answered, "A man can receive nothing unless it has been given him from heaven. ²⁸ You yourselves testify that I said, 'I am not the Christ,' but, 'I have been sent before him.' ²⁹ He who has the bride is the bridegroom; but the friend of the bridegroom, who stands and hears him, rejoices greatly because of the bridegroom's voice. Therefore my joy is made full. ³⁰ He must increase, but I must decrease.

1. Invite the Holy Spirit into this reading, asking the Author of Scripture to speak to you through His Word
2. Read today's passage as many times as you need, take your time
3. Write down (below) what the Lord is saying to you today
4. Live with this Word in your heart through the day

_____

_____

Sunday, January 12, 2025
THE BAPTISM OF THE LORD

First Reading: Isaiah 42: 1-4, 6-7

¹ "Behold, my servant, whom I uphold,
my chosen, in whom my soul delights:
I have put my Spirit on him.
He will bring justice to the nations.
² He will not shout,
nor raise his voice,
nor cause it to be heard in the street.

³ He won't break a bruised reed.
He won't quench a dimly burning wick.
He will faithfully bring justice.
⁴ He will not fail nor be discouraged,
until he has set justice in the earth,
and the islands wait for his law."
⁶ "I, Yahweh, have called you in righteousness.
I will hold your hand.
I will keep you,
and make you a covenant for the people,
as a light for the nations,
⁷ to open the blind eyes,
to bring the prisoners out of the dungeon,
and those who sit in darkness out of the prison.

Responsorial Psalm: Psalms 104: 1b-4, 24-25, 27-30

¹ᵇ Yahweh, my God, you are very great.
You are clothed with honor and majesty.
² He covers himself with light as with a garment.
He stretches out the heavens like a curtain.
³ He lays the beams of his rooms in the waters.
He makes the clouds his chariot.
He walks on the wings of the wind.
⁴ He makes his messengers winds,
and his servants flames of fire.
²⁴ Yahweh, how many are your works!
In wisdom, you have made them all.
The earth is full of your riches.
²⁵ There is the sea, great and wide,
in which are innumerable living things,
both small and large animals.
²⁷ These all wait for you,
that you may give them their food in due season.
²⁸ You give to them; they gather.
You open your hand; they are satisfied with good.
²⁹ You hide your face; they are troubled.
You take away their breath; they die and return to the dust.
³⁰ You send out your Spirit and they are created.
You renew the face of the ground.

Second Reading: Titus 2: 11-14; 3: 4-7

[11] For the grace of God has appeared, bringing salvation to all men, [12] instructing us to the intent that, denying ungodliness and worldly lusts, we would live soberly, righteously, and godly in this present age; [13] looking for the blessed hope and appearing of the glory of our great God and Savior, Jesus Christ, [14] who gave himself for us, that he might redeem us from all iniquity and purify for himself a people for his own possession, zealous for good works.
[4] But when the kindness of God our Savior and his love toward mankind appeared, [5] not by works of righteousness which we did ourselves, but according to his mercy, he saved us through the washing of regeneration and renewing by the Holy Spirit, [6] whom he poured out on us richly through Jesus Christ our Savior; [7] that being justified by his grace, we might be made heirs according to the hope of eternal life.

Gospel: Luke 3: 15-16, 21-22

[15] As the people were in expectation, and all men reasoned in their hearts concerning John, whether perhaps he was the Christ, [16] John answered them all, "I indeed baptize you with water, but he comes who is mightier than I, the strap of whose sandals I am not worthy to loosen. He will baptize you in the Holy Spirit and fire.
[21] Now when all the people were baptized, Jesus also had been baptized and was praying. The sky was opened, [22] and the Holy Spirit descended in a bodily form like a dove on him; and a voice came out of the sky, saying "You are my beloved Son. In you I am well pleased."

1. Invite the Holy Spirit into this reading, asking the Author of Scripture to speak to you through His Word
2. Read today's passage as many times as you need, take your time
3. Write down (below) what the Lord is saying to you today
4. Live with this Word in your heart through the day

_____

_____

Monday, January 13, 2025
Saint Hilary, Bishop and Doctor of the Church

First Reading: Hebrews 1: 1-6

¹ God, having in the past spoken to the fathers through the prophets at many times and in various ways, ² has at the end of these days spoken to us by his Son, whom he appointed heir of all things, through whom also he made the worlds. ³ His Son is the radiance of his glory, the very image of his substance, and upholding all things by the word of his power, who, when he had by himself purified us of our sins, sat down on the right hand of the Majesty on high, ⁴ having become as much better than the angels as the more excellent name he has inherited is better than theirs. ⁵ For to which of the angels did he say at any time,
"You are my Son.
Today I have become your father?"
and again,
"I will be to him a Father,
and he will be to me a Son?"
⁶ When he again brings in the firstborn into the world he says, "Let all the angels of God worship him."

Responsorial Psalm: Psalms 97: 1 and 2b, 6 and 7c, 9

¹ Yahweh reigns!
Let the earth rejoice!
Let the multitude of islands be glad!
² Clouds and darkness are around him.
Righteousness and justice are the foundation of his throne.
⁶ The heavens declare his righteousness.
All the peoples have seen his glory.
⁷ᶜ Worship him, all you gods!
⁹ For you, Yahweh, are most high above all the earth.
You are exalted far above all gods.

Gospel: Mark 1: 14-20

¹⁴ Now after John was taken into custody, Jesus came into Galilee, preaching the Good News of God's Kingdom, ¹⁵ and saying, "The time is fulfilled, and God's Kingdom is at hand! Repent, and believe in the Good News."
¹⁶ Passing along by the sea of Galilee, he saw Simon and Andrew, the brother of Simon, casting a net into the sea, for they were fishermen. ¹⁷ Jesus said to them, "Come after me, and I will make you into fishers for men."
¹⁸ Immediately they left their nets, and followed him.

¹⁹ Going on a little further from there, he saw James the son of Zebedee, and John his brother, who were also in the boat mending the nets. ²⁰ Immediately he called them, and they left their father, Zebedee, in the boat with the hired servants, and went after him.

1. Invite the Holy Spirit into this reading, asking the Author of Scripture to speak to you through His Word
2. Read today's passage as many times as you need, take your time
3. Write down (below) what the Lord is saying to you today
4. Live with this Word in your heart through the day

_____

_____

Tuesday, January 14, 2025

First Reading: Hebrews 2: 5-12

⁵ For he didn't subject the world to come, of which we speak, to angels. ⁶ But one has somewhere testified, saying,
"What is man, that you think of him?
Or the son of man, that you care for him?
⁷ You made him a little lower than the angels.
You crowned him with glory and honor.±
⁸ You have put all things in subjection under his feet."*
For in that he subjected all things to him, he left nothing that is not subject to him. But now we don't yet see all things subjected to him. ⁹ But we see him who has been made a little lower than the angels, Jesus, because of the suffering of death crowned with glory and honor, that by the grace of God he should taste of death for everyone. ¹⁰ For it became him, for whom are all things and through whom are all things, in bringing many children to glory, to make the author of their salvation perfect through sufferings. ¹¹ For both he who sanctifies and those who are sanctified are all from one, for which cause he is not ashamed to call them brothers,± ¹² saying,
"I will declare your name to my brothers.
Among the congregation I will sing your praise."

Responsorial Psalm: Psalms 8: 2ab and 5-9

² From the lips of babes and infants you have established strength,

because of your adversaries, that you might silence the enemy and the avenger.
⁵ For you have made him a little lower than the angels,
and crowned him with glory and honor.
⁶ You make him ruler over the works of your hands.
You have put all things under his feet:
⁷ All sheep and cattle,
yes, and the animals of the field,
⁸ the birds of the sky, the fish of the sea,
and whatever passes through the paths of the seas.
⁹ Yahweh, our Lord,
how majestic is your name in all the earth!

Gospel: Mark 1: 21-28

²¹ They went into Capernaum, and immediately on the Sabbath day he entered into the synagogue and taught. ²² They were astonished at his teaching, for he taught them as having authority, and not as the scribes. ²³ Immediately there was in their synagogue a man with an unclean spirit, and he cried out, ²⁴ saying, "Ha! What do we have to do with you, Jesus, you Nazarene? Have you come to destroy us? I know who you are: the Holy One of God!"
²⁵ Jesus rebuked him, saying, "Be quiet, and come out of him!"
²⁶ The unclean spirit, convulsing him and crying with a loud voice, came out of him. ²⁷ They were all amazed, so that they questioned among themselves, saying, "What is this? A new teaching? For with authority he commands even the unclean spirits, and they obey him!" ²⁸ The report of him went out immediately everywhere into all the region of Galilee and its surrounding area.

1. Invite the Holy Spirit into this reading, asking the Author of Scripture to speak to you through His Word
2. Read today's passage as many times as you need, take your time
3. Write down (below) what the Lord is saying to you today
4. Live with this Word in your heart through the day

_____

_____

Wednesday, January 15, 2025

First Reading: Hebrews 2: 14-18

14 Since then the children have shared in flesh and blood, he also himself in the same way partook of the same, that through death he might bring to nothing him who had the power of death, that is, the devil, 15 and might deliver all of them who through fear of death were all their lifetime subject to bondage. 16 For most certainly, he doesn't give help to angels, but he gives help to the offspring§ of Abraham. 17 Therefore he was obligated in all things to be made like his brothers, that he might become a merciful and faithful high priest in things pertaining to God, to make atonement for the sins of the people. 18 For in that he himself has suffered being tempted, he is able to help those who are tempted.

Responsorial Psalm: Psalms 105: 1-4, 6-9

1 Give thanks to Yahweh! Call on his name!
Make his doings known among the peoples.
2 Sing to him, sing praises to him!
Tell of all his marvelous works.
3 Glory in his holy name.
Let the heart of those who seek Yahweh rejoice.
4 Seek Yahweh and his strength.
Seek his face forever more.
6 you offspring of Abraham, his servant,
you children of Jacob, his chosen ones.
7 He is Yahweh, our God.
His judgments are in all the earth.
8 He has remembered his covenant forever,
the word which he commanded to a thousand generations,
9 the covenant which he made with Abraham,
his oath to Isaac,

Gospel: Mark 1: 29-39

29 Immediately, when they had come out of the synagogue, they came into the house of Simon and Andrew, with James and John. 30 Now Simon's wife's mother lay sick with a fever, and immediately they told him about her. 31 He came and took her by the hand and raised her up. The fever left her immediately,‡ and she served them.
32 At evening, when the sun had set, they brought to him all who were sick and those who were possessed by demons. 33 All the city was gathered together at the door. 34 He healed many who were sick with various diseases and cast out many demons. He didn't allow the demons to speak, because they knew him.

35 Early in the morning, while it was still dark, he rose up and went out, and departed into a deserted place, and prayed there. 36 Simon and those who were with him searched for him. 37 They found him and told him, "Everyone is looking for you."
38 He said to them, "Let's go elsewhere into the next towns, that I may preach there also, because I came out for this reason." 39 He went into their synagogues throughout all Galilee, preaching and casting out demons.

1. Invite the Holy Spirit into this reading, asking the Author of Scripture to speak to you through His Word
2. Read today's passage as many times as you need, take your time
3. Write down (below) what the Lord is saying to you today
4. Live with this Word in your heart through the day

Thursday, January 16, 2025

First Reading: Hebrews 3: 7-14

7 Therefore, even as the Holy Spirit says,
"Today if you will hear his voice,
8 don't harden your hearts as in the rebellion,
in the day of the trial in the wilderness,
9 where your fathers tested me and tried me,
and saw my deeds for forty years.
10 Therefore I was displeased with that generation,
and said, 'They always err in their heart,
but they didn't know my ways.'
11 As I swore in my wrath,
'They will not enter into my rest.' "*
12 Beware, brothers, lest perhaps there might be in any one of you an evil heart of unbelief, in falling away from the living God; 13 but exhort one another day by day, so long as it is called "today", lest any one of you be hardened by the deceitfulness of sin. 14 For we have become partakers of Christ, if we hold the beginning of our confidence firm to the end

Responsorial Psalm: Psalms 95: 6-11

⁶ Oh come, let's worship and bow down.
Let's kneel before Yahweh, our Maker,
⁷ for he is our God.
We are the people of his pasture,
and the sheep in his care.
Today, oh that you would hear his voice!
⁸ Don't harden your heart, as at Meribah,
as in the day of Massah in the wilderness,
⁹ when your fathers tempted me,
tested me, and saw my work.
¹⁰ Forty long years I was grieved with that generation,
and said, "They are a people who err in their heart.
They have not known my ways."
¹¹ Therefore I swore in my wrath,
"They won't enter into my rest."

Gospel: Mark 1: 40-45

⁴⁰ A leper came to him, begging him, kneeling down to him, and saying to him, "If you want to, you can make me clean." ⁴¹ Being moved with compassion, he stretched out his hand, and touched him, and said to him, "I want to. Be made clean." ⁴² When he had said this, immediately the leprosy departed from him and he was made clean. ⁴³ He strictly warned him and immediately sent him out, ⁴⁴ and said to him, "See that you say nothing to anybody, but go show yourself to the priest and offer for your cleansing the things which Moses commanded, for a testimony to them." ⁴⁵ But he went out, and began to proclaim it much, and to spread about the matter, so that Jesus could no more openly enter into a city, but was outside in desert places. People came to him from everywhere.

1. Invite the Holy Spirit into this reading, asking the Author of Scripture to speak to you through His Word
2. Read today's passage as many times as you need, take your time
3. Write down (below) what the Lord is saying to you today
4. Live with this Word in your heart through the day

Friday, January 17, 2025
Saint Anthony, Abbot

First Reading: Hebrews 4: 1-5, 11

¹ Let's fear therefore, lest perhaps anyone of you should seem to have come short of a promise of entering into his rest. ² For indeed we have had good news preached to us, even as they also did, but the word they heard didn't profit them, because it wasn't mixed with faith by those who heard. ³ For we who have believed do enter into that rest, even as he has said, "As I swore in my wrath, they will not enter into my rest;" although the works were finished from the foundation of the world. ⁴ For he has said this somewhere about the seventh day, "God rested on the seventh day from all his works;" ⁵ and in this place again, "They will not enter into my rest."
¹¹ Let's therefore give diligence to enter into that rest, lest anyone fall after the same example of disobedience.

Responsorial Psalm: Psalms 78: 3 and 4bc, 6c-7, 8

³ which we have heard and known,
and our fathers have told us.
⁴ᵇᶜ telling to the generation to come the praises of Yahweh,
his strength, and his wondrous deeds that he has done.
⁶ who should arise and tell their children,
⁷ that they might set their hope in God,
and not forget God's deeds,
but keep his commandments,
⁸ and might not be as their fathers—
a stubborn and rebellious generation,
a generation that didn't make their hearts loyal,
whose spirit was not steadfast with God.

Gospel: Mark 2: 1-12

¹ When he entered again into Capernaum after some days, it was heard that he was at home. ² Immediately many were gathered together, so that there was no more room, not even around the door; and he spoke the word to them. ³ Four people came, carrying a paralytic to him. ⁴ When they could not come near to him for the crowd, they removed the roof where he was. When they had broken it up, they let down the mat that the paralytic was lying on. ⁵ Jesus, seeing their faith, said to the paralytic, "Son, your sins are forgiven you."

⁶ But there were some of the scribes sitting there and reasoning in their hearts, ⁷ "Why does this man speak blasphemies like that? Who can forgive sins but God alone?"
⁸ Immediately Jesus, perceiving in his spirit that they so reasoned within themselves, said to them, "Why do you reason these things in your hearts? ⁹ Which is easier, to tell the paralytic, 'Your sins are forgiven;' or to say, 'Arise, and take up your bed, and walk'? ¹⁰ But that you may know that the Son of Man has authority on earth to forgive sins"—he said to the paralytic— ¹¹ "I tell you, arise, take up your mat, and go to your house."
¹² He arose, and immediately took up the mat and went out in front of them all, so that they were all amazed and glorified God, saying, "We never saw anything like this!"

1. Invite the Holy Spirit into this reading, asking the Author of Scripture to speak to you through His Word
2. Read today's passage as many times as you need, take your time
3. Write down (below) what the Lord is saying to you today
4. Live with this Word in your heart through the day

_____

_____

Saturday, January 18, 2025

First Reading: Hebrews 4: 12-16

¹² For the word of God is living and active, and sharper than any two-edged sword, piercing even to the dividing of soul and spirit, of both joints and marrow, and is able to discern the thoughts and intentions of the heart. ¹³ There is no creature that is hidden from his sight, but all things are naked and laid open before the eyes of him to whom we must give an account.
¹⁴ Having then a great high priest who has passed through the heavens, Jesus, the Son of God, let's hold tightly to our confession. ¹⁵ For we don't have a high priest who can't be touched with the feeling of our infirmities, but one who has been in all points tempted like we are, yet without sin. ¹⁶ Let's therefore draw near with boldness to the throne of grace, that we may receive mercy and may find grace for help in time of need.

Responsorial Psalm: Psalms 19: 8, 9, 10

⁸ Yahweh's precepts are right, rejoicing the heart.
Yahweh's commandment is pure, enlightening the eyes.

⁹ The fear of Yahweh is clean, enduring forever.
Yahweh's ordinances are true, and righteous altogether.
¹⁰ They are more to be desired than gold, yes, than much fine gold,
sweeter also than honey and the extract of the honeycomb.

Gospel: Mark 2: 13-17

¹³ He went out again by the seaside. All the multitude came to him, and he taught them. ¹⁴ As he passed by, he saw Levi the son of Alphaeus sitting at the tax office. He said to him, "Follow me." And he arose and followed him.
¹⁵ He was reclining at the table in his house, and many tax collectors and sinners sat down with Jesus and his disciples, for there were many, and they followed him. ¹⁶ The scribes and the Pharisees, when they saw that he was eating with the sinners and tax collectors, said to his disciples, "Why is it that he eats and drinks with tax collectors and sinners?"
¹⁷ When Jesus heard it, he said to them, "Those who are healthy have no need for a physician, but those who are sick. I came not to call the righteous, but sinners to repentance."

1. Invite the Holy Spirit into this reading, asking the Author of Scripture to speak to you through His Word
2. Read today's passage as many times as you need, take your time
3. Write down (below) what the Lord is saying to you today
4. Live with this Word in your heart through the day

_____

_____

Sunday, January 19, 2025
SECOND SUNDAY IN ORDINARY TIME

First Reading: Isaiah 62: 1-5

¹ For Zion's sake I will not hold my peace,
and for Jerusalem's sake I will not rest,
until her righteousness shines out like the dawn,
and her salvation like a burning lamp.
² The nations will see your righteousness,
and all kings your glory.

You will be called by a new name,
which Yahweh's mouth will name.
³ You will also be a crown of beauty in Yahweh's hand,
and a royal diadem in your God's hand.
⁴ You will not be called Forsaken any more,
nor will your land be called Desolate any more;
but you will be called Hephzibah,⸸
and your land Beulah;⸸
for Yahweh delights in you,
and your land will be married.
⁵ For as a young man marries a virgin,
so your sons will marry you.
As a bridegroom rejoices over his bride,
so your God will rejoice over you.

Responsorial Psalm: Psalms 96: 1-3, 7-10

¹ Sing to Yahweh a new song!
Sing to Yahweh, all the earth.
² Sing to Yahweh!
Bless his name!
Proclaim his salvation from day to day!
³ Declare his glory among the nations,
his marvelous works among all the peoples.
⁷ Ascribe to Yahweh, you families of nations,
ascribe to Yahweh glory and strength.
⁸ Ascribe to Yahweh the glory due to his name.
Bring an offering, and come into his courts.
⁹ Worship Yahweh in holy array.
Tremble before him, all the earth.
¹⁰ Say among the nations, "Yahweh reigns."
The world is also established.
It can't be moved.
He will judge the peoples with equity.

Second Reading: First Corinthians 12: 4-11

⁴ Now there are various kinds of gifts, but the same Spirit. ⁵ There are various kinds of service, and the same Lord. ⁶ There are various kinds of workings, but the same God who works all things in all. ⁷ But to each one is given the manifestation of the Spirit for the profit

of all. ⁸ For to one is given through the Spirit the word of wisdom, and to another the word of knowledge according to the same Spirit, ⁹ to another faith by the same Spirit, and to another gifts of healings by the same Spirit, ¹⁰ and to another workings of miracles, and to another prophecy, and to another discerning of spirits, to another different kinds of languages, and to another the interpretation of languages. ¹¹ But the one and the same Spirit produces all of these, distributing to each one separately as he desires.

Gospel: John 2: 1-11

¹ The third day, there was a wedding in Cana of Galilee. Jesus' mother was there. ² Jesus also was invited, with his disciples, to the wedding. ³ When the wine ran out, Jesus' mother said to him, "They have no wine."
⁴ Jesus said to her, "Woman, what does that have to do with you and me? My hour has not yet come."
⁵ His mother said to the servants, "Whatever he says to you, do it."
⁶ Now there were six water pots of stone set there after the Jews' way of purifying, containing two or three metretes apiece. ⁷ Jesus said to them, "Fill the water pots with water." So they filled them up to the brim. ⁸ He said to them, "Now draw some out, and take it to the ruler of the feast." So they took it. ⁹ When the ruler of the feast tasted the water now become wine, and didn't know where it came from (but the servants who had drawn the water knew), the ruler of the feast called the bridegroom ¹⁰ and said to him, "Everyone serves the good wine first, and when the guests have drunk freely, then that which is worse. You have kept the good wine until now!" ¹¹ This beginning of his signs Jesus did in Cana of Galilee, and revealed his glory; and his disciples believed in him.

1. Invite the Holy Spirit into this reading, asking the Author of Scripture to speak to you through His Word
2. Read today's passage as many times as you need, take your time
3. Write down (below) what the Lord is saying to you today
4. Live with this Word in your heart through the day

_____

_____

Monday, January 20, 2025
Saint Fabian, Pope and Martyr; Saint Sebastian, Martyr

First Reading: Hebrews 5: 1-10

¹ For every high priest, being taken from among men, is appointed for men in things pertaining to God, that he may offer both gifts and sacrifices for sins. ² The high priest can deal gently with those who are ignorant and going astray, because he himself is also surrounded with weakness. ³ Because of this, he must offer sacrifices for sins for the people, as well as for himself. ⁴ Nobody takes this honor on himself, but he is called by God, just like Aaron was. ⁵ So also Christ didn't glorify himself to be made a high priest, but it was he who said to him,
"You are my Son.
Today I have become your father."*
⁶ As he says also in another place,
"You are a priest forever,
after the order of Melchizedek."*
⁷ He, in the days of his flesh, having offered up prayers and petitions with strong crying and tears to him who was able to save him from death, and having been heard for his godly fear, ⁸ though he was a Son, yet learned obedience by the things which he suffered. ⁹ Having been made perfect, he became to all of those who obey him the author of eternal salvation, ¹⁰ named by God a high priest after the order of Melchizedek.

Responsorial Psalm: Psalms 110: 1, 2, 3, 4

¹ Yahweh says to my Lord, "Sit at my right hand,
until I make your enemies your footstool for your feet."
² Yahweh will send out the rod of your strength out of Zion.
Rule among your enemies.
³ Your people offer themselves willingly in the day of your power, in holy array.
Out of the womb of the morning, you have the dew of your youth.
⁴ Yahweh has sworn, and will not change his mind:
"You are a priest forever in the order of Melchizedek."

Gospel: Mark 2: 18-22

¹⁸ John's disciples and the Pharisees were fasting, and they came and asked him, "Why do John's disciples and the disciples of the Pharisees fast, but your disciples don't fast?" ¹⁹ Jesus said to them, "Can the groomsmen fast while the bridegroom is with them? As long as they have the bridegroom with them, they can't fast. ²⁰ But the days will come when the bridegroom will be taken away from them, and then they will fast in that day. ²¹ No one sews a piece of unshrunk cloth on an old garment, or else the patch shrinks and the new tears away from the old, and a worse hole is made. ²² No one puts new wine into old

wineskins; or else the new wine will burst the skins, and the wine pours out, and the skins will be destroyed; but they put new wine into fresh wineskins."

1. Invite the Holy Spirit into this reading, asking the Author of Scripture to speak to you through His Word
2. Read today's passage as many times as you need, take your time
3. Write down (below) what the Lord is saying to you today
4. Live with this Word in your heart through the day

___

Tuesday, January 21, 2025
Saint Agnes, Virgin and Martyr

First Reading: Hebrews 6: 10-20

[10] For God is not unrighteous, so as to forget your work and the labor of love which you showed toward his name, in that you served the saints, and still do serve them. [11] We desire that each one of you may show the same diligence to the fullness of hope even to the end, [12] that you won't be sluggish, but imitators of those who through faith and perseverance inherited the promises.
[13] For when God made a promise to Abraham, since he could swear by no one greater, he swore by himself, [14] saying, "Surely blessing I will bless you, and multiplying I will multiply you." [15] Thus, having patiently endured, he obtained the promise. [16] For men indeed swear by a greater one, and in every dispute of theirs the oath is final for confirmation. [17] In this way God, being determined to show more abundantly to the heirs of the promise the immutability of his counsel, interposed with an oath, [18] that by two immutable things, in which it is impossible for God to lie, we may have a strong encouragement, who have fled for refuge to take hold of the hope set before us. [19] This hope we have as an anchor of the soul, a hope both sure and steadfast and entering into that which is within the veil, [20] where as a forerunner Jesus entered for us, having become a high priest forever after the order of Melchizedek.

Responsorial Psalm: Psalms 111: 1-2, 4-5, 9 and 10c

[1] Praise Yah!
I will give thanks to Yahweh with my whole heart,

in the council of the upright, and in the congregation.
² Yahweh's works are great,
pondered by all those who delight in them.
⁴ He has caused his wonderful works to be remembered.
Yahweh is gracious and merciful.
⁵ He has given food to those who fear him.
He always remembers his covenant.
⁹ He has sent redemption to his people.
He has ordained his covenant forever.
His name is holy and awesome!
¹⁰ᶜ His praise endures forever!

Gospel: Mark 2: 23-28

²³ He was going on the Sabbath day through the grain fields; and his disciples began, as they went, to pluck the ears of grain. ²⁴ The Pharisees said to him, "Behold, why do they do that which is not lawful on the Sabbath day?"
²⁵ He said to them, "Did you never read what David did when he had need and was hungry— he, and those who were with him? ²⁶ How he entered into God's house at the time of Abiathar the high priest, and ate the show bread, which is not lawful to eat except for the priests, and gave also to those who were with him?"
²⁷ He said to them, "The Sabbath was made for man, not man for the Sabbath. ²⁸ Therefore the Son of Man is lord even of the Sabbath."

1. Invite the Holy Spirit into this reading, asking the Author of Scripture to speak to you through His Word
2. Read today's passage as many times as you need, take your time
3. Write down (below) what the Lord is saying to you today
4. Live with this Word in your heart through the day

_____

_____

Wednesday, January 22, 2025
Day of Prayer for the Legal Protection of Unborn Children

First Reading: Hebrews 7: 1-3, 15-17

¹ For this Melchizedek, king of Salem, priest of God Most High, who met Abraham returning from the slaughter of the kings and blessed him, ² to whom also Abraham divided a tenth part of all (being first, by interpretation, "king of righteousness", and then also "king of Salem", which means "king of peace", ³ without father, without mother, without genealogy, having neither beginning of days nor end of life, but made like the Son of God), remains a priest continually.

¹⁵ This is yet more abundantly evident, if after the likeness of Melchizedek there arises another priest, ¹⁶ who has been made, not after the law of a fleshly commandment, but after the power of an endless life; ¹⁷ for it is testified,
"You are a priest forever, according to the order of Melchizedek."

Responsorial Psalm: Psalms 110: 1, 2, 3, 4

¹ Yahweh says to my Lord, "Sit at my right hand,
until I make your enemies your footstool for your feet."
² Yahweh will send out the rod of your strength out of Zion.
Rule among your enemies.
³ Your people offer themselves willingly in the day of your power, in holy array.
Out of the womb of the morning, you have the dew of your youth.
⁴ Yahweh has sworn, and will not change his mind:
"You are a priest forever in the order of Melchizedek."

Gospel: Mark 3: 1-6

¹ He entered again into the synagogue, and there was a man there whose hand was withered. ² They watched him, whether he would heal him on the Sabbath day, that they might accuse him. ³ He said to the man whose hand was withered, "Stand up." ⁴ He said to them, "Is it lawful on the Sabbath day to do good or to do harm? To save a life or to kill?" But they were silent. ⁵ When he had looked around at them with anger, being grieved at the hardening of their hearts, he said to the man, "Stretch out your hand." He stretched it out, and his hand was restored as healthy as the other. ⁶ The Pharisees went out, and immediately conspired with the Herodians against him, how they might destroy him.

1. Invite the Holy Spirit into this reading, asking the Author of Scripture to speak to you through His Word
2. Read today's passage as many times as you need, take your time
3. Write down (below) what the Lord is saying to you today
4. Live with this Word in your heart through the day

Thursday, January 23, 2025
Saint Vincent, Deacon and Martyr; Saint Marianne Cope, Virgin

First Reading: Hebrews 7: 25 – 8: 6

²⁵ Therefore he is also able to save to the uttermost those who draw near to God through him, seeing that he lives forever to make intercession for them.
²⁶ For such a high priest was fitting for us: holy, guiltless, undefiled, separated from sinners, and made higher than the heavens; ²⁷ who doesn't need, like those high priests, to offer up sacrifices daily, first for his own sins, and then for the sins of the people. For he did this once for all, when he offered up himself. ²⁸ For the law appoints men as high priests who have weakness, but the word of the oath, which came after the law, appoints a Son forever who has been perfected.
¹ Now in the things which we are saying, the main point is this: we have such a high priest, who sat down on the right hand of the throne of the Majesty in the heavens, ² a servant of the sanctuary and of the true tabernacle which the Lord pitched, not man. ³ For every high priest is appointed to offer both gifts and sacrifices. Therefore it is necessary that this high priest also have something to offer. ⁴ For if he were on earth, he would not be a priest at all, seeing there are priests who offer the gifts according to the law, ⁵ who serve a copy and shadow of the heavenly things, even as Moses was warned by God when he was about to make the tabernacle, for he said, "See, you shall make everything according to the pattern that was shown to you on the mountain."* ⁶ But now he has obtained a more excellent ministry, by as much as he is also the mediator of a better covenant, which on better promises has been given as law.

Responsorial Psalm: Psalms 40: 7-10, 17

⁷ Then I said, "Behold, I have come.
It is written about me in the book in the scroll.
⁸ I delight to do your will, my God.
Yes, your law is within my heart."
⁹ I have proclaimed glad news of righteousness in the great assembly.
Behold, I will not seal my lips, Yahweh, you know.
¹⁰ I have not hidden your righteousness within my heart.
I have declared your faithfulness and your salvation.

I have not concealed your loving kindness and your truth from the great assembly.
¹⁷ But I am poor and needy.
May the Lord think about me.
You are my help and my deliverer.
Don't delay, my God.

Gospel: Mark 3: 7-12

⁷ Jesus withdrew to the sea with his disciples; and a great multitude followed him from Galilee, from Judea, ⁸ from Jerusalem, from Idumaea, beyond the Jordan, and those from around Tyre and Sidon. A great multitude, hearing what great things he did, came to him. ⁹ He spoke to his disciples that a little boat should stay near him because of the crowd, so that they wouldn't press on him. ¹⁰ For he had healed many, so that as many as had diseases pressed on him that they might touch him. ¹¹ The unclean spirits, whenever they saw him, fell down before him and cried, "You are the Son of God!" ¹² He sternly warned them that they should not make him known.

1. Invite the Holy Spirit into this reading, asking the Author of Scripture to speak to you through His Word
2. Read today's passage as many times as you need, take your time
3. Write down (below) what the Lord is saying to you today
4. Live with this Word in your heart through the day

_____

_____

Friday, January 24, 2025
Saint Francis de Sales, Bishop and Doctor of the Church

First Reading: Hebrews 8: 6-13

⁶ But now he has obtained a more excellent ministry, by as much as he is also the mediator of a better covenant, which on better promises has been given as law.
⁷ For if that first covenant had been faultless, then no place would have been sought for a second. ⁸ For finding fault with them, he said,
"Behold,‡ the days are coming", says the Lord,
"that I will make a new covenant with the house of Israel and with the house of Judah;
⁹ not according to the covenant that I made with their fathers

in the day that I took them by the hand to lead them out of the land of Egypt;
for they didn't continue in my covenant,
and I disregarded them," says the Lord.
¹⁰ "For this is the covenant that I will make with the house of Israel
after those days," says the Lord:
"I will put my laws into their mind;
I will also write them on their heart.
I will be their God,
and they will be my people.
¹¹ They will not teach every man his fellow citizen‡
and every man his brother, saying, 'Know the Lord,'
for all will know me,
from their least to their greatest.
¹² For I will be merciful to their unrighteousness.
I will remember their sins and lawless deeds no more."*
¹³ In that he says, "A new covenant", he has made the first obsolete. But that which is becoming obsolete and grows aged is near to vanishing away.

Responsorial Psalm: Psalms 85: 8 and 10-13

⁸ I will hear what God, Yahweh, will speak,
for he will speak peace to his people, his saints;
but let them not turn again to folly.
¹⁰ Mercy and truth meet together.
Righteousness and peace have kissed each other.
¹¹ Truth springs out of the earth.
Righteousness has looked down from heaven.
¹² Yes, Yahweh will give that which is good.
Our land will yield its increase.
¹³ Righteousness goes before him,
and prepares the way for his steps.

Gospel: Mark 3: 13-19

¹³ He went up into the mountain and called to himself those whom he wanted, and they went to him. ¹⁴ He appointed twelve, that they might be with him, and that he might send them out to preach ¹⁵ and to have authority to heal sicknesses and to cast out demons: ¹⁶ Simon (to whom he gave the name Peter); ¹⁷ James the son of Zebedee; and John, the brother of James, (whom he called Boanerges, which means, Sons of

Thunder); ¹⁸ Andrew; Philip; Bartholomew; Matthew; Thomas; James, the son of Alphaeus; Thaddaeus; Simon the Zealot; ¹⁹ and Judas Iscariot, who also betrayed him. Then he came into a house.

1. Invite the Holy Spirit into this reading, asking the Author of Scripture to speak to you through His Word
2. Read today's passage as many times as you need, take your time
3. Write down (below) what the Lord is saying to you today
4. Live with this Word in your heart through the day

_____

_____

Saturday, January 25, 2025
The Conversion of Saint Paul the Apostle

First Reading: Acts 22: 3-16

³ "I am indeed a Jew, born in Tarsus of Cilicia, but brought up in this city at the feet of Gamaliel, instructed according to the strict tradition of the law of our fathers, being zealous for God, even as you all are today. ⁴ I persecuted this Way to the death, binding and delivering into prisons both men and women, ⁵ as also the high priest and all the council of the elders testify, from whom also I received letters to the brothers, and traveled to Damascus to bring them also who were there to Jerusalem in bonds to be punished.

⁶ "As I made my journey and came close to Damascus, about noon suddenly a great light shone around me from the sky. ⁷ I fell to the ground and heard a voice saying to me, 'Saul, Saul, why are you persecuting me?' ⁸ I answered, 'Who are you, Lord?' He said to me, 'I am Jesus of Nazareth, whom you persecute.'

⁹ "Those who were with me indeed saw the light and were afraid, but they didn't understand the voice of him who spoke to me. ¹⁰ I said, 'What shall I do, Lord?' The Lord said to me, 'Arise, and go into Damascus. There you will be told about all things which are appointed for you to do.' ¹¹ When I couldn't see for the glory of that light, being led by the hand of those who were with me, I came into Damascus.

¹² "One Ananias, a devout man according to the law, well reported of by all the Jews who lived in Damascus, ¹³ came to me, and standing by me said to me, 'Brother Saul, receive your sight!' In that very hour I looked up at him. ¹⁴ He said, 'The God of our fathers has appointed you to know his will, and to see the Righteous One, and to hear a voice from his mouth. ¹⁵ For you will be a witness for him to all men of what you have seen and

heard. ¹⁶ Now why do you wait? Arise, be baptized, and wash away your sins, calling on the name of the Lord.'

Responsorial Psalm: Psalms 117: 1bc, 2

¹ Praise Yahweh, all you nations!
Extol him, all you peoples!
² For his loving kindness is great toward us.
Yahweh's faithfulness endures forever.
Praise Yah!

Gospel: Mark 16: 15-18

¹⁵ He said to them, "Go into all the world and preach the Good News to the whole creation. ¹⁶ He who believes and is baptized will be saved; but he who disbelieves will be condemned. ¹⁷ These signs will accompany those who believe: in my name they will cast out demons; they will speak with new languages; ¹⁸ they will take up serpents; and if they drink any deadly thing, it will in no way hurt them; they will lay hands on the sick, and they will recover."

1. Invite the Holy Spirit into this reading, asking the Author of Scripture to speak to you through His Word
2. Read today's passage as many times as you need, take your time
3. Write down (below) what the Lord is saying to you today
4. Live with this Word in your heart through the day

_____

_____

Sunday, January 26, 2025
THIRD SUNDAY IN ORDINARY TIME

First Reading: Nehemiah 8: 2-4a, 5-6, 8-10

² Ezra the priest brought the law before the assembly, both men and women, and all who could hear with understanding, on the first day of the seventh month. ³ He read from it before the wide place that was in front of the water gate from early morning until midday, in the presence of the men and the women, and of those who could understand. The ears

of all the people were attentive to the book of the law. ⁴ᵃ Ezra the scribe stood on a pulpit of wood, which they had made for the purpose; ⁵ Ezra opened the book in the sight of all the people (for he was above all the people), and when he opened it, all the people stood up. ⁶ Then Ezra blessed Yahweh, the great God.
All the people answered, "Amen, Amen," with the lifting up of their hands. They bowed their heads, and worshiped Yahweh with their faces to the ground.
⁸ They read in the book, in the law of God, distinctly; and they gave the sense, so that they understood the reading.
⁹ Nehemiah, who was the governor, Ezra the priest and scribe, and the Levites who taught the people said to all the people, "Today is holy to Yahweh your God. Don't mourn, nor weep." For all the people wept when they heard the words of the law. ¹⁰ Then he said to them, "Go your way. Eat the fat, drink the sweet, and send portions to him for whom nothing is prepared, for today is holy to our Lord. Don't be grieved, for the joy of Yahweh is your strength."

Responsorial Psalm: Psalms 19: 8, 9, 10, 15

⁸ Yahweh's precepts are right, rejoicing the heart.
Yahweh's commandment is pure, enlightening the eyes.
⁹ The fear of Yahweh is clean, enduring forever.
Yahweh's ordinances are true, and righteous altogether.
¹⁰ They are more to be desired than gold, yes, than much fine gold,
sweeter also than honey and the extract of the honeycomb.
¹⁵ Let the words of my mouth and the meditation of my heart
be acceptable in your sight,
Yahweh, my rock, and my redeemer.

Second Reading: First Corinthians 12: 12-14, 27

¹² For as the body is one and has many members, and all the members of the body, being many, are one body; so also is Christ. ¹³ For in one Spirit we were all baptized into one body, whether Jews or Greeks, whether bond or free; and were all given to drink into one Spirit.
¹⁴ For the body is not one member, but many.
²⁷ Now you are the body of Christ, and members individually.

Gospel: Luke 1: 1-4; 4: 14-21

¹ Since many have undertaken to set in order a narrative concerning those matters which have been fulfilled among us, ² even as those who from the beginning were eyewitnesses and servants of the word delivered them to us, ³ it seemed good to me also, having traced

the course of all things accurately from the first, to write to you in order, most excellent Theophilus; ⁴ that you might know the certainty concerning the things in which you were instructed.

¹⁴ Jesus returned in the power of the Spirit into Galilee, and news about him spread through all the surrounding area. ¹⁵ He taught in their synagogues, being glorified by all.

¹⁶ He came to Nazareth, where he had been brought up. He entered, as was his custom, into the synagogue on the Sabbath day, and stood up to read. ¹⁷ The book of the prophet Isaiah was handed to him. He opened the book, and found the place where it was written,

¹⁸ "The Spirit of the Lord is on me,
because he has anointed me to preach good news to the poor.
He has sent me to heal the broken hearted,±
to proclaim release to the captives,
recovering of sight to the blind,
to deliver those who are crushed,
¹⁹ and to proclaim the acceptable year of the Lord."±

²⁰ He closed the book, gave it back to the attendant, and sat down. The eyes of all in the synagogue were fastened on him. ²¹ He began to tell them, "Today, this Scripture has been fulfilled in your hearing."

1. Invite the Holy Spirit into this reading, asking the Author of Scripture to speak to you through His Word
2. Read today's passage as many times as you need, take your time
3. Write down (below) what the Lord is saying to you today
4. Live with this Word in your heart through the day

Monday, January 27, 2025
Saint Angela Merici, Virgin

First Reading: Hebrews 9: 15, 24-28

¹⁵ For this reason he is the mediator of a new covenant, since a death has occurred for the redemption of the transgressions that were under the first covenant, that those who have been called may receive the promise of the eternal inheritance.

²⁴ For Christ hasn't entered into holy places made with hands, which are representations of the true, but into heaven itself, now to appear in the presence of God for us; ²⁵ nor yet

that he should offer himself often, as the high priest enters into the holy place year by year with blood not his own, 26 or else he must have suffered often since the foundation of the world. But now once at the end of the ages, he has been revealed to put away sin by the sacrifice of himself. 27 Inasmuch as it is appointed for men to die once, and after this, judgment, 28 so Christ also, having been offered once to bear the sins of many, will appear a second time, not to deal with sin, but to save those who are eagerly waiting for him.

Responsorial Psalm: Psalms 98: 1-6

1 Sing to Yahweh a new song,
for he has done marvelous things!
His right hand and his holy arm have worked salvation for him.
2 Yahweh has made known his salvation.
He has openly shown his righteousness in the sight of the nations.
3 He has remembered his loving kindness and his faithfulness toward the house of Israel.
All the ends of the earth have seen the salvation of our God.
4 Make a joyful noise to Yahweh, all the earth!
Burst out and sing for joy, yes, sing praises!
5 Sing praises to Yahweh with the harp,
with the harp and the voice of melody.
6 With trumpets and sound of the ram's horn,
make a joyful noise before the King, Yahweh.

Gospel: Mark 3: 22-30

22 The scribes who came down from Jerusalem said, "He has Beelzebul," and, "By the prince of the demons he casts out the demons."
23 He summoned them and said to them in parables, "How can Satan cast out Satan? 24 If a kingdom is divided against itself, that kingdom cannot stand. 25 If a house is divided against itself, that house cannot stand. 26 If Satan has risen up against himself, and is divided, he can't stand, but has an end. 27 But no one can enter into the house of the strong man to plunder unless he first binds the strong man; then he will plunder his house.
28 "Most certainly I tell you, all sins of the descendants of man will be forgiven, including their blasphemies with which they may blaspheme; 29 but whoever may blaspheme against the Holy Spirit never has forgiveness, but is subject to eternal condemnation." 30 —because they said, "He has an unclean spirit."

1. Invite the Holy Spirit into this reading, asking the Author of Scripture to speak to you through His Word
2. Read today's passage as many times as you need, take your time

3. Write down (below) what the Lord is saying to you today
4. Live with this Word in your heart through the day

_____

_____

Tuesday, January 28, 2025
Saint Thomas Aquinas, Priest and Doctor of the Church

First Reading: Hebrews 10: 1-10

¹ For the law, having a shadow of the good to come, not the very image of the things, can never with the same sacrifices year by year, which they offer continually, make perfect those who draw near. ² Or else wouldn't they have ceased to be offered, because the worshipers, having been once cleansed, would have had no more consciousness of sins? ³ But in those sacrifices there is a yearly reminder of sins. ⁴ For it is impossible that the blood of bulls and goats should take away sins. ⁵ Therefore when he comes into the world, he says,
"You didn't desire sacrifice and offering,
but you prepared a body for me.
⁶ You had no pleasure in whole burnt offerings and sacrifices for sin.
⁷ Then I said, 'Behold, I have come (in the scroll of the book it is written of me)
to do your will, O God.' "
⁸ Previously saying, "Sacrifices and offerings and whole burnt offerings and sacrifices for sin you didn't desire, neither had pleasure in them" (those which are offered according to the law), ⁹ then he has said, "Behold, I have come to do your will." He takes away the first, that he may establish the second, ¹⁰ by which will we have been sanctified through the offering of the body of Jesus Christ once for all.

Responsorial Psalm: Psalms 40: 2 and 4ab, 7-8a, 10, 11

² He brought me up also out of a horrible pit,
out of the miry clay.
He set my feet on a rock,
and gave me a firm place to stand.
⁴ Blessed is the man who makes Yahweh his trust,
and doesn't respect the proud, nor such as turn away to lies.
⁷ Then I said, "Behold, I have come.

It is written about me in the book in the scroll.
⁸ᵃ I delight to do your will, my God.
¹⁰ I have not hidden your righteousness within my heart.
I have declared your faithfulness and your salvation.
I have not concealed your loving kindness and your truth from the great assembly.
¹¹ Don't withhold your tender mercies from me, Yahweh.
Let your loving kindness and your truth continually preserve me.

Gospel: Mark 3: 31-35

³¹ His mother and his brothers came, and standing outside, they sent to him, calling him. ³² A multitude was sitting around him, and they told him, "Behold, your mother, your brothers, and your sisters‡ are outside looking for you."
³³ He answered them, "Who are my mother and my brothers?" ³⁴ Looking around at those who sat around him, he said, "Behold, my mother and my brothers! ³⁵ For whoever does the will of God is my brother, my sister, and mother."

1. Invite the Holy Spirit into this reading, asking the Author of Scripture to speak to you through His Word
2. Read today's passage as many times as you need, take your time
3. Write down (below) what the Lord is saying to you today
4. Live with this Word in your heart through the day

_____

_____

Wednesday, January 29, 2025

First Reading: Hebrews 10: 11-18

¹¹ Every priest indeed stands day by day serving and offering often the same sacrifices, which can never take away sins, ¹² but he, when he had offered one sacrifice for sins forever, sat down on the right hand of God, ¹³ from that time waiting until his enemies are made the footstool of his feet. ¹⁴ For by one offering he has perfected forever those who are being sanctified. ¹⁵ The Holy Spirit also testifies to us, for after saying,
¹⁶ "This is the covenant that I will make with them
after those days," says the Lord,
"I will put my laws on their heart,

I will also write them on their mind;"*
then he says,
¹⁷ "I will remember their sins and their iniquities no more."*
¹⁸ Now where remission of these is, there is no more offering for sin.

Responsorial Psalm: Psalms 110: 1, 2, 3, 4

¹ Yahweh says to my Lord, "Sit at my right hand,
until I make your enemies your footstool for your feet."
² Yahweh will send out the rod of your strength out of Zion.
Rule among your enemies.
³ Your people offer themselves willingly in the day of your power, in holy array.
Out of the womb of the morning, you have the dew of your youth.
⁴ Yahweh has sworn, and will not change his mind:
"You are a priest forever in the order of Melchizedek."

Gospel: Mark 4: 1-20

¹ Again he began to teach by the seaside. A great multitude was gathered to him, so that he entered into a boat in the sea and sat down. All the multitude were on the land by the sea. ² He taught them many things in parables, and told them in his teaching, ³ "Listen! Behold, the farmer went out to sow. ⁴ As he sowed, some seed fell by the road, and the birds* came and devoured it. ⁵ Others fell on the rocky ground, where it had little soil, and immediately it sprang up, because it had no depth of soil. ⁶ When the sun had risen, it was scorched; and because it had no root, it withered away. ⁷ Others fell among the thorns, and the thorns grew up and choked it, and it yielded no fruit. ⁸ Others fell into the good ground and yielded fruit, growing up and increasing. Some produced thirty times, some sixty times, and some one hundred times as much." ⁹ He said, "Whoever has ears to hear, let him hear."
¹⁰ When he was alone, those who were around him with the twelve asked him about the parables. ¹¹ He said to them, "To you is given the mystery of God's Kingdom, but to those who are outside, all things are done in parables, ¹² that 'seeing they may see and not perceive, and hearing they may hear and not understand, lest perhaps they should turn again, and their sins should be forgiven them.' "*
¹³ He said to them, "Don't you understand this parable? How will you understand all of the parables? ¹⁴ The farmer sows the word. ¹⁵ The ones by the road are the ones where the word is sown; and when they have heard, immediately Satan comes and takes away the word which has been sown in them. ¹⁶ These in the same way are those who are sown on the rocky places, who, when they have heard the word, immediately receive it with joy. ¹⁷ They have no root in themselves, but are short-lived. When oppression or

persecution arises because of the word, immediately they stumble. ¹⁸ Others are those who are sown among the thorns. These are those who have heard the word, ¹⁹ and the cares of this age, and the deceitfulness of riches, and the lusts of other things entering in choke the word, and it becomes unfruitful. ²⁰ Those which were sown on the good ground are those who hear the word, accept it, and bear fruit, some thirty times, some sixty times, and some one hundred times."

1. Invite the Holy Spirit into this reading, asking the Author of Scripture to speak to you through His Word
2. Read today's passage as many times as you need, take your time
3. Write down (below) what the Lord is saying to you today
4. Live with this Word in your heart through the day

Thursday, January 30, 2025

First Reading: Hebrews 10: 19-25

¹⁹ Having therefore, brothers, boldness to enter into the holy place by the blood of Jesus, ²⁰ by the way which he dedicated for us, a new and living way, through the veil, that is to say, his flesh, ²¹ and having a great priest over God's house, ²² let's draw near with a true heart in fullness of faith, having our hearts sprinkled from an evil conscience and having our body washed with pure water, ²³ let's hold fast the confession of our hope without wavering; for he who promised is faithful.
²⁴ Let's consider how to provoke one another to love and good works, ²⁵ not forsaking our own assembling together, as the custom of some is, but exhorting one another, and so much the more as you see the Day approaching.

Responsorial Psalm: Psalms 24: 1-6

¹ The earth is Yahweh's, with its fullness;
the world, and those who dwell in it.
² For he has founded it on the seas,
and established it on the floods.
³ Who may ascend to Yahweh's hill?
Who may stand in his holy place?

⁴ He who has clean hands and a pure heart;
who has not lifted up his soul to falsehood,
and has not sworn deceitfully.
⁵ He shall receive a blessing from Yahweh,
righteousness from the God of his salvation.
⁶ This is the generation of those who seek Him,
who seek your face—even Jacob.

Gospel: Mark 4: 21-25

²¹ He said to them, "Is a lamp brought to be put under a basket ǂ or under a bed? Isn't it put on a stand? ²² For there is nothing hidden except that it should be made known, neither was anything made secret but that it should come to light. ²³ If any man has ears to hear, let him hear."
²⁴ He said to them, "Take heed what you hear. With whatever measure you measure, it will be measured to you; and more will be given to you who hear. ²⁵ For whoever has, to him more will be given; and he who doesn't have, even that which he has will be taken away from him."

1. Invite the Holy Spirit into this reading, asking the Author of Scripture to speak to you through His Word
2. Read today's passage as many times as you need, take your time
3. Write down (below) what the Lord is saying to you today
4. Live with this Word in your heart through the day

Friday, January 31, 2025
Saint John Bosco, Priest

First Reading: Hebrews 10: 32-39

³² But remember the former days, in which, after you were enlightened, you endured a great struggle with sufferings: ³³ partly, being exposed to both reproaches and oppressions, and partly, becoming partakers with those who were treated so. ³⁴ For you both had compassion on me in my chains and joyfully accepted the plundering of your possessions, knowing that you have for yourselves a better possession and an enduring one in the

heavens. ³⁵ Therefore don't throw away your boldness, which has a great reward. ³⁶ For you need endurance so that, having done the will of God, you may receive the promise.
³⁷ "In a very little while,
he who comes will come and will not wait.
³⁸ But the righteous one will live by faith.
If he shrinks back, my soul has no pleasure in him."
³⁹ But we are not of those who shrink back to destruction, but of those who have faith to the saving of the soul.

Responsorial Psalm: Psalms 37: 3-6, 23-24, 39-40

³ Trust in Yahweh, and do good.
Dwell in the land, and enjoy safe pasture.
⁴ Also delight yourself in Yahweh,
and he will give you the desires of your heart.
⁵ Commit your way to Yahweh.
Trust also in him, and he will do this:
⁶ he will make your righteousness shine out like light,
and your justice as the noon day sun.
²³ A man's steps are established by Yahweh.
He delights in his way.
²⁴ Though he stumble, he shall not fall,
for Yahweh holds him up with his hand.
³⁹ But the salvation of the righteous is from Yahweh.
He is their stronghold in the time of trouble.
⁴⁰ Yahweh helps them and rescues them.
He rescues them from the wicked and saves them,
because they have taken refuge in him.

Gospel: Mark 4: 26-34

²⁶ He said, "God's Kingdom is as if a man should cast seed on the earth, ²⁷ and should sleep and rise night and day, and the seed should spring up and grow, though he doesn't know how. ²⁸ For the earth bears fruit by itself: first the blade, then the ear, then the full grain in the ear. ²⁹ But when the fruit is ripe, immediately he puts in the sickle, because the harvest has come."
³⁰ He said, "How will we liken God's Kingdom? Or with what parable will we illustrate it? ³¹ It's like a grain of mustard seed, which, when it is sown in the earth, though it is less than all the seeds that are on the earth, ³² yet when it is sown, grows up and becomes

greater than all the herbs, and puts out great branches, so that the birds of the sky can lodge under its shadow."

33 With many such parables he spoke the word to them, as they were able to hear it. 34 Without a parable he didn't speak to them; but privately to his own disciples he explained everything.

1. Invite the Holy Spirit into this reading, asking the Author of Scripture to speak to you through His Word
2. Read today's passage as many times as you need, take your time
3. Write down (below) what the Lord is saying to you today
4. Live with this Word in your heart through the day

_____

_____

Saturday, February 1, 2025

First Reading: Hebrews 11: 1-2, 8-19

1 Now faith is assurance of things hoped for, proof of things not seen. 2 For by this, the elders obtained approval.
8 By faith Abraham, when he was called, obeyed to go out to the place which he was to receive for an inheritance. He went out, not knowing where he went. 9 By faith he lived as an alien in the land of promise, as in a land not his own, dwelling in tents with Isaac and Jacob, the heirs with him of the same promise. 10 For he was looking for the city which has foundations, whose builder and maker is God.
11 By faith even Sarah herself received power to conceive, and she bore a child when she was past age, since she counted him faithful who had promised. 12 Therefore as many as the stars of the sky in multitude, and as innumerable as the sand which is by the sea shore, were fathered by one man, and him as good as dead.
13 These all died in faith, not having received the promises, but having seen╪ them and embraced them from afar, and having confessed that they were strangers and pilgrims on the earth. 14 For those who say such things make it clear that they are seeking a country of their own. 15 If indeed they had been thinking of that country from which they went out, they would have had enough time to return. 16 But now they desire a better country, that is, a heavenly one. Therefore God is not ashamed of them, to be called their God, for he has prepared a city for them.

¹⁷ By faith, Abraham, being tested, offered up Isaac. Yes, he who had gladly received the promises was offering up his only born§ son, ¹⁸ to whom it was said, "Your offspring will be accounted as from Isaac," ᵃ ¹⁹ concluding that God is able to raise up even from the dead. Figuratively speaking, he also did receive him back from the dead.

Responsorial Psalm: Luke 1: 69-75

⁶⁹ and has raised up a horn of salvation for us in the house of his servant David
⁷⁰ (as he spoke by the mouth of his holy prophets who have been from of old),
⁷¹ salvation from our enemies and from the hand of all who hate us;
⁷² to show mercy toward our fathers,
to remember his holy covenant,
⁷³ the oath which he swore to Abraham our father,
⁷⁴ to grant to us that we, being delivered out of the hand of our enemies,
should serve him without fear,
⁷⁵ in holiness and righteousness before him all the days of our life.

Gospel: Mark 4: 35-41

³⁵ On that day, when evening had come, he said to them, "Let's go over to the other side." ³⁶ Leaving the multitude, they took him with them, even as he was, in the boat. Other small boats were also with him. ³⁷ A big wind storm arose, and the waves beat into the boat, so much that the boat was already filled. ³⁸ He himself was in the stern, asleep on the cushion; and they woke him up and asked him, "Teacher, don't you care that we are dying?" ³⁹ He awoke and rebuked the wind, and said to the sea, "Peace! Be still!" The wind ceased and there was a great calm. ⁴⁰ He said to them, "Why are you so afraid? How is it that you have no faith?"
⁴¹ They were greatly afraid and said to one another, "Who then is this, that even the wind and the sea obey him?"

1. Invite the Holy Spirit into this reading, asking the Author of Scripture to speak to you through His Word
2. Read today's passage as many times as you need, take your time
3. Write down (below) what the Lord is saying to you today
4. Live with this Word in your heart through the day

Sunday, February 2, 2025
THE PRESENTATION OF THE LORD

First Reading: Malachi 3: 1-4

¹ "Behold, I send my messenger, and he will prepare the way before me! The Lord, whom you seek, will suddenly come to his temple. Behold, the messenger of the covenant, whom you desire, is coming!" says Yahweh of Armies. ² "But who can endure the day of his coming? And who will stand when he appears? For he is like a refiner's fire, and like launderers' soap; ³ and he will sit as a refiner and purifier of silver, and he will purify the sons of Levi, and refine them as gold and silver; and they shall offer to Yahweh offerings in righteousness. ⁴ Then the offering of Judah and Jerusalem will be pleasant to Yahweh as in the days of old and as in ancient years.

Responsorial Psalm: Psalms 24: 7-10

⁷ Lift up your heads, you gates!
Be lifted up, you everlasting doors,
and the King of glory will come in.
⁸ Who is the King of glory?
Yahweh strong and mighty,
Yahweh mighty in battle.
⁹ Lift up your heads, you gates;
yes, lift them up, you everlasting doors,
and the King of glory will come in.
¹⁰ Who is this King of glory?
Yahweh of Armies is the King of glory!

Second Reading: Hebrews 2: 14-18

¹⁴ Since then the children have shared in flesh and blood, he also himself in the same way partook of the same, that through death he might bring to nothing him who had the power of death, that is, the devil, ¹⁵ and might deliver all of them who through fear of death were all their lifetime subject to bondage. ¹⁶ For most certainly, he doesn't give help to angels, but he gives help to the offspring§ of Abraham. ¹⁷ Therefore he was obligated in all things to be made like his brothers, that he might become a merciful and faithful high priest in things pertaining to God, to make atonement for the sins of the people. ¹⁸ For in that he himself has suffered being tempted, he is able to help those who are tempted.

Gospel: Luke 2: 22-32

22 When the days of their purification according to the law of Moses were fulfilled, they brought him up to Jerusalem to present him to the Lord 23 (as it is written in the law of the Lord, "Every male who opens the womb shall be called holy to the Lord"), 24 and to offer a sacrifice according to that which is said in the law of the Lord, "A pair of turtledoves, or two young pigeons."

25 Behold, there was a man in Jerusalem whose name was Simeon. This man was righteous and devout, looking for the consolation of Israel, and the Holy Spirit was on him. 26 It had been revealed to him by the Holy Spirit that he should not see death before he had seen the Lord's Christ. 27 He came in the Spirit into the temple. When the parents brought in the child, Jesus, that they might do concerning him according to the custom of the law, 28 then he received him into his arms and blessed God, and said,

29 "Now you are releasing your servant, Master,
according to your word, in peace;
30 for my eyes have seen your salvation,
31 which you have prepared before the face of all peoples;
32 a light for revelation to the nations,
and the glory of your people Israel."

1. Invite the Holy Spirit into this reading, asking the Author of Scripture to speak to you through His Word
2. Read today's passage as many times as you need, take your time
3. Write down (below) what the Lord is saying to you today
4. Live with this Word in your heart through the day

_____

_____

Monday, February 3, 2025
Saint Blaise, Bishop and Martyr; Saint Ansgar, Bishop

First Reading: Hebrews 11: 32-40

32 What more shall I say? For the time would fail me if I told of Gideon, Barak, Samson, Jephthah, David, Samuel, and the prophets— 33 who through faith subdued kingdoms, worked out righteousness, obtained promises, stopped the mouths of lions, 34 quenched

the power of fire,⁎ escaped the edge of the sword,⁎ from weakness were made strong, grew mighty in war, and caused foreign armies to flee. ³⁵ Women received their dead by resurrection.⁎ Others were tortured, not accepting their deliverance, that they might obtain a better resurrection. ³⁶ Others were tried by mocking and scourging, yes, moreover by bonds and imprisonment. ³⁷ They were stoned.⁎ They were sawn apart. They were tempted. They were slain with the sword.⁎ They went around in sheep skins and in goat skins; being destitute, afflicted, ill-treated— ³⁸ of whom the world was not worthy—wandering in deserts, mountains, caves, and the holes of the earth.

³⁹ These all, having been commended for their faith, didn't receive the promise, ⁴⁰ God having provided some better thing concerning us, so that apart from us they should not be made perfect.

Responsorial Psalm: Psalms 31: 20- 24

²⁰ In the shelter of your presence you will hide them from the plotting of man.
You will keep them secretly in a dwelling away from the strife of tongues.
²¹ Praise be to Yahweh,
for he has shown me his marvelous loving kindness in a strong city.
²² As for me, I said in my haste, "I am cut off from before your eyes."
Nevertheless you heard the voice of my petitions when I cried to you.
²³ Oh love Yahweh, all you his saints!
Yahweh preserves the faithful,
and fully recompenses him who behaves arrogantly.
²⁴ Be strong, and let your heart take courage,
all you who hope in Yahweh.

Gospel: Mark 5: 1-20

¹ They came to the other side of the sea, into the country of the Gadarenes. ² When he had come out of the boat, immediately a man with an unclean spirit met him out of the tombs. ³ He lived in the tombs. Nobody could bind him any more, not even with chains, ⁴ because he had been often bound with fetters and chains, and the chains had been torn apart by him, and the fetters broken in pieces. Nobody had the strength to tame him. ⁵ Always, night and day, in the tombs and in the mountains, he was crying out, and cutting himself with stones. ⁶ When he saw Jesus from afar, he ran and bowed down to him, ⁷ and crying out with a loud voice, he said, "What have I to do with you, Jesus, you Son of the Most High God? I adjure you by God, don't torment me." ⁸ For he said to him, "Come out of the man, you unclean spirit!"
⁹ He asked him, "What is your name?"

He said to him, "My name is Legion, for we are many." ¹⁰ He begged him much that he would not send them away out of the country. ¹¹ Now on the mountainside there was a great herd of pigs feeding. ¹² All the demons begged him, saying, "Send us into the pigs, that we may enter into them."

¹³ At once Jesus gave them permission. The unclean spirits came out and entered into the pigs. The herd of about two thousand rushed down the steep bank into the sea, and they were drowned in the sea. ¹⁴ Those who fed the pigs fled, and told it in the city and in the country.

The people came to see what it was that had happened. ¹⁵ They came to Jesus, and saw him who had been possessed by demons sitting, clothed, and in his right mind, even him who had the legion; and they were afraid. ¹⁶ Those who saw it declared to them what happened to him who was possessed by demons, and about the pigs. ¹⁷ They began to beg him to depart from their region.

¹⁸ As he was entering into the boat, he who had been possessed by demons begged him that he might be with him. ¹⁹ He didn't allow him, but said to him, "Go to your house, to your friends, and tell them what great things the Lord has done for you and how he had mercy on you."

²⁰ He went his way, and began to proclaim in Decapolis how Jesus had done great things for him, and everyone marveled.

1. Invite the Holy Spirit into this reading, asking the Author of Scripture to speak to you through His Word
2. Read today's passage as many times as you need, take your time
3. Write down (below) what the Lord is saying to you today
4. Live with this Word in your heart through the day

_____

_____

Tuesday, February 4, 2025

First Reading: Hebrews 12: 1-4

¹ Therefore let's also, seeing we are surrounded by so great a cloud of witnesses, lay aside every weight and the sin which so easily entangles us, and let's run with perseverance the race that is set before us, ² looking to Jesus, the author and perfecter of faith, who for the joy that was set before him endured the cross, despising its shame, and has sat down at the right hand of the throne of God.

³ For consider him who has endured such contradiction of sinners against himself, that you don't grow weary, fainting in your souls. ⁴ You have not yet resisted to blood, striving against sin.

Responsorial Psalm: Psalms 22: 26b-28 and 30-31

²⁶ᵇThey shall praise Yahweh who seek after him.
Let your hearts live forever.
²⁷ All the ends of the earth shall remember and turn to Yahweh.
All the relatives of the nations shall worship before you.
²⁸ For the kingdom is Yahweh's.
He is the ruler over the nations.
³⁰ Posterity shall serve him.
Future generations shall be told about the Lord.
³¹ They shall come and shall declare his righteousness to a people that shall be born,
for he has done it.

Gospel: Mark 5: 21-43

²¹ When Jesus had crossed back over in the boat to the other side, a great multitude was gathered to him; and he was by the sea. ²² Behold, one of the rulers of the synagogue, Jairus by name, came; and seeing him, he fell at his feet ²³ and begged him much, saying, "My little daughter is at the point of death. Please come and lay your hands on her, that she may be made healthy, and live."
²⁴ He went with him, and a great multitude followed him, and they pressed upon him on all sides. ²⁵ A certain woman who had a discharge of blood for twelve years, ²⁶ and had suffered many things by many physicians, and had spent all that she had, and was no better, but rather grew worse, ²⁷ having heard the things concerning Jesus, came up behind him in the crowd and touched his clothes. ²⁸ For she said, "If I just touch his clothes, I will be made well." ²⁹ Immediately the flow of her blood was dried up, and she felt in her body that she was healed of her affliction.
³⁰ Immediately Jesus, perceiving in himself that the power had gone out from him, turned around in the crowd and asked, "Who touched my clothes?"
³¹ His disciples said to him, "You see the multitude pressing against you, and you say, 'Who touched me?' "
³² He looked around to see her who had done this thing. ³³ But the woman, fearing and trembling, knowing what had been done to her, came and fell down before him, and told him all the truth.
³⁴ He said to her, "Daughter, your faith has made you well. Go in peace, and be cured of your disease."

35 While he was still speaking, people came from the synagogue ruler's house, saying, "Your daughter is dead. Why bother the Teacher any more?"
36 But Jesus, when he heard the message spoken, immediately said to the ruler of the synagogue, "Don't be afraid, only believe." 37 He allowed no one to follow him except Peter, James, and John the brother of James. 38 He came to the synagogue ruler's house, and he saw an uproar, weeping, and great wailing. 39 When he had entered in, he said to them, "Why do you make an uproar and weep? The child is not dead, but is asleep."
40 They ridiculed him. But he, having put them all out, took the father of the child, her mother, and those who were with him, and went in where the child was lying. 41 Taking the child by the hand, he said to her, "Talitha cumi!" which means, being interpreted, "Girl, I tell you, get up!" 42 Immediately the girl rose up and walked, for she was twelve years old. They were amazed with great amazement. 43 He strictly ordered them that no one should know this, and commanded that something should be given to her to eat.

1. Invite the Holy Spirit into this reading, asking the Author of Scripture to speak to you through His Word
2. Read today's passage as many times as you need, take your time
3. Write down (below) what the Lord is saying to you today
4. Live with this Word in your heart through the day

Wednesday, February 5, 2025
Saint Agatha, Virgin and Martyr

First Reading: Hebrews 12: 4-7, 11-15

4 You have not yet resisted to blood, striving against sin. 5 You have forgotten the exhortation which reasons with you as with children,
"My son, don't take lightly the chastening of the Lord,
nor faint when you are reproved by him;
6 for whom the Lord loves, he disciplines,
and chastises every son whom he receives."
7 It is for discipline that you endure. God deals with you as with children, for what son is there whom his father doesn't discipline?
11 All chastening seems for the present to be not joyous but grievous; yet afterward it yields the peaceful fruit of righteousness to those who have been trained by it. 12 Therefore lift up

the hands that hang down and the feeble knees, * ¹³ and make straight paths for your feet,* so what is lame may not be dislocated, but rather be healed.
¹⁴ Follow after peace with all men, and the sanctification without which no man will see the Lord, ¹⁵ looking carefully lest there be any man who falls short of the grace of God, lest any root of bitterness springing up trouble you and many be defiled by it,

Responsorial Psalm: Psalms 103: 1-2, 13-14, 17-18a

¹ Praise Yahweh, my soul!
All that is within me, praise his holy name!
² Praise Yahweh, my soul,
and don't forget all his benefits,
¹³ Like a father has compassion on his children,
so Yahweh has compassion on those who fear him.
¹⁴ For he knows how we are made.
He remembers that we are dust.
¹⁷ But Yahweh's loving kindness is from everlasting to everlasting with those who fear him,
his righteousness to children's children,
¹⁸ᵃ to those who keep his covenant,

Gospel: Mark 6: 1-6

¹ He went out from there. He came into his own country, and his disciples followed him. ² When the Sabbath had come, he began to teach in the synagogue, and many hearing him were astonished, saying, "Where did this man get these things?" and, "What is the wisdom that is given to this man, that such mighty works come about by his hands? ³ Isn't this the carpenter, the son of Mary and brother of James, Joses, Judah, and Simon? Aren't his sisters here with us?" So they were offended at him.
⁴ Jesus said to them, "A prophet is not without honor, except in his own country, and among his own relatives, and in his own house." ⁵ He could do no mighty work there, except that he laid his hands on a few sick people and healed them. ⁶ He marveled because of their unbelief.
He went around the villages teaching.

1. Invite the Holy Spirit into this reading, asking the Author of Scripture to speak to you through His Word
2. Read today's passage as many times as you need, take your time
3. Write down (below) what the Lord is saying to you today
4. Live with this Word in your heart through the day

Thursday, February 6, 2025
Saint Paul Miki and Companions, Martyrs

First Reading: Hebrews 12: 18-19, 21-24

18 For you have not come to a mountain that might be touched and that burned with fire, and to blackness, darkness, storm, 19 the sound of a trumpet, and the voice of words; which those who heard it begged that not one more word should be spoken to them,
21 So fearful was the appearance that Moses said, "I am terrified and trembling."*
22 But you have come to Mount Zion and to the city of the living God, the heavenly Jerusalem, and to innumerable multitudes of angels, 23 to the festal gathering and assembly of the firstborn who are enrolled in heaven, to God the Judge of all, to the spirits of just men made perfect, 24 to Jesus, the mediator of a new covenant,* and to the blood of sprinkling that speaks better than that of Abel.

Responsorial Psalm: Psalms 48: 2-4, 9-11

2 Beautiful in elevation, the joy of the whole earth,
is Mount Zion, on the north sides,
the city of the great King.
3 God has shown himself in her citadels as a refuge.
4 For, behold, the kings assembled themselves,
they passed by together.
9 We have thought about your loving kindness, God,
in the middle of your temple.
10 As is your name, God,
so is your praise to the ends of the earth.
Your right hand is full of righteousness.
11 Let Mount Zion be glad!
Let the daughters of Judah rejoice because of your judgments.

Gospel: Mark 6: 7-13

7 He called to himself the twelve, and began to send them out two by two; and he gave them authority over the unclean spirits. 8 He commanded them that they should take nothing for

their journey, except a staff only: no bread, no wallet, no money in their purse, ⁹ but to wear sandals, and not put on two tunics. ¹⁰ He said to them, "Wherever you enter into a house, stay there until you depart from there. ¹¹ Whoever will not receive you nor hear you, as you depart from there, shake off the dust that is under your feet for a testimony against them. Assuredly, I tell you, it will be more tolerable for Sodom and Gomorrah in the day of judgment than for that city!"

¹² They went out and preached that people should repent. ¹³ They cast out many demons, and anointed many with oil who were sick and healed them.

1. Invite the Holy Spirit into this reading, asking the Author of Scripture to speak to you through His Word
2. Read today's passage as many times as you need, take your time
3. Write down (below) what the Lord is saying to you today
4. Live with this Word in your heart through the day

Friday, February 7, 2025

First Reading: Hebrews 13: 1-8

¹ Let brotherly love continue. ² Don't forget to show hospitality to strangers, for in doing so, some have entertained angels without knowing it. ³ Remember those who are in bonds, as bound with them, and those who are ill-treated, since you are also in the body. ⁴ Let marriage be held in honor among all, and let the bed be undefiled; but God will judge the sexually immoral and adulterers.
⁵ Be free from the love of money, content with such things as you have, for he has said, "I will in no way leave you, neither will I in any way forsake you." ⁶ So that with good courage we say,
"The Lord is my helper. I will not fear.
What can man do to me?"
⁷ Remember your leaders, men who spoke to you the word of God, and considering the results of their conduct, imitate their faith. ⁸ Jesus Christ is the same yesterday, today, and forever.

Responsorial Psalm: Psalms 27: 1, 3, 5, 8b-9abc

¹ Yahweh is my light and my salvation.
Whom shall I fear?
Yahweh is the strength of my life.
Of whom shall I be afraid?
³ Though an army should encamp against me,
my heart shall not fear.
Though war should rise against me,
even then I will be confident.
⁵ For in the day of trouble, he will keep me secretly in his pavilion.
In the secret place of his tabernacle, he will hide me.
He will lift me up on a rock.
⁸ᵇ my heart said to you, "I will seek your face, Yahweh."
⁹ Don't hide your face from me.
Don't put your servant away in anger.
You have been my help.
Don't abandon me,
neither forsake me, God of my salvation.

Gospel: Mark 6: 14-29

¹⁴ King Herod heard this, for his name had become known, and he said, "John the Baptizer has risen from the dead, and therefore these powers are at work in him." ¹⁵ But others said, "He is Elijah." Others said, "He is a prophet, or like one of the prophets." ¹⁶ But Herod, when he heard this, said, "This is John, whom I beheaded. He has risen from the dead." ¹⁷ For Herod himself had sent out and arrested John and bound him in prison for the sake of Herodias, his brother Philip's wife, for he had married her. ¹⁸ For John had said to Herod, "It is not lawful for you to have your brother's wife." ¹⁹ Herodias set herself against him and desired to kill him, but she couldn't, ²⁰ for Herod feared John, knowing that he was a righteous and holy man, and kept him safe. When he heard him, he did many things, and he heard him gladly.
²¹ Then a convenient day came when Herod on his birthday made a supper for his nobles, the high officers, and the chief men of Galilee. ²² When the daughter of Herodias herself came in and danced, she pleased Herod and those sitting with him. The king said to the young lady, "Ask me whatever you want, and I will give it to you." ²³ He swore to her, "Whatever you ask of me, I will give you, up to half of my kingdom."
²⁴ She went out and said to her mother, "What shall I ask?"
She said, "The head of John the Baptizer."
²⁵ She came in immediately with haste to the king and requested, "I want you to give me right now the head of John the Baptizer on a platter."

26 The king was exceedingly sorry, but for the sake of his oaths and of his dinner guests, he didn't wish to refuse her. 27 Immediately the king sent out a soldier of his guard and commanded to bring John's head; and he went and beheaded him in the prison, 28 and brought his head on a platter, and gave it to the young lady; and the young lady gave it to her mother.
29 When his disciples heard this, they came and took up his corpse and laid it in a tomb.

1. Invite the Holy Spirit into this reading, asking the Author of Scripture to speak to you through His Word
2. Read today's passage as many times as you need, take your time
3. Write down (below) what the Lord is saying to you today
4. Live with this Word in your heart through the day

Saturday, February 8, 2025
Saint Jerome Emiliani; Saint Josephine Bakhita, Virgin; BVM

First Reading: Hebrews 13: 15-17, 20-21

15 Through him, then, let's offer up a sacrifice of praise to God ⃰ continually, that is, the fruit of lips which proclaim allegiance to his name. 16 But don't forget to be doing good and sharing, for with such sacrifices God is well pleased.
17 Obey your leaders and submit to them, for they watch on behalf of your souls, as those who will give account, that they may do this with joy and not with groaning, for that would be unprofitable for you.
20 Now may the God of peace, who brought again from the dead the great shepherd of the sheep with the blood of an eternal covenant, our Lord Jesus, 21 make you complete in every good work to do his will, working in you that which is well pleasing in his sight, through Jesus Christ, to whom be the glory forever and ever. Amen.

Responsorial Psalm: Psalms 23: 1-6

1 Yahweh is my shepherd;
I shall lack nothing.
2 He makes me lie down in green pastures.
He leads me beside still waters.

3 He restores my soul.
He guides me in the paths of righteousness for his name's sake.
4 Even though I walk through the valley of the shadow of death,
I will fear no evil, for you are with me.
Your rod and your staff,
they comfort me.
5 You prepare a table before me
in the presence of my enemies.
You anoint my head with oil.
My cup runs over.
6 Surely goodness and loving kindness shall follow me all the days of my life,
and I will dwell in Yahweh's house forever.

Gospel: Mark 6: 30-34

30 The apostles gathered themselves together to Jesus, and they told him all things, whatever they had done, and whatever they had taught. 31 He said to them, "Come away into a deserted place, and rest awhile." For there were many coming and going, and they had no leisure so much as to eat. 32 They went away in the boat to a deserted place by themselves. 33 They saw them going, and many recognized him and ran there on foot from all the cities. They arrived before them and came together to him. 34 Jesus came out, saw a great multitude, and he had compassion on them because they were like sheep without a shepherd; and he began to teach them many things.

1. Invite the Holy Spirit into this reading, asking the Author of Scripture to speak to you through His Word
2. Read today's passage as many times as you need, take your time
3. Write down (below) what the Lord is saying to you today
4. Live with this Word in your heart through the day

Sunday, February 9, 2025
FIFTH SUNDAY IN ORDINARY TIME

First Reading: Isaiah 6: 1-2a, 3-8

¹ In the year that King Uzziah died, I saw the Lord sitting on a throne, high and lifted up; and his train filled the temple. ²ᵃ Above him stood the seraphim. ³ One called to another, and said,

"Holy, holy, holy, is Yahweh of Armies!
The whole earth is full of his glory!"

⁴ The foundations of the thresholds shook at the voice of him who called, and the house was filled with smoke. ⁵ Then I said, "Woe is me! For I am undone, because I am a man of unclean lips and I live among a people of unclean lips, for my eyes have seen the King, Yahweh of Armies!"

⁶ Then one of the seraphim flew to me, having a live coal in his hand, which he had taken with the tongs from off the altar. ⁷ He touched my mouth with it, and said, "Behold, this has touched your lips; and your iniquity is taken away, and your sin forgiven."

⁸ I heard the Lord's voice, saying, "Whom shall I send, and who will go for us?"
Then I said, "Here I am. Send me!"

Responsorial Psalm: Psalms 138: 1-5, 7c-8

¹ I will give you thanks with my whole heart.
Before the gods,⸸ I will sing praises to you.
² I will bow down toward your holy temple,
and give thanks to your Name for your loving kindness and for your truth;
for you have exalted your Name and your Word above all.
³ In the day that I called, you answered me.
You encouraged me with strength in my soul.
⁴ All the kings of the earth will give you thanks, Yahweh,
for they have heard the words of your mouth.
⁵ Yes, they will sing of the ways of Yahweh,
for Yahweh's glory is great!
⁷ᶜ Your right hand will save me.
⁸ Yahweh will fulfill that which concerns me.
Your loving kindness, Yahweh, endures forever.
Don't forsake the works of your own hands.

Second Reading: First Corinthians 15: 1-11

¹ Now I declare to you, brothers, the Good News which I preached to you, which also you received, in which you also stand, ² by which also you are saved, if you hold firmly the word which I preached to you—unless you believed in vain.

³ For I delivered to you first of all that which I also received: that Christ died for our sins according to the Scriptures, ⁴ that he was buried, that he was raised on the third day

according to the Scriptures, ⁵ and that he appeared to Cephas, then to the twelve. ⁶ Then he appeared to over five hundred brothers at once, most of whom remain until now, but some have also fallen asleep. ⁷ Then he appeared to James, then to all the apostles, ⁸ and last of all, as to the child born at the wrong time, he appeared to me also. ⁹ For I am the least of the apostles, who is not worthy to be called an apostle, because I persecuted the assembly of God. ¹⁰ But by the grace of God I am what I am. His grace which was given to me was not futile, but I worked more than all of them; yet not I, but the grace of God which was with me. ¹¹ Whether then it is I or they, so we preach, and so you believed.

Gospel: Luke 5: 1-11

¹ Now while the multitude pressed on him and heard the word of God, he was standing by the lake of Gennesaret. ² He saw two boats standing by the lake, but the fishermen had gone out of them and were washing their nets. ³ He entered into one of the boats, which was Simon's, and asked him to put out a little from the land. He sat down and taught the multitudes from the boat.
⁴ When he had finished speaking, he said to Simon, "Put out into the deep and let down your nets for a catch."
⁵ Simon answered him, "Master, we worked all night and caught nothing; but at your word I will let down the net." ⁶ When they had done this, they caught a great multitude of fish, and their net was breaking. ⁷ They beckoned to their partners in the other boat, that they should come and help them. They came and filled both boats, so that they began to sink. ⁸ But Simon Peter, when he saw it, fell down at Jesus' knees, saying, "Depart from me, for I am a sinful man, Lord." ⁹ For he was amazed, and all who were with him, at the catch of fish which they had caught; ¹⁰ and so also were James and John, sons of Zebedee, who were partners with Simon.
Jesus said to Simon, "Don't be afraid. From now on you will be catching people alive."
¹¹ When they had brought their boats to land, they left everything, and followed him.

1. Invite the Holy Spirit into this reading, asking the Author of Scripture to speak to you through His Word
2. Read today's passage as many times as you need, take your time
3. Write down (below) what the Lord is saying to you today
4. Live with this Word in your heart through the day

Monday, February 10, 2025
Saint Scholastica, Virgin

First Reading: Genesis 1: 1-19

¹ In the beginning, God created the heavens and the earth. ² The earth was formless and empty. Darkness was on the surface of the deep and God's Spirit was hovering over the surface of the waters.
³ God said, "Let there be light," and there was light. ⁴ God saw the light, and saw that it was good. God divided the light from the darkness. ⁵ God called the light "day", and the darkness he called "night". There was evening and there was morning, the first day.
⁶ God said, "Let there be an expanse in the middle of the waters, and let it divide the waters from the waters." ⁷ God made the expanse, and divided the waters which were under the expanse from the waters which were above the expanse; and it was so. ⁸ God called the expanse "sky". There was evening and there was morning, a second day.
⁹ God said, "Let the waters under the sky be gathered together to one place, and let the dry land appear;" and it was so. ¹⁰ God called the dry land "earth", and the gathering together of the waters he called "seas". God saw that it was good. ¹¹ God said, "Let the earth yield grass, herbs yielding seeds, and fruit trees bearing fruit after their kind, with their seeds in it, on the earth;" and it was so. ¹² The earth yielded grass, herbs yielding seed after their kind, and trees bearing fruit, with their seeds in it, after their kind; and God saw that it was good. ¹³ There was evening and there was morning, a third day.
¹⁴ God said, "Let there be lights in the expanse of the sky to divide the day from the night; and let them be for signs to mark seasons, days, and years; ¹⁵ and let them be for lights in the expanse of the sky to give light on the earth;" and it was so. ¹⁶ God made the two great lights: the greater light to rule the day, and the lesser light to rule the night. He also made the stars. ¹⁷ God set them in the expanse of the sky to give light to the earth, ¹⁸ and to rule over the day and over the night, and to divide the light from the darkness. God saw that it was good. ¹⁹ There was evening and there was morning, a fourth day.

Responsorial Psalm: Psalms 104: 1-2a, 5-6, 10 and 12, 24 and 35c

¹ Bless Yahweh, my soul.
Yahweh, my God, you are very great.
You are clothed with honor and majesty.
²ᵃ He covers himself with light as with a garment.
⁵ He laid the foundations of the earth,
that it should not be moved forever.
⁶ You covered it with the deep as with a cloak.
The waters stood above the mountains.

¹⁰ He sends springs into the valleys.
They run among the mountains.
¹² The birds of the sky nest by them.
They sing among the branches.
²⁴ Yahweh, how many are your works!
In wisdom, you have made them all.
The earth is full of your riches.
³⁵ᶜ Bless Yahweh, my soul.
Praise Yah!

Gospel: Mark 6: 53-56

⁵³ When they had crossed over, they came to land at Gennesaret and moored to the shore. ⁵⁴ When they had come out of the boat, immediately the people recognized him, ⁵⁵ and ran around that whole region, and began to bring those who were sick on their mats to where they heard he was. ⁵⁶ Wherever he entered—into villages, or into cities, or into the country—they laid the sick in the marketplaces and begged him that they might just touch the fringe⸸ of his garment; and as many as touched him were made well.

1. Invite the Holy Spirit into this reading, asking the Author of Scripture to speak to you through His Word
2. Read today's passage as many times as you need, take your time
3. Write down (below) what the Lord is saying to you today
4. Live with this Word in your heart through the day

_____

_____

Tuesday, February 11, 2025
Our Lady of Lourdes

First Reading: Genesis 1: 20 – 2: 4a

²⁰ God said, "Let the waters abound with living creatures, and let birds fly above the earth in the open expanse of the sky." ²¹ God created the large sea creatures and every living creature that moves, with which the waters swarmed, after their kind, and every winged bird after its kind. God saw that it was good. ²² God blessed them, saying, "Be fruitful, and

multiply, and fill the waters in the seas, and let birds multiply on the earth." 23 There was evening and there was morning, a fifth day.

24 God said, "Let the earth produce living creatures after their kind, livestock, creeping things, and animals of the earth after their kind;" and it was so. 25 God made the animals of the earth after their kind, and the livestock after their kind, and everything that creeps on the ground after its kind. God saw that it was good.

26 God said, "Let's make man in our image, after our likeness. Let them have dominion over the fish of the sea, and over the birds of the sky, and over the livestock, and over all the earth, and over every creeping thing that creeps on the earth." 27 God created man in his own image. In God's image he created him; male and female he created them. 28 God blessed them. God said to them, "Be fruitful, multiply, fill the earth, and subdue it. Have dominion over the fish of the sea, over the birds of the sky, and over every living thing that moves on the earth." 29 God said, "Behold,‡ I have given you every herb yielding seed, which is on the surface of all the earth, and every tree, which bears fruit yielding seed. It will be your food. 30 To every animal of the earth, and to every bird of the sky, and to everything that creeps on the earth, in which there is life, I have given every green herb for food;" and it was so.

31 God saw everything that he had made, and, behold, it was very good. There was evening and there was morning, a sixth day.

1 The heavens, the earth, and all their vast array were finished. 2 On the seventh day God finished his work which he had done; and he rested on the seventh day from all his work which he had done. 3 God blessed the seventh day, and made it holy, because he rested in it from all his work of creation which he had done.

4a This is the history of the generations of the heavens and of the earth when they were created,

Responsorial Psalm: Psalms 8: 4-9

4 what is man, that you think of him?
What is the son of man, that you care for him?
5 For you have made him a little lower than the angels,‡
and crowned him with glory and honor.
6 You make him ruler over the works of your hands.
You have put all things under his feet:
7 All sheep and cattle,
yes, and the animals of the field,
8 the birds of the sky, the fish of the sea,
and whatever passes through the paths of the seas.
9 Yahweh, our Lord,
how majestic is your name in all the earth!

Gospel: Mark 7: 1-13

¹ Then the Pharisees and some of the scribes gathered together to him, having come from Jerusalem. ² Now when they saw some of his disciples eating bread with defiled, that is unwashed, hands, they found fault. ³ (For the Pharisees and all the Jews don't eat unless they wash their hands and forearms, holding to the tradition of the elders. ⁴ They don't eat when they come from the marketplace unless they bathe themselves, and there are many other things which they have received to hold to: washings of cups, pitchers, bronze vessels, and couches.) ⁵ The Pharisees and the scribes asked him, "Why don't your disciples walk according to the tradition of the elders, but eat their bread with unwashed hands?"
⁶ He answered them, "Well did Isaiah prophesy of you hypocrites, as it is written,
'This people honors me with their lips,
but their heart is far from me.
⁷ They worship me in vain,
teaching as doctrines the commandments of men.'
⁸ "For you set aside the commandment of God, and hold tightly to the tradition of men—the washing of pitchers and cups, and you do many other such things." ⁹ He said to them, "Full well do you reject the commandment of God, that you may keep your tradition. ¹⁰ For Moses said, 'Honor your father and your mother;' and, 'He who speaks evil of father or mother, let him be put to death.' ¹¹ But you say, 'If a man tells his father or his mother, "Whatever profit you might have received from me is Corban,"' that is to say, given to God, ¹² "then you no longer allow him to do anything for his father or his mother, ¹³ making void the word of God by your tradition which you have handed down. You do many things like this."

1. Invite the Holy Spirit into this reading, asking the Author of Scripture to speak to you through His Word
2. Read today's passage as many times as you need, take your time
3. Write down (below) what the Lord is saying to you today
4. Live with this Word in your heart through the day

_____
_____

Wednesday, February 12, 2025

First Reading: Genesis 2: 4b-9, 15-17

⁴ᵇ in the day that Yahweh⁺ God made the earth and the heavens. ⁵ No plant of the field was yet in the earth, and no herb of the field had yet sprung up; for Yahweh God had not caused it to rain on the earth. There was not a man to till the ground, ⁶ but a mist went up from the earth, and watered the whole surface of the ground. ⁷ Yahweh God formed man from the dust of the ground, and breathed into his nostrils the breath of life; and man became a living soul. ⁸ Yahweh God planted a garden eastward, in Eden, and there he put the man whom he had formed. ⁹ Out of the ground Yahweh God made every tree to grow that is pleasant to the sight, and good for food, including the tree of life in the middle of the garden and the tree of the knowledge of good and evil.

¹⁵ Yahweh God took the man, and put him into the garden of Eden to cultivate and keep it. ¹⁶ Yahweh God commanded the man, saying, "You may freely eat of every tree of the garden; ¹⁷ but you shall not eat of the tree of the knowledge of good and evil; for in the day that you eat of it, you will surely die."

Responsorial Psalm: Psalms 104: 1-2a, 27-28, 29bc-30

¹ Bless Yahweh, my soul.
Yahweh, my God, you are very great.
You are clothed with honor and majesty.
²ᵃ He covers himself with light as with a garment.
²⁷ These all wait for you,
that you may give them their food in due season.
²⁸ You give to them; they gather.
You open your hand; they are satisfied with good.
²⁹ᵇᶜ You take away their breath; they die and return to the dust.
³⁰ You send out your Spirit and they are created.
You renew the face of the ground.

Gospel: Mark 7: 14-23

¹⁴ He called all the multitude to himself and said to them, "Hear me, all of you, and understand. ¹⁵ There is nothing from outside of the man that going into him can defile him; but the things which proceed out of the man are those that defile the man. ¹⁶ If anyone has ears to hear, let him hear!"⁺
¹⁷ When he had entered into a house away from the multitude, his disciples asked him about the parable. ¹⁸ He said to them, "Are you also without understanding? Don't you perceive that whatever goes into the man from outside can't defile him, ¹⁹ because it doesn't go into his heart, but into his stomach, then into the latrine, making all foods clean?"§ ²⁰ He said, "That which proceeds out of the man, that defiles the man. ²¹ For from within, out of

the hearts of men, proceed evil thoughts, adulteries, sexual sins, murders, thefts, 22 covetings, wickedness, deceit, lustful desires, an evil eye, blasphemy, pride, and foolishness. 23 All these evil things come from within and defile the man."

1. Invite the Holy Spirit into this reading, asking the Author of Scripture to speak to you through His Word
2. Read today's passage as many times as you need, take your time
3. Write down (below) what the Lord is saying to you today
4. Live with this Word in your heart through the day

_____

_____

Thursday, February 13, 2025

First Reading: Genesis 2: 18-25

18 Yahweh God said, "It is not good for the man to be alone. I will make him a helper comparable to§ him." 19 Out of the ground Yahweh God formed every animal of the field, and every bird of the sky, and brought them to the man to see what he would call them. Whatever the man called every living creature became its name. 20 The man gave names to all livestock, and to the birds of the sky, and to every animal of the field; but for man there was not found a helper comparable to him. 21 Yahweh God caused the man to fall into a deep sleep. As the man slept, he took one of his ribs, and closed up the flesh in its place. 22 Yahweh God made a woman from the rib which he had taken from the man, and brought her to the man. 23 The man said, "This is now bone of my bones, and flesh of my flesh. She will be called 'woman,' because she was taken out of Man." 24 Therefore a man will leave his father and his mother, and will join with his wife, and they will be one flesh. 25 The man and his wife were both naked, and they were not ashamed.

Responsorial Psalm: Psalms 128: 1-5

1 Blessed is everyone who fears Yahweh,
who walks in his ways.
2 For you will eat the labor of your hands.
You will be happy, and it will be well with you.
3 Your wife will be as a fruitful vine in the innermost parts of your house,
your children like olive shoots around your table.

⁴ Behold, this is how the man who fears Yahweh is blessed.
⁵ May Yahweh bless you out of Zion,
and may you see the good of Jerusalem all the days of your life.

Gospel: Mark 7: 24-30

²⁴ From there he arose and went away into the borders of Tyre and Sidon. He entered into a house and didn't want anyone to know it, but he couldn't escape notice. ²⁵ For a woman whose little daughter had an unclean spirit, having heard of him, came and fell down at his feet. ²⁶ Now the woman was a Greek, a Syrophoenician by race. She begged him that he would cast the demon out of her daughter. ²⁷ But Jesus said to her, "Let the children be filled first, for it is not appropriate to take the children's bread and throw it to the dogs."
²⁸ But she answered him, "Yes, Lord. Yet even the dogs under the table eat the children's crumbs."
²⁹ He said to her, "For this saying, go your way. The demon has gone out of your daughter."
³⁰ She went away to her house, and found the child having been laid on the bed, with the demon gone out.

1. Invite the Holy Spirit into this reading, asking the Author of Scripture to speak to you through His Word
2. Read today's passage as many times as you need, take your time
3. Write down (below) what the Lord is saying to you today
4. Live with this Word in your heart through the day

_____

_____

Friday, February 14, 2025
Saints Cyril, Monk, and Methodius, Bishop

First Reading: Genesis 3: 1-8

¹ Now the serpent was more subtle than any animal of the field which Yahweh God had made. He said to the woman, "Has God really said, 'You shall not eat of any tree of the garden'?"
² The woman said to the serpent, "We may eat fruit from the trees of the garden, ³ but not the fruit of the tree which is in the middle of the garden. God has said, 'You shall not eat of it. You shall not touch it, lest you die.'"

⁴ The serpent said to the woman, "You won't really die, ⁵ for God knows that in the day you eat it, your eyes will be opened, and you will be like God, knowing good and evil." ⁶ When the woman saw that the tree was good for food, and that it was a delight to the eyes, and that the tree was to be desired to make one wise, she took some of its fruit, and ate. Then she gave some to her husband with her, and he ate it, too. ⁷ Their eyes were opened, and they both knew that they were naked. They sewed fig leaves together, and made coverings for themselves. ⁸ They heard Yahweh God's voice walking in the garden in the cool of the day, and the man and his wife hid themselves from the presence of Yahweh God among the trees of the garden.

Responsorial Psalm: Psalms 32: 1-2, 5- 7

¹ Blessed is he whose disobedience is forgiven,
whose sin is covered.
² Blessed is the man to whom Yahweh doesn't impute iniquity,
in whose spirit there is no deceit.
⁵ I acknowledged my sin to you.
I didn't hide my iniquity.
I said, I will confess my transgressions to Yahweh,
and you forgave the iniquity of my sin.
⁶ For this, let everyone who is godly pray to you in a time when you may be found.
Surely when the great waters overflow, they shall not reach to him.
⁷ You are my hiding place.
You will preserve me from trouble.
You will surround me with songs of deliverance.

Gospel: Mark 7: 31-37

³¹ Again he departed from the borders of Tyre and Sidon, and came to the sea of Galilee through the middle of the region of Decapolis. ³² They brought to him one who was deaf and had an impediment in his speech. They begged him to lay his hand on him. ³³ He took him aside from the multitude privately and put his fingers into his ears; and he spat and touched his tongue. ³⁴ Looking up to heaven, he sighed, and said to him, "Ephphatha!" that is, "Be opened!" ³⁵ Immediately his ears were opened, and the impediment of his tongue was released, and he spoke clearly. ³⁶ He commanded them that they should tell no one, but the more he commanded them, so much the more widely they proclaimed it. ³⁷ They were astonished beyond measure, saying, "He has done all things well. He makes even the deaf hear and the mute speak!"

1. Invite the Holy Spirit into this reading, asking the Author of Scripture to speak to you through His Word
2. Read today's passage as many times as you need, take your time
3. Write down (below) what the Lord is saying to you today
4. Live with this Word in your heart through the day

_____

_____

Saturday, February 15, 2025

First Reading: Genesis 3: 9-24

⁹ Yahweh God called to the man, and said to him, "Where are you?"
¹⁰ The man said, "I heard your voice in the garden, and I was afraid, because I was naked; so I hid myself."
¹¹ God said, "Who told you that you were naked? Have you eaten from the tree that I commanded you not to eat from?"
¹² The man said, "The woman whom you gave to be with me, she gave me fruit from the tree, and I ate it."
¹³ Yahweh God said to the woman, "What have you done?"
The woman said, "The serpent deceived me, and I ate."
¹⁴ Yahweh God said to the serpent,
"Because you have done this,
you are cursed above all livestock,
and above every animal of the field.
You shall go on your belly
and you shall eat dust all the days of your life.
¹⁵ I will put hostility between you and the woman,
and between your offspring and her offspring.
He will bruise your head,
and you will bruise his heel."
¹⁶ To the woman he said,
"I will greatly multiply your pain in childbirth.
You will bear children in pain.
Your desire will be for your husband,
and he will rule over you."
¹⁷ To Adam he said,

"Because you have listened to your wife's voice,
and have eaten from the tree,
about which I commanded you, saying, 'You shall not eat of it,'
the ground is cursed for your sake.
You will eat from it with much labor all the days of your life.
¹⁸ It will yield thorns and thistles to you;
and you will eat the herb of the field.
¹⁹ You will eat bread by the sweat of your face until you return to the ground,
for you were taken out of it.
For you are dust,
and you shall return to dust."
²⁰ The man called his wife Eve because she would be the mother of all the living. ²¹ Yahweh God made garments of animal skins for Adam and for his wife, and clothed them.
²² Yahweh God said, "Behold, the man has become like one of us, knowing good and evil. Now, lest he reach out his hand, and also take of the tree of life, and eat, and live forever—" ²³ Therefore Yahweh God sent him out from the garden of Eden, to till the ground from which he was taken. ²⁴ So he drove out the man; and he placed cherubim‡ at the east of the garden of Eden, and a flaming sword which turned every way, to guard the way to the tree of life.

Responsorial Psalm: Psalms 90: 2-6, 12-13

² Before the mountains were born,
before you had formed the earth and the world,
even from everlasting to everlasting, you are God.
³ You turn man to destruction, saying,
"Return, you children of men."
⁴ For a thousand years in your sight are just like yesterday when it is past,
like a watch in the night.
⁵ You sweep them away as they sleep.
In the morning they sprout like new grass.
⁶ In the morning it sprouts and springs up.
By evening, it is withered and dry.
¹² So teach us to count our days,
that we may gain a heart of wisdom.
¹³ Relent, Yahweh!§
How long?
Have compassion on your servants!

Gospel: Mark 8: 1-10

¹ In those days, when there was a very great multitude, and they had nothing to eat, Jesus called his disciples to himself and said to them, ² "I have compassion on the multitude, because they have stayed with me now three days and have nothing to eat. ³ If I send them away fasting to their home, they will faint on the way, for some of them have come a long way."
⁴ His disciples answered him, "From where could one satisfy these people with bread here in a deserted place?"
⁵ He asked them, "How many loaves do you have?"
They said, "Seven."
⁶ He commanded the multitude to sit down on the ground, and he took the seven loaves. Having given thanks, he broke them and gave them to his disciples to serve, and they served the multitude. ⁷ They also had a few small fish. Having blessed them, he said to serve these also. ⁸ They ate and were filled. They took up seven baskets of broken pieces that were left over. ⁹ Those who had eaten were about four thousand. Then he sent them away.
¹⁰ Immediately he entered into the boat with his disciples and came into the region of Dalmanutha.

1. Invite the Holy Spirit into this reading, asking the Author of Scripture to speak to you through His Word
2. Read today's passage as many times as you need, take your time
3. Write down (below) what the Lord is saying to you today
4. Live with this Word in your heart through the day

Sunday, February 16, 2025
SIXTH SUNDAY IN ORDINARY TIME

First Reading: Jeremiah 17: 5-8

⁵ Yahweh says:
"Cursed is the man who trusts in man,
relies on strength of flesh,
and whose heart departs from Yahweh.
⁶ For he will be like a bush in the desert,

and will not see when good comes,
but will inhabit the parched places in the wilderness,
an uninhabited salt land.
⁷ "Blessed is the man who trusts in Yahweh,
and whose confidence is in Yahweh.
⁸ For he will be as a tree planted by the waters,
who spreads out its roots by the river,
and will not fear when heat comes,
but its leaf will be green,
and will not be concerned in the year of drought.
It won't cease from yielding fruit.

Responsorial Psalm: Psalms 1: 1-4 and 6

¹ Blessed is the man who doesn't walk in the counsel of the wicked,
nor stand on the path of sinners,
nor sit in the seat of scoffers;
² but his delight is in Yahweh's⁺ law.
On his law he meditates day and night.
³ He will be like a tree planted by the streams of water,
that produces its fruit in its season,
whose leaf also does not wither.
Whatever he does shall prosper.
⁴ The wicked are not so,
but are like the chaff which the wind drives away.
⁶ For Yahweh knows the way of the righteous,
but the way of the wicked shall perish.

Second Reading: First Corinthians 15: 12, 16-20

¹² Now if Christ is preached, that he has been raised from the dead, how do some among you say that there is no resurrection of the dead?
¹⁶ For if the dead aren't raised, neither has Christ been raised. ¹⁷ If Christ has not been raised, your faith is vain; you are still in your sins. ¹⁸ Then they also who are fallen asleep in Christ have perished. ¹⁹ If we have only hoped in Christ in this life, we are of all men most pitiable.
²⁰ But now Christ has been raised from the dead. He became the first fruit of those who are asleep.

Gospel: Luke 6: 17, 20-26

¹⁷ He came down with them and stood on a level place, with a crowd of his disciples and a great number of the people from all Judea and Jerusalem and the sea coast of Tyre and Sidon, who came to hear him and to be healed of their diseases,
²⁰ He lifted up his eyes to his disciples, and said:
"Blessed are you who are poor,
for God's Kingdom is yours.
²¹ Blessed are you who hunger now,
for you will be filled.
Blessed are you who weep now,
for you will laugh.
²² Blessed are you when men hate you, and when they exclude and mock you, and throw out your name as evil, for the Son of Man's sake.
²³ Rejoice in that day and leap for joy, for behold, your reward is great in heaven, for their fathers did the same thing to the prophets.
²⁴ "But woe to you who are rich!
For you have received your consolation.
²⁵ Woe to you, you who are full now,
for you will be hungry.
Woe to you who laugh now,
for you will mourn and weep.
²⁶ Woe,‡ when‡ men speak well of you,
for their fathers did the same thing to the false prophets.

1. Invite the Holy Spirit into this reading, asking the Author of Scripture to speak to you through His Word
2. Read today's passage as many times as you need, take your time
3. Write down (below) what the Lord is saying to you today
4. Live with this Word in your heart through the day

_____

_____

Monday, February 17, 2025
The Seven Holy Founders of the Servite Order

First Reading: Genesis 4: 1-15, 25

¹ The man knew⁺ Eve his wife. She conceived,⁺ and gave birth to Cain, and said, "I have gotten a man with Yahweh's help." ² Again she gave birth, to Cain's brother Abel. Abel was a keeper of sheep, but Cain was a tiller of the ground. ³ As time passed, Cain brought an offering to Yahweh from the fruit of the ground. ⁴ Abel also brought some of the firstborn of his flock and of its fat. Yahweh respected Abel and his offering, ⁵ but he didn't respect Cain and his offering. Cain was very angry, and the expression on his face fell. ⁶ Yahweh said to Cain, "Why are you angry? Why has the expression of your face fallen? ⁷ If you do well, won't it be lifted up? If you don't do well, sin crouches at the door. Its desire is for you, but you are to rule over it." ⁸ Cain said to Abel, his brother, "Let's go into the field." While they were in the field, Cain rose up against Abel, his brother, and killed him.

⁹ Yahweh said to Cain, "Where is Abel, your brother?"

He said, "I don't know. Am I my brother's keeper?"

¹⁰ Yahweh said, "What have you done? The voice of your brother's blood cries to me from the ground. ¹¹ Now you are cursed because of the ground, which has opened its mouth to receive your brother's blood from your hand. ¹² From now on, when you till the ground, it won't yield its strength to you. You will be a fugitive and a wanderer in the earth."

¹³ Cain said to Yahweh, "My punishment is greater than I can bear. ¹⁴ Behold, you have driven me out today from the surface of the ground. I will be hidden from your face, and I will be a fugitive and a wanderer in the earth. Whoever finds me will kill me."

¹⁵ Yahweh said to him, "Therefore whoever slays Cain, vengeance will be taken on him sevenfold." Yahweh appointed a sign for Cain, so that anyone finding him would not strike him.

²⁵ Adam knew his wife again. She gave birth to a son, and named him Seth, saying, "for God has given me another child instead of Abel, for Cain killed him."

Responsorial Psalm: Psalms 50: 1 and 8, 16bc-17, 20-21

¹ The Mighty One, God, Yahweh, speaks,
and calls the earth from sunrise to sunset.
⁸ I don't rebuke you for your sacrifices.
Your burnt offerings are continually before me.
¹⁶ᵇᶜ "What right do you have to declare my statutes,
that you have taken my covenant on your lips,
¹⁷ since you hate instruction,
and throw my words behind you?
²⁰ You sit and speak against your brother.
You slander your own mother's son.
²¹ You have done these things, and I kept silent.
You thought that I was just like you.
I will rebuke you, and accuse you in front of your eyes.

Gospel: Mark 8: 11-13

¹¹ The Pharisees came out and began to question him, seeking from him a sign from heaven and testing him. ¹² He sighed deeply in his spirit and said, "Why does this generation⸱ seek a sign? Most certainly I tell you, no sign will be given to this generation."
¹³ He left them, and again entering into the boat, departed to the other side

1. Invite the Holy Spirit into this reading, asking the Author of Scripture to speak to you through His Word
2. Read today's passage as many times as you need, take your time
3. Write down (below) what the Lord is saying to you today
4. Live with this Word in your heart through the day

Tuesday, February 18, 2025

First Reading: Genesis 6: 5-8; 7: 1-5, 10

⁵ Yahweh saw that the wickedness of man was great in the earth, and that every imagination of the thoughts of man's heart was continually only evil. ⁶ Yahweh was sorry that he had made man on the earth, and it grieved him in his heart. ⁷ Yahweh said, "I will destroy man whom I have created from the surface of the ground—man, along with animals, creeping things, and birds of the sky—for I am sorry that I have made them." ⁸ But Noah found favor in Yahweh's eyes.
¹ Yahweh said to Noah, "Come with all of your household into the ship, for I have seen your righteousness before me in this generation. ² You shall take seven pairs of every clean animal with you, the male and his female. Of the animals that are not clean, take two, the male and his female. ³ Also of the birds of the sky, seven and seven, male and female, to keep seed alive on the surface of all the earth. ⁴ In seven days, I will cause it to rain on the earth for forty days and forty nights. I will destroy every living thing that I have made from the surface of the ground."
⁵ Noah did everything that Yahweh commanded him.
¹⁰ After the seven days, the floodwaters came on the earth.

Responsorial Psalm: Psalms 29: 1-4 and 9c-10

¹ Ascribe to Yahweh, you sons of the mighty,
ascribe to Yahweh glory and strength.
² Ascribe to Yahweh the glory due to his name.
Worship Yahweh in holy array.
³ Yahweh's voice is on the waters.
The God of glory thunders, even Yahweh on many waters.
⁴ Yahweh's voice is powerful.
Yahweh's voice is full of majesty.
9c In his temple everything says, "Glory!"
¹⁰ Yahweh sat enthroned at the Flood.
Yes, Yahweh sits as King forever.

Gospel: Mark 8: 14-21

¹⁴ They forgot to take bread; and they didn't have more than one loaf in the boat with them. ¹⁵ He warned them, saying, "Take heed: beware of the yeast of the Pharisees and the yeast of Herod."
¹⁶ They reasoned with one another, saying, "It's because we have no bread."
¹⁷ Jesus, perceiving it, said to them, "Why do you reason that it's because you have no bread? Don't you perceive yet or understand? Is your heart still hardened? ¹⁸ Having eyes, don't you see? Having ears, don't you hear? Don't you remember? ¹⁹ When I broke the five loaves among the five thousand, how many baskets full of broken pieces did you take up?"
They told him, "Twelve."
²⁰ "When the seven loaves fed the four thousand, how many baskets full of broken pieces did you take up?"
They told him, "Seven."
²¹ He asked them, "Don't you understand yet?"

1. Invite the Holy Spirit into this reading, asking the Author of Scripture to speak to you through His Word
2. Read today's passage as many times as you need, take your time
3. Write down (below) what the Lord is saying to you today
4. Live with this Word in your heart through the day

Wednesday, February 19, 2025

First Reading: Genesis 8: 6-13, 20-22

⁶ At the end of forty days, Noah opened the window of the ship which he had made, ⁷ and he sent out a raven. It went back and forth, until the waters were dried up from the earth. ⁸ He himself sent out a dove to see if the waters were abated from the surface of the ground, ⁹ but the dove found no place to rest her foot, and she returned into the ship to him, for the waters were on the surface of the whole earth. He put out his hand, and took her, and brought her to him into the ship. ¹⁰ He waited yet another seven days; and again he sent the dove out of the ship. ¹¹ The dove came back to him at evening and, behold, in her mouth was a freshly plucked olive leaf. So Noah knew that the waters were abated from the earth. ¹² He waited yet another seven days, and sent out the dove; and she didn't return to him any more.
¹³ In the six hundred first year, in the first month, the first day of the month, the waters were dried up from the earth. Noah removed the covering of the ship, and looked. He saw that the surface of the ground was dry.
²⁰ Noah built an altar to Yahweh, and took of every clean animal, and of every clean bird, and offered burnt offerings on the altar. ²¹ Yahweh smelled the pleasant aroma. Yahweh said in his heart, "I will not again curse the ground any more for man's sake because the imagination of man's heart is evil from his youth. I will never again strike every living thing, as I have done. ²² While the earth remains, seed time and harvest, and cold and heat, and summer and winter, and day and night will not cease."

Responsorial Psalm: Psalms 116: 12-15, 18-19

¹² What will I give to Yahweh for all his benefits toward me?
¹³ I will take the cup of salvation, and call on Yahweh's name.
¹⁴ I will pay my vows to Yahweh,
yes, in the presence of all his people.
¹⁵ Precious in Yahweh's sight is the death of his saints.
¹⁸ I will pay my vows to Yahweh,
yes, in the presence of all his people,
¹⁹ in the courts of Yahweh's house,
in the middle of you, Jerusalem.
Praise Yah!

Gospel: Mark 8: 22-26

22 He came to Bethsaida. They brought a blind man to him and begged him to touch him. 23 He took hold of the blind man by the hand, and brought him out of the village. When he had spat on his eyes, and laid his hands on him, he asked him if he saw anything.
24 He looked up, and said, "I see men, but I see them like walking trees."
25 Then again he laid his hands on his eyes. He looked intently, and was restored, and saw everyone clearly. 26 He sent him away to his house, saying, "Don't enter into the village, nor tell anyone in the village."

1. Invite the Holy Spirit into this reading, asking the Author of Scripture to speak to you through His Word
2. Read today's passage as many times as you need, take your time
3. Write down (below) what the Lord is saying to you today
4. Live with this Word in your heart through the day

Thursday, February 20, 2025

First Reading: Genesis 9: 1-13

1 God blessed Noah and his sons, and said to them, "Be fruitful, multiply, and replenish the earth. 2 The fear of you and the dread of you will be on every animal of the earth, and on every bird of the sky. Everything that moves along the ground, and all the fish of the sea, are delivered into your hand. 3 Every moving thing that lives will be food for you. As I gave you the green herb, I have given everything to you. 4 But flesh with its life, that is, its blood, you shall not eat. 5 I will surely require accounting for your life's blood. At the hand of every animal I will require it. At the hand of man, even at the hand of every man's brother, I will require the life of man. 6 Whoever sheds man's blood, his blood will be shed by man, for God made man in his own image. 7 Be fruitful and multiply. Increase abundantly in the earth, and multiply in it."
8 God spoke to Noah and to his sons with him, saying, 9 "As for me, behold, I establish my covenant with you, and with your offspring after you, 10 and with every living creature that is with you: the birds, the livestock, and every animal of the earth with you, of all that go out of the ship, even every animal of the earth. 11 I will establish my covenant with you: All flesh will not be cut off any more by the waters of the flood. There will never again be a flood to destroy the earth." 12 God said, "This is the token of the covenant which I make between me and you and every living creature that is with you, for perpetual

generations: ¹³ I set my rainbow in the cloud, and it will be a sign of a covenant between me and the earth.

Responsorial Psalm: Psalms 102: 16-23

¹⁶ For Yahweh has built up Zion.
He has appeared in his glory.
¹⁷ He has responded to the prayer of the destitute,
and has not despised their prayer.
¹⁸ This will be written for the generation to come.
A people which will be created will praise Yah,
¹⁹ for he has looked down from the height of his sanctuary.
From heaven, Yahweh saw the earth,
²⁰ to hear the groans of the prisoner,
to free those who are condemned to death,
²¹ that men may declare Yahweh's name in Zion,
and his praise in Jerusalem,
²² when the peoples are gathered together,
the kingdoms, to serve Yahweh.
²³ He weakened my strength along the course.
He shortened my days.

Gospel: Mark 8: 27-33

²⁷ Jesus went out, with his disciples, into the villages of Caesarea Philippi. On the way he asked his disciples, "Who do men say that I am?"
²⁸ They told him, "John the Baptizer, and others say Elijah, but others, one of the prophets."
²⁹ He said to them, "But who do you say that I am?"
Peter answered, "You are the Christ."
³⁰ He commanded them that they should tell no one about him. ³¹ He began to teach them that the Son of Man must suffer many things, and be rejected by the elders, the chief priests, and the scribes, and be killed, and after three days rise again. ³² He spoke to them openly. Peter took him and began to rebuke him. ³³ But he, turning around and seeing his disciples, rebuked Peter, and said, "Get behind me, Satan! For you have in mind not the things of God, but the things of men."

1. Invite the Holy Spirit into this reading, asking the Author of Scripture to speak to you through His Word
2. Read today's passage as many times as you need, take your time
3. Write down (below) what the Lord is saying to you today

4. Live with this Word in your heart through the day

Friday, February 21, 2025

First Reading: Genesis 11: 1-9

¹ The whole earth was of one language and of one speech. ² As they traveled east, they found a plain in the land of Shinar, and they lived there. ³ They said to one another, "Come, let's make bricks, and burn them thoroughly." They had brick for stone, and they used tar for mortar. ⁴ They said, "Come, let's build ourselves a city, and a tower whose top reaches to the sky, and let's make a name for ourselves, lest we be scattered abroad on the surface of the whole earth."
⁵ Yahweh came down to see the city and the tower, which the children of men built. ⁶ Yahweh said, "Behold, they are one people, and they all have one language, and this is what they begin to do. Now nothing will be withheld from them, which they intend to do. ⁷ Come, let's go down, and there confuse their language, that they may not understand one another's speech." ⁸ So Yahweh scattered them abroad from there on the surface of all the earth. They stopped building the city. ⁹ Therefore its name was called Babel, because there Yahweh confused the language of all the earth. From there, Yahweh scattered them abroad on the surface of all the earth.

Responsorial Psalm: Psalms 33: 10-15

¹⁰ Yahweh brings the counsel of the nations to nothing.
He makes the thoughts of the peoples to be of no effect.
¹¹ The counsel of Yahweh stands fast forever,
the thoughts of his heart to all generations.
¹² Blessed is the nation whose God is Yahweh,
the people whom he has chosen for his own inheritance.
¹³ Yahweh looks from heaven.
He sees all the sons of men.
¹⁴ From the place of his habitation he looks out on all the inhabitants of the earth,
¹⁵ he who fashions all of their hearts;
and he considers all of their works.

Gospel: Mark 8: 34 – 9:1

34 He called the multitude to himself with his disciples and said to them, "Whoever wants to come after me, let him deny himself, and take up his cross, and follow me. 35 For whoever wants to save his life will lose it; and whoever will lose his life for my sake and the sake of the Good News will save it. 36 For what does it profit a man to gain the whole world and forfeit his life? 37 For what will a man give in exchange for his life? 38 For whoever will be ashamed of me and of my words in this adulterous and sinful generation, the Son of Man also will be ashamed of him when he comes in his Father's glory with the holy angels." 1 He said to them, "Most certainly I tell you, there are some standing here who will in no way taste death until they see God's Kingdom come with power."

1. Invite the Holy Spirit into this reading, asking the Author of Scripture to speak to you through His Word
2. Read today's passage as many times as you need, take your time
3. Write down (below) what the Lord is saying to you today
4. Live with this Word in your heart through the day

_____

_____

Saturday, February 22, 2025
The Chair of Saint Peter the Apostle

First Reading: First Peter 5: 1-4

¹ Therefore I exhort the elders among you, as a fellow elder and a witness of the sufferings of Christ, and who will also share in the glory that will be revealed: ² shepherd the flock of God which is among you, exercising the oversight, not under compulsion, but voluntarily; not for dishonest gain, but willingly; ³ not as lording it over those entrusted to you, but making yourselves examples to the flock. ⁴ When the chief Shepherd is revealed, you will receive the crown of glory that doesn't fade away.

Responsorial Psalm: Psalms 23: 1-3a, 4, 5, 6

¹ Yahweh is my shepherd;
I shall lack nothing.
² He makes me lie down in green pastures.

He leads me beside still waters.
³ᵃ He restores my soul.
⁴ Even though I walk through the valley of the shadow of death,
I will fear no evil, for you are with me.
Your rod and your staff,
they comfort me.
⁵ You prepare a table before me
in the presence of my enemies.
You anoint my head with oil.
My cup runs over.
⁶ Surely goodness and loving kindness shall follow me all the days of my life,
and I will dwell in Yahweh's house forever.

Gospel: Matthew 16: 13-19

¹³ Now when Jesus came into the parts of Caesarea Philippi, he asked his disciples, saying, "Who do men say that I, the Son of Man, am?"
¹⁴ They said, "Some say John the Baptizer, some, Elijah, and others, Jeremiah or one of the prophets."
¹⁵ He said to them, "But who do you say that I am?"
¹⁶ Simon Peter answered, "You are the Christ, the Son of the living God."
¹⁷ Jesus answered him, "Blessed are you, Simon Bar Jonah, for flesh and blood has not revealed this to you, but my Father who is in heaven. ¹⁸ I also tell you that you are Peter,‡ and on this rock ‡ I will build my assembly, and the gates of Hades§ will not prevail against it. ¹⁹ I will give to you the keys of the Kingdom of Heaven, and whatever you bind on earth will have been bound in heaven; and whatever you release on earth will have been released in heaven."

1. Invite the Holy Spirit into this reading, asking the Author of Scripture to speak to you through His Word
2. Read today's passage as many times as you need, take your time
3. Write down (below) what the Lord is saying to you today
4. Live with this Word in your heart through the day

_____

_____

Sunday, February 23, 2025

SEVENTH SUNDAY IN ORDINARY TIME

First Reading: First Samuel 26: 2, 7-9, 12-13, 22-23

2 Then Saul arose and went down to the wilderness of Ziph, having three thousand chosen men of Israel with him, to seek David in the wilderness of Ziph.
7 So David and Abishai came to the people by night; and, behold, Saul lay sleeping within the place of the wagons, with his spear stuck in the ground at his head; and Abner and the people lay around him. 8 Then Abishai said to David, "God has delivered up your enemy into your hand today. Now therefore please let me strike him with the spear to the earth at one stroke, and I will not strike him the second time."
9 David said to Abishai, "Don't destroy him, for who can stretch out his hand against Yahweh's anointed, and be guiltless?"
12 So David took the spear and the jar of water from Saul's head, and they went away. No man saw it, or knew it, nor did any awake; for they were all asleep, because a deep sleep from Yahweh had fallen on them. 13 Then David went over to the other side, and stood on the top of the mountain far away, a great space being between them;
22 David answered, "Behold the spear, O king! Let one of the young men come over and get it. 23 Yahweh will render to every man his righteousness and his faithfulness; because Yahweh delivered you into my hand today, and I wouldn't stretch out my hand against Yahweh's anointed.

Responsorial Psalm: Psalms 103: 1-4, 8, 10, 12-13

1 Praise Yahweh, my soul!
All that is within me, praise his holy name!
2 Praise Yahweh, my soul,
and don't forget all his benefits,
3 who forgives all your sins,
who heals all your diseases,
4 who redeems your life from destruction,
who crowns you with loving kindness and tender mercies,
8 Yahweh is merciful and gracious,
slow to anger, and abundant in loving kindness.
10 He has not dealt with us according to our sins,
nor repaid us for our iniquities.
12 As far as the east is from the west,
so far has he removed our transgressions from us.
13 Like a father has compassion on his children,
so Yahweh has compassion on those who fear him.

Second Reading: First Corinthians 15: 45-49

45 So also it is written, "The first man Adam became a living soul." ∗ The last Adam became a life-giving spirit. 46 However, that which is spiritual isn't first, but that which is natural, then that which is spiritual. 47 The first man is of the earth, made of dust. The second man is the Lord from heaven. 48 As is the one made of dust, such are those who are also made of dust; and as is the heavenly, such are they also that are heavenly. 49 As we have borne the image of those made of dust, let's± also bear the image of the heavenly.

Gospel: Luke 6: 27-38

27 "But I tell you who hear: love your enemies, do good to those who hate you, 28 bless those who curse you, and pray for those who mistreat you. 29 To him who strikes you on the cheek, offer also the other; and from him who takes away your cloak, don't withhold your coat also. 30 Give to everyone who asks you, and don't ask him who takes away your goods to give them back again.
31 "As you would like people to do to you, do exactly so to them.
32 "If you love those who love you, what credit is that to you? For even sinners love those who love them. 33 If you do good to those who do good to you, what credit is that to you? For even sinners do the same. 34 If you lend to those from whom you hope to receive, what credit is that to you? Even sinners lend to sinners, to receive back as much. 35 But love your enemies, and do good, and lend, expecting nothing back; and your reward will be great, and you will be children of the Most High; for he is kind toward the unthankful and evil.
36 "Therefore be merciful,
even as your Father is also merciful.
37 Don't judge,
and you won't be judged.
Don't condemn,
and you won't be condemned.
Set free,
and you will be set free.
38 "Give, and it will be given to you: good measure, pressed down, shaken together, and running over, will be given to you.§ For with the same measure you measure it will be measured back to you."

1. Invite the Holy Spirit into this reading, asking the Author of Scripture to speak to you through His Word
2. Read today's passage as many times as you need, take your time
3. Write down (below) what the Lord is saying to you today
4. Live with this Word in your heart through the day

Monday, February 24, 2025

First Reading: Sirach 1: 1-10

¹ All wisdom comes from the Lord,
and is with him forever.
² Who can count the sand of the seas,
the drops of rain,
and the days of eternity?
³ Who will search out the height of the sky,
the breadth of the earth, the deep,
and wisdom?
⁴ Wisdom has been created before all things,
and the understanding of prudence from everlasting. 5 ‡
⁶ To whom has the root of wisdom been revealed?
Who has known her shrewd counsels? 7 ‡
⁸ There is one wise, greatly to be feared,
sitting upon his throne: the Lord.
⁹ He created her.
He saw and measured her.
He poured her out upon all his works.
¹⁰ She is with all flesh according to his gift.
He gave her freely to those who love him.

Responsorial Psalm: Psalms 93: 1-2, 5

¹ Yahweh reigns!
He is clothed with majesty!
Yahweh is armed with strength.
The world also is established.
It can't be moved.
² Your throne is established from long ago.
You are from everlasting.
⁵ Your statutes stand firm.

Holiness adorns your house,
Yahweh, forever more.

Gospel: Mark 9: 14-29

14 Coming to the disciples, he saw a great multitude around them, and scribes questioning them. 15 Immediately all the multitude, when they saw him, were greatly amazed, and running to him, greeted him. 16 He asked the scribes, "What are you asking them?"
17 One of the multitude answered, "Teacher, I brought to you my son, who has a mute spirit; 18 and wherever it seizes him, it throws him down; and he foams at the mouth, grinds his teeth, and becomes rigid. I asked your disciples to cast it out, and they weren't able."
19 He answered him, "Unbelieving generation, how long shall I be with you? How long shall I bear with you? Bring him to me."
20 They brought him to him, and when he saw him, immediately the spirit convulsed him and he fell on the ground, wallowing and foaming at the mouth.
21 He asked his father, "How long has it been since this has been happening to him?"
He said, "From childhood. 22 Often it has cast him both into the fire and into the water to destroy him. But if you can do anything, have compassion on us and help us."
23 Jesus said to him, "If you can believe, all things are possible to him who believes."
24 Immediately the father of the child cried out with tears, "I believe. Help my unbelief!"
25 When Jesus saw that a multitude came running together, he rebuked the unclean spirit, saying to him, "You mute and deaf spirit, I command you, come out of him, and never enter him again!"
26 After crying out and convulsing him greatly, it came out of him. The boy became like one dead, so much that most of them said, "He is dead." 27 But Jesus took him by the hand and raised him up; and he arose.
28 When he had come into the house, his disciples asked him privately, "Why couldn't we cast it out?"
29 He said to them, "This kind can come out by nothing but by prayer and fasting."

1. Invite the Holy Spirit into this reading, asking the Author of Scripture to speak to you through His Word
2. Read today's passage as many times as you need, take your time
3. Write down (below) what the Lord is saying to you today
4. Live with this Word in your heart through the day

Tuesday, February 25, 2025

First Reading: Sirach 2: 1-11

¹ My son, if you come to serve the Lord,
prepare your soul for temptation.
² Set your heart aright, constantly endure,
and don't make haste in time of calamity.
³ Cling to him, and don't depart,
that you may be increased at your latter end.
⁴ Accept whatever is brought upon you,
and be patient when you suffer humiliation.
⁵ For gold is tried in the fire,
and acceptable men in the furnace of humiliation.
⁶ Put your trust in him, and he will help you.
Make your ways straight, and set your hope on him.
⁷ All you who fear the Lord, wait for his mercy.
Don't turn aside, lest you fall.
⁸ All you who fear the Lord, put your trust in him,
and your reward will not fail.
⁹ All you who fear the Lord, hope for good things,
and for eternal gladness and mercy.
¹⁰ Look at the generations of old, and see:
Who ever put his trust in the Lord, and was ashamed?
Or who remained in his fear, and was forsaken?
Or who called upon him, and he neglected him?
¹¹ For the Lord is full of compassion and mercy.
He forgives sins and saves in time of affliction.

Responsorial Psalm: Psalms 37: 3-4, 18-19, 27-28, 39-40

³ Trust in Yahweh, and do good.
Dwell in the land, and enjoy safe pasture.
⁴ Also delight yourself in Yahweh,
and he will give you the desires of your heart.
¹⁸ Yahweh knows the days of the perfect.
Their inheritance shall be forever.
¹⁹ They shall not be disappointed in the time of evil.
In the days of famine they shall be satisfied.
²⁷ Depart from evil, and do good.

Live securely forever.
28 For Yahweh loves justice,
and doesn't forsake his saints.
They are preserved forever,
but the children of the wicked shall be cut off.
39 But the salvation of the righteous is from Yahweh.
He is their stronghold in the time of trouble.
40 Yahweh helps them and rescues them.
He rescues them from the wicked and saves them,
because they have taken refuge in him.

Gospel: Mark 9: 30-37

30 They went out from there and passed through Galilee. He didn't want anyone to know it, 31 for he was teaching his disciples, and said to them, "The Son of Man is being handed over to the hands of men, and they will kill him; and when he is killed, on the third day he will rise again."
32 But they didn't understand the saying, and were afraid to ask him.
33 He came to Capernaum, and when he was in the house he asked them, "What were you arguing among yourselves on the way?"
34 But they were silent, for they had disputed with one another on the way about who was the greatest.
35 He sat down and called the twelve; and he said to them, "If any man wants to be first, he shall be last of all, and servant of all." 36 He took a little child and set him in the middle of them. Taking him in his arms, he said to them, 37 "Whoever receives one such little child in my name receives me; and whoever receives me, doesn't receive me, but him who sent me."

1. Invite the Holy Spirit into this reading, asking the Author of Scripture to speak to you through His Word
2. Read today's passage as many times as you need, take your time
3. Write down (below) what the Lord is saying to you today
4. Live with this Word in your heart through the day

_____

_____

Wednesday, February 26, 2025

First Reading: Sirach 4: 11-19

¹¹ Wisdom exalts her sons,
and takes hold of those who seek her.
¹² He who loves her loves life.
Those who seek her early will be filled with gladness.
¹³ He who holds her fast will inherit glory.
Where⸸ he enters, the Lord will bless.
¹⁴ Those who serve her minister to the Holy One.
The Lord loves those who love her.
¹⁵ He who listens to her will judge the nations.
He who heeds her will dwell securely.
¹⁶ If he trusts her, he will inherit her,
and his generations will possess her.
¹⁷ For at the first she will walk with him in crooked ways,
and will bring fear and dread upon him,
and torment him with her discipline,
until she may trust his soul, and try him by her judgments.
¹⁸ Then she will return him again to the straight way,
and will gladden him, and reveal to him her secrets.
¹⁹ If he goes astray, she will forsake him,
and hand him over to his fall.

Responsorial Psalm: Psalms 119: 165, 168, 171, 172, 174, 175

¹⁶⁵ Those who love your law have great peace.
Nothing causes them to stumble.
¹⁶⁸ I have obeyed your precepts and your testimonies,
for all my ways are before you.
¹⁷¹ Let my lips utter praise,
for you teach me your statutes.
¹⁷² Let my tongue sing of your word,
for all your commandments are righteousness.
¹⁷⁴ I have longed for your salvation, Yahweh.
Your law is my delight.
¹⁷⁵ Let my soul live, that I may praise you.
Let your ordinances help me.

Gospel: Mark 9: 38-40

⁳⁸ John said to him, "Teacher, we saw someone who doesn't follow us casting out demons in your name; and we forbade him, because he doesn't follow us." ³⁹ But Jesus said, "Don't forbid him, for there is no one who will do a mighty work in my name and be able quickly to speak evil of me. ⁴⁰ For whoever is not against us is on our side.

1. Invite the Holy Spirit into this reading, asking the Author of Scripture to speak to you through His Word
2. Read today's passage as many times as you need, take your time
3. Write down (below) what the Lord is saying to you today
4. Live with this Word in your heart through the day

Thursday, February 27, 2025
Saint Gregory of Narek, Abbot and Doctor of the Church

First Reading: Sirach 5: 1-8

¹ Don't set your heart upon your goods.
Don't say, "They are sufficient for me."
² Don't follow your own mind and your strength
to walk in the desires of your heart.
³ Don't say, "Who will have dominion over me?"
for the Lord will surely take vengeance on you.
⁴ Don't say, "I sinned, and what happened to me?"
for the Lord is patient.
⁵ Don't be so confident of atonement
that you add sin upon sins.
⁶ Don't say, "His compassion is great.
He will be pacified for the multitude of my sins,"
for mercy and wrath are with him,
and his indignation will rest on sinners.
⁷ Don't wait to turn to the Lord.
Don't put off from day to day;
for suddenly the wrath of the Lord will come on you,

and you will perish in the time of vengeance.
⁸ Don't set your heart upon unrighteous gains,
for you will profit nothing in the day of calamity.

Responsorial Psalm: Psalms 1: 1-4 and 6

¹ Blessed is the man who doesn't walk in the counsel of the wicked,
nor stand on the path of sinners,
nor sit in the seat of scoffers;
² but his delight is in Yahweh's⁺ law.
On his law he meditates day and night.
³ He will be like a tree planted by the streams of water,
that produces its fruit in its season,
whose leaf also does not wither.
Whatever he does shall prosper.
⁴ The wicked are not so,
but are like the chaff which the wind drives away.
⁶ For Yahweh knows the way of the righteous,
but the way of the wicked shall perish.

Gospel: Mark 9: 41-50

⁴¹ For whoever will give you a cup of water to drink in my name because you are Christ's, most certainly I tell you, he will in no way lose his reward. ⁴² "Whoever will cause one of these little ones who believe in me to stumble, it would be better for him if he were thrown into the sea with a millstone hung around his neck. ⁴³ If your hand causes you to stumble, cut it off. It is better for you to enter into life maimed, rather than having your two hands to go into Gehenna,⁺ into the unquenchable fire, ⁴⁴ 'where their worm doesn't die, and the fire is not quenched.' ⁺ ⁴⁵ If your foot causes you to stumble, cut it off. It is better for you to enter into life lame, rather than having your two feet to be cast into Gehenna, § into the fire that will never be quenched— ⁴⁶ 'where their worm doesn't die, and the fire is not quenched.' ⁺ ⁴⁷ If your eye causes you to stumble, throw it out. It is better for you to enter into God's Kingdom with one eye, rather than having two eyes to be cast into the Gehenna⁺ of fire, ⁴⁸ 'where their worm doesn't die, and the fire is not quenched.' ⁺ ⁴⁹ For everyone will be salted with fire, and every sacrifice will be seasoned with salt. ⁵⁰ Salt is good, but if the salt has lost its saltiness, with what will you season it? Have salt in yourselves, and be at peace with one another."

1. Invite the Holy Spirit into this reading, asking the Author of Scripture to speak to you through His Word

2. Read today's passage as many times as you need, take your time
3. Write down (below) what the Lord is saying to you today
4. Live with this Word in your heart through the day

_____

_____

Friday, February 28, 2025

First Reading: Sirach 6: 5-17

⁵ Sweet words will multiply a man's friends.
A gracious tongue will multiply courtesies.
⁶ Let those that are at peace with you be many,
but your advisers one of a thousand.
⁷ If you want to gain a friend, get him in a time of testing,
and don't be in a hurry to trust him.
⁸ For there is a friend just for an occasion.
He won't continue in the day of your affliction.
⁹ And there is a friend who turns into an enemy.
He will discover strife to your reproach.
¹⁰ And there is a friend who is a companion at the table,
but he won't continue in the day of your affliction.
¹¹ In your prosperity he will be as yourself,
and will be bold over your servants.
¹² If you are brought low, he will be against you,
and will hide himself from your face.
¹³ Separate yourself from your enemies,
and beware of your friends.
¹⁴ A faithful friend is a strong defense.
He who has found him has found a treasure.
¹⁵ There is nothing that can be taken in exchange for a faithful friend.
His excellency is beyond price.
¹⁶ A faithful friend is a life-saving medicine.
Those who fear the Lord will find him.
¹⁷ He who fears the Lord directs his friendship properly;
for as he is, so is his neighbor also.

Responsorial Psalm: Psalms 119: 12, 16, 18, 27, 34, 35

¹² Blessed are you, Yahweh.
Teach me your statutes.
¹⁶ I will delight myself in your statutes.
I will not forget your word.
¹⁸ Open my eyes,
that I may see wondrous things out of your law.
²⁷ Let me understand the teaching of your precepts!
Then I will meditate on your wondrous works.
³⁴ Give me understanding, and I will keep your law.
Yes, I will obey it with my whole heart.
³⁵ Direct me in the path of your commandments,
for I delight in them.

Gospel: Mark 10: 1-12

¹ He arose from there and came into the borders of Judea and beyond the Jordan. Multitudes came together to him again. As he usually did, he was again teaching them.
² Pharisees came to him testing him, and asked him, "Is it lawful for a man to divorce his wife?"
³ He answered, "What did Moses command you?"
⁴ They said, "Moses allowed a certificate of divorce to be written, and to divorce her."
⁵ But Jesus said to them, "For your hardness of heart, he wrote you this commandment. ⁶ But from the beginning of the creation, God made them male and female. ⁷ For this cause a man will leave his father and mother, and will join to his wife, ⁸ and the two will become one flesh, so that they are no longer two, but one flesh. ⁹ What therefore God has joined together, let no man separate."
¹⁰ In the house, his disciples asked him again about the same matter. ¹¹ He said to them, "Whoever divorces his wife and marries another commits adultery against her. ¹² If a woman herself divorces her husband and marries another, she commits adultery."

1. Invite the Holy Spirit into this reading, asking the Author of Scripture to speak to you through His Word
2. Read today's passage as many times as you need, take your time
3. Write down (below) what the Lord is saying to you today
4. Live with this Word in your heart through the day

_____

_____

Saturday, March 1, 2025

First Reading: Sirach 17: 1-15

¹ The Lord created mankind out of earth,
and turned them back to it again.
² He gave them days by number, and a set time,
and gave them authority over the things that are on it.
³ He endowed them with strength proper to them,
and made them according to his own image.
⁴ He put the fear of man upon all flesh,
and gave him dominion over beasts and birds. 5 ‡
⁶ He gave them counsel, tongue, eyes,
ears, and heart to have understanding.
⁷ He filled them with the knowledge of wisdom,
and showed them good and evil.
⁸ He set his eye upon their hearts,
to show them the majesty of his works. 9 ‡
¹⁰ And they will praise his holy name,
& that they may declare the majesty of his works.
¹¹ He added to them knowledge,
and gave them a law of life for a heritage.
¹² He made an everlasting covenant with them,
and showed them his decrees.
¹³ Their eyes saw the majesty of his glory.
Their ears heard the glory of his voice.
¹⁴ He said to them, "Beware of all unrighteousness."
So he gave them commandment, each man concerning his neighbor.
¹⁵ Their ways are ever before him.
They will not be hidden from his eyes.

Responsorial Psalm: Psalms 103: 13-18

¹³ Like a father has compassion on his children,
so Yahweh has compassion on those who fear him.
¹⁴ For he knows how we are made.
He remembers that we are dust.
¹⁵ As for man, his days are like grass.
As a flower of the field, so he flourishes.
¹⁶ For the wind passes over it, and it is gone.

Its place remembers it no more.
17 But Yahweh's loving kindness is from everlasting to everlasting with those who fear him, his righteousness to children's children,
18 to those who keep his covenant,
to those who remember to obey his precepts.

Gospel: Mark 10: 13-16

13 They were bringing to him little children, that he should touch them, but the disciples rebuked those who were bringing them. 14 But when Jesus saw it, he was moved with indignation and said to them, "Allow the little children to come to me! Don't forbid them, for God's Kingdom belongs to such as these. 15 Most certainly I tell you, whoever will not receive God's Kingdom like a little child, he will in no way enter into it." 16 He took them in his arms and blessed them, laying his hands on them.

1. Invite the Holy Spirit into this reading, asking the Author of Scripture to speak to you through His Word
2. Read today's passage as many times as you need, take your time
3. Write down (below) what the Lord is saying to you today
4. Live with this Word in your heart through the day

_____

_____

Sunday, March 2, 2025
EIGHTH SUNDAY IN ORDINARY TIME

First Reading: Sirach 27: 4-7

4 In the shaking of a sieve, the refuse remains,
so does the filth of man in his thoughts.
5 The furnace tests the potter's vessels;
so the test of a person is in his thoughts.
6 The fruit of a tree discloses its cultivation,
so is the utterance of the thought of a person's heart.
7 Praise no man before you hear his thoughts,
for this is how people are tested.

Responsorial Psalm: Psalms 92: 2-3, 13-15

2 to proclaim your loving kindness in the morning,
and your faithfulness every night,
3 with the ten-stringed lute, with the harp,
and with the melody of the lyre.
13 They are planted in Yahweh's house.
They will flourish in our God's courts.
14 They will still produce fruit in old age.
They will be full of sap and green,
15 to show that Yahweh is upright.
He is my rock,
and there is no unrighteousness in him.

Second Reading: First Corinthians 15: 54-58

54 But when this perishable body will have become imperishable, and this mortal will have put on immortality, then what is written will happen: "Death is swallowed up in victory."*
55 "Death, where is your sting?
Hades,‡ where is your victory?"*
56 The sting of death is sin, and the power of sin is the law. 57 But thanks be to God, who gives us the victory through our Lord Jesus Christ. 58 Therefore, my beloved brothers, be steadfast, immovable, always abounding in the Lord's work, because you know that your labor is not in vain in the Lord.

Gospel: Luke 6: 39-45

39 He spoke a parable to them. "Can the blind guide the blind? Won't they both fall into a pit? 40 A disciple is not above his teacher, but everyone when he is fully trained will be like his teacher. 41 Why do you see the speck of chaff that is in your brother's eye, but don't consider the beam that is in your own eye? 42 Or how can you tell your brother, 'Brother, let me remove the speck of chaff that is in your eye,' when you yourself don't see the beam that is in your own eye? You hypocrite! First remove the beam from your own eye, and then you can see clearly to remove the speck of chaff that is in your brother's eye.
43 "For there is no good tree that produces rotten fruit, nor again a rotten tree that produces good fruit. 44 For each tree is known by its own fruit. For people don't gather figs from thorns, nor do they gather grapes from a bramble bush. 45 The good man out of the good treasure of his heart brings out that which is good, and the evil man out of the evil treasure of his heart brings out that which is evil, for out of the abundance of the heart, his mouth speaks.

1. Invite the Holy Spirit into this reading, asking the Author of Scripture to speak to you through His Word
2. Read today's passage as many times as you need, take your time
3. Write down (below) what the Lord is saying to you today
4. Live with this Word in your heart through the day

_____

_____

Monday, March 3, 2025
Saint Katharine Drexel, Virgin

First Reading: Sirach 17: 20-24

20 Their iniquities are not hidden from him.
All their sins are before the Lord. 21 ‡
22 With him the alms of a man is as a signet.
He will keep a man's kindness as the pupil of the eye.‡
23 Afterwards he will rise up and repay them,
and render their repayment upon their head.
24 However to those who repent he grants a return.
He comforts those who are losing hope.

Responsorial Psalm: Psalms 32: 1-2, 5-7

1 Blessed is he whose disobedience is forgiven,
whose sin is covered.
2 Blessed is the man to whom Yahweh doesn't impute iniquity,
in whose spirit there is no deceit.
5 I acknowledged my sin to you.
I didn't hide my iniquity.
I said, I will confess my transgressions to Yahweh,
and you forgave the iniquity of my sin.
6 For this, let everyone who is godly pray to you in a time when you may be found.
Surely when the great waters overflow, they shall not reach to him.
7 You are my hiding place.
You will preserve me from trouble.

You will surround me with songs of deliverance.

Gospel: Mark 10: 17-27

17 As he was going out into the way, one ran to him, knelt before him, and asked him, "Good Teacher, what shall I do that I may inherit eternal life?"
18 Jesus said to him, "Why do you call me good? No one is good except one—God. 19 You know the commandments: 'Do not murder,' 'Do not commit adultery,' 'Do not steal,' 'Do not give false testimony,' 'Do not defraud,' 'Honor your father and mother.' "*
20 He said to him, "Teacher, I have observed all these things from my youth."
21 Jesus looking at him loved him, and said to him, "One thing you lack. Go, sell whatever you have and give to the poor, and you will have treasure in heaven; and come, follow me, taking up the cross."
22 But his face fell at that saying, and he went away sorrowful, for he was one who had great possessions.
23 Jesus looked around and said to his disciples, "How difficult it is for those who have riches to enter into God's Kingdom!"
24 The disciples were amazed at his words. But Jesus answered again, "Children, how hard it is for those who trust in riches to enter into God's Kingdom! 25 It is easier for a camel to go through a needle's eye than for a rich man to enter into God's Kingdom."
26 They were exceedingly astonished, saying to him, "Then who can be saved?"
27 Jesus, looking at them, said, "With men it is impossible, but not with God, for all things are possible with God."

1. Invite the Holy Spirit into this reading, asking the Author of Scripture to speak to you through His Word
2. Read today's passage as many times as you need, take your time
3. Write down (below) what the Lord is saying to you today
4. Live with this Word in your heart through the day

_____

_____

Tuesday, March 4, 2025
Saint Casimir

First Reading: Sirach 35: 1-12

¹ He who keeps the law multiplies offerings.
He who heeds the commandments sacrifices a peace offering.
² He who returns a kindness offers fine flour.
He who gives alms sacrifices a thank offering.
³ To depart from wickedness pleases the Lord.
To depart from unrighteousness is an atoning sacrifice.
⁴ See that you don't appear in the presence of the Lord empty.
⁵ For all these things are done because of the commandment.
⁶ The offering of the righteous enriches the altar.
The sweet fragrance of it is before the Most High.
⁷ The sacrifice of a righteous man is acceptable.
It won't be forgotten.
⁸ Glorify the Lord with generosity.
Don't reduce the first fruits of your hands.
⁹ In every gift show a cheerful countenance,
And dedicate your tithe with gladness.
¹⁰ Give to the Most High according as he has given.
As your hand has found, give generously.
¹¹ For the Lord repays,
and he will repay you sevenfold.
¹² Don't plan to bribe him with gifts, for he will not receive them.
Don't set your mind on an unrighteous sacrifice,
For the Lord is the judge,
and with him is no respect of persons.

Responsorial Psalm: Psalms 50: 5-8, 14 and 23

⁵ "Gather my saints together to me,
those who have made a covenant with me by sacrifice."
⁶ The heavens shall declare his righteousness,
for God himself is judge.
⁷ "Hear, my people, and I will speak.
Israel, I will testify against you.
I am God, your God.
⁸ I don't rebuke you for your sacrifices.
Your burnt offerings are continually before me.
¹⁴ Offer to God the sacrifice of thanksgiving.
Pay your vows to the Most High.
²³ Whoever offers the sacrifice of thanksgiving glorifies me,
and prepares his way so that I will show God's salvation to him."

Gospel: Mark 10: 28-31

28 Peter began to tell him, "Behold, we have left all and have followed you."
29 Jesus said, "Most certainly I tell you, there is no one who has left house, or brothers, or sisters, or father, or mother, or wife, or children, or land, for my sake, and for the sake of the Good News, 30 but he will receive one hundred times more now in this time: houses, brothers, sisters, mothers, children, and land, with persecutions; and in the age to come eternal life. 31 But many who are first will be last, and the last first."

1. Invite the Holy Spirit into this reading, asking the Author of Scripture to speak to you through His Word
2. Read today's passage as many times as you need, take your time
3. Write down (below) what the Lord is saying to you today
4. Live with this Word in your heart through the day

_____

_____

Wednesday, March 5, 2025
Ash Wednesday

First Reading: Joel 2: 12-18

12 "Yet even now," says Yahweh, "turn to me with all your heart,
and with fasting, and with weeping, and with mourning."
13 Tear your heart and not your garments,
and turn to Yahweh, your God;
for he is gracious and merciful,
slow to anger, and abundant in loving kindness,
and relents from sending calamity.
14 Who knows? He may turn and relent,
and leave a blessing behind him,
even a meal offering and a drink offering to Yahweh, your God.
15 Blow the trumpet in Zion!
Sanctify a fast.
Call a solemn assembly.
16 Gather the people.

Sanctify the assembly.
Assemble the elders.
Gather the children, and those who nurse from breasts.
Let the bridegroom go out of his room,
and the bride out of her chamber.
[17] Let the priests, the ministers of Yahweh, weep between the porch and the altar,
and let them say, "Spare your people, Yahweh,
and don't give your heritage to reproach,
that the nations should rule over them.
Why should they say among the peoples,
'Where is their God?' "
[18] Then Yahweh was jealous for his land,
and had pity on his people.

Responsorial Psalm: Psalms 51: 3-6ab, 12-14 and 17

[3] For I know my transgressions.
My sin is constantly before me.
[4] Against you, and you only, I have sinned,
and done that which is evil in your sight,
so you may be proved right when you speak,
and justified when you judge.
[5] Behold, I was born in iniquity.
My mother conceived me in sin.
[6] Behold, you desire truth in the inward parts.
You teach me wisdom in the inmost place.
[12] Restore to me the joy of your salvation.
Uphold me with a willing spirit.
[13] Then I will teach transgressors your ways.
Sinners will be converted to you.
[14] Deliver me from the guilt of bloodshed, O God, the God of my salvation.
My tongue will sing aloud of your righteousness.
[17] The sacrifices of God are a broken spirit.
O God, you will not despise a broken and contrite heart.

Second Reading: Second Corinthians 5: 20 – 6:2

[20] We are therefore ambassadors on behalf of Christ, as though God were entreating by us: we beg you on behalf of Christ, be reconciled to God. [21] For him who knew no sin he made to be sin on our behalf, so that in him we might become the righteousness of God.

¹ Working together, we entreat also that you do not receive the grace of God in vain. ² For he says,
"At an acceptable time I listened to you.
In a day of salvation I helped you."
Behold, now is the acceptable time. Behold, now is the day of salvation.

Gospel: Matthew 6: 1-6, 16-18

¹ "Be careful that you don't do your charitable giving before men, to be seen by them, or else you have no reward from your Father who is in heaven. ² Therefore, when you do merciful deeds, don't sound a trumpet before yourself, as the hypocrites do in the synagogues and in the streets, that they may get glory from men. Most certainly I tell you, they have received their reward. ³ But when you do merciful deeds, don't let your left hand know what your right hand does, ⁴ so that your merciful deeds may be in secret, then your Father who sees in secret will reward you openly.
⁵ "When you pray, you shall not be as the hypocrites, for they love to stand and pray in the synagogues and in the corners of the streets, that they may be seen by men. Most certainly, I tell you, they have received their reward. ⁶ But you, when you pray, enter into your inner room, and having shut your door, pray to your Father who is in secret; and your Father who sees in secret will reward you openly.
¹⁶ "Moreover when you fast, don't be like the hypocrites, with sad faces. For they disfigure their faces that they may be seen by men to be fasting. Most certainly I tell you, they have received their reward. ¹⁷ But you, when you fast, anoint your head and wash your face, ¹⁸ so that you are not seen by men to be fasting, but by your Father who is in secret; and your Father, who sees in secret, will reward you.

1. Invite the Holy Spirit into this reading, asking the Author of Scripture to speak to you through His Word
2. Read today's passage as many times as you need, take your time
3. Write down (below) what the Lord is saying to you today
4. Live with this Word in your heart through the day

Thursday, March 6, 2025

First Reading: Deuteronomy 30: 15-20

¹⁵ Behold, I have set before you today life and prosperity, and death and evil. ¹⁶ For I command you today to love Yahweh your God, to walk in his ways and to keep his commandments, his statutes, and his ordinances, that you may live and multiply, and that Yahweh your God may bless you in the land where you go in to possess it. ¹⁷ But if your heart turns away, and you will not hear, but are drawn away and worship other gods, and serve them, ¹⁸ I declare to you today that you will surely perish. You will not prolong your days in the land where you pass over the Jordan to go in to possess it. ¹⁹ I call heaven and earth to witness against you today that I have set before you life and death, the blessing and the curse. Therefore choose life, that you may live, you and your descendants, ²⁰ to love Yahweh your God, to obey his voice, and to cling to him; for he is your life, and the length of your days, that you may dwell in the land which Yahweh swore to your fathers, to Abraham, to Isaac, and to Jacob, to give them.

Responsorial Psalm: Psalms 1: 1-4 and 6

¹ Blessed is the man who doesn't walk in the counsel of the wicked,
nor stand on the path of sinners,
nor sit in the seat of scoffers;
² but his delight is in Yahweh's± law.
On his law he meditates day and night.
³ He will be like a tree planted by the streams of water,
that produces its fruit in its season,
whose leaf also does not wither.
Whatever he does shall prosper.
⁴ The wicked are not so,
but are like the chaff which the wind drives away.
⁶ For Yahweh knows the way of the righteous,
but the way of the wicked shall perish.

Gospel: Luke 9: 22-25

²² saying, "The Son of Man must suffer many things, and be rejected by the elders, chief priests, and scribes, and be killed, and the third day be raised up."
²³ He said to all, "If anyone desires to come after me, let him deny himself, take up his cross,§ and follow me. ²⁴ For whoever desires to save his life will lose it, but whoever will lose his life for my sake will save it. ²⁵ For what does it profit a man if he gains the whole world, and loses or forfeits his own self?

1. Invite the Holy Spirit into this reading, asking the Author of Scripture to speak to you through His Word
2. Read today's passage as many times as you need, take your time
3. Write down (below) what the Lord is saying to you today
4. Live with this Word in your heart through the day

___

___

Friday, March 7, 2025
Saints Perpetua and Felicity, Martyrs

First Reading: Isaiah 58: 1-9a

¹ "Cry aloud! Don't spare!
Lift up your voice like a trumpet!
Declare to my people their disobedience,
and to the house of Jacob their sins.
² Yet they seek me daily,
and delight to know my ways.
As a nation that did righteousness,
and didn't forsake the ordinance of their God,
they ask of me righteous judgments.
They delight to draw near to God.
³ 'Why have we fasted,' they say, 'and you don't see?
Why have we afflicted our soul, and you don't notice?'
"Behold, in the day of your fast you find pleasure,
and oppress all your laborers.
⁴ Behold, you fast for strife and contention,
and to strike with the fist of wickedness.
You don't fast today so as to make your voice to be heard on high.
⁵ Is this the fast that I have chosen?
A day for a man to humble his soul?
Is it to bow down his head like a reed,
and to spread sackcloth and ashes under himself?
Will you call this a fast,
and an acceptable day to Yahweh?
⁶ "Isn't this the fast that I have chosen:

to release the bonds of wickedness,
to undo the straps of the yoke,
to let the oppressed go free,
and that you break every yoke?
7 Isn't it to distribute your bread to the hungry,
and that you bring the poor who are cast out to your house?
When you see the naked,
that you cover him;
and that you not hide yourself from your own flesh?
8 Then your light will break out as the morning,
and your healing will appear quickly;
then your righteousness shall go before you,
and Yahweh's glory will be your rear guard.
9 Then you will call, and Yahweh will answer.
You will cry for help, and he will say, 'Here I am.'

Responsorial Psalm: Psalms 51: 3-6ab, 18-19

3 For I know my transgressions.
My sin is constantly before me.
4 Against you, and you only, I have sinned,
and done that which is evil in your sight,
so you may be proved right when you speak,
and justified when you judge.
5 Behold, I was born in iniquity.
My mother conceived me in sin.
6a Behold, you desire truth in the inward parts.
18 Do well in your good pleasure to Zion.
Build the walls of Jerusalem.
19 Then you will delight in the sacrifices of righteousness,
in burnt offerings and in whole burnt offerings.
Then they will offer bulls on your altar.

Gospel: Matthew 9: 14-15

14 Then John's disciples came to him, saying, "Why do we and the Pharisees fast often, but your disciples don't fast?"
15 Jesus said to them, "Can the friends of the bridegroom mourn as long as the bridegroom is with them? But the days will come when the bridegroom will be taken away from them, and then they will fast.

1. Invite the Holy Spirit into this reading, asking the Author of Scripture to speak to you through His Word
2. Read today's passage as many times as you need, take your time
3. Write down (below) what the Lord is saying to you today
4. Live with this Word in your heart through the day

_____

_____

Saturday, March 8, 2025
Saint John of God, Religious

First Reading: Isaiah 58: 9b-14

9b"If you take away from among you the yoke,
finger pointing,
and speaking wickedly;
10 and if you pour out your soul to the hungry,
and satisfy the afflicted soul,
then your light will rise in darkness,
and your obscurity will be as the noonday;
11 and Yahweh will guide you continually,
satisfy your soul in dry places,
and make your bones strong.
You will be like a watered garden,
and like a spring of water
whose waters don't fail.
12 Those who will be of you will build the old waste places.
You will raise up the foundations of many generations.
You will be called Repairer of the Breach,
Restorer of Paths with Dwellings.
13 "If you turn away your foot from the Sabbath,
from doing your pleasure on my holy day,
and call the Sabbath a delight,
and the holy of Yahweh honorable,
and honor it,
not doing your own ways,

nor finding your own pleasure,
nor speaking your own words,
¹⁴ then you will delight yourself in Yahweh,
and I will make you to ride on the high places of the earth,
and I will feed you with the heritage of Jacob your father;"
for Yahweh's mouth has spoken it.

Responsorial Psalm: Psalms 86: 1-6

¹ Hear, Yahweh, and answer me,
for I am poor and needy.
² Preserve my soul, for I am godly.
You, my God, save your servant who trusts in you.
³ Be merciful to me, Lord,
for I call to you all day long.
⁴ Bring joy to the soul of your servant,
for to you, Lord, do I lift up my soul.
⁵ For you, Lord, are good, and ready to forgive,
abundant in loving kindness to all those who call on you.
⁶ Hear, Yahweh, my prayer.
Listen to the voice of my petitions.

Gospel: Luke 5: 27-32

²⁷ After these things he went out and saw a tax collector named Levi sitting at the tax office, and said to him, "Follow me!"
²⁸ He left everything, and rose up and followed him. ²⁹ Levi made a great feast for him in his house. There was a great crowd of tax collectors and others who were reclining with them. ³⁰ Their scribes and the Pharisees murmured against his disciples, saying, "Why do you eat and drink with the tax collectors and sinners?"
³¹ Jesus answered them, "Those who are healthy have no need for a physician, but those who are sick do. ³² I have not come to call the righteous, but sinners, to repentance."

1. Invite the Holy Spirit into this reading, asking the Author of Scripture to speak to you through His Word
2. Read today's passage as many times as you need, take your time
3. Write down (below) what the Lord is saying to you today
4. Live with this Word in your heart through the day

Sunday, March 9, 2025
FIRST SUNDAY OF LENT

First Reading: Deuteronomy 26: 4-10

⁴ The priest shall take the basket out of your hand, and set it down before Yahweh your God's altar. ⁵ You shall answer and say before Yahweh your God, "My father⁺ was a Syrian ready to perish. He went down into Egypt, and lived there, few in number. There he became a great, mighty, and populous nation. ⁶ The Egyptians mistreated us, afflicted us, and imposed hard labor on us. ⁷ Then we cried to Yahweh, the God of our fathers. Yahweh heard our voice, and saw our affliction, our toil, and our oppression. ⁸ Yahweh brought us out of Egypt with a mighty hand, with an outstretched arm, with great terror, with signs, and with wonders; ⁹ and he has brought us into this place, and has given us this land, a land flowing with milk and honey. ¹⁰ Now, behold, I have brought the first of the fruit of the ground, which you, Yahweh, have given me." You shall set it down before Yahweh your God, and worship before Yahweh your God.

Responsorial Psalm: Psalms 91: 1-2, 10-15

¹ He who dwells in the secret place of the Most High
will rest in the shadow of the Almighty.
² I will say of Yahweh, "He is my refuge and my fortress;
my God, in whom I trust."
¹⁰ no evil shall happen to you,
neither shall any plague come near your dwelling.
¹¹ For he will put his angels in charge of you,
to guard you in all your ways.
¹² They will bear you up in their hands,
so that you won't dash your foot against a stone.
¹³ You will tread on the lion and cobra.
You will trample the young lion and the serpent underfoot.
¹⁴ "Because he has set his love on me, therefore I will deliver him.
I will set him on high, because he has known my name.
¹⁵ He will call on me, and I will answer him.
I will be with him in trouble.

I will deliver him, and honor him.

Second Reading: Romans 10: 8-13

8 But what does it say? "The word is near you, in your mouth and in your heart;"* that is, the word of faith which we preach: 9 that if you will confess with your mouth that Jesus is Lord and believe in your heart that God raised him from the dead, you will be saved. 10 For with the heart one believes resulting in righteousness; and with the mouth confession is made resulting in salvation. 11 For the Scripture says, "Whoever believes in him will not be disappointed."*
12 For there is no distinction between Jew and Greek; for the same Lord is Lord of all, and is rich to all who call on him. 13 For, "Whoever will call on the name of the Lord will be saved."

Gospel: Luke 4: 1-13

1 Jesus, full of the Holy Spirit, returned from the Jordan and was led by the Spirit into the wilderness 2 for forty days, being tempted by the devil. He ate nothing in those days. Afterward, when they were completed, he was hungry.
3 The devil said to him, "If you are the Son of God, command this stone to become bread."
4 Jesus answered him, saying, "It is written, 'Man shall not live by bread alone, but by every word of God.' "*
5 The devil, leading him up on a high mountain, showed him all the kingdoms of the world in a moment of time. 6 The devil said to him, "I will give you all this authority and their glory, for it has been delivered to me, and I give it to whomever I want. 7 If you therefore will worship before me, it will all be yours."
8 Jesus answered him, "Get behind me, Satan! For it is written, 'You shall worship the Lord your God, and you shall serve him only.' "*
9 He led him to Jerusalem and set him on the pinnacle of the temple, and said to him, "If you are the Son of God, cast yourself down from here, 10 for it is written,
'He will put his angels in charge of you, to guard you;'
11 and,
'On their hands they will bear you up,
lest perhaps you dash your foot against a stone.' "*
12 Jesus answering, said to him, "It has been said, 'You shall not tempt the Lord your God.' "*
13 When the devil had completed every temptation, he departed from him until another time.

1. Invite the Holy Spirit into this reading, asking the Author of Scripture to speak to you through His Word
2. Read today's passage as many times as you need, take your time
3. Write down (below) what the Lord is saying to you today
4. Live with this Word in your heart through the day

Monday, March 10, 2025

First Reading: Leviticus 19: 1-2, 11-18

1 Yahweh spoke to Moses, saying, 2 "Speak to all the congregation of the children of Israel, and tell them, 'You shall be holy; for I, Yahweh your God, am holy.
11 " 'You shall not steal.
" 'You shall not lie.
" 'You shall not deceive one another.
12 " 'You shall not swear by my name falsely, and profane the name of your God. I am Yahweh.
13 " 'You shall not oppress your neighbor, nor rob him.
" 'The wages of a hired servant shall not remain with you all night until the morning.
14 " 'You shall not curse the deaf, nor put a stumbling block before the blind; but you shall fear your God. I am Yahweh.
15 " 'You shall do no injustice in judgment. You shall not be partial to the poor, nor show favoritism to the great; but you shall judge your neighbor in righteousness.
16 " 'You shall not go around as a slanderer among your people.
" 'You shall not endanger the life± of your neighbor. I am Yahweh.
17 " 'You shall not hate your brother in your heart. You shall surely rebuke your neighbor, and not bear sin because of him.
18 " 'You shall not take vengeance, nor bear any grudge against the children of your people; but you shall love your neighbor as yourself. I am Yahweh.

Responsorial Psalm: Psalms 19: 8-10

8 Yahweh's precepts are right, rejoicing the heart.
Yahweh's commandment is pure, enlightening the eyes.
9 The fear of Yahweh is clean, enduring forever.

Yahweh's ordinances are true, and righteous altogether.
¹⁰ They are more to be desired than gold, yes, than much fine gold,
sweeter also than honey and the extract of the honeycomb.

Gospel: Matthew 25: 31-46

³¹ "But when the Son of Man comes in his glory, and all the holy angels with him, then he will sit on the throne of his glory. ³² Before him all the nations will be gathered, and he will separate them one from another, as a shepherd separates the sheep from the goats. ³³ He will set the sheep on his right hand, but the goats on the left. ³⁴ Then the King will tell those on his right hand, 'Come, blessed of my Father, inherit the Kingdom prepared for you from the foundation of the world; ³⁵ for I was hungry and you gave me food to eat. I was thirsty and you gave me drink. I was a stranger and you took me in. ³⁶ I was naked and you clothed me. I was sick and you visited me. I was in prison and you came to me.'
³⁷ "Then the righteous will answer him, saying, 'Lord, when did we see you hungry and feed you, or thirsty and give you a drink? ³⁸ When did we see you as a stranger and take you in, or naked and clothe you? ³⁹ When did we see you sick or in prison and come to you?'
⁴⁰ "The King will answer them, 'Most certainly I tell you, because you did it to one of the least of these my brothers,§ you did it to me.' ⁴¹ Then he will say also to those on the left hand, 'Depart from me, you cursed, into the eternal fire which is prepared for the devil and his angels; ⁴² for I was hungry, and you didn't give me food to eat; I was thirsty, and you gave me no drink; ⁴³ I was a stranger, and you didn't take me in; naked, and you didn't clothe me; sick, and in prison, and you didn't visit me.'
⁴⁴ "Then they will also answer, saying, 'Lord, when did we see you hungry, or thirsty, or a stranger, or naked, or sick, or in prison, and didn't help you?'
⁴⁵ "Then he will answer them, saying, 'Most certainly I tell you, because you didn't do it to one of the least of these, you didn't do it to me.' ⁴⁶ These will go away into eternal punishment, but the righteous into eternal life."

1. Invite the Holy Spirit into this reading, asking the Author of Scripture to speak to you through His Word
2. Read today's passage as many times as you need, take your time
3. Write down (below) what the Lord is saying to you today
4. Live with this Word in your heart through the day

Tuesday, March 11, 2025

First Reading: Isaiah 55: 10-11

¹⁰ For as the rain comes down and the snow from the sky,
and doesn't return there, but waters the earth,
and makes it grow and bud,
and gives seed to the sower and bread to the eater;
¹¹ so is my word that goes out of my mouth:
it will not return to me void,
but it will accomplish that which I please,
and it will prosper in the thing I sent it to do.

Responsorial Psalm: Psalms 34: 4-7, 16-19

⁴ I sought Yahweh, and he answered me,
and delivered me from all my fears.
⁵ They looked to him, and were radiant.
Their faces shall never be covered with shame.
⁶ This poor man cried, and Yahweh heard him,
and saved him out of all his troubles.
⁷ Yahweh's angel encamps around those who fear him,
and delivers them.
¹⁶ Yahweh's face is against those who do evil,
to cut off their memory from the earth.
¹⁷ The righteous cry, and Yahweh hears,
and delivers them out of all their troubles.
¹⁸ Yahweh is near to those who have a broken heart,
and saves those who have a crushed spirit.
¹⁹ Many are the afflictions of the righteous,
but Yahweh delivers him out of them all.

Gospel: Matthew 6: 7-15

⁷ In praying, don't use vain repetitions as the Gentiles do; for they think that they will be heard for their much speaking. ⁸ Therefore don't be like them, for your Father knows what things you need before you ask him. ⁹ Pray like this:
" 'Our Father in heaven, may your name be kept holy.
¹⁰ Let your Kingdom come.
Let your will be done on earth as it is in heaven.

¹¹ Give us today our daily bread.
¹² Forgive us our debts,
as we also forgive our debtors.
¹³ Bring us not into temptation,
but deliver us from the evil one.
For yours is the Kingdom, the power, and the glory forever. Amen.'
¹⁴ "For if you forgive men their trespasses, your heavenly Father will also forgive you. ¹⁵ But if you don't forgive men their trespasses, neither will your Father forgive your trespasses.

1. Invite the Holy Spirit into this reading, asking the Author of Scripture to speak to you through His Word
2. Read today's passage as many times as you need, take your time
3. Write down (below) what the Lord is saying to you today
4. Live with this Word in your heart through the day

Wednesday, March 12, 2025

First Reading: Jonah 3: 1-10

¹ Yahweh's word came to Jonah the second time, saying, ² "Arise, go to Nineveh, that great city, and preach to it the message that I give you."
³ So Jonah arose, and went to Nineveh, according to Yahweh's word. Now Nineveh was an exceedingly great city, three days' journey across. ⁴ Jonah began to enter into the city a day's journey, and he cried out, and said, "In forty days, Nineveh will be overthrown!"
⁵ The people of Nineveh believed God; and they proclaimed a fast and put on sackcloth, from their greatest even to their least. ⁶ The news reached the king of Nineveh, and he arose from his throne, took off his royal robe, covered himself with sackcloth, and sat in ashes. ⁷ He made a proclamation and published through Nineveh by the decree of the king and his nobles, saying, "Let neither man nor animal, herd nor flock, taste anything; let them not feed, nor drink water; ⁸ but let them be covered with sackcloth, both man and animal, and let them cry mightily to God. Yes, let them turn everyone from his evil way and from the violence that is in his hands. ⁹ Who knows whether God will not turn and relent, and turn away from his fierce anger, so that we might not perish?"
¹⁰ God saw their works, that they turned from their evil way. God relented of the disaster which he said he would do to them, and he didn't do it.

Responsorial Psalm: Psalms 51: 3-4, 12-13, 18-19

³ For I know my transgressions.
My sin is constantly before me.
⁴ Against you, and you only, I have sinned,
and done that which is evil in your sight,
so you may be proved right when you speak,
and justified when you judge.
¹² Restore to me the joy of your salvation.
Uphold me with a willing spirit.
¹³ Then I will teach transgressors your ways.
Sinners will be converted to you.
¹⁸ Do well in your good pleasure to Zion.
Build the walls of Jerusalem.
¹⁹ Then you will delight in the sacrifices of righteousness,
in burnt offerings and in whole burnt offerings.
Then they will offer bulls on your altar.

Gospel: Luke 11: 29-32

²⁹ When the multitudes were gathering together to him, he began to say, "This is an evil generation. It seeks after a sign. No sign will be given to it but the sign of Jonah the prophet. ³⁰ For even as Jonah became a sign to the Ninevites, so the Son of Man will also be to this generation. ³¹ The Queen of the South will rise up in the judgment with the men of this generation and will condemn them, for she came from the ends of the earth to hear the wisdom of Solomon; and behold, one greater than Solomon is here. ³² The men of Nineveh will stand up in the judgment with this generation, and will condemn it, for they repented at the preaching of Jonah; and behold, one greater than Jonah is here.

1. Invite the Holy Spirit into this reading, asking the Author of Scripture to speak to you through His Word
2. Read today's passage as many times as you need, take your time
3. Write down (below) what the Lord is saying to you today
4. Live with this Word in your heart through the day

_____

_____

Thursday, March 13, 2025

First Reading: Esther: 31-40

³¹ She implored the Lord God of Israel, and said, "O my Lord, you alone are our king. Help me. I am destitute, and have no helper but you, ³² for my danger is near at hand§. ³³ I have heard from my birth in the tribe of my kindred that you, Lord, took Israel out of all the nations, and our fathers out of all their kindred for a perpetual inheritance, and have done for them all that you have said. ³⁴ And now we have sinned before you, and you have delivered us into the hands of our enemies, ³⁵ because we honored their gods. You are righteous, O Lord. ³⁶ But now they have not been content with the bitterness of our slavery, but have laid their hands on the hands of their idols ³⁷ to abolish the decree of your mouth, and utterly to destroy your inheritance, and to stop the mouth of those who praise you, and to extinguish the glory of your house and your altar, ³⁸ and to open the mouth of the Gentiles to speak the‡ praises of vanities, and that a mortal king should be admired forever. ³⁹ O Lord, don't surrender your sceptre to those who don't exist, and don't let them laugh at our fall, but turn their counsel against themselves, and make an example of him who has begun to injure us. ⁴⁰ Remember us, O Lord!

Responsorial Psalm: Psalms 138: 1-3, 7c-8

¹ I will give you thanks with my whole heart.
Before the gods,‡ I will sing praises to you.
² I will bow down toward your holy temple,
and give thanks to your Name for your loving kindness and for your truth;
for you have exalted your Name and your Word above all.
³ In the day that I called, you answered me.
You encouraged me with strength in my soul.
⁷ᶜ Your right hand will save me.
⁸ Yahweh will fulfill that which concerns me.
Your loving kindness, Yahweh, endures forever.
Don't forsake the works of your own hands.

Gospel: Matthew 7: 7-12

⁷ "Ask, and it will be given you. Seek, and you will find. Knock, and it will be opened for you. ⁸ For everyone who asks receives. He who seeks finds. To him who knocks it will be opened. ⁹ Or who is there among you who, if his son asks him for bread, will give him a stone? ¹⁰ Or if he asks for a fish, who will give him a serpent? ¹¹ If you then, being evil, know how to give good gifts to your children, how much more will your Father who is in

heaven give good things to those who ask him! ¹² Therefore, whatever you desire for men to do to you, you shall also do to them; for this is the law and the prophets.

1. Invite the Holy Spirit into this reading, asking the Author of Scripture to speak to you through His Word
2. Read today's passage as many times as you need, take your time
3. Write down (below) what the Lord is saying to you today
4. Live with this Word in your heart through the day

_____

_____

Friday, March 14, 2025

First Reading: Ezekiel 18: 21-28

²¹ "But if the wicked turns from all his sins that he has committed, and keeps all my statutes, and does that which is lawful and right, he shall surely live. He shall not die. ²² None of his transgressions that he has committed will be remembered against him. In his righteousness that he has done, he shall live. ²³ Have I any pleasure in the death of the wicked?" says the Lord Yahweh, "and not rather that he should return from his way, and live?
²⁴ "But when the righteous turns away from his righteousness, and commits iniquity, and does according to all the abominations that the wicked man does, should he live? None of his righteous deeds that he has done will be remembered. In his trespass that he has trespassed, and in his sin that he has sinned, in them he shall die.
²⁵ "Yet you say, 'The way of the Lord is not equal.' Hear now, house of Israel: Is my way not equal? Aren't your ways unequal? ²⁶ When the righteous man turns away from his righteousness, and commits iniquity, and dies in it, then he dies in his iniquity that he has done. ²⁷ Again, when the wicked man turns away from his wickedness that he has committed, and does that which is lawful and right, he will save his soul alive. ²⁸ Because he considers, and turns away from all his transgressions that he has committed, he shall surely live. He shall not die.

Responsorial Psalm: Psalms 130: 1-8

¹ Out of the depths I have cried to you, Yahweh.
² Lord, hear my voice.

Let your ears be attentive to the voice of my petitions.
3 If you, Yah, kept a record of sins,
Lord, who could stand?
4 But there is forgiveness with you,
therefore you are feared.
5 I wait for Yahweh.
My soul waits.
I hope in his word.
6 My soul longs for the Lord more than watchmen long for the morning,
more than watchmen for the morning.
7 Israel, hope in Yahweh,
for there is loving kindness with Yahweh.
Abundant redemption is with him.
8 He will redeem Israel from all their sins.

Gospel: Matthew 5: 20-26

20 For I tell you that unless your righteousness exceeds that of the scribes and Pharisees, there is no way you will enter into the Kingdom of Heaven.
21 "You have heard that it was said to the ancient ones, 'You shall not murder;' and 'Whoever murders will be in danger of the judgment.' 22 But I tell you that everyone who is angry with his brother without a cause will be in danger of the judgment. Whoever says to his brother, 'Raca!' will be in danger of the council. Whoever says, 'You fool!' will be in danger of the fire of Gehenna.
23 "If therefore you are offering your gift at the altar, and there remember that your brother has anything against you, 24 leave your gift there before the altar, and go your way. First be reconciled to your brother, and then come and offer your gift. 25 Agree with your adversary quickly while you are with him on the way; lest perhaps the prosecutor deliver you to the judge, and the judge deliver you to the officer, and you be cast into prison. 26 Most certainly I tell you, you shall by no means get out of there until you have paid the last penny.

1. Invite the Holy Spirit into this reading, asking the Author of Scripture to speak to you through His Word
2. Read today's passage as many times as you need, take your time
3. Write down (below) what the Lord is saying to you today
4. Live with this Word in your heart through the day

_____

_____

Saturday, March 15, 2025

First Reading: Deuteronomy 26: 16-19

16 Today Yahweh your God commands you to do these statutes and ordinances. You shall therefore keep and do them with all your heart and with all your soul. 17 You have declared today that Yahweh is your God, and that you would walk in his ways, keep his statutes, his commandments, and his ordinances, and listen to his voice. 18 Yahweh has declared today that you are a people for his own possession, as he has promised you, and that you should keep all his commandments. 19 He will make you high above all nations that he has made, in praise, in name, and in honor, and that you may be a holy people to Yahweh your God, as he has spoken.

Responsorial Psalm: Psalms 119: 1-2, 4-5, 7-8

1 Blessed are those whose ways are blameless,
who walk according to Yahweh's law.
2 Blessed are those who keep his statutes,
who seek him with their whole heart.
4 You have commanded your precepts,
that we should fully obey them.
5 Oh that my ways were steadfast
to obey your statutes!
7 I will give thanks to you with uprightness of heart,
when I learn your righteous judgments.
8 I will observe your statutes.
Don't utterly forsake me.

Gospel: Matthew 5: 43-48

43 "You have heard that it was said, 'You shall love your neighbor‡ and hate your enemy.'‡ 44 But I tell you, love your enemies, bless those who curse you, do good to those who hate you, and pray for those who mistreat you and persecute you, 45 that you may be children of your Father who is in heaven. For he makes his sun to rise on the evil and the good, and sends rain on the just and the unjust. 46 For if you love those who love you, what reward do you have? Don't even the tax collectors do the same? 47 If you only greet your friends, what more do you do than others? Don't even the tax collectors§ do the same? 48 Therefore you shall be perfect, just as your Father in heaven is perfect.

1. Invite the Holy Spirit into this reading, asking the Author of Scripture to speak to you through His Word
2. Read today's passage as many times as you need, take your time
3. Write down (below) what the Lord is saying to you today
4. Live with this Word in your heart through the day

_____

_____

Sunday, March 16, 2025
SECOND SUNDAY OF LENT

First Reading: Genesis 15: 5-12, 17-18

5 Yahweh brought him outside, and said, "Look now toward the sky, and count the stars, if you are able to count them." He said to Abram, "So your offspring will be." 6 He believed in Yahweh, who credited it to him for righteousness. 7 He said to Abram, "I am Yahweh who brought you out of Ur of the Chaldees, to give you this land to inherit it."
8 He said, "Lord Yahweh, how will I know that I will inherit it?"
9 He said to him, "Bring me a heifer three years old, a female goat three years old, a ram three years old, a turtledove, and a young pigeon." 10 He brought him all these, and divided them in the middle, and laid each half opposite the other; but he didn't divide the birds. 11 The birds of prey came down on the carcasses, and Abram drove them away.
12 When the sun was going down, a deep sleep fell on Abram. Now terror and great darkness fell on him.
17 It came to pass that, when the sun went down, and it was dark, behold, a smoking furnace and a flaming torch passed between these pieces. 18 In that day Yahweh made a covenant with Abram, saying, "I have given this land to your offspring, from the river of Egypt to the great river, the river Euphrates:

Responsorial Psalm: Psalms 27: 1, 7-9, 13-14

1 Yahweh is my light and my salvation.
Whom shall I fear?
Yahweh is the strength of my life.
Of whom shall I be afraid?
7 Hear, Yahweh, when I cry with my voice.
Have mercy also on me, and answer me.

⁸ When you said, "Seek my face,"
my heart said to you, "I will seek your face, Yahweh."
⁹ Don't hide your face from me.
Don't put your servant away in anger.
You have been my help.
Don't abandon me,
neither forsake me, God of my salvation.
¹³ I am still confident of this:
I will see the goodness of Yahweh in the land of the living.
¹⁴ Wait for Yahweh.
Be strong, and let your heart take courage.
Yes, wait for Yahweh.

Second Reading: Philippians 3: 17 – 4: 1

¹⁷ Brothers, be imitators together of me, and note those who walk this way, even as you have us for an example. ¹⁸ For many walk, of whom I told you often, and now tell you even weeping, as the enemies of the cross of Christ, ¹⁹ whose end is destruction, whose god is the belly, and whose glory is in their shame, who think about earthly things. ²⁰ For our citizenship is in heaven, from where we also wait for a Savior, the Lord Jesus Christ, ²¹ who will change the body of our humiliation to be conformed to the body of his glory, according to the working by which he is able even to subject all things to himself.
¹ Therefore, my brothers, beloved and longed for, my joy and crown, stand firm in the Lord in this way, my beloved.

Gospel: Luke 9: 28-36

²⁸ About eight days after these sayings, he took with him Peter, John, and James, and went up onto the mountain to pray. ²⁹ As he was praying, the appearance of his face was altered, and his clothing became white and dazzling. ³⁰ Behold, two men were talking with him, who were Moses and Elijah, ³¹ who appeared in glory and spoke of his departure, which he was about to accomplish at Jerusalem.
³² Now Peter and those who were with him were heavy with sleep, but when they were fully awake, they saw his glory, and the two men who stood with him. ³³ As they were parting from him, Peter said to Jesus, "Master, it is good for us to be here. Let's make three tents: one for you, one for Moses, and one for Elijah," not knowing what he said.
³⁴ While he said these things, a cloud came and overshadowed them, and they were afraid as they entered into the cloud. ³⁵ A voice came out of the cloud, saying, "This is my beloved Son. Listen to him!" ³⁶ When the voice came, Jesus was found alone. They were silent, and told no one in those days any of the things which they had seen.

1. Invite the Holy Spirit into this reading, asking the Author of Scripture to speak to you through His Word
2. Read today's passage as many times as you need, take your time
3. Write down (below) what the Lord is saying to you today
4. Live with this Word in your heart through the day

_____

_____

Monday, March 17, 2025
Saint Patrick, Bishop

First Reading: Daniel 9: 4b-10

4b "Oh, Lord, the great and dreadful God, who keeps covenant and loving kindness with those who love him and keep his commandments, 5 we have sinned, and have dealt perversely, and have done wickedly, and have rebelled, even turning aside from your precepts and from your ordinances. 6 We haven't listened to your servants the prophets, who spoke in your name to our kings, our princes, and our fathers, and to all the people of the land.
7 "Lord, righteousness belongs to you, but to us confusion of face, as it is today; to the men of Judah, and to the inhabitants of Jerusalem, and to all Israel, who are near and who are far off, through all the countries where you have driven them, because of their trespass that they have trespassed against you. 8 Lord, to us belongs confusion of face, to our kings, to our princes, and to our fathers, because we have sinned against you. 9 To the Lord our God belong mercies and forgiveness, for we have rebelled against him. 10 We haven't obeyed Yahweh our God's voice, to walk in his laws, which he set before us by his servants the prophets.

Responsorial Psalm: Psalms 79: 8, 9, 11 and 13

8 Don't hold the iniquities of our forefathers against us.
Let your tender mercies speedily meet us,
for we are in desperate need.
9 Help us, God of our salvation, for the glory of your name.
Deliver us, and forgive our sins, for your name's sake.
11 Let the sighing of the prisoner come before you.

According to the greatness of your power, preserve those who are sentenced to death.
¹³ So we, your people and sheep of your pasture,
will give you thanks forever.
We will praise you forever, to all generations.

Gospel: Luke 6: 36-38

³⁶ "Therefore be merciful,
even as your Father is also merciful.
³⁷ Don't judge,
and you won't be judged.
Don't condemn,
and you won't be condemned.
Set free,
and you will be set free.
³⁸ "Give, and it will be given to you: good measure, pressed down, shaken together, and running over, will be given to you.§ For with the same measure you measure it will be measured back to you."

1. Invite the Holy Spirit into this reading, asking the Author of Scripture to speak to you through His Word
2. Read today's passage as many times as you need, take your time
3. Write down (below) what the Lord is saying to you today
4. Live with this Word in your heart through the day

_____

_____

Tuesday, March 18, 2025
Saint Cyril of Jerusalem, Bishop and Doctor of the Church

First Reading: Isaiah 1: 10, 16-20

¹⁰ Hear Yahweh's word, you rulers of Sodom!
Listen to the law of our God,§ you people of Gomorrah!
¹⁶ Wash yourselves. Make yourself clean.
Put away the evil of your doings from before my eyes.
Cease to do evil.

¹⁷ Learn to do well.
Seek justice.
Relieve the oppressed.
Defend the fatherless.
Plead for the widow."
¹⁸ "Come now, and let's reason together," says Yahweh:
"Though your sins are as scarlet, they shall be as white as snow.
Though they are red like crimson, they shall be as wool.
¹⁹ If you are willing and obedient,
you will eat the good of the land;
²⁰ but if you refuse and rebel, you will be devoured with the sword;
for Yahweh's mouth has spoken it."

Responsorial Psalm: Psalms 50: 8-9, 16bc-17, 21 and 23

⁸ I don't rebuke you for your sacrifices.
Your burnt offerings are continually before me.
⁹ I have no need for a bull from your stall,
nor male goats from your pens.
¹⁶ᵇ "What right do you have to declare my statutes,
that you have taken my covenant on your lips,
¹⁷ since you hate instruction,
and throw my words behind you?
²¹ You have done these things, and I kept silent.
You thought that I was just like you.
I will rebuke you, and accuse you in front of your eyes.
²³ Whoever offers the sacrifice of thanksgiving glorifies me,
and prepares his way so that I will show God's salvation to him."

Gospel: Matthew 23: 1-12

¹ Then Jesus spoke to the multitudes and to his disciples, ² saying, "The scribes and the Pharisees sit on Moses' seat. ³ All things therefore whatever they tell you to observe, observe and do, but don't do their works; for they say, and don't do. ⁴ For they bind heavy burdens that are grievous to be borne, and lay them on men's shoulders; but they themselves will not lift a finger to help them. ⁵ But they do all their works to be seen by men. They make their phylacteries‡ broad and enlarge the fringes‡ of their garments, ⁶ and love the place of honor at feasts, the best seats in the synagogues, ⁷ the salutations in the marketplaces, and to be called 'Rabbi, Rabbi'§ by men. ⁸ But you are not to be called 'Rabbi', for one is your teacher, the Christ, and all of you are brothers. ⁹ Call no man on the

earth your father, for one is your Father, he who is in heaven. ¹⁰ Neither be called masters, for one is your master, the Christ. ¹¹ But he who is greatest among you will be your servant. ¹² Whoever exalts himself will be humbled, and whoever humbles himself will be exalted.

1. Invite the Holy Spirit into this reading, asking the Author of Scripture to speak to you through His Word
2. Read today's passage as many times as you need, take your time
3. Write down (below) what the Lord is saying to you today
4. Live with this Word in your heart through the day

Wednesday, March 19, 2025
SAINT JOSEPH, SPOUSE OF THE BLESSED VIRGIN MARY

First Reading: Second Samuel 7: 4-5a, 12-14a, 16

⁴ That same night, Yahweh's word came to Nathan, saying, ⁵ᵃ "Go and tell my servant David, 'Yahweh says,
¹² When your days are fulfilled and you sleep with your fathers, I will set up your offspring after you, who will proceed out of your body, and I will establish his kingdom. ¹³ He will build a house for my name, and I will establish the throne of his kingdom forever. ¹⁴ᵃ I will be his father, and he will be my son.
¹⁶ Your house and your kingdom will be made sure forever before you. Your throne will be established forever."'

Responsorial Psalm: Psalms 89: 2-5, 27 and 29

² I indeed declare, "Love stands firm forever.
You established the heavens.
Your faithfulness is in them."
³ "I have made a covenant with my chosen one,
I have sworn to David, my servant,
⁴ 'I will establish your offspring forever,
and build up your throne to all generations.'"
⁵ The heavens will praise your wonders, Yahweh,

your faithfulness also in the assembly of the holy ones.
²⁷ I will also appoint him my firstborn,
the highest of the kings of the earth.
²⁹ I will also make his offspring endure forever,
and his throne as the days of heaven.

Second Reading: Romans 4: 13, 16-18, 22

¹³ For the promise to Abraham and to his offspring that he would be heir of the world wasn't through the law, but through the righteousness of faith.
¹⁶ For this cause it is of faith, that it may be according to grace, to the end that the promise may be sure to all the offspring, not to that only which is of the law, but to that also which is of the faith of Abraham, who is the father of us all. ¹⁷ As it is written, "I have made you a father of many nations." This is in the presence of him whom he believed: God, who gives life to the dead, and calls the things that are not, as though they were. ¹⁸ Against hope, Abraham in hope believed, to the end that he might become a father of many nations, according to that which had been spoken, "So will your offspring be." ²² Therefore it also was "credited to him for righteousness."

Gospel: Matthew 1: 16, 18-21, 24

¹⁶ Jacob became the father of Joseph, the husband of Mary, from whom was born Jesus, who is called Christ.
¹⁸ Now the birth of Jesus Christ was like this: After his mother, Mary, was engaged to Joseph, before they came together, she was found pregnant by the Holy Spirit. ¹⁹ Joseph, her husband, being a righteous man, and not willing to make her a public example, intended to put her away secretly. ²⁰ But when he thought about these things, behold, an angel of the Lord appeared to him in a dream, saying, "Joseph, son of David, don't be afraid to take to yourself Mary as your wife, for that which is conceived in her is of the Holy Spirit. ²¹ She shall give birth to a son. You shall name him Jesus, for it is he who shall save his people from their sins."
²⁴ Joseph arose from his sleep, and did as the angel of the Lord commanded him, and took his wife to himself; ²⁵ and didn't know her sexually until she had given birth to her firstborn son. He named him Jesus.

1. Invite the Holy Spirit into this reading, asking the Author of Scripture to speak to you through His Word
2. Read today's passage as many times as you need, take your time
3. Write down (below) what the Lord is saying to you today
4. Live with this Word in your heart through the day

Thursday, March 20, 2025

First Reading: Jeremiah 17: 5-10

⁵ Yahweh says:
"Cursed is the man who trusts in man,
relies on strength of flesh,
and whose heart departs from Yahweh.
⁶ For he will be like a bush in the desert,
and will not see when good comes,
but will inhabit the parched places in the wilderness,
an uninhabited salt land.
⁷ "Blessed is the man who trusts in Yahweh,
and whose confidence is in Yahweh.
⁸ For he will be as a tree planted by the waters,
who spreads out its roots by the river,
and will not fear when heat comes,
but its leaf will be green,
and will not be concerned in the year of drought.
It won't cease from yielding fruit.
⁹ The heart is deceitful above all things
and it is exceedingly corrupt.
Who can know it?
¹⁰ "I, Yahweh, search the mind.
I try the heart,
even to give every man according to his ways,
according to the fruit of his doings."

Responsorial Psalm: Psalms 1: 1-4 and 6

¹ Blessed is the man who doesn't walk in the counsel of the wicked,
nor stand on the path of sinners,
nor sit in the seat of scoffers;
² but his delight is in Yahweh's law.

On his law he meditates day and night.
³ He will be like a tree planted by the streams of water,
that produces its fruit in its season,
whose leaf also does not wither.
Whatever he does shall prosper.
⁴ The wicked are not so,
but are like the chaff which the wind drives away.
⁶ For Yahweh knows the way of the righteous,
but the way of the wicked shall perish.

Gospel: Luke 16: 19-31

¹⁹ "Now there was a certain rich man, and he was clothed in purple and fine linen, living in luxury every day. ²⁰ A certain beggar, named Lazarus, was taken to his gate, full of sores, ²¹ and desiring to be fed with the crumbs that fell from the rich man's table. Yes, even the dogs came and licked his sores. ²² The beggar died, and he was carried away by the angels to Abraham's bosom. The rich man also died and was buried. ²³ In Hades, he lifted up his eyes, being in torment, and saw Abraham far off, and Lazarus at his bosom. ²⁴ He cried and said, 'Father Abraham, have mercy on me, and send Lazarus, that he may dip the tip of his finger in water and cool my tongue! For I am in anguish in this flame.'

²⁵ "But Abraham said, 'Son, remember that you, in your lifetime, received your good things, and Lazarus, in the same way, bad things. But here he is now comforted and you are in anguish. ²⁶ Besides all this, between us and you there is a great gulf fixed, that those who want to pass from here to you are not able, and that no one may cross over from there to us.'

²⁷ "He said, 'I ask you therefore, father, that you would send him to my father's house— ²⁸ for I have five brothers—that he may testify to them, so they won't also come into this place of torment.'

²⁹ "But Abraham said to him, 'They have Moses and the prophets. Let them listen to them.'
³⁰ "He said, 'No, father Abraham, but if one goes to them from the dead, they will repent.'
³¹ "He said to him, 'If they don't listen to Moses and the prophets, neither will they be persuaded if one rises from the dead.' "

1. Invite the Holy Spirit into this reading, asking the Author of Scripture to speak to you through His Word
2. Read today's passage as many times as you need, take your time
3. Write down (below) what the Lord is saying to you today
4. Live with this Word in your heart through the day

Friday, March 21, 2025

First Reading: Genesis 37: 3-4, 12-13a, 17b-28

3 Now Israel loved Joseph more than all his children, because he was the son of his old age, and he made him a tunic of many colors. 4 His brothers saw that their father loved him more than all his brothers, and they hated him, and couldn't speak peaceably to him.
12 His brothers went to feed their father's flock in Shechem. 13a Israel said to Joseph, "Aren't your brothers feeding the flock in Shechem? Come, and I will send you to them."
17b Joseph went after his brothers, and found them in Dothan. 18 They saw him afar off, and before he came near to them, they conspired against him to kill him. 19 They said to one another, "Behold, this dreamer comes. 20 Come now therefore, and let's kill him, and cast him into one of the pits, and we will say, 'An evil animal has devoured him.' We will see what will become of his dreams."
21 Reuben heard it, and delivered him out of their hand, and said, "Let's not take his life." 22 Reuben said to them, "Shed no blood. Throw him into this pit that is in the wilderness, but lay no hand on him"—that he might deliver him out of their hand, to restore him to his father. 23 When Joseph came to his brothers, they stripped Joseph of his tunic, the tunic of many colors that was on him; 24 and they took him, and threw him into the pit. The pit was empty. There was no water in it.
25 They sat down to eat bread, and they lifted up their eyes and looked, and saw a caravan of Ishmaelites was coming from Gilead, with their camels bearing spices and balm and myrrh, going to carry it down to Egypt. 26 Judah said to his brothers, "What profit is it if we kill our brother and conceal his blood? 27 Come, and let's sell him to the Ishmaelites, and not let our hand be on him; for he is our brother, our flesh." His brothers listened to him. 28 Midianites who were merchants passed by, and they drew and lifted up Joseph out of the pit, and sold Joseph to the Ishmaelites for twenty pieces of silver. The merchants brought Joseph into Egypt.

Responsorial Psalm: Psalms 105: 16-21

16 He called for a famine on the land.
He destroyed the food supplies.
17 He sent a man before them.
Joseph was sold for a slave.

¹⁸ They bruised his feet with shackles.
His neck was locked in irons,
¹⁹ until the time that his word happened,
and Yahweh's word proved him true.
²⁰ The king sent and freed him,
even the ruler of peoples, and let him go free.
²¹ He made him lord of his house,
and ruler of all of his possessions,

Gospel: Matthew 21: 33-43, 45-46

³³ "Hear another parable. There was a man who was a master of a household who planted a vineyard, set a hedge about it, dug a wine press in it, built a tower, leased it out to farmers, and went into another country. ³⁴ When the season for the fruit came near, he sent his servants to the farmers to receive his fruit. ³⁵ The farmers took his servants, beat one, killed another, and stoned another. ³⁶ Again, he sent other servants more than the first; and they treated them the same way. ³⁷ But afterward he sent to them his son, saying, 'They will respect my son.' ³⁸ But the farmers, when they saw the son, said among themselves, 'This is the heir. Come, let's kill him and seize his inheritance.' ³⁹ So they took him and threw him out of the vineyard, then killed him. ⁴⁰ When therefore the lord of the vineyard comes, what will he do to those farmers?"
⁴¹ They told him, "He will miserably destroy those miserable men, and will lease out the vineyard to other farmers who will give him the fruit in its season."
⁴² Jesus said to them, "Did you never read in the Scriptures,
'The stone which the builders rejected
was made the head of the corner.
This was from the Lord.
It is marvelous in our eyes'?*
⁴³ "Therefore I tell you, God's Kingdom will be taken away from you and will be given to a nation producing its fruit.
⁴⁵ When the chief priests and the Pharisees heard his parables, they perceived that he spoke about them. ⁴⁶ When they sought to seize him, they feared the multitudes, because they considered him to be a prophet.

1. Invite the Holy Spirit into this reading, asking the Author of Scripture to speak to you through His Word
2. Read today's passage as many times as you need, take your time
3. Write down (below) what the Lord is saying to you today
4. Live with this Word in your heart through the day

Saturday, March 22, 2025

First Reading: Micah 7: 14-15, 18-20

¹⁴ Shepherd your people with your staff,
the flock of your heritage,
who dwell by themselves in a forest.
Let them feed in the middle of fertile pasture land,
in Bashan and Gilead, as in the days of old.
¹⁵ "As in the days of your coming out of the land of Egypt,
I will show them marvelous things."
¹⁸ Who is a God like you, who pardons iniquity,
and passes over the disobedience of the remnant of his heritage?
He doesn't retain his anger forever,
because he delights in loving kindness.
¹⁹ He will again have compassion on us.
He will tread our iniquities under foot.
You will cast all their sins into the depths of the sea.
²⁰ You will give truth to Jacob,
and mercy to Abraham,
as you have sworn to our fathers from the days of old.

Responsorial Psalm: Psalms 103: 1-4, 9-12

¹ Praise Yahweh, my soul!
All that is within me, praise his holy name!
² Praise Yahweh, my soul,
and don't forget all his benefits,
³ who forgives all your sins,
who heals all your diseases,
⁴ who redeems your life from destruction,
who crowns you with loving kindness and tender mercies,
⁹ He will not always accuse;
neither will he stay angry forever.
¹⁰ He has not dealt with us according to our sins,

nor repaid us for our iniquities.
¹¹ For as the heavens are high above the earth,
so great is his loving kindness toward those who fear him.
¹² As far as the east is from the west,
so far has he removed our transgressions from us.

Gospel: Luke 15: 1-3, 11-32

¹ Now all the tax collectors and sinners were coming close to him to hear him. ² The Pharisees and the scribes murmured, saying, "This man welcomes sinners, and eats with them."
³ He told them this parable
¹¹ He said, "A certain man had two sons. ¹² The younger of them said to his father, 'Father, give me my share of your property.' So he divided his livelihood between them. ¹³ Not many days after, the younger son gathered all of this together and traveled into a far country. There he wasted his property with riotous living. ¹⁴ When he had spent all of it, there arose a severe famine in that country, and he began to be in need. ¹⁵ He went and joined himself to one of the citizens of that country, and he sent him into his fields to feed pigs. ¹⁶ He wanted to fill his belly with the pods that the pigs ate, but no one gave him any. ¹⁷ But when he came to himself, he said, 'How many hired servants of my father's have bread enough to spare, and I'm dying with hunger! ¹⁸ I will get up and go to my father, and will tell him, "Father, I have sinned against heaven and in your sight. ¹⁹ I am no more worthy to be called your son. Make me as one of your hired servants."'
²⁰ "He arose and came to his father. But while he was still far off, his father saw him and was moved with compassion, and ran, fell on his neck, and kissed him. ²¹ The son said to him, 'Father, I have sinned against heaven and in your sight. I am no longer worthy to be called your son.'
²² "But the father said to his servants, 'Bring out the best robe and put it on him. Put a ring on his hand and sandals on his feet. ²³ Bring the fattened calf, kill it, and let's eat and celebrate; ²⁴ for this, my son, was dead and is alive again. He was lost and is found.' Then they began to celebrate.
²⁵ "Now his elder son was in the field. As he came near to the house, he heard music and dancing. ²⁶ He called one of the servants to him and asked what was going on. ²⁷ He said to him, 'Your brother has come, and your father has killed the fattened calf, because he has received him back safe and healthy.' ²⁸ But he was angry and would not go in. Therefore his father came out and begged him. ²⁹ But he answered his father, 'Behold, these many years I have served you, and I never disobeyed a commandment of yours, but you never gave me a goat, that I might celebrate with my friends. ³⁰ But when this your son came, who has devoured your living with prostitutes, you killed the fattened calf for him.'

³¹ "He said to him, 'Son, you are always with me, and all that is mine is yours. ³² But it was appropriate to celebrate and be glad, for this, your brother, was dead, and is alive again. He was lost, and is found.'"

1. Invite the Holy Spirit into this reading, asking the Author of Scripture to speak to you through His Word
2. Read today's passage as many times as you need, take your time
3. Write down (below) what the Lord is saying to you today
4. Live with this Word in your heart through the day

_____

_____

Sunday, March 23, 2025
THIRD SUNDAY OF LENT

First Reading: Exodus 3: 1-8a, 13-15

¹ Now Moses was keeping the flock of Jethro, his father-in-law, the priest of Midian, and he led the flock to the back of the wilderness, and came to God's mountain, to Horeb. ² Yahweh's⁺ angel appeared to him in a flame of fire out of the middle of a bush. He looked, and behold, the bush burned with fire, and the bush was not consumed. ³ Moses said, "I will go now, and see this great sight, why the bush is not burned."
⁴ When Yahweh saw that he came over to see, God called to him out of the middle of the bush, and said, "Moses! Moses!"
He said, "Here I am."
⁵ He said, "Don't come close. Take off your sandals, for the place you are standing on is holy ground." ⁶ Moreover he said, "I am the God of your father, the God of Abraham, the God of Isaac, and the God of Jacob."
Moses hid his face because he was afraid to look at God.
⁷ Yahweh said, "I have surely seen the affliction of my people who are in Egypt, and have heard their cry because of their taskmasters, for I know their sorrows. ⁸ I have come down to deliver them out of the hand of the Egyptians, and to bring them up out of that land to a good and large land, to a land flowing with milk and honey;
¹³ Moses said to God, "Behold, when I come to the children of Israel, and tell them, 'The God of your fathers has sent me to you,' and they ask me, 'What is his name?' what should I tell them?"

¹⁴ God said to Moses, "I AM WHO I AM," and he said, "You shall tell the children of Israel this: 'I AM has sent me to you.' " ¹⁵ God said moreover to Moses, "You shall tell the children of Israel this, 'Yahweh, the God of your fathers, the God of Abraham, the God of Isaac, and the God of Jacob, has sent me to you.' This is my name forever, and this is my memorial to all generations.

Responsorial Psalm: Psalms 103: 1-4, 6-8, 11

¹ Praise Yahweh, my soul!
All that is within me, praise his holy name!
² Praise Yahweh, my soul,
and don't forget all his benefits,
³ who forgives all your sins,
who heals all your diseases,
⁴ who redeems your life from destruction,
who crowns you with loving kindness and tender mercies,
⁶ Yahweh executes righteous acts,
and justice for all who are oppressed.
⁷ He made known his ways to Moses,
his deeds to the children of Israel.
⁸ Yahweh is merciful and gracious,
slow to anger, and abundant in loving kindness.
¹¹ For as the heavens are high above the earth,
so great is his loving kindness toward those who fear him.

Second Reading: First Corinthians 10: 1-6, 10-12

¹ Now I would not have you ignorant, brothers, that our fathers were all under the cloud, and all passed through the sea; ² and were all baptized into Moses in the cloud and in the sea; ³ and all ate the same spiritual food; ⁴ and all drank the same spiritual drink. For they drank of a spiritual rock that followed them, and the rock was Christ. ⁵ However with most of them, God was not well pleased, for they were overthrown in the wilderness.
⁶ Now these things were our examples, to the intent we should not lust after evil things as they also lusted.
¹⁰ Don't grumble, as some of them also grumbled, and perished by the destroyer. ¹¹ Now all these things happened to them by way of example, and they were written for our admonition, on whom the ends of the ages have come. ¹² Therefore let him who thinks he stands be careful that he doesn't fall.

Gospel: Luke 13: 1-9

¹ Now there were some present at the same time who told him about the Galileans whose blood Pilate had mixed with their sacrifices. ² Jesus answered them, "Do you think that these Galileans were worse sinners than all the other Galileans, because they suffered such things? ³ I tell you, no, but unless you repent, you will all perish in the same way. ⁴ Or those eighteen on whom the tower in Siloam fell and killed them—do you think that they were worse offenders than all the men who dwell in Jerusalem? ⁵ I tell you, no, but, unless you repent, you will all perish in the same way."
⁶ He spoke this parable. "A certain man had a fig tree planted in his vineyard, and he came seeking fruit on it and found none. ⁷ He said to the vine dresser, 'Behold, these three years I have come looking for fruit on this fig tree, and found none. Cut it down! Why does it waste the soil?' ⁸ He answered, 'Lord, leave it alone this year also, until I dig around it and fertilize it. ⁹ If it bears fruit, fine; but if not, after that, you can cut it down.' "

1. Invite the Holy Spirit into this reading, asking the Author of Scripture to speak to you through His Word
2. Read today's passage as many times as you need, take your time
3. Write down (below) what the Lord is saying to you today
4. Live with this Word in your heart through the day

_____

_____

Monday, March 24, 2025

First Reading: Second Kings 5: 1-15

¹ Now Naaman, captain of the army of the king of Syria, was a great man with his master, and honorable, because by him Yahweh had given victory to Syria; he was also a mighty man of valor, but he was a leper. ² The Syrians had gone out in bands, and had brought away captive out of the land of Israel a little girl, and she waited on Naaman's wife. ³ She said to her mistress, "I wish that my lord were with the prophet who is in Samaria! Then he would heal him of his leprosy."
⁴ Someone went in and told his lord, saying, "The girl who is from the land of Israel said this."
⁵ The king of Syria said, "Go now, and I will send a letter to the king of Israel."
He departed, and took with him ten talents‡ of silver, six thousand pieces of gold, and ten changes of clothing. ⁶ He brought the letter to the king of Israel, saying, "Now when this

letter has come to you, behold, I have sent Naaman my servant to you, that you may heal him of his leprosy."

7 When the king of Israel had read the letter, he tore his clothes and said, "Am I God, to kill and to make alive, that this man sends to me to heal a man of his leprosy? But please consider and see how he seeks a quarrel against me."

8 It was so, when Elisha the man of God heard that the king of Israel had torn his clothes, that he sent to the king, saying, "Why have you torn your clothes? Let him come now to me, and he shall know that there is a prophet in Israel."

9 So Naaman came with his horses and with his chariots, and stood at the door of the house of Elisha. 10 Elisha sent a messenger to him, saying, "Go and wash in the Jordan seven times, and your flesh shall come again to you, and you shall be clean."

11 But Naaman was angry, and went away and said, "Behold, I thought, 'He will surely come out to me, and stand, and call on the name of Yahweh his God, and wave his hand over the place, and heal the leper.' 12 Aren't Abanah and Pharpar, the rivers of Damascus, better than all the waters of Israel? Couldn't I wash in them and be clean?" So he turned and went away in a rage.

13 His servants came near and spoke to him, and said, "My father, if the prophet had asked you do some great thing, wouldn't you have done it? How much rather then, when he says to you, 'Wash, and be clean'?"

14 Then went he down and dipped himself seven times in the Jordan, according to the saying of the man of God; and his flesh was restored like the flesh of a little child, and he was clean. 15 He returned to the man of God, he and all his company, and came, and stood before him; and he said, "See now, I know that there is no God in all the earth, but in Israel. Now therefore, please take a gift from your servant."

Responsorial Psalm: Psalms 42: 2, 3; 43: 3, 4

2 My soul thirsts for God, for the living God.
When shall I come and appear before God?
3 My tears have been my food day and night,
while they continually ask me, "Where is your God?"
3 Oh, send out your light and your truth.
Let them lead me.
Let them bring me to your holy hill,
to your tents.
4 Then I will go to the altar of God,
to God, my exceeding joy.
I will praise you on the harp, God, my God.

Gospel: Luke 4: 24-30

24 He said, "Most certainly I tell you, no prophet is acceptable in his hometown. 25 But truly I tell you, there were many widows in Israel in the days of Elijah, when the sky was shut up three years and six months, when a great famine came over all the land. 26 Elijah was sent to none of them, except to Zarephath, in the land of Sidon, to a woman who was a widow. 27 There were many lepers in Israel in the time of Elisha the prophet, yet not one of them was cleansed, except Naaman, the Syrian."
28 They were all filled with wrath in the synagogue as they heard these things. 29 They rose up, threw him out of the city, and led him to the brow of the hill that their city was built on, that they might throw him off the cliff. 30 But he, passing through the middle of them, went his way.

1. Invite the Holy Spirit into this reading, asking the Author of Scripture to speak to you through His Word
2. Read today's passage as many times as you need, take your time
3. Write down (below) what the Lord is saying to you today
4. Live with this Word in your heart through the day

_____

_____

Tuesday, March 25, 2025
THE ANNUNCIATION OF THE LORD

First Reading: Isaiah 7: 10-14; 8: 10

10 Yahweh spoke again to Ahaz, saying, 11 "Ask a sign of Yahweh your God; ask it either in the depth, or in the height above."
12 But Ahaz said, "I won't ask. I won't tempt Yahweh."
13 He said, "Listen now, house of David. Is it not enough for you to try the patience of men, that you will try the patience of my God also? 14 Therefore the Lord himself will give you a sign. Behold, the virgin will conceive, and bear a son, and shall call his name Immanuel.
10 Take counsel together, and it will be brought to nothing; speak the word, and it will not stand, for God is with us."

Responsorial Psalm: Psalms 40: 7-11

7 Then I said, "Behold, I have come.

It is written about me in the book in the scroll.
⁸ I delight to do your will, my God.
Yes, your law is within my heart."
⁹ I have proclaimed glad news of righteousness in the great assembly.
Behold, I will not seal my lips, Yahweh, you know.
¹⁰ I have not hidden your righteousness within my heart.
I have declared your faithfulness and your salvation.
I have not concealed your loving kindness and your truth from the great assembly.
¹¹ Don't withhold your tender mercies from me, Yahweh.
Let your loving kindness and your truth continually preserve me.

Second Reading: Hebrews 10: 4-10

⁴ For it is impossible that the blood of bulls and goats should take away sins. ⁵ Therefore when he comes into the world, he says,
"You didn't desire sacrifice and offering,
but you prepared a body for me.
⁶ You had no pleasure in whole burnt offerings and sacrifices for sin.
⁷ Then I said, 'Behold, I have come (in the scroll of the book it is written of me)
to do your will, O God.' "
⁸ Previously saying, "Sacrifices and offerings and whole burnt offerings and sacrifices for sin you didn't desire, neither had pleasure in them" (those which are offered according to the law), ⁹ then he has said, "Behold, I have come to do your will." He takes away the first, that he may establish the second, ¹⁰ by which will we have been sanctified through the offering of the body of Jesus Christ once for all.

Gospel: Luke 1: 26-38

²⁶ Now in the sixth month, the angel Gabriel was sent from God to a city of Galilee named Nazareth, ²⁷ to a virgin pledged to be married to a man whose name was Joseph, of David's house. The virgin's name was Mary. ²⁸ Having come in, the angel said to her, "Rejoice, you highly favored one! The Lord is with you. Blessed are you among women!"
²⁹ But when she saw him, she was greatly troubled at the saying, and considered what kind of salutation this might be. ³⁰ The angel said to her, "Don't be afraid, Mary, for you have found favor with God. ³¹ Behold, you will conceive in your womb and give birth to a son, and shall name him 'Jesus.' ³² He will be great and will be called the Son of the Most High. The Lord God will give him the throne of his father David, ³³ and he will reign over the house of Jacob forever. There will be no end to his Kingdom."
³⁴ Mary said to the angel, "How can this be, seeing I am a virgin?"

35 The angel answered her, "The Holy Spirit will come on you, and the power of the Most High will overshadow you. Therefore also the holy one who is born from you will be called the Son of God. 36 Behold, Elizabeth your relative also has conceived a son in her old age; and this is the sixth month with her who was called barren. 37 For nothing spoken by God is impossible."±
38 Mary said, "Behold, the servant of the Lord; let it be done to me according to your word." Then the angel departed from her.

1. Invite the Holy Spirit into this reading, asking the Author of Scripture to speak to you through His Word
2. Read today's passage as many times as you need, take your time
3. Write down (below) what the Lord is saying to you today
4. Live with this Word in your heart through the day

Wednesday, March 26, 2025

First Reading: Deuteronomy 4:1, 5-9

1 Now, Israel, listen to the statutes and to the ordinances which I teach you, to do them, that you may live and go in and possess the land which Yahweh, the God of your fathers, gives you.
5 Behold, I have taught you statutes and ordinances, even as Yahweh my God commanded me, that you should do so in the middle of the land where you go in to possess it. 6 Keep therefore and do them; for this is your wisdom and your understanding in the sight of the peoples who shall hear all these statutes and say, "Surely this great nation is a wise and understanding people." 7 For what great nation is there that has a god so near to them as Yahweh our God is whenever we call on him? 8 What great nation is there that has statutes and ordinances so righteous as all this law which I set before you today?
9 Only be careful, and keep your soul diligently, lest you forget the things which your eyes saw, and lest they depart from your heart all the days of your life; but make them known to your children and your children's children

Responsorial Psalm: Psalms 147: 12-13, 15-16, 19-20

12 Praise Yahweh, Jerusalem!

Praise your God, Zion!
¹³ For he has strengthened the bars of your gates.
He has blessed your children within you.
¹⁵ He sends out his commandment to the earth.
His word runs very swiftly.
¹⁶ He gives snow like wool,
and scatters frost like ashes.
¹⁹ He shows his word to Jacob,
his statutes and his ordinances to Israel.
²⁰ He has not done this for just any nation.
They don't know his ordinances.
Praise Yah!

Gospel: Matthew 5: 17-19

¹⁷ "Don't think that I came to destroy the law or the prophets. I didn't come to destroy, but to fulfill. ¹⁸ For most certainly, I tell you, until heaven and earth pass away, not even one smallest letter⁺ or one tiny pen stroke§ shall in any way pass away from the law, until all things are accomplished. ¹⁹ Therefore, whoever shall break one of these least commandments and teach others to do so, shall be called least in the Kingdom of Heaven; but whoever shall do and teach them shall be called great in the Kingdom of Heaven.

1. Invite the Holy Spirit into this reading, asking the Author of Scripture to speak to you through His Word
2. Read today's passage as many times as you need, take your time
3. Write down (below) what the Lord is saying to you today
4. Live with this Word in your heart through the day

Thursday, March 27, 2025

First Reading: Jeremiah 7: 23-28

²³ but this thing I commanded them, saying, 'Listen to my voice, and I will be your God, and you shall be my people. Walk in all the way that I command you, that it may be well with you.' ²⁴ But they didn't listen or turn their ear, but walked in their own counsels and

in the stubbornness of their evil heart, and went backward, and not forward. 25 Since the day that your fathers came out of the land of Egypt to this day, I have sent to you all my servants the prophets, daily rising up early and sending them. 26 Yet they didn't listen to me or incline their ear, but made their neck stiff. They did worse than their fathers.

27 "You shall speak all these words to them, but they will not listen to you. You shall also call to them, but they will not answer you. 28 You shall tell them, 'This is the nation that has not listened to Yahweh their God's voice, nor received instruction. Truth has perished, and is cut off from their mouth.'

Responsorial Psalm: Psalms 95: 1-2, 6-9

1 Oh come, let's sing to Yahweh.
Let's shout aloud to the rock of our salvation!
2 Let's come before his presence with thanksgiving.
Let's extol him with songs!
6 Oh come, let's worship and bow down.
Let's kneel before Yahweh, our Maker,
7 for he is our God.
We are the people of his pasture,
and the sheep in his care.
Today, oh that you would hear his voice!
8 Don't harden your heart, as at Meribah,
as in the day of Massah in the wilderness,
9 when your fathers tempted me,
tested me, and saw my work.

Gospel: Luke 11: 14-23

14 He was casting out a demon, and it was mute. When the demon had gone out, the mute man spoke; and the multitudes marveled. 15 But some of them said, "He casts out demons by Beelzebul, the prince of the demons." 16 Others, testing him, sought from him a sign from heaven. 17 But he, knowing their thoughts, said to them, "Every kingdom divided against itself is brought to desolation. A house divided against itself falls. 18 If Satan also is divided against himself, how will his kingdom stand? For you say that I cast out demons by Beelzebul. 19 But if I cast out demons by Beelzebul, by whom do your children cast them out? Therefore they will be your judges. 20 But if I by God's finger cast out demons, then God's Kingdom has come to you.
21 "When the strong man, fully armed, guards his own dwelling, his goods are safe. 22 But when someone stronger attacks him and overcomes him, he takes from him his whole armor in which he trusted, and divides his plunder.

²³ "He who is not with me is against me. He who doesn't gather with me scatters.

1. Invite the Holy Spirit into this reading, asking the Author of Scripture to speak to you through His Word
2. Read today's passage as many times as you need, take your time
3. Write down (below) what the Lord is saying to you today
4. Live with this Word in your heart through the day

_____

_____

Friday, March 28, 2025

First Reading: Hosea 14: 2-10

² Take words with you, and return to Yahweh.
Tell him, "Forgive all our sins,
and accept that which is good;
so we offer bulls as we vowed of our lips.
³ Assyria can't save us.
We won't ride on horses;
neither will we say any more to the work of our hands, 'Our gods!'
for in you the fatherless finds mercy."

⁴ "I will heal their waywardness.
I will love them freely;
for my anger is turned away from them.
⁵ I will be like the dew to Israel.
He will blossom like the lily,
and send down his roots like Lebanon.
⁶ His branches will spread,
and his beauty will be like the olive tree,
and his fragrance like Lebanon.
⁷ Men will dwell in his shade.
They will revive like the grain,
and blossom like the vine.
Their fragrance will be like the wine of Lebanon.
⁸ Ephraim, what have I to do any more with idols?

I answer, and will take care of him.
I am like a green cypress tree;
from me your fruit is found."
⁹ Who is wise, that he may understand these things?
Who is prudent, that he may know them?
For the ways of Yahweh are right,
and the righteous walk in them,
but the rebellious stumble in them.

Responsorial Psalm: Psalms 81: 6c-11ab, 14 and 16

⁶ His hands were freed from the basket.
⁷ You called in trouble, and I delivered you.
I answered you in the secret place of thunder.
I tested you at the waters of Meribah."
⁸ "Hear, my people, and I will testify to you,
Israel, if you would listen to me!
⁹ There shall be no strange god in you,
neither shall you worship any foreign god.
¹⁰ I am Yahweh, your God,
who brought you up out of the land of Egypt.
Open your mouth wide, and I will fill it.
¹¹ But my people didn't listen to my voice.
Israel desired none of me.
¹⁴ I would soon subdue their enemies,
and turn my hand against their adversaries.
¹⁶ But he would have also fed them with the finest of the wheat.
I will satisfy you with honey out of the rock."

Gospel: Mark 12: 28-34

²⁸ One of the scribes came and heard them questioning together, and knowing that he had answered them well, asked him, "Which commandment is the greatest of all?"
²⁹ Jesus answered, "The greatest is: 'Hear, Israel, the Lord our God, the Lord is one. ³⁰ You shall love the Lord your God with all your heart, with all your soul, with all your mind, and with all your strength.' This is the first commandment. ³¹ The second is like this: 'You shall love your neighbor as yourself.' There is no other commandment greater than these."
³² The scribe said to him, "Truly, teacher, you have said well that he is one, and there is none other but he; ³³ and to love him with all the heart, with all the understanding, all the

soul, and with all the strength, and to love his neighbor as himself, is more important than all whole burnt offerings and sacrifices."

34 When Jesus saw that he answered wisely, he said to him, "You are not far from God's Kingdom."

No one dared ask him any question after that.

1. Invite the Holy Spirit into this reading, asking the Author of Scripture to speak to you through His Word
2. Read today's passage as many times as you need, take your time
3. Write down (below) what the Lord is saying to you today
4. Live with this Word in your heart through the day

___

___

Saturday, March 29, 2025

First Reading: Hosea 6: 1-6

1 "Come! Let's return to Yahweh;
for he has torn us to pieces,
and he will heal us;
he has injured us,
and he will bind up our wounds.
2 After two days he will revive us.
On the third day he will raise us up,
and we will live before him.
3 Let's acknowledge Yahweh.
Let's press on to know Yahweh.
As surely as the sun rises,
Yahweh will appear.
He will come to us like the rain,
like the spring rain that waters the earth."
4 "Ephraim, what shall I do to you?
Judah, what shall I do to you?
For your love is like a morning cloud,
and like the dew that disappears early.
5 Therefore I have cut them to pieces with the prophets;

I killed them with the words of my mouth.
Your judgments are like a flash of lightning.
⁶ For I desire mercy, and not sacrifice;
and the knowledge of God more than burnt offerings.

Responsorial Psalm: Psalms 51: 3-4, 18-19

³ For I know my transgressions.
My sin is constantly before me.
⁴ Against you, and you only, I have sinned,
and done that which is evil in your sight,
so you may be proved right when you speak,
and justified when you judge.
¹⁸ Do well in your good pleasure to Zion.
Build the walls of Jerusalem.
¹⁹ Then you will delight in the sacrifices of righteousness,
in burnt offerings and in whole burnt offerings.
Then they will offer bulls on your altar.

Gospel: Luke 18: 9-14

⁹ He also spoke this parable to certain people who were convinced of their own righteousness, and who despised all others: ¹⁰ "Two men went up into the temple to pray; one was a Pharisee, and the other was a tax collector. ¹¹ The Pharisee stood and prayed by himself like this: 'God, I thank you that I am not like the rest of men: extortionists, unrighteous, adulterers, or even like this tax collector. ¹² I fast twice a week. I give tithes of all that I get.' ¹³ But the tax collector, standing far away, wouldn't even lift up his eyes to heaven, but beat his chest, saying, 'God, be merciful to me, a sinner!' ¹⁴ I tell you, this man went down to his house justified rather than the other; for everyone who exalts himself will be humbled, but he who humbles himself will be exalted."

1. Invite the Holy Spirit into this reading, asking the Author of Scripture to speak to you through His Word
2. Read today's passage as many times as you need, take your time
3. Write down (below) what the Lord is saying to you today
4. Live with this Word in your heart through the day

Sunday, March 30, 2025
FOURTH SUNDAY OF LENT

First Reading: Joshua 5: 9a, 10-12

⁹ Yahweh said to Joshua, "Today I have rolled away the reproach of Egypt from you." Therefore the name of that place was called Gilgal‡ to this day. ¹⁰ The children of Israel encamped in Gilgal. They kept the Passover on the fourteenth day of the month at evening in the plains of Jericho. ¹¹ They ate unleavened cakes and parched grain of the produce of the land on the next day after the Passover, in the same day. ¹² The manna ceased on the next day, after they had eaten of the produce of the land. The children of Israel didn't have manna any more, but they ate of the fruit of the land of Canaan that year.

Responsorial Psalm: Psalms 34: 2-7

² My soul shall boast in Yahweh.
The humble shall hear of it and be glad.
³ Oh magnify Yahweh with me.
Let's exalt his name together.
⁴ I sought Yahweh, and he answered me,
and delivered me from all my fears.
⁵ They looked to him, and were radiant.
Their faces shall never be covered with shame.
⁶ This poor man cried, and Yahweh heard him,
and saved him out of all his troubles.
⁷ Yahweh's angel encamps around those who fear him,
and delivers them.

Second Reading: Second Corinthians 5: 17-21

¹⁷ Therefore if anyone is in Christ, he is a new creation. The old things have passed away. Behold,‡ all things have become new. ¹⁸ But all things are of God, who reconciled us to himself through Jesus Christ, and gave to us the ministry of reconciliation; ¹⁹ namely, that God was in Christ reconciling the world to himself, not reckoning to them their trespasses, and having committed to us the word of reconciliation.
²⁰ We are therefore ambassadors on behalf of Christ, as though God were entreating by us: we beg you on behalf of Christ, be reconciled to God. ²¹ For him who knew no sin he made to be sin on our behalf, so that in him we might become the righteousness of God.

Gospel: Luke 15: 1-3,11-32

¹ Now all the tax collectors and sinners were coming close to him to hear him. ² The Pharisees and the scribes murmured, saying, "This man welcomes sinners, and eats with them."
³ He told them this parable
¹¹ He said, "A certain man had two sons. ¹² The younger of them said to his father, 'Father, give me my share of your property.' So he divided his livelihood between them. ¹³ Not many days after, the younger son gathered all of this together and traveled into a far country. There he wasted his property with riotous living. ¹⁴ When he had spent all of it, there arose a severe famine in that country, and he began to be in need. ¹⁵ He went and joined himself to one of the citizens of that country, and he sent him into his fields to feed pigs. ¹⁶ He wanted to fill his belly with the pods that the pigs ate, but no one gave him any. ¹⁷ But when he came to himself, he said, 'How many hired servants of my father's have bread enough to spare, and I'm dying with hunger! ¹⁸ I will get up and go to my father, and will tell him, "Father, I have sinned against heaven and in your sight. ¹⁹ I am no more worthy to be called your son. Make me as one of your hired servants."'
²⁰ "He arose and came to his father. But while he was still far off, his father saw him and was moved with compassion, and ran, fell on his neck, and kissed him. ²¹ The son said to him, 'Father, I have sinned against heaven and in your sight. I am no longer worthy to be called your son.'
²² "But the father said to his servants, 'Bring out the best robe and put it on him. Put a ring on his hand and sandals on his feet. ²³ Bring the fattened calf, kill it, and let's eat and celebrate; ²⁴ for this, my son, was dead and is alive again. He was lost and is found.' Then they began to celebrate.
²⁵ "Now his elder son was in the field. As he came near to the house, he heard music and dancing. ²⁶ He called one of the servants to him and asked what was going on. ²⁷ He said to him, 'Your brother has come, and your father has killed the fattened calf, because he has received him back safe and healthy.' ²⁸ But he was angry and would not go in. Therefore his father came out and begged him. ²⁹ But he answered his father, 'Behold, these many years I have served you, and I never disobeyed a commandment of yours, but you never gave me a goat, that I might celebrate with my friends. ³⁰ But when this your son came, who has devoured your living with prostitutes, you killed the fattened calf for him.'
³¹ "He said to him, 'Son, you are always with me, and all that is mine is yours. ³² But it was appropriate to celebrate and be glad, for this, your brother, was dead, and is alive again. He was lost, and is found.'"

1. Invite the Holy Spirit into this reading, asking the Author of Scripture to speak to you through His Word
2. Read today's passage as many times as you need, take your time
3. Write down (below) what the Lord is saying to you today

4. Live with this Word in your heart through the day

_____

_____

Monday, March 31, 2025

First Reading: Isaiah 65: 17-21

¹⁷ "For, behold, I create new heavens and a new earth;
and the former things will not be remembered,
nor come into mind.
¹⁸ But be glad and rejoice forever in that which I create;
for, behold, I create Jerusalem to be a delight,
and her people a joy.
¹⁹ I will rejoice in Jerusalem,
and delight in my people;
and the voice of weeping and the voice of crying
will be heard in her no more.
²⁰ "No more will there be an infant who only lives a few days,
nor an old man who has not filled his days;
for the child will die one hundred years old,
and the sinner being one hundred years old will be accursed.
²¹ They will build houses and inhabit them.
They will plant vineyards and eat their fruit.

Responsorial Psalm: Psalms 30: 2 and 4-6, 11-12

² Yahweh my God, I cried to you,
and you have healed me.
⁴ Sing praise to Yahweh, you saints of his.
Give thanks to his holy name.
⁵ For his anger is but for a moment.
His favor is for a lifetime.
Weeping may stay for the night,
but joy comes in the morning.
⁶ As for me, I said in my prosperity,
"I shall never be moved."

¹¹ You have turned my mourning into dancing for me.
You have removed my sackcloth, and clothed me with gladness,
¹² to the end that my heart may sing praise to you, and not be silent.
Yahweh my God, I will give thanks to you forever!

Gospel: John 4: 43-54

⁴³ After the two days he went out from there and went into Galilee. ⁴⁴ For Jesus himself testified that a prophet has no honor in his own country. ⁴⁵ So when he came into Galilee, the Galileans received him, having seen all the things that he did in Jerusalem at the feast, for they also went to the feast. ⁴⁶ Jesus came therefore again to Cana of Galilee, where he made the water into wine. There was a certain nobleman whose son was sick at Capernaum. ⁴⁷ When he heard that Jesus had come out of Judea into Galilee, he went to him and begged him that he would come down and heal his son, for he was at the point of death. ⁴⁸ Jesus therefore said to him, "Unless you see signs and wonders, you will in no way believe."
⁴⁹ The nobleman said to him, "Sir, come down before my child dies."
⁵⁰ Jesus said to him, "Go your way. Your son lives." The man believed the word that Jesus spoke to him, and he went his way. ⁵¹ As he was going down, his servants met him and reported, saying "Your child lives!" ⁵² So he inquired of them the hour when he began to get better. They said therefore to him, "Yesterday at the seventh hour,§ the fever left him." ⁵³ So the father knew that it was at that hour in which Jesus said to him, "Your son lives." He believed, as did his whole house. ⁵⁴ This is again the second sign that Jesus did, having come out of Judea into Galilee.

1. Invite the Holy Spirit into this reading, asking the Author of Scripture to speak to you through His Word
2. Read today's passage as many times as you need, take your time
3. Write down (below) what the Lord is saying to you today
4. Live with this Word in your heart through the day

___

Tuesday, April 1, 2025

First Reading: Ezekiel 47: 1-9, 12

¹ He brought me back to the door of the temple; and behold, waters flowed out from under the threshold of the temple eastward, for the front of the temple faced toward the east. The waters came down from underneath, from the right side of the temple, on the south of the altar. ² Then he brought me out by the way of the gate northward, and led me around by the way outside to the outer gate, by the way of the gate that looks toward the east. Behold, waters ran out on the right side.

³ When the man went out eastward with the line in his hand, he measured one thousand cubits,¹ and he caused me to pass through the waters, waters that were to the ankles. ⁴ Again he measured one thousand, and caused me to pass through the waters, waters that were to the knees. Again he measured one thousand, and caused me to pass through waters that were to the waist. ⁵ Afterward he measured one thousand; and it was a river that I could not pass through, for the waters had risen, waters to swim in, a river that could not be walked through.

⁶ He said to me, "Son of man, have you seen this?"

Then he brought me and caused me to return to the bank of the river. ⁷ Now when I had returned, behold, on the bank of the river were very many trees on the one side and on the other. ⁸ Then he said to me, "These waters flow out toward the eastern region and will go down into the Arabah. Then they will go toward the sea and flow into the sea which will be made to flow out; and the waters will be healed. ⁹ It will happen that every living creature which swarms, in every place where the rivers come, will live. Then there will be a very great multitude of fish; for these waters have come there, and the waters of the sea will be healed, and everything will live wherever the river comes.

¹² By the river banks, on both sides, will grow every tree for food, whose leaf won't wither, neither will its fruit fail. It will produce new fruit every month, because its waters issue out of the sanctuary. Its fruit will be for food, and its leaf for healing."

Responsorial Psalm: Psalms 46: 2-3, 5-6, 8-9

² Therefore we won't be afraid, though the earth changes,
though the mountains are shaken into the heart of the seas;
³ though its waters roar and are troubled,
though the mountains tremble with their swelling.
⁵ God is within her. She shall not be moved.
God will help her at dawn.
⁶ The nations raged. The kingdoms were moved.
He lifted his voice and the earth melted.
⁸ Come, see Yahweh's works,
what desolations he has made in the earth.
⁹ He makes wars cease to the end of the earth.
He breaks the bow, and shatters the spear.

He burns the chariots in the fire.

Gospel: John 5: 1-16

¹ After these things, there was a feast of the Jews, and Jesus went up to Jerusalem. ² Now in Jerusalem by the sheep gate, there is a pool, which is called in Hebrew, "Bethesda", having five porches. ³ In these lay a great multitude of those who were sick, blind, lame, or paralyzed, waiting for the moving of the water; ⁴ for an angel went down at certain times into the pool and stirred up the water. Whoever stepped in first after the stirring of the water was healed of whatever disease he had. ⁵ A certain man was there who had been sick for thirty-eight years. ⁶ When Jesus saw him lying there, and knew that he had been sick for a long time, he asked him, "Do you want to be made well?"
⁷ The sick man answered him, "Sir, I have no one to put me into the pool when the water is stirred up, but while I'm coming, another steps down before me."
⁸ Jesus said to him, "Arise, take up your mat, and walk."
⁹ Immediately, the man was made well, and took up his mat and walked. Now that day was a Sabbath. ¹⁰ So the Jews said to him who was cured, "It is the Sabbath. It is not lawful for you to carry the mat."
¹¹ He answered them, "He who made me well said to me, 'Take up your mat and walk.'"
¹² Then they asked him, "Who is the man who said to you, 'Take up your mat and walk'?"
¹³ But he who was healed didn't know who it was, for Jesus had withdrawn, a crowd being in the place.
¹⁴ Afterward Jesus found him in the temple and said to him, "Behold, you are made well. Sin no more, so that nothing worse happens to you."
¹⁵ The man went away, and told the Jews that it was Jesus who had made him well. ¹⁶ For this cause the Jews persecuted Jesus and sought to kill him, because he did these things on the Sabbath.

1. Invite the Holy Spirit into this reading, asking the Author of Scripture to speak to you through His Word
2. Read today's passage as many times as you need, take your time
3. Write down (below) what the Lord is saying to you today
4. Live with this Word in your heart through the day

_____

_____

Wednesday, April 2, 2025

Saint Francis of Paola, Hermit

First Reading: Isaiah 49: 8-15

8 Yahweh says, "I have answered you in an acceptable time.
I have helped you in a day of salvation.
I will preserve you and give you for a covenant of the people,
to raise up the land, to make them inherit the desolate heritage,
9 saying to those who are bound, 'Come out!';
to those who are in darkness, 'Show yourselves!'
"They shall feed along the paths,
and their pasture shall be on all treeless heights.
10 They shall not hunger nor thirst;
neither shall the heat nor sun strike them,
for he who has mercy on them will lead them.
He will guide them by springs of water.
11 I will make all my mountains a road,
and my highways shall be exalted.
12 Behold, these shall come from afar,
and behold, these from the north and from the west,
and these from the land of Sinim."
13 Sing, heavens, and be joyful, earth!
Break out into singing, mountains!
For Yahweh has comforted his people,
and will have compassion on his afflicted.
14 But Zion said, "Yahweh has forsaken me,
and the Lord has forgotten me."
15 "Can a woman forget her nursing child,
that she should not have compassion on the son of her womb?
Yes, these may forget,
yet I will not forget you!

Responsorial Psalm: Psalms 145: 8-9, 13cd-14, 17-18

8 Yahweh is gracious, merciful,
slow to anger, and of great loving kindness.
9 Yahweh is good to all.
His tender mercies are over all his works.
13c Yahweh is faithful in all his words,
and loving in all his deeds.‡

¹⁴ Yahweh upholds all who fall,
and raises up all those who are bowed down.
¹⁷ Yahweh is righteous in all his ways,
and gracious in all his works.
¹⁸ Yahweh is near to all those who call on him,
to all who call on him in truth.

Gospel: John 5: 17-30

¹⁷ But Jesus answered them, "My Father is still working, so I am working, too."
¹⁸ For this cause therefore the Jews sought all the more to kill him, because he not only broke the Sabbath, but also called God his own Father, making himself equal with God. ¹⁹ Jesus therefore answered them, "Most certainly, I tell you, the Son can do nothing of himself, but what he sees the Father doing. For whatever things he does, these the Son also does likewise. ²⁰ For the Father has affection for the Son, and shows him all things that he himself does. He will show him greater works than these, that you may marvel. ²¹ For as the Father raises the dead and gives them life, even so the Son also gives life to whom he desires. ²² For the Father judges no one, but he has given all judgment to the Son, ²³ that all may honor the Son, even as they honor the Father. He who doesn't honor the Son doesn't honor the Father who sent him.
²⁴ "Most certainly I tell you, he who hears my word and believes him who sent me has eternal life, and doesn't come into judgment, but has passed out of death into life. ²⁵ Most certainly I tell you, the hour comes, and now is, when the dead will hear the Son of God's voice; and those who hear will live. ²⁶ For as the Father has life in himself, even so he gave to the Son also to have life in himself. ²⁷ He also gave him authority to execute judgment, because he is a son of man. ²⁸ Don't marvel at this, for the hour comes in which all who are in the tombs will hear his voice ²⁹ and will come out; those who have done good, to the resurrection of life; and those who have done evil, to the resurrection of judgment. ³⁰ I can of myself do nothing. As I hear, I judge; and my judgment is righteous, because I don't seek my own will, but the will of my Father who sent me.

1. Invite the Holy Spirit into this reading, asking the Author of Scripture to speak to you through His Word
2. Read today's passage as many times as you need, take your time
3. Write down (below) what the Lord is saying to you today
4. Live with this Word in your heart through the day

_____

_____

Thursday, April 3, 2025

First Reading: Exodus 32: 7-14

⁷ Yahweh spoke to Moses, "Go, get down; for your people, whom you brought up out of the land of Egypt, have corrupted themselves! ⁸ They have turned away quickly out of the way which I commanded them. They have made themselves a molded calf, and have worshiped it, and have sacrificed to it, and said, 'These are your gods, Israel, which brought you up out of the land of Egypt.' "
⁹ Yahweh said to Moses, "I have seen these people, and behold, they are a stiff-necked people. ¹⁰ Now therefore leave me alone, that my wrath may burn hot against them, and that I may consume them; and I will make of you a great nation."
¹¹ Moses begged Yahweh his God, and said, "Yahweh, why does your wrath burn hot against your people, that you have brought out of the land of Egypt with great power and with a mighty hand? ¹² Why should the Egyptians talk, saying, 'He brought them out for evil, to kill them in the mountains, and to consume them from the surface of the earth'? Turn from your fierce wrath, and turn away from this evil against your people. ¹³ Remember Abraham, Isaac, and Israel, your servants, to whom you swore by your own self, and said to them, 'I will multiply your offspring‡ as the stars of the sky, and all this land that I have spoken of I will give to your offspring, and they shall inherit it forever.' "
¹⁴ So Yahweh turned away from the evil which he said he would do to his people.

Responsorial Psalm: Psalms 106: 19-23

¹⁹ They made a calf in Horeb,
and worshiped a molten image.
²⁰ Thus they exchanged their glory
for an image of a bull that eats grass.
²¹ They forgot God, their Savior,
who had done great things in Egypt,
²² wondrous works in the land of Ham,
and awesome things by the Red Sea.
²³ Therefore he said that he would destroy them,
had Moses, his chosen, not stood before him in the breach,
to turn away his wrath, so that he wouldn't destroy them.

Gospel: John 5: 31-47

³¹ "If I testify about myself, my witness is not valid. ³² It is another who testifies about me. I know that the testimony which he testifies about me is true. ³³ You have sent to John, and

he has testified to the truth. 34 But the testimony which I receive is not from man. However, I say these things that you may be saved. 35 He was the burning and shining lamp, and you were willing to rejoice for a while in his light. 36 But the testimony which I have is greater than that of John; for the works which the Father gave me to accomplish, the very works that I do, testify about me, that the Father has sent me. 37 The Father himself, who sent me, has testified about me. You have neither heard his voice at any time, nor seen his form. 38 You don't have his word living in you, because you don't believe him whom he sent.

39 "You search the Scriptures, because you think that in them you have eternal life; and these are they which testify about me. 40 Yet you will not come to me, that you may have life. 41 I don't receive glory from men. 42 But I know you, that you don't have God's love in yourselves. 43 I have come in my Father's name, and you don't receive me. If another comes in his own name, you will receive him. 44 How can you believe, who receive glory from one another, and you don't seek the glory that comes from the only God?

45 "Don't think that I will accuse you to the Father. There is one who accuses you, even Moses, on whom you have set your hope. 46 For if you believed Moses, you would believe me; for he wrote about me. 47 But if you don't believe his writings, how will you believe my words?"

1. Invite the Holy Spirit into this reading, asking the Author of Scripture to speak to you through His Word
2. Read today's passage as many times as you need, take your time
3. Write down (below) what the Lord is saying to you today
4. Live with this Word in your heart through the day

_____

_____

Friday, April 4, 2025
Saint Isidore, Bishop and Doctor of the Church

First Reading: Wisdom 2: 1a, 12-22

1 For they said within themselves, with unsound reasoning,
"Our life is short and sorrowful.
12 But let's lie in wait for the righteous man,
because he annoys us,
is contrary to our works,

reproaches us with sins against the law,
and charges us with sins against our training.
[13] He professes to have knowledge of God,
and calls himself a child of the Lord.
[14] He became to us a reproof of our thoughts.
[15] He is grievous to us even to look at,
because his life is unlike other men's,
and his paths are strange.
[16] We were regarded by him as something worthless,
and he abstains from our ways as from uncleanness.
He calls the latter end of the righteous happy.
He boasts that God is his father.
[17] Let's see if his words are true.
Let's test what will happen at the end of his life.
[18] For if the righteous man is God's son, he will uphold him,
and he will deliver him out of the hand of his adversaries.
[19] Let's test him with insult and torture,
that we may find out how gentle he is,
and test his patience.
[20] Let's condemn him to a shameful death,
for he will be protected, according to his words."
[21] Thus they reasoned, and they were led astray;
for their wickedness blinded them,
[22] and they didn't know the mysteries of God,
neither did they hope for wages of holiness,
nor did they discern that there is a prize for blameless souls.

Responsorial Psalm: Psalms 34: 17-21

[17] The righteous cry, and Yahweh hears,
and delivers them out of all their troubles.
[18] Yahweh is near to those who have a broken heart,
and saves those who have a crushed spirit.
[19] Many are the afflictions of the righteous,
but Yahweh delivers him out of them all.
[20] He protects all of his bones.
Not one of them is broken.
[21] Evil shall kill the wicked.
Those who hate the righteous shall be condemned.

Gospel: John 7: 1-2, 10, 25-30

¹ After these things, Jesus was walking in Galilee, for he wouldn't walk in Judea, because the Jews sought to kill him. ² Now the feast of the Jews, the Feast of Booths, was at hand. ¹⁰ But when his brothers had gone up to the feast, then he also went up, not publicly, but as it were in secret.
²⁵ Therefore some of them of Jerusalem said, "Isn't this he whom they seek to kill? ²⁶ Behold, he speaks openly, and they say nothing to him. Can it be that the rulers indeed know that this is truly the Christ? ²⁷ However, we know where this man comes from, but when the Christ comes, no one will know where he comes from."
²⁸ Jesus therefore cried out in the temple, teaching and saying, "You both know me, and know where I am from. I have not come of myself, but he who sent me is true, whom you don't know. ²⁹ I know him, because I am from him, and he sent me."
³⁰ They sought therefore to take him; but no one laid a hand on him, because his hour had not yet come.

1. Invite the Holy Spirit into this reading, asking the Author of Scripture to speak to you through His Word
2. Read today's passage as many times as you need, take your time
3. Write down (below) what the Lord is saying to you today
4. Live with this Word in your heart through the day

___

___

Saturday, April 5, 2025
Saint Vincent Ferrer, Priest

First Reading: Jeremiah 11: 18-20

¹⁸ Yahweh gave me knowledge of it, and I knew it. Then you showed me their doings. ¹⁹ But I was like a gentle lamb that is led to the slaughter. I didn't know that they had devised plans against me, saying,
"Let's destroy the tree with its fruit,
and let's cut him off from the land of the living,
that his name may be no more remembered."
²⁰ But, Yahweh of Armies, who judges righteously,
who tests the heart and the mind,

I will see your vengeance on them;
for to you I have revealed my cause.

Responsorial Psalm: Psalms 7: 2-3, 9bc-10, 11-12

² lest they tear apart my soul like a lion,
ripping it in pieces, while there is no one to deliver.
³ Yahweh, my God, if I have done this,
if there is iniquity in my hands,
⁹ Oh let the wickedness of the wicked come to an end,
but establish the righteous;
their minds and hearts are searched by the righteous God.
¹⁰ My shield is with God,
who saves the upright in heart.
¹¹ God is a righteous judge,
yes, a God who has indignation every day.
¹² If a man doesn't repent, he will sharpen his sword;
he has bent and strung his bow.

Gospel: John 7: 40-53

⁴⁰ Many of the multitude therefore, when they heard these words, said, "This is truly the prophet." ⁴¹ Others said, "This is the Christ." But some said, "What, does the Christ come out of Galilee? ⁴² Hasn't the Scripture said that the Christ comes of the offspring of David, and from Bethlehem, the village where David was?" ⁴³ So a division arose in the multitude because of him. ⁴⁴ Some of them would have arrested him, but no one laid hands on him. ⁴⁵ The officers therefore came to the chief priests and Pharisees; and they said to them, "Why didn't you bring him?"
⁴⁶ The officers answered, "No man ever spoke like this man!"
⁴⁷ The Pharisees therefore answered them, "You aren't also led astray, are you? ⁴⁸ Have any of the rulers or any of the Pharisees believed in him? ⁴⁹ But this multitude that doesn't know the law is cursed."
⁵⁰ Nicodemus (he who came to him by night, being one of them) said to them, ⁵¹ "Does our law judge a man unless it first hears from him personally and knows what he does?"
⁵² They answered him, "Are you also from Galilee? Search and see that no prophet has arisen out of Galilee."
⁵³ Everyone went to his own house,

1. Invite the Holy Spirit into this reading, asking the Author of Scripture to speak to you through His Word

2. Read today's passage as many times as you need, take your time
3. Write down (below) what the Lord is saying to you today
4. Live with this Word in your heart through the day

_____

_____

Sunday, April 6, 2025
FIFTH SUNDAY OF LENT

First Reading: Isaiah 43: 16-21

¹⁶ Yahweh, who makes a way in the sea,
and a path in the mighty waters,
¹⁷ who brings out the chariot and horse,
the army and the mighty man
(they lie down together, they shall not rise;
they are extinct, they are quenched like a wick) says:
¹⁸ "Don't remember the former things,
and don't consider the things of old.
¹⁹ Behold, I will do a new thing.
It springs out now.
Don't you know it?
I will even make a way in the wilderness,
and rivers in the desert.
²⁰ The animals of the field, the jackals and the ostriches, shall honor me,
because I give water in the wilderness and rivers in the desert,
to give drink to my people, my chosen,
²¹ the people which I formed for myself,
that they might declare my praise.

Responsorial Psalm: Psalms 126: 1-6

¹ When Yahweh brought back those who returned to Zion,
we were like those who dream.
² Then our mouth was filled with laughter,
and our tongue with singing.
Then they said among the nations,

"Yahweh has done great things for them."
³ Yahweh has done great things for us,
and we are glad.
⁴ Restore our fortunes again, Yahweh,
like the streams in the Negev.
⁵ Those who sow in tears will reap in joy.
⁶ He who goes out weeping, carrying seed for sowing,
will certainly come again with joy, carrying his sheaves.

Second Reading: Philippians 3: 8-14

⁸ Yes most certainly, and I count all things to be a loss for the excellency of the knowledge of Christ Jesus, my Lord, for whom I suffered the loss of all things, and count them nothing but refuse, that I may gain Christ ⁹ and be found in him, not having a righteousness of my own, that which is of the law, but that which is through faith in Christ, the righteousness which is from God by faith, ¹⁰ that I may know him and the power of his resurrection, and the fellowship of his sufferings, becoming conformed to his death, ¹¹ if by any means I may attain to the resurrection from the dead. ¹² Not that I have already obtained, or am already made perfect; but I press on, that I may take hold of that for which also I was taken hold of by Christ Jesus.
¹³ Brothers, I don't regard myself as yet having taken hold, but one thing I do: forgetting the things which are behind and stretching forward to the things which are before, ¹⁴ I press on toward the goal for the prize of the high calling of God in Christ Jesus.

Gospel: John 8: 1-11

¹ but Jesus went to the Mount of Olives.
² Now very early in the morning, he came again into the temple, and all the people came to him. He sat down and taught them. ³ The scribes and the Pharisees brought a woman taken in adultry. Having set her in the middle, ⁴ they told him, "Teacher, we found this woman in adultry, in the very act. ⁵ Now in our law, Moses commanded us to stone such women.* What then do you say about her?" ⁶ They said this testing him, that they might have something to accuse him of.
But Jesus stooped down and wrote on the ground with his finger. ⁷ But when they continued asking him, he looked up and said to them, "He who is without sin among you, let him throw the first stone at her." ⁸ Again he stooped down and wrote on the ground with his finger.
⁹ They, when they heard it, being convicted by their conscience, went out one by one, beginning from the oldest, even to the last. Jesus was left alone with the woman where she

was, in the middle. ¹⁰ Jesus, standing up, saw her and said, "Woman, where are your accusers? Did no one condemn you?"

¹¹ She said, "No one, Lord."

Jesus said, "Neither do I condemn you. Go your way. From now on, sin no more."

1. Invite the Holy Spirit into this reading, asking the Author of Scripture to speak to you through His Word
2. Read today's passage as many times as you need, take your time
3. Write down (below) what the Lord is saying to you today
4. Live with this Word in your heart through the day

Monday, April 7, 2025
Saint John Baptist de la Salle, Priest

First Reading: Daniel 13: 41c-62

⁴¹ Then the assembly believed them, as those who were elders of the people and judges; so they condemned her to death.

⁴² Then Susanna cried out with a loud voice, and said, "O everlasting God, you know the secrets, and know all things before they happen. ⁴³ You know that they have testified falsely against me. Behold, I must die, even though I never did such things as these men have maliciously invented against me."

⁴⁴ The Lord heard her voice. ⁴⁵ Therefore when she was led away to be put to death, God raised up the holy spirit of a young youth, whose name was Daniel. ⁴⁶ He cried with a loud voice, "I am clear from the blood of this woman!"

⁴⁷ Then all the people turned them toward him, and said, "What do these words that you have spoken mean?"

⁴⁸ So he, standing in the midst of them, said, "Are you all such fools, you sons of Israel, that without examination or knowledge of the truth you have condemned a daughter of Israel? ⁴⁹ Return again to the place of judgment; for these have testified falsely against her."

⁵⁰ Therefore all the people turned again in haste, and the elders said to him, "Come, sit down among us, and show it to us, seeing God has given you the honor of an elder."

⁵¹ Then Daniel said to them, "Put them far apart from each another, and I will examine them." ⁵² So when they were put apart one from another, he called one of them, and said to him, "O you who have become old in wickedness, now your sins have returned which you

have committed before, ⁵³ in pronouncing unjust judgment, condemning the innocent, and letting the guilty go free; although the Lord says, 'You shall not kill the innocent and righteous.' ⁵⁴ Now then, if you saw her, tell me, under which tree did you see them companying together?"

He answered, "Under a mastick tree."

⁵⁵ And Daniel said, "You have certainly lied against your own head; for even now the angel of God has received the sentence of God and will cut you in two." ⁵⁶ So he put him aside, and commanded to bring the other, and said to him, "O you seed of Canaan, and not of Judah, beauty has deceived you, and lust has perverted your heart. ⁵⁷ Thus you have dealt with the daughters of Israel, and they for fear were intimate with you; but the daughter of Judah would not tolerate your wickedness. ⁵⁸ Now therefore tell me, under which tree did you take them being intimate together?"

He answered, "Under an evergreen oak tree."

⁵⁹ Then Daniel said to him, "You have also certainly lied against your own head; for the angel of God waits with the sword to cut you in two, that he may destroy you."

⁶⁰ With that, all the assembly cried out with a loud voice, and blessed God, who saves those who hope in him. ⁶¹ Then they arose against the two elders, for Daniel had convicted them of false testimony out of their own mouth. ⁶² According to the law of Moses they did to them what they maliciously intended to do to their neighbor. They put them to death, and the innocent blood was saved the same day.

Responsorial Psalm: Psalms 23: 1-6

¹ Yahweh is my shepherd;
I shall lack nothing.
² He makes me lie down in green pastures.
He leads me beside still waters.
³ He restores my soul.
He guides me in the paths of righteousness for his name's sake.
⁴ Even though I walk through the valley of the shadow of death,
I will fear no evil, for you are with me.
Your rod and your staff,
they comfort me.
⁵ You prepare a table before me
in the presence of my enemies.
You anoint my head with oil.
My cup runs over.
⁶ Surely goodness and loving kindness shall follow me all the days of my life,
and I will dwell in Yahweh's house forever.

Gospel: John 8: 12-20

¹² Again, therefore, Jesus spoke to them, saying, "I am the light of the world. He who follows me will not walk in the darkness, but will have the light of life."
¹³ The Pharisees therefore said to him, "You testify about yourself. Your testimony is not valid."
¹⁴ Jesus answered them, "Even if I testify about myself, my testimony is true, for I know where I came from, and where I am going; but you don't know where I came from, or where I am going. ¹⁵ You judge according to the flesh. I judge no one. ¹⁶ Even if I do judge, my judgment is true, for I am not alone, but I am with the Father who sent me. ¹⁷ It's also written in your law that the testimony of two people is valid. ¹⁸ I am one who testifies about myself, and the Father who sent me testifies about me."
¹⁹ They said therefore to him, "Where is your Father?"
Jesus answered, "You know neither me nor my Father. If you knew me, you would know my Father also." ²⁰ Jesus spoke these words in the treasury, as he taught in the temple. Yet no one arrested him, because his hour had not yet come.

1. Invite the Holy Spirit into this reading, asking the Author of Scripture to speak to you through His Word
2. Read today's passage as many times as you need, take your time
3. Write down (below) what the Lord is saying to you today
4. Live with this Word in your heart through the day

_____

_____

Tuesday, April 8, 2025

First Reading: Numbers 21: 4-9

⁴ They traveled from Mount Hor by the way to the Red Sea, to go around the land of Edom. The soul of the people was very discouraged because of the journey. ⁵ The people spoke against God and against Moses: "Why have you brought us up out of Egypt to die in the wilderness? For there is no bread, there is no water, and our soul loathes this disgusting food!"
⁶ Yahweh sent venomous snakes among the people, and they bit the people. Many people of Israel died. ⁷ The people came to Moses, and said, "We have sinned, because we have

spoken against Yahweh and against you. Pray to Yahweh, that he take away the serpents from us." Moses prayed for the people.

⁸ Yahweh said to Moses, "Make a venomous snake, and set it on a pole. It shall happen that everyone who is bitten, when he sees it, shall live." ⁹ Moses made a serpent of bronze, and set it on the pole. If a serpent had bitten any man, when he looked at the serpent of bronze, he lived.

Responsorial Psalm: Psalms 102: 2-3, 16-21

² Don't hide your face from me in the day of my distress.
Turn your ear to me.
Answer me quickly in the day when I call.
³ For my days consume away like smoke.
My bones are burned as a torch.
¹⁶ For Yahweh has built up Zion.
He has appeared in his glory.
¹⁷ He has responded to the prayer of the destitute,
and has not despised their prayer.
¹⁸ This will be written for the generation to come.
A people which will be created will praise Yah,
¹⁹ for he has looked down from the height of his sanctuary.
From heaven, Yahweh saw the earth,
²⁰ to hear the groans of the prisoner,
to free those who are condemned to death,
²¹ that men may declare Yahweh's name in Zion,
and his praise in Jerusalem,

Gospel: John 8: 21-30

²¹ Jesus said therefore again to them, "I am going away, and you will seek me, and you will die in your sins. Where I go, you can't come."

²² The Jews therefore said, "Will he kill himself, because he says, 'Where I am going, you can't come'?"

²³ He said to them, "You are from beneath. I am from above. You are of this world. I am not of this world. ²⁴ I said therefore to you that you will die in your sins; for unless you believe that I am⁺ he, you will die in your sins."

²⁵ They said therefore to him, "Who are you?"

Jesus said to them, "Just what I have been saying to you from the beginning. ²⁶ I have many things to speak and to judge concerning you. However, he who sent me is true; and the things which I heard from him, these I say to the world."

27 They didn't understand that he spoke to them about the Father. 28 Jesus therefore said to them, "When you have lifted up the Son of Man, then you will know that I am he, and I do nothing of myself, but as my Father taught me, I say these things. 29 He who sent me is with me. The Father hasn't left me alone, for I always do the things that are pleasing to him."

30 As he spoke these things, many believed in him.

1. Invite the Holy Spirit into this reading, asking the Author of Scripture to speak to you through His Word
2. Read today's passage as many times as you need, take your time
3. Write down (below) what the Lord is saying to you today
4. Live with this Word in your heart through the day

Wednesday, April 9, 2025

First Reading: Daniel 3: 14-20, 91-92, 95

14 Nebuchadnezzar answered them, "Is it on purpose, Shadrach, Meshach, and Abednego, that you don't serve my god, nor worship the golden image which I have set up? 15 Now if you are ready whenever you hear the sound of the horn, flute, zither, lyre, harp, pipe, and all kinds of music to fall down and worship the image which I have made, good; but if you don't worship, you shall be cast the same hour into the middle of a burning fiery furnace. Who is that god who will deliver you out of my hands?"

16 Shadrach, Meshach, and Abednego answered the king, "Nebuchadnezzar, we have no need to answer you in this matter. 17 If it happens, our God whom we serve is able to deliver us from the burning fiery furnace; and he will deliver us out of your hand, O king. 18 But if not, let it be known to you, O king, that we will not serve your gods or worship the golden image which you have set up."

19 Then Nebuchadnezzar was full of fury, and the form of his appearance was changed against Shadrach, Meshach, and Abednego. He spoke, and commanded that they should heat the furnace seven times more than it was usually heated. 20 He commanded certain mighty men who were in his army to bind Shadrach, Meshach, and Abednego, and to cast them into the burning fiery furnace.

91 ‡ Then Nebuchadnezzar the king was astonished and rose up in haste. He spoke and said to his counselors, "Didn't we cast three men bound into the middle of the fire?"

They answered the king, "True, O king."

⁹² He answered, "Look, I see four men loose, walking in the middle of the fire, and they are unharmed. The appearance of the fourth is like a son of the gods."

⁹⁵ Nebuchadnezzar spoke and said, "Blessed be the God of Shadrach, Meshach, and Abednego, who has sent his angel and delivered his servants who trusted in him, and have changed the king's word, and have yielded their bodies, that they might not serve nor worship any god, except their own God.

Responsorial Psalm: Daniel 3: 52, 53, 54, 55, 56

⁵² "Blessed are you, O Lord, you God of our fathers, to be praised and exalted above all forever! ⁵³ Blessed is your glorious and holy name, to be praised and exalted above all forever! ⁵⁴ Blessed are you in the temple of your holy glory, to be praised and glorified above all forever! ⁵⁵ Blessed are you who see the depths and sit upon the cherubim, to be praised and exalted above all forever. ⁵⁶ Blessed are you on the throne of your kingdom, to be praised and extolled above all forever!

Gospel: John 8: 31-42

³¹ Jesus therefore said to those Jews who had believed him, "If you remain in my word, then you are truly my disciples. ³² You will know the truth, and the truth will make you free."

³³ They answered him, "We are Abraham's offspring, and have never been in bondage to anyone. How do you say, 'You will be made free'?"

³⁴ Jesus answered them, "Most certainly I tell you, everyone who commits sin is the bondservant of sin. ³⁵ A bondservant doesn't live in the house forever. A son remains forever. ³⁶ If therefore the Son makes you free, you will be free indeed. ³⁷ I know that you are Abraham's offspring, yet you seek to kill me, because my word finds no place in you. ³⁸ I say the things which I have seen with my Father; and you also do the things which you have seen with your father."

³⁹ They answered him, "Our father is Abraham."

Jesus said to them, "If you were Abraham's children, you would do the works of Abraham. ⁴⁰ But now you seek to kill me, a man who has told you the truth which I heard from God. Abraham didn't do this. ⁴¹ You do the works of your father."

They said to him, "We were not born of sexual immorality. We have one Father, God."

⁴² Therefore Jesus said to them, "If God were your father, you would love me, for I came out and have come from God. For I haven't come of myself, but he sent me.

1. Invite the Holy Spirit into this reading, asking the Author of Scripture to speak to you through His Word
2. Read today's passage as many times as you need, take your time
3. Write down (below) what the Lord is saying to you today
4. Live with this Word in your heart through the day

_____

_____

Thursday, April 10, 2025

First Reading: Genesis 17: 3-9

3 Abram fell on his face. God talked with him, saying, 4 "As for me, behold, my covenant is with you. You will be the father of a multitude of nations. 5 Your name will no more be called Abram, but your name will be Abraham; for I have made you the father of a multitude of nations. 6 I will make you exceedingly fruitful, and I will make nations of you. Kings will come out of you. 7 I will establish my covenant between me and you and your offspring after you throughout their generations for an everlasting covenant, to be a God to you and to your offspring after you. 8 I will give to you, and to your offspring after you, the land where you are traveling, all the land of Canaan, for an everlasting possession. I will be their God."
9 God said to Abraham, "As for you, you shall keep my covenant, you and your offspring after you throughout their generations.

Responsorial Psalm: Psalms 105: 4-9

4 Seek Yahweh and his strength.
Seek his face forever more.
5 Remember his marvelous works that he has done:
his wonders, and the judgments of his mouth,
6 you offspring of Abraham, his servant,
you children of Jacob, his chosen ones.
7 He is Yahweh, our God.
His judgments are in all the earth.
8 He has remembered his covenant forever,
the word which he commanded to a thousand generations,
9 the covenant which he made with Abraham,

his oath to Isaac,

Gospel: John 8: 51-59

⁵¹ Most certainly, I tell you, if a person keeps my word, he will never see death."
⁵² Then the Jews said to him, "Now we know that you have a demon. Abraham died, as did the prophets; and you say, 'If a man keeps my word, he will never taste of death.' ⁵³ Are you greater than our father Abraham, who died? The prophets died. Who do you make yourself out to be?"
⁵⁴ Jesus answered, "If I glorify myself, my glory is nothing. It is my Father who glorifies me, of whom you say that he is our God. ⁵⁵ You have not known him, but I know him. If I said, 'I don't know him,' I would be like you, a liar. But I know him and keep his word. ⁵⁶ Your father Abraham rejoiced to see my day. He saw it and was glad."
⁵⁷ The Jews therefore said to him, "You are not yet fifty years old! Have you seen Abraham?"
⁵⁸ Jesus said to them, "Most certainly, I tell you, before Abraham came into existence, I AM.*"
⁵⁹ Therefore they took up stones to throw at him, but Jesus hid himself and went out of the temple, having gone through the middle of them, and so passed by.

1. Invite the Holy Spirit into this reading, asking the Author of Scripture to speak to you through His Word
2. Read today's passage as many times as you need, take your time
3. Write down (below) what the Lord is saying to you today
4. Live with this Word in your heart through the day

Friday, April 11, 2025
Saint Stanislaus, Bishop and Martyr

First Reading: Jeremiah 20: 10-13

¹⁰ For I have heard the defaming of many:
"Terror on every side!
Denounce, and we will denounce him!"
say all my familiar friends,
those who watch for my fall.

"Perhaps he will be persuaded,
and we will prevail against him,
and we will take our revenge on him."
¹¹ But Yahweh is with me as an awesome mighty one.
Therefore my persecutors will stumble,
and they won't prevail.
They will be utterly disappointed
because they have not dealt wisely,
even with an everlasting dishonor which will never be forgotten.
¹² But Yahweh of Armies, who tests the righteous,
who sees the heart and the mind,
let me see your vengeance on them,
for I have revealed my cause to you.
¹³ Sing to Yahweh!
Praise Yahweh,
for he has delivered the soul of the needy from the hand of evildoers.

Responsorial Psalm: Psalms 18: 2-7

² Yahweh is my rock, my fortress, and my deliverer;
my God, my rock, in whom I take refuge;
my shield, and the horn of my salvation, my high tower.
³ I call on Yahweh, who is worthy to be praised;
and I am saved from my enemies.
⁴ The cords of death surrounded me.
The floods of ungodliness made me afraid.
⁵ The cords of Sheol were around me.
The snares of death came on me.
⁶ In my distress I called on Yahweh,
and cried to my God.
He heard my voice out of his temple.
My cry before him came into his ears.
⁷ Then the earth shook and trembled.
The foundations also of the mountains quaked and were shaken,
because he was angry.

Gospel: John 10: 31-42

³¹ Therefore the Jews took up stones again to stone him. ³² Jesus answered them, "I have shown you many good works from my Father. For which of those works do you stone me?"

33 The Jews answered him, "We don't stone you for a good work, but for blasphemy, because you, being a man, make yourself God."
34 Jesus answered them, "Isn't it written in your law, 'I said, you are gods'? 35 If he called them gods, to whom the word of God came (and the Scripture can't be broken), 36 do you say of him whom the Father sanctified and sent into the world, 'You blaspheme,' because I said, 'I am the Son of God'? 37 If I don't do the works of my Father, don't believe me. 38 But if I do them, though you don't believe me, believe the works, that you may know and believe that the Father is in me, and I in the Father."
39 They sought again to seize him, and he went out of their hand. 40 He went away again beyond the Jordan into the place where John was baptizing at first, and he stayed there. 41 Many came to him. They said, "John indeed did no sign, but everything that John said about this man is true." 42 Many believed in him there.

1. Invite the Holy Spirit into this reading, asking the Author of Scripture to speak to you through His Word
2. Read today's passage as many times as you need, take your time
3. Write down (below) what the Lord is saying to you today
4. Live with this Word in your heart through the day

Saturday, April 12, 2025

First Reading: Ezekiel 37: 21-28

21 Say to them, 'The Lord Yahweh says: "Behold, I will take the children of Israel from among the nations where they have gone, and will gather them on every side, and bring them into their own land. 22 I will make them one nation in the land, on the mountains of Israel. One king will be king to them all. They will no longer be two nations. They won't be divided into two kingdoms any more at all. 23 They won't defile themselves any more with their idols, nor with their detestable things, nor with any of their transgressions; but I will save them out of all their dwelling places in which they have sinned, and will cleanse them. So they will be my people, and I will be their God.
24 " ' "My servant David will be king over them. They all will have one shepherd. They will also walk in my ordinances and observe my statutes, and do them. 25 They will dwell in the land that I have given to Jacob my servant, in which your fathers lived. They will dwell therein, they, and their children, and their children's children, forever. David my servant

will be their prince forever. ²⁶ Moreover I will make a covenant of peace with them. It will be an everlasting covenant with them. I will place them, multiply them, and will set my sanctuary among them forever more. ²⁷ My tent also will be with them. I will be their God, and they will be my people. ²⁸ The nations will know that I am Yahweh who sanctifies Israel, when my sanctuary is among them forever more." ' "

Responsorial Psalm: Jeremiah 31: 10, 11-12, 13

¹⁰ "Hear Yahweh's word, you nations,
and declare it in the distant islands. Say,
'He who scattered Israel will gather him,
and keep him, as a shepherd does his flock.'
¹¹ For Yahweh has ransomed Jacob,
and redeemed him from the hand of him who was stronger than he.
¹² They will come and sing in the height of Zion,
and will flow to the goodness of Yahweh,
to the grain, to the new wine, to the oil,
and to the young of the flock and of the herd.
Their soul will be as a watered garden.
They will not sorrow any more at all.
¹³ Then the virgin will rejoice in the dance,
the young men and the old together;
for I will turn their mourning into joy,

Gospel: John 11: 45-56

⁴⁵ Therefore many of the Jews who came to Mary and saw what Jesus did believed in him. ⁴⁶ But some of them went away to the Pharisees and told them the things which Jesus had done. ⁴⁷ The chief priests therefore and the Pharisees gathered a council, and said, "What are we doing? For this man does many signs. ⁴⁸ If we leave him alone like this, everyone will believe in him, and the Romans will come and take away both our place and our nation."
⁴⁹ But a certain one of them, Caiaphas, being high priest that year, said to them, "You know nothing at all, ⁵⁰ nor do you consider that it is advantageous for us that one man should die for the people, and that the whole nation not perish." ⁵¹ Now he didn't say this of himself, but being high priest that year, he prophesied that Jesus would die for the nation, ⁵² and not for the nation only, but that he might also gather together into one the children of God who are scattered abroad. ⁵³ So from that day forward they took counsel that they might put him to death. ⁵⁴ Jesus therefore walked no more openly among the Jews, but departed

from there into the country near the wilderness, to a city called Ephraim. He stayed there with his disciples.
55 Now the Passover of the Jews was at hand. Many went up from the country to Jerusalem before the Passover, to purify themselves. 56 Then they sought for Jesus and spoke with one another as they stood in the temple, "What do you think—that he isn't coming to the feast at all?"

1. Invite the Holy Spirit into this reading, asking the Author of Scripture to speak to you through His Word
2. Read today's passage as many times as you need, take your time
3. Write down (below) what the Lord is saying to you today
4. Live with this Word in your heart through the day

Sunday, April 13, 2025
PALM SUNDAY OF THE PASSION OF THE LORD

Procession: Luke 19: 28-40

28 Having said these things, he went on ahead, going up to Jerusalem.
29 When he came near to Bethsphage‡ and Bethany, at the mountain that is called Olivet, he sent two of his disciples, 30 saying, "Go your way into the village on the other side, in which, as you enter, you will find a colt tied, which no man has ever sat upon. Untie it and bring it. 31 If anyone asks you, 'Why are you untying it?' say to him: 'The Lord needs it.'"
32 Those who were sent went away and found things just as he had told them. 33 As they were untying the colt, its owners said to them, "Why are you untying the colt?" 34 They said, "The Lord needs it." 35 Then they brought it to Jesus. They threw their cloaks on the colt and sat Jesus on them. 36 As he went, they spread their cloaks on the road.
37 As he was now getting near, at the descent of the Mount of Olives, the whole multitude of the disciples began to rejoice and praise God with a loud voice for all the mighty works which they had seen, 38 saying, "Blessed is the King who comes in the name of the Lord!⁑ Peace in heaven, and glory in the highest!"
39 Some of the Pharisees from the multitude said to him, "Teacher, rebuke your disciples!"
40 He answered them, "I tell you that if these were silent, the stones would cry out."

First Reading: Isaiah 50: 4-7

⁴ The Lord Yahweh has given me the tongue of those who are taught,
that I may know how to sustain with words him who is weary.
He awakens morning by morning,
he awakens my ear to hear as those who are taught.
⁵ The Lord Yahweh has opened my ear.
I was not rebellious.
I have not turned back.
⁶ I gave my back to those who beat me,
and my cheeks to those who plucked off the hair.
I didn't hide my face from shame and spitting.
⁷ For the Lord Yahweh will help me.
Therefore I have not been confounded.
Therefore I have set my face like a flint,
and I know that I won't be disappointed.

Responsorial Psalm: Psalms 22: 8-9, 17-20, 23-24

⁸ "He trusts in Yahweh.
Let him deliver him.
Let him rescue him, since he delights in him."
⁹ But you brought me out of the womb.
You made me trust while at my mother's breasts.
¹⁷ I can count all of my bones.
They look and stare at me.
¹⁸ They divide my garments among them.
They cast lots for my clothing.
¹⁹ But don't be far off, Yahweh.
You are my help. Hurry to help me!
²⁰ Deliver my soul from the sword,
my precious life from the power of the dog.
²³ You who fear Yahweh, praise him!
All you descendants of Jacob, glorify him!
Stand in awe of him, all you descendants of Israel!
²⁴ For he has not despised nor abhorred the affliction of the afflicted,
neither has he hidden his face from him;
but when he cried to him, he heard.

Second Reading: Philippians 2:6-11

⁶ who, existing in the form of God, didn't consider equality with God a thing to be grasped, ⁷ but emptied himself, taking the form of a servant, being made in the likeness of men. ⁸ And being found in human form, he humbled himself, becoming obedient to the point of death, yes, the death of the cross. ⁹ Therefore God also highly exalted him, and gave to him the name which is above every name, ¹⁰ that at the name of Jesus every knee should bow, of those in heaven, those on earth, and those under the earth, ¹¹ and that every tongue should confess that Jesus Christ is Lord, to the glory of God the Father.

Gospel: Luke 22: 14 – 23: 56

¹⁴ When the hour had come, he sat down with the twelve apostles. ¹⁵ He said to them, "I have earnestly desired to eat this Passover with you before I suffer, ¹⁶ for I tell you, I will no longer by any means eat of it until it is fulfilled in God's Kingdom." ¹⁷ He received a cup, and when he had given thanks, he said, "Take this and share it among yourselves, ¹⁸ for I tell you, I will not drink at all again from the fruit of the vine, until God's Kingdom comes." ¹⁹ He took bread, and when he had given thanks, he broke and gave it to them, saying, "This is my body which is given for you. Do this in memory of me." ²⁰ Likewise, he took the cup after supper, saying, "This cup is the new covenant in my blood, which is poured out for you. ²¹ But behold, the hand of him who betrays me is with me on the table. ²² The Son of Man indeed goes as it has been determined, but woe to that man through whom he is betrayed!"

²³ They began to question among themselves which of them it was who would do this thing.
²⁴ A dispute also arose among them, which of them was considered to be greatest. ²⁵ He said to them, "The kings of the nations lord it over them, and those who have authority over them are called 'benefactors.' ²⁶ But not so with you. Rather, the one who is greater among you, let him become as the younger, and one who is governing, as one who serves. ²⁷ For who is greater, one who sits at the table, or one who serves? Isn't it he who sits at the table? But I am among you as one who serves.

²⁸ "But you are those who have continued with me in my trials. ²⁹ I confer on you a kingdom, even as my Father conferred on me, ³⁰ that you may eat and drink at my table in my Kingdom. You will sit on thrones, judging the twelve tribes of Israel."

³¹ The Lord said, "Simon, Simon, behold, Satan asked to have all of you, that he might sift you as wheat, ³² but I prayed for you, that your faith wouldn't fail. You, when once you have turned again, establish your brothers."±

³³ He said to him, "Lord, I am ready to go with you both to prison and to death!"

³⁴ He said, "I tell you, Peter, the rooster will by no means crow today until you deny that you know me three times."

³⁵ He said to them, "When I sent you out without purse, bag, and sandals, did you lack anything?"

They said, "Nothing."

36 Then he said to them, "But now, whoever has a purse, let him take it, and likewise a bag. Whoever has none, let him sell his cloak, and buy a sword. 37 For I tell you that this which is written must still be fulfilled in me: 'He was counted with transgressors.'* For that which concerns me is being fulfilled."

38 They said, "Lord, behold, here are two swords."

He said to them, "That is enough."

39 He came out and went, as his custom was, to the Mount of Olives. His disciples also followed him. 40 When he was at the place, he said to them, "Pray that you don't enter into temptation."

41 He was withdrawn from them about a stone's throw, and he knelt down and prayed, 42 saying, "Father, if you are willing, remove this cup from me. Nevertheless, not my will, but yours, be done."

43 An angel from heaven appeared to him, strengthening him. 44 Being in agony, he prayed more earnestly. His sweat became like great drops of blood falling down on the ground.

45 When he rose up from his prayer, he came to the disciples and found them sleeping because of grief, 46 and said to them, "Why do you sleep? Rise and pray that you may not enter into temptation."

47 While he was still speaking, a crowd appeared. He who was called Judas, one of the twelve, was leading them. He came near to Jesus to kiss him. 48 But Jesus said to him, "Judas, do you betray the Son of Man with a kiss?"

49 When those who were around him saw what was about to happen, they said to him, "Lord, shall we strike with the sword?" 50 A certain one of them struck the servant of the high priest, and cut off his right ear.

51 But Jesus answered, "Let me at least do this"—and he touched his ear and healed him. 52 Jesus said to the chief priests, captains of the temple, and elders, who had come against him, "Have you come out as against a robber, with swords and clubs? 53 When I was with you in the temple daily, you didn't stretch out your hands against me. But this is your hour, and the power of darkness."

54 They seized him and led him away, and brought him into the high priest's house. But Peter followed from a distance. 55 When they had kindled a fire in the middle of the courtyard and had sat down together, Peter sat among them. 56 A certain servant girl saw him as he sat in the light, and looking intently at him, said, "This man also was with him."

57 He denied Jesus, saying, "Woman, I don't know him."

58 After a little while someone else saw him and said, "You also are one of them!"

But Peter answered, "Man, I am not!"

59 After about one hour passed, another confidently affirmed, saying, "Truly this man also was with him, for he is a Galilean!"

60 But Peter said, "Man, I don't know what you are talking about!" Immediately, while he was still speaking, a rooster crowed. 61 The Lord turned and looked at Peter. Then Peter

remembered the Lord's word, how he said to him, "Before the rooster crows you will deny me three times." ⁶² He went out, and wept bitterly.

⁶³ The men who held Jesus mocked him and beat him. ⁶⁴ Having blindfolded him, they struck him on the face and asked him, "Prophesy! Who is the one who struck you?" ⁶⁵ They spoke many other things against him, insulting him.

⁶⁶ As soon as it was day, the assembly of the elders of the people were gathered together, both chief priests and scribes, and they led him away into their council, saying, ⁶⁷ "If you are the Christ, tell us."

But he said to them, "If I tell you, you won't believe, ⁶⁸ and if I ask, you will in no way answer me or let me go. ⁶⁹ From now on, the Son of Man will be seated at the right hand of the power of God."

⁷⁰ They all said, "Are you then the Son of God?"

He said to them, "You say it, because I am."

⁷¹ They said, "Why do we need any more witness? For we ourselves have heard from his own mouth!"

¹ The whole company of them rose up and brought him before Pilate. ² They began to accuse him, saying, "We found this man perverting the nation, forbidding paying taxes to Caesar, and saying that he himself is Christ, a king."

³ Pilate asked him, "Are you the King of the Jews?"

He answered him, "So you say."

⁴ Pilate said to the chief priests and the multitudes, "I find no basis for a charge against this man."

⁵ But they insisted, saying, "He stirs up the people, teaching throughout all Judea, beginning from Galilee even to this place."

⁶ But when Pilate heard Galilee mentioned, he asked if the man was a Galilean. ⁷ When he found out that he was in Herod's jurisdiction, he sent him to Herod, who was also in Jerusalem during those days.

⁸ Now when Herod saw Jesus, he was exceedingly glad, for he had wanted to see him for a long time, because he had heard many things about him. He hoped to see some miracle done by him. ⁹ He questioned him with many words, but he gave no answers. ¹⁰ The chief priests and the scribes stood, vehemently accusing him. ¹¹ Herod with his soldiers humiliated him and mocked him. Dressing him in luxurious clothing, they sent him back to Pilate. ¹² Herod and Pilate became friends with each other that very day, for before that they were enemies with each other.

¹³ Pilate called together the chief priests, the rulers, and the people, ¹⁴ and said to them, "You brought this man to me as one that perverts the people, and behold, having examined him before you, I found no basis for a charge against this man concerning those things of which you accuse him. ¹⁵ Neither has Herod, for I sent you to him, and see, nothing worthy of death has been done by him. ¹⁶ I will therefore chastise him and release him."

¹⁷ Now he had to release one prisoner to them at the feast.† ¹⁸ But they all cried out together, saying, "Away with this man! Release to us Barabbas!"— ¹⁹ one who was thrown into prison for a certain revolt in the city, and for murder.

²⁰ Then Pilate spoke to them again, wanting to release Jesus, ²¹ but they shouted, saying, "Crucify! Crucify him!"

²² He said to them the third time, "Why? What evil has this man done? I have found no capital crime in him. I will therefore chastise him and release him." ²³ But they were urgent with loud voices, asking that he might be crucified. Their voices and the voices of the chief priests prevailed. ²⁴ Pilate decreed that what they asked for should be done. ²⁵ He released him who had been thrown into prison for insurrection and murder, for whom they asked, but he delivered Jesus up to their will.

²⁶ When they led him away, they grabbed one Simon of Cyrene, coming from the country, and laid the cross on him to carry it after Jesus. ²⁷ A great multitude of the people followed him, including women who also mourned and lamented him. ²⁸ But Jesus, turning to them, said, "Daughters of Jerusalem, don't weep for me, but weep for yourselves and for your children. ²⁹ For behold, the days are coming in which they will say, 'Blessed are the barren, the wombs that never bore, and the breasts that never nursed.' ³⁰ Then they will begin to tell the mountains, 'Fall on us!' and tell the hills, 'Cover us.'* ³¹ For if they do these things in the green tree, what will be done in the dry?"

³² There were also others, two criminals, led with him to be put to death. ³³ When they came to the place that is called "The Skull", they crucified him there with the criminals, one on the right and the other on the left.

³⁴ Jesus said, "Father, forgive them, for they don't know what they are doing."

Dividing his garments among them, they cast lots. ³⁵ The people stood watching. The rulers with them also scoffed at him, saying, "He saved others. Let him save himself, if this is the Christ of God, his chosen one!"

³⁶ The soldiers also mocked him, coming to him and offering him vinegar, ³⁷ and saying, "If you are the King of the Jews, save yourself!"

³⁸ An inscription was also written over him in letters of Greek, Latin, and Hebrew: "THIS IS THE KING OF THE JEWS."

³⁹ One of the criminals who was hanged insulted him, saying, "If you are the Christ, save yourself and us!"

⁴⁰ But the other answered, and rebuking him said, "Don't you even fear God, seeing you are under the same condemnation? ⁴¹ And we indeed justly, for we receive the due reward for our deeds, but this man has done nothing wrong." ⁴² He said to Jesus, "Lord, remember me when you come into your Kingdom."

⁴³ Jesus said to him, "Assuredly I tell you, today you will be with me in Paradise."

⁴⁴ It was now about the sixth hour,‡ and darkness came over the whole land until the ninth hour.§ ⁴⁵ The sun was darkened, and the veil of the temple was torn in two. ⁴⁶ Jesus, crying

with a loud voice, said, "Father, into your hands I commit my spirit!" Having said this, he breathed his last.

47 When the centurion saw what was done, he glorified God, saying, "Certainly this was a righteous man." 48 All the multitudes that came together to see this, when they saw the things that were done, returned home beating their chests. 49 All his acquaintances and the women who followed with him from Galilee stood at a distance, watching these things.

50 Behold, there was a man named Joseph, who was a member of the council, a good and righteous man 51 (he had not consented to their counsel and deed), from Arimathaea, a city of the Jews, who was also waiting for God's Kingdom. 52 This man went to Pilate, and asked for Jesus' body. 53 He took it down and wrapped it in a linen cloth, and laid him in a tomb that was cut in stone, where no one had ever been laid. 54 It was the day of the Preparation, and the Sabbath was drawing near. 55 The women who had come with him out of Galilee followed after, and saw the tomb and how his body was laid. 56 They returned and prepared spices and ointments. On the Sabbath they rested according to the commandment.

1. Invite the Holy Spirit into this reading, asking the Author of Scripture to speak to you through His Word
2. Read today's passage as many times as you need, take your time
3. Write down (below) what the Lord is saying to you today
4. Live with this Word in your heart through the day

Monday, April 14, 2025
Monday of Holy Week

First Reading: Isaiah 42: 1-7

1 "Behold, my servant, whom I uphold,
my chosen, in whom my soul delights:
I have put my Spirit on him.
He will bring justice to the nations.
2 He will not shout,
nor raise his voice,
nor cause it to be heard in the street.
3 He won't break a bruised reed.
He won't quench a dimly burning wick.

He will faithfully bring justice.
⁴ He will not fail nor be discouraged,
until he has set justice in the earth,
and the islands wait for his law."
⁵ God Yahweh,
he who created the heavens and stretched them out,
he who spread out the earth and that which comes out of it,
he who gives breath to its people and spirit to those who walk in it, says:
⁶ "I, Yahweh, have called you in righteousness.
I will hold your hand.
I will keep you,
and make you a covenant for the people,
as a light for the nations,
⁷ to open the blind eyes,
to bring the prisoners out of the dungeon,
and those who sit in darkness out of the prison.

Responsorial Psalm: Psalms 27: 1, 2, 3, 13-14

¹ Yahweh is my light and my salvation.
Whom shall I fear?
Yahweh is the strength of my life.
Of whom shall I be afraid?
² When evildoers came at me to eat up my flesh,
even my adversaries and my foes, they stumbled and fell.
³ Though an army should encamp against me,
my heart shall not fear.
Though war should rise against me,
even then I will be confident.
¹³ I am still confident of this:
I will see the goodness of Yahweh in the land of the living.
¹⁴ Wait for Yahweh.
Be strong, and let your heart take courage.
Yes, wait for Yahweh.

Gospel: John 12: 1-11

¹ Then, six days before the Passover, Jesus came to Bethany, where Lazarus was, who had been dead, whom he raised from the dead. ² So they made him a supper there. Martha served, but Lazarus was one of those who sat at the table with him. ³ Therefore Mary took

a pound⸸ of ointment of pure nard, very precious, and anointed Jesus' feet and wiped his feet with her hair. The house was filled with the fragrance of the ointment.

⁴ Then Judas Iscariot, Simon's son, one of his disciples, who would betray him, said, ⁵ "Why wasn't this ointment sold for three hundred denarii⸸ and given to the poor?" ⁶ Now he said this, not because he cared for the poor, but because he was a thief, and having the money box, used to steal what was put into it.

⁷ But Jesus said, "Leave her alone. She has kept this for the day of my burial. ⁸ For you always have the poor with you, but you don't always have me."

⁹ A large crowd therefore of the Jews learned that he was there; and they came, not for Jesus' sake only, but that they might see Lazarus also, whom he had raised from the dead. ¹⁰ But the chief priests conspired to put Lazarus to death also, ¹¹ because on account of him many of the Jews went away and believed in Jesus.

1. Invite the Holy Spirit into this reading, asking the Author of Scripture to speak to you through His Word
2. Read today's passage as many times as you need, take your time
3. Write down (below) what the Lord is saying to you today
4. Live with this Word in your heart through the day

Tuesday, April 15, 2025
Tuesday of Holy Week

First Reading: Isaiah 49: 1-6

¹ Listen, islands, to me.
Listen, you peoples, from afar:
Yahweh has called me from the womb;
from the inside of my mother, he has mentioned my name.
² He has made my mouth like a sharp sword.
He has hidden me in the shadow of his hand.
He has made me a polished shaft.
He has kept me close in his quiver.
³ He said to me, "You are my servant,
Israel, in whom I will be glorified."
⁴ But I said, "I have labored in vain.

I have spent my strength in vain for nothing;
yet surely the justice due to me is with Yahweh,
and my reward with my God."
⁵ Now Yahweh, he who formed me from the womb to be his servant,
says to bring Jacob again to him,
and to gather Israel to him,
for I am honorable in Yahweh's eyes,
and my God has become my strength.
⁶ Indeed, he says, "It is too light a thing that you should be my servant to raise up the tribes of Jacob,
and to restore the preserved of Israel.
I will also give you as a light to the nations,
that you may be my salvation to the end of the earth."

Responsorial Psalm: Psalms 71: 1-6, 15 and 17

¹ In you, Yahweh, I take refuge.
Never let me be disappointed.
² Deliver me in your righteousness, and rescue me.
Turn your ear to me, and save me.
³ Be to me a rock of refuge to which I may always go.
Give the command to save me,
for you are my rock and my fortress.
⁴ Rescue me, my God, from the hand of the wicked,
from the hand of the unrighteous and cruel man.
⁵ For you are my hope, Lord Yahweh,
my confidence from my youth.
⁶ I have relied on you from the womb.
You are he who took me out of my mother's womb.
I will always praise you.
¹⁵ My mouth will tell about your righteousness,
and of your salvation all day,
though I don't know its full measure.
¹⁷ God, you have taught me from my youth.
Until now, I have declared your wondrous works.

Gospel: John 13: 21-33, 36-38

²¹ When Jesus had said this, he was troubled in spirit, and testified, "Most certainly I tell you that one of you will betray me."

²² The disciples looked at one another, perplexed about whom he spoke. ²³ One of his disciples, whom Jesus loved, was at the table, leaning against Jesus' chest. ²⁴ Simon Peter therefore beckoned to him, and said to him, "Tell us who it is of whom he speaks."

²⁵ He, leaning back, as he was, on Jesus' chest, asked him, "Lord, who is it?"

²⁶ Jesus therefore answered, "It is he to whom I will give this piece of bread when I have dipped it." So when he had dipped the piece of bread, he gave it to Judas, the son of Simon Iscariot. ²⁷ After the piece of bread, then Satan entered into him.

Then Jesus said to him, "What you do, do quickly."

²⁸ Now nobody at the table knew why he said this to him. ²⁹ For some thought, because Judas had the money box, that Jesus said to him, "Buy what things we need for the feast," or that he should give something to the poor. ³⁰ Therefore having received that morsel, he went out immediately. It was night.

³¹ When he had gone out, Jesus said, "Now the Son of Man has been glorified, and God has been glorified in him. ³² If God has been glorified in him, God will also glorify him in himself, and he will glorify him immediately. ³³ Little children, I will be with you a little while longer. You will seek me, and as I said to the Jews, 'Where I am going, you can't come,' so now I tell you.

³⁶ Simon Peter said to him, "Lord, where are you going?"

Jesus answered, "Where I am going, you can't follow now, but you will follow afterwards."

³⁷ Peter said to him, "Lord, why can't I follow you now? I will lay down my life for you."

³⁸ Jesus answered him, "Will you lay down your life for me? Most certainly I tell you, the rooster won't crow until you have denied me three times.

1. Invite the Holy Spirit into this reading, asking the Author of Scripture to speak to you through His Word
2. Read today's passage as many times as you need, take your time
3. Write down (below) what the Lord is saying to you today
4. Live with this Word in your heart through the day

_____

_____

Wednesday, April 16, 2025
Wednesday of Holy Week

First Reading: Isaiah 50: 4-9a

⁴ The Lord Yahweh has given me the tongue of those who are taught,

that I may know how to sustain with words him who is weary.
He awakens morning by morning,
he awakens my ear to hear as those who are taught.
⁵ The Lord Yahweh has opened my ear.
I was not rebellious.
I have not turned back.
⁶ I gave my back to those who beat me,
and my cheeks to those who plucked off the hair.
I didn't hide my face from shame and spitting.
⁷ For the Lord Yahweh will help me.
Therefore I have not been confounded.
Therefore I have set my face like a flint,
and I know that I won't be disappointed.
⁸ He who justifies me is near.
Who will bring charges against me?
Let us stand up together.
Who is my adversary?
Let him come near to me.
⁹ Behold, the Lord Yahweh will help me!
Who is he who will condemn me?

Responsorial Psalm: Psalms 69: 8-10, 21-22, 31 and 33-34

⁸ I have become a stranger to my brothers,
an alien to my mother's children.
⁹ For the zeal of your house consumes me.
The reproaches of those who reproach you have fallen on me.
¹⁰ When I wept and I fasted,
that was to my reproach.
²¹ They also gave me poison for my food.
In my thirst, they gave me vinegar to drink.
²² Let their table before them become a snare.
May it become a retribution and a trap.
³¹ It will please Yahweh better than an ox,
or a bull that has horns and hoofs.
³³ For Yahweh hears the needy,
and doesn't despise his captive people.
³⁴ Let heaven and earth praise him;
the seas, and everything that moves therein!

Gospel: Matthew 26: 14-25

¹⁴ Then one of the twelve, who was called Judas Iscariot, went to the chief priests ¹⁵ and said, "What are you willing to give me if I deliver him to you?" So they weighed out for him thirty pieces of silver. ¹⁶ From that time he sought opportunity to betray him.
¹⁷ Now on the first day of unleavened bread, the disciples came to Jesus, saying to him, "Where do you want us to prepare for you to eat the Passover?"
¹⁸ He said, "Go into the city to a certain person, and tell him, 'The Teacher says, "My time is at hand. I will keep the Passover at your house with my disciples." ' "
¹⁹ The disciples did as Jesus commanded them, and they prepared the Passover.
²⁰ Now when evening had come, he was reclining at the table with the twelve disciples. ²¹ As they were eating, he said, "Most certainly I tell you that one of you will betray me."
²² They were exceedingly sorrowful, and each began to ask him, "It isn't me, is it, Lord?"
²³ He answered, "He who dipped his hand with me in the dish will betray me. ²⁴ The Son of Man goes even as it is written of him, but woe to that man through whom the Son of Man is betrayed! It would be better for that man if he had not been born."
²⁵ Judas, who betrayed him, answered, "It isn't me, is it, Rabbi?"
He said to him, "You said it."

1. Invite the Holy Spirit into this reading, asking the Author of Scripture to speak to you through His Word
2. Read today's passage as many times as you need, take your time
3. Write down (below) what the Lord is saying to you today
4. Live with this Word in your heart through the day

_____

_____

Thursday, April 17, 2025
Thursday of Holy Week (Holy Thursday)

First Reading: Exodus 12: 1-8, 11-14

¹ Yahweh spoke to Moses and Aaron in the land of Egypt, saying, ² "This month shall be to you the beginning of months. It shall be the first month of the year to you. ³ Speak to all the congregation of Israel, saying, 'On the tenth day of this month, they shall take to them every man a lamb, according to their fathers' houses, a lamb for a household; ⁴ and if the household is too little for a lamb, then he and his neighbor next to his house shall take one

according to the number of the souls. You shall make your count for the lamb according to what everyone can eat. 5 Your lamb shall be without defect, a male a year old. You shall take it from the sheep or from the goats. 6 You shall keep it until the fourteenth day of the same month; and the whole assembly of the congregation of Israel shall kill it at evening. 7 They shall take some of the blood, and put it on the two door posts and on the lintel, on the houses in which they shall eat it. 8 They shall eat the meat in that night, roasted with fire, with unleavened bread. They shall eat it with bitter herbs.

11 This is how you shall eat it: with your belt on your waist, your sandals on your feet, and your staff in your hand; and you shall eat it in haste: it is Yahweh's Passover. 12 For I will go through the land of Egypt in that night, and will strike all the firstborn in the land of Egypt, both man and animal. I will execute judgments against all the gods of Egypt. I am Yahweh. 13 The blood shall be to you for a token on the houses where you are. When I see the blood, I will pass over you, and no plague will be on you to destroy you when I strike the land of Egypt. 14 This day shall be a memorial for you. You shall keep it as a feast to Yahweh. You shall keep it as a feast throughout your generations by an ordinance forever.

Responsorial Psalm: Psalms 116: 12-13, 15-18

12 What will I give to Yahweh for all his benefits toward me?
13 I will take the cup of salvation, and call on Yahweh's name.
15 Precious in Yahweh's sight is the death of his saints.
16 Yahweh, truly I am your servant.
I am your servant, the son of your servant girl.
You have freed me from my chains.
17 I will offer to you the sacrifice of thanksgiving,
and will call on Yahweh's name.
18 I will pay my vows to Yahweh,
yes, in the presence of all his people,

Second Reading: First Corinthians 11: 23-26

23 For I received from the Lord that which also I delivered to you, that the Lord Jesus on the night in which he was betrayed took bread. 24 When he had given thanks, he broke it and said, "Take, eat. This is my body, which is broken for you. Do this in memory of me." 25 In the same way he also took the cup after supper, saying, "This cup is the new covenant in my blood. Do this, as often as you drink, in memory of me." 26 For as often as you eat this bread and drink this cup, you proclaim the Lord's death until he comes.

Gospel: John 13: 1-15

¹ Now before the feast of the Passover, Jesus, knowing that his time had come that he would depart from this world to the Father, having loved his own who were in the world, he loved them to the end. ² During supper, the devil having already put into the heart of Judas Iscariot, Simon's son, to betray him, ³ Jesus, knowing that the Father had given all things into his hands, and that he came from God and was going to God, ⁴ arose from supper, and laid aside his outer garments. He took a towel and wrapped a towel around his waist. ⁵ Then he poured water into the basin, and began to wash the disciples' feet and to wipe them with the towel that was wrapped around him. ⁶ Then he came to Simon Peter. He said to him, "Lord, do you wash my feet?"

⁷ Jesus answered him, "You don't know what I am doing now, but you will understand later."

⁸ Peter said to him, "You will never wash my feet!"

Jesus answered him, "If I don't wash you, you have no part with me."

⁹ Simon Peter said to him, "Lord, not my feet only, but also my hands and my head!"

¹⁰ Jesus said to him, "Someone who has bathed only needs to have his feet washed, but is completely clean. You are clean, but not all of you." ¹¹ For he knew him who would betray him; therefore he said, "You are not all clean." ¹² So when he had washed their feet, put his outer garment back on, and sat down again, he said to them, "Do you know what I have done to you? ¹³ You call me, 'Teacher' and 'Lord.' You say so correctly, for so I am. ¹⁴ If I then, the Lord and the Teacher, have washed your feet, you also ought to wash one another's feet. ¹⁵ For I have given you an example, that you should also do as I have done to you.

1. Invite the Holy Spirit into this reading, asking the Author of Scripture to speak to you through His Word
2. Read today's passage as many times as you need, take your time
3. Write down (below) what the Lord is saying to you today
4. Live with this Word in your heart through the day

Friday, April 18, 2025
Friday of the Passion of the Lord (Good Friday)

First Reading: Isaiah 52: 13 – 53: 12

¹³ Behold, my servant will deal wisely.

He will be exalted and lifted up,
and will be very high.
¹⁴ Just as many were astonished at you—
his appearance was marred more than any man, and his form more than the sons of men—
¹⁵ so he will cleanse‡ many nations.
Kings will shut their mouths at him;
for they will see that which had not been told them,
and they will understand that which they had not heard.
¹ Who has believed our message?
To whom has Yahweh's arm been revealed?
² For he grew up before him as a tender plant,
and as a root out of dry ground.
He has no good looks or majesty.
When we see him, there is no beauty that we should desire him.
³ He was despised
and rejected by men,
a man of suffering
and acquainted with disease.
He was despised as one from whom men hide their face;
and we didn't respect him.
⁴ Surely he has borne our sickness
and carried our suffering;
yet we considered him plagued,
struck by God, and afflicted.
⁵ But he was pierced for our transgressions.
He was crushed for our iniquities.
The punishment that brought our peace was on him;
and by his wounds we are healed.
⁶ All we like sheep have gone astray.
Everyone has turned to his own way;
and Yahweh has laid on him the iniquity of us all.
⁷ He was oppressed,
yet when he was afflicted he didn't open his mouth.
As a lamb that is led to the slaughter,
and as a sheep that before its shearers is silent,
so he didn't open his mouth.
⁸ He was taken away by oppression and judgment.
As for his generation,
who considered that he was cut off out of the land of the living
and stricken for the disobedience of my people?

⁹ They made his grave with the wicked,
and with a rich man in his death,
although he had done no violence,
nor was any deceit in his mouth.
¹⁰ Yet it pleased Yahweh to bruise him.
He has caused him to suffer.
When you make his soul an offering for sin,
he will see his offspring.
He will prolong his days
and Yahweh's pleasure will prosper in his hand.
¹¹ After the suffering of his soul,
he will see the light‡ and be satisfied.
My righteous servant will justify many by the knowledge of himself;
and he will bear their iniquities.
¹² Therefore I will give him a portion with the great.
He will divide the plunder with the strong,
because he poured out his soul to death
and was counted with the transgressors;
yet he bore the sins of many
and made intercession for the transgressors.

Responsorial Psalm: Psalms 31: 2, 6, 12-13, 15-16, 17

² Bow down your ear to me.
Deliver me speedily.
Be to me a strong rock,
a house of defense to save me.
⁶ I hate those who regard lying vanities,
but I trust in Yahweh.
¹² I am forgotten from their hearts like a dead man.
I am like broken pottery.
¹³ For I have heard the slander of many, terror on every side,
while they conspire together against me,
they plot to take away my life.
¹⁵ My times are in your hand.
Deliver me from the hand of my enemies, and from those who persecute me.
¹⁶ Make your face to shine on your servant.
Save me in your loving kindness.
¹⁷ Let me not be disappointed, Yahweh, for I have called on you.
Let the wicked be disappointed.

Let them be silent in Sheol.†

Second Reading: Hebrews 4: 14-16; 5: 7-9

14 Having then a great high priest who has passed through the heavens, Jesus, the Son of God, let's hold tightly to our confession. 15 For we don't have a high priest who can't be touched with the feeling of our infirmities, but one who has been in all points tempted like we are, yet without sin. 16 Let's therefore draw near with boldness to the throne of grace, that we may receive mercy and may find grace for help in time of need.

7 He, in the days of his flesh, having offered up prayers and petitions with strong crying and tears to him who was able to save him from death, and having been heard for his godly fear, 8 though he was a Son, yet learned obedience by the things which he suffered. 9 Having been made perfect, he became to all of those who obey him the author of eternal salvation

Gospel: John 18: 1 – 19: 42

1 When Jesus had spoken these words, he went out with his disciples over the brook Kidron, where there was a garden, into which he and his disciples entered. 2 Now Judas, who betrayed him, also knew the place, for Jesus often met there with his disciples. 3 Judas then, having taken a detachment of soldiers and officers from the chief priests and the Pharisees, came there with lanterns, torches, and weapons. 4 Jesus therefore, knowing all the things that were happening to him, went out and said to them, "Who are you looking for?"

5 They answered him, "Jesus of Nazareth."

Jesus said to them, "I am he."

Judas also, who betrayed him, was standing with them. 6 When therefore he said to them, "I am he," they went backward and fell to the ground.

7 Again therefore he asked them, "Who are you looking for?"

They said, "Jesus of Nazareth."

8 Jesus answered, "I told you that I am he. If therefore you seek me, let these go their way," 9 that the word might be fulfilled which he spoke, "Of those whom you have given me, I have lost none."*

10 Simon Peter therefore, having a sword, drew it, struck the high priest's servant, and cut off his right ear. The servant's name was Malchus. 11 Jesus therefore said to Peter, "Put the sword into its sheath. The cup which the Father has given me, shall I not surely drink it?"

12 So the detachment, the commanding officer, and the officers of the Jews seized Jesus and bound him, 13 and led him to Annas first, for he was father-in-law to Caiaphas, who was high priest that year. 14 Now it was Caiaphas who advised the Jews that it was expedient that one man should perish for the people.

¹⁵ Simon Peter followed Jesus, as did another disciple. Now that disciple was known to the high priest, and entered in with Jesus into the court of the high priest; ¹⁶ but Peter was standing at the door outside. So the other disciple, who was known to the high priest, went out and spoke to her who kept the door, and brought in Peter. ¹⁷ Then the maid who kept the door said to Peter, "Are you also one of this man's disciples?"

He said, "I am not."

¹⁸ Now the servants and the officers were standing there, having made a fire of coals, for it was cold. They were warming themselves. Peter was with them, standing and warming himself.

¹⁹ The high priest therefore asked Jesus about his disciples and about his teaching.

²⁰ Jesus answered him, "I spoke openly to the world. I always taught in synagogues and in the temple, where the Jews always meet. I said nothing in secret. ²¹ Why do you ask me? Ask those who have heard me what I said to them. Behold, they know the things which I said."

²² When he had said this, one of the officers standing by slapped Jesus with his hand, saying, "Do you answer the high priest like that?"

²³ Jesus answered him, "If I have spoken evil, testify of the evil; but if well, why do you beat me?"

²⁴ Annas sent him bound to Caiaphas, the high priest.

²⁵ Now Simon Peter was standing and warming himself. They said therefore to him, "You aren't also one of his disciples, are you?"

He denied it and said, "I am not."

²⁶ One of the servants of the high priest, being a relative of him whose ear Peter had cut off, said, "Didn't I see you in the garden with him?"

²⁷ Peter therefore denied it again, and immediately the rooster crowed.

²⁸ They led Jesus therefore from Caiaphas into the Praetorium. It was early, and they themselves didn't enter into the Praetorium, that they might not be defiled, but might eat the Passover. ²⁹ Pilate therefore went out to them and said, "What accusation do you bring against this man?"

³⁰ They answered him, "If this man weren't an evildoer, we wouldn't have delivered him up to you."

³¹ Pilate therefore said to them, "Take him yourselves, and judge him according to your law."

Therefore the Jews said to him, "It is illegal for us to put anyone to death," ³² that the word of Jesus might be fulfilled, which he spoke, signifying by what kind of death he should die.

³³ Pilate therefore entered again into the Praetorium, called Jesus, and said to him, "Are you the King of the Jews?"

³⁴ Jesus answered him, "Do you say this by yourself, or did others tell you about me?"

³⁵ Pilate answered, "I'm not a Jew, am I? Your own nation and the chief priests delivered you to me. What have you done?"

36 Jesus answered, "My Kingdom is not of this world. If my Kingdom were of this world, then my servants would fight, that I wouldn't be delivered to the Jews. But now my Kingdom is not from here."

37 Pilate therefore said to him, "Are you a king then?"

Jesus answered, "You say that I am a king. For this reason I have been born, and for this reason I have come into the world, that I should testify to the truth. Everyone who is of the truth listens to my voice."

38 Pilate said to him, "What is truth?"

When he had said this, he went out again to the Jews, and said to them, "I find no basis for a charge against him. 39 But you have a custom that I should release someone to you at the Passover. Therefore, do you want me to release to you the King of the Jews?"

40 Then they all shouted again, saying, "Not this man, but Barabbas!" Now Barabbas was a robber.

1 So Pilate then took Jesus and flogged him. 2 The soldiers twisted thorns into a crown and put it on his head, and dressed him in a purple garment. 3 They kept saying, "Hail, King of the Jews!" and they kept slapping him.

4 Then Pilate went out again, and said to them, "Behold, I bring him out to you, that you may know that I find no basis for a charge against him."

5 Jesus therefore came out, wearing the crown of thorns and the purple garment. Pilate said to them, "Behold, the man!"

6 When therefore the chief priests and the officers saw him, they shouted, saying, "Crucify! Crucify!"

Pilate said to them, "Take him yourselves and crucify him, for I find no basis for a charge against him."

7 The Jews answered him, "We have a law, and by our law he ought to die, because he made himself the Son of God."

8 When therefore Pilate heard this saying, he was more afraid. 9 He entered into the Praetorium again, and said to Jesus, "Where are you from?" But Jesus gave him no answer. 10 Pilate therefore said to him, "Aren't you speaking to me? Don't you know that I have power to release you and have power to crucify you?"

11 Jesus answered, "You would have no power at all against me, unless it were given to you from above. Therefore he who delivered me to you has greater sin."

12 At this, Pilate was seeking to release him, but the Jews cried out, saying, "If you release this man, you aren't Caesar's friend! Everyone who makes himself a king speaks against Caesar!"

13 When Pilate therefore heard these words, he brought Jesus out and sat down on the judgment seat at a place called "The Pavement", but in Hebrew, "Gabbatha." 14 Now it was the Preparation Day of the Passover, at about the sixth hour. He said to the Jews, "Behold, your King!"

15 They cried out, "Away with him! Away with him! Crucify him!"

Pilate said to them, "Shall I crucify your King?"

The chief priests answered, "We have no king but Caesar!"

16 So then he delivered him to them to be crucified. So they took Jesus and led him away. 17 He went out, bearing his cross, to the place called "The Place of a Skull", which is called in Hebrew, "Golgotha", 18 where they crucified him, and with him two others, on either side one, and Jesus in the middle. 19 Pilate wrote a title also, and put it on the cross. There was written, "JESUS OF NAZARETH, THE KING OF THE JEWS." 20 Therefore many of the Jews read this title, for the place where Jesus was crucified was near the city; and it was written in Hebrew, in Latin, and in Greek. 21 The chief priests of the Jews therefore said to Pilate, "Don't write, 'The King of the Jews,' but, 'he said, "I am King of the Jews." ' "

22 Pilate answered, "What I have written, I have written."

23 Then the soldiers, when they had crucified Jesus, took his garments and made four parts, to every soldier a part; and also the tunic. Now the tunic was without seam, woven from the top throughout. 24 Then they said to one another, "Let's not tear it, but cast lots for it to decide whose it will be," that the Scripture might be fulfilled, which says,

"They parted my garments among them.

They cast lots for my clothing."∗

Therefore the soldiers did these things.

25 But standing by Jesus' cross were his mother, his mother's sister, Mary the wife of Clopas, and Mary Magdalene. 26 Therefore when Jesus saw his mother, and the disciple whom he loved standing there, he said to his mother, "Woman, behold, your son!" 27 Then he said to the disciple, "Behold, your mother!" From that hour, the disciple took her to his own home. 28 After this, Jesus, seeing± that all things were now finished, that the Scripture might be fulfilled, said, "I am thirsty!" 29 Now a vessel full of vinegar was set there; so they put a sponge full of the vinegar on hyssop, and held it at his mouth. 30 When Jesus therefore had received the vinegar, he said, "It is finished!" Then he bowed his head and gave up his spirit.

31 Therefore the Jews, because it was the Preparation Day, so that the bodies wouldn't remain on the cross on the Sabbath (for that Sabbath was a special one), asked of Pilate that their legs might be broken and that they might be taken away. 32 Therefore the soldiers came and broke the legs of the first and of the other who was crucified with him; 33 but when they came to Jesus and saw that he was already dead, they didn't break his legs. 34 However, one of the soldiers pierced his side with a spear, and immediately blood and water came out. 35 He who has seen has testified, and his testimony is true. He knows that he tells the truth, that you may believe. 36 For these things happened that the Scripture might be fulfilled, "A bone of him will not be broken."∗ 37 Again another Scripture says, "They will look on him whom they pierced."∗

38 After these things, Joseph of Arimathaea, being a disciple of Jesus, but secretly for fear of the Jews, asked of Pilate that he might take away Jesus' body. Pilate gave him

permission. He came therefore and took away his body. ³⁹ Nicodemus, who at first came to Jesus by night, also came bringing a mixture of myrrh and aloes, about a hundred Roman pounds.§ ⁴⁰ So they took Jesus' body, and bound it in linen cloths with the spices, as the custom of the Jews is to bury. ⁴¹ Now in the place where he was crucified there was a garden. In the garden was a new tomb in which no man had ever yet been laid. ⁴² Then, because of the Jews' Preparation Day (for the tomb was near at hand), they laid Jesus there.

1. Invite the Holy Spirit into this reading, asking the Author of Scripture to speak to you through His Word
2. Read today's passage as many times as you need, take your time
3. Write down (below) what the Lord is saying to you today
4. Live with this Word in your heart through the day

Saturday, April 19, 2025
Holy Saturday

First Reading: Genesis 1: 1, 26-31a

¹ In the beginning, God‡ created the heavens and the earth.
²⁶ God said, "Let's make man in our image, after our likeness. Let them have dominion over the fish of the sea, and over the birds of the sky, and over the livestock, and over all the earth, and over every creeping thing that creeps on the earth." ²⁷ God created man in his own image. In God's image he created him; male and female he created them. ²⁸ God blessed them. God said to them, "Be fruitful, multiply, fill the earth, and subdue it. Have dominion over the fish of the sea, over the birds of the sky, and over every living thing that moves on the earth." ²⁹ God said, "Behold,‡ I have given you every herb yielding seed, which is on the surface of all the earth, and every tree, which bears fruit yielding seed. It will be your food. ³⁰ To every animal of the earth, and to every bird of the sky, and to everything that creeps on the earth, in which there is life, I have given every green herb for food;" and it was so.
³¹ God saw everything that he had made, and, behold, it was very good.

Responsorial Psalm: Psalms 104: 1-2, 5-6, 10, 12, 13-14, 24, 35

¹ Bless Yahweh, my soul.

Yahweh, my God, you are very great.
You are clothed with honor and majesty.
² He covers himself with light as with a garment.
He stretches out the heavens like a curtain.
⁵ He laid the foundations of the earth,
that it should not be moved forever.
⁶ You covered it with the deep as with a cloak.
The waters stood above the mountains.
¹⁰ He sends springs into the valleys.
They run among the mountains.
¹² The birds of the sky nest by them.
They sing among the branches.
¹³ He waters the mountains from his rooms.
The earth is filled with the fruit of your works.
¹⁴ He causes the grass to grow for the livestock,
and plants for man to cultivate,
that he may produce food out of the earth:
²⁴ Yahweh, how many are your works!
In wisdom, you have made them all.
The earth is full of your riches.
³⁵ Let sinners be consumed out of the earth.
Let the wicked be no more.
Bless Yahweh, my soul.
Praise Yah!

Second Reading: Genesis 22: 1-2, 9, 10-13, 15-18

¹ After these things, God tested Abraham, and said to him, "Abraham!"
He said, "Here I am."
² He said, "Now take your son, your only son, Isaac, whom you love, and go into the land of Moriah. Offer him there as a burnt offering on one of the mountains which I will tell you of."
⁹ They came to the place which God had told him of. Abraham built the altar there, and laid the wood in order, bound Isaac his son, and laid him on the altar, on the wood. ¹⁰ Abraham stretched out his hand, and took the knife to kill his son.
¹¹ Yahweh's angel called to him out of the sky, and said, "Abraham, Abraham!"
He said, "Here I am."
¹² He said, "Don't lay your hand on the boy or do anything to him. For now I know that you fear God, since you have not withheld your son, your only son, from me."

¹³ Abraham lifted up his eyes, and looked, and saw that behind him was a ram caught in the thicket by his horns. Abraham went and took the ram, and offered him up for a burnt offering instead of his son.

¹⁵ Yahweh's angel called to Abraham a second time out of the sky, ¹⁶ and said, " 'I have sworn by myself,' says Yahweh, 'because you have done this thing, and have not withheld your son, your only son, ¹⁷ that I will bless you greatly, and I will multiply your offspring greatly like the stars of the heavens, and like the sand which is on the seashore. Your offspring will possess the gate of his enemies. ¹⁸ All the nations of the earth will be blessed by your offspring, because you have obeyed my voice.' "

Responsorial Psalm: Psalms 16: 5, 8, 9-10, 11

⁵ Yahweh assigned my portion and my cup.
You made my lot secure.
⁸ I have set Yahweh always before me.
Because he is at my right hand, I shall not be moved.
⁹ Therefore my heart is glad, and my tongue rejoices.
My body shall also dwell in safety.
¹⁰ For you will not leave my soul in Sheol,‡
neither will you allow your holy one to see corruption.
¹¹ You will show me the path of life.
In your presence is fullness of joy.
In your right hand there are pleasures forever more.

Third Reading: Exodus 14: 15 – 15: 1

¹⁵ Yahweh said to Moses, "Why do you cry to me? Speak to the children of Israel, that they go forward. ¹⁶ Lift up your rod, and stretch out your hand over the sea and divide it. Then the children of Israel shall go into the middle of the sea on dry ground. ¹⁷ Behold, I myself will harden the hearts of the Egyptians, and they will go in after them. I will get myself honor over Pharaoh, and over all his armies, over his chariots, and over his horsemen. ¹⁸ The Egyptians shall know that I am Yahweh when I have gotten myself honor over Pharaoh, over his chariots, and over his horsemen." ¹⁹ The angel of God, who went before the camp of Israel, moved and went behind them; and the pillar of cloud moved from before them, and stood behind them. ²⁰ It came between the camp of Egypt and the camp of Israel. There was the cloud and the darkness, yet it gave light by night. One didn't come near the other all night.
²¹ Moses stretched out his hand over the sea, and Yahweh caused the sea to go back by a strong east wind all night, and made the sea dry land, and the waters were divided. ²² The children of Israel went into the middle of the sea on the dry ground; and the waters were a

wall to them on their right hand and on their left. ²³ The Egyptians pursued, and went in after them into the middle of the sea: all of Pharaoh's horses, his chariots, and his horsemen. ²⁴ In the morning watch, Yahweh looked out on the Egyptian army through the pillar of fire and of cloud, and confused the Egyptian army. ²⁵ He took off their chariot wheels, and they drove them heavily; so that the Egyptians said, "Let's flee from the face of Israel, for Yahweh fights for them against the Egyptians!"

²⁶ Yahweh said to Moses, "Stretch out your hand over the sea, that the waters may come again on the Egyptians, on their chariots, and on their horsemen." ²⁷ Moses stretched out his hand over the sea, and the sea returned to its strength when the morning appeared; and the Egyptians fled against it. Yahweh overthrew the Egyptians in the middle of the sea. ²⁸ The waters returned, and covered the chariots and the horsemen, even all Pharaoh's army that went in after them into the sea. There remained not so much as one of them. ²⁹ But the children of Israel walked on dry land in the middle of the sea, and the waters were a wall to them on their right hand and on their left. ³⁰ Thus Yahweh saved Israel that day out of the hand of the Egyptians; and Israel saw the Egyptians dead on the seashore. ³¹ Israel saw the great work which Yahweh did to the Egyptians, and the people feared Yahweh; and they believed in Yahweh and in his servant Moses.

¹ Then Moses and the children of Israel sang this song to Yahweh, and said,
"I will sing to Yahweh, for he has triumphed gloriously.
He has thrown the horse and his rider into the sea.

Responsorial Psalm: Exodus 15: 1-6, 17-18

¹ Then Moses and the children of Israel sang this song to Yahweh, and said,
"I will sing to Yahweh, for he has triumphed gloriously.
He has thrown the horse and his rider into the sea.
² Yah is my strength and song.
He has become my salvation.
This is my God, and I will praise him;
my father's God, and I will exalt him.
³ Yahweh is a man of war.
Yahweh is his name.
⁴ He has cast Pharaoh's chariots and his army into the sea.
His chosen captains are sunk in the Red Sea.
⁵ The deeps cover them.
They went down into the depths like a stone.
⁶ Your right hand, Yahweh, is glorious in power.
Your right hand, Yahweh, dashes the enemy in pieces.
¹⁷ You will bring them in, and plant them in the mountain of your inheritance,
the place, Yahweh, which you have made for yourself to dwell in:

the sanctuary, Lord, which your hands have established.
¹⁸ Yahweh will reign forever and ever."

Fourth Reading: Isaiah 54: 5-14

⁵ For your Maker is your husband; Yahweh of Armies is his name.
The Holy One of Israel is your Redeemer.
He will be called the God of the whole earth.
⁶ For Yahweh has called you as a wife forsaken and grieved in spirit,
even a wife of youth, when she is cast off," says your God.
⁷ "For a small moment I have forsaken you,
but I will gather you with great mercies.
⁸ In overflowing wrath I hid my face from you for a moment,
but with everlasting loving kindness I will have mercy on you," says Yahweh your Redeemer.
⁹ "For this is like the waters of Noah to me;
for as I have sworn that the waters of Noah will no more go over the earth,
so I have sworn that I will not be angry with you, nor rebuke you.
¹⁰ For the mountains may depart,
and the hills be removed,
but my loving kindness will not depart from you,
and my covenant of peace will not be removed,"
says Yahweh who has mercy on you.
¹¹ "You afflicted, tossed with storms, and not comforted,
behold, I will set your stones in beautiful colors,
and lay your foundations with sapphires.
¹² I will make your pinnacles of rubies,
your gates of sparkling jewels,
and all your walls of precious stones.
¹³ All your children will be taught by Yahweh,
and your children's peace will be great.
¹⁴ You will be established in righteousness.
You will be far from oppression,
for you will not be afraid,
and far from terror,
for it shall not come near you.

Responsorial Psalm: Psalms 30: 2, 4, 5-6, 11-12

² Yahweh my God, I cried to you,

and you have healed me.
⁴ Sing praise to Yahweh, you saints of his.
Give thanks to his holy name.
⁵ For his anger is but for a moment.
His favor is for a lifetime.
Weeping may stay for the night,
but joy comes in the morning.
⁶ As for me, I said in my prosperity,
"I shall never be moved."
¹¹ You have turned my mourning into dancing for me.
You have removed my sackcloth, and clothed me with gladness,
¹² to the end that my heart may sing praise to you, and not be silent.
Yahweh my God, I will give thanks to you forever!

Fifth Reading: Isaiah 55: 1-11

¹ "Hey! Come, everyone who thirsts, to the waters!
Come, he who has no money, buy, and eat!
Yes, come, buy wine and milk without money and without price.
² Why do you spend money for that which is not bread,
and your labor for that which doesn't satisfy?
Listen diligently to me, and eat that which is good,
and let your soul delight itself in richness.
³ Turn your ear, and come to me.
Hear, and your soul will live.
I will make an everlasting covenant with you, even the sure mercies of David.
⁴ Behold, I have given him for a witness to the peoples,
a leader and commander to the peoples.
⁵ Behold, you shall call a nation that you don't know;
and a nation that didn't know you shall run to you,
because of Yahweh your God,
and for the Holy One of Israel;
for he has glorified you."
⁶ Seek Yahweh while he may be found.
Call on him while he is near.
⁷ Let the wicked forsake his way,
and the unrighteous man his thoughts.
Let him return to Yahweh, and he will have mercy on him,
to our God, for he will freely pardon.
⁸ "For my thoughts are not your thoughts,

and your ways are not my ways," says Yahweh.
9 "For as the heavens are higher than the earth,
so are my ways higher than your ways,
and my thoughts than your thoughts.
10 For as the rain comes down and the snow from the sky,
and doesn't return there, but waters the earth,
and makes it grow and bud,
and gives seed to the sower and bread to the eater;
11 so is my word that goes out of my mouth:
it will not return to me void,
but it will accomplish that which I please,
and it will prosper in the thing I sent it to do.

Responsorial Psalm: Isaiah 12: 2-3, 4, 5-6

2 Behold, God is my salvation. I will trust, and will not be afraid; for Yah, Yahweh, is my strength and song; and he has become my salvation." 3 Therefore with joy you will draw water out of the wells of salvation.
4 In that day you will say, "Give thanks to Yahweh! Call on his name! Declare his doings among the peoples! Proclaim that his name is exalted!
5 Sing to Yahweh, for he has done excellent things! Let this be known in all the earth! 6 Cry aloud and shout, you inhabitant of Zion, for the Holy One of Israel is great among you!"

Sixth Reading: Baruch 3: 9-15, 32 – 4: 4

9 Hear, O Israel, the commandments of life! Give ear to understand wisdom! 10 How is it, O Israel, that you are in your enemies' land, that you have become old in a strange country, that you are defiled with the dead, 11 that you are counted with those who are in Hades? 12 You have forsaken the fountain of wisdom. 13 If you had walked in the way of God, you would have dwelled in peace forever. 14 Learn where there is wisdom, where there is strength, and where there is understanding, that you may also know where there is length of days and life, where there is the light of the eyes and peace. 15 Who has found out her place? Who has come into her treasuries?
32 But he that knows all things knows her, he found her out with his understanding. He who prepared the earth for all time has filled it with four-footed beasts. 33 It is he who sends forth the light, and it goes. He called it, and it obeyed him with fear. 34 The stars shone in their watches, and were glad. When he called them, they said, "Here we are." They shone with gladness to him who made them. 35 This is our God. No other can be compared to him. 36 He has found out all the way of knowledge, and has given it to Jacob his servant and to Israel who is loved by him. 37 Afterward she appeared upon earth, and lived with men.

¹ This is the book of God's commandments and the law that endures forever. All those who hold it fast will live, but those who leave it will die. ² Turn, O Jacob, and take hold of it. Walk toward the shining of its light. ³ Don't give your glory to another, nor the things that are to your advantage to a foreign nation. ⁴ O Israel, we are happy; for the things that are pleasing to God are made known to us.

Responsorial Psalm: Psalms 19: 8, 9, 10, 11

⁸ Yahweh's precepts are right, rejoicing the heart.
Yahweh's commandment is pure, enlightening the eyes.
⁹ The fear of Yahweh is clean, enduring forever.
Yahweh's ordinances are true, and righteous altogether.
¹⁰ They are more to be desired than gold, yes, than much fine gold,
sweeter also than honey and the extract of the honeycomb.
¹¹ Moreover your servant is warned by them.
In keeping them there is great reward.

Seventh Reading: Ezekiel 36: 16-17a, 18-28

¹⁶ Moreover Yahweh's word came to me, saying, ¹⁷ "Son of man, when the house of Israel lived in their own land, they defiled it by their ways and by their deeds.
¹⁸ Therefore I poured out my wrath on them for the blood which they had poured out on the land, and because they had defiled it with their idols. ¹⁹ I scattered them among the nations, and they were dispersed through the countries. I judged them according to their way and according to their deeds. ²⁰ When they came to the nations where they went, they profaned my holy name, in that men said of them, 'These are Yahweh's people, and have left his land.' ²¹ But I had respect for my holy name, which the house of Israel had profaned among the nations where they went.
²² "Therefore tell the house of Israel, 'The Lord Yahweh says: "I don't do this for your sake, house of Israel, but for my holy name, which you have profaned among the nations where you went. ²³ I will sanctify my great name, which has been profaned among the nations, which you have profaned among them. Then the nations will know that I am Yahweh," says the Lord Yahweh, "when I am proven holy in you before their eyes.
²⁴ " ' "For I will take you from among the nations and gather you out of all the countries, and will bring you into your own land. ²⁵ I will sprinkle clean water on you, and you will be clean. I will cleanse you from all your filthiness and from all your idols. ²⁶ I will also give you a new heart, and I will put a new spirit within you. I will take away the stony heart out of your flesh, and I will give you a heart of flesh. ²⁷ I will put my Spirit within you, and cause you to walk in my statutes. You will keep my ordinances and do them. ²⁸ You will dwell in the land that I gave to your fathers. You will be my people, and I will be your God.

Responsorial Psalm: Psalms 42: 3, 5; 43: 3, 4

3 My tears have been my food day and night,
while they continually ask me, "Where is your God?"
5 Why are you in despair, my soul?
Why are you disturbed within me?
Hope in God!
For I shall still praise him for the saving help of his presence.
3 Oh, send out your light and your truth.
Let them lead me.
Let them bring me to your holy hill,
to your tents.
4 Then I will go to the altar of God,
to God, my exceeding joy.
I will praise you on the harp, God, my God.

Epistle Reading: Romans 6: 3-11

3 Or don't you know that all of us who were baptized into Christ Jesus were baptized into his death? 4 We were buried therefore with him through baptism into death, that just as Christ was raised from the dead through the glory of the Father, so we also might walk in newness of life.
5 For if we have become united with him in the likeness of his death, we will also be part of his resurrection; 6 knowing this, that our old man was crucified with him, that the body of sin might be done away with, so that we would no longer be in bondage to sin. 7 For he who has died has been freed from sin. 8 But if we died with Christ, we believe that we will also live with him, 9 knowing that Christ, being raised from the dead, dies no more. Death no longer has dominion over him! 10 For the death that he died, he died to sin one time; but the life that he lives, he lives to God. 11 Thus consider yourselves also to be dead to sin, but alive to God in Christ Jesus our Lord.

Responsorial Psalm: Psalms 118: 1-2, 16-17, 22-23

1 Give thanks to Yahweh, for he is good,
for his loving kindness endures forever.
2 Let Israel now say
that his loving kindness endures forever.
16 The right hand of Yahweh is exalted!
The right hand of Yahweh does valiantly!"

¹⁷ I will not die, but live,
and declare Yah's works.
²² The stone which the builders rejected
has become the cornerstone.‡
²³ This is Yahweh's doing.
It is marvelous in our eyes.

Gospel: Luke 24: 1-12

¹ But on the first day of the week, at early dawn, they and some others came to the tomb, bringing the spices which they had prepared. ² They found the stone rolled away from the tomb. ³ They entered in, and didn't find the Lord Jesus' body. ⁴ While they were greatly perplexed about this, behold, two men stood by them in dazzling clothing. ⁵ Becoming terrified, they bowed their faces down to the earth.
The men said to them, "Why do you seek the living among the dead? ⁶ He isn't here, but is risen. Remember what he told you when he was still in Galilee, ⁷ saying that the Son of Man must be delivered up into the hands of sinful men and be crucified, and the third day rise again?"
⁸ They remembered his words, ⁹ returned from the tomb, and told all these things to the eleven and to all the rest. ¹⁰ Now they were Mary Magdalene, Joanna, and Mary the mother of James. The other women with them told these things to the apostles. ¹¹ These words seemed to them to be nonsense, and they didn't believe them. ¹² But Peter got up and ran to the tomb. Stooping and looking in, he saw the strips of linen lying by themselves, and he departed to his home, wondering what had happened.

1. Invite the Holy Spirit into this reading, asking the Author of Scripture to speak to you through His Word
2. Read today's passage as many times as you need, take your time
3. Write down (below) what the Lord is saying to you today
4. Live with this Word in your heart through the day

Sunday, April 20, 2025
EASTER SUNDAY OF THE RESURRECTION OF THE LORD

First Reading: Acts 10: 34a, 37-43

³⁴ᵃ Peter opened his mouth and said,
³⁷ you yourselves know what happened, which was proclaimed throughout all Judea, beginning from Galilee, after the baptism which John preached; ³⁸ how God anointed Jesus of Nazareth with the Holy Spirit and with power, who went about doing good and healing all who were oppressed by the devil, for God was with him. ³⁹ We are witnesses of everything he did both in the country of the Jews and in Jerusalem; whom they also⁺ killed, hanging him on a tree. ⁴⁰ God raised him up the third day and gave him to be revealed, ⁴¹ not to all the people, but to witnesses who were chosen before by God, to us, who ate and drank with him after he rose from the dead. ⁴² He commanded us to preach to the people and to testify that this is he who is appointed by God as the Judge of the living and the dead. ⁴³ All the prophets testify about him, that through his name everyone who believes in him will receive remission of sins."

Responsorial Psalm: Psalms 118: 1-2, 16-17, 22-23

¹ Give thanks to Yahweh, for he is good,
for his loving kindness endures forever.
² Let Israel now say
that his loving kindness endures forever.
¹⁶ The right hand of Yahweh is exalted!
The right hand of Yahweh does valiantly!"
¹⁷ I will not die, but live,
and declare Yah's works.
²² The stone which the builders rejected
has become the cornerstone.⁺
²³ This is Yahweh's doing.
It is marvelous in our eyes.

Second Reading: Colossians 3: 1-4

¹ If then you were raised together with Christ, seek the things that are above, where Christ is, seated on the right hand of God. ² Set your mind on the things that are above, not on the things that are on the earth. ³ For you died, and your life is hidden with Christ in God. ⁴ When Christ, our life, is revealed, then you will also be revealed with him in glory.

Gospel: John 20: 1-9

¹ Now on the first day of the week, Mary Magdalene went early, while it was still dark, to the tomb, and saw that the stone had been taken away from the tomb. ² Therefore she ran

and came to Simon Peter and to the other disciple whom Jesus loved, and said to them, "They have taken away the Lord out of the tomb, and we don't know where they have laid him!"

³ Therefore Peter and the other disciple went out, and they went toward the tomb. ⁴ They both ran together. The other disciple outran Peter and came to the tomb first. ⁵ Stooping and looking in, he saw the linen cloths lying there; yet he didn't enter in. ⁶ Then Simon Peter came, following him, and entered into the tomb. He saw the linen cloths lying, ⁷ and the cloth that had been on his head, not lying with the linen cloths, but rolled up in a place by itself. ⁸ So then the other disciple who came first to the tomb also entered in, and he saw and believed. ⁹ For as yet they didn't know the Scripture, that he must rise from the dead.

1. Invite the Holy Spirit into this reading, asking the Author of Scripture to speak to you through His Word
2. Read today's passage as many times as you need, take your time
3. Write down (below) what the Lord is saying to you today
4. Live with this Word in your heart through the day

_____

_____

Monday, April 21, 2025
Easter Monday

First Reading: Acts 2: 14, 22-33

¹⁴ But Peter, standing up with the eleven, lifted up his voice and spoke out to them, "You men of Judea and all you who dwell at Jerusalem, let this be known to you, and listen to my words.
²² "Men of Israel, hear these words! Jesus of Nazareth, a man approved by God to you by mighty works and wonders and signs which God did by him among you, even as you yourselves know, ²³ him, being delivered up by the determined counsel and foreknowledge of God, you have taken by the hand of lawless men, crucified and killed; ²⁴ whom God raised up, having freed him from the agony of death, because it was not possible that he should be held by it. ²⁵ For David says concerning him,
'I saw the Lord always before my face,
for he is on my right hand, that I should not be moved.
²⁶ Therefore my heart was glad, and my tongue rejoiced.
Moreover my flesh also will dwell in hope,

27 because you will not leave my soul in Hades,‡
neither will you allow your Holy One to see decay.
28 You made known to me the ways of life.
You will make me full of gladness with your presence.'*
29 "Brothers, I may tell you freely of the patriarch David, that he both died and was buried, and his tomb is with us to this day. 30 Therefore, being a prophet, and knowing that God had sworn with an oath to him that of the fruit of his body, according to the flesh, he would raise up the Christ§ to sit on his throne, 31 he foreseeing this, spoke about the resurrection of the Christ, that his soul wasn't left in Hades,‡ and his flesh didn't see decay. 32 This Jesus God raised up, to which we all are witnesses. 33 Being therefore exalted by the right hand of God, and having received from the Father the promise of the Holy Spirit, he has poured out this which you now see and hear.

Responsorial Psalm: Psalms 16: 1-2a and 5, 7-8, 9-10, 11

1 Preserve me, God, for I take refuge in you.
2a My soul, you have said to Yahweh,
5 Yahweh assigned my portion and my cup.
You made my lot secure.
7 I will bless Yahweh, who has given me counsel.
Yes, my heart instructs me in the night seasons.
8 I have set Yahweh always before me.
Because he is at my right hand, I shall not be moved.
9 Therefore my heart is glad, and my tongue rejoices.
My body shall also dwell in safety.
10 For you will not leave my soul in Sheol,‡
neither will you allow your holy one to see corruption.
11 You will show me the path of life.
In your presence is fullness of joy.
In your right hand there are pleasures forever more.

Gospel: Matthew 28: 8-15

8 They departed quickly from the tomb with fear and great joy, and ran to bring his disciples word. 9 As they went to tell his disciples, behold, Jesus met them, saying, "Rejoice!"
They came and took hold of his feet, and worshiped him.
10 Then Jesus said to them, "Don't be afraid. Go tell my brothers ‡ that they should go into Galilee, and there they will see me."
11 Now while they were going, behold, some of the guards came into the city and told the chief priests all the things that had happened. 12 When they were assembled with the elders

and had taken counsel, they gave a large amount of silver to the soldiers, ¹³ saying, "Say that his disciples came by night and stole him away while we slept. ¹⁴ If this comes to the governor's ears, we will persuade him and make you free of worry." ¹⁵ So they took the money and did as they were told. This saying was spread abroad among the Jews, and continues until today.

1. Invite the Holy Spirit into this reading, asking the Author of Scripture to speak to you through His Word
2. Read today's passage as many times as you need, take your time
3. Write down (below) what the Lord is saying to you today
4. Live with this Word in your heart through the day

Tuesday, April 22, 2025
Tuesday within the Octave of Easter

First Reading: Acts 2: 36-41

³⁶ "Let all the house of Israel therefore know certainly that God has made him both Lord and Christ, this Jesus whom you crucified."
³⁷ Now when they heard this, they were cut to the heart, and said to Peter and the rest of the apostles, "Brothers, what shall we do?"
³⁸ Peter said to them, "Repent and be baptized, every one of you, in the name of Jesus Christ for the forgiveness of sins, and you will receive the gift of the Holy Spirit. ³⁹ For the promise is to you and to your children, and to all who are far off, even as many as the Lord our God will call to himself." ⁴⁰ With many other words he testified and exhorted them, saying, "Save yourselves from this crooked generation!"
⁴¹ Then those who gladly received his word were baptized. There were added that day about three thousand souls.

Responsorial Psalm: Psalms 33: 4-5, 18-19, 20 and 22

⁴ For Yahweh's word is right.
All his work is done in faithfulness.
⁵ He loves righteousness and justice.
The earth is full of the loving kindness of Yahweh.

¹⁸ Behold, Yahweh's eye is on those who fear him,
on those who hope in his loving kindness,
¹⁹ to deliver their soul from death,
to keep them alive in famine.
²⁰ Our soul has waited for Yahweh.
He is our help and our shield.
²² Let your loving kindness be on us, Yahweh,
since we have hoped in you.

Gospel: John 20: 11-18

¹¹ But Mary was standing outside at the tomb weeping. So as she wept, she stooped and looked into the tomb, ¹² and she saw two angels in white sitting, one at the head and one at the feet, where the body of Jesus had lain. ¹³ They asked her, "Woman, why are you weeping?"
She said to them, "Because they have taken away my Lord, and I don't know where they have laid him." ¹⁴ When she had said this, she turned around and saw Jesus standing, and didn't know that it was Jesus.
¹⁵ Jesus said to her, "Woman, why are you weeping? Who are you looking for?"
She, supposing him to be the gardener, said to him, "Sir, if you have carried him away, tell me where you have laid him, and I will take him away."
¹⁶ Jesus said to her, "Mary."
She turned and said to him, "Rabboni!"⁺ which is to say, "Teacher!"⁺
¹⁷ Jesus said to her, "Don't hold me, for I haven't yet ascended to my Father; but go to my brothers and tell them, 'I am ascending to my Father and your Father, to my God and your God.'"
¹⁸ Mary Magdalene came and told the disciples that she had seen the Lord, and that he had said these things to her.

1. Invite the Holy Spirit into this reading, asking the Author of Scripture to speak to you through His Word
2. Read today's passage as many times as you need, take your time
3. Write down (below) what the Lord is saying to you today
4. Live with this Word in your heart through the day

Wednesday, April 23, 2025
Wednesday within the Octave of Easter

First Reading: Acts 3: 1-10

¹ Peter and John were going up into the temple at the hour of prayer, the ninth hour. ² A certain man who was lame from his mother's womb was being carried, whom they laid daily at the door of the temple which is called Beautiful, to ask gifts for the needy of those who entered into the temple. ³ Seeing Peter and John about to go into the temple, he asked to receive gifts for the needy. ⁴ Peter, fastening his eyes on him, with John, said, "Look at us." ⁵ He listened to them, expecting to receive something from them. ⁶ But Peter said, "I have no silver or gold, but what I have, that I give you. In the name of Jesus Christ of Nazareth, get up and walk!" ⁷ He took him by the right hand and raised him up. Immediately his feet and his ankle bones received strength. ⁸ Leaping up, he stood and began to walk. He entered with them into the temple, walking, leaping, and praising God. ⁹ All the people saw him walking and praising God. ¹⁰ They recognized him, that it was he who used to sit begging for gifts for the needy at the Beautiful Gate of the temple. They were filled with wonder and amazement at what had happened to him.

Responsorial Psalm: Psalms 105: 1-4, 6-9

¹ Give thanks to Yahweh! Call on his name!
Make his doings known among the peoples.
² Sing to him, sing praises to him!
Tell of all his marvelous works.
³ Glory in his holy name.
Let the heart of those who seek Yahweh rejoice.
⁴ Seek Yahweh and his strength.
Seek his face forever more.
⁶ you offspring of Abraham, his servant,
you children of Jacob, his chosen ones.
⁷ He is Yahweh, our God.
His judgments are in all the earth.
⁸ He has remembered his covenant forever,
the word which he commanded to a thousand generations,
⁹ the covenant which he made with Abraham,
his oath to Isaac,

Gospel: Luke 24: 13-35

¹³ Behold, two of them were going that very day to a village named Emmaus, which was sixty stadia¹ from Jerusalem. ¹⁴ They talked with each other about all of these things which had happened. ¹⁵ While they talked and questioned together, Jesus himself came near, and went with them. ¹⁶ But their eyes were kept from recognizing him. ¹⁷ He said to them, "What are you talking about as you walk, and are sad?"

¹⁸ One of them, named Cleopas, answered him, "Are you the only stranger in Jerusalem who doesn't know the things which have happened there in these days?"

¹⁹ He said to them, "What things?"

They said to him, "The things concerning Jesus the Nazarene, who was a prophet mighty in deed and word before God and all the people; ²⁰ and how the chief priests and our rulers delivered him up to be condemned to death, and crucified him. ²¹ But we were hoping that it was he who would redeem Israel. Yes, and besides all this, it is now the third day since these things happened. ²² Also, certain women of our company amazed us, having arrived early at the tomb; ²³ and when they didn't find his body, they came saying that they had also seen a vision of angels, who said that he was alive. ²⁴ Some of us went to the tomb and found it just like the women had said, but they didn't see him."

²⁵ He said to them, "Foolish people, and slow of heart to believe in all that the prophets have spoken! ²⁶ Didn't the Christ have to suffer these things and to enter into his glory?" ²⁷ Beginning from Moses and from all the prophets, he explained to them in all the Scriptures the things concerning himself.

²⁸ They came near to the village where they were going, and he acted like he would go further.

²⁹ They urged him, saying, "Stay with us, for it is almost evening, and the day is almost over."

He went in to stay with them. ³⁰ When he had sat down at the table with them, he took the bread and gave thanks. Breaking it, he gave it to them. ³¹ Their eyes were opened and they recognized him; then he vanished out of their sight. ³² They said to one another, "Weren't our hearts burning within us while he spoke to us along the way, and while he opened the Scriptures to us?" ³³ They rose up that very hour, returned to Jerusalem, and found the eleven gathered together, and those who were with them, ³⁴ saying, "The Lord is risen indeed, and has appeared to Simon!" ³⁵ They related the things that happened along the way, and how he was recognized by them in the breaking of the bread.

1. Invite the Holy Spirit into this reading, asking the Author of Scripture to speak to you through His Word
2. Read today's passage as many times as you need, take your time
3. Write down (below) what the Lord is saying to you today
4. Live with this Word in your heart through the day

Thursday, April 24, 2025
Thursday within the Octave of Easter

First Reading: Acts 3: 11-26

¹¹ As the lame man who was healed held on to Peter and John, all the people ran together to them in the porch that is called Solomon's, greatly wondering.
¹² When Peter saw it, he responded to the people, "You men of Israel, why do you marvel at this man? Why do you fasten your eyes on us, as though by our own power or godliness we had made him walk? ¹³ The God of Abraham, Isaac, and Jacob, the God of our fathers, has glorified his Servant Jesus, whom you delivered up and denied in the presence of Pilate, when he had determined to release him. ¹⁴ But you denied the Holy and Righteous One and asked for a murderer to be granted to you, ¹⁵ and killed the Prince of life, whom God raised from the dead, to which we are witnesses. ¹⁶ By faith in his name, his name has made this man strong, whom you see and know. Yes, the faith which is through him has given him this perfect soundness in the presence of you all.
¹⁷ "Now, brothers, I know that you did this in ignorance, as did also your rulers. ¹⁸ But the things which God announced by the mouth of all his prophets, that Christ should suffer, he thus fulfilled.
¹⁹ "Repent therefore, and turn again, that your sins may be blotted out, so that there may come times of refreshing from the presence of the Lord, ²⁰ and that he may send Christ Jesus, who was ordained for you before, ²¹ whom heaven must receive until the times of restoration of all things, which God spoke long ago by the mouth of his holy prophets. ²² For Moses indeed said to the fathers, 'The Lord God will raise up a prophet for you from among your brothers, like me. You shall listen to him in all things whatever he says to you. ²³ It will be that every soul that will not listen to that prophet will be utterly destroyed from among the people.' ²⁴ Yes, and all the prophets from Samuel and those who followed after, as many as have spoken, also told of these days. ²⁵ You are the children of the prophets, and of the covenant which God made with our fathers, saying to Abraham, 'All the families of the earth will be blessed through your offspring.' ²⁶ God, having raised up his servant Jesus, sent him to you first to bless you, in turning away every one of you from your wickedness."

Responsorial Psalm: Psalms 8: 2ab and 5-9

² From the lips of babes and infants you have established strength,
because of your adversaries, that you might silence the enemy and the avenger.
⁵ For you have made him a little lower than the angels,†
and crowned him with glory and honor.
⁶ You make him ruler over the works of your hands.
You have put all things under his feet:
⁷ All sheep and cattle,
yes, and the animals of the field,
⁸ the birds of the sky, the fish of the sea,
and whatever passes through the paths of the seas.
⁹ Yahweh, our Lord,
how majestic is your name in all the earth!

Gospel: Luke 24: 35-48

³⁵ They related the things that happened along the way, and how he was recognized by them in the breaking of the bread.
³⁶ As they said these things, Jesus himself stood among them, and said to them, "Peace be to you."
³⁷ But they were terrified and filled with fear, and supposed that they had seen a spirit.
³⁸ He said to them, "Why are you troubled? Why do doubts arise in your hearts? ³⁹ See my hands and my feet, that it is truly me. Touch me and see, for a spirit doesn't have flesh and bones, as you see that I have." ⁴⁰ When he had said this, he showed them his hands and his feet. ⁴¹ While they still didn't believe for joy, and wondered, he said to them, "Do you have anything here to eat?"
⁴² They gave him a piece of a broiled fish and some honeycomb. ⁴³ He took them, and ate in front of them. ⁴⁴ He said to them, "This is what I told you while I was still with you, that all things which are written in the law of Moses, the prophets, and the psalms concerning me must be fulfilled."
⁴⁵ Then he opened their minds, that they might understand the Scriptures. ⁴⁶ He said to them, "Thus it is written, and thus it was necessary for the Christ to suffer and to rise from the dead the third day, ⁴⁷ and that repentance and remission of sins should be preached in his name to all the nations, beginning at Jerusalem. ⁴⁸ You are witnesses of these things.

1. Invite the Holy Spirit into this reading, asking the Author of Scripture to speak to you through His Word
2. Read today's passage as many times as you need, take your time
3. Write down (below) what the Lord is saying to you today
4. Live with this Word in your heart through the day

Friday, April 25, 2025
Friday within the Octave of Easter

First Reading: Acts 4: 1-12

¹ As they spoke to the people, the priests and the captain of the temple and the Sadducees came to them, ² being upset because they taught the people and proclaimed in Jesus the resurrection from the dead. ³ They laid hands on them, and put them in custody until the next day, for it was now evening. ⁴ But many of those who heard the word believed, and the number of the men came to be about five thousand.
⁵ In the morning, their rulers, elders, and scribes were gathered together in Jerusalem. ⁶ Annas the high priest was there, with Caiaphas, John, Alexander, and as many as were relatives of the high priest. ⁷ When they had stood Peter and John in the middle of them, they inquired, "By what power, or in what name, have you done this?"
⁸ Then Peter, filled with the Holy Spirit, said to them, "You rulers of the people and elders of Israel, ⁹ if we are examined today concerning a good deed done to a crippled man, by what means this man has been healed, ¹⁰ may it be known to you all, and to all the people of Israel, that in the name of Jesus Christ of Nazareth, whom you crucified, whom God raised from the dead, this man stands here before you whole in him. ¹¹ He is 'the stone which was regarded as worthless by you, the builders, which has become the head of the corner.'✱ ¹² There is salvation in no one else, for there is no other name under heaven that is given among men, by which we must be saved!"

Responsorial Psalm: Psalms 118: 1-2 and 4, 22-27a

¹ Give thanks to Yahweh, for he is good,
for his loving kindness endures forever.
² Let Israel now say
that his loving kindness endures forever.
⁴ Now let those who fear Yahweh say
that his loving kindness endures forever.
²² The stone which the builders rejected
has become the cornerstone.‡
²³ This is Yahweh's doing.
It is marvelous in our eyes.

²⁴ This is the day that Yahweh has made.
We will rejoice and be glad in it!
²⁵ Save us now, we beg you, Yahweh!
Yahweh, we beg you, send prosperity now.
²⁶ Blessed is he who comes in Yahweh's name!
We have blessed you out of Yahweh's house.
²⁷ᵃ Yahweh is God, and he has given us light.

Gospel: John 21: 1-14

¹ After these things, Jesus revealed himself again to the disciples at the sea of Tiberias. He revealed himself this way. ² Simon Peter, Thomas called Didymus, Nathanael of Cana in Galilee, and the sons of Zebedee, and two others of his disciples were together. ³ Simon Peter said to them, "I'm going fishing."
They told him, "We are also coming with you." They immediately went out and entered into the boat. That night, they caught nothing. ⁴ But when day had already come, Jesus stood on the beach; yet the disciples didn't know that it was Jesus. ⁵ Jesus therefore said to them, "Children, have you anything to eat?"
They answered him, "No."
⁶ He said to them, "Cast the net on the right side of the boat, and you will find some."
They cast it therefore, and now they weren't able to draw it in for the multitude of fish. ⁷ That disciple therefore whom Jesus loved said to Peter, "It's the Lord!"
So when Simon Peter heard that it was the Lord, he wrapped his coat around himself (for he was naked), and threw himself into the sea. ⁸ But the other disciples came in the little boat (for they were not far from the land, but about two hundred cubits away), dragging the net full of fish. ⁹ So when they got out on the land, they saw a fire of coals there, with fish and bread laid on it. ¹⁰ Jesus said to them, "Bring some of the fish which you have just caught."
¹¹ Simon Peter went up, and drew the net to land, full of one hundred fifty-three great fish. Even though there were so many, the net wasn't torn.
¹² Jesus said to them, "Come and eat breakfast!"
None of the disciples dared inquire of him, "Who are you?" knowing that it was the Lord.
¹³ Then Jesus came and took the bread, gave it to them, and the fish likewise. ¹⁴ This is now the third time that Jesus was revealed to his disciples after he had risen from the dead.

1. Invite the Holy Spirit into this reading, asking the Author of Scripture to speak to you through His Word
2. Read today's passage as many times as you need, take your time
3. Write down (below) what the Lord is saying to you today
4. Live with this Word in your heart through the day

Saturday, April 26, 2025
Saturday within the Octave of Easter

First Reading: Acts 4: 13-21

[13] Now when they saw the boldness of Peter and John, and had perceived that they were unlearned and ignorant men, they marveled. They recognized that they had been with Jesus. [14] Seeing the man who was healed standing with them, they could say nothing against it. [15] But when they had commanded them to go aside out of the council, they conferred among themselves, [16] saying, "What shall we do to these men? Because indeed a notable miracle has been done through them, as can be plainly seen by all who dwell in Jerusalem, and we can't deny it. [17] But so that this spreads no further among the people, let's threaten them, that from now on they don't speak to anyone in this name." [18] They called them, and commanded them not to speak at all nor teach in the name of Jesus.
[19] But Peter and John answered them, "Whether it is right in the sight of God to listen to you rather than to God, judge for yourselves, [20] for we can't help telling the things which we saw and heard."
[21] When they had further threatened them, they let them go, finding no way to punish them, because of the people; for everyone glorified God for that which was done.

Responsorial Psalm: Psalms 118: 1 and 14-21

[1] Give thanks to Yahweh, for he is good,
for his loving kindness endures forever.
[14] Yah is my strength and song.
He has become my salvation.
[15] The voice of rejoicing and salvation is in the tents of the righteous.
"The right hand of Yahweh does valiantly.
[16] The right hand of Yahweh is exalted!
The right hand of Yahweh does valiantly!"
[17] I will not die, but live,
and declare Yah's works.
[18] Yah has punished me severely,
but he has not given me over to death.

¹⁹ Open to me the gates of righteousness.
I will enter into them.
I will give thanks to Yah.
²⁰ This is the gate of Yahweh;
the righteous will enter into it.
²¹ I will give thanks to you, for you have answered me,
and have become my salvation.

Gospel: Mark 16: 9-15

⁹ §Now when he had risen early on the first day of the week, he appeared first to Mary Magdalene, from whom he had cast out seven demons. ¹⁰ She went and told those who had been with him, as they mourned and wept. ¹¹ When they heard that he was alive and had been seen by her, they disbelieved.
¹² After these things he was revealed in another form to two of them as they walked, on their way into the country. ¹³ They went away and told it to the rest. They didn't believe them, either.
¹⁴ Afterward he was revealed to the eleven themselves as they sat at the table; and he rebuked them for their unbelief and hardness of heart, because they didn't believe those who had seen him after he had risen. ¹⁵ He said to them, "Go into all the world and preach the Good News to the whole creation.

1. Invite the Holy Spirit into this reading, asking the Author of Scripture to speak to you through His Word
2. Read today's passage as many times as you need, take your time
3. Write down (below) what the Lord is saying to you today
4. Live with this Word in your heart through the day

Sunday, April 27, 2025
SECOND SUNDAY OF EASTER
SUNDAY OF DIVINE MERCY

First Reading: Acts 5: 12-16

¹² By the hands of the apostles many signs and wonders were done among the people. They were all with one accord in Solomon's porch. ¹³ None of the rest dared to join them; however, the people honored them. ¹⁴ More believers were added to the Lord, multitudes of both men and women. ¹⁵ They even carried out the sick into the streets and laid them on cots and mattresses, so that as Peter came by, at least his shadow might overshadow some of them. ¹⁶ The multitude also came together from the cities around Jerusalem, bringing sick people and those who were tormented by unclean spirits; and they were all healed.

Responsorial Psalm: Psalms 118: 2-4, 13-15, 22-24

² Let Israel now say
that his loving kindness endures forever.
³ Let the house of Aaron now say
that his loving kindness endures forever.
⁴ Now let those who fear Yahweh say
that his loving kindness endures forever.
¹³ You pushed me back hard, to make me fall,
but Yahweh helped me.
¹⁴ Yah is my strength and song.
He has become my salvation.
¹⁵ The voice of rejoicing and salvation is in the tents of the righteous.
"The right hand of Yahweh does valiantly.
²² The stone which the builders rejected
has become the cornerstone.‡
²³ This is Yahweh's doing.
It is marvelous in our eyes.
²⁴ This is the day that Yahweh has made.
We will rejoice and be glad in it!

Second Reading: Revelation 1: 9-11a, 12-13, 17-19

⁹ I John, your brother and partner with you in the oppression, Kingdom, and perseverance in Christ Jesus, was on the isle that is called Patmos because of God's Word and the testimony of Jesus Christ. ¹⁰ I was in the Spirit on the Lord's day, and I heard behind me a loud voice, like a trumpet ¹¹ª saying,§ "What you see, write in a book and send to the seven assemblies
¹² I turned to see the voice that spoke with me. Having turned, I saw seven golden lamp stands. ¹³ And among the lamp stands was one like a son of man,* clothed with a robe reaching down to his feet, and with a golden sash around his chest.
¹⁷ When I saw him, I fell at his feet like a dead man.

He laid his right hand on me, saying, "Don't be afraid. I am the first and the last, ⁱ⁸ and the Living one. I was dead, and behold, I am alive forever and ever. Amen. I have the keys of Death and of Hades.‡ ¹⁹ Write therefore the things which you have seen, and the things which are, and the things which will happen hereafter.

Gospel: John 20:19-31

¹⁹ When therefore it was evening on that day, the first day of the week, and when the doors were locked where the disciples were assembled, for fear of the Jews, Jesus came and stood in the middle and said to them, "Peace be to you."
²⁰ When he had said this, he showed them his hands and his side. The disciples therefore were glad when they saw the Lord. ²¹ Jesus therefore said to them again, "Peace be to you. As the Father has sent me, even so I send you." ²² When he had said this, he breathed on them, and said to them, "Receive the Holy Spirit! ²³ If you forgive anyone's sins, they have been forgiven them. If you retain anyone's sins, they have been retained."
²⁴ But Thomas, one of the twelve, called Didymus,§ wasn't with them when Jesus came. ²⁵ The other disciples therefore said to him, "We have seen the Lord!"
But he said to them, "Unless I see in his hands the print of the nails, put my finger into the print of the nails, and put my hand into his side, I will not believe."
²⁶ After eight days, again his disciples were inside and Thomas was with them. Jesus came, the doors being locked, and stood in the middle, and said, "Peace be to you." ²⁷ Then he said to Thomas, "Reach here your finger, and see my hands. Reach here your hand, and put it into my side. Don't be unbelieving, but believing."
²⁸ Thomas answered him, "My Lord and my God!"
²⁹ Jesus said to him, "Because you have seen me,‡ you have believed. Blessed are those who have not seen and have believed."
³⁰ Therefore Jesus did many other signs in the presence of his disciples, which are not written in this book; ³¹ but these are written that you may believe that Jesus is the Christ, the Son of God, and that believing you may have life in his name.

1. Invite the Holy Spirit into this reading, asking the Author of Scripture to speak to you through His Word
2. Read today's passage as many times as you need, take your time
3. Write down (below) what the Lord is saying to you today
4. Live with this Word in your heart through the day

_____

_____

Monday, April 28, 2025
Saint Peter Chanel, Priest and Martyr; Saint Louis Grignion de Montfort, Priest

First Reading: Acts 4: 23-31

²³ Being let go, they came to their own company and reported all that the chief priests and the elders had said to them. ²⁴ When they heard it, they lifted up their voice to God with one accord and said, "O Lord, you are God, who made the heaven, the earth, the sea, and all that is in them; ²⁵ who by the mouth of your servant David, said,
'Why do the nations rage,
and the peoples plot a vain thing?
²⁶ The kings of the earth take a stand,
and the rulers plot together,
against the Lord, and against his Christ.'‡*
²⁷ "For truly,‡ both Herod and Pontius Pilate, with the Gentiles and the people of Israel, were gathered together against your holy servant Jesus, whom you anointed, ²⁸ to do whatever your hand and your counsel foreordained to happen. ²⁹ Now, Lord, look at their threats, and grant to your servants to speak your word with all boldness, ³⁰ while you stretch out your hand to heal; and that signs and wonders may be done through the name of your holy Servant Jesus."
³¹ When they had prayed, the place was shaken where they were gathered together. They were all filled with the Holy Spirit, and they spoke the word of God with boldness.

Responsorial Psalm: Psalms 2: 1-9

¹ Why do the nations rage,
and the peoples plot a vain thing?
² The kings of the earth take a stand,
and the rulers take counsel together,
against Yahweh, and against his Anointed,‡ saying,
³ "Let's break their bonds apart,
and cast their cords from us."
⁴ He who sits in the heavens will laugh.
The Lord‡ will have them in derision.
⁵ Then he will speak to them in his anger,
and terrify them in his wrath:
⁶ "Yet I have set my King on my holy hill of Zion."
⁷ I will tell of the decree:
Yahweh said to me, "You are my son.
Today I have become your father.

⁸ Ask of me, and I will give the nations for your inheritance,
the uttermost parts of the earth for your possession.
⁹ You shall break them with a rod of iron.
You shall dash them in pieces like a potter's vessel."

Gospel: John 3: 1-8

¹ Now there was a man of the Pharisees named Nicodemus, a ruler of the Jews. ² He came to Jesus by night and said to him, "Rabbi, we know that you are a teacher come from God, for no one can do these signs that you do, unless God is with him." ³ Jesus answered him, "Most certainly I tell you, unless one is born anew, he can't see God's Kingdom." ⁴ Nicodemus said to him, "How can a man be born when he is old? Can he enter a second time into his mother's womb and be born?" ⁵ Jesus answered, "Most certainly I tell you, unless one is born of water and Spirit, he can't enter into God's Kingdom. ⁶ That which is born of the flesh is flesh. That which is born of the Spirit is spirit. ⁷ Don't marvel that I said to you, 'You must be born anew.' ⁸ The wind blows where it wants to, and you hear its sound, but don't know where it comes from and where it is going. So is everyone who is born of the Spirit."

1. Invite the Holy Spirit into this reading, asking the Author of Scripture to speak to you through His Word
2. Read today's passage as many times as you need, take your time
3. Write down (below) what the Lord is saying to you today
4. Live with this Word in your heart through the day

_____

_____

Tuesday, April 29, 2025
Saint Catherine of Siena, Virgin and Doctor of the Church

First Reading: Acts 4: 32-37

³² The multitude of those who believed were of one heart and soul. Not one of them claimed that anything of the things which he possessed was his own, but they had all things in common. ³³ With great power, the apostles gave their testimony of the resurrection of the Lord Jesus. Great grace was on them all. ³⁴ For neither was there among them any who

lacked, for as many as were owners of lands or houses sold them, and brought the proceeds of the things that were sold, ³⁵ and laid them at the apostles' feet; and distribution was made to each, according as anyone had need.

³⁶ Joses, who by the apostles was also called Barnabas (which is, being interpreted, Son of Encouragement), a Levite, a man of Cyprus by race, ³⁷ having a field, sold it and brought the money and laid it at the apostles' feet.

Responsorial Psalm: Psalms 93: 1-2, 5

¹ Yahweh reigns!
He is clothed with majesty!
Yahweh is armed with strength.
The world also is established.
It can't be moved.
² Your throne is established from long ago.
You are from everlasting.
⁵ Your statutes stand firm.
Holiness adorns your house,
Yahweh, forever more.

Gospel: John 3: 7b-15

⁷ᵇ 'You must be born anew.' ⁸ The wind‡ blows where it wants to, and you hear its sound, but don't know where it comes from and where it is going. So is everyone who is born of the Spirit."

⁹ Nicodemus answered him, "How can these things be?"

¹⁰ Jesus answered him, "Are you the teacher of Israel, and don't understand these things? ¹¹ Most certainly I tell you, we speak that which we know and testify of that which we have seen, and you don't receive our witness. ¹² If I told you earthly things and you don't believe, how will you believe if I tell you heavenly things? ¹³ No one has ascended into heaven but he who descended out of heaven, the Son of Man, who is in heaven. ¹⁴ As Moses lifted up the serpent in the wilderness, even so must the Son of Man be lifted up, ¹⁵ that whoever believes in him should not perish, but have eternal life.

1. Invite the Holy Spirit into this reading, asking the Author of Scripture to speak to you through His Word
2. Read today's passage as many times as you need, take your time
3. Write down (below) what the Lord is saying to you today
4. Live with this Word in your heart through the day

Wednesday, April 30, 2025
Saint Pius V, Pope

First Reading: Acts 5: 17-26

17 But the high priest rose up, and all those who were with him (which is the sect of the Sadducees), and they were filled with jealousy 18 and laid hands on the apostles, then put them in public custody. 19 But an angel of the Lord opened the prison doors by night, and brought them out and said, 20 "Go stand and speak in the temple to the people all the words of this life."
21 When they heard this, they entered into the temple about daybreak and taught. But the high priest and those who were with him came and called the council together, with all the senate of the children of Israel, and sent to the prison to have them brought. 22 But the officers who came didn't find them in the prison. They returned and reported, 23 "We found the prison shut and locked, and the guards standing before the doors, but when we opened them, we found no one inside!"
24 Now when the high priest, the captain of the temple, and the chief priests heard these words, they were very perplexed about them and what might become of this. 25 One came and told them, "Behold, the men whom you put in prison are in the temple, standing and teaching the people." 26 Then the captain went with the officers, and brought them without violence, for they were afraid that the people might stone them.

Responsorial Psalm: Psalms 34: 2-9

2 My soul shall boast in Yahweh.
The humble shall hear of it and be glad.
3 Oh magnify Yahweh with me.
Let's exalt his name together.
4 I sought Yahweh, and he answered me,
and delivered me from all my fears.
5 They looked to him, and were radiant.
Their faces shall never be covered with shame.
6 This poor man cried, and Yahweh heard him,
and saved him out of all his troubles.
7 Yahweh's angel encamps around those who fear him,

and delivers them.
⁸ Oh taste and see that Yahweh is good.
Blessed is the man who takes refuge in him.
⁹ Oh fear Yahweh, you his saints,
for there is no lack with those who fear him.

Gospel: John 3: 16-21

¹⁶ For God so loved the world, that he gave his only born§ Son, that whoever believes in him should not perish, but have eternal life. ¹⁷ For God didn't send his Son into the world to judge the world, but that the world should be saved through him. ¹⁸ He who believes in him is not judged. He who doesn't believe has been judged already, because he has not believed in the name of the only born Son of God. ¹⁹ This is the judgment, that the light has come into the world, and men loved the darkness rather than the light, for their works were evil. ²⁰ For everyone who does evil hates the light and doesn't come to the light, lest his works would be exposed. ²¹ But he who does the truth comes to the light, that his works may be revealed, that they have been done in God."

1. Invite the Holy Spirit into this reading, asking the Author of Scripture to speak to you through His Word
2. Read today's passage as many times as you need, take your time
3. Write down (below) what the Lord is saying to you today
4. Live with this Word in your heart through the day

Thursday, May 1, 2025
Saint Joseph the Worker

First Reading: Acts 5: 27-33

²⁷ When they had brought them, they set them before the council. The high priest questioned them, ²⁸ saying, "Didn't we strictly command you not to teach in this name? Behold, you have filled Jerusalem with your teaching, and intend to bring this man's blood on us."
²⁹ But Peter and the apostles answered, "We must obey God rather than men. ³⁰ The God of our fathers raised up Jesus, whom you killed, hanging him on a tree. ³¹ God exalted him

with his right hand to be a Prince and a Savior, to give repentance to Israel, and remission of sins. ³² We are his witnesses of these things; and so also is the Holy Spirit, whom God has given to those who obey him."

³³ But they, when they heard this, were cut to the heart, and were determined to kill them.

Responsorial Psalm: Psalms 34: 2 and 9, 17-18, 19-20

² My soul shall boast in Yahweh.
The humble shall hear of it and be glad.
⁹ Oh fear Yahweh, you his saints,
for there is no lack with those who fear him.
¹⁷ The righteous cry, and Yahweh hears,
and delivers them out of all their troubles.
¹⁸ Yahweh is near to those who have a broken heart,
and saves those who have a crushed spirit.
¹⁹ Many are the afflictions of the righteous,
but Yahweh delivers him out of them all.
²⁰ He protects all of his bones.
Not one of them is broken.

Gospel: John 3: 31-36

³¹ "He who comes from above is above all. He who is from the earth belongs to the earth and speaks of the earth. He who comes from heaven is above all. ³² What he has seen and heard, of that he testifies; and no one receives his witness. ³³ He who has received his witness has set his seal to this, that God is true. ³⁴ For he whom God has sent speaks the words of God; for God gives the Spirit without measure. ³⁵ The Father loves the Son, and has given all things into his hand. ³⁶ One who believes in the Son has eternal life, but one who disobeys⁺ the Son won't see life, but the wrath of God remains on him."

1. Invite the Holy Spirit into this reading, asking the Author of Scripture to speak to you through His Word
2. Read today's passage as many times as you need, take your time
3. Write down (below) what the Lord is saying to you today
4. Live with this Word in your heart through the day

Friday, May 2, 2025
Saint Athanasius, Bishop and Doctor of the Church

First Reading: Acts 5: 34-42

34 But one stood up in the council, a Pharisee named Gamaliel, a teacher of the law, honored by all the people, and commanded to put the apostles out for a little while. 35 He said to them, "You men of Israel, be careful concerning these men, what you are about to do. 36 For before these days Theudas rose up, making himself out to be somebody; to whom a number of men, about four hundred, joined themselves. He was slain; and all, as many as obeyed him, were dispersed and came to nothing. 37 After this man, Judas of Galilee rose up in the days of the enrollment, and drew away some people after him. He also perished, and all, as many as obeyed him, were scattered abroad. 38 Now I tell you, withdraw from these men and leave them alone. For if this counsel or this work is of men, it will be overthrown. 39 But if it is of God, you will not be able to overthrow it, and you would be found even to be fighting against God!"

40 They agreed with him. Summoning the apostles, they beat them and commanded them not to speak in the name of Jesus, and let them go. 41 They therefore departed from the presence of the council, rejoicing that they were counted worthy to suffer dishonor for Jesus' name.

42 Every day, in the temple and at home, they never stopped teaching and preaching Jesus, the Christ.

Responsorial Psalm: Psalms 27: 1, 4, 13-14

1 Yahweh is my light and my salvation.
Whom shall I fear?
Yahweh is the strength of my life.
Of whom shall I be afraid?
4 One thing I have asked of Yahweh, that I will seek after:
that I may dwell in Yahweh's house all the days of my life,
to see Yahweh's beauty,
and to inquire in his temple.
13 I am still confident of this:
I will see the goodness of Yahweh in the land of the living.
14 Wait for Yahweh.
Be strong, and let your heart take courage.
Yes, wait for Yahweh.

Gospel: John 6: 1-15

¹ After these things, Jesus went away to the other side of the sea of Galilee, which is also called the Sea of Tiberias. ² A great multitude followed him, because they saw his signs which he did on those who were sick. ³ Jesus went up into the mountain, and he sat there with his disciples. ⁴ Now the Passover, the feast of the Jews, was at hand. ⁵ Jesus therefore, lifting up his eyes and seeing that a great multitude was coming to him, said to Philip, "Where are we to buy bread, that these may eat?" ⁶ He said this to test him, for he himself knew what he would do.

⁷ Philip answered him, "Two hundred denarii worth of bread is not sufficient for them, that every one of them may receive a little."

⁸ One of his disciples, Andrew, Simon Peter's brother, said to him, ⁹ "There is a boy here who has five barley loaves and two fish, but what are these among so many?"

¹⁰ Jesus said, "Have the people sit down." Now there was much grass in that place. So the men sat down, in number about five thousand. ¹¹ Jesus took the loaves, and having given thanks, he distributed to the disciples, and the disciples to those who were sitting down, likewise also of the fish as much as they desired. ¹² When they were filled, he said to his disciples, "Gather up the broken pieces which are left over, that nothing be lost." ¹³ So they gathered them up, and filled twelve baskets with broken pieces from the five barley loaves, which were left over by those who had eaten. ¹⁴ When therefore the people saw the sign which Jesus did, they said, "This is truly the prophet who comes into the world." ¹⁵ Jesus therefore, perceiving that they were about to come and take him by force to make him king, withdrew again to the mountain by himself.

1. Invite the Holy Spirit into this reading, asking the Author of Scripture to speak to you through His Word
2. Read today's passage as many times as you need, take your time
3. Write down (below) what the Lord is saying to you today
4. Live with this Word in your heart through the day

Saturday, May 3, 2025
Saints Philip and James, Apostles

First Reading: First Corinthians 15: 1-8

¹ Now I declare to you, brothers, the Good News which I preached to you, which also you received, in which you also stand, ² by which also you are saved, if you hold firmly the word which I preached to you—unless you believed in vain.
³ For I delivered to you first of all that which I also received: that Christ died for our sins according to the Scriptures, ⁴ that he was buried, that he was raised on the third day according to the Scriptures, ⁵ and that he appeared to Cephas, then to the twelve. ⁶ Then he appeared to over five hundred brothers at once, most of whom remain until now, but some have also fallen asleep. ⁷ Then he appeared to James, then to all the apostles, ⁸ and last of all, as to the child born at the wrong time, he appeared to me also.

Responsorial Psalm: Psalms 19: 2-3, 4-5

² Day after day they pour out speech,
and night after night they display knowledge.
³ There is no speech nor language
where their voice is not heard.
⁴ Their voice has gone out through all the earth,
their words to the end of the world.
In them he has set a tent for the sun,
⁵ which is as a bridegroom coming out of his room,
like a strong man rejoicing to run his course.

Gospel: John 14: 6-14

⁶ Jesus said to him, "I am the way, the truth, and the life. No one comes to the Father, except through me. ⁷ If you had known me, you would have known my Father also. From now on, you know him and have seen him."
⁸ Philip said to him, "Lord, show us the Father, and that will be enough for us."
⁹ Jesus said to him, "Have I been with you such a long time, and do you not know me, Philip? He who has seen me has seen the Father. How do you say, 'Show us the Father'? ¹⁰ Don't you believe that I am in the Father, and the Father in me? The words that I tell you, I speak not from myself; but the Father who lives in me does his works. ¹¹ Believe me that I am in the Father, and the Father in me; or else believe me for the very works' sake. ¹² Most certainly I tell you, he who believes in me, the works that I do, he will do also; and he will do greater works than these, because I am going to my Father. ¹³ Whatever you will ask in my name, I will do it, that the Father may be glorified in the Son. ¹⁴ If you will ask anything in my name, I will do it.

1. Invite the Holy Spirit into this reading, asking the Author of Scripture to speak to you through His Word

2. Read today's passage as many times as you need, take your time
3. Write down (below) what the Lord is saying to you today
4. Live with this Word in your heart through the day

Sunday, May 4, 2025
THIRD SUNDAY OF EASTER

First Reading: Acts 5: 27-32, 40b-41

27 When they had brought them, they set them before the council. The high priest questioned them, 28 saying, "Didn't we strictly command you not to teach in this name? Behold, you have filled Jerusalem with your teaching, and intend to bring this man's blood on us."
29 But Peter and the apostles answered, "We must obey God rather than men. 30 The God of our fathers raised up Jesus, whom you killed, hanging him on a tree. 31 God exalted him with his right hand to be a Prince and a Savior, to give repentance to Israel, and remission of sins. 32 We are his witnesses of these things; and so also is the Holy Spirit, whom God has given to those who obey him."
40b Summoning the apostles, they beat them and commanded them not to speak in the name of Jesus, and let them go. 41 They therefore departed from the presence of the council, rejoicing that they were counted worthy to suffer dishonor for Jesus' name.

Responsorial Psalm: Psalms 30: 2 and 4, 5-6, 11-12

2 Yahweh my God, I cried to you,
and you have healed me.
4 Sing praise to Yahweh, you saints of his.
Give thanks to his holy name.
5 For his anger is but for a moment.
His favor is for a lifetime.
Weeping may stay for the night,
but joy comes in the morning.
6 As for me, I said in my prosperity,
"I shall never be moved."
11 You have turned my mourning into dancing for me.

You have removed my sackcloth, and clothed me with gladness,
¹² to the end that my heart may sing praise to you, and not be silent.
Yahweh my God, I will give thanks to you forever!

Second Reading: Revelation 5: 11-14

¹¹ I looked, and I heard something like a voice of many angels around the throne, the living creatures, and the elders. The number of them was ten thousands of ten thousands, and thousands of thousands, ¹² saying with a loud voice, "Worthy is the Lamb who has been killed to receive the power, wealth, wisdom, strength, honor, glory, and blessing!"
¹³ I heard every created thing which is in heaven, on the earth, under the earth, on the sea, and everything in them, saying, "To him who sits on the throne and to the Lamb be the blessing, the honor, the glory, and the dominion, forever and ever! Amen!"‡
¹⁴ The four living creatures said, "Amen!" Then the‡ elders fell down and worshiped.

Gospel: John 21: 1-19

¹ After these things, Jesus revealed himself again to the disciples at the sea of Tiberias. He revealed himself this way. ² Simon Peter, Thomas called Didymus,‡ Nathanael of Cana in Galilee, and the sons of Zebedee, and two others of his disciples were together. ³ Simon Peter said to them, "I'm going fishing."
They told him, "We are also coming with you." They immediately went out and entered into the boat. That night, they caught nothing. ⁴ But when day had already come, Jesus stood on the beach; yet the disciples didn't know that it was Jesus. ⁵ Jesus therefore said to them, "Children, have you anything to eat?"
They answered him, "No."
⁶ He said to them, "Cast the net on the right side of the boat, and you will find some."
They cast it therefore, and now they weren't able to draw it in for the multitude of fish. ⁷ That disciple therefore whom Jesus loved said to Peter, "It's the Lord!"
So when Simon Peter heard that it was the Lord, he wrapped his coat around himself (for he was naked), and threw himself into the sea. ⁸ But the other disciples came in the little boat (for they were not far from the land, but about two hundred cubits‡ away), dragging the net full of fish. ⁹ So when they got out on the land, they saw a fire of coals there, with fish and bread laid on it. ¹⁰ Jesus said to them, "Bring some of the fish which you have just caught."
¹¹ Simon Peter went up, and drew the net to land, full of one hundred fifty-three great fish. Even though there were so many, the net wasn't torn.
¹² Jesus said to them, "Come and eat breakfast!"
None of the disciples dared inquire of him, "Who are you?" knowing that it was the Lord.

¹³ Then Jesus came and took the bread, gave it to them, and the fish likewise. ¹⁴ This is now the third time that Jesus was revealed to his disciples after he had risen from the dead. ¹⁵ So when they had eaten their breakfast, Jesus said to Simon Peter, "Simon, son of Jonah, do you love me more than these?"

He said to him, "Yes, Lord; you know that I have affection for you."

He said to him, "Feed my lambs." ¹⁶ He said to him again a second time, "Simon, son of Jonah, do you love me?"

He said to him, "Yes, Lord; you know that I have affection for you."

He said to him, "Tend my sheep." ¹⁷ He said to him the third time, "Simon, son of Jonah, do you have affection for me?"

Peter was grieved because he asked him the third time, "Do you have affection for me?" He said to him, "Lord, you know everything. You know that I have affection for you."

Jesus said to him, "Feed my sheep. ¹⁸ Most certainly I tell you, when you were young, you dressed yourself and walked where you wanted to. But when you are old, you will stretch out your hands, and another will dress you and carry you where you don't want to go."

¹⁹ Now he said this, signifying by what kind of death he would glorify God. When he had said this, he said to him, "Follow me."

1. Invite the Holy Spirit into this reading, asking the Author of Scripture to speak to you through His Word
2. Read today's passage as many times as you need, take your time
3. Write down (below) what the Lord is saying to you today
4. Live with this Word in your heart through the day

_____

_____

Monday, May 5, 2025

First Reading: Acts 6: 8-15

⁸ Stephen, full of faith and power, performed great wonders and signs among the people. ⁹ But some of those who were of the synagogue called "The Libertines", and of the Cyrenians, of the Alexandrians, and of those of Cilicia and Asia arose, disputing with Stephen. ¹⁰ They weren't able to withstand the wisdom and the Spirit by which he spoke. ¹¹ Then they secretly induced men to say, "We have heard him speak blasphemous words against Moses and God." ¹² They stirred up the people, the elders, and the scribes, and came against him and seized him, then brought him in to the council, ¹³ and set up false

witnesses who said, "This man never stops speaking blasphemous words against this holy place and the law. ¹⁴ For we have heard him say that this Jesus of Nazareth will destroy this place, and will change the customs which Moses delivered to us." ¹⁵ All who sat in the council, fastening their eyes on him, saw his face like it was the face of an angel.

Responsorial Psalm: Psalms 119: 23-24, 26-27, 29-30

²³ Though princes sit and slander me,
your servant will meditate on your statutes.
²⁴ Indeed your statutes are my delight,
and my counselors.
²⁶ I declared my ways, and you answered me.
Teach me your statutes.
²⁷ Let me understand the teaching of your precepts!
Then I will meditate on your wondrous works.
²⁹ Keep me from the way of deceit.
Grant me your law graciously!
³⁰ I have chosen the way of truth.
I have set your ordinances before me.

Gospel: John 6: 22-29

²² On the next day, the multitude that stood on the other side of the sea saw that there was no other boat there, except the one in which his disciples had embarked, and that Jesus hadn't entered with his disciples into the boat, but his disciples had gone away alone. ²³ However, boats from Tiberias came near to the place where they ate the bread after the Lord had given thanks. ²⁴ When the multitude therefore saw that Jesus wasn't there, nor his disciples, they themselves got into the boats and came to Capernaum, seeking Jesus. ²⁵ When they found him on the other side of the sea, they asked him, "Rabbi, when did you come here?"
²⁶ Jesus answered them, "Most certainly I tell you, you seek me, not because you saw signs, but because you ate of the loaves and were filled. ²⁷ Don't work for the food which perishes, but for the food which remains to eternal life, which the Son of Man will give to you. For God the Father has sealed him."
²⁸ They said therefore to him, "What must we do, that we may work the works of God?"
²⁹ Jesus answered them, "This is the work of God, that you believe in him whom he has sent."

1. Invite the Holy Spirit into this reading, asking the Author of Scripture to speak to you through His Word

2. Read today's passage as many times as you need, take your time
3. Write down (below) what the Lord is saying to you today
4. Live with this Word in your heart through the day

_____

_____

Tuesday, May 6, 2025

First Reading: Acts 7: 51-60

51 "You stiff-necked and uncircumcised in heart and ears, you always resist the Holy Spirit! As your fathers did, so you do. 52 Which of the prophets didn't your fathers persecute? They killed those who foretold the coming of the Righteous One, of whom you have now become betrayers and murderers. 53 You received the law as it was ordained by angels, and didn't keep it!"
54 Now when they heard these things, they were cut to the heart, and they gnashed at him with their teeth. 55 But he, being full of the Holy Spirit, looked up steadfastly into heaven and saw the glory of God, and Jesus standing on the right hand of God, 56 and said, "Behold, I see the heavens opened and the Son of Man standing at the right hand of God!"
57 But they cried out with a loud voice and stopped their ears, then rushed at him with one accord. 58 They threw him out of the city and stoned him. The witnesses placed their garments at the feet of a young man named Saul. 59 They stoned Stephen as he called out, saying, "Lord Jesus, receive my spirit!" 60 He kneeled down and cried with a loud voice, "Lord, don't hold this sin against them!" When he had said this, he fell asleep.

Responsorial Psalm: Psalms 31: 3-4, 6 and 7b and 8a, 17 and 21ab

3 For you are my rock and my fortress,
therefore for your name's sake lead me and guide me.
4 Pluck me out of the net that they have laid secretly for me,
for you are my stronghold.
6 I hate those who regard lying vanities,
but I trust in Yahweh.
7 I will be glad and rejoice in your loving kindness,
for you have seen my affliction.
8a You have not shut me up into the hand of the enemy.
17 Let me not be disappointed, Yahweh, for I have called on you.

Let the wicked be disappointed.
Let them be silent in Sheol.
²¹ Praise be to Yahweh,
for he has shown me his marvelous loving kindness in a strong city.

Gospel: John 6: 30-35

³⁰ They said therefore to him, "What then do you do for a sign, that we may see and believe you? What work do you do? ³¹ Our fathers ate the manna in the wilderness. As it is written, 'He gave them bread out of heaven to eat.' "
³² Jesus therefore said to them, "Most certainly, I tell you, it wasn't Moses who gave you the bread out of heaven, but my Father gives you the true bread out of heaven. ³³ For the bread of God is that which comes down out of heaven and gives life to the world."
³⁴ They said therefore to him, "Lord, always give us this bread."
³⁵ Jesus said to them, "I am the bread of life. Whoever comes to me will not be hungry, and whoever believes in me will never be thirsty.

1. Invite the Holy Spirit into this reading, asking the Author of Scripture to speak to you through His Word
2. Read today's passage as many times as you need, take your time
3. Write down (below) what the Lord is saying to you today
4. Live with this Word in your heart through the day

Wednesday, May 7, 2025

First Reading: Acts 8: 1b-8

¹ᵇ A great persecution arose against the assembly which was in Jerusalem in that day. They were all scattered abroad throughout the regions of Judea and Samaria, except for the apostles. ² Devout men buried Stephen and lamented greatly over him. ³ But Saul ravaged the assembly, entering into every house and dragged both men and women off to prison. ⁴ Therefore those who were scattered abroad went around preaching the word. ⁵ Philip went down to the city of Samaria and proclaimed to them the Christ. ⁶ The multitudes listened with one accord to the things that were spoken by Philip when they heard and saw the signs which he did. ⁷ For unclean spirits came out of many of those who

had them. They came out, crying with a loud voice. Many who had been paralyzed and lame were healed. ⁸ There was great joy in that city.

Responsorial Psalm: Psalms 66: 1-3a, 4-5, 6-7a

¹ Make a joyful shout to God, all the earth!
² Sing to the glory of his name!
Offer glory and praise!
³ᵃ Tell God, "How awesome are your deeds!
⁴ All the earth will worship you,
and will sing to you;
they will sing to your name."
⁵ Come, and see God's deeds—
awesome work on behalf of the children of men.
⁶ He turned the sea into dry land.
They went through the river on foot.
There, we rejoiced in him.
⁷ᵃ He rules by his might forever.

Gospel: John 6: 35-40

³⁵ Jesus said to them, "I am the bread of life. Whoever comes to me will not be hungry, and whoever believes in me will never be thirsty. ³⁶ But I told you that you have seen me, and yet you don't believe. ³⁷ All those whom the Father gives me will come to me. He who comes to me I will in no way throw out. ³⁸ For I have come down from heaven, not to do my own will, but the will of him who sent me. ³⁹ This is the will of my Father who sent me, that of all he has given to me I should lose nothing, but should raise him up at the last day. ⁴⁰ This is the will of the one who sent me, that everyone who sees the Son and believes in him should have eternal life; and I will raise him up at the last day."

1. Invite the Holy Spirit into this reading, asking the Author of Scripture to speak to you through His Word
2. Read today's passage as many times as you need, take your time
3. Write down (below) what the Lord is saying to you today
4. Live with this Word in your heart through the day

_____

_____

Thursday, May 8, 2025

First Reading: Acts 8: 26-40

²⁶ Then an angel of the Lord spoke to Philip, saying, "Arise, and go toward the south to the way that goes down from Jerusalem to Gaza. This is a desert."
²⁷ He arose and went; and behold, there was a man of Ethiopia, a eunuch of great authority under Candace, queen of the Ethiopians, who was over all her treasure, who had come to Jerusalem to worship. ²⁸ He was returning and sitting in his chariot, and was reading the prophet Isaiah.
²⁹ The Spirit said to Philip, "Go near, and join yourself to this chariot."
³⁰ Philip ran to him, and heard him reading Isaiah the prophet, and said, "Do you understand what you are reading?"
³¹ He said, "How can I, unless someone explains it to me?" He begged Philip to come up and sit with him. ³² Now the passage of the Scripture which he was reading was this,
"He was led as a sheep to the slaughter.
As a lamb before his shearer is silent,
so he doesn't open his mouth.
³³ In his humiliation, his judgment was taken away.
Who will declare His generation?
For his life is taken from the earth."˃
³⁴ The eunuch answered Philip, "Who is the prophet talking about? About himself, or about someone else?"
³⁵ Philip opened his mouth, and beginning from this Scripture, preached to him about Jesus. ³⁶ As they went on the way, they came to some water; and the eunuch said, "Behold, here is water. What is keeping me from being baptized?"
³⁷ ⸱ ³⁸ He commanded the chariot to stand still, and they both went down into the water, both Philip and the eunuch, and he baptized him.
³⁹ When they came up out of the water, the Spirit of the Lord caught Philip away, and the eunuch didn't see him any more, for he went on his way rejoicing. ⁴⁰ But Philip was found at Azotus. Passing through, he preached the Good News to all the cities until he came to Caesarea.

Responsorial Psalm: Psalms 66: 8-9, 16-17, 20

⁸ Praise our God, you peoples!
Make the sound of his praise heard,
⁹ who preserves our life among the living,
and doesn't allow our feet to be moved.
¹⁶ Come and hear, all you who fear God.

I will declare what he has done for my soul.
¹⁷ I cried to him with my mouth.
He was extolled with my tongue.
²⁰ Blessed be God, who has not turned away my prayer,
nor his loving kindness from me.

Gospel: John 6: 44-51

⁴⁴ No one can come to me unless the Father who sent me draws him; and I will raise him up in the last day. ⁴⁵ It is written in the prophets, 'They will all be taught by God.' ⁎ Therefore everyone who hears from the Father and has learned, comes to me. ⁴⁶ Not that anyone has seen the Father, except he who is from God. He has seen the Father. ⁴⁷ Most certainly, I tell you, he who believes in me has eternal life. ⁴⁸ I am the bread of life. ⁴⁹ Your fathers ate the manna in the wilderness and they died. ⁵⁰ This is the bread which comes down out of heaven, that anyone may eat of it and not die. ⁵¹ I am the living bread which came down out of heaven. If anyone eats of this bread, he will live forever. Yes, the bread which I will give for the life of the world is my flesh."

1. Invite the Holy Spirit into this reading, asking the Author of Scripture to speak to you through His Word
2. Read today's passage as many times as you need, take your time
3. Write down (below) what the Lord is saying to you today
4. Live with this Word in your heart through the day

_____

_____

Friday, May 9, 2025

First Reading: Acts 9: 1-20

¹ But Saul, still breathing threats and slaughter against the disciples of the Lord, went to the high priest ² and asked for letters from him to the synagogues of Damascus, that if he found any who were of the Way, whether men or women, he might bring them bound to Jerusalem. ³ As he traveled, he got close to Damascus, and suddenly a light from the sky shone around him. ⁴ He fell on the earth, and heard a voice saying to him, "Saul, Saul, why do you persecute me?"
⁵ He said, "Who are you, Lord?"

The Lord said, "I am Jesus, whom you are persecuting.‡ 6 But‡ rise up and enter into the city, then you will be told what you must do."

⁷ The men who traveled with him stood speechless, hearing the sound, but seeing no one. ⁸ Saul arose from the ground, and when his eyes were opened, he saw no one. They led him by the hand and brought him into Damascus. ⁹ He was without sight for three days, and neither ate nor drank.

¹⁰ Now there was a certain disciple at Damascus named Ananias. The Lord said to him in a vision, "Ananias!"

He said, "Behold, it's me, Lord."

¹¹ The Lord said to him, "Arise and go to the street which is called Straight, and inquire in the house of Judah§ for one named Saul, a man of Tarsus. For behold, he is praying, ¹² and in a vision he has seen a man named Ananias coming in and laying his hands on him, that he might receive his sight."

¹³ But Ananias answered, "Lord, I have heard from many about this man, how much evil he did to your saints at Jerusalem. ¹⁴ Here he has authority from the chief priests to bind all who call on your name."

¹⁵ But the Lord said to him, "Go your way, for he is my chosen vessel to bear my name before the nations and kings, and the children of Israel. ¹⁶ For I will show him how many things he must suffer for my name's sake."

¹⁷ Ananias departed and entered into the house. Laying his hands on him, he said, "Brother Saul, the Lord, who appeared to you on the road by which you came, has sent me that you may receive your sight and be filled with the Holy Spirit." ¹⁸ Immediately something like scales fell from his eyes, and he received his sight. He arose and was baptized. ¹⁹ He took food and was strengthened.

Saul stayed several days with the disciples who were at Damascus. ²⁰ Immediately in the synagogues he proclaimed the Christ, that he is the Son of God.

Responsorial Psalm: Psalms 117: 1, 2

¹ Praise Yahweh, all you nations!
Extol him, all you peoples!
² For his loving kindness is great toward us.
Yahweh's faithfulness endures forever.
Praise Yah!

Gospel: John 6: 52-59

⁵² The Jews therefore contended with one another, saying, "How can this man give us his flesh to eat?"

53 Jesus therefore said to them, "Most certainly I tell you, unless you eat the flesh of the Son of Man and drink his blood, you don't have life in yourselves. 54 He who eats my flesh and drinks my blood has eternal life, and I will raise him up at the last day. 55 For my flesh is food indeed, and my blood is drink indeed. 56 He who eats my flesh and drinks my blood lives in me, and I in him. 57 As the living Father sent me, and I live because of the Father, so he who feeds on me will also live because of me. 58 This is the bread which came down out of heaven—not as our fathers ate the manna and died. He who eats this bread will live forever." 59 He said these things in the synagogue, as he taught in Capernaum.

1. Invite the Holy Spirit into this reading, asking the Author of Scripture to speak to you through His Word
2. Read today's passage as many times as you need, take your time
3. Write down (below) what the Lord is saying to you today
4. Live with this Word in your heart through the day

_____

_____

Saturday, May 10, 2025
Saint John of Avila, Priest and Doctor of the Church;
USA: Saint Damien de Veuster, Priest

First Reading: Acts 9: 31-42

31 So the assemblies throughout all Judea, Galilee, and Samaria had peace and were built up. They were multiplied, walking in the fear of the Lord and in the comfort of the Holy Spirit.
32 As Peter went throughout all those parts, he came down also to the saints who lived at Lydda. 33 There he found a certain man named Aeneas, who had been bedridden for eight years because he was paralyzed. 34 Peter said to him, "Aeneas, Jesus Christ heals you. Get up and make your bed!" Immediately he arose. 35 All who lived at Lydda and in Sharon saw him, and they turned to the Lord.
36 Now there was at Joppa a certain disciple named Tabitha, which when translated means Dorcas.‡ This woman was full of good works and acts of mercy which she did. 37 In those days, she became sick and died. When they had washed her, they laid her in an upper room. 38 As Lydda was near Joppa, the disciples, hearing that Peter was there, sent two men§ to him, imploring him not to delay in coming to them. 39 Peter got up and went with them. When he had come, they brought him into the upper room. All the widows stood by

him weeping, and showing the tunics and other garments which Dorcas had made while she was with them. ⁴⁰ Peter sent them all out, and knelt down and prayed. Turning to the body, he said, "Tabitha, get up!" She opened her eyes, and when she saw Peter, she sat up. ⁴¹ He gave her his hand and raised her up. Calling the saints and widows, he presented her alive. ⁴² This became known throughout all Joppa, and many believed in the Lord. ⁴³ He stayed many days in Joppa with a tanner named Simon.

Responsorial Psalm: Psalms 116: 12-13, 14-15, 16-17

¹² What will I give to Yahweh for all his benefits toward me?
¹³ I will take the cup of salvation, and call on Yahweh's name.
¹⁴ I will pay my vows to Yahweh,
yes, in the presence of all his people.
¹⁵ Precious in Yahweh's sight is the death of his saints.
¹⁶ Yahweh, truly I am your servant.
I am your servant, the son of your servant girl.
You have freed me from my chains.
¹⁷ I will offer to you the sacrifice of thanksgiving,
and will call on Yahweh's name.

Gospel: John 6: 60-69

⁶⁰ Therefore many of his disciples, when they heard this, said, "This is a hard saying! Who can listen to it?"
⁶¹ But Jesus knowing in himself that his disciples murmured at this, said to them, "Does this cause you to stumble? ⁶² Then what if you would see the Son of Man ascending to where he was before? ⁶³ It is the spirit who gives life. The flesh profits nothing. The words that I speak to you are spirit, and are life. ⁶⁴ But there are some of you who don't believe." For Jesus knew from the beginning who they were who didn't believe, and who it was who would betray him. ⁶⁵ He said, "For this cause I have said to you that no one can come to me, unless it is given to him by my Father."
⁶⁶ At this, many of his disciples went back and walked no more with him. ⁶⁷ Jesus said therefore to the twelve, "You don't also want to go away, do you?"
⁶⁸ Simon Peter answered him, "Lord, to whom would we go? You have the words of eternal life. ⁶⁹ We have come to believe and know that you are the Christ, the Son of the living God."

1. Invite the Holy Spirit into this reading, asking the Author of Scripture to speak to you through His Word
2. Read today's passage as many times as you need, take your time
3. Write down (below) what the Lord is saying to you today

4. Live with this Word in your heart through the day

_____

_____

Sunday, May 11, 2025
FOURTH SUNDAY OF EASTER

First Reading: Acts 13: 14, 43-52

14 But they, passing on from Perga, came to Antioch of Pisidia. They went into the synagogue on the Sabbath day and sat down.
43 Now when the synagogue broke up, many of the Jews and of the devout proselytes followed Paul and Barnabas; who, speaking to them, urged them to continue in the grace of God.
44 The next Sabbath, almost the whole city was gathered together to hear the word of God. 45 But when the Jews saw the multitudes, they were filled with jealousy, and contradicted the things which were spoken by Paul, and blasphemed.
46 Paul and Barnabas spoke out boldly, and said, "It was necessary that God's word should be spoken to you first. Since indeed you thrust it from yourselves, and judge yourselves unworthy of eternal life, behold, we turn to the Gentiles. 47 For so has the Lord commanded us, saying,
'I have set you as a light for the Gentiles,
that you should bring salvation to the uttermost parts of the earth.' "
48 As the Gentiles heard this, they were glad and glorified the word of God. As many as were appointed to eternal life believed. 49 The Lord's word was spread abroad throughout all the region. 50 But the Jews stirred up the devout and prominent women and the chief men of the city, and stirred up a persecution against Paul and Barnabas, and threw them out of their borders. 51 But they shook off the dust of their feet against them, and came to Iconium. 52 The disciples were filled with joy and with the Holy Spirit.

Responsorial Psalm: Psalms 100: 1-2, 3, 5

1 Shout for joy to Yahweh, all you lands!
2 Serve Yahweh with gladness.
Come before his presence with singing.
3 Know that Yahweh, he is God.
It is he who has made us, and we are his.

We are his people, and the sheep of his pasture.
5 For Yahweh is good.
His loving kindness endures forever,
his faithfulness to all generations.

Second Reading: Revelation 7: 9, 14b-17

9 After these things I looked, and behold, a great multitude which no man could count, out of every nation and of all tribes, peoples, and languages, standing before the throne and before the Lamb, dressed in white robes, with palm branches in their hands.
14b He said to me, "These are those who came out of the great suffering. They washed their robes and made them white in the Lamb's blood. 15 Therefore they are before the throne of God, and they serve him day and night in his temple. He who sits on the throne will spread his tabernacle over them. 16 They will never be hungry or thirsty any more. The sun won't beat on them, nor any heat; 17 for the Lamb who is in the middle of the throne shepherds them and leads them to springs of life-giving waters. And God will wipe away every tear from their eyes."

Gospel: John 10: 27-30

27 My sheep hear my voice, and I know them, and they follow me. 28 I give eternal life to them. They will never perish, and no one will snatch them out of my hand. 29 My Father who has given them to me is greater than all. No one is able to snatch them out of my Father's hand. 30 I and the Father are one."

1. Invite the Holy Spirit into this reading, asking the Author of Scripture to speak to you through His Word
2. Read today's passage as many times as you need, take your time
3. Write down (below) what the Lord is saying to you today
4. Live with this Word in your heart through the day

Monday, May 12, 2025
Saints Nereus and Achilleus, Martyrs; Saint Pancras, Martyr

First Reading: Acts 11: 1-18

¹ Now the apostles and the brothers† who were in Judea heard that the Gentiles had also received the word of God. ² When Peter had come up to Jerusalem, those who were of the circumcision contended with him, ³ saying, "You went in to uncircumcised men and ate with them!"
⁴ But Peter began, and explained to them in order, saying, ⁵ "I was in the city of Joppa praying, and in a trance I saw a vision: a certain container descending, like it was a great sheet let down from heaven by four corners. It came as far as me. ⁶ When I had looked intently at it, I considered, and saw the four-footed animals of the earth, wild animals, creeping things, and birds of the sky. ⁷ I also heard a voice saying to me, 'Rise, Peter, kill and eat!' ⁸ But I said, 'Not so, Lord, for nothing unholy or unclean has ever entered into my mouth.' ⁹ But a voice answered me the second time out of heaven, 'What God has cleansed, don't you call unclean.' ¹⁰ This was done three times, and all were drawn up again into heaven. ¹¹ Behold, immediately three men stood before the house where I was, having been sent from Caesarea to me. ¹² The Spirit told me to go with them without discriminating. These six brothers also accompanied me, and we entered into the man's house. ¹³ He told us how he had seen the angel standing in his house and saying to him, 'Send to Joppa and get Simon, who is called Peter, ¹⁴ who will speak to you words by which you will be saved, you and all your house.' ¹⁵ As I began to speak, the Holy Spirit fell on them, even as on us at the beginning. ¹⁶ I remembered the word of the Lord, how he said, 'John indeed baptized in water, but you will be baptized in the Holy Spirit.' ¹⁷ If then God gave to them the same gift as us when we believed in the Lord Jesus Christ, who was I, that I could withstand God?"
¹⁸ When they heard these things, they held their peace and glorified God, saying, "Then God has also granted to the Gentiles repentance to life!"

Responsorial Psalm: Psalms 42: 2-3; 43: 3-4

² My soul thirsts for God, for the living God.
When shall I come and appear before God?
³ My tears have been my food day and night,
while they continually ask me, "Where is your God?"
³ Oh, send out your light and your truth.
Let them lead me.
Let them bring me to your holy hill,
to your tents.
⁴ Then I will go to the altar of God,
to God, my exceeding joy.
I will praise you on the harp, God, my God.

Gospel: John 10: 1-10

¹ "Most certainly, I tell you, one who doesn't enter by the door into the sheep fold, but climbs up some other way, is a thief and a robber. ² But one who enters in by the door is the shepherd of the sheep. ³ The gatekeeper opens the gate for him, and the sheep listen to his voice. He calls his own sheep by name and leads them out. ⁴ Whenever he brings out his own sheep, he goes before them; and the sheep follow him, for they know his voice. ⁵ They will by no means follow a stranger, but will flee from him; for they don't know the voice of strangers." ⁶ Jesus spoke this parable to them, but they didn't understand what he was telling them.

⁷ Jesus therefore said to them again, "Most certainly, I tell you, I am the sheep's door. ⁸ All who came before me are thieves and robbers, but the sheep didn't listen to them. ⁹ I am the door. If anyone enters in by me, he will be saved, and will go in and go out and will find pasture. ¹⁰ The thief only comes to steal, kill, and destroy. I came that they may have life, and may have it abundantly.

1. Invite the Holy Spirit into this reading, asking the Author of Scripture to speak to you through His Word
2. Read today's passage as many times as you need, take your time
3. Write down (below) what the Lord is saying to you today
4. Live with this Word in your heart through the day

_____

_____

Tuesday, May 13, 2025
Our Lady of Fatima

First Reading: Acts 11: 19-26

¹⁹ They therefore who were scattered abroad by the oppression that arose about Stephen traveled as far as Phoenicia, Cyprus, and Antioch, speaking the word to no one except to Jews only. ²⁰ But there were some of them, men of Cyprus and Cyrene, who, when they had come to Antioch, spoke to the Hellenists,‡ preaching the Lord Jesus. ²¹ The hand of the Lord was with them, and a great number believed and turned to the Lord. ²² The report concerning them came to the ears of the assembly which was in Jerusalem. They sent out Barnabas to go as far as Antioch, ²³ who, when he had come, and had seen the grace of God, was glad. He exhorted them all, that with purpose of heart they should remain near to the

Lord. 24 For he was a good man, and full of the Holy Spirit and of faith, and many people were added to the Lord.
25 Barnabas went out to Tarsus to look for Saul. 26 When he had found him, he brought him to Antioch. For a whole year they were gathered together with the assembly, and taught many people. The disciples were first called Christians in Antioch.

Responsorial Psalm: Psalms 87: 1-3, 4-5, 6-7

1 His foundation is in the holy mountains.
2 Yahweh loves the gates of Zion more than all the dwellings of Jacob.
3 Glorious things are spoken about you, city of God.
4 I will record Rahab‡ and Babylon among those who acknowledge me.
Behold, Philistia, Tyre, and also Ethiopia:
"This one was born there."
5 Yes, of Zion it will be said, "This one and that one was born in her;"
the Most High himself will establish her.
6 Yahweh will count, when he writes up the peoples,
"This one was born there."
7 Those who sing as well as those who dance say,
"All my springs are in you."

Gospel: John 10: 22-30

22 It was the Feast of the Dedication‡ at Jerusalem. 23 It was winter, and Jesus was walking in the temple, in Solomon's porch. 24 The Jews therefore came around him and said to him, "How long will you hold us in suspense? If you are the Christ, tell us plainly."
25 Jesus answered them, "I told you, and you don't believe. The works that I do in my Father's name, these testify about me. 26 But you don't believe, because you are not of my sheep, as I told you. 27 My sheep hear my voice, and I know them, and they follow me. 28 I give eternal life to them. They will never perish, and no one will snatch them out of my hand. 29 My Father who has given them to me is greater than all. No one is able to snatch them out of my Father's hand. 30 I and the Father are one."

1. Invite the Holy Spirit into this reading, asking the Author of Scripture to speak to you through His Word
2. Read today's passage as many times as you need, take your time
3. Write down (below) what the Lord is saying to you today
4. Live with this Word in your heart through the day

Wednesday, May 14, 2025
Saint Matthias, Apostle

First Reading: Acts 1: 15-17, 20-26

[15] In these days, Peter stood up in the middle of the disciples (and the number of names was about one hundred twenty), and said, [16] "Brothers, it was necessary that this Scripture should be fulfilled, which the Holy Spirit spoke before by the mouth of David concerning Judas, who was guide to those who took Jesus. [17] For he was counted with us, and received his portion in this ministry.
[20] For it is written in the book of Psalms,
'Let his habitation be made desolate.
Let no one dwell in it;'* and, 'Let another take his office.'*
[21] "Of the men therefore who have accompanied us all the time that the Lord Jesus went in and out among us, [22] beginning from the baptism of John to the day that he was received up from us, of these one must become a witness with us of his resurrection."
[23] They put forward two: Joseph called Barsabbas, who was also called Justus, and Matthias. [24] They prayed and said, "You, Lord, who know the hearts of all men, show which one of these two you have chosen [25] to take part in this ministry and apostleship from which Judas fell away, that he might go to his own place." [26] They drew lots for them, and the lot fell on Matthias; and he was counted with the eleven apostles.

Responsorial Psalm: Psalms 113: 1-8

[1] Praise Yah!
Praise, you servants of Yahweh,
praise Yahweh's name.
[2] Blessed be Yahweh's name,
from this time forward and forever more.
[3] From the rising of the sun to its going down,
Yahweh's name is to be praised.
[4] Yahweh is high above all nations,
his glory above the heavens.
[5] Who is like Yahweh, our God,
who has his seat on high,

⁶ who stoops down to see in heaven and in the earth?
⁷ He raises up the poor out of the dust,
and lifts up the needy from the ash heap,
⁸ that he may set him with princes,
even with the princes of his people.

Gospel: John 15: 9-17

⁹ Even as the Father has loved me, I also have loved you. Remain in my love. ¹⁰ If you keep my commandments, you will remain in my love, even as I have kept my Father's commandments and remain in his love. ¹¹ I have spoken these things to you, that my joy may remain in you, and that your joy may be made full.
¹² "This is my commandment, that you love one another, even as I have loved you. ¹³ Greater love has no one than this, that someone lay down his life for his friends. ¹⁴ You are my friends if you do whatever I command you. ¹⁵ No longer do I call you servants, for the servant doesn't know what his lord does. But I have called you friends, for everything that I heard from my Father, I have made known to you. ¹⁶ You didn't choose me, but I chose you and appointed you, that you should go and bear fruit, and that your fruit should remain; that whatever you will ask of the Father in my name, he may give it to you.
¹⁷ "I command these things to you, that you may love one another.

1. Invite the Holy Spirit into this reading, asking the Author of Scripture to speak to you through His Word
2. Read today's passage as many times as you need, take your time
3. Write down (below) what the Lord is saying to you today
4. Live with this Word in your heart through the day

Thursday, May 15, 2025
Saint Isidore

First Reading: Acts 13: 13-25

¹³ Now Paul and his company set sail from Paphos and came to Perga in Pamphylia. John departed from them and returned to Jerusalem. ¹⁴ But they, passing on from Perga, came

to Antioch of Pisidia. They went into the synagogue on the Sabbath day and sat down. ¹⁵ After the reading of the law and the prophets, the rulers of the synagogue sent to them, saying, "Brothers, if you have any word of exhortation for the people, speak."

¹⁶ Paul stood up, and gesturing with his hand said, "Men of Israel, and you who fear God, listen. ¹⁷ The God of this people‡ chose our fathers, and exalted the people when they stayed as aliens in the land of Egypt, and with an uplifted arm, he led them out of it. ¹⁸ For a period of about forty years he put up with them in the wilderness. ¹⁹ When he had destroyed seven nations in the land of Canaan, he gave them their land for an inheritance for about four hundred fifty years. ²⁰ After these things, he gave them judges until Samuel the prophet. ²¹ Afterward they asked for a king, and God gave to them Saul the son of Kish, a man of the tribe of Benjamin, for forty years. ²² When he had removed him, he raised up David to be their king, to whom he also testified, 'I have found David the son of Jesse, a man after my heart, who will do all my will.' ²³ From this man's offspring, God has brought salvation‡ to Israel according to his promise, ²⁴ before his coming, when John had first preached the baptism of repentance to Israel.§ ²⁵ As John was fulfilling his course, he said, 'What do you suppose that I am? I am not he. But behold, one comes after me, the sandals of whose feet I am not worthy to untie.'

Responsorial Psalm: Psalms 89: 2-3, 21-22, 25 and 27

² I indeed declare, "Love stands firm forever.
You established the heavens.
Your faithfulness is in them."
³ "I have made a covenant with my chosen one,
I have sworn to David, my servant,
²¹ with whom my hand shall be established.
My arm will also strengthen him.
²² No enemy will tax him.
No wicked man will oppress him.
²⁵ I will set his hand also on the sea,
and his right hand on the rivers.
²⁷ I will also appoint him my firstborn,
the highest of the kings of the earth.

Gospel: John 13: 16-20

¹⁶ Most certainly I tell you, a servant is not greater than his lord, neither is one who is sent greater than he who sent him. ¹⁷ If you know these things, blessed are you if you do them. ¹⁸ I don't speak concerning all of you. I know whom I have chosen; but that the Scripture may be fulfilled, 'He who eats bread with me has lifted up his heel against

me.'" ¹⁹ From now on, I tell you before it happens, that when it happens, you may believe that I am he. ²⁰ Most certainly I tell you, he who receives whomever I send, receives me; and he who receives me, receives him who sent me."

1. Invite the Holy Spirit into this reading, asking the Author of Scripture to speak to you through His Word
2. Read today's passage as many times as you need, take your time
3. Write down (below) what the Lord is saying to you today
4. Live with this Word in your heart through the day

_____

_____

Friday, May 16, 2025

First Reading: Acts 13: 26-33

²⁶ "Brothers, children of the stock of Abraham, and those among you who fear God, the word of this salvation is sent out to you. ²⁷ For those who dwell in Jerusalem, and their rulers, because they didn't know him, nor the voices of the prophets which are read every Sabbath, fulfilled them by condemning him. ²⁸ Though they found no cause for death, they still asked Pilate to have him killed. ²⁹ When they had fulfilled all things that were written about him, they took him down from the tree and laid him in a tomb. ³⁰ But God raised him from the dead, ³¹ and he was seen for many days by those who came up with him from Galilee to Jerusalem, who are his witnesses to the people. ³² We bring you good news of the promise made to the fathers, ³³ that God has fulfilled this to us, their children, in that he raised up Jesus. As it is also written in the second psalm,
'You are my Son.
Today I have become your father.'

Responsorial Psalm: Psalms 2: 6-7, 8-9, 10-11ab

⁶ "Yet I have set my King on my holy hill of Zion."
⁷ I will tell of the decree:
Yahweh said to me, "You are my son.
Today I have become your father.
⁸ Ask of me, and I will give the nations for your inheritance,
the uttermost parts of the earth for your possession.

⁹ You shall break them with a rod of iron.
You shall dash them in pieces like a potter's vessel."
¹⁰ Now therefore be wise, you kings.
Be instructed, you judges of the earth.
¹¹ Serve Yahweh with fear,
and rejoice with trembling.

Gospel: John 14: 1-6

¹ "Don't let your heart be troubled. Believe in God. Believe also in me. ² In my Father's house are many homes. If it weren't so, I would have told you. I am going to prepare a place for you. ³ If I go and prepare a place for you, I will come again and will receive you to myself; that where I am, you may be there also. ⁴ You know where I go, and you know the way."
⁵ Thomas said to him, "Lord, we don't know where you are going. How can we know the way?"
⁶ Jesus said to him, "I am the way, the truth, and the life. No one comes to the Father, except through me.

1. Invite the Holy Spirit into this reading, asking the Author of Scripture to speak to you through His Word
2. Read today's passage as many times as you need, take your time
3. Write down (below) what the Lord is saying to you today
4. Live with this Word in your heart through the day

_____

_____

Saturday, May 17, 2025

First Reading: Acts 13: 44-52

⁴⁴ The next Sabbath, almost the whole city was gathered together to hear the word of God. ⁴⁵ But when the Jews saw the multitudes, they were filled with jealousy, and contradicted the things which were spoken by Paul, and blasphemed.
⁴⁶ Paul and Barnabas spoke out boldly, and said, "It was necessary that God's word should be spoken to you first. Since indeed you thrust it from yourselves, and judge yourselves

unworthy of eternal life, behold, we turn to the Gentiles. ⁴⁷ For so has the Lord commanded us, saying,
'I have set you as a light for the Gentiles,
that you should bring salvation to the uttermost parts of the earth.' " ⸰
⁴⁸ As the Gentiles heard this, they were glad and glorified the word of God. As many as were appointed to eternal life believed. ⁴⁹ The Lord's word was spread abroad throughout all the region. ⁵⁰ But the Jews stirred up the devout and prominent women and the chief men of the city, and stirred up a persecution against Paul and Barnabas, and threw them out of their borders. ⁵¹ But they shook off the dust of their feet against them, and came to Iconium. ⁵² The disciples were filled with joy and with the Holy Spirit.

Responsorial Psalm: Psalms 98: 1-4

¹ Sing to Yahweh a new song,
for he has done marvelous things!
His right hand and his holy arm have worked salvation for him.
² Yahweh has made known his salvation.
He has openly shown his righteousness in the sight of the nations.
³ He has remembered his loving kindness and his faithfulness toward the house of Israel.
All the ends of the earth have seen the salvation of our God.
⁴ Make a joyful noise to Yahweh, all the earth!
Burst out and sing for joy, yes, sing praises!

Gospel: John 14: 7-14

⁷ If you had known me, you would have known my Father also. From now on, you know him and have seen him."
⁸ Philip said to him, "Lord, show us the Father, and that will be enough for us."
⁹ Jesus said to him, "Have I been with you such a long time, and do you not know me, Philip? He who has seen me has seen the Father. How do you say, 'Show us the Father'? ¹⁰ Don't you believe that I am in the Father, and the Father in me? The words that I tell you, I speak not from myself; but the Father who lives in me does his works. ¹¹ Believe me that I am in the Father, and the Father in me; or else believe me for the very works' sake. ¹² Most certainly I tell you, he who believes in me, the works that I do, he will do also; and he will do greater works than these, because I am going to my Father. ¹³ Whatever you will ask in my name, I will do it, that the Father may be glorified in the Son. ¹⁴ If you will ask anything in my name, I will do it.

1. Invite the Holy Spirit into this reading, asking the Author of Scripture to speak to you through His Word

2. Read today's passage as many times as you need, take your time
3. Write down (below) what the Lord is saying to you today
4. Live with this Word in your heart through the day

___

___

Sunday, May 18, 2025
FIFTH SUNDAY OF EASTER

First Reading: Acts 14: 21-27

²¹ When they had preached the Good News to that city and had made many disciples, they returned to Lystra, Iconium, and Antioch, ²² strengthening the souls of the disciples, exhorting them to continue in the faith, and that through many afflictions we must enter into God's Kingdom. ²³ When they had appointed elders for them in every assembly, and had prayed with fasting, they commended them to the Lord on whom they had believed. ²⁴ They passed through Pisidia and came to Pamphylia. ²⁵ When they had spoken the word in Perga, they went down to Attalia. ²⁶ From there they sailed to Antioch, from where they had been committed to the grace of God for the work which they had fulfilled. ²⁷ When they had arrived and had gathered the assembly together, they reported all the things that God had done with them, and that he had opened a door of faith to the nations.

Responsorial Psalm: Psalms 145: 8-13

⁸ Yahweh is gracious, merciful,
slow to anger, and of great loving kindness.
⁹ Yahweh is good to all.
His tender mercies are over all his works.
¹⁰ All your works will give thanks to you, Yahweh.
Your saints will extol you.
¹¹ They will speak of the glory of your kingdom,
and talk about your power,
¹² to make known to the sons of men his mighty acts,
the glory of the majesty of his kingdom.
¹³ Your kingdom is an everlasting kingdom.
Your dominion endures throughout all generations.
Yahweh is faithful in all his words,

and loving in all his deeds.

Second Reading: Revelation 21: 1-5a

¹ I saw a new heaven and a new earth, for the first heaven and the first earth have passed away, and the sea is no more. ² I saw the holy city, New Jerusalem, coming down out of heaven from God, prepared like a bride adorned for her husband. ³ I heard a loud voice out of heaven saying, "Behold, God's dwelling is with people; and he will dwell with them, and they will be his people, and God himself will be with them as their God. ⁴ He will wipe away every tear from their eyes. Death will be no more; neither will there be mourning, nor crying, nor pain any more. The first things have passed away."
⁵ᵃ He who sits on the throne said, "Behold, I am making all things new."

Gospel: John 13: 31-33a, 34-35

³¹ When he had gone out, Jesus said, "Now the Son of Man has been glorified, and God has been glorified in him. ³² If God has been glorified in him, God will also glorify him in himself, and he will glorify him immediately. ³³ᵃ Little children, I will be with you a little while longer.
³⁴ A new commandment I give to you, that you love one another. Just as I have loved you, you also love one another. ³⁵ By this everyone will know that you are my disciples, if you have love for one another."

1. Invite the Holy Spirit into this reading, asking the Author of Scripture to speak to you through His Word
2. Read today's passage as many times as you need, take your time
3. Write down (below) what the Lord is saying to you today
4. Live with this Word in your heart through the day

Monday, May 19, 2025

First Reading: Acts 14: 5-18

⁵ When some of both the Gentiles and the Jews, with their rulers, made a violent attempt to mistreat and stone them, ⁶ they became aware of it and fled to the cities of Lycaonia, Lystra, Derbe, and the surrounding region. ⁷ There they preached the Good News.
⁸ At Lystra a certain man sat, impotent in his feet, a cripple from his mother's womb, who never had walked.

Responsorial Psalm: Psalms 115: 1-2, 3-4, 15-16

¹ Not to us, Yahweh, not to us,
but to your name give glory,
for your loving kindness, and for your truth's sake.
² Why should the nations say,
"Where is their God, now?"
³ But our God is in the heavens.
He does whatever he pleases.
⁴ Their idols are silver and gold,
the work of men's hands.
¹⁵ Blessed are you by Yahweh,
who made heaven and earth.
¹⁶ The heavens are Yahweh's heavens,
but he has given the earth to the children of men.

Gospel: John 14: 21-26

²¹ One who has my commandments and keeps them, that person is one who loves me. One who loves me will be loved by my Father, and I will love him, and will reveal myself to him."
²² Judas (not Iscariot) said to him, "Lord, what has happened that you are about to reveal yourself to us, and not to the world?"
²³ Jesus answered him, "If a man loves me, he will keep my word. My Father will love him, and we will come to him and make our home with him. ²⁴ He who doesn't love me doesn't keep my words. The word which you hear isn't mine, but the Father's who sent me.
²⁵ "I have said these things to you while still living with you. ²⁶ But the Counselor, the Holy Spirit, whom the Father will send in my name, will teach you all things, and will remind you of all that I said to you.

1. Invite the Holy Spirit into this reading, asking the Author of Scripture to speak to you through His Word
2. Read today's passage as many times as you need, take your time
3. Write down (below) what the Lord is saying to you today
4. Live with this Word in your heart through the day

Tuesday, May 20, 2025
Saint Bernardine of Siena, Priest

First Reading: Acts 14: 19-28

19 But some Jews from Antioch and Iconium came there, and having persuaded the multitudes, they stoned Paul and dragged him out of the city, supposing that he was dead. 20 But as the disciples stood around him, he rose up, and entered into the city. On the next day he went out with Barnabas to Derbe.
21 When they had preached the Good News to that city and had made many disciples, they returned to Lystra, Iconium, and Antioch, 22 strengthening the souls of the disciples, exhorting them to continue in the faith, and that through many afflictions we must enter into God's Kingdom. 23 When they had appointed elders for them in every assembly, and had prayed with fasting, they commended them to the Lord on whom they had believed.
24 They passed through Pisidia and came to Pamphylia. 25 When they had spoken the word in Perga, they went down to Attalia. 26 From there they sailed to Antioch, from where they had been committed to the grace of God for the work which they had fulfilled. 27 When they had arrived and had gathered the assembly together, they reported all the things that God had done with them, and that he had opened a door of faith to the nations. 28 They stayed there with the disciples for a long time.

Responsorial Psalm: Psalms 145: 10-11, 12-13ab, 21

10 All your works will give thanks to you, Yahweh.
Your saints will extol you.
11 They will speak of the glory of your kingdom,
and talk about your power,
12 to make known to the sons of men his mighty acts,
the glory of the majesty of his kingdom.
13ab Your kingdom is an everlasting kingdom.
Your dominion endures throughout all generations.
21 My mouth will speak the praise of Yahweh.
Let all flesh bless his holy name forever and ever.

Gospel: John 14: 27-31a

²⁷ Peace I leave with you. My peace I give to you; not as the world gives, I give to you. Don't let your heart be troubled, neither let it be fearful. ²⁸ You heard how I told you, 'I am going away, and I will come back to you.' If you loved me, you would have rejoiced because I said 'I am going to my Father;' for the Father is greater than I. ²⁹ Now I have told you before it happens so that when it happens, you may believe. ³⁰ I will no more speak much with you, for the prince of the world comes, and he has nothing in me. ³¹ᵃ But that the world may know that I love the Father, and as the Father commanded me, even so I do.

1. Invite the Holy Spirit into this reading, asking the Author of Scripture to speak to you through His Word
2. Read today's passage as many times as you need, take your time
3. Write down (below) what the Lord is saying to you today
4. Live with this Word in your heart through the day

Wednesday, May 21, 2025
Saint Christopher Magallanes, Priest, and Companions, Martyrs

First Reading: Acts 15: 1-6

¹ Some men came down from Judea and taught the brothers, "Unless you are circumcised after the custom of Moses, you can't be saved." ² Therefore when Paul and Barnabas had no small discord and discussion with them, they appointed Paul, Barnabas, and some others of them to go up to Jerusalem to the apostles and elders about this question. ³ They, being sent on their way by the assembly, passed through both Phoenicia and Samaria, declaring the conversion of the Gentiles. They caused great joy to all the brothers. ⁴ When they had come to Jerusalem, they were received by the assembly and the apostles and the elders, and they reported everything that God had done with them.
⁵ But some of the sect of the Pharisees who believed rose up, saying, "It is necessary to circumcise them, and to command them to keep the law of Moses."
⁶ The apostles and the elders were gathered together to see about this matter.

Responsorial Psalm: Psalms 122: 1-5

¹ I was glad when they said to me,
"Let's go to Yahweh's house!"
² Our feet are standing within your gates, Jerusalem!
³ Jerusalem is built as a city that is compact together,
⁴ where the tribes go up, even Yah's tribes,
according to an ordinance for Israel,
to give thanks to Yahweh's name.
⁵ For there are set thrones for judgment,
the thrones of David's house.

Gospel: John 15: 1-8

¹ "I am the true vine, and my Father is the farmer. ² Every branch in me that doesn't bear fruit, he takes away. Every branch that bears fruit, he prunes, that it may bear more fruit. ³ You are already pruned clean because of the word which I have spoken to you. ⁴ Remain in me, and I in you. As the branch can't bear fruit by itself unless it remains in the vine, so neither can you, unless you remain in me. ⁵ I am the vine. You are the branches. He who remains in me and I in him bears much fruit, for apart from me you can do nothing. ⁶ If a man doesn't remain in me, he is thrown out as a branch and is withered; and they gather them, throw them into the fire, and they are burned. ⁷ If you remain in me, and my words remain in you, you will ask whatever you desire, and it will be done for you. ⁸ "In this my Father is glorified, that you bear much fruit; and so you will be my disciples.

1. Invite the Holy Spirit into this reading, asking the Author of Scripture to speak to you through His Word
2. Read today's passage as many times as you need, take your time
3. Write down (below) what the Lord is saying to you today
4. Live with this Word in your heart through the day

Thursday, May 22, 2025
Saint Rita of Cascia, Religious

First Reading: Acts 15: 7-21

⁷ When there had been much discussion, Peter rose up and said to them, "Brothers, you know that a good while ago God made a choice among you that by my mouth the nations should hear the word of the Good News and believe. ⁸ God, who knows the heart, testified about them, giving them the Holy Spirit, just like he did to us. ⁹ He made no distinction between us and them, cleansing their hearts by faith. ¹⁰ Now therefore why do you tempt God, that you should put a yoke on the neck of the disciples which neither our fathers nor we were able to bear? ¹¹ But we believe that we are saved through the grace of the Lord Jesus,‡ just as they are."

¹² All the multitude kept silence, and they listened to Barnabas and Paul reporting what signs and wonders God had done among the nations through them. ¹³ After they were silent, James answered, "Brothers, listen to me. ¹⁴ Simeon has reported how God first visited the nations to take out of them a people for his name. ¹⁵ This agrees with the words of the prophets. As it is written,

¹⁶ 'After these things I will return.
I will again build the tabernacle of David, which has fallen.
I will again build its ruins.
I will set it up ¹⁷ that the rest of men may seek after the Lord:
all the Gentiles who are called by my name,
says the Lord, who does all these things.'*

¹⁸ "All of God's works are known to him from eternity. ¹⁹ Therefore my judgment is that we don't trouble those from among the Gentiles who turn to God, ²⁰ but that we write to them that they abstain from the pollution of idols, from sexual immorality, from what is strangled, and from blood. ²¹ For Moses from generations of old has in every city those who preach him, being read in the synagogues every Sabbath."

Responsorial Psalm: Psalms 96: 1-3, 10

¹ Sing to Yahweh a new song!
Sing to Yahweh, all the earth.
² Sing to Yahweh!
Bless his name!
Proclaim his salvation from day to day!
³ Declare his glory among the nations,
his marvelous works among all the peoples.
¹⁰ Say among the nations, "Yahweh reigns."
The world is also established.
It can't be moved.
He will judge the peoples with equity.

Gospel: John 15: 9-11

⁹ Even as the Father has loved me, I also have loved you. Remain in my love. ¹⁰ If you keep my commandments, you will remain in my love, even as I have kept my Father's commandments and remain in his love. ¹¹ I have spoken these things to you, that my joy may remain in you, and that your joy may be made full.

1. Invite the Holy Spirit into this reading, asking the Author of Scripture to speak to you through His Word
2. Read today's passage as many times as you need, take your time
3. Write down (below) what the Lord is saying to you today
4. Live with this Word in your heart through the day

Friday, May 23, 2025

First Reading: Acts 15: 22-31

²² Then it seemed good to the apostles and the elders, with the whole assembly, to choose men out of their company, and send them to Antioch with Paul and Barnabas: Judas called Barsabbas, and Silas, chief men among the brothers. ²³ They wrote these things by their hand:
"The apostles, the elders, and the brothers, to the brothers who are of the Gentiles in Antioch, Syria, and Cilicia: greetings. ²⁴ Because we have heard that some who went out from us have troubled you with words, unsettling your souls, saying, 'You must be circumcised and keep the law,' to whom we gave no commandment; ²⁵ it seemed good to us, having come to one accord, to choose out men and send them to you with our beloved Barnabas and Paul, ²⁶ men who have risked their lives for the name of our Lord Jesus Christ. ²⁷ We have sent therefore Judas and Silas, who themselves will also tell you the same things by word of mouth. ²⁸ For it seemed good to the Holy Spirit, and to us, to lay no greater burden on you than these necessary things: ²⁹ that you abstain from things sacrificed to idols, from blood, from things strangled, and from sexual immorality, from which if you keep yourselves, it will be well with you. Farewell."
³⁰ So, when they were sent off, they came to Antioch. Having gathered the multitude together, they delivered the letter. ³¹ When they had read it, they rejoiced over the encouragement.

Responsorial Psalm: Psalms 57: 8-9, 10

⁸ Wake up, my glory! Wake up, lute and harp!
I will wake up the dawn.
⁹ I will give thanks to you, Lord, among the peoples.
I will sing praises to you among the nations.
¹⁰ For your great loving kindness reaches to the heavens,
and your truth to the skies.

Gospel: John 15: 12-17

¹² "This is my commandment, that you love one another, even as I have loved you. ¹³ Greater love has no one than this, that someone lay down his life for his friends. ¹⁴ You are my friends if you do whatever I command you. ¹⁵ No longer do I call you servants, for the servant doesn't know what his lord does. But I have called you friends, for everything that I heard from my Father, I have made known to you. ¹⁶ You didn't choose me, but I chose you and appointed you, that you should go and bear fruit, and that your fruit should remain; that whatever you will ask of the Father in my name, he may give it to you.
¹⁷ "I command these things to you, that you may love one another.

1. Invite the Holy Spirit into this reading, asking the Author of Scripture to speak to you through His Word
2. Read today's passage as many times as you need, take your time
3. Write down (below) what the Lord is saying to you today
4. Live with this Word in your heart through the day

_____

_____

Saturday, May 24, 2025

First Reading: Acts 16: 1-10

¹ He came to Derbe and Lystra; and behold, a certain disciple was there, named Timothy, the son of a Jewess who believed, but his father was a Greek. ² The brothers who were at Lystra and Iconium gave a good testimony about him. ³ Paul wanted to have him go out with him, and he took and circumcised him because of the Jews who were in those parts,

for they all knew that his father was a Greek. ⁴ As they went on their way through the cities, they delivered the decrees to them to keep which had been ordained by the apostles and elders who were at Jerusalem. ⁵ So the assemblies were strengthened in the faith, and increased in number daily.

⁶ When they had gone through the region of Phrygia and Galatia, they were forbidden by the Holy Spirit to speak the word in Asia. ⁷ When they had come opposite Mysia, they tried to go into Bithynia, but the Spirit didn't allow them. ⁸ Passing by Mysia, they came down to Troas. ⁹ A vision appeared to Paul in the night. There was a man of Macedonia standing, begging him and saying, "Come over into Macedonia and help us." ¹⁰ When he had seen the vision, immediately we sought to go out to Macedonia, concluding that the Lord had called us to preach the Good News to them.

Responsorial Psalm: Psalms 100: 2, 3, 5

² Serve Yahweh with gladness.
Come before his presence with singing.
³ Know that Yahweh, he is God.
It is he who has made us, and we are his.
We are his people, and the sheep of his pasture.
⁵ For Yahweh is good.
His loving kindness endures forever,
his faithfulness to all generations.

Gospel: John 15: 18-21

¹⁸ If the world hates you, you know that it has hated me before it hated you. ¹⁹ If you were of the world, the world would love its own. But because you are not of the world, since I chose you out of the world, therefore the world hates you. ²⁰ Remember the word that I said to you: 'A servant is not greater than his lord.' If they persecuted me, they will also persecute you. If they kept my word, they will also keep yours. ²¹ But they will do all these things to you for my name's sake, because they don't know him who sent me.

1. Invite the Holy Spirit into this reading, asking the Author of Scripture to speak to you through His Word
2. Read today's passage as many times as you need, take your time
3. Write down (below) what the Lord is saying to you today
4. Live with this Word in your heart through the day

_____

_____

Sunday, May 25, 2025
SIXTH SUNDAY OF EASTER

First Reading: Acts 15: 1-2, 22-29

¹ Some men came down from Judea and taught the brothers, "Unless you are circumcised after the custom of Moses, you can't be saved." ² Therefore when Paul and Barnabas had no small discord and discussion with them, they appointed Paul, Barnabas, and some others of them to go up to Jerusalem to the apostles and elders about this question.

²² Then it seemed good to the apostles and the elders, with the whole assembly, to choose men out of their company, and send them to Antioch with Paul and Barnabas: Judas called Barsabbas, and Silas, chief men among the brothers. ²³ They wrote these things by their hand:

"The apostles, the elders, and the brothers, to the brothers who are of the Gentiles in Antioch, Syria, and Cilicia: greetings. ²⁴ Because we have heard that some who went out from us have troubled you with words, unsettling your souls, saying, 'You must be circumcised and keep the law,' to whom we gave no commandment; ²⁵ it seemed good to us, having come to one accord, to choose out men and send them to you with our beloved Barnabas and Paul, ²⁶ men who have risked their lives for the name of our Lord Jesus Christ. ²⁷ We have sent therefore Judas and Silas, who themselves will also tell you the same things by word of mouth. ²⁸ For it seemed good to the Holy Spirit, and to us, to lay no greater burden on you than these necessary things: ²⁹ that you abstain from things sacrificed to idols, from blood, from things strangled, and from sexual immorality, from which if you keep yourselves, it will be well with you. Farewell."

Responsorial Psalm: Psalms 67: 2-3, 5, 6

² That your way may be known on earth,
and your salvation among all nations,
³ let the peoples praise you, God.
Let all the peoples praise you.
⁵ Let the peoples praise you, God.
Let all the peoples praise you.
⁶ The earth has yielded its increase.
God, even our own God, will bless us.

Second Reading: Revelation 21: 10-14, 22-23

¹⁰ He carried me away in the Spirit to a great and high mountain, and showed me the holy city, Jerusalem, coming down out of heaven from God, ¹¹ having the glory of God. Her light

was like a most precious stone, like a jasper stone, clear as crystal; 12 having a great and high wall with twelve gates, and at the gates twelve angels, and names written on them, which are the names of the twelve tribes of the children of Israel. 13 On the east were three gates, and on the north three gates, and on the south three gates, and on the west three gates. 14 The wall of the city had twelve foundations, and on them twelve names of the twelve Apostles of the Lamb.

22 I saw no temple in it, for the Lord God the Almighty and the Lamb are its temple. 23 The city has no need for the sun or moon to shine, for the very glory of God illuminated it and its lamp is the Lamb.

Gospel: John 14: 23-29

23 Jesus answered him, "If a man loves me, he will keep my word. My Father will love him, and we will come to him and make our home with him. 24 He who doesn't love me doesn't keep my words. The word which you hear isn't mine, but the Father's who sent me.
25 "I have said these things to you while still living with you. 26 But the Counselor, the Holy Spirit, whom the Father will send in my name, will teach you all things, and will remind you of all that I said to you. 27 Peace I leave with you. My peace I give to you; not as the world gives, I give to you. Don't let your heart be troubled, neither let it be fearful. 28 You heard how I told you, 'I am going away, and I will come back to you.' If you loved me, you would have rejoiced because I said 'I am going to my Father;' for the Father is greater than I. 29 Now I have told you before it happens so that when it happens, you may believe.

1. Invite the Holy Spirit into this reading, asking the Author of Scripture to speak to you through His Word
2. Read today's passage as many times as you need, take your time
3. Write down (below) what the Lord is saying to you today
4. Live with this Word in your heart through the day

Monday, May 26, 2025
Saint Philip Neri, Priest

First Reading: Acts 16: 11-15

¹¹ Setting sail therefore from Troas, we made a straight course to Samothrace, and the day following to Neapolis; ¹² and from there to Philippi, which is a city of Macedonia, the foremost of the district, a Roman colony. We were staying some days in this city.

¹³ On the Sabbath day we went outside of the city by a riverside, where we supposed there was a place of prayer, and we sat down and spoke to the women who had come together. ¹⁴ A certain woman named Lydia, a seller of purple, of the city of Thyatira, one who worshiped God, heard us. The Lord opened her heart to listen to the things which were spoken by Paul. ¹⁵ When she and her household were baptized, she begged us, saying, "If you have judged me to be faithful to the Lord, come into my house and stay." So she persuaded us.

Responsorial Psalm: Psalms 149: 1b-2, 3-4, 5-6a and 9b

¹ᵇ Sing to Yahweh a new song,
his praise in the assembly of the saints.
² Let Israel rejoice in him who made them.
Let the children of Zion be joyful in their King.
³ Let them praise his name in the dance!
Let them sing praises to him with tambourine and harp!
⁴ For Yahweh takes pleasure in his people.
He crowns the humble with salvation.
⁵ Let the saints rejoice in honor.
Let them sing for joy on their beds.
⁶ᵃ May the high praises of God be in their mouths,
⁹ᵇ All his saints have this honor.
Praise Yah!

Gospel: John 15: 26 – 16: 4

²⁶ "When the Counselor⸸ has come, whom I will send to you from the Father, the Spirit of truth, who proceeds from the Father, he will testify about me. ²⁷ You will also testify, because you have been with me from the beginning.

¹ "I have said these things to you so that you wouldn't be caused to stumble. ² They will put you out of the synagogues. Yes, the time is coming that whoever kills you will think that he offers service to God. ³ They will do these things⸸ because they have not known the Father nor me. ⁴ But I have told you these things so that when the time comes, you may remember that I told you about them. I didn't tell you these things from the beginning, because I was with you.

1. Invite the Holy Spirit into this reading, asking the Author of Scripture to speak to you through His Word

2. Read today's passage as many times as you need, take your time
3. Write down (below) what the Lord is saying to you today
4. Live with this Word in your heart through the day

_____

_____

Tuesday, May 27, 2025
Saint Augustine of Canterbury, Bishop

First Reading: Acts 16: 22-34

22 The multitude rose up together against them and the magistrates tore their clothes from them, then commanded them to be beaten with rods. 23 When they had laid many stripes on them, they threw them into prison, charging the jailer to keep them safely. 24 Having received such a command, he threw them into the inner prison and secured their feet in the stocks.
25 But about midnight Paul and Silas were praying and singing hymns to God, and the prisoners were listening to them. 26 Suddenly there was a great earthquake, so that the foundations of the prison were shaken; and immediately all the doors were opened, and everyone's bonds were loosened. 27 The jailer, being roused out of sleep and seeing the prison doors open, drew his sword and was about to kill himself, supposing that the prisoners had escaped. 28 But Paul cried with a loud voice, saying, "Don't harm yourself, for we are all here!"
29 He called for lights, sprang in, fell down trembling before Paul and Silas, 30 brought them out, and said, "Sirs, what must I do to be saved?"
31 They said, "Believe in the Lord Jesus Christ, and you will be saved, you and your household." 32 They spoke the word of the Lord to him, and to all who were in his house.
33 He took them the same hour of the night and washed their stripes, and was immediately baptized, he and all his household. 34 He brought them up into his house and set food before them, and rejoiced greatly with all his household, having believed in God.

Responsorial Psalm: Psalms 138: 1-3, 7c-8

1 I will give you thanks with my whole heart.
Before the gods,‡ I will sing praises to you.
2 I will bow down toward your holy temple,
and give thanks to your Name for your loving kindness and for your truth;

for you have exalted your Name and your Word above all.
³ In the day that I called, you answered me.
You encouraged me with strength in my soul.
⁷ᶜ Your right hand will save me.
⁸ Yahweh will fulfill that which concerns me.
Your loving kindness, Yahweh, endures forever.
Don't forsake the works of your own hands.

Gospel: John 16: 5-11

⁵ But now I am going to him who sent me, and none of you asks me, 'Where are you going?' ⁶ But because I have told you these things, sorrow has filled your heart. ⁷ Nevertheless I tell you the truth: It is to your advantage that I go away; for if I don't go away, the Counselor won't come to you. But if I go, I will send him to you. ⁸ When he has come, he will convict the world about sin, about righteousness, and about judgment; ⁹ about sin, because they don't believe in me; ¹⁰ about righteousness, because I am going to my Father, and you won't see me any more; ¹¹ about judgment, because the prince of this world has been judged.

1. Invite the Holy Spirit into this reading, asking the Author of Scripture to speak to you through His Word
2. Read today's passage as many times as you need, take your time
3. Write down (below) what the Lord is saying to you today
4. Live with this Word in your heart through the day

_____

_____

Wednesday, May 28, 2025

First Reading: Acts 17: 15, 22 – 18: 1

¹⁵ But those who escorted Paul brought him as far as Athens. Receiving a commandment to Silas and Timothy that they should come to him very quickly, they departed.
²² Paul stood in the middle of the Areopagus and said, "You men of Athens, I perceive that you are very religious in all things. ²³ For as I passed along and observed the objects of your worship, I also found an altar with this inscription: 'TO AN UNKNOWN GOD.' What therefore you worship in ignorance, I announce to you. ²⁴ The God who made the world

and all things in it, he, being Lord of heaven and earth, doesn't dwell in temples made with hands. 25 He isn't served by men's hands, as though he needed anything, seeing he himself gives to all life and breath and all things. 26 He made from one blood every nation of men to dwell on all the surface of the earth, having determined appointed seasons and the boundaries of their dwellings, 27 that they should seek the Lord, if perhaps they might reach out for him and find him, though he is not far from each one of us. 28 'For in him we live, move, and have our being.' As some of your own poets have said, 'For we are also his offspring.' 29 Being then the offspring of God, we ought not to think that the Divine Nature is like gold, or silver, or stone, engraved by art and design of man. 30 The times of ignorance therefore God overlooked. But now he commands that all people everywhere should repent, 31 because he has appointed a day in which he will judge the world in righteousness by the man whom he has ordained; of which he has given assurance to all men, in that he has raised him from the dead."

32 Now when they heard of the resurrection of the dead, some mocked; but others said, "We want to hear you again concerning this."

33 Thus Paul went out from among them. 34 But certain men joined with him and believed, including Dionysius the Areopagite, and a woman named Damaris, and others with them.

1 After these things Paul departed from Athens and came to Corinth.

Responsorial Psalm: Psalms 148: 1-2, 11-14

1 Praise Yah!
Praise Yahweh from the heavens!
Praise him in the heights!
2 Praise him, all his angels!
Praise him, all his army!
11 kings of the earth and all peoples,
princes and all judges of the earth,
12 both young men and maidens,
old men and children.
13 Let them praise Yahweh's name,
for his name alone is exalted.
His glory is above the earth and the heavens.
14 He has lifted up the horn of his people,
the praise of all his saints,
even of the children of Israel, a people near to him.
Praise Yah!

Gospel: John 16: 12-15

¹² "I still have many things to tell you, but you can't bear them now. ¹³ However, when he, the Spirit of truth, has come, he will guide you into all truth, for he will not speak from himself; but whatever he hears, he will speak. He will declare to you things that are coming. ¹⁴ He will glorify me, for he will take from what is mine and will declare it to you. ¹⁵ All things that the Father has are mine; therefore I said that he takes⸸ of mine and will declare it to you.

1. Invite the Holy Spirit into this reading, asking the Author of Scripture to speak to you through His Word
2. Read today's passage as many times as you need, take your time
3. Write down (below) what the Lord is saying to you today
4. Live with this Word in your heart through the day

Thursday, May 29, 2025
Saint Paul VI, Pope

First Reading: Acts 18: 1-8

¹ After these things Paul departed from Athens and came to Corinth. ² He found a certain Jew named Aquila, a man of Pontus by race, who had recently come from Italy with his wife Priscilla, because Claudius had commanded all the Jews to depart from Rome. He came to them, ³ and because he practiced the same trade, he lived with them and worked, for by trade they were tent makers. ⁴ He reasoned in the synagogue every Sabbath and persuaded Jews and Greeks.
⁵ When Silas and Timothy came down from Macedonia, Paul was compelled by the Spirit, testifying to the Jews that Jesus was the Christ. ⁶ When they opposed him and blasphemed, he shook out his clothing and said to them, "Your blood be on your own heads! I am clean. From now on, I will go to the Gentiles!"
⁷ He departed there and went into the house of a certain man named Justus, one who worshiped God, whose house was next door to the synagogue. ⁸ Crispus, the ruler of the synagogue, believed in the Lord with all his house. Many of the Corinthians, when they heard, believed and were baptized.

Responsorial Psalm: Psalms 98: 1-4

¹ Sing to Yahweh a new song,
for he has done marvelous things!
His right hand and his holy arm have worked salvation for him.
² Yahweh has made known his salvation.
He has openly shown his righteousness in the sight of the nations.
³ He has remembered his loving kindness and his faithfulness toward the house of Israel.
All the ends of the earth have seen the salvation of our God.
⁴ Make a joyful noise to Yahweh, all the earth!
Burst out and sing for joy, yes, sing praises!

Gospel: John 16: 16-20

¹⁶ "A little while, and you will not see me. Again a little while, and you will see me."
¹⁷ Some of his disciples therefore said to one another, "What is this that he says to us, 'A little while, and you won't see me, and again a little while, and you will see me;' and, 'Because I go to the Father'?" ¹⁸ They said therefore, "What is this that he says, 'A little while'? We don't know what he is saying."
¹⁹ Therefore Jesus perceived that they wanted to ask him, and he said to them, "Do you inquire among yourselves concerning this, that I said, 'A little while, and you won't see me, and again a little while, and you will see me'? ²⁰ Most certainly I tell you that you will weep and lament, but the world will rejoice. You will be sorrowful, but your sorrow will be turned into joy.

1. Invite the Holy Spirit into this reading, asking the Author of Scripture to speak to you through His Word
2. Read today's passage as many times as you need, take your time
3. Write down (below) what the Lord is saying to you today
4. Live with this Word in your heart through the day

_____
_____

Friday, May 30, 2025

First Reading: Acts 18: 9-18

⁹ The Lord said to Paul in the night by a vision, "Don't be afraid, but speak and don't be silent; ¹⁰ for I am with you, and no one will attack you to harm you, for I have many people in this city."

¹¹ He lived there a year and six months, teaching the word of God among them. ¹² But when Gallio was proconsul of Achaia, the Jews with one accord rose up against Paul and brought him before the judgment seat, ¹³ saying, "This man persuades men to worship God contrary to the law."

¹⁴ But when Paul was about to open his mouth, Gallio said to the Jews, "If indeed it were a matter of wrong or of wicked crime, you Jews, it would be reasonable that I should bear with you; ¹⁵ but if they are questions about words and names and your own law, look to it yourselves. For I don't want to be a judge of these matters." ¹⁶ So he drove them from the judgment seat.

¹⁷ Then all the Greeks seized Sosthenes, the ruler of the synagogue, and beat him before the judgment seat. Gallio didn't care about any of these things.

¹⁸ Paul, having stayed after this many more days, took his leave of the brothers,‡ and sailed from there for Syria, together with Priscilla and Aquila. He shaved his head in Cenchreae, for he had a vow.

Responsorial Psalm: Psalms 47: 2-7

² For Yahweh Most High is awesome.
He is a great King over all the earth.
³ He subdues nations under us,
and peoples under our feet.
⁴ He chooses our inheritance for us,
the glory of Jacob whom he loved.
⁵ God has gone up with a shout,
Yahweh with the sound of a trumpet.
⁶ Sing praises to God! Sing praises!
Sing praises to our King! Sing praises!
⁷ For God is the King of all the earth.
Sing praises with understanding.

Gospel: John 16: 20-23

²⁰ Most certainly I tell you that you will weep and lament, but the world will rejoice. You will be sorrowful, but your sorrow will be turned into joy. ²¹ A woman, when she gives birth, has sorrow because her time has come. But when she has delivered the child, she doesn't remember the anguish any more, for the joy that a human being is born into the

world. ²² Therefore you now have sorrow, but I will see you again, and your heart will rejoice, and no one will take your joy away from you.
²³ "In that day you will ask me no questions. Most certainly I tell you, whatever you may ask of the Father in my name, he will give it to you.

1. Invite the Holy Spirit into this reading, asking the Author of Scripture to speak to you through His Word
2. Read today's passage as many times as you need, take your time
3. Write down (below) what the Lord is saying to you today
4. Live with this Word in your heart through the day

Saturday, May 31, 2025
The Visitation of the Blessed Virgin Mary

First Reading: Zephaniah 3: 14-18a

¹⁴ Sing, daughter of Zion! Shout, Israel! Be glad and rejoice with all your heart, daughter of Jerusalem. ¹⁵ Yahweh has taken away your judgments. He has thrown out your enemy. The King of Israel, Yahweh, is among you. You will not be afraid of evil any more. ¹⁶ In that day, it will be said to Jerusalem, "Don't be afraid, Zion. Don't let your hands be weak." ¹⁷ Yahweh, your God, is among you, a mighty one who will save. He will rejoice over you with joy. He will calm you in his love. He will rejoice over you with singing. ¹⁸ᵃ I will remove those who grieve about the appointed feasts from you.

Responsorial Psalm: Isaiah 12: 2-3, 4bcd, 5-6

² Behold, God is my salvation. I will trust, and will not be afraid; for Yah, Yahweh, is my strength and song; and he has become my salvation." ³ Therefore with joy you will draw water out of the wells of salvation. ⁴ᵇ "Give thanks to Yahweh! Call on his name! Declare his doings among the peoples! Proclaim that his name is exalted! ⁵ Sing to Yahweh, for he has done excellent things! Let this be known in all the earth! ⁶ Cry aloud and shout, you inhabitant of Zion, for the Holy One of Israel is great among you!".

Gospel: Luke 1: 39-56

³⁹ Mary arose in those days and went into the hill country with haste, into a city of Judah, ⁴⁰ and entered into the house of Zacharias and greeted Elizabeth. ⁴¹ When Elizabeth heard Mary's greeting, the baby leaped in her womb; and Elizabeth was filled with the Holy Spirit. ⁴² She called out with a loud voice and said, "Blessed are you among women, and blessed is the fruit of your womb! ⁴³ Why am I so favored, that the mother of my Lord should come to me? ⁴⁴ For behold, when the voice of your greeting came into my ears, the baby leaped in my womb for joy! ⁴⁵ Blessed is she who believed, for there will be a fulfillment of the things which have been spoken to her from the Lord!"

⁴⁶ Mary said,

"My soul magnifies the Lord.

⁴⁷ My spirit has rejoiced in God my Savior,

⁴⁸ for he has looked at the humble state of his servant.

For behold, from now on, all generations will call me blessed.

⁴⁹ For he who is mighty has done great things for me.

Holy is his name.

⁵⁰ His mercy is for generations and generations on those who fear him.

⁵¹ He has shown strength with his arm.

He has scattered the proud in the imagination of their hearts.

⁵² He has put down princes from their thrones,

and has exalted the lowly.

⁵³ He has filled the hungry with good things.

He has sent the rich away empty.

⁵⁴ He has given help to Israel, his servant, that he might remember mercy,

⁵⁵ as he spoke to our fathers,

to Abraham and his offspring§ forever."

⁵⁶ Mary stayed with her about three months, and then returned to her house.

1. Invite the Holy Spirit into this reading, asking the Author of Scripture to speak to you through His Word
2. Read today's passage as many times as you need, take your time
3. Write down (below) what the Lord is saying to you today
4. Live with this Word in your heart through the day

_____

_____

Sunday, June 1, 2025
Ascension of the Lord Solemnity (Seventh Sunday of Easter)

First Reading: Acts 1: 1-11

¹ The first book I wrote, Theophilus, concerned all that Jesus began both to do and to teach, ² until the day in which he was received up, after he had given commandment through the Holy Spirit to the apostles whom he had chosen. ³ To these he also showed himself alive after he suffered, by many proofs, appearing to them over a period of forty days and speaking about God's Kingdom. ⁴ Being assembled together with them, he commanded them, "Don't depart from Jerusalem, but wait for the promise of the Father, which you heard from me. ⁵ For John indeed baptized in water, but you will be baptized in the Holy Spirit not many days from now."

⁶ Therefore, when they had come together, they asked him, "Lord, are you now restoring the kingdom to Israel?"

⁷ He said to them, "It isn't for you to know times or seasons which the Father has set within his own authority. ⁸ But you will receive power when the Holy Spirit has come upon you. You will be witnesses to me in Jerusalem, in all Judea and Samaria, and to the uttermost parts of the earth."

⁹ When he had said these things, as they were looking, he was taken up, and a cloud received him out of their sight. ¹⁰ While they were looking steadfastly into the sky as he went, behold, two men stood by them in white clothing, ¹¹ who also said, "You men of Galilee, why do you stand looking into the sky? This Jesus, who was received up from you into the sky, will come back in the same way as you saw him going into the sky."

Responsorial Psalm: Psalms 47: 2-3, 6-7, 8-9

² For Yahweh Most High is awesome.
He is a great King over all the earth.
³ He subdues nations under us,
and peoples under our feet.
⁶ Sing praises to God! Sing praises!
Sing praises to our King! Sing praises!
⁷ For God is the King of all the earth.
Sing praises with understanding.
⁸ God reigns over the nations.
God sits on his holy throne.
⁹ The princes of the peoples are gathered together,
the people of the God of Abraham.
For the shields of the earth belong to God.
He is greatly exalted!

Second Reading: Ephesians 1: 17-23

¹⁷ that the God of our Lord Jesus Christ, the Father of glory, may give to you a spirit of wisdom and revelation in the knowledge of him, ¹⁸ having the eyes of your hearts‡ enlightened, that you may know what is the hope of his calling, and what are the riches of the glory of his inheritance in the saints, ¹⁹ and what is the exceeding greatness of his power toward us who believe, according to that working of the strength of his might ²⁰ which he worked in Christ when he raised him from the dead and made him to sit at his right hand in the heavenly places, ²¹ far above all rule, authority, power, dominion, and every name that is named, not only in this age, but also in that which is to come. ²² He put all things in subjection under his feet, and gave him to be head over all things for the assembly, ²³ which is his body, the fullness of him who fills all in all.

Gospel: Luke 24: 46-53

⁴⁶ He said to them, "Thus it is written, and thus it was necessary for the Christ to suffer and to rise from the dead the third day, ⁴⁷ and that repentance and remission of sins should be preached in his name to all the nations, beginning at Jerusalem. ⁴⁸ You are witnesses of these things. ⁴⁹ Behold, I send out the promise of my Father on you. But wait in the city of Jerusalem until you are clothed with power from on high."
⁵⁰ He led them out as far as Bethany, and he lifted up his hands and blessed them. ⁵¹ While he blessed them, he withdrew from them and was carried up into heaven. ⁵² They worshiped him and returned to Jerusalem with great joy, ⁵³ and were continually in the temple, praising and blessing God. Amen.

1. Invite the Holy Spirit into this reading, asking the Author of Scripture to speak to you through His Word
2. Read today's passage as many times as you need, take your time
3. Write down (below) what the Lord is saying to you today
4. Live with this Word in your heart through the day

Monday, June 2, 2025
Saints Marcellinus and Peter, Martyrs

First Reading: Acts 19: 1-8

¹ While Apollos was at Corinth, Paul, having passed through the upper country, came to Ephesus and found certain disciples. ² He said to them, "Did you receive the Holy Spirit when you believed?"

They said to him, "No, we haven't even heard that there is a Holy Spirit."

³ He said, "Into what then were you baptized?"

They said, "Into John's baptism."

⁴ Paul said, "John indeed baptized with the baptism of repentance, saying to the people that they should believe in the one who would come after him, that is, in Christ Jesus."[1]

⁵ When they heard this, they were baptized in the name of the Lord Jesus. ⁶ When Paul had laid his hands on them, the Holy Spirit came on them and they spoke with other languages and prophesied. ⁷ They were about twelve men in all.

⁸ He entered into the synagogue and spoke boldly for a period of three months, reasoning and persuading about the things concerning God's Kingdom.

Responsorial Psalm: Psalms 68: 2-3ab, 4-5acd, 6-7ab

² As smoke is driven away,
so drive them away.
As wax melts before the fire,
so let the wicked perish at the presence of God.
³ But let the righteous be glad.
Let them rejoice before God.
⁴ Sing to God! Sing praises to his name!
Extol him who rides on the clouds:
to Yah, his name!
Rejoice before him!
⁵ A father of the fatherless, and a defender of the widows,
is God in his holy habitation.
⁶ God sets the lonely in families.
He brings out the prisoners with singing,
but the rebellious dwell in a sun-scorched land.
⁷ God, when you went out before your people,
when you marched through the wilderness…

Gospel: John 16: 29-33

²⁹ His disciples said to him, "Behold, now you are speaking plainly, and using no figures of speech. ³⁰ Now we know that you know all things, and don't need for anyone to question you. By this we believe that you came from God."

[31] Jesus answered them, "Do you now believe? [32] Behold, the time is coming, yes, and has now come, that you will be scattered, everyone to his own place, and you will leave me alone. Yet I am not alone, because the Father is with me. [33] I have told you these things, that in me you may have peace. In the world you have trouble; but cheer up! I have overcome the world."

1. Invite the Holy Spirit into this reading, asking the Author of Scripture to speak to you through His Word
2. Read today's passage as many times as you need, take your time
3. Write down (below) what the Lord is saying to you today
4. Live with this Word in your heart through the day

Tuesday, June 3, 2025
Saint Charles Lwanga and Companions, Martyrs

First Reading: Acts 20: 17-27

[17] From Miletus he sent to Ephesus and called to himself the elders of the assembly. [18] When they had come to him, he said to them, "You yourselves know, from the first day that I set foot in Asia, how I was with you all the time, [19] serving the Lord with all humility, with many tears, and with trials which happened to me by the plots of the Jews; [20] how I didn't shrink from declaring to you anything that was profitable, teaching you publicly and from house to house, [21] testifying both to Jews and to Greeks repentance toward God and faith toward our Lord Jesus. [22] Now, behold, I go bound by the Spirit to Jerusalem, not knowing what will happen to me there; [23] except that the Holy Spirit testifies in every city, saying that bonds and afflictions wait for me. [24] But these things don't count; nor do I hold my life dear to myself, so that I may finish my race with joy, and the ministry which I received from the Lord Jesus, to fully testify to the Good News of the grace of God.
[25] "Now, behold, I know that you all, among whom I went about preaching God's Kingdom, will see my face no more. [26] Therefore I testify to you today that I am clean from the blood of all men, [27] for I didn't shrink from declaring to you the whole counsel of God.

Responsorial Psalm: Psalms 68: 10-11, 20-21

[10] Your congregation lived therein.

You, God, prepared your goodness for the poor.
¹¹ The Lord announced the word.
The ones who proclaim it are a great company.
²⁰ God is to us a God of deliverance.
To Yahweh, the Lord, belongs escape from death.
²¹ But God will strike through the head of his enemies,
the hairy scalp of such a one as still continues in his guiltiness.

Gospel: John 17: 1-11a

¹ Jesus said these things, then lifting up his eyes to heaven, he said, "Father, the time has come. Glorify your Son, that your Son may also glorify you; ² even as you gave him authority over all flesh, so he will give eternal life to all whom you have given him. ³ This is eternal life, that they should know you, the only true God, and him whom you sent, Jesus Christ. ⁴ I glorified you on the earth. I have accomplished the work which you have given me to do. ⁵ Now, Father, glorify me with your own self with the glory which I had with you before the world existed.
⁶ "I revealed your name to the people whom you have given me out of the world. They were yours, and you have given them to me. They have kept your word. ⁷ Now they have known that all things whatever you have given me are from you, ⁸ for the words which you have given me I have given to them; and they received them, and knew for sure that I came from you. They have believed that you sent me. ⁹ I pray for them. I don't pray for the world, but for those whom you have given me, for they are yours. ¹⁰ All things that are mine are yours, and yours are mine, and I am glorified in them. ¹¹ᵃ I am no more in the world, but these are in the world, and I am coming to you.

1. Invite the Holy Spirit into this reading, asking the Author of Scripture to speak to you through His Word
2. Read today's passage as many times as you need, take your time
3. Write down (below) what the Lord is saying to you today
4. Live with this Word in your heart through the day

_____

_____

Wednesday, June 4, 2025

First Reading: Acts 20: 28-38

²⁸ Take heed, therefore, to yourselves and to all the flock, in which the Holy Spirit has made you overseers, to shepherd the assembly of the Lord and§ God which he purchased with his own blood. ²⁹ For I know that after my departure, vicious wolves will enter in among you, not sparing the flock. ³⁰ Men will arise from among your own selves, speaking perverse things, to draw away the disciples after them. ³¹ Therefore watch, remembering that for a period of three years I didn't cease to admonish everyone night and day with tears. ³² Now, brothers,‡ I entrust you to God and to the word of his grace, which is able to build up and to give you the inheritance among all those who are sanctified. ³³ I coveted no one's silver, gold, or clothing. ³⁴ You yourselves know that these hands served my necessities, and those who were with me. ³⁵ In all things I gave you an example, that so laboring you ought to help the weak, and to remember the words of the Lord Jesus, that he himself said, 'It is more blessed to give than to receive.' "

³⁶ When he had spoken these things, he knelt down and prayed with them all. ³⁷ They all wept freely, and fell on Paul's neck and kissed him, ³⁸ sorrowing most of all because of the word which he had spoken, that they should see his face no more. Then they accompanied him to the ship.

Responsorial Psalm: Psalms 68: 29-30, 33-35

²⁹ Because of your temple at Jerusalem,
kings shall bring presents to you.
³⁰ Rebuke the wild animal of the reeds,
the multitude of the bulls with the calves of the peoples.
Trample under foot the bars of silver.
Scatter the nations who delight in war.
³³ to him who rides on the heaven of heavens, which are of old;
behold, he utters his voice, a mighty voice.
³⁴ Ascribe strength to God!
His excellency is over Israel,
his strength is in the skies.
³⁵ You are awesome, God, in your sanctuaries.
The God of Israel gives strength and power to his people.
Praise be to God!

Gospel: John 17: 11b-19

¹¹ᵇ Holy Father, keep them through your name which you have given me, that they may be one, even as we are. ¹² While I was with them in the world, I kept them in your name. I have kept those whom you have given me. None of them is lost except the son of

destruction, that the Scripture might be fulfilled. ¹³ But now I come to you, and I say these things in the world, that they may have my joy made full in themselves. ¹⁴ I have given them your word. The world hated them because they are not of the world, even as I am not of the world. ¹⁵ I pray not that you would take them from the world, but that you would keep them from the evil one. ¹⁶ They are not of the world, even as I am not of the world. ¹⁷ Sanctify them in your truth. Your word is truth. ¹⁸ As you sent me into the world, even so I have sent them into the world. ¹⁹ For their sakes I sanctify myself, that they themselves also may be sanctified in truth.

1. Invite the Holy Spirit into this reading, asking the Author of Scripture to speak to you through His Word
2. Read today's passage as many times as you need, take your time
3. Write down (below) what the Lord is saying to you today
4. Live with this Word in your heart through the day

_____

_____

Thursday, June 5, 2025
Saint Boniface, Bishop and Martyr

First Reading: Acts 22: 30; 23: 6-11

³⁰ But on the next day, desiring to know the truth about why he was accused by the Jews, he freed him from the bonds and commanded the chief priests and all the council to come together, and brought Paul down and set him before them.
⁶ But when Paul perceived that the one part were Sadducees and the other Pharisees, he cried out in the council, "Men and brothers, I am a Pharisee, a son of Pharisees. Concerning the hope and resurrection of the dead I am being judged!"
⁷ When he had said this, an argument arose between the Pharisees and Sadducees, and the crowd was divided. ⁸ For the Sadducees say that there is no resurrection, nor angel, nor spirit; but the Pharisees confess all of these. ⁹ A great clamor arose, and some of the scribes of the Pharisees' part stood up, and contended, saying, "We find no evil in this man. But if a spirit or angel has spoken to him, let's not fight against God!"
¹⁰ When a great argument arose, the commanding officer, fearing that Paul would be torn in pieces by them, commanded the soldiers to go down and take him by force from among them and bring him into the barracks.

¹¹ The following night, the Lord stood by him and said, "Cheer up, Paul, for as you have testified about me at Jerusalem, so you must testify also at Rome."

Responsorial Psalm: Psalms 16: 1-2a and 5, 7-8, 9-10, 11

¹ Preserve me, God, for I take refuge in you.
²ᵃ My soul, you have said to Yahweh, "You are my Lord.
⁵ Yahweh assigned my portion and my cup.
You made my lot secure.
⁷ I will bless Yahweh, who has given me counsel.
Yes, my heart instructs me in the night seasons.
⁸ I have set Yahweh always before me.
Because he is at my right hand, I shall not be moved.
⁹ Therefore my heart is glad, and my tongue rejoices.
My body shall also dwell in safety.
¹⁰ For you will not leave my soul in Sheol,‡
neither will you allow your holy one to see corruption.
¹¹ You will show me the path of life.
In your presence is fullness of joy.
In your right hand there are pleasures forever more.

Gospel: John 17: 20-26

²⁰ "Not for these only do I pray, but for those also who will believe in me through their word, ²¹ that they may all be one; even as you, Father, are in me, and I in you, that they also may be one in us; that the world may believe that you sent me. ²² The glory which you have given me, I have given to them, that they may be one, even as we are one, ²³ I in them, and you in me, that they may be perfected into one, that the world may know that you sent me and loved them, even as you loved me. ²⁴ Father, I desire that they also whom you have given me be with me where I am, that they may see my glory which you have given me, for you loved me before the foundation of the world. ²⁵ Righteous Father, the world hasn't known you, but I knew you; and these knew that you sent me. ²⁶ I made known to them your name, and will make it known; that the love with which you loved me may be in them, and I in them."

1. Invite the Holy Spirit into this reading, asking the Author of Scripture to speak to you through His Word
2. Read today's passage as many times as you need, take your time
3. Write down (below) what the Lord is saying to you today
4. Live with this Word in your heart through the day

Friday, June 6, 2025
Saint Norbert, Bishop

First Reading: Acts 25: 13b-21

¹³ᵇ King Agrippa and Bernice arrived at Caesarea and greeted Festus. ¹⁴ As he stayed there many days, Festus laid Paul's case before the king, saying, "There is a certain man left a prisoner by Felix; ¹⁵ about whom, when I was at Jerusalem, the chief priests and the elders of the Jews informed me, asking for a sentence against him. ¹⁶ I answered them that it is not the custom of the Romans to give up any man to destruction before the accused has met the accusers face to face and has had opportunity to make his defense concerning the matter laid against him. ¹⁷ When therefore they had come together here, I didn't delay, but on the next day sat on the judgment seat and commanded the man to be brought. ¹⁸ When the accusers stood up, they brought no charges against him of such things as I supposed; ¹⁹ but had certain questions against him about their own religion and about one Jesus, who was dead, whom Paul affirmed to be alive. ²⁰ Being perplexed how to inquire concerning these things, I asked whether he was willing to go to Jerusalem and there be judged concerning these matters. ²¹ But when Paul had appealed to be kept for the decision of the emperor, I commanded him to be kept until I could send him to Caesar."

Responsorial Psalm: Psalms 103: 1-2, 11-12, 19-20ab

¹ Praise Yahweh, my soul!
All that is within me, praise his holy name!
² Praise Yahweh, my soul,
and don't forget all his benefits,
¹¹ For as the heavens are high above the earth,
so great is his loving kindness toward those who fear him.
¹² As far as the east is from the west,
so far has he removed our transgressions from us.
¹⁹ Yahweh has established his throne in the heavens.
His kingdom rules over all.
²⁰ᵃᵇ Praise Yahweh, you angels of his,
who are mighty in strength, who fulfill his word,

Gospel: John 21: 15-19

¹⁵ So when they had eaten their breakfast, Jesus said to Simon Peter, "Simon, son of Jonah, do you love me more than these?"
He said to him, "Yes, Lord; you know that I have affection for you."
He said to him, "Feed my lambs." ¹⁶ He said to him again a second time, "Simon, son of Jonah, do you love me?"
He said to him, "Yes, Lord; you know that I have affection for you."
He said to him, "Tend my sheep." ¹⁷ He said to him the third time, "Simon, son of Jonah, do you have affection for me?"
Peter was grieved because he asked him the third time, "Do you have affection for me?" He said to him, "Lord, you know everything. You know that I have affection for you."
Jesus said to him, "Feed my sheep. ¹⁸ Most certainly I tell you, when you were young, you dressed yourself and walked where you wanted to. But when you are old, you will stretch out your hands, and another will dress you and carry you where you don't want to go."
¹⁹ Now he said this, signifying by what kind of death he would glorify God. When he had said this, he said to him, "Follow me."

1. Invite the Holy Spirit into this reading, asking the Author of Scripture to speak to you through His Word
2. Read today's passage as many times as you need, take your time
3. Write down (below) what the Lord is saying to you today
4. Live with this Word in your heart through the day

___
___

Saturday, June 7, 2025

First Reading: Acts 28: 16-20, 30-31

¹⁶ When we entered into Rome, the centurion delivered the prisoners to the captain of the guard, but Paul was allowed to stay by himself with the soldier who guarded him.
¹⁷ After three days Paul called together those who were the leaders of the Jews. When they had come together, he said to them, "I, brothers, though I had done nothing against the people or the customs of our fathers, still was delivered prisoner from Jerusalem into the hands of the Romans, ¹⁸ who, when they had examined me, desired to set me free, because

there was no cause of death in me. ¹⁹ But when the Jews spoke against it, I was constrained to appeal to Caesar, not that I had anything about which to accuse my nation. ²⁰ For this cause therefore I asked to see you and to speak with you. For because of the hope of Israel I am bound with this chain."

³⁰ Paul stayed two whole years in his own rented house and received all who were coming to him, ³¹ preaching God's Kingdom and teaching the things concerning the Lord Jesus Christ with all boldness, without hindrance.

Responsorial Psalm: Psalms 11: 4, 5 and 7

⁴ Yahweh is in his holy temple.
Yahweh is on his throne in heaven.
His eyes observe.
His eyes examine the children of men.
⁵ Yahweh examines the righteous,
but his soul hates the wicked and him who loves violence.
⁷ For Yahweh is righteous.
He loves righteousness.
The upright shall see his face.

Gospel: John 21: 20-25

²⁰ Then Peter, turning around, saw a disciple following. This was the disciple whom Jesus loved, the one who had also leaned on Jesus' chest at the supper and asked, "Lord, who is going to betray you?" ²¹ Peter, seeing him, said to Jesus, "Lord, what about this man?"
²² Jesus said to him, "If I desire that he stay until I come, what is that to you? You follow me." ²³ This saying therefore went out among the brothers§ that this disciple wouldn't die. Yet Jesus didn't say to him that he wouldn't die, but, "If I desire that he stay until I come, what is that to you?"
²⁴ This is the disciple who testifies about these things, and wrote these things. We know that his witness is true. ²⁵ There are also many other things which Jesus did, which if they would all be written, I suppose that even the world itself wouldn't have room for the books that would be written.

1. Invite the Holy Spirit into this reading, asking the Author of Scripture to speak to you through His Word
2. Read today's passage as many times as you need, take your time
3. Write down (below) what the Lord is saying to you today
4. Live with this Word in your heart through the day

Sunday, June 8, 2025
PENTECOST SUNDAY

First Reading: Acts 2: 1-11

¹ Now when the day of Pentecost had come, they were all with one accord in one place. ² Suddenly there came from the sky a sound like the rushing of a mighty wind, and it filled all the house where they were sitting. ³ Tongues like fire appeared and were distributed to them, and one sat on each of them. ⁴ They were all filled with the Holy Spirit and began to speak with other languages, as the Spirit gave them the ability to speak.
⁵ Now there were dwelling in Jerusalem Jews, devout men, from every nation under the sky. ⁶ When this sound was heard, the multitude came together and were bewildered, because everyone heard them speaking in his own language. ⁷ They were all amazed and marveled, saying to one another, "Behold, aren't all these who speak Galileans? ⁸ How do we hear, everyone in our own native language? ⁹ Parthians, Medes, Elamites, and people from Mesopotamia, Judea, Cappadocia, Pontus, Asia, ¹⁰ Phrygia, Pamphylia, Egypt, the parts of Libya around Cyrene, visitors from Rome, both Jews and proselytes, ¹¹ Cretans and Arabians—we hear them speaking in our languages the mighty works of God!"

Responsorial Psalm: Psalms 104: 1, 24, 29-30, 31, 34

¹ Bless Yahweh, my soul.
Yahweh, my God, you are very great.
You are clothed with honor and majesty.
²⁴ Yahweh, how many are your works!
In wisdom, you have made them all.
The earth is full of your riches.
²⁹ You hide your face; they are troubled.
You take away their breath; they die and return to the dust.
³⁰ You send out your Spirit and they are created.
You renew the face of the ground.
³¹ Let Yahweh's glory endure forever.
Let Yahweh rejoice in his works.
³⁴ Let my meditation be sweet to him.
I will rejoice in Yahweh.

Second Reading: Romans 8: 8-17

8 Those who are in the flesh can't please God.
9 But you are not in the flesh but in the Spirit, if it is so that the Spirit of God dwells in you. But if any man doesn't have the Spirit of Christ, he is not his. 10 If Christ is in you, the body is dead because of sin, but the spirit is alive because of righteousness. 11 But if the Spirit of him who raised up Jesus from the dead dwells in you, he who raised up Christ Jesus from the dead will also give life to your mortal bodies through his Spirit who dwells in you.
12 So then, brothers, we are debtors, not to the flesh, to live after the flesh. 13 For if you live after the flesh, you must die; but if by the Spirit you put to death the deeds of the body, you will live. 14 For as many as are led by the Spirit of God, these are children of God. 15 For you didn't receive the spirit of bondage again to fear, but you received the Spirit of adoption, by whom we cry, "Abba! Father!"
16 The Spirit himself testifies with our spirit that we are children of God; 17 and if children, then heirs—heirs of God and joint heirs with Christ, if indeed we suffer with him, that we may also be glorified with him.
18 For I consider that the sufferings of this present time are not worthy to be compared with the glory which will be revealed toward us.

Gospel: John 20: 19-23

19 When therefore it was evening on that day, the first day of the week, and when the doors were locked where the disciples were assembled, for fear of the Jews, Jesus came and stood in the middle and said to them, "Peace be to you."
20 When he had said this, he showed them his hands and his side. The disciples therefore were glad when they saw the Lord. 21 Jesus therefore said to them again, "Peace be to you. As the Father has sent me, even so I send you." 22 When he had said this, he breathed on them, and said to them, "Receive the Holy Spirit! 23 If you forgive anyone's sins, they have been forgiven them. If you retain anyone's sins, they have been retained."

1. Invite the Holy Spirit into this reading, asking the Author of Scripture to speak to you through His Word
2. Read today's passage as many times as you need, take your time
3. Write down (below) what the Lord is saying to you today
4. Live with this Word in your heart through the day

_____

_____

Monday, June 9, 2025
The Blessed Virgin Mary, Mother of the Church

First Reading: Acts 1: 12-14

[12] Then they returned to Jerusalem from the mountain called Olivet, which is near Jerusalem, a Sabbath day's journey away. [13] When they had come in, they went up into the upper room where they were staying, that is Peter, John, James, Andrew, Philip, Thomas, Bartholomew, Matthew, James the son of Alphaeus, Simon the Zealot, and Judas the son of James. [14] All these with one accord continued steadfastly in prayer and supplication, along with the women and Mary the mother of Jesus, and with his brothers.

Responsorial Psalm: Psalms 34: 2-9

[2] My soul shall boast in Yahweh.
The humble shall hear of it and be glad.
[3] Oh magnify Yahweh with me.
Let's exalt his name together.
[4] I sought Yahweh, and he answered me,
and delivered me from all my fears.
[5] They looked to him, and were radiant.
Their faces shall never be covered with shame.
[6] This poor man cried, and Yahweh heard him,
and saved him out of all his troubles.
[7] Yahweh's angel encamps around those who fear him,
and delivers them.
[8] Oh taste and see that Yahweh is good.
Blessed is the man who takes refuge in him.
[9] Oh fear Yahweh, you his saints,
for there is no lack with those who fear him.

Gospel: John 19: 25-34

[25] But standing by Jesus' cross were his mother, his mother's sister, Mary the wife of Clopas, and Mary Magdalene. [26] Therefore when Jesus saw his mother, and the disciple whom he loved standing there, he said to his mother, "Woman, behold, your son!" [27] Then he said to the disciple, "Behold, your mother!" From that hour, the disciple took her to his own home. [28] After this, Jesus, seeing‡ that all things were now finished, that the Scripture might be fulfilled, said, "I am thirsty!" [29] Now a vessel full of vinegar was set there; so they put a sponge full of the vinegar on hyssop, and held it at his mouth. [30] When Jesus therefore had

received the vinegar, he said, "It is finished!" Then he bowed his head and gave up his spirit.
31 Therefore the Jews, because it was the Preparation Day, so that the bodies wouldn't remain on the cross on the Sabbath (for that Sabbath was a special one), asked of Pilate that their legs might be broken and that they might be taken away. 32 Therefore the soldiers came and broke the legs of the first and of the other who was crucified with him; 33 but when they came to Jesus and saw that he was already dead, they didn't break his legs. 34 However, one of the soldiers pierced his side with a spear, and immediately blood and water came out.

1. Invite the Holy Spirit into this reading, asking the Author of Scripture to speak to you through His Word
2. Read today's passage as many times as you need, take your time
3. Write down (below) what the Lord is saying to you today
4. Live with this Word in your heart through the day

Tuesday, June 10, 2025

First Reading: Second Corinthians 1: 18-22

18 But as God is faithful, our word toward you was not "Yes and no." 19 For the Son of God, Jesus Christ, who was preached among you by us—by me, Silvanus, and Timothy—was not "Yes and no," but in him is "Yes." 20 For however many are the promises of God, in him is the "Yes." Therefore also through him is the "Amen", to the glory of God through us.
21 Now he who establishes us with you in Christ and anointed us is God, 22 who also sealed us and gave us the down payment of the Spirit in our hearts.

Responsorial Psalm: Psalms 119: 129, 130, 131, 132, 133, 135

129 Your testimonies are wonderful,
therefore my soul keeps them.
130 The entrance of your words gives light.
It gives understanding to the simple.
131 I opened my mouth wide and panted,
for I longed for your commandments.

¹³² Turn to me, and have mercy on me,
as you always do to those who love your name.
¹³³ Establish my footsteps in your word.
Don't let any iniquity have dominion over me.
¹³⁵ Make your face shine on your servant.
Teach me your statutes.

Gospel: Matthew 5: 13-16

¹³ "You are the salt of the earth, but if the salt has lost its flavor, with what will it be salted? It is then good for nothing, but to be cast out and trodden under the feet of men.
¹⁴ You are the light of the world. A city located on a hill can't be hidden. ¹⁵ Neither do you light a lamp and put it under a measuring basket, but on a stand; and it shines to all who are in the house. ¹⁶ Even so, let your light shine before men, that they may see your good works and glorify your Father who is in heaven.

1. Invite the Holy Spirit into this reading, asking the Author of Scripture to speak to you through His Word
2. Read today's passage as many times as you need, take your time
3. Write down (below) what the Lord is saying to you today
4. Live with this Word in your heart through the day

Wednesday, June 11, 2025
Saint Barnabas, Apostle

First Reading: Acts 11: 21-26; 13: 1-3

²¹ The hand of the Lord was with them, and a great number believed and turned to the Lord. ²² The report concerning them came to the ears of the assembly which was in Jerusalem. They sent out Barnabas to go as far as Antioch, ²³ who, when he had come, and had seen the grace of God, was glad. He exhorted them all, that with purpose of heart they should remain near to the Lord. ²⁴ For he was a good man, and full of the Holy Spirit and of faith, and many people were added to the Lord.

25 Barnabas went out to Tarsus to look for Saul. 26 When he had found him, he brought him to Antioch. For a whole year they were gathered together with the assembly, and taught many people. The disciples were first called Christians in Antioch.

1 Now in the assembly that was at Antioch there were some prophets and teachers: Barnabas, Simeon who was called Niger, Lucius of Cyrene, Manaen the foster brother of Herod the tetrarch, and Saul. 2 As they served the Lord and fasted, the Holy Spirit said, "Separate Barnabas and Saul for me, for the work to which I have called them."
3 Then, when they had fasted and prayed and laid their hands on them, they sent them away.

Responsorial Psalm: Psalms 98: 1, 2-3ab, 3cd-4, 5-6

1 Sing to Yahweh a new song,
for he has done marvelous things!
His right hand and his holy arm have worked salvation for him.
2 Yahweh has made known his salvation.
He has openly shown his righteousness in the sight of the nations.
3 He has remembered his loving kindness and his faithfulness toward the house of Israel.
All the ends of the earth have seen the salvation of our God.
4 Make a joyful noise to Yahweh, all the earth!
Burst out and sing for joy, yes, sing praises!
5 Sing praises to Yahweh with the harp,
with the harp and the voice of melody.
6 With trumpets and sound of the ram's horn,
make a joyful noise before the King, Yahweh.

Gospel: Matthew 5: 17-19

17 "Don't think that I came to destroy the law or the prophets. I didn't come to destroy, but to fulfill. 18 For most certainly, I tell you, until heaven and earth pass away, not even one smallest letter‡ or one tiny pen stroke§ shall in any way pass away from the law, until all things are accomplished. 19 Therefore, whoever shall break one of these least commandments and teach others to do so, shall be called least in the Kingdom of Heaven; but whoever shall do and teach them shall be called great in the Kingdom of Heaven.

1. Invite the Holy Spirit into this reading, asking the Author of Scripture to speak to you through His Word
2. Read today's passage as many times as you need, take your time
3. Write down (below) what the Lord is saying to you today
4. Live with this Word in your heart through the day

Thursday, June 12, 2025

First Reading: Second Corinthians 3: 15 – 4: 1, 3-6

15 But to this day, when Moses is read, a veil lies on their heart. 16 But whenever someone turns to the Lord, the veil is taken away. 17 Now the Lord is the Spirit; and where the Spirit of the Lord is, there is liberty. 18 But we all, with unveiled face seeing the glory of the Lord as in a mirror, are transformed into the same image from glory to glory, even as from the Lord, the Spirit.
1 Therefore, seeing we have this ministry, even as we obtained mercy, we don't faint.
3 Even if our Good News is veiled, it is veiled in those who are dying, 4 in whom the god of this world has blinded the minds of the unbelieving, that the light of the Good News of the glory of Christ, who is the image of God, should not dawn on them. 5 For we don't preach ourselves, but Christ Jesus as Lord, and ourselves as your servants for Jesus' sake, 6 seeing it is God who said, "Light will shine out of darkness," who has shone in our hearts to give the light of the knowledge of the glory of God in the face of Jesus Christ.

Responsorial Psalm: Psalms 85: 9ab and 10, 11-12, 13

9 Surely his salvation is near those who fear him,
that glory may dwell in our land.
10 Mercy and truth meet together.
Righteousness and peace have kissed each other.
11 Truth springs out of the earth.
Righteousness has looked down from heaven.
12 Yes, Yahweh will give that which is good.
Our land will yield its increase.
13 Righteousness goes before him,
and prepares the way for his steps.

Gospel: Matthew 5: 20-26

20 For I tell you that unless your righteousness exceeds that of the scribes and Pharisees, there is no way you will enter into the Kingdom of Heaven.

21 "You have heard that it was said to the ancient ones, 'You shall not murder;' and 'Whoever murders will be in danger of the judgment.' 22 But I tell you that everyone who is angry with his brother without a cause will be in danger of the judgment. Whoever says to his brother, 'Raca!' will be in danger of the council. Whoever says, 'You fool!' will be in danger of the fire of Gehenna.

23 "If therefore you are offering your gift at the altar, and there remember that your brother has anything against you, 24 leave your gift there before the altar, and go your way. First be reconciled to your brother, and then come and offer your gift. 25 Agree with your adversary quickly while you are with him on the way; lest perhaps the prosecutor deliver you to the judge, and the judge deliver you to the officer, and you be cast into prison. 26 Most certainly I tell you, you shall by no means get out of there until you have paid the last penny.

1. Invite the Holy Spirit into this reading, asking the Author of Scripture to speak to you through His Word
2. Read today's passage as many times as you need, take your time
3. Write down (below) what the Lord is saying to you today
4. Live with this Word in your heart through the day

Friday, June 13, 2025
Saint Anthony of Padua, Priest and Doctor of the Church

First Reading: Second Corinthians 4: 7-15

7 But we have this treasure in clay vessels, that the exceeding greatness of the power may be of God and not from ourselves. 8 We are pressed on every side, yet not crushed; perplexed, yet not to despair; 9 pursued, yet not forsaken; struck down, yet not destroyed; 10 always carrying in the body the putting to death of the Lord Jesus, that the life of Jesus may also be revealed in our body. 11 For we who live are always delivered to death for Jesus' sake, that the life also of Jesus may be revealed in our mortal flesh. 12 So then death works in us, but life in you.
13 But having the same spirit of faith, according to that which is written, "I believed, and therefore I spoke." We also believe, and therefore we also speak, 14 knowing that he who raised the Lord Jesus will raise us also with Jesus, and will present us with you. 15 For all things are for your sakes, that the grace, being multiplied through the many, may cause the thanksgiving to abound to the glory of God.

Responsorial Psalm: Psalms 116: 10-11, 15-16, 17-18

¹⁰ I believed, therefore I said,
"I was greatly afflicted."
¹¹ I said in my haste,
"All people are liars."
¹⁵ Precious in Yahweh's sight is the death of his saints.
¹⁶ Yahweh, truly I am your servant.
I am your servant, the son of your servant girl.
You have freed me from my chains.
¹⁷ I will offer to you the sacrifice of thanksgiving,
and will call on Yahweh's name.
¹⁸ I will pay my vows to Yahweh,
yes, in the presence of all his people,

Gospel: Matthew 5: 27-32

²⁷ "You have heard that it was said, ‡ 'You shall not commit adultery;'* ²⁸ but I tell you that everyone who gazes at a woman to lust after her has committed adultery with her already in his heart. ²⁹ If your right eye causes you to stumble, pluck it out and throw it away from you. For it is more profitable for you that one of your members should perish than for your whole body to be cast into Gehenna.§ ³⁰ If your right hand causes you to stumble, cut it off, and throw it away from you. For it is more profitable for you that one of your members should perish, than for your whole body to be cast into Gehenna.‡

³¹ "It was also said, 'Whoever shall put away his wife, let him give her a writing of divorce,'* ³² but I tell you that whoever puts away his wife, except for the cause of sexual immorality, makes her an adulteress; and whoever marries her when she is put away commits adultery.

1. Invite the Holy Spirit into this reading, asking the Author of Scripture to speak to you through His Word
2. Read today's passage as many times as you need, take your time
3. Write down (below) what the Lord is saying to you today
4. Live with this Word in your heart through the day

Saturday, June 14, 2025

First Reading: Second Corinthians 5: 14-21

14 For the love of Christ compels us; because we judge thus: that one died for all, therefore all died. 15 He died for all, that those who live should no longer live to themselves, but to him who for their sakes died and rose again.

16 Therefore we know no one according to the flesh from now on. Even though we have known Christ according to the flesh, yet now we know him so no more. 17 Therefore if anyone is in Christ, he is a new creation. The old things have passed away. Behold, all things have become new. 18 But all things are of God, who reconciled us to himself through Jesus Christ, and gave to us the ministry of reconciliation; 19 namely, that God was in Christ reconciling the world to himself, not reckoning to them their trespasses, and having committed to us the word of reconciliation.

20 We are therefore ambassadors on behalf of Christ, as though God were entreating by us: we beg you on behalf of Christ, be reconciled to God. 21 For him who knew no sin he made to be sin on our behalf, so that in him we might become the righteousness of God.

Responsorial Psalm: Psalms 103: 1-4, 9-12

1 Praise Yahweh, my soul!
All that is within me, praise his holy name!
2 Praise Yahweh, my soul,
and don't forget all his benefits,
3 who forgives all your sins,
who heals all your diseases,
4 who redeems your life from destruction,
who crowns you with loving kindness and tender mercies,
9 He will not always accuse;
neither will he stay angry forever.
10 He has not dealt with us according to our sins,
nor repaid us for our iniquities.
11 For as the heavens are high above the earth,
so great is his loving kindness toward those who fear him.
12 As far as the east is from the west,
so far has he removed our transgressions from us.

Gospel: Matthew 5: 33-37

33 "Again you have heard that it was said to the ancient ones, 'You shall not make false vows, but shall perform to the Lord your vows,' 34 but I tell you, don't swear at all: neither by heaven, for it is the throne of God; 35 nor by the earth, for it is the footstool of his feet; nor by Jerusalem, for it is the city of the great King. 36 Neither shall you swear by your head, for you can't make one hair white or black. 37 But let your 'Yes' be 'Yes' and your 'No' be 'No.' Whatever is more than these is of the evil one.

1. Invite the Holy Spirit into this reading, asking the Author of Scripture to speak to you through His Word
2. Read today's passage as many times as you need, take your time
3. Write down (below) what the Lord is saying to you today
4. Live with this Word in your heart through the day

Sunday, June 15, 2025

First Reading: Proverbs 8: 22-31

22 "Yahweh possessed me in the beginning of his work,
before his deeds of old.
23 I was set up from everlasting, from the beginning,
before the earth existed.
24 When there were no depths, I was born,
when there were no springs abounding with water.
25 Before the mountains were settled in place,
before the hills, I was born;
26 while as yet he had not made the earth, nor the fields,
nor the beginning of the dust of the world.
27 When he established the heavens, I was there.
When he set a circle on the surface of the deep,
28 when he established the clouds above,
when the springs of the deep became strong,
29 when he gave to the sea its boundary,
that the waters should not violate his commandment,
when he marked out the foundations of the earth,
30 then I was the craftsman by his side.

I was a delight day by day,
always rejoicing before him,
31 rejoicing in his whole world.
My delight was with the sons of men.

Responsorial Psalm: Psalms 8: 4-9

4 what is man, that you think of him?
What is the son of man, that you care for him?
5 For you have made him a little lower than the angels,‡
and crowned him with glory and honor.
6 You make him ruler over the works of your hands.
You have put all things under his feet:
7 All sheep and cattle,
yes, and the animals of the field,
8 the birds of the sky, the fish of the sea,
and whatever passes through the paths of the seas.
9 Yahweh, our Lord,
how majestic is your name in all the earth!

Second Reading: Romans 5: 1-5

1 Being therefore justified by faith, we have peace with God through our Lord Jesus Christ; 2 through whom we also have our access by faith into this grace in which we stand. We rejoice in hope of the glory of God. 3 Not only this, but we also rejoice in our sufferings, knowing that suffering produces perseverance; 4 and perseverance, proven character; and proven character, hope; 5 and hope doesn't disappoint us, because God's love has been poured into our hearts through the Holy Spirit who was given to us.

Gospel: John 16: 12-15

12 "I still have many things to tell you, but you can't bear them now. 13 However, when he, the Spirit of truth, has come, he will guide you into all truth, for he will not speak from himself; but whatever he hears, he will speak. He will declare to you things that are coming. 14 He will glorify me, for he will take from what is mine and will declare it to you. 15 All things that the Father has are mine; therefore I said that he takes‡ of mine and will declare it to you.

1. Invite the Holy Spirit into this reading, asking the Author of Scripture to speak to you through His Word

2. Read today's passage as many times as you need, take your time
3. Write down (below) what the Lord is saying to you today
4. Live with this Word in your heart through the day

_____

_____

Monday, June 16, 2025

First Reading: Second Corinthians 6: 1-10

¹ Working together, we entreat also that you do not receive the grace of God in vain. ² For he says,
"At an acceptable time I listened to you.
In a day of salvation I helped you."
Behold, now is the acceptable time. Behold, now is the day of salvation. ³ We give no occasion of stumbling in anything, that our service may not be blamed, ⁴ but in everything commending ourselves as servants of God: in great endurance, in afflictions, in hardships, in distresses, ⁵ in beatings, in imprisonments, in riots, in labors, in watchings, in fastings, ⁶ in pureness, in knowledge, in perseverance, in kindness, in the Holy Spirit, in sincere love, ⁷ in the word of truth, in the power of God, by the armor of righteousness on the right hand and on the left, ⁸ by glory and dishonor, by evil report and good report, as deceivers and yet true, ⁹ as unknown and yet well known, as dying and behold—we live, as punished and not killed, ¹⁰ as sorrowful yet always rejoicing, as poor yet making many rich, as having nothing and yet possessing all things.

Responsorial Psalm: Psalms 98: 1, 2b, 3-4

¹ Sing to Yahweh a new song,
for he has done marvelous things!
His right hand and his holy arm have worked salvation for him.
²ᵇ He has openly shown his righteousness in the sight of the nations.
³ He has remembered his loving kindness and his faithfulness toward the house of Israel.
All the ends of the earth have seen the salvation of our God.
⁴ Make a joyful noise to Yahweh, all the earth!
Burst out and sing for joy, yes, sing praises!

Gospel: Matthew 5: 38-42

³⁸ "You have heard that it was said, 'An eye for an eye, and a tooth for a tooth.' ³⁹ But I tell you, don't resist him who is evil; but whoever strikes you on your right cheek, turn to him the other also. ⁴⁰ If anyone sues you to take away your coat, let him have your cloak also. ⁴¹ Whoever compels you to go one mile, go with him two. ⁴² Give to him who asks you, and don't turn away him who desires to borrow from you.

1. Invite the Holy Spirit into this reading, asking the Author of Scripture to speak to you through His Word
2. Read today's passage as many times as you need, take your time
3. Write down (below) what the Lord is saying to you today
4. Live with this Word in your heart through the day

Tuesday, June 17, 2025

First Reading: Second Corinthians 8: 1-9

¹ Moreover, brothers, we make known to you the grace of God which has been given in the assemblies of Macedonia, ² how in a severe ordeal of affliction, the abundance of their joy and their deep poverty abounded to the riches of their generosity. ³ For according to their power, I testify, yes and beyond their power, they gave of their own accord, ⁴ begging us with much entreaty to receive this grace and the fellowship in the service to the saints. ⁵ This was not as we had expected, but first they gave their own selves to the Lord, and to us through the will of God. ⁶ So we urged Titus, that as he had made a beginning before, so he would also complete in you this grace. ⁷ But as you abound in everything—in faith, utterance, knowledge, all earnestness, and in your love to us—see that you also abound in this grace.
⁸ I speak not by way of commandment, but as proving through the earnestness of others the sincerity also of your love. ⁹ For you know the grace of our Lord Jesus Christ, that though he was rich, yet for your sakes he became poor, that you through his poverty might become rich.

Responsorial Psalm: Psalms 146: 2, 5-9a

² While I live, I will praise Yahweh.

I will sing praises to my God as long as I exist.
⁵ Happy is he who has the God of Jacob for his help,
whose hope is in Yahweh, his God,
⁶ who made heaven and earth,
the sea, and all that is in them;
who keeps truth forever;
⁷ who executes justice for the oppressed;
who gives food to the hungry.
Yahweh frees the prisoners.
⁸ Yahweh opens the eyes of the blind.
Yahweh raises up those who are bowed down.
Yahweh loves the righteous.
⁹ᵃ Yahweh preserves the foreigners.

Gospel: Matthew 5: 43-48

⁴³ "You have heard that it was said, 'You shall love your neighbor ⃰ and hate your enemy.'⃰ ⁴⁴ But I tell you, love your enemies, bless those who curse you, do good to those who hate you, and pray for those who mistreat you and persecute you, ⁴⁵ that you may be children of your Father who is in heaven. For he makes his sun to rise on the evil and the good, and sends rain on the just and the unjust. ⁴⁶ For if you love those who love you, what reward do you have? Don't even the tax collectors do the same? ⁴⁷ If you only greet your friends, what more do you do than others? Don't even the tax collectors§ do the same? ⁴⁸ Therefore you shall be perfect, just as your Father in heaven is perfect.

1. Invite the Holy Spirit into this reading, asking the Author of Scripture to speak to you through His Word
2. Read today's passage as many times as you need, take your time
3. Write down (below) what the Lord is saying to you today
4. Live with this Word in your heart through the day

Wednesday, June 18, 2025

First Reading: Second Corinthians 9: 6-11

⁶ Remember this: he who sows sparingly will also reap sparingly. He who sows bountifully will also reap bountifully. ⁷ Let each man give according as he has determined in his heart, not grudgingly or under compulsion, for God loves a cheerful giver. ⁸ And God is able to make all grace abound to you, that you, always having all sufficiency in everything, may abound to every good work. ⁹ As it is written,
"He has scattered abroad. He has given to the poor.
His righteousness remains forever."
¹⁰ Now may he who supplies seed to the sower and bread for food, supply and multiply your seed for sowing, and increase the fruits of your righteousness, ¹¹ you being enriched in everything for all generosity, which produces thanksgiving to God through us.

Responsorial Psalm: Psalms 112: 1bc-4, 9

¹ᵇ Blessed is the man who fears Yahweh,
who delights greatly in his commandments.
² His offspring will be mighty in the land.
The generation of the upright will be blessed.
³ Wealth and riches are in his house.
His righteousness endures forever.
⁴ Light dawns in the darkness for the upright,
gracious, merciful, and righteous.
⁹ He has dispersed, he has given to the poor.
His righteousness endures forever.
His horn will be exalted with honor.

Gospel: Matthew 6: 1-6, 16-18

¹ "Be careful that you don't do your charitable giving before men, to be seen by them, or else you have no reward from your Father who is in heaven. ² Therefore, when you do merciful deeds, don't sound a trumpet before yourself, as the hypocrites do in the synagogues and in the streets, that they may get glory from men. Most certainly I tell you, they have received their reward. ³ But when you do merciful deeds, don't let your left hand know what your right hand does, ⁴ so that your merciful deeds may be in secret, then your Father who sees in secret will reward you openly.
⁵ "When you pray, you shall not be as the hypocrites, for they love to stand and pray in the synagogues and in the corners of the streets, that they may be seen by men. Most certainly, I tell you, they have received their reward. ⁶ But you, when you pray, enter into your inner room, and having shut your door, pray to your Father who is in secret; and your Father who sees in secret will reward you openly.

¹⁶ "Moreover when you fast, don't be like the hypocrites, with sad faces. For they disfigure their faces that they may be seen by men to be fasting. Most certainly I tell you, they have received their reward. ¹⁷ But you, when you fast, anoint your head and wash your face, ¹⁸ so that you are not seen by men to be fasting, but by your Father who is in secret; and your Father, who sees in secret, will reward you.

1. Invite the Holy Spirit into this reading, asking the Author of Scripture to speak to you through His Word
2. Read today's passage as many times as you need, take your time
3. Write down (below) what the Lord is saying to you today
4. Live with this Word in your heart through the day

Thursday, June 19, 2025
Saint Romuald, Abbot

First Reading: Second Corinthians 11: 1-11

¹ I wish that you would bear with me in a little foolishness, but indeed you do bear with me. ² For I am jealous over you with a godly jealousy. For I promised you in marriage to one husband, that I might present you as a pure virgin to Christ. ³ But I am afraid that somehow, as the serpent deceived Eve in his craftiness, so your minds might be corrupted from the simplicity that is in Christ. ⁴ For if he who comes preaches another Jesus whom we didn't preach, or if you receive a different spirit which you didn't receive, or a different "good news" which you didn't accept, you put up with that well enough. ⁵ For I reckon that I am not at all behind the very best apostles. ⁶ But though I am unskilled in speech, yet I am not unskilled in knowledge. No, in every way we have been revealed to you in all things. ⁷ Or did I commit a sin in humbling myself that you might be exalted, because I preached to you God's Good News free of charge? ⁸ I robbed other assemblies, taking wages from them that I might serve you. ⁹ When I was present with you and was in need, I wasn't a burden on anyone, for the brothers, when they came from Macedonia, supplied the measure of my need. In everything I kept myself from being burdensome to you, and I will continue to do so. ¹⁰ As the truth of Christ is in me, no one will stop me from this boasting in the regions of Achaia. ¹¹ Why? Because I don't love you? God knows.

Responsorial Psalm: Psalms 111: 1b-2, 3-4, 7-8

¹ᵇ I will give thanks to Yahweh with my whole heart,
in the council of the upright, and in the congregation.
² Yahweh's works are great,
pondered by all those who delight in them.
³ His work is honor and majesty.
His righteousness endures forever.
⁴ He has caused his wonderful works to be remembered.
Yahweh is gracious and merciful.
⁷ The works of his hands are truth and justice.
All his precepts are sure.
⁸ They are established forever and ever.
They are done in truth and uprightness.

Gospel: Matthew 6: 7-15

⁷ In praying, don't use vain repetitions as the Gentiles do; for they think that they will be heard for their much speaking. ⁸ Therefore don't be like them, for your Father knows what things you need before you ask him. ⁹ Pray like this:
" 'Our Father in heaven, may your name be kept holy.
¹⁰ Let your Kingdom come.
Let your will be done on earth as it is in heaven.
¹¹ Give us today our daily bread.
¹² Forgive us our debts,
as we also forgive our debtors.
¹³ Bring us not into temptation,
but deliver us from the evil one.
For yours is the Kingdom, the power, and the glory forever. Amen.'
¹⁴ "For if you forgive men their trespasses, your heavenly Father will also forgive you. ¹⁵ But if you don't forgive men their trespasses, neither will your Father forgive your trespasses.

1. Invite the Holy Spirit into this reading, asking the Author of Scripture to speak to you through His Word
2. Read today's passage as many times as you need, take your time
3. Write down (below) what the Lord is saying to you today
4. Live with this Word in your heart through the day

_____

_____

Friday, June 20, 2025

First Reading: Second Corinthians 11: 18, 21-30

¹⁸ Seeing that many boast after the flesh, I will also boast.
²¹ To my shame, I speak as though we had been weak. Yet in whatever way anyone is bold (I speak in foolishness), I am bold also. ²² Are they Hebrews? So am I. Are they Israelites? So am I. Are they the offspring⸸ of Abraham? So am I. ²³ Are they servants of Christ? (I speak as one beside himself.) I am more so: in labors more abundantly, in prisons more abundantly, in stripes above measure, and in deaths often. ²⁴ Five times I received forty stripes minus one from the Jews. ²⁵ Three times I was beaten with rods. Once I was stoned. Three times I suffered shipwreck. I have been a night and a day in the deep. ²⁶ I have been in travels often, perils of rivers, perils of robbers, perils from my countrymen, perils from the Gentiles, perils in the city, perils in the wilderness, perils in the sea, perils among false brothers; ²⁷ in labor and travail, in watchings often, in hunger and thirst, in fastings often, and in cold and nakedness.
²⁸ Besides those things that are outside, there is that which presses on me daily: anxiety for all the assemblies. ²⁹ Who is weak, and I am not weak? Who is caused to stumble, and I don't burn with indignation?
³⁰ If I must boast, I will boast of the things that concern my weakness.

Responsorial Psalm: Psalms 34: 2-7

² My soul shall boast in Yahweh.
The humble shall hear of it and be glad.
³ Oh magnify Yahweh with me.
Let's exalt his name together.
⁴ I sought Yahweh, and he answered me,
and delivered me from all my fears.
⁵ They looked to him, and were radiant.
Their faces shall never be covered with shame.
⁶ This poor man cried, and Yahweh heard him,
and saved him out of all his troubles.
⁷ Yahweh's angel encamps around those who fear him,
and delivers them.

Gospel: Matthew 6: 19-23

¹⁹ "Don't lay up treasures for yourselves on the earth, where moth and rust consume, and where thieves break through and steal; ²⁰ but lay up for yourselves treasures in heaven,

where neither moth nor rust consume, and where thieves don't break through and steal; 21 for where your treasure is, there your heart will be also.

22 "The lamp of the body is the eye. If therefore your eye is sound, your whole body will be full of light. 23 But if your eye is evil, your whole body will be full of darkness. If therefore the light that is in you is darkness, how great is the darkness!

1. Invite the Holy Spirit into this reading, asking the Author of Scripture to speak to you through His Word
2. Read today's passage as many times as you need, take your time
3. Write down (below) what the Lord is saying to you today
4. Live with this Word in your heart through the day

Saturday, June 21, 2025
Saint Aloysius Gonzaga, Religious

First Reading: Second Corinthians 12: 1-10

1 It is doubtless not profitable for me to boast, but I will come to visions and revelations of the Lord. 2 I know a man in Christ who was caught up into the third heaven fourteen years ago—whether in the body, I don't know, or whether out of the body, I don't know; God knows. 3 I know such a man (whether in the body, or outside of the body, I don't know; God knows), 4 how he was caught up into Paradise and heard unspeakable words, which it is not lawful for a man to utter. 5 On behalf of such a one I will boast, but on my own behalf I will not boast, except in my weaknesses. 6 For if I would desire to boast, I will not be foolish; for I will speak the truth. But I refrain, so that no man may think more of me than that which he sees in me or hears from me. 7 By reason of the exceeding greatness of the revelations, that I should not be exalted excessively, a thorn in the flesh was given to me: a messenger of Satan to torment me, that I should not be exalted excessively. 8 Concerning this thing, I begged the Lord three times that it might depart from me. 9 He has said to me, "My grace is sufficient for you, for my power is made perfect in weakness." Most gladly therefore I will rather glory in my weaknesses, that the power of Christ may rest on me. 10 Therefore I take pleasure in weaknesses, in injuries, in necessities, in persecutions, and in distresses, for Christ's sake. For when I am weak, then am I strong.

Responsorial Psalm: Psalms 34: 8-13

⁸ Oh taste and see that Yahweh is good.
Blessed is the man who takes refuge in him.
⁹ Oh fear Yahweh, you his saints,
for there is no lack with those who fear him.
¹⁰ The young lions do lack, and suffer hunger,
but those who seek Yahweh shall not lack any good thing.
¹¹ Come, you children, listen to me.
I will teach you the fear of Yahweh.
¹² Who is someone who desires life,
and loves many days, that he may see good?
¹³ Keep your tongue from evil,
and your lips from speaking lies.

Gospel: Matthew 6: 24-34

²⁴ "No one can serve two masters, for either he will hate the one and love the other, or else he will be devoted to one and despise the other. You can't serve both God and Mammon. ²⁵ Therefore I tell you, don't be anxious for your life: what you will eat, or what you will drink; nor yet for your body, what you will wear. Isn't life more than food, and the body more than clothing? ²⁶ See the birds of the sky, that they don't sow, neither do they reap, nor gather into barns. Your heavenly Father feeds them. Aren't you of much more value than they?

²⁷ "Which of you by being anxious, can add one moment§ to his lifespan? ²⁸ Why are you anxious about clothing? Consider the lilies of the field, how they grow. They don't toil, neither do they spin, ²⁹ yet I tell you that even Solomon in all his glory was not dressed like one of these. ³⁰ But if God so clothes the grass of the field, which today exists and tomorrow is thrown into the oven, won't he much more clothe you, you of little faith?

³¹ "Therefore don't be anxious, saying, 'What will we eat?', 'What will we drink?' or, 'With what will we be clothed?' ³² For the Gentiles seek after all these things; for your heavenly Father knows that you need all these things. ³³ But seek first God's Kingdom and his righteousness; and all these things will be given to you as well. ³⁴ Therefore don't be anxious for tomorrow, for tomorrow will be anxious for itself. Each day's own evil is sufficient.

1. Invite the Holy Spirit into this reading, asking the Author of Scripture to speak to you through His Word
2. Read today's passage as many times as you need, take your time
3. Write down (below) what the Lord is saying to you today
4. Live with this Word in your heart through the day

Sunday, June 22, 2025
THE MOST HOLY BODY AND BLOOD OF CHRIST
Corpus Christi

First Reading: Genesis 14: 18-20

18 Melchizedek king of Salem brought out bread and wine. He was priest of God Most High. 19 He blessed him, and said, "Blessed be Abram of God Most High, possessor of heaven and earth. 20 Blessed be God Most High, who has delivered your enemies into your hand."
Abram gave him a tenth of all.

Responsorial Psalm: Psalms 110: 1, 2, 3, 4

1 Yahweh says to my Lord, "Sit at my right hand,
until I make your enemies your footstool for your feet."
2 Yahweh will send out the rod of your strength out of Zion.
Rule among your enemies.
3 Your people offer themselves willingly in the day of your power, in holy array.
Out of the womb of the morning, you have the dew of your youth.
4 Yahweh has sworn, and will not change his mind:
"You are a priest forever in the order of Melchizedek."

Second Reading: First Corinthians 11: 23-26

23 For I received from the Lord that which also I delivered to you, that the Lord Jesus on the night in which he was betrayed took bread. 24 When he had given thanks, he broke it and said, "Take, eat. This is my body, which is broken for you. Do this in memory of me." 25 In the same way he also took the cup after supper, saying, "This cup is the new covenant in my blood. Do this, as often as you drink, in memory of me." 26 For as often as you eat this bread and drink this cup, you proclaim the Lord's death until he comes.

Gospel: Luke 9: 11b-17

¹¹ᵇ He welcomed them, spoke to them of God's Kingdom, and he cured those who needed healing. ¹² The day began to wear away; and the twelve came and said to him, "Send the multitude away, that they may go into the surrounding villages and farms and lodge and get food, for we are here in a deserted place."

¹³ But he said to them, "You give them something to eat."

They said, "We have no more than five loaves and two fish, unless we should go and buy food for all these people." ¹⁴ For they were about five thousand men.

He said to his disciples, "Make them sit down in groups of about fifty each." ¹⁵ They did so, and made them all sit down. ¹⁶ He took the five loaves and the two fish, and looking up to the sky, he blessed them, broke them, and gave them to the disciples to set before the multitude. ¹⁷ They ate and were all filled. They gathered up twelve baskets of broken pieces that were left over.

1. Invite the Holy Spirit into this reading, asking the Author of Scripture to speak to you through His Word
2. Read today's passage as many times as you need, take your time
3. Write down (below) what the Lord is saying to you today
4. Live with this Word in your heart through the day

_____

_____

Monday, June 23, 2025

First Reading: Genesis 12: 1-9

¹ Now Yahweh said to Abram, "Leave your country, and your relatives, and your father's house, and go to the land that I will show you. ² I will make of you a great nation. I will bless you and make your name great. You will be a blessing. ³ I will bless those who bless you, and I will curse him who treats you with contempt. All the families of the earth will be blessed through you."

⁴ So Abram went, as Yahweh had told him. Lot went with him. Abram was seventy-five years old when he departed from Haran. ⁵ Abram took Sarai his wife, Lot his brother's son, all their possessions that they had gathered, and the people whom they had acquired in Haran, and they went to go into the land of Canaan. They entered into the land of Canaan. ⁶ Abram passed through the land to the place of Shechem, to the oak of Moreh. At that time, Canaanites were in the land.

⁷ Yahweh appeared to Abram and said, "I will give this land to your offspring."‡

He built an altar there to Yahweh, who had appeared to him. ⁸ He left from there to go to the mountain on the east of Bethel and pitched his tent, having Bethel on the west, and Ai on the east. There he built an altar to Yahweh and called on Yahweh's name. ⁹ Abram traveled, still going on toward the South.

Responsorial Psalm: Psalms 33: 12-13, 18-20 and 22

¹² Blessed is the nation whose God is Yahweh,
the people whom he has chosen for his own inheritance.
¹³ Yahweh looks from heaven.
He sees all the sons of men.
¹⁸ Behold, Yahweh's eye is on those who fear him,
on those who hope in his loving kindness,
¹⁹ to deliver their soul from death,
to keep them alive in famine.
²⁰ Our soul has waited for Yahweh.
He is our help and our shield.
²² Let your loving kindness be on us, Yahweh,
since we have hoped in you.

Gospel: Matthew 7: 1-5

¹ "Don't judge, so that you won't be judged. ² For with whatever judgment you judge, you will be judged; and with whatever measure you measure, it will be measured to you. ³ Why do you see the speck that is in your brother's eye, but don't consider the beam that is in your own eye? ⁴ Or how will you tell your brother, 'Let me remove the speck from your eye,' and behold, the beam is in your own eye? ⁵ You hypocrite! First remove the beam out of your own eye, and then you can see clearly to remove the speck out of your brother's eye.

1. Invite the Holy Spirit into this reading, asking the Author of Scripture to speak to you through His Word
2. Read today's passage as many times as you need, take your time
3. Write down (below) what the Lord is saying to you today
4. Live with this Word in your heart through the day

_____

_____

Tuesday, June 24, 2025
THE NATIVITY OF SAINT JOHN THE BAPTIST

First Reading: Isaiah 49: 1-6

¹ Listen, islands, to me.
Listen, you peoples, from afar:
Yahweh has called me from the womb;
from the inside of my mother, he has mentioned my name.
² He has made my mouth like a sharp sword.
He has hidden me in the shadow of his hand.
He has made me a polished shaft.
He has kept me close in his quiver.
³ He said to me, "You are my servant,
Israel, in whom I will be glorified."
⁴ But I said, "I have labored in vain.
I have spent my strength in vain for nothing;
yet surely the justice due to me is with Yahweh,
and my reward with my God."
⁵ Now Yahweh, he who formed me from the womb to be his servant,
says to bring Jacob again to him,
and to gather Israel to him,
for I am honorable in Yahweh's eyes,
and my God has become my strength.
⁶ Indeed, he says, "It is too light a thing that you should be my servant to raise up the tribes of Jacob,
and to restore the preserved of Israel.
I will also give you as a light to the nations,
that you may be my salvation to the end of the earth."

Responsorial Psalm: Psalms 139: 1b-3, 13-15

¹ Yahweh, you have searched me,
and you know me.
² You know my sitting down and my rising up.
You perceive my thoughts from afar.
³ You search out my path and my lying down,
and are acquainted with all my ways.
¹³ For you formed my inmost being.
You knit me together in my mother's womb.

¹⁴ I will give thanks to you,
for I am fearfully and wonderfully made.
Your works are wonderful.
My soul knows that very well.
¹⁵ My frame wasn't hidden from you,
when I was made in secret,
woven together in the depths of the earth.

Second Reading: Acts 13: 22-26

²² When he had removed him, he raised up David to be their king, to whom he also testified, 'I have found David the son of Jesse, a man after my heart, who will do all my will.' ²³ From this man's offspring, God has brought salvation‡ to Israel according to his promise, ²⁴ before his coming, when John had first preached the baptism of repentance to Israel.§ ²⁵ As John was fulfilling his course, he said, 'What do you suppose that I am? I am not he. But behold, one comes after me, the sandals of whose feet I am not worthy to untie.' ²⁶ "Brothers, children of the stock of Abraham, and those among you who fear God, the word of this salvation is sent out to you.

Gospel: Luke 1: 57-66, 80

⁵⁷ Now the time that Elizabeth should give birth was fulfilled, and she gave birth to a son. ⁵⁸ Her neighbors and her relatives heard that the Lord had magnified his mercy toward her, and they rejoiced with her. ⁵⁹ On the eighth day, they came to circumcise the child; and they would have called him Zacharias, after the name of his father. ⁶⁰ His mother answered, "Not so; but he will be called John."
⁶¹ They said to her, "There is no one among your relatives who is called by this name." ⁶² They made signs to his father, what he would have him called.
⁶³ He asked for a writing tablet, and wrote, "His name is John."
They all marveled. ⁶⁴ His mouth was opened immediately and his tongue freed, and he spoke, blessing God. ⁶⁵ Fear came on all who lived around them, and all these sayings were talked about throughout all the hill country of Judea. ⁶⁶ All who heard them laid them up in their heart, saying, "What then will this child be?" The hand of the Lord was with him.
⁸⁰ The child was growing and becoming strong in spirit, and was in the desert until the day of his public appearance to Israel.

1. Invite the Holy Spirit into this reading, asking the Author of Scripture to speak to you through His Word
2. Read today's passage as many times as you need, take your time
3. Write down (below) what the Lord is saying to you today

4. Live with this Word in your heart through the day

_____

_____

Wednesday, June 25, 2025

First Reading: Genesis 15: 1-12, 17-18

¹ After these things Yahweh's word came to Abram in a vision, saying, "Don't be afraid, Abram. I am your shield, your exceedingly great reward."
² Abram said, "Lord Yahweh, what will you give me, since I go childless, and he who will inherit my estate is Eliezer of Damascus?" ³ Abram said, "Behold, you have given no children to me: and, behold, one born in my house is my heir."
⁴ Behold, Yahweh's word came to him, saying, "This man will not be your heir, but he who will come out of your own body will be your heir." ⁵ Yahweh brought him outside, and said, "Look now toward the sky, and count the stars, if you are able to count them." He said to Abram, "So your offspring will be." ⁶ He believed in Yahweh, who credited it to him for righteousness. ⁷ He said to Abram, "I am Yahweh who brought you out of Ur of the Chaldees, to give you this land to inherit it."
⁸ He said, "Lord Yahweh, how will I know that I will inherit it?"
⁹ He said to him, "Bring me a heifer three years old, a female goat three years old, a ram three years old, a turtledove, and a young pigeon." ¹⁰ He brought him all these, and divided them in the middle, and laid each half opposite the other; but he didn't divide the birds. ¹¹ The birds of prey came down on the carcasses, and Abram drove them away.
¹² When the sun was going down, a deep sleep fell on Abram. Now terror and great darkness fell on him.
¹⁷ It came to pass that, when the sun went down, and it was dark, behold, a smoking furnace and a flaming torch passed between these pieces. ¹⁸ In that day Yahweh made a covenant with Abram, saying, "I have given this land to your offspring, from the river of Egypt to the great river, the river Euphrates

Responsorial Psalm: Psalms 105: 1-4, 6-9

¹ Give thanks to Yahweh! Call on his name!
Make his doings known among the peoples.
² Sing to him, sing praises to him!
Tell of all his marvelous works.

³ Glory in his holy name.
Let the heart of those who seek Yahweh rejoice.
⁴ Seek Yahweh and his strength.
Seek his face forever more.
⁶ you offspring of Abraham, his servant,
you children of Jacob, his chosen ones.
⁷ He is Yahweh, our God.
His judgments are in all the earth.
⁸ He has remembered his covenant forever,
the word which he commanded to a thousand generations,
⁹ the covenant which he made with Abraham,
his oath to Isaac,

Gospel: Matthew 7: 15-20

¹⁵ "Beware of false prophets, who come to you in sheep's clothing, but inwardly are ravening wolves. ¹⁶ By their fruits you will know them. Do you gather grapes from thorns or figs from thistles? ¹⁷ Even so, every good tree produces good fruit, but the corrupt tree produces evil fruit. ¹⁸ A good tree can't produce evil fruit, neither can a corrupt tree produce good fruit. ¹⁹ Every tree that doesn't grow good fruit is cut down and thrown into the fire. ²⁰ Therefore by their fruits you will know them.

1. Invite the Holy Spirit into this reading, asking the Author of Scripture to speak to you through His Word
2. Read today's passage as many times as you need, take your time
3. Write down (below) what the Lord is saying to you today
4. Live with this Word in your heart through the day

_____

_____

Thursday, June 26, 2025

First Reading: Genesis 16: 6b-12, 15-16

⁶ᵇ Do to her whatever is good in your eyes." Sarai dealt harshly with her, and she fled from her face.

⁷ Yahweh's angel found her by a fountain of water in the wilderness, by the fountain on the way to Shur. ⁸ He said, "Hagar, Sarai's servant, where did you come from? Where are you going?"

She said, "I am fleeing from the face of my mistress Sarai."

⁹ Yahweh's angel said to her, "Return to your mistress, and submit yourself under her hands." ¹⁰ Yahweh's angel said to her, "I will greatly multiply your offspring, that they will not be counted for multitude." ¹¹ Yahweh's angel said to her, "Behold, you are with child, and will bear a son. You shall call his name Ishmael, because Yahweh has heard your affliction. ¹² He will be like a wild donkey among men. His hand will be against every man, and every man's hand against him. He will live opposed to all of his brothers."

¹³ She called the name of Yahweh who spoke to her, "You are a God who sees," for she said, "Have I even stayed alive after seeing him?" ¹⁴ Therefore the well was called Beer Lahai Roi.¹ Behold, it is between Kadesh and Bered.

¹⁵ Hagar bore a son for Abram. Abram called the name of his son, whom Hagar bore, Ishmael. ¹⁶ Abram was eighty-six years old when Hagar bore Ishmael to Abram.

Responsorial Psalm: Psalms 106: 1b-5

¹ᵇ Give thanks to Yahweh, for he is good,
for his loving kindness endures forever.
² Who can utter the mighty acts of Yahweh,
or fully declare all his praise?
³ Blessed are those who keep justice.
Blessed is one who does what is right at all times.
⁴ Remember me, Yahweh, with the favor that you show to your people.
Visit me with your salvation,
⁵ that I may see the prosperity of your chosen,
that I may rejoice in the gladness of your nation,
that I may glory with your inheritance.

Gospel: Matthew 7: 21-29

²¹ "Not everyone who says to me, 'Lord, Lord,' will enter into the Kingdom of Heaven, but he who does the will of my Father who is in heaven. ²² Many will tell me in that day, 'Lord, Lord, didn't we prophesy in your name, in your name cast out demons, and in your name do many mighty works?' ²³ Then I will tell them, 'I never knew you. Depart from me, you who work iniquity.'

²⁴ "Everyone therefore who hears these words of mine and does them, I will liken him to a wise man who built his house on a rock. ²⁵ The rain came down, the floods came, and the winds blew and beat on that house; and it didn't fall, for it was founded on the

rock. 26 Everyone who hears these words of mine and doesn't do them will be like a foolish man who built his house on the sand. 27 The rain came down, the floods came, and the winds blew and beat on that house; and it fell—and its fall was great."

28 When Jesus had finished saying these things, the multitudes were astonished at his teaching, 29 for he taught them with authority, and not like the scribes.

1. Invite the Holy Spirit into this reading, asking the Author of Scripture to speak to you through His Word
2. Read today's passage as many times as you need, take your time
3. Write down (below) what the Lord is saying to you today
4. Live with this Word in your heart through the day

Friday, June 27, 2025
THE MOST SACRED HEART OF JESUS

First Reading: Ezekiel 34: 11-16

11 " 'For the Lord Yahweh says: "Behold, I myself, even I, will search for my sheep, and will seek them out. 12 As a shepherd seeks out his flock in the day that he is among his sheep that are scattered abroad, so I will seek out my sheep. I will deliver them out of all places where they have been scattered in the cloudy and dark day. 13 I will bring them out from the peoples, and gather them from the countries, and will bring them into their own land. I will feed them on the mountains of Israel, by the watercourses, and in all the inhabited places of the country. 14 I will feed them with good pasture, and their fold will be on the mountains of the height of Israel. There they will lie down in a good fold. They will feed on rich pasture on the mountains of Israel. 15 I myself will be the shepherd of my sheep, and I will cause them to lie down," says the Lord Yahweh. 16 "I will seek that which was lost, and will bring back that which was driven away, and will bind up that which was broken, and will strengthen that which was sick; but I will destroy the fat and the strong. I will feed them in justice." '

Responsorial Psalm: Psalms 23: 1-6

1 Yahweh is my shepherd;
I shall lack nothing.

² He makes me lie down in green pastures.
He leads me beside still waters.
³ He restores my soul.
He guides me in the paths of righteousness for his name's sake.
⁴ Even though I walk through the valley of the shadow of death,
I will fear no evil, for you are with me.
Your rod and your staff,
they comfort me.
⁵ You prepare a table before me
in the presence of my enemies.
You anoint my head with oil.
My cup runs over.
⁶ Surely goodness and loving kindness shall follow me all the days of my life,
and I will dwell in Yahweh's house forever.

Second Reading: Romans 5: 5-11

⁵ and hope doesn't disappoint us, because God's love has been poured into our hearts through the Holy Spirit who was given to us.
⁶ For while we were yet weak, at the right time Christ died for the ungodly. ⁷ For one will hardly die for a righteous man. Yet perhaps for a good person someone would even dare to die. ⁸ But God commends his own love toward us, in that while we were yet sinners, Christ died for us.
⁹ Much more then, being now justified by his blood, we will be saved from God's wrath through him. ¹⁰ For if while we were enemies, we were reconciled to God through the death of his Son, much more, being reconciled, we will be saved by his life.
¹¹ Not only so, but we also rejoice in God through our Lord Jesus Christ, through whom we have now received the reconciliation.

Gospel: Luke 15: 3-7

³ He told them this parable: ⁴ "Which of you men, if you had one hundred sheep and lost one of them, wouldn't leave the ninety-nine in the wilderness and go after the one that was lost, until he found it? ⁵ When he has found it, he carries it on his shoulders, rejoicing. ⁶ When he comes home, he calls together his friends and his neighbors, saying to them, 'Rejoice with me, for I have found my sheep which was lost!' ⁷ I tell you that even so there will be more joy in heaven over one sinner who repents, than over ninety-nine righteous people who need no repentance.

1. Invite the Holy Spirit into this reading, asking the Author of Scripture to speak to you through His Word
2. Read today's passage as many times as you need, take your time
3. Write down (below) what the Lord is saying to you today
4. Live with this Word in your heart through the day

Saturday, June 28, 2025
The Immaculate Heart of the Blessed Virgin Mary; Saint Irenaeus, Bishop, Martyr, and Doctor of the Church

First Reading: Genesis 18: 1-15

¹ Yahweh appeared to him by the oaks of Mamre, as he sat in the tent door in the heat of the day. ² He lifted up his eyes and looked, and saw that three men stood near him. When he saw them, he ran to meet them from the tent door, and bowed himself to the earth, ³ and said, "My lord, if now I have found favor in your sight, please don't go away from your servant. ⁴ Now let a little water be fetched, wash your feet, and rest yourselves under the tree. ⁵ I will get a piece of bread so you can refresh your heart. After that you may go your way, now that you have come to your servant."
They said, "Very well, do as you have said."
⁶ Abraham hurried into the tent to Sarah, and said, "Quickly prepare three seahs of fine meal, knead it, and make cakes." ⁷ Abraham ran to the herd, and fetched a tender and good calf, and gave it to the servant. He hurried to dress it. ⁸ He took butter, milk, and the calf which he had dressed, and set it before them. He stood by them under the tree, and they ate.
⁹ They asked him, "Where is Sarah, your wife?"
He said, "There, in the tent."
¹⁰ He said, "I will certainly return to you at about this time next year; and behold, Sarah your wife will have a son."
Sarah heard in the tent door, which was behind him. ¹¹ Now Abraham and Sarah were old, well advanced in age. Sarah had passed the age of childbearing. ¹² Sarah laughed within herself, saying, "After I have grown old will I have pleasure, my lord being old also?"
¹³ Yahweh said to Abraham, "Why did Sarah laugh, saying, 'Will I really bear a child when I am old?' ¹⁴ Is anything too hard for Yahweh? At the set time I will return to you, when the season comes around, and Sarah will have a son."

¹⁵ Then Sarah denied it, saying, "I didn't laugh," for she was afraid.
He said, "No, but you did laugh."

Responsorial Psalm: Luke 1: 46-47, 48-49, 50 and 53, 54-55

⁴⁶ Mary said,
"My soul magnifies the Lord.
⁴⁷ My spirit has rejoiced in God my Savior,
⁴⁸ for he has looked at the humble state of his servant.
For behold, from now on, all generations will call me blessed.
⁴⁹ For he who is mighty has done great things for me.
Holy is his name.
⁵⁰ His mercy is for generations and generations on those who fear him.
⁵³ He has filled the hungry with good things.
He has sent the rich away empty.
⁵⁴ He has given help to Israel, his servant, that he might remember mercy,
⁵⁵ as he spoke to our fathers,
to Abraham and his offspring§ forever."

Gospel: Luke 2: 41-51

⁴¹ His parents went every year to Jerusalem at the feast of the Passover. ⁴² When he was twelve years old, they went up to Jerusalem according to the custom of the feast; ⁴³ and when they had fulfilled the days, as they were returning, the boy Jesus stayed behind in Jerusalem. Joseph and his mother didn't know it, ⁴⁴ but supposing him to be in the company, they went a day's journey; and they looked for him among their relatives and acquaintances. ⁴⁵ When they didn't find him, they returned to Jerusalem, looking for him. ⁴⁶ After three days they found him in the temple, sitting in the middle of the teachers, both listening to them and asking them questions. ⁴⁷ All who heard him were amazed at his understanding and his answers. ⁴⁸ When they saw him, they were astonished; and his mother said to him, "Son, why have you treated us this way? Behold, your father and I were anxiously looking for you."
⁴⁹ He said to them, "Why were you looking for me? Didn't you know that I must be in my Father's house?" ⁵⁰ They didn't understand the saying which he spoke to them. ⁵¹ And he went down with them and came to Nazareth. He was subject to them, and his mother kept all these sayings in her heart.

1. Invite the Holy Spirit into this reading, asking the Author of Scripture to speak to you through His Word
2. Read today's passage as many times as you need, take your time

3. Write down (below) what the Lord is saying to you today
4. Live with this Word in your heart through the day

___

Sunday, June 29, 2025
SAINTS PETER AND PAUL, APOSTLES

First Reading: Acts 12: 1-11

¹ Now about that time, King Herod stretched out his hands to oppress some of the assembly. ² He killed James, the brother of John, with the sword. ³ When he saw that it pleased the Jews, he proceeded to seize Peter also. This was during the days of unleavened bread. ⁴ When he had arrested him, he put him in prison and delivered him to four squads of four soldiers each to guard him, intending to bring him out to the people after the Passover. ⁵ Peter therefore was kept in the prison, but constant prayer was made by the assembly to God for him. ⁶ The same night when Herod was about to bring him out, Peter was sleeping between two soldiers, bound with two chains. Guards in front of the door kept the prison.
⁷ And behold, an angel of the Lord stood by him, and a light shone in the cell. He struck Peter on the side and woke him up, saying, "Stand up quickly!" His chains fell off his hands. ⁸ The angel said to him, "Get dressed and put on your sandals." He did so. He said to him, "Put on your cloak and follow me." ⁹ And he went out and followed him. He didn't know that what was being done by the angel was real, but thought he saw a vision. ¹⁰ When they were past the first and the second guard, they came to the iron gate that leads into the city, which opened to them by itself. They went out and went down one street, and immediately the angel departed from him.
¹¹ When Peter had come to himself, he said, "Now I truly know that the Lord has sent out his angel and delivered me out of the hand of Herod, and from everything the Jewish people were expecting."

Responsorial Psalm: Psalms 34: 2-9

² My soul shall boast in Yahweh.
The humble shall hear of it and be glad.
³ Oh magnify Yahweh with me.
Let's exalt his name together.

⁴ I sought Yahweh, and he answered me,
and delivered me from all my fears.
⁵ They looked to him, and were radiant.
Their faces shall never be covered with shame.
⁶ This poor man cried, and Yahweh heard him,
and saved him out of all his troubles.
⁷ Yahweh's angel encamps around those who fear him,
and delivers them.
⁸ Oh taste and see that Yahweh is good.
Blessed is the man who takes refuge in him.
⁹ Oh fear Yahweh, you his saints,
for there is no lack with those who fear him.

Second Reading: Second Timothy 4: 6-8, 17-18

⁶ For I am already being offered, and the time of my departure has come. ⁷ I have fought the good fight. I have finished the course. I have kept the faith. ⁸ From now on, the crown of righteousness is stored up for me, which the Lord, the righteous judge, will give to me on that day; and not to me only, but also to all those who have loved his appearing.
¹⁷ But the Lord stood by me and strengthened me, that through me the message might be fully proclaimed, and that all the Gentiles might hear. So I was delivered out of the mouth of the lion. ¹⁸ And the Lord will deliver me from every evil work and will preserve me for his heavenly Kingdom. To him be the glory forever and ever. Amen.

Gospel: Matthew 16: 13-19

¹³ Now when Jesus came into the parts of Caesarea Philippi, he asked his disciples, saying, "Who do men say that I, the Son of Man, am?"
¹⁴ They said, "Some say John the Baptizer, some, Elijah, and others, Jeremiah or one of the prophets."
¹⁵ He said to them, "But who do you say that I am?"
¹⁶ Simon Peter answered, "You are the Christ, the Son of the living God."
¹⁷ Jesus answered him, "Blessed are you, Simon Bar Jonah, for flesh and blood has not revealed this to you, but my Father who is in heaven. ¹⁸ I also tell you that you are Peter,⁺ and on this rock ⁺ I will build my assembly, and the gates of Hades§ will not prevail against it. ¹⁹ I will give to you the keys of the Kingdom of Heaven, and whatever you bind on earth will have been bound in heaven; and whatever you release on earth will have been released in heaven."

1. Invite the Holy Spirit into this reading, asking the Author of Scripture to speak to you through His Word
2. Read today's passage as many times as you need, take your time
3. Write down (below) what the Lord is saying to you today
4. Live with this Word in your heart through the day

Monday, June 30, 2025
The First Martyrs of the Holy Roman Church

First Reading: Genesis 18: 16-33

16 The men rose up from there, and looked toward Sodom. Abraham went with them to see them on their way. 17 Yahweh said, "Will I hide from Abraham what I do, 18 since Abraham will surely become a great and mighty nation, and all the nations of the earth will be blessed in him? 19 For I have known him, to the end that he may command his children and his household after him, that they may keep the way of Yahweh, to do righteousness and justice; to the end that Yahweh may bring on Abraham that which he has spoken of him." 20 Yahweh said, "Because the cry of Sodom and Gomorrah is great, and because their sin is very grievous, 21 I will go down now, and see whether their deeds are as bad as the reports which have come to me. If not, I will know."

22 The men turned from there, and went toward Sodom, but Abraham stood yet before Yahweh. 23 Abraham came near, and said, "Will you consume the righteous with the wicked? 24 What if there are fifty righteous within the city? Will you consume and not spare the place for the fifty righteous who are in it? 25 May it be far from you to do things like that, to kill the righteous with the wicked, so that the righteous should be like the wicked. May that be far from you. Shouldn't the Judge of all the earth do right?"

26 Yahweh said, "If I find in Sodom fifty righteous within the city, then I will spare the whole place for their sake." 27 Abraham answered, "See now, I have taken it on myself to speak to the Lord, although I am dust and ashes. 28 What if there will lack five of the fifty righteous? Will you destroy all the city for lack of five?"

He said, "I will not destroy it if I find forty-five there."

29 He spoke to him yet again, and said, "What if there are forty found there?"

He said, "I will not do it for the forty's sake."

30 He said, "Oh don't let the Lord be angry, and I will speak. What if there are thirty found there?"

He said, "I will not do it if I find thirty there."
³¹ He said, "See now, I have taken it on myself to speak to the Lord. What if there are twenty found there?"
He said, "I will not destroy it for the twenty's sake."
³² He said, "Oh don't let the Lord be angry, and I will speak just once more. What if ten are found there?"
He said, "I will not destroy it for the ten's sake."
³³ Yahweh went his way as soon as he had finished communing with Abraham, and Abraham returned to his place.

Responsorial Psalm: Psalms 103: 1b-2, 3-4, 8-9, 10-11

¹ᵇ All that is within me, praise his holy name!
² Praise Yahweh, my soul,
and don't forget all his benefits,
³ who forgives all your sins,
who heals all your diseases,
⁴ who redeems your life from destruction,
who crowns you with loving kindness and tender mercies,
⁸ Yahweh is merciful and gracious,
slow to anger, and abundant in loving kindness.
⁹ He will not always accuse;
neither will he stay angry forever.
¹⁰ He has not dealt with us according to our sins,
nor repaid us for our iniquities.
¹¹ For as the heavens are high above the earth,
so great is his loving kindness toward those who fear him.

Gospel: Matthew 8: 18-22

¹⁸ Now when Jesus saw great multitudes around him, he gave the order to depart to the other side.
¹⁹ A scribe came and said to him, "Teacher, I will follow you wherever you go."
²⁰ Jesus said to him, "The foxes have holes and the birds of the sky have nests, but the Son of Man has nowhere to lay his head."
²¹ Another of his disciples said to him, "Lord, allow me first to go and bury my father."
²² But Jesus said to him, "Follow me, and leave the dead to bury their own dead."

1. Invite the Holy Spirit into this reading, asking the Author of Scripture to speak to you through His Word

2. Read today's passage as many times as you need, take your time
3. Write down (below) what the Lord is saying to you today
4. Live with this Word in your heart through the day

Tuesday, July 1, 2025
Saint Junípero Serra, Priest

First Reading: Genesis 19: 15-29

¹⁵ When the morning came, then the angels hurried Lot, saying, "Get up! Take your wife and your two daughters who are here, lest you be consumed in the iniquity of the city." ¹⁶ But he lingered; and the men grabbed his hand, his wife's hand, and his two daughters' hands, Yahweh being merciful to him; and they took him out, and set him outside of the city. ¹⁷ It came to pass, when they had taken them out, that he said, "Escape for your life! Don't look behind you, and don't stay anywhere in the plain. Escape to the mountains, lest you be consumed!"
¹⁸ Lot said to them, "Oh, not so, my lord. ¹⁹ See now, your servant has found favor in your sight, and you have magnified your loving kindness, which you have shown to me in saving my life. I can't escape to the mountain, lest evil overtake me, and I die. ²⁰ See now, this city is near to flee to, and it is a little one. Oh let me escape there (isn't it a little one?), and my soul will live."
²¹ He said to him, "Behold, I have granted your request concerning this thing also, that I will not overthrow the city of which you have spoken. ²² Hurry, escape there, for I can't do anything until you get there." Therefore the name of the city was called Zoar.‡
²³ The sun had risen on the earth when Lot came to Zoar. ²⁴ Then Yahweh rained on Sodom and on Gomorrah sulfur and fire from Yahweh out of the sky. ²⁵ He overthrew those cities, all the plain, all the inhabitants of the cities, and that which grew on the ground. ²⁶ But Lot's wife looked back from behind him, and she became a pillar of salt.
²⁷ Abraham went up early in the morning to the place where he had stood before Yahweh. ²⁸ He looked toward Sodom and Gomorrah, and toward all the land of the plain, and saw that the smoke of the land went up as the smoke of a furnace.
²⁹ When God destroyed the cities of the plain, God remembered Abraham, and sent Lot out of the middle of the overthrow, when he overthrew the cities in which Lot lived.

Responsorial Psalm: Psalms 26: 2-3, 9-10, 11-12

² Examine me, Yahweh, and prove me.
Try my heart and my mind.
³ For your loving kindness is before my eyes.
I have walked in your truth.
⁹ Don't gather my soul with sinners,
nor my life with bloodthirsty men
¹⁰ in whose hands is wickedness;
their right hand is full of bribes.
¹¹ But as for me, I will walk in my integrity.
Redeem me, and be merciful to me.
¹² My foot stands in an even place.
In the congregations I will bless Yahweh.

Gospel: Matthew 8: 23-27

²³ When he got into a boat, his disciples followed him. ²⁴ Behold, a violent storm came up on the sea, so much that the boat was covered with the waves; but he was asleep. ²⁵ The disciples came to him and woke him up, saying, "Save us, Lord! We are dying!"
²⁶ He said to them, "Why are you fearful, O you of little faith?" Then he got up, rebuked the wind and the sea, and there was a great calm.
²⁷ The men marveled, saying, "What kind of man is this, that even the wind and the sea obey him?"

1. Invite the Holy Spirit into this reading, asking the Author of Scripture to speak to you through His Word
2. Read today's passage as many times as you need, take your time
3. Write down (below) what the Lord is saying to you today
4. Live with this Word in your heart through the day

Wednesday, July 2, 2025

First Reading: Genesis 21: 5, 8-20a

⁵ Abraham was one hundred years old when his son, Isaac, was born to him.

⁸ The child grew and was weaned. Abraham made a great feast on the day that Isaac was weaned. ⁹ Sarah saw the son of Hagar the Egyptian, whom she had borne to Abraham, mocking. ¹⁰ Therefore she said to Abraham, "Cast out this servant and her son! For the son of this servant will not be heir with my son, Isaac."

¹¹ The thing was very grievous in Abraham's sight on account of his son. ¹² God said to Abraham, "Don't let it be grievous in your sight because of the boy, and because of your servant. In all that Sarah says to you, listen to her voice. For your offspring will be named through Isaac. ¹³ I will also make a nation of the son of the servant, because he is your child." ¹⁴ Abraham rose up early in the morning, and took bread and a container of water, and gave it to Hagar, putting it on her shoulder; and gave her the child, and sent her away. She departed, and wandered in the wilderness of Beersheba. ¹⁵ The water in the container was spent, and she put the child under one of the shrubs. ¹⁶ She went and sat down opposite him, a good way off, about a bow shot away. For she said, "Don't let me see the death of the child." She sat opposite him, and lifted up her voice, and wept. ¹⁷ God heard the voice of the boy.

The angel of God called to Hagar out of the sky, and said to her, "What troubles you, Hagar? Don't be afraid. For God has heard the voice of the boy where he is. ¹⁸ Get up, lift up the boy, and hold him with your hand. For I will make him a great nation."

¹⁹ God opened her eyes, and she saw a well of water. She went, filled the container with water, and gave the boy a drink.

²⁰ᵃ God was with the boy, and he grew.

Responsorial Psalm: Psalms 34: 7-8, 10-11, 12-13

⁷ Yahweh's angel encamps around those who fear him,
and delivers them.
⁸ Oh taste and see that Yahweh is good.
Blessed is the man who takes refuge in him.
¹⁰ The young lions do lack, and suffer hunger,
but those who seek Yahweh shall not lack any good thing.
¹¹ Come, you children, listen to me.
I will teach you the fear of Yahweh.
¹² Who is someone who desires life,
and loves many days, that he may see good?
¹³ Keep your tongue from evil,
and your lips from speaking lies.

Gospel: Matthew 8: 28-34

²⁸ When he came to the other side, into the country of the Gergesenes,⁺ two people possessed by demons met him there, coming out of the tombs, exceedingly fierce, so that nobody could pass that way. ²⁹ Behold, they cried out, saying, "What do we have to do with you, Jesus, Son of God? Have you come here to torment us before the time?" ³⁰ Now there was a herd of many pigs feeding far away from them. ³¹ The demons begged him, saying, "If you cast us out, permit us to go away into the herd of pigs."
³² He said to them, "Go!"
They came out and went into the herd of pigs; and behold, the whole herd of pigs rushed down the cliff into the sea and died in the water. ³³ Those who fed them fled and went away into the city and told everything, including what happened to those who were possessed with demons. ³⁴ Behold, all the city came out to meet Jesus. When they saw him, they begged that he would depart from their borders.

1. Invite the Holy Spirit into this reading, asking the Author of Scripture to speak to you through His Word
2. Read today's passage as many times as you need, take your time
3. Write down (below) what the Lord is saying to you today
4. Live with this Word in your heart through the day

___

___

Thursday, July 3, 2025
Saint Thomas, Apostle

First Reading: Ephesians 2: 19-22

¹⁹ So then you are no longer strangers and foreigners, but you are fellow citizens with the saints and of the household of God, ²⁰ being built on the foundation of the apostles and prophets, Christ Jesus himself being the chief cornerstone; ²¹ in whom the whole building, fitted together, grows into a holy temple in the Lord; ²² in whom you also are built together for a habitation of God in the Spirit.

Responsorial Psalm: Psalms 117: 1bc, 2

¹ Praise Yahweh, all you nations!
Extol him, all you peoples!
² For his loving kindness is great toward us.

Yahweh's faithfulness endures forever.
Praise Yah!

Gospel: John 20: 24-29

24 But Thomas, one of the twelve, called Didymus,§ wasn't with them when Jesus came. 25 The other disciples therefore said to him, "We have seen the Lord!"
But he said to them, "Unless I see in his hands the print of the nails, put my finger into the print of the nails, and put my hand into his side, I will not believe."
26 After eight days, again his disciples were inside and Thomas was with them. Jesus came, the doors being locked, and stood in the middle, and said, "Peace be to you." 27 Then he said to Thomas, "Reach here your finger, and see my hands. Reach here your hand, and put it into my side. Don't be unbelieving, but believing."
28 Thomas answered him, "My Lord and my God!"
29 Jesus said to him, "Because you have seen me,‡ you have believed. Blessed are those who have not seen and have believed."

1. Invite the Holy Spirit into this reading, asking the Author of Scripture to speak to you through His Word
2. Read today's passage as many times as you need, take your time
3. Write down (below) what the Lord is saying to you today
4. Live with this Word in your heart through the day

Friday, July 4, 2025
USA: Independence Day

First Reading: Genesis 23: 1-4, 19; 24: 1-8, 62-67

1 Sarah lived one hundred twenty-seven years. This was the length of Sarah's life. 2 Sarah died in Kiriath Arba (also called Hebron), in the land of Canaan. Abraham came to mourn for Sarah, and to weep for her. 3 Abraham rose up from before his dead and spoke to the children of Heth, saying, 4 "I am a stranger and a foreigner living with you. Give me a possession of a burying-place with you, that I may bury my dead out of my sight."
19 After this, Abraham buried Sarah his wife in the cave of the field of Machpelah before Mamre (that is, Hebron), in the land of Canaan.

¹Abraham was old, and well advanced in age. Yahweh had blessed Abraham in all things. ² Abraham said to his servant, the elder of his house, who ruled over all that he had, "Please put your hand under my thigh. ³ I will make you swear by Yahweh, the God of heaven and the God of the earth, that you shall not take a wife for my son of the daughters of the Canaanites, among whom I live. ⁴ But you shall go to my country, and to my relatives, and take a wife for my son Isaac."

⁵ The servant said to him, "What if the woman isn't willing to follow me to this land? Must I bring your son again to the land you came from?"

⁶ Abraham said to him, "Beware that you don't bring my son there again. ⁷ Yahweh, the God of heaven—who took me from my father's house, and from the land of my birth, who spoke to me, and who swore to me, saying, 'I will give this land to your offspring—he will send his angel before you, and you shall take a wife for my son from there. ⁸ If the woman isn't willing to follow you, then you shall be clear from this oath to me. Only you shall not bring my son there again."

⁶² Isaac came from the way of Beer Lahai Roi, for he lived in the land of the South. ⁶³ Isaac went out to meditate in the field at the evening. He lifted up his eyes and looked. Behold, there were camels coming. ⁶⁴ Rebekah lifted up her eyes, and when she saw Isaac, she got off the camel. ⁶⁵ She said to the servant, "Who is the man who is walking in the field to meet us?"

The servant said, "It is my master."

She took her veil, and covered herself. ⁶⁶ The servant told Isaac all the things that he had done. ⁶⁷ Isaac brought her into his mother Sarah's tent, and took Rebekah, and she became his wife. He loved her. So Isaac was comforted after his mother's death.

Responsorial Psalm: Psalms 106: 1b-5

¹ᵇ Give thanks to Yahweh, for he is good,
for his loving kindness endures forever.
² Who can utter the mighty acts of Yahweh,
or fully declare all his praise?
³ Blessed are those who keep justice.
Blessed is one who does what is right at all times.
⁴ Remember me, Yahweh, with the favor that you show to your people.
Visit me with your salvation,
⁵ that I may see the prosperity of your chosen,
that I may rejoice in the gladness of your nation,
that I may glory with your inheritance.

Gospel: Matthew 9: 9-13

⁹ As Jesus passed by from there, he saw a man called Matthew sitting at the tax collection office. He said to him, "Follow me." He got up and followed him. ¹⁰ As he sat in the house, behold, many tax collectors and sinners came and sat down with Jesus and his disciples. ¹¹ When the Pharisees saw it, they said to his disciples, "Why does your teacher eat with tax collectors and sinners?"

¹² When Jesus heard it, he said to them, "Those who are healthy have no need for a physician, but those who are sick do. ¹³ But you go and learn what this means: 'I desire mercy, and not sacrifice,' for I came not to call the righteous, but sinners to repentance."

1. Invite the Holy Spirit into this reading, asking the Author of Scripture to speak to you through His Word
2. Read today's passage as many times as you need, take your time
3. Write down (below) what the Lord is saying to you today
4. Live with this Word in your heart through the day

Saturday, July 5, 2025
Saint Anthony Zaccaria, Priest;
Saint Elizabeth of Portugal

First Reading: Genesis 27: 1-5, 15-29

¹ When Isaac was old, and his eyes were dim, so that he could not see, he called Esau his elder son, and said to him, "My son?"
He said to him, "Here I am."
² He said, "See now, I am old. I don't know the day of my death. ³ Now therefore, please take your weapons, your quiver and your bow, and go out to the field, and get me venison. ⁴ Make me savory food, such as I love, and bring it to me, that I may eat, and that my soul may bless you before I die."
⁵ Rebekah heard when Isaac spoke to Esau his son. Esau went to the field to hunt for venison, and to bring it.
¹⁵ Rebekah took the good clothes of Esau, her elder son, which were with her in the house, and put them on Jacob, her younger son. ¹⁶ She put the skins of the young goats on his hands, and on the smooth of his neck. ¹⁷ She gave the savory food and the bread, which she had prepared, into the hand of her son Jacob.
¹⁸ He came to his father, and said, "My father?"

He said, "Here I am. Who are you, my son?"
¹⁹ Jacob said to his father, "I am Esau your firstborn. I have done what you asked me to do. Please arise, sit and eat of my venison, that your soul may bless me."
²⁰ Isaac said to his son, "How is it that you have found it so quickly, my son?"
He said, "Because Yahweh your God gave me success."
²¹ Isaac said to Jacob, "Please come near, that I may feel you, my son, whether you are really my son Esau or not."
²² Jacob went near to Isaac his father. He felt him, and said, "The voice is Jacob's voice, but the hands are the hands of Esau." ²³ He didn't recognize him, because his hands were hairy, like his brother Esau's hands. So he blessed him. ²⁴ He said, "Are you really my son Esau?"
He said, "I am."
²⁵ He said, "Bring it near to me, and I will eat of my son's venison, that my soul may bless you."
He brought it near to him, and he ate. He brought him wine, and he drank. ²⁶ His father Isaac said to him, "Come near now, and kiss me, my son." ²⁷ He came near, and kissed him. He smelled the smell of his clothing, and blessed him, and said,

"Behold, the smell of my son
is as the smell of a field which Yahweh has blessed.
²⁸ God give you of the dew of the sky,
of the fatness of the earth,
and plenty of grain and new wine.
²⁹ Let peoples serve you,
and nations bow down to you.
Be lord over your brothers.
Let your mother's sons bow down to you.
Cursed be everyone who curses you.
Blessed be everyone who blesses you."

Responsorial Psalm: Psalms 135: 1b-2, 3-4, 5-6

¹ᵇ Praise Yahweh's name!
Praise him, you servants of Yahweh,
² you who stand in Yahweh's house,
in the courts of our God's house.
³ Praise Yah, for Yahweh is good.
Sing praises to his name, for that is pleasant.
⁴ For Yah has chosen Jacob for himself,
Israel for his own possession.
⁵ For I know that Yahweh is great,
that our Lord is above all gods.

⁶ Whatever Yahweh pleased, that he has done,
in heaven and in earth, in the seas and in all deeps.

Gospel: Matthew 9: 14-17

¹⁴ Then John's disciples came to him, saying, "Why do we and the Pharisees fast often, but your disciples don't fast?"
¹⁵ Jesus said to them, "Can the friends of the bridegroom mourn as long as the bridegroom is with them? But the days will come when the bridegroom will be taken away from them, and then they will fast. ¹⁶ No one puts a piece of unshrunk cloth on an old garment; for the patch would tear away from the garment, and a worse hole is made. ¹⁷ Neither do people put new wine into old wine skins, or else the skins would burst, and the wine be spilled, and the skins ruined. No, they put new wine into fresh wine skins, and both are preserved."

1. Invite the Holy Spirit into this reading, asking the Author of Scripture to speak to you through His Word
2. Read today's passage as many times as you need, take your time
3. Write down (below) what the Lord is saying to you today
4. Live with this Word in your heart through the day

Sunday, July 6, 2025
FOURTEENTH SUNDAY IN ORDINARY TIME

First Reading: Isaiah 66: 10-14c

¹⁰ "Rejoice with Jerusalem, and be glad for her, all you who love her.
Rejoice for joy with her, all you who mourn over her;
¹¹ that you may nurse and be satisfied at the comforting breasts;
that you may drink deeply,
and be delighted with the abundance of her glory."
¹² For Yahweh says, "Behold, I will extend peace to her like a river,
and the glory of the nations like an overflowing stream,
and you will nurse.
You will be carried on her side,
and will be dandled on her knees.

¹³ As one whom his mother comforts,
so I will comfort you.
You will be comforted in Jerusalem."
¹⁴ You will see it, and your heart shall rejoice,
and your bones will flourish like the tender grass.
Yahweh's hand will be known among his servants;

Responsorial Psalm: Psalms 66: 1-7, 16 and 20

¹ Make a joyful shout to God, all the earth!
² Sing to the glory of his name!
Offer glory and praise!
³ Tell God, "How awesome are your deeds!
Through the greatness of your power, your enemies submit themselves to you.
⁴ All the earth will worship you,
and will sing to you;
they will sing to your name."
⁵ Come, and see God's deeds—
awesome work on behalf of the children of men.
⁶ He turned the sea into dry land.
They went through the river on foot.
There, we rejoiced in him.
⁷ He rules by his might forever.
His eyes watch the nations.
Don't let the rebellious rise up against him.
¹⁶ Come and hear, all you who fear God.
I will declare what he has done for my soul.
²⁰ Blessed be God, who has not turned away my prayer,
nor his loving kindness from me.

Second Reading: Galatians 6: 14-18

¹⁴ But far be it from me to boast except in the cross of our Lord Jesus Christ, through which the world has been crucified to me, and I to the world. ¹⁵ For in Christ Jesus neither is circumcision anything, nor uncircumcision, but a new creation. ¹⁶ As many as walk by this rule, peace and mercy be on them, and on God's Israel.
¹⁷ From now on, let no one cause me any trouble, for I bear the marks of the Lord Jesus branded on my body.
¹⁸ The grace of our Lord Jesus Christ be with your spirit, brothers. Amen.

Gospel: Luke 10: 1-12, 17-20

¹ Now after these things, the Lord also appointed seventy others, and sent them two by two ahead of him into every city and place where he was about to come. ² Then he said to them, "The harvest is indeed plentiful, but the laborers are few. Pray therefore to the Lord of the harvest, that he may send out laborers into his harvest. ³ Go your ways. Behold, I send you out as lambs among wolves. ⁴ Carry no purse, nor wallet, nor sandals. Greet no one on the way. ⁵ Into whatever house you enter, first say, 'Peace be to this house.' ⁶ If a son of peace is there, your peace will rest on him; but if not, it will return to you. ⁷ Remain in that same house, eating and drinking the things they give, for the laborer is worthy of his wages. Don't go from house to house. ⁸ Into whatever city you enter and they receive you, eat the things that are set before you. ⁹ Heal the sick who are there and tell them, 'God's Kingdom has come near to you.' ¹⁰ But into whatever city you enter and they don't receive you, go out into its streets and say, ¹¹ 'Even the dust from your city that clings to us, we wipe off against you. Nevertheless know this, that God's Kingdom has come near to you.' ¹² I tell you, it will be more tolerable in that day for Sodom than for that city.
¹⁷ The seventy returned with joy, saying, "Lord, even the demons are subject to us in your name!"
¹⁸ He said to them, "I saw Satan having fallen like lightning from heaven. ¹⁹ Behold, I give you authority to tread on serpents and scorpions, and over all the power of the enemy. Nothing will in any way hurt you. ²⁰ Nevertheless, don't rejoice in this, that the spirits are subject to you, but rejoice that your names are written in heaven."

1. Invite the Holy Spirit into this reading, asking the Author of Scripture to speak to you through His Word
2. Read today's passage as many times as you need, take your time
3. Write down (below) what the Lord is saying to you today
4. Live with this Word in your heart through the day

Monday, July 7, 2025

First Reading: Genesis 28: 10-22a

¹⁰ Jacob went out from Beersheba, and went toward Haran. ¹¹ He came to a certain place, and stayed there all night, because the sun had set. He took one of the stones of the place,

and put it under his head, and lay down in that place to sleep. ¹² He dreamed and saw a stairway set upon the earth, and its top reached to heaven. Behold, the angels of God were ascending and descending on it. ¹³ Behold, Yahweh stood above it, and said, "I am Yahweh, the God of Abraham your father, and the God of Isaac. I will give the land you lie on to you and to your offspring. ¹⁴ Your offspring will be as the dust of the earth, and you will spread abroad to the west, and to the east, and to the north, and to the south. In you and in your offspring, all the families of the earth will be blessed. ¹⁵ Behold, I am with you, and will keep you, wherever you go, and will bring you again into this land. For I will not leave you until I have done that which I have spoken of to you."

¹⁶ Jacob awakened out of his sleep, and he said, "Surely Yahweh is in this place, and I didn't know it." ¹⁷ He was afraid, and said, "How awesome this place is! This is none other than God's house, and this is the gate of heaven."

¹⁸ Jacob rose up early in the morning, and took the stone that he had put under his head, and set it up for a pillar, and poured oil on its top. ¹⁹ He called the name of that place Bethel, but the name of the city was Luz at the first. ²⁰ Jacob vowed a vow, saying, "If God will be with me, and will keep me in this way that I go, and will give me bread to eat, and clothing to put on, ²¹ so that I come again to my father's house in peace, and Yahweh will be my God, ²²ᵃ then this stone, which I have set up for a pillar, will be God's house.

Responsorial Psalm: Psalms 91: 1-2, 3-4, 14-15ab

¹ He who dwells in the secret place of the Most High
will rest in the shadow of the Almighty.
² I will say of Yahweh, "He is my refuge and my fortress;
my God, in whom I trust."
³ For he will deliver you from the snare of the fowler,
and from the deadly pestilence.
⁴ He will cover you with his feathers.
Under his wings you will take refuge.
His faithfulness is your shield and rampart.
¹⁴ "Because he has set his love on me, therefore I will deliver him.
I will set him on high, because he has known my name.
¹⁵ He will call on me, and I will answer him.
I will be with him in trouble.

Gospel: Matthew 9: 18-26

¹⁸ While he told these things to them, behold, a ruler came and worshiped him, saying, "My daughter has just died, but come and lay your hand on her, and she will live."

19 Jesus got up and followed him, as did his disciples. 20 Behold, a woman who had a discharge of blood for twelve years came behind him, and touched the fringe‡ of his garment; 21 for she said within herself, "If I just touch his garment, I will be made well." 22 But Jesus, turning around and seeing her, said, "Daughter, cheer up! Your faith has made you well." And the woman was made well from that hour.
23 When Jesus came into the ruler's house and saw the flute players and the crowd in noisy disorder, 24 he said to them, "Make room, because the girl isn't dead, but sleeping."
They were ridiculing him. 25 But when the crowd was sent out, he entered in, took her by the hand, and the girl arose. 26 The report of this went out into all that land.

1. Invite the Holy Spirit into this reading, asking the Author of Scripture to speak to you through His Word
2. Read today's passage as many times as you need, take your time
3. Write down (below) what the Lord is saying to you today
4. Live with this Word in your heart through the day

Tuesday, July 8, 2025

First Reading: Genesis 32: 23-32

23 He took them, and sent them over the stream, and sent over that which he had. 24 Jacob was left alone, and wrestled with a man there until the breaking of the day. 25 When he saw that he didn't prevail against him, the man touched the hollow of his thigh, and the hollow of Jacob's thigh was strained as he wrestled. 26 The man said, "Let me go, for the day breaks."
Jacob said, "I won't let you go unless you bless me."
27 He said to him, "What is your name?"
He said, "Jacob".
28 He said, "Your name will no longer be called Jacob, but Israel; for you have fought with God and with men, and have prevailed."
29 Jacob asked him, "Please tell me your name."
He said, "Why is it that you ask what my name is?" So he blessed him there.
30 Jacob called the name of the place Peniel;‡ for he said, "I have seen God face to face, and my life is preserved." 31 The sun rose on him as he passed over Peniel, and he limped because of his thigh. 32 Therefore the children of Israel don't eat the sinew of the hip, which

is on the hollow of the thigh, to this day, because he touched the hollow of Jacob's thigh in the sinew of the hip.

Responsorial Psalm: Psalms 17: 1b, 2-3, 6-7ab, 8b and 15

¹ᵇ Give ear to my prayer that doesn't go out of deceitful lips.
² Let my sentence come out of your presence.
Let your eyes look on equity.
³ You have proved my heart.
You have visited me in the night.
You have tried me, and found nothing.
I have resolved that my mouth shall not disobey.
⁶ I have called on you, for you will answer me, God.
Turn your ear to me.
Hear my speech.
⁷ Show your marvelous loving kindness,
you who save those who take refuge by your right hand from their enemies.
⁸ᵇ Hide me under the shadow of your wings,
¹⁵ As for me, I shall see your face in righteousness.
I shall be satisfied, when I awake, with seeing your form.

Gospel: Matthew 9: 32-38

³² As they went out, behold, a mute man who was demon possessed was brought to him. ³³ When the demon was cast out, the mute man spoke. The multitudes marveled, saying, "Nothing like this has ever been seen in Israel!"
³⁴ But the Pharisees said, "By the prince of the demons, he casts out demons."
³⁵ Jesus went about all the cities and the villages, teaching in their synagogues and preaching the Good News of the Kingdom, and healing every disease and every sickness among the people. ³⁶ But when he saw the multitudes, he was moved with compassion for them because they were harassed§ and scattered, like sheep without a shepherd. ³⁷ Then he said to his disciples, "The harvest indeed is plentiful, but the laborers are few. ³⁸ Pray therefore that the Lord of the harvest will send out laborers into his harvest."

1. Invite the Holy Spirit into this reading, asking the Author of Scripture to speak to you through His Word
2. Read today's passage as many times as you need, take your time
3. Write down (below) what the Lord is saying to you today
4. Live with this Word in your heart through the day

Wednesday, July 9, 2025
Saint Augustine Zhao Rong, Priest, and Companions, Martyrs

First Reading: Genesis 41: 55-57; 42: 5-7a, 17-24a

55 When all the land of Egypt was famished, the people cried to Pharaoh for bread, and Pharaoh said to all the Egyptians, "Go to Joseph. What he says to you, do." 56 The famine was over all the surface of the earth. Joseph opened all the store houses, and sold to the Egyptians. The famine was severe in the land of Egypt. 57 All countries came into Egypt, to Joseph, to buy grain, because the famine was severe in all the earth.

5 The sons of Israel came to buy among those who came, for the famine was in the land of Canaan. 6 Joseph was the governor over the land. It was he who sold to all the people of the land. Joseph's brothers came, and bowed themselves down to him with their faces to the earth. 7a Joseph saw his brothers, and he recognized them, but acted like a stranger to them, and spoke roughly with them. He said to them, "Where did you come from?"

17 He put them all together into custody for three days.

18 Joseph said to them the third day, "Do this, and live, for I fear God. 19 If you are honest men, then let one of your brothers be bound in your prison; but you go, carry grain for the famine of your houses. 20 Bring your youngest brother to me; so will your words be verified, and you won't die."

They did so. 21 They said to one another, "We are certainly guilty concerning our brother, in that we saw the distress of his soul, when he begged us, and we wouldn't listen. Therefore this distress has come upon us." 22 Reuben answered them, saying, "Didn't I tell you, saying, 'Don't sin against the child,' and you wouldn't listen? Therefore also, behold, his blood is required." 23 They didn't know that Joseph understood them; for there was an interpreter between them. 24a He turned himself away from them, and wept.

Responsorial Psalm: Psalms 33: 2-3, 10-11, 18-19

2 Give thanks to Yahweh with the lyre.
Sing praises to him with the harp of ten strings.
3 Sing to him a new song.
Play skillfully with a shout of joy!
10 Yahweh brings the counsel of the nations to nothing.
He makes the thoughts of the peoples to be of no effect.

¹¹ The counsel of Yahweh stands fast forever,
the thoughts of his heart to all generations.
¹⁸ Behold, Yahweh's eye is on those who fear him,
on those who hope in his loving kindness,
¹⁹ to deliver their soul from death,
to keep them alive in famine.

Gospel: Matthew 10: 1-7

¹ He called to himself his twelve disciples, and gave them authority over unclean spirits, to cast them out, and to heal every disease and every sickness. ² Now the names of the twelve apostles are these. The first, Simon, who is called Peter; Andrew, his brother; James the son of Zebedee; John, his brother; ³ Philip; Bartholomew; Thomas; Matthew the tax collector; James the son of Alphaeus; Lebbaeus, who was also called⸤ Thaddaeus; ⁴ Simon the Zealot; and Judas Iscariot, who also betrayed him.
⁵ Jesus sent these twelve out and commanded them, saying, "Don't go among the Gentiles, and don't enter into any city of the Samaritans. ⁶ Rather, go to the lost sheep of the house of Israel. ⁷ As you go, preach, saying, 'The Kingdom of Heaven is at hand!'

1. Invite the Holy Spirit into this reading, asking the Author of Scripture to speak to you through His Word
2. Read today's passage as many times as you need, take your time
3. Write down (below) what the Lord is saying to you today
4. Live with this Word in your heart through the day

_____

_____

Thursday, July 10, 2025

First Reading: Genesis 44: 18-21, 23-29; 45: 1-5

¹⁸ Then Judah came near to him, and said, "Oh, my lord, please let your servant speak a word in my lord's ears, and don't let your anger burn against your servant; for you are even as Pharaoh. ¹⁹ My lord asked his servants, saying, 'Have you a father, or a brother?' ²⁰ We said to my lord, 'We have a father, an old man, and a child of his old age, a little one; and his brother is dead, and he alone is left of his mother; and his father loves him.' ²¹ You said to your servants, 'Bring him down to me, that I may set my eyes on him.'

²³ You said to your servants, 'Unless your youngest brother comes down with you, you will see my face no more.' ²⁴ When we came up to your servant my father, we told him the words of my lord. ²⁵ Our father said, 'Go again and buy us a little food.' ²⁶ We said, 'We can't go down. If our youngest brother is with us, then we will go down: for we may not see the man's face, unless our youngest brother is with us.' ²⁷ Your servant, my father, said to us, 'You know that my wife bore me two sons. ²⁸ One went out from me, and I said, "Surely he is torn in pieces;" and I haven't seen him since. ²⁹ If you take this one also from me, and harm happens to him, you will bring down my gray hairs with sorrow to Sheol.'

¹ Then Joseph couldn't control himself before all those who stood before him, and he called out, "Cause everyone to go out from me!" No one else stood with him, while Joseph made himself known to his brothers. ² He wept aloud. The Egyptians heard, and the house of Pharaoh heard. ³ Joseph said to his brothers, "I am Joseph! Does my father still live?"

His brothers couldn't answer him; for they were terrified at his presence. ⁴ Joseph said to his brothers, "Come near to me, please."

They came near. He said, "I am Joseph, your brother, whom you sold into Egypt. ⁵ Now don't be grieved, nor angry with yourselves, that you sold me here, for God sent me before you to preserve life.

Responsorial Psalm: Psalms 105: 16-21

¹⁶ He called for a famine on the land.
He destroyed the food supplies.
¹⁷ He sent a man before them.
Joseph was sold for a slave.
¹⁸ They bruised his feet with shackles.
His neck was locked in irons,
¹⁹ until the time that his word happened,
and Yahweh's word proved him true.
²⁰ The king sent and freed him,
even the ruler of peoples, and let him go free.
²¹ He made him lord of his house,
and ruler of all of his possessions,

Gospel: Matthew 10: 7-15

⁷ As you go, preach, saying, 'The Kingdom of Heaven is at hand!' ⁸ Heal the sick, cleanse the lepers,‡ and cast out demons. Freely you received, so freely give. ⁹ Don't take any gold, silver, or brass in your money belts. ¹⁰ Take no bag for your journey, neither two coats, nor sandals, nor staff: for the laborer is worthy of his food. ¹¹ Into whatever city or village you enter, find out who in it is worthy, and stay there until you go on. ¹² As you enter into the

household, greet it. ¹³ If the household is worthy, let your peace come on it, but if it isn't worthy, let your peace return to you. ¹⁴ Whoever doesn't receive you or hear your words, as you go out of that house or that city, shake the dust off your feet. ¹⁵ Most certainly I tell you, it will be more tolerable for the land of Sodom and Gomorrah in the day of judgment than for that city.

1. Invite the Holy Spirit into this reading, asking the Author of Scripture to speak to you through His Word
2. Read today's passage as many times as you need, take your time
3. Write down (below) what the Lord is saying to you today
4. Live with this Word in your heart through the day

Friday, July 11, 2025
Saint Benedict, Abbot

First Reading: Genesis 46: 1-7, 28-30

¹ Israel traveled with all that he had, and came to Beersheba, and offered sacrifices to the God of his father, Isaac. ² God spoke to Israel in the visions of the night, and said, "Jacob, Jacob!"
He said, "Here I am."
³ He said, "I am God, the God of your father. Don't be afraid to go down into Egypt, for there I will make of you a great nation. ⁴ I will go down with you into Egypt. I will also surely bring you up again. Joseph's hand will close your eyes."
⁵ Jacob rose up from Beersheba, and the sons of Israel carried Jacob, their father, their little ones, and their wives, in the wagons which Pharaoh had sent to carry him. ⁶ They took their livestock, and their goods, which they had gotten in the land of Canaan, and came into Egypt—Jacob, and all his offspring with him, ⁷ his sons, and his sons' sons with him, his daughters, and his sons' daughters, and he brought all his offspring with him into Egypt.
²⁸ Jacob sent Judah before him to Joseph, to show the way before him to Goshen, and they came into the land of Goshen. ²⁹ Joseph prepared his chariot, and went up to meet Israel, his father, in Goshen. He presented himself to him, and fell on his neck, and wept on his neck a good while. ³⁰ Israel said to Joseph, "Now let me die, since I have seen your face, that you are still alive."

Responsorial Psalm: Psalms 37: 3-4, 18-19, 27-28, 39-40

3 Trust in Yahweh, and do good.
Dwell in the land, and enjoy safe pasture.
4 Also delight yourself in Yahweh,
and he will give you the desires of your heart.
18 Yahweh knows the days of the perfect.
Their inheritance shall be forever.
19 They shall not be disappointed in the time of evil.
In the days of famine they shall be satisfied.
27 Depart from evil, and do good.
Live securely forever.
28 For Yahweh loves justice,
and doesn't forsake his saints.
They are preserved forever,
39 But the salvation of the righteous is from Yahweh.
He is their stronghold in the time of trouble.
40 Yahweh helps them and rescues them.
He rescues them from the wicked and saves them,
because they have taken refuge in him.

Gospel: Matthew 10: 16-23

16 "Behold, I send you out as sheep among wolves. Therefore be wise as serpents and harmless as doves. 17 But beware of men, for they will deliver you up to councils, and in their synagogues they will scourge you. 18 Yes, and you will be brought before governors and kings for my sake, for a testimony to them and to the nations. 19 But when they deliver you up, don't be anxious how or what you will say, for it will be given you in that hour what you will say. 20 For it is not you who speak, but the Spirit of your Father who speaks in you. 21 "Brother will deliver up brother to death, and the father his child. Children will rise up against parents and cause them to be put to death. 22 You will be hated by all men for my name's sake, but he who endures to the end will be saved. 23 But when they persecute you in this city, flee into the next, for most certainly I tell you, you will not have gone through the cities of Israel until the Son of Man has come.

1. Invite the Holy Spirit into this reading, asking the Author of Scripture to speak to you through His Word
2. Read today's passage as many times as you need, take your time
3. Write down (below) what the Lord is saying to you today

4. Live with this Word in your heart through the day

_____

_____

Saturday, July 12, 2025

First Reading: Genesis 49: 29-32; 50: 15-26a

29 He instructed them, and said to them, "I am to be gathered to my people. Bury me with my fathers in the cave that is in the field of Ephron the Hittite, 30 in the cave that is in the field of Machpelah, which is before Mamre, in the land of Canaan, which Abraham bought with the field from Ephron the Hittite as a burial place. 31 There they buried Abraham and Sarah, his wife. There they buried Isaac and Rebekah, his wife, and there I buried Leah: 32 the field and the cave that is therein, which was purchased from the children of Heth." 33 When Jacob finished charging his sons, he gathered up his feet into the bed, breathed his last breath, and was gathered to his people.
15 When Joseph's brothers saw that their father was dead, they said, "It may be that Joseph will hate us, and will fully pay us back for all the evil which we did to him." 16 They sent a message to Joseph, saying, "Your father commanded before he died, saying, 17 'You shall tell Joseph, "Now please forgive the disobedience of your brothers, and their sin, because they did evil to you." ' Now, please forgive the disobedience of the servants of the God of your father." Joseph wept when they spoke to him. 18 His brothers also went and fell down before his face; and they said, "Behold, we are your servants." 19 Joseph said to them, "Don't be afraid, for am I in the place of God? 20 As for you, you meant evil against me, but God meant it for good, to save many people alive, as is happening today. 21 Now therefore don't be afraid. I will provide for you and your little ones." He comforted them, and spoke kindly to them.
22 Joseph lived in Egypt, he, and his father's house. Joseph lived one hundred ten years. 23 Joseph saw Ephraim's children to the third generation. The children also of Machir, the son of Manasseh, were born on Joseph's knees. 24 Joseph said to his brothers, "I am dying, but God will surely visit you, and bring you up out of this land to the land which he swore to Abraham, to Isaac, and to Jacob." 25 Joseph took an oath from the children of Israel, saying, "God will surely visit you, and you shall carry up my bones from here." 26 So Joseph died, being one hundred ten years old, and they embalmed him, and he was put in a coffin in Egypt.

Responsorial Psalm: Psalms 105: 1-2, 3-4, 6-7

¹ Give thanks to Yahweh! Call on his name!
Make his doings known among the peoples.
² Sing to him, sing praises to him!
Tell of all his marvelous works.
³ Glory in his holy name.
Let the heart of those who seek Yahweh rejoice.
⁴ Seek Yahweh and his strength.
Seek his face forever more.
⁶ you offspring of Abraham, his servant,
you children of Jacob, his chosen ones.
⁷ He is Yahweh, our God.
His judgments are in all the earth.

Gospel: Matthew 10: 24-33

²⁴ "A disciple is not above his teacher, nor a servant above his lord. ²⁵ It is enough for the disciple that he be like his teacher, and the servant like his lord. If they have called the master of the house Beelzebul, how much more those of his household! ²⁶ Therefore don't be afraid of them, for there is nothing covered that will not be revealed, or hidden that will not be known. ²⁷ What I tell you in the darkness, speak in the light; and what you hear whispered in the ear, proclaim on the housetops. ²⁸ Don't be afraid of those who kill the body, but are not able to kill the soul. Rather, fear him who is able to destroy both soul and body in Gehenna.

²⁹ "Aren't two sparrows sold for an assarion coin? Not one of them falls to the ground apart from your Father's will. ³⁰ But the very hairs of your head are all numbered. ³¹ Therefore don't be afraid. You are of more value than many sparrows. ³² Everyone therefore who confesses me before men, I will also confess him before my Father who is in heaven. ³³ But whoever denies me before men, I will also deny him before my Father who is in heaven.

1. Invite the Holy Spirit into this reading, asking the Author of Scripture to speak to you through His Word
2. Read today's passage as many times as you need, take your time
3. Write down (below) what the Lord is saying to you today
4. Live with this Word in your heart through the day

Sunday, July 13, 2025
FIFTEENTH SUNDAY IN ORDINARY TIME

First Reading: Deuteronomy 30: 10-14

10 if you will obey Yahweh your God's voice, to keep his commandments and his statutes which are written in this book of the law, if you turn to Yahweh your God with all your heart and with all your soul.
11 For this commandment which I command you today is not too hard for you or too distant. 12 It is not in heaven, that you should say, "Who will go up for us to heaven, bring it to us, and proclaim it to us, that we may do it?" 13 Neither is it beyond the sea, that you should say, "Who will go over the sea for us, bring it to us, and proclaim it to us, that we may do it?" 14 But the word is very near to you, in your mouth and in your heart, that you may do it.

Responsorial Psalm: Psalms 19: 8, 9, 10, 11

8 Yahweh's precepts are right, rejoicing the heart.
Yahweh's commandment is pure, enlightening the eyes.
9 The fear of Yahweh is clean, enduring forever.
Yahweh's ordinances are true, and righteous altogether.
10 They are more to be desired than gold, yes, than much fine gold,
sweeter also than honey and the extract of the honeycomb.
11 Moreover your servant is warned by them.
In keeping them there is great reward.

Second Reading: Colossians 1: 15-20

15 He is the image of the invisible God, the firstborn of all creation. 16 For by him all things were created in the heavens and on the earth, visible things and invisible things, whether thrones or dominions or principalities or powers. All things have been created through him and for him. 17 He is before all things, and in him all things are held together. 18 He is the head of the body, the assembly, who is the beginning, the firstborn from the dead, that in all things he might have the preeminence. 19 For all the fullness was pleased to dwell in him, 20 and through him to reconcile all things to himself by him, whether things on the earth or things in the heavens, having made peace through the blood of his cross.

Gospel: Luke 10: 25-37

²⁵ Behold, a certain lawyer stood up and tested him, saying, "Teacher, what shall I do to inherit eternal life?"
²⁶ He said to him, "What is written in the law? How do you read it?"
²⁷ He answered, "You shall love the Lord your God with all your heart, with all your soul, with all your strength, and with all your mind; and your neighbor as yourself."
²⁸ He said to him, "You have answered correctly. Do this, and you will live."
²⁹ But he, desiring to justify himself, asked Jesus, "Who is my neighbor?"
³⁰ Jesus answered, "A certain man was going down from Jerusalem to Jericho, and he fell among robbers, who both stripped him and beat him, and departed, leaving him half dead. ³¹ By chance a certain priest was going down that way. When he saw him, he passed by on the other side. ³² In the same way a Levite also, when he came to the place and saw him, passed by on the other side. ³³ But a certain Samaritan, as he traveled, came where he was. When he saw him, he was moved with compassion, ³⁴ came to him, and bound up his wounds, pouring on oil and wine. He set him on his own animal, brought him to an inn, and took care of him. ³⁵ On the next day, when he departed, he took out two denarii, gave them to the host, and said to him, 'Take care of him. Whatever you spend beyond that, I will repay you when I return.' ³⁶ Now which of these three do you think seemed to be a neighbor to him who fell among the robbers?"
³⁷ He said, "He who showed mercy on him."
Then Jesus said to him, "Go and do likewise."

1. Invite the Holy Spirit into this reading, asking the Author of Scripture to speak to you through His Word
2. Read today's passage as many times as you need, take your time
3. Write down (below) what the Lord is saying to you today
4. Live with this Word in your heart through the day

Monday, July 14, 2025
Saint Kateri Tekakwitha, Virgin

First Reading: Exodus 1: 8-14, 22

⁸ Now there arose a new king over Egypt, who didn't know Joseph. ⁹ He said to his people, "Behold, the people of the children of Israel are more and mightier than we. ¹⁰ Come, let's deal wisely with them, lest they multiply, and it happen that when any war breaks out, they

also join themselves to our enemies and fight against us, and escape out of the land." 11 Therefore they set taskmasters over them to afflict them with their burdens. They built storage cities for Pharaoh: Pithom and Raamses. 12 But the more they afflicted them, the more they multiplied and the more they spread out. They started to dread the children of Israel. 13 The Egyptians ruthlessly made the children of Israel serve, 14 and they made their lives bitter with hard service in mortar and in brick, and in all kinds of service in the field, all their service, in which they ruthlessly made them serve.

22 Pharaoh commanded all his people, saying, "You shall cast every son who is born into the river, and every daughter you shall save alive."

Responsorial Psalm: Psalms 124: 1b-8

1 If it had not been Yahweh who was on our side,
let Israel now say,
2 if it had not been Yahweh who was on our side,
when men rose up against us,
3 then they would have swallowed us up alive,
when their wrath was kindled against us,
4 then the waters would have overwhelmed us,
the stream would have gone over our soul.
5 Then the proud waters would have gone over our soul.
6 Blessed be Yahweh,
who has not given us as a prey to their teeth.
7 Our soul has escaped like a bird out of the fowler's snare.
The snare is broken, and we have escaped.
8 Our help is in Yahweh's name,
who made heaven and earth.

Gospel: Matthew 10: 34 – 11: 1

34 "Don't think that I came to send peace on the earth. I didn't come to send peace, but a sword. 35 For I came to set a man at odds against his father, and a daughter against her mother, and a daughter-in-law against her mother-in-law. 36 A man's foes will be those of his own household." 37 He who loves father or mother more than me is not worthy of me; and he who loves son or daughter more than me isn't worthy of me. 38 He who doesn't take his cross and follow after me isn't worthy of me. 39 He who seeks his life will lose it; and he who loses his life for my sake will find it.

40 "He who receives you receives me, and he who receives me receives him who sent me. 41 He who receives a prophet in the name of a prophet will receive a prophet's reward. He who receives a righteous man in the name of a righteous man will receive a righteous

man's reward. ⁴² Whoever gives one of these little ones just a cup of cold water to drink in the name of a disciple, most certainly I tell you, he will in no way lose his reward."
¹ When Jesus had finished directing his twelve disciples, he departed from there to teach and preach in their cities.

1. Invite the Holy Spirit into this reading, asking the Author of Scripture to speak to you through His Word
2. Read today's passage as many times as you need, take your time
3. Write down (below) what the Lord is saying to you today
4. Live with this Word in your heart through the day

Tuesday, July 15, 2025
Saint Bonaventure, Bishop and Doctor of the Church

First Reading: Exodus 2: 1-15a

¹ A man of the house of Levi went and took a daughter of Levi as his wife. ² The woman conceived and bore a son. When she saw that he was a fine child, she hid him three months. ³ When she could no longer hide him, she took a papyrus basket for him, and coated it with tar and with pitch. She put the child in it, and laid it in the reeds by the river's bank. ⁴ His sister stood far off, to see what would be done to him. ⁵ Pharaoh's daughter came down to bathe at the river. Her maidens walked along by the riverside. She saw the basket among the reeds, and sent her servant to get it. ⁶ She opened it, and saw the child, and behold, the baby cried. She had compassion on him, and said, "This is one of the Hebrews' children."
⁷ Then his sister said to Pharaoh's daughter, "Should I go and call a nurse for you from the Hebrew women, that she may nurse the child for you?"
⁸ Pharaoh's daughter said to her, "Go."
The young woman went and called the child's mother. ⁹ Pharaoh's daughter said to her, "Take this child away, and nurse him for me, and I will give you your wages."
The woman took the child, and nursed it. ¹⁰ The child grew, and she brought him to Pharaoh's daughter, and he became her son. She named him Moses,‡ and said, "Because I drew him out of the water."
¹¹ In those days, when Moses had grown up, he went out to his brothers and saw their burdens. He saw an Egyptian striking a Hebrew, one of his brothers. ¹² He looked this way

and that way, and when he saw that there was no one, he killed the Egyptian, and hid him in the sand.

13 He went out the second day, and behold, two men of the Hebrews were fighting with each other. He said to him who did the wrong, "Why do you strike your fellow?"

14 He said, "Who made you a prince and a judge over us? Do you plan to kill me, as you killed the Egyptian?"

Moses was afraid, and said, "Surely this thing is known." 15a Now when Pharaoh heard this thing, he sought to kill Moses.

Responsorial Psalm: Psalms 69: 3, 14, 30-31, 33-34

3 I am weary with my crying.
My throat is dry.
My eyes fail looking for my God.
14 Deliver me out of the mire, and don't let me sink.
Let me be delivered from those who hate me, and out of the deep waters.
30 I will praise the name of God with a song,
and will magnify him with thanksgiving.
31 It will please Yahweh better than an ox,
or a bull that has horns and hoofs.
33 For Yahweh hears the needy,
and doesn't despise his captive people.
34 Let heaven and earth praise him;
the seas, and everything that moves therein!

Gospel: Matthew 11: 20-24

20 Then he began to denounce the cities in which most of his mighty works had been done, because they didn't repent. 21 "Woe to you, Chorazin! Woe to you, Bethsaida! For if the mighty works had been done in Tyre and Sidon which were done in you, they would have repented long ago in sackcloth and ashes. 22 But I tell you, it will be more tolerable for Tyre and Sidon on the day of judgment than for you. 23 You, Capernaum, who are exalted to heaven, you will go down to Hades. § For if the mighty works had been done in Sodom which were done in you, it would have remained until today. 24 But I tell you that it will be more tolerable for the land of Sodom on the day of judgment, than for you."

1. Invite the Holy Spirit into this reading, asking the Author of Scripture to speak to you through His Word
2. Read today's passage as many times as you need, take your time
3. Write down (below) what the Lord is saying to you today

4. Live with this Word in your heart through the day

Wednesday, July 16, 2025
Our Lady of Mount Carmel

First Reading: Exodus 3: 1-6, 9-12

¹ Now Moses was keeping the flock of Jethro, his father-in-law, the priest of Midian, and he led the flock to the back of the wilderness, and came to God's mountain, to Horeb. ² Yahweh's angel appeared to him in a flame of fire out of the middle of a bush. He looked, and behold, the bush burned with fire, and the bush was not consumed. ³ Moses said, "I will go now, and see this great sight, why the bush is not burned."
⁴ When Yahweh saw that he came over to see, God called to him out of the middle of the bush, and said, "Moses! Moses!"
He said, "Here I am."
⁵ He said, "Don't come close. Take off your sandals, for the place you are standing on is holy ground." ⁶ Moreover he said, "I am the God of your father, the God of Abraham, the God of Isaac, and the God of Jacob."
Moses hid his face because he was afraid to look at God.
⁹ Now, behold, the cry of the children of Israel has come to me. Moreover I have seen the oppression with which the Egyptians oppress them. ¹⁰ Come now therefore, and I will send you to Pharaoh, that you may bring my people, the children of Israel, out of Egypt."
¹¹ Moses said to God, "Who am I, that I should go to Pharaoh, and that I should bring the children of Israel out of Egypt?"
¹² He said, "Certainly I will be with you. This will be the token to you, that I have sent you: when you have brought the people out of Egypt, you shall serve God on this mountain."

Responsorial Psalm: Psalms 103: 1b-2, 3-4, 6-7

¹ᵇ All that is within me, praise his holy name!
² Praise Yahweh, my soul,
and don't forget all his benefits,
³ who forgives all your sins,
who heals all your diseases,
⁴ who redeems your life from destruction,

who crowns you with loving kindness and tender mercies,
⁶ Yahweh executes righteous acts,
and justice for all who are oppressed.
⁷ He made known his ways to Moses,
his deeds to the children of Israel.

Gospel: Matthew 11: 25-27

²⁵ At that time, Jesus answered, "I thank you, Father, Lord of heaven and earth, that you hid these things from the wise and understanding, and revealed them to infants. ²⁶ Yes, Father, for so it was well-pleasing in your sight. ²⁷ All things have been delivered to me by my Father. No one knows the Son, except the Father; neither does anyone know the Father, except the Son and he to whom the Son desires to reveal him.

1. Invite the Holy Spirit into this reading, asking the Author of Scripture to speak to you through His Word
2. Read today's passage as many times as you need, take your time
3. Write down (below) what the Lord is saying to you today
4. Live with this Word in your heart through the day

___

Thursday, July 17, 2025

First Reading: Exodus 3: 13-20

¹³ Moses said to God, "Behold, when I come to the children of Israel, and tell them, 'The God of your fathers has sent me to you,' and they ask me, 'What is his name?' what should I tell them?"
¹⁴ God said to Moses, "I AM WHO I AM," and he said, "You shall tell the children of Israel this: 'I AM has sent me to you.' " ¹⁵ God said moreover to Moses, "You shall tell the children of Israel this, 'Yahweh, the God of your fathers, the God of Abraham, the God of Isaac, and the God of Jacob, has sent me to you.' This is my name forever, and this is my memorial to all generations. ¹⁶ Go and gather the elders of Israel together, and tell them, 'Yahweh, the God of your fathers, the God of Abraham, of Isaac, and of Jacob, has appeared to me, saying, "I have surely visited you, and seen that which is done to you in Egypt. ¹⁷ I have said, I will bring you up out of the affliction of Egypt to the land of the Canaanite, the Hittite,

the Amorite, the Perizzite, the Hivite, and the Jebusite, to a land flowing with milk and honey." ' ¹⁸ They will listen to your voice. You shall come, you and the elders of Israel, to the king of Egypt, and you shall tell him, 'Yahweh, the God of the Hebrews, has met with us. Now please let us go three days' journey into the wilderness, that we may sacrifice to Yahweh, our God.' ¹⁹ I know that the king of Egypt won't give you permission to go, no, not by a mighty hand. ²⁰ I will reach out my hand and strike Egypt with all my wonders which I will do among them, and after that he will let you go.

Responsorial Psalm: Psalms 105: 1 and 5, 8-9, 24-27

¹ Give thanks to Yahweh! Call on his name!
Make his doings known among the peoples.
⁵ Remember his marvelous works that he has done:
his wonders, and the judgments of his mouth,
⁸ He has remembered his covenant forever,
the word which he commanded to a thousand generations,
⁹ the covenant which he made with Abraham,
his oath to Isaac,
²⁴ He increased his people greatly,
and made them stronger than their adversaries.
²⁵ He turned their heart to hate his people,
to conspire against his servants.
²⁶ He sent Moses, his servant,
and Aaron, whom he had chosen.
²⁷ They performed miracles among them,
and wonders in the land of Ham.

Gospel: Matthew 11: 28-30

²⁸ "Come to me, all you who labor and are heavily burdened, and I will give you rest. ²⁹ Take my yoke upon you and learn from me, for I am gentle and humble in heart; and you will find rest for your souls. ³⁰ For my yoke is easy, and my burden is light."

1. Invite the Holy Spirit into this reading, asking the Author of Scripture to speak to you through His Word
2. Read today's passage as many times as you need, take your time
3. Write down (below) what the Lord is saying to you today
4. Live with this Word in your heart through the day

Friday, July 18, 2025
Saint Camillus de Lellis, Priest

First Reading: Exodus 11: 10 – 12: 14

¹⁰ Moses and Aaron did all these wonders before Pharaoh, but Yahweh hardened Pharaoh's heart, and he didn't let the children of Israel go out of his land.
¹ Yahweh spoke to Moses and Aaron in the land of Egypt, saying, ² "This month shall be to you the beginning of months. It shall be the first month of the year to you. ³ Speak to all the congregation of Israel, saying, 'On the tenth day of this month, they shall take to them every man a lamb, according to their fathers' houses, a lamb for a household; ⁴ and if the household is too little for a lamb, then he and his neighbor next to his house shall take one according to the number of the souls. You shall make your count for the lamb according to what everyone can eat. ⁵ Your lamb shall be without defect, a male a year old. You shall take it from the sheep or from the goats. ⁶ You shall keep it until the fourteenth day of the same month; and the whole assembly of the congregation of Israel shall kill it at evening. ⁷ They shall take some of the blood, and put it on the two door posts and on the lintel, on the houses in which they shall eat it. ⁸ They shall eat the meat in that night, roasted with fire, with unleavened bread. They shall eat it with bitter herbs. ⁹ Don't eat it raw, nor boiled at all with water, but roasted with fire; with its head, its legs and its inner parts. ¹⁰ You shall let nothing of it remain until the morning; but that which remains of it until the morning you shall burn with fire. ¹¹ This is how you shall eat it: with your belt on your waist, your sandals on your feet, and your staff in your hand; and you shall eat it in haste: it is Yahweh's Passover. ¹² For I will go through the land of Egypt in that night, and will strike all the firstborn in the land of Egypt, both man and animal. I will execute judgments against all the gods of Egypt. I am Yahweh. ¹³ The blood shall be to you for a token on the houses where you are. When I see the blood, I will pass over you, and no plague will be on you to destroy you when I strike the land of Egypt. ¹⁴ This day shall be a memorial for you. You shall keep it as a feast to Yahweh. You shall keep it as a feast throughout your generations by an ordinance forever.

Responsorial Psalm: Psalms 116: 12-13, 15 and 16bc, 17-18

¹² What will I give to Yahweh for all his benefits toward me?
¹³ I will take the cup of salvation, and call on Yahweh's name.

¹⁵ Precious in Yahweh's sight is the death of his saints.
¹⁶ᵇ I am your servant, the son of your servant girl.
You have freed me from my chains.
¹⁷ I will offer to you the sacrifice of thanksgiving,
and will call on Yahweh's name.
¹⁸ I will pay my vows to Yahweh,
yes, in the presence of all his people,

Gospel: Matthew 12: 1-8

¹ At that time, Jesus went on the Sabbath day through the grain fields. His disciples were hungry and began to pluck heads of grain and to eat. ² But the Pharisees, when they saw it, said to him, "Behold, your disciples do what is not lawful to do on the Sabbath."
³ But he said to them, "Haven't you read what David did when he was hungry, and those who were with him: ⁴ how he entered into God's house and ate the show bread, which was not lawful for him to eat, nor for those who were with him, but only for the priests?* ⁵ Or have you not read in the law that on the Sabbath day the priests in the temple profane the Sabbath and are guiltless? ⁶ But I tell you that one greater than the temple is here. ⁷ But if you had known what this means, 'I desire mercy, and not sacrifice,'* you wouldn't have condemned the guiltless. ⁸ For the Son of Man is Lord of the Sabbath."

1. Invite the Holy Spirit into this reading, asking the Author of Scripture to speak to you through His Word
2. Read today's passage as many times as you need, take your time
3. Write down (below) what the Lord is saying to you today
4. Live with this Word in your heart through the day

___

___

Saturday, July 19, 2025

First Reading: Exodus 12: 37-42

³⁷ The children of Israel traveled from Rameses to Succoth, about six hundred thousand on foot who were men, in addition to children. ³⁸ A mixed multitude went up also with them, with flocks, herds, and even very much livestock. ³⁹ They baked unleavened cakes of the dough which they brought out of Egypt; for it wasn't leavened, because they were thrust

out of Egypt, and couldn't wait, and they had not prepared any food for themselves. ⁴⁰ Now the time that the children of Israel lived in Egypt was four hundred thirty years. ⁴¹ At the end of four hundred thirty years, to the day, all of Yahweh's armies went out from the land of Egypt. ⁴² It is a night to be much observed to Yahweh for bringing them out from the land of Egypt. This is that night of Yahweh, to be much observed by all the children of Israel throughout their generations.

Responsorial Psalm: Psalms 136: 1 and 23-24, 10-12, 13-15

¹ Give thanks to Yahweh, for he is good,
for his loving kindness endures forever.
²³ who remembered us in our low estate,
for his loving kindness endures forever;
²⁴ and has delivered us from our adversaries,
for his loving kindness endures forever;
¹⁰ to him who struck down the Egyptian firstborn,
for his loving kindness endures forever;
¹¹ and brought out Israel from among them,
for his loving kindness endures forever;
¹² with a strong hand, and with an outstretched arm,
for his loving kindness endures forever;
¹³ to him who divided the Red Sea apart,
for his loving kindness endures forever;
¹⁴ and made Israel to pass through the middle of it,
for his loving kindness endures forever;
¹⁵ but overthrew Pharaoh and his army in the Red Sea,
for his loving kindness endures forever;

Gospel: Matthew 12: 14-21

¹⁴ But the Pharisees went out and conspired against him, how they might destroy him.
¹⁵ Jesus, perceiving that, withdrew from there. Great multitudes followed him; and he healed them all, ¹⁶ and commanded them that they should not make him known, ¹⁷ that it might be fulfilled which was spoken through Isaiah the prophet, saying,
¹⁸ "Behold, my servant whom I have chosen,
my beloved in whom my soul is well pleased.
I will put my Spirit on him.
He will proclaim justice to the nations.
¹⁹ He will not strive, nor shout,
neither will anyone hear his voice in the streets.

²⁰ He won't break a bruised reed.
He won't quench a smoking flax,
until he leads justice to victory.
²¹ In his name, the nations will hope."

1. Invite the Holy Spirit into this reading, asking the Author of Scripture to speak to you through His Word
2. Read today's passage as many times as you need, take your time
3. Write down (below) what the Lord is saying to you today
4. Live with this Word in your heart through the day

Sunday, July 20, 2025
SIXTEENTH SUNDAY IN ORDINARY TIME

First Reading: Genesis 18: 1-10a

¹ Yahweh appeared to him by the oaks of Mamre, as he sat in the tent door in the heat of the day. ² He lifted up his eyes and looked, and saw that three men stood near him. When he saw them, he ran to meet them from the tent door, and bowed himself to the earth, ³ and said, "My lord, if now I have found favor in your sight, please don't go away from your servant. ⁴ Now let a little water be fetched, wash your feet, and rest yourselves under the tree. ⁵ I will get a piece of bread so you can refresh your heart. After that you may go your way, now that you have come to your servant."
They said, "Very well, do as you have said."
⁶ Abraham hurried into the tent to Sarah, and said, "Quickly prepare three seahs of fine meal, knead it, and make cakes." ⁷ Abraham ran to the herd, and fetched a tender and good calf, and gave it to the servant. He hurried to dress it. ⁸ He took butter, milk, and the calf which he had dressed, and set it before them. He stood by them under the tree, and they ate.
⁹ They asked him, "Where is Sarah, your wife?"
He said, "There, in the tent."
¹⁰ᵃ He said, "I will certainly return to you at about this time next year; and behold, Sarah your wife will have a son."

Responsorial Psalm: Psalms 15: 2-5

² He who walks blamelessly and does what is right,
and speaks truth in his heart;
³ he who doesn't slander with his tongue,
nor does evil to his friend,
nor casts slurs against his fellow man;
⁴ in whose eyes a vile man is despised,
but who honors those who fear Yahweh;
he who keeps an oath even when it hurts, and doesn't change;
⁵ he who doesn't lend out his money for usury,
nor take a bribe against the innocent.
He who does these things shall never be shaken.

Second Reading: Colossians 1: 24-28

²⁴ Now I rejoice in my sufferings for your sake, and fill up on my part that which is lacking of the afflictions of Christ in my flesh for his body's sake, which is the assembly, ²⁵ of which I was made a servant according to the stewardship of God which was given me toward you to fulfill the word of God, ²⁶ the mystery which has been hidden for ages and generations. But now it has been revealed to his saints, ²⁷ to whom God was pleased to make known what are the riches of the glory of this mystery among the Gentiles, which is Christ in you, the hope of glory. ²⁸ We proclaim him, admonishing every man and teaching every man in all wisdom, that we may present every man perfect in Christ Jesus;

Gospel: Luke 10: 38-42

³⁸ As they went on their way, he entered into a certain village, and a certain woman named Martha received him into her house. ³⁹ She had a sister called Mary, who also sat at Jesus' feet and heard his word. ⁴⁰ But Martha was distracted with much serving, and she came up to him, and said, "Lord, don't you care that my sister left me to serve alone? Ask her therefore to help me."
⁴¹ Jesus answered her, "Martha, Martha, you are anxious and troubled about many things, ⁴² but one thing is needed. Mary has chosen the good part, which will not be taken away from her."

1. Invite the Holy Spirit into this reading, asking the Author of Scripture to speak to you through His Word
2. Read today's passage as many times as you need, take your time
3. Write down (below) what the Lord is saying to you today
4. Live with this Word in your heart through the day

Monday, July 21, 2025
Saint Lawrence of Brindisi, Priest and Doctor of the Church

First Reading: Exodus 14: 5-18

⁵ The king of Egypt was told that the people had fled; and the heart of Pharaoh and of his servants was changed toward the people, and they said, "What is this we have done, that we have let Israel go from serving us?" ⁶ He prepared his chariot, and took his army with him; ⁷ and he took six hundred chosen chariots, and all the chariots of Egypt, with captains over all of them. ⁸ Yahweh hardened the heart of Pharaoh king of Egypt, and he pursued the children of Israel; for the children of Israel went out with a high hand. ⁹ The Egyptians pursued them. All the horses and chariots of Pharaoh, his horsemen, and his army overtook them encamping by the sea, beside Pihahiroth, before Baal Zephon.

¹⁰ When Pharaoh came near, the children of Israel lifted up their eyes, and behold, the Egyptians were marching after them; and they were very afraid. The children of Israel cried out to Yahweh. ¹¹ They said to Moses, "Because there were no graves in Egypt, have you taken us away to die in the wilderness? Why have you treated us this way, to bring us out of Egypt? ¹² Isn't this the word that we spoke to you in Egypt, saying, 'Leave us alone, that we may serve the Egyptians'? For it would have been better for us to serve the Egyptians than to die in the wilderness."

¹³ Moses said to the people, "Don't be afraid. Stand still, and see the salvation of Yahweh, which he will work for you today; for you will never again see the Egyptians whom you have seen today. ¹⁴ Yahweh will fight for you, and you shall be still."

¹⁵ Yahweh said to Moses, "Why do you cry to me? Speak to the children of Israel, that they go forward. ¹⁶ Lift up your rod, and stretch out your hand over the sea and divide it. Then the children of Israel shall go into the middle of the sea on dry ground. ¹⁷ Behold, I myself will harden the hearts of the Egyptians, and they will go in after them. I will get myself honor over Pharaoh, and over all his armies, over his chariots, and over his horsemen. ¹⁸ The Egyptians shall know that I am Yahweh when I have gotten myself honor over Pharaoh, over his chariots, and over his horsemen."

Responsorial Psalm: Exodus 15: 1bc-2, 3-4, 5-6

¹ᵇ "I will sing to Yahweh, for he has triumphed gloriously.

He has thrown the horse and his rider into the sea.
² Yah is my strength and song.
He has become my salvation.
This is my God, and I will praise him;
my father's God, and I will exalt him.
³ Yahweh is a man of war.
Yahweh is his name.
⁴ He has cast Pharaoh's chariots and his army into the sea.
His chosen captains are sunk in the Red Sea.
⁵ The deeps cover them.
They went down into the depths like a stone.
⁶ Your right hand, Yahweh, is glorious in power.
Your right hand, Yahweh, dashes the enemy in pieces.

Gospel: Matthew 12: 38-42

³⁸ Then certain of the scribes and Pharisees answered, "Teacher, we want to see a sign from you." ³⁹ But he answered them, "An evil and adulterous generation seeks after a sign, but no sign will be given to it but the sign of Jonah the prophet. ⁴⁰ For as Jonah was three days and three nights in the belly of the huge fish, so will the Son of Man be three days and three nights in the heart of the earth. ⁴¹ The men of Nineveh will stand up in the judgment with this generation and will condemn it, for they repented at the preaching of Jonah; and behold, someone greater than Jonah is here. ⁴² The Queen of the South will rise up in the judgment with this generation and will condemn it, for she came from the ends of the earth to hear the wisdom of Solomon; and behold, someone greater than Solomon is here.

1. Invite the Holy Spirit into this reading, asking the Author of Scripture to speak to you through His Word
2. Read today's passage as many times as you need, take your time
3. Write down (below) what the Lord is saying to you today
4. Live with this Word in your heart through the day

___

___

Tuesday, July 22, 2025
Saint Mary Magdalene

First Reading: Exodus 14: 21 – 15: 1

21 Moses stretched out his hand over the sea, and Yahweh caused the sea to go back by a strong east wind all night, and made the sea dry land, and the waters were divided. 22 The children of Israel went into the middle of the sea on the dry ground; and the waters were a wall to them on their right hand and on their left. 23 The Egyptians pursued, and went in after them into the middle of the sea: all of Pharaoh's horses, his chariots, and his horsemen. 24 In the morning watch, Yahweh looked out on the Egyptian army through the pillar of fire and of cloud, and confused the Egyptian army. 25 He took off their chariot wheels, and they drove them heavily; so that the Egyptians said, "Let's flee from the face of Israel, for Yahweh fights for them against the Egyptians!"
26 Yahweh said to Moses, "Stretch out your hand over the sea, that the waters may come again on the Egyptians, on their chariots, and on their horsemen." 27 Moses stretched out his hand over the sea, and the sea returned to its strength when the morning appeared; and the Egyptians fled against it. Yahweh overthrew the Egyptians in the middle of the sea. 28 The waters returned, and covered the chariots and the horsemen, even all Pharaoh's army that went in after them into the sea. There remained not so much as one of them. 29 But the children of Israel walked on dry land in the middle of the sea, and the waters were a wall to them on their right hand and on their left. 30 Thus Yahweh saved Israel that day out of the hand of the Egyptians; and Israel saw the Egyptians dead on the seashore. 31 Israel saw the great work which Yahweh did to the Egyptians, and the people feared Yahweh; and they believed in Yahweh and in his servant Moses.
1 Then Moses and the children of Israel sang this song to Yahweh, and said,
"I will sing to Yahweh, for he has triumphed gloriously.
He has thrown the horse and his rider into the sea.

Responsorial Psalm: Exodus 15: 8-9, 10 and 12, 17

8 With the blast of your nostrils, the waters were piled up.
The floods stood upright as a heap.
The deeps were congealed in the heart of the sea.
9 The enemy said, 'I will pursue. I will overtake. I will divide the plunder.
My desire will be satisfied on them.
I will draw my sword. My hand will destroy them.'
10 You blew with your wind.
The sea covered them.
They sank like lead in the mighty waters.
12 You stretched out your right hand.
The earth swallowed them.

¹⁷ You will bring them in, and plant them in the mountain of your inheritance,
the place, Yahweh, which you have made for yourself to dwell in:
the sanctuary, Lord, which your hands have established.

Gospel: John 20: 1-2, 11-18

¹ Now on the first day of the week, Mary Magdalene went early, while it was still dark, to the tomb, and saw that the stone had been taken away from the tomb. ² Therefore she ran and came to Simon Peter and to the other disciple whom Jesus loved, and said to them, "They have taken away the Lord out of the tomb, and we don't know where they have laid him!"
¹¹ But Mary was standing outside at the tomb weeping. So as she wept, she stooped and looked into the tomb, ¹² and she saw two angels in white sitting, one at the head and one at the feet, where the body of Jesus had lain. ¹³ They asked her, "Woman, why are you weeping?"
She said to them, "Because they have taken away my Lord, and I don't know where they have laid him." ¹⁴ When she had said this, she turned around and saw Jesus standing, and didn't know that it was Jesus.
¹⁵ Jesus said to her, "Woman, why are you weeping? Who are you looking for?"
She, supposing him to be the gardener, said to him, "Sir, if you have carried him away, tell me where you have laid him, and I will take him away."
¹⁶ Jesus said to her, "Mary."
She turned and said to him, "Rabboni!"⸸ which is to say, "Teacher!"⸸
¹⁷ Jesus said to her, "Don't hold me, for I haven't yet ascended to my Father; but go to my brothers and tell them, 'I am ascending to my Father and your Father, to my God and your God.'"
¹⁸ Mary Magdalene came and told the disciples that she had seen the Lord, and that he had said these things to her.

1. Invite the Holy Spirit into this reading, asking the Author of Scripture to speak to you through His Word
2. Read today's passage as many times as you need, take your time
3. Write down (below) what the Lord is saying to you today
4. Live with this Word in your heart through the day

_____

_____

Wednesday, July 23, 2025
Saint Bridget, Religious

First Reading: Exodus 16: 1-5, 9-15

¹ They took their journey from Elim, and all the congregation of the children of Israel came to the wilderness of Sin, which is between Elim and Sinai, on the fifteenth day of the second month after their departing out of the land of Egypt. ² The whole congregation of the children of Israel murmured against Moses and against Aaron in the wilderness; ³ and the children of Israel said to them, "We wish that we had died by Yahweh's hand in the land of Egypt, when we sat by the meat pots, when we ate our fill of bread, for you have brought us out into this wilderness to kill this whole assembly with hunger."
⁴ Then Yahweh said to Moses, "Behold, I will rain bread from the sky for you, and the people shall go out and gather a day's portion every day, that I may test them, whether they will walk in my law or not. ⁵ It shall come to pass on the sixth day, that they shall prepare that which they bring in, and it shall be twice as much as they gather daily."
⁹ Moses said to Aaron, "Tell all the congregation of the children of Israel, 'Come close to Yahweh, for he has heard your murmurings.' " ¹⁰ As Aaron spoke to the whole congregation of the children of Israel, they looked toward the wilderness, and behold, Yahweh's glory appeared in the cloud. ¹¹ Yahweh spoke to Moses, saying, ¹² "I have heard the murmurings of the children of Israel. Speak to them, saying, 'At evening you shall eat meat, and in the morning you shall be filled with bread. Then you will know that I am Yahweh your God.' "
¹³ In the evening, quail came up and covered the camp; and in the morning the dew lay around the camp. ¹⁴ When the dew that lay had gone, behold, on the surface of the wilderness was a small round thing, small as the frost on the ground. ¹⁵ When the children of Israel saw it, they said to one another, "What is it?" For they didn't know what it was. Moses said to them, "It is the bread which Yahweh has given you to eat.

Responsorial Psalm: Psalms 78: 18-19, 23-24, 25-26, 27-28

¹⁸ They tempted God in their heart
by asking food according to their desire.
¹⁹ Yes, they spoke against God.
They said, "Can God prepare a table in the wilderness?
²³ Yet he commanded the skies above,
and opened the doors of heaven.
²⁴ He rained down manna on them to eat,
and gave them food from the sky.
²⁵ Man ate the bread of angels.
He sent them food to the full.

²⁶ He caused the east wind to blow in the sky.
By his power he guided the south wind.
²⁷ He also rained meat on them as the dust,
winged birds as the sand of the seas.
²⁸ He let them fall in the middle of their camp,
around their habitations.

Gospel: Matthew 13: 1-9

¹ On that day Jesus went out of the house and sat by the seaside. ² Great multitudes gathered to him, so that he entered into a boat and sat; and all the multitude stood on the beach. ³ He spoke to them many things in parables, saying, "Behold, a farmer went out to sow. ⁴ As he sowed, some seeds fell by the roadside, and the birds came and devoured them. ⁵ Others fell on rocky ground, where they didn't have much soil, and immediately they sprang up, because they had no depth of earth. ⁶ When the sun had risen, they were scorched. Because they had no root, they withered away. ⁷ Others fell among thorns. The thorns grew up and choked them. ⁸ Others fell on good soil and yielded fruit: some one hundred times as much, some sixty, and some thirty. ⁹ He who has ears to hear, let him hear."

1. Invite the Holy Spirit into this reading, asking the Author of Scripture to speak to you through His Word
2. Read today's passage as many times as you need, take your time
3. Write down (below) what the Lord is saying to you today
4. Live with this Word in your heart through the day

Thursday, July 24, 2025
Saint Sharbel Makhlūf, Priest

First Reading: Exodus 19: 1-2, 9-11, 16-20b

¹ In the third month after the children of Israel had gone out of the land of Egypt, on that same day they came into the wilderness of Sinai. ² When they had departed from Rephidim, and had come to the wilderness of Sinai, they encamped in the wilderness; and there Israel encamped before the mountain.

⁹ Yahweh said to Moses, "Behold, I come to you in a thick cloud, that the people may hear when I speak with you, and may also believe you forever." Moses told the words of the people to Yahweh. ¹⁰ Yahweh said to Moses, "Go to the people, and sanctify them today and tomorrow, and let them wash their garments, ¹¹ and be ready for the third day; for on the third day Yahweh will come down in the sight of all the people on Mount Sinai.

¹⁶ On the third day, when it was morning, there were thunders and lightnings, and a thick cloud on the mountain, and the sound of an exceedingly loud trumpet; and all the people who were in the camp trembled. ¹⁷ Moses led the people out of the camp to meet God; and they stood at the lower part of the mountain. ¹⁸ All of Mount Sinai smoked, because Yahweh descended on it in fire; and its smoke ascended like the smoke of a furnace, and the whole mountain quaked greatly. ¹⁹ When the sound of the trumpet grew louder and louder, Moses spoke, and God answered him by a voice. ²⁰ Yahweh came down on Mount Sinai, to the top of the mountain. Yahweh called Moses to the top of the mountain, and Moses went up.

Responsorial Psalm: Daniel 3: 52, 53, 54, 55, 56

⁵² "Blessed are you, O Lord, you God of our fathers, to be praised and exalted above all forever! ⁵³ Blessed is your glorious and holy name, to be praised and exalted above all forever! ⁵⁴ Blessed are you in the temple of your holy glory, to be praised and glorified above all forever! ⁵⁵ Blessed are you who see the depths and sit upon the cherubim, to be praised and exalted above all forever. ⁵⁶ Blessed are you on the throne of your kingdom, to be praised and extolled above all forever!

Gospel: Matthew 13: 10-17

¹⁰ The disciples came, and said to him, "Why do you speak to them in parables?"
¹¹ He answered them, "To you it is given to know the mysteries of the Kingdom of Heaven, but it is not given to them. ¹² For whoever has, to him will be given, and he will have abundance; but whoever doesn't have, from him will be taken away even that which he has. ¹³ Therefore I speak to them in parables, because seeing they don't see, and hearing, they don't hear, neither do they understand. ¹⁴ In them the prophecy of Isaiah is fulfilled, which says,
'By hearing you will hear, and will in no way understand;
Seeing you will see,
and will in no way perceive;
¹⁵ for this people's heart has grown callous, their ears are dull of hearing,
and they have closed their eyes;
or else perhaps they might perceive with their eyes, hear with their ears,
understand with their heart, and would turn again,
and I would heal them.'

16 "But blessed are your eyes, for they see; and your ears, for they hear. 17 For most certainly I tell you that many prophets and righteous men desired to see the things which you see, and didn't see them; and to hear the things which you hear, and didn't hear them.

1. Invite the Holy Spirit into this reading, asking the Author of Scripture to speak to you through His Word
2. Read today's passage as many times as you need, take your time
3. Write down (below) what the Lord is saying to you today
4. Live with this Word in your heart through the day

Friday, July 25, 2025
Saint James, Apostle

First Reading: Second Corinthians 4: 7-15

7 But we have this treasure in clay vessels, that the exceeding greatness of the power may be of God and not from ourselves. 8 We are pressed on every side, yet not crushed; perplexed, yet not to despair; 9 pursued, yet not forsaken; struck down, yet not destroyed; 10 always carrying in the body the putting to death of the Lord Jesus, that the life of Jesus may also be revealed in our body. 11 For we who live are always delivered to death for Jesus' sake, that the life also of Jesus may be revealed in our mortal flesh. 12 So then death works in us, but life in you.
13 But having the same spirit of faith, according to that which is written, "I believed, and therefore I spoke." We also believe, and therefore we also speak, 14 knowing that he who raised the Lord Jesus will raise us also with Jesus, and will present us with you. 15 For all things are for your sakes, that the grace, being multiplied through the many, may cause the thanksgiving to abound to the glory of God.

Responsorial Psalm: Psalms 126: 1bc-6

1 When Yahweh brought back those who returned to Zion,
we were like those who dream.
2 Then our mouth was filled with laughter,
and our tongue with singing.
Then they said among the nations,

"Yahweh has done great things for them."
³ Yahweh has done great things for us,
and we are glad.
⁴ Restore our fortunes again, Yahweh,
like the streams in the Negev.
⁵ Those who sow in tears will reap in joy.
⁶ He who goes out weeping, carrying seed for sowing,
will certainly come again with joy, carrying his sheaves.

Gospel: Matthew 20: 20-28

²⁰ Then the mother of the sons of Zebedee came to him with her sons, kneeling and asking a certain thing of him. ²¹ He said to her, "What do you want?"
She said to him, "Command that these, my two sons, may sit, one on your right hand and one on your left hand, in your Kingdom."
²² But Jesus answered, "You don't know what you are asking. Are you able to drink the cup that I am about to drink, and be baptized with the baptism that I am baptized with?"
They said to him, "We are able."
²³ He said to them, "You will indeed drink my cup, and be baptized with the baptism that I am baptized with; but to sit on my right hand and on my left hand is not mine to give, but it is for whom it has been prepared by my Father."
²⁴ When the ten heard it, they were indignant with the two brothers.
²⁵ But Jesus summoned them, and said, "You know that the rulers of the nations lord it over them, and their great ones exercise authority over them. ²⁶ It shall not be so among you; but whoever desires to become great among you shall be your servant. ²⁷ Whoever desires to be first among you shall be your bondservant, ²⁸ even as the Son of Man came not to be served, but to serve, and to give his life as a ransom for many."

1. Invite the Holy Spirit into this reading, asking the Author of Scripture to speak to you through His Word
2. Read today's passage as many times as you need, take your time
3. Write down (below) what the Lord is saying to you today
4. Live with this Word in your heart through the day

_____

_____

Saturday, July 26, 2025

Saints Joachim and Anne, Parents of the Blessed Virgin Mary

First Reading: Exodus 24: 3-8

3 Moses came and told the people all Yahweh's words, and all the ordinances; and all the people answered with one voice, and said, "All the words which Yahweh has spoken will we do."
4 Moses wrote all Yahweh's words, then rose up early in the morning and built an altar at the base of the mountain, with twelve pillars for the twelve tribes of Israel. 5 He sent young men of the children of Israel, who offered burnt offerings and sacrificed peace offerings of cattle to Yahweh. 6 Moses took half of the blood and put it in basins, and half of the blood he sprinkled on the altar. 7 He took the book of the covenant and read it in the hearing of the people, and they said, "We will do all that Yahweh has said, and be obedient."
8 Moses took the blood, and sprinkled it on the people, and said, "Look, this is the blood of the covenant, which Yahweh has made with you concerning all these words."

Responsorial Psalm: Psalms 50: 1b-2, 5-6, 14-15

1 The Mighty One, God, Yahweh, speaks,
and calls the earth from sunrise to sunset.
2 Out of Zion, the perfection of beauty,
God shines out.
5 "Gather my saints together to me,
those who have made a covenant with me by sacrifice."
6 The heavens shall declare his righteousness,
for God himself is judge.
14 Offer to God the sacrifice of thanksgiving.
Pay your vows to the Most High.
15 Call on me in the day of trouble.
I will deliver you, and you will honor me."

Gospel: Matthew 13: 24-30

24 He set another parable before them, saying, "The Kingdom of Heaven is like a man who sowed good seed in his field, 25 but while people slept, his enemy came and sowed darnel weeds[1] also among the wheat, and went away. 26 But when the blade sprang up and produced grain, then the darnel weeds appeared also. 27 The servants of the householder came and said to him, 'Sir, didn't you sow good seed in your field? Where did these darnel weeds come from?'
28 "He said to them, 'An enemy has done this.'

"The servants asked him, 'Do you want us to go and gather them up?' 29 "But he said, 'No, lest perhaps while you gather up the darnel weeds, you root up the wheat with them. 30 Let both grow together until the harvest, and in the harvest time I will tell the reapers, "First, gather up the darnel weeds, and bind them in bundles to burn them; but gather the wheat into my barn." ' "

1. Invite the Holy Spirit into this reading, asking the Author of Scripture to speak to you through His Word
2. Read today's passage as many times as you need, take your time
3. Write down (below) what the Lord is saying to you today
4. Live with this Word in your heart through the day

Sunday, July 27, 2025
SEVENTEENTH SUNDAY IN ORDINARY TIME

First Reading: Genesis 18: 20-32

20 Yahweh said, "Because the cry of Sodom and Gomorrah is great, and because their sin is very grievous, 21 I will go down now, and see whether their deeds are as bad as the reports which have come to me. If not, I will know."

22 The men turned from there, and went toward Sodom, but Abraham stood yet before Yahweh. 23 Abraham came near, and said, "Will you consume the righteous with the wicked? 24 What if there are fifty righteous within the city? Will you consume and not spare the place for the fifty righteous who are in it? 25 May it be far from you to do things like that, to kill the righteous with the wicked, so that the righteous should be like the wicked. May that be far from you. Shouldn't the Judge of all the earth do right?"

26 Yahweh said, "If I find in Sodom fifty righteous within the city, then I will spare the whole place for their sake." 27 Abraham answered, "See now, I have taken it on myself to speak to the Lord, although I am dust and ashes. 28 What if there will lack five of the fifty righteous? Will you destroy all the city for lack of five?"

He said, "I will not destroy it if I find forty-five there."

29 He spoke to him yet again, and said, "What if there are forty found there?"

He said, "I will not do it for the forty's sake."

30 He said, "Oh don't let the Lord be angry, and I will speak. What if there are thirty found there?"

He said, "I will not do it if I find thirty there."
³¹ He said, "See now, I have taken it on myself to speak to the Lord. What if there are twenty found there?"
He said, "I will not destroy it for the twenty's sake."
³² He said, "Oh don't let the Lord be angry, and I will speak just once more. What if ten are found there?"
He said, "I will not destroy it for the ten's sake."

Responsorial Psalm: Psalms 138: 1-2, 2-3, 6-7, 7-8

¹ I will give you thanks with my whole heart.
Before the gods,¹ I will sing praises to you.
² I will bow down toward your holy temple,
and give thanks to your Name for your loving kindness and for your truth;
for you have exalted your Name and your Word above all.
³ In the day that I called, you answered me.
You encouraged me with strength in my soul.
⁶ For though Yahweh is high, yet he looks after the lowly;
but he knows the proud from afar.
⁷ Though I walk in the middle of trouble, you will revive me.
You will stretch out your hand against the wrath of my enemies.
Your right hand will save me.
⁸ Yahweh will fulfill that which concerns me.
Your loving kindness, Yahweh, endures forever.
Don't forsake the works of your own hands.

Second Reading: Colossians 2: 12-14

¹² having been buried with him in baptism, in which you were also raised with him through faith in the working of God, who raised him from the dead. ¹³ You were dead through your trespasses and the uncircumcision of your flesh. He made you alive together with him, having forgiven us all our trespasses, ¹⁴ wiping out the handwriting in ordinances which was against us. He has taken it out of the way, nailing it to the cross.

Gospel: Luke 11: 1-13

¹ When he finished praying in a certain place, one of his disciples said to him, "Lord, teach us to pray, just as John also taught his disciples."
² He said to them, "When you pray, say,
'Our Father in heaven,

may your name be kept holy.
May your Kingdom come.
May your will be done on earth, as it is in heaven.
³ Give us day by day our daily bread.
⁴ Forgive us our sins,
for we ourselves also forgive everyone who is indebted to us.
Bring us not into temptation,
but deliver us from the evil one.' "

⁵ He said to them, "Which of you, if you go to a friend at midnight and tell him, 'Friend, lend me three loaves of bread, ⁶ for a friend of mine has come to me from a journey, and I have nothing to set before him,' ⁷ and he from within will answer and say, 'Don't bother me. The door is now shut, and my children are with me in bed. I can't get up and give it to you'? ⁸ I tell you, although he will not rise and give it to him because he is his friend, yet because of his persistence, he will get up and give him as many as he needs.

⁹ "I tell you, keep asking, and it will be given you. Keep seeking, and you will find. Keep knocking, and it will be opened to you. ¹⁰ For everyone who asks receives. He who seeks finds. To him who knocks it will be opened.

¹¹ "Which of you fathers, if your son asks for bread, will give him a stone? Or if he asks for a fish, he won't give him a snake instead of a fish, will he? ¹² Or if he asks for an egg, he won't give him a scorpion, will he? ¹³ If you then, being evil, know how to give good gifts to your children, how much more will your heavenly Father give the Holy Spirit to those who ask him?"

1. Invite the Holy Spirit into this reading, asking the Author of Scripture to speak to you through His Word
2. Read today's passage as many times as you need, take your time
3. Write down (below) what the Lord is saying to you today
4. Live with this Word in your heart through the day

_____

_____

Monday, July 28, 2025

First Reading: Exodus 32: 15-24, 30-34

¹⁵ Moses turned, and went down from the mountain, with the two tablets of the covenant in his hand; tablets that were written on both their sides. They were written on one side

and on the other. ¹⁶ The tablets were the work of God, and the writing was the writing of God, engraved on the tablets.

¹⁷ When Joshua heard the noise of the people as they shouted, he said to Moses, "There is the noise of war in the camp."

¹⁸ He said, "It isn't the voice of those who shout for victory. It is not the voice of those who cry for being overcome; but the noise of those who sing that I hear." ¹⁹ As soon as he came near to the camp, he saw the calf and the dancing. Then Moses' anger grew hot, and he threw the tablets out of his hands, and broke them beneath the mountain. ²⁰ He took the calf which they had made, and burned it with fire, ground it to powder, and scattered it on the water, and made the children of Israel drink it.

²¹ Moses said to Aaron, "What did these people do to you, that you have brought a great sin on them?"

²² Aaron said, "Don't let the anger of my lord grow hot. You know the people, that they are set on evil. ²³ For they said to me, 'Make us gods, which shall go before us. As for this Moses, the man who brought us up out of the land of Egypt, we don't know what has become of him.' ²⁴ I said to them, 'Whoever has any gold, let them take it off.' So they gave it to me; and I threw it into the fire, and out came this calf."

³⁰ On the next day, Moses said to the people, "You have sinned a great sin. Now I will go up to Yahweh. Perhaps I shall make atonement for your sin."

³¹ Moses returned to Yahweh, and said, "Oh, this people have sinned a great sin, and have made themselves gods of gold. ³² Yet now, if you will, forgive their sin—and if not, please blot me out of your book which you have written."

³³ Yahweh said to Moses, "Whoever has sinned against me, I will blot him out of my book. ³⁴ Now go, lead the people to the place of which I have spoken to you. Behold, my angel shall go before you. Nevertheless, in the day when I punish, I will punish them for their sin."

Responsorial Psalm: Psalms 106: 19-20, 21-22, 23

¹⁹ They made a calf in Horeb,
and worshiped a molten image.
²⁰ Thus they exchanged their glory
for an image of a bull that eats grass.
²¹ They forgot God, their Savior,
who had done great things in Egypt,
²² wondrous works in the land of Ham,
and awesome things by the Red Sea.
²³ Therefore he said that he would destroy them,
had Moses, his chosen, not stood before him in the breach,
to turn away his wrath, so that he wouldn't destroy them.

Gospel: Matthew 13: 31-35

31 He set another parable before them, saying, "The Kingdom of Heaven is like a grain of mustard seed which a man took, and sowed in his field, 32 which indeed is smaller than all seeds. But when it is grown, it is greater than the herbs and becomes a tree, so that the birds of the air come and lodge in its branches."
33 He spoke another parable to them. "The Kingdom of Heaven is like yeast which a woman took and hid in three measures± of meal, until it was all leavened."
34 Jesus spoke all these things in parables to the multitudes; and without a parable, he didn't speak to them, 35 that it might be fulfilled which was spoken through the prophet, saying,
"I will open my mouth in parables;
I will utter things hidden from the foundation of the world."

1. Invite the Holy Spirit into this reading, asking the Author of Scripture to speak to you through His Word
2. Read today's passage as many times as you need, take your time
3. Write down (below) what the Lord is saying to you today
4. Live with this Word in your heart through the day

___

___

Tuesday, July 29, 2025
Saints Martha, Mary, and Lazarus

First Reading: Exodus 33: 7-11; 34: 5b-9, 28

7 Now Moses used to take the tent and pitch it outside the camp, far away from the camp, and he called it "The Tent of Meeting." Everyone who sought Yahweh went out to the Tent of Meeting, which was outside the camp. 8 When Moses went out to the Tent, all the people rose up, and stood, everyone at their tent door, and watched Moses, until he had gone into the Tent. 9 When Moses entered into the Tent, the pillar of cloud descended, stood at the door of the Tent, and Yahweh spoke with Moses. 10 All the people saw the pillar of cloud stand at the door of the Tent, and all the people rose up and worshiped, everyone at their tent door. 11 Yahweh spoke to Moses face to face, as a man speaks to his friend. He turned

again into the camp, but his servant Joshua, the son of Nun, a young man, didn't depart from the Tent.

⁵ Yahweh descended in the cloud, and stood with him there, and proclaimed Yahweh's name. ⁶ Yahweh passed by before him, and proclaimed, "Yahweh! Yahweh, a merciful and gracious God, slow to anger, and abundant in loving kindness and truth, ⁷ keeping loving kindness for thousands, forgiving iniquity and disobedience and sin; and who will by no means clear the guilty, visiting the iniquity of the fathers on the children, and on the children's children, on the third and on the fourth generation."

⁸ Moses hurried and bowed his head toward the earth, and worshiped. ⁹ He said, "If now I have found favor in your sight, Lord, please let the Lord go among us, even though this is a stiff-necked people; pardon our iniquity and our sin, and take us for your inheritance."

²⁸ He was there with Yahweh forty days and forty nights; he neither ate bread, nor drank water. He wrote on the tablets the words of the covenant, the ten commandments.

Responsorial Psalm: Psalms 103: 6-7, 8-9, 10-11, 12-13

⁶ Yahweh executes righteous acts,
and justice for all who are oppressed.
⁷ He made known his ways to Moses,
his deeds to the children of Israel.
⁸ Yahweh is merciful and gracious,
slow to anger, and abundant in loving kindness.
⁹ He will not always accuse;
neither will he stay angry forever.
¹⁰ He has not dealt with us according to our sins,
nor repaid us for our iniquities.
¹¹ For as the heavens are high above the earth,
so great is his loving kindness toward those who fear him.
¹² As far as the east is from the west,
so far has he removed our transgressions from us.
¹³ Like a father has compassion on his children,
so Yahweh has compassion on those who fear him.

Gospel: John 11: 19-27

¹⁹ Many of the Jews had joined the women around Martha and Mary, to console them concerning their brother. ²⁰ Then when Martha heard that Jesus was coming, she went and met him, but Mary stayed in the house. ²¹ Therefore Martha said to Jesus, "Lord, if you would have been here, my brother wouldn't have died. ²² Even now I know that whatever you ask of God, God will give you."

²³ Jesus said to her, "Your brother will rise again."
²⁴ Martha said to him, "I know that he will rise again in the resurrection at the last day."
²⁵ Jesus said to her, "I am the resurrection and the life. He who believes in me will still live, even if he dies. ²⁶ Whoever lives and believes in me will never die. Do you believe this?"
²⁷ She said to him, "Yes, Lord. I have come to believe that you are the Christ, God's Son, he who comes into the world."

1. Invite the Holy Spirit into this reading, asking the Author of Scripture to speak to you through His Word
2. Read today's passage as many times as you need, take your time
3. Write down (below) what the Lord is saying to you today
4. Live with this Word in your heart through the day

Wednesday, July 30, 2025
Saint Peter Chrysologus, Bishop and Doctor of the Church

First Reading: Exodus 34: 29-35

²⁹ When Moses came down from Mount Sinai with the two tablets of the covenant in Moses' hand, when he came down from the mountain, Moses didn't know that the skin of his face shone by reason of his speaking with him. ³⁰ When Aaron and all the children of Israel saw Moses, behold, the skin of his face shone; and they were afraid to come near him. ³¹ Moses called to them, and Aaron and all the rulers of the congregation returned to him; and Moses spoke to them. ³² Afterward all the children of Israel came near, and he gave them all the commandments that Yahweh had spoken with him on Mount Sinai. ³³ When Moses was done speaking with them, he put a veil on his face. ³⁴ But when Moses went in before Yahweh to speak with him, he took the veil off, until he came out; and he came out, and spoke to the children of Israel that which he was commanded. ³⁵ The children of Israel saw Moses' face, that the skin of Moses' face shone; so Moses put the veil on his face again, until he went in to speak with him.

Responsorial Psalm: Psalms 99: 5, 6, 7, 9

⁵ Exalt Yahweh our God.
Worship at his footstool.

He is Holy!
⁶ Moses and Aaron were among his priests,
Samuel was among those who call on his name.
They called on Yahweh, and he answered them.
⁷ He spoke to them in the pillar of cloud.
They kept his testimonies,
the statute that he gave them.
⁹ Exalt Yahweh, our God.
Worship at his holy hill,
for Yahweh, our God, is holy!

Gospel: Matthew 13: 44-46

⁴⁴ "Again, the Kingdom of Heaven is like treasure hidden in the field, which a man found and hid. In his joy, he goes and sells all that he has and buys that field.
⁴⁵ "Again, the Kingdom of Heaven is like a man who is a merchant seeking fine pearls, ⁴⁶ who having found one pearl of great price, he went and sold all that he had and bought it.

1. Invite the Holy Spirit into this reading, asking the Author of Scripture to speak to you through His Word
2. Read today's passage as many times as you need, take your time
3. Write down (below) what the Lord is saying to you today
4. Live with this Word in your heart through the day

Thursday, July 31, 2025
Saint Ignatius of Loyola, Priest

First Reading: Exodus 40: 16-21, 34-38

¹⁶ Moses did so. According to all that Yahweh commanded him, so he did.
¹⁷ In the first month in the second year, on the first day of the month, the tabernacle was raised up. ¹⁸ Moses raised up the tabernacle, and laid its sockets, and set up its boards, and put in its bars, and raised up its pillars. ¹⁹ He spread the covering over the tent, and put the roof of the tabernacle above on it, as Yahweh commanded Moses. ²⁰ He took and put the

covenant into the ark, and set the poles on the ark, and put the mercy seat above on the ark. 21 He brought the ark into the tabernacle, and set up the veil of the screen, and screened the ark of the covenant, as Yahweh commanded Moses.

34 Then the cloud covered the Tent of Meeting, and Yahweh's glory filled the tabernacle. 35 Moses wasn't able to enter into the Tent of Meeting, because the cloud stayed on it, and Yahweh's glory filled the tabernacle. 36 When the cloud was taken up from over the tabernacle, the children of Israel went onward, throughout all their journeys; 37 but if the cloud wasn't taken up, then they didn't travel until the day that it was taken up. 38 For the cloud of Yahweh was on the tabernacle by day, and there was fire in the cloud by night, in the sight of all the house of Israel, throughout all their journeys.

Responsorial Psalm: Psalms 84: 3, 4, 5-6a and 8a, 11

3 Yes, the sparrow has found a home,
and the swallow a nest for herself, where she may have her young,
near your altars, Yahweh of Armies, my King, and my God.
4 Blessed are those who dwell in your house.
They are always praising you.
5 Blessed are those whose strength is in you,
who have set their hearts on a pilgrimage.
6a Passing through the valley of Weeping, they make it a place of springs.
8a Listen, God of Jacob.
11 For Yahweh God is a sun and a shield.
Yahweh will give grace and glory.
He withholds no good thing from those who walk blamelessly.

Gospel: Matthew 13: 47-53

47 "Again, the Kingdom of Heaven is like a dragnet that was cast into the sea and gathered some fish of every kind, 48 which, when it was filled, fishermen drew up on the beach. They sat down and gathered the good into containers, but the bad they threw away. 49 So it will be in the end of the world.§ The angels will come and separate the wicked from among the righteous, 50 and will cast them into the furnace of fire. There will be weeping and gnashing of teeth." 51 Jesus said to them, "Have you understood all these things?"
They answered him, "Yes, Lord."
52 He said to them, "Therefore every scribe who has been made a disciple in the Kingdom of Heaven is like a man who is a householder, who brings out of his treasure new and old things."
53 When Jesus had finished these parables, he departed from there.

1. Invite the Holy Spirit into this reading, asking the Author of Scripture to speak to you through His Word
2. Read today's passage as many times as you need, take your time
3. Write down (below) what the Lord is saying to you today
4. Live with this Word in your heart through the day

Friday, August 1, 2025
Saint Alphonsus Liguori, Bishop and Doctor of the Church

First Reading: Leviticus 23: 1, 4-11, 15-16, 27, 34b-37

¹ Yahweh spoke to Moses, saying,
⁴ " 'These are the set feasts of Yahweh, even holy convocations, which you shall proclaim in their appointed season. ⁵ In the first month, on the fourteenth day of the month in the evening, is Yahweh's Passover. ⁶ On the fifteenth day of the same month is the feast of unleavened bread to Yahweh. Seven days you shall eat unleavened bread. ⁷ In the first day you shall have a holy convocation. You shall do no regular work. ⁸ But you shall offer an offering made by fire to Yahweh seven days. In the seventh day is a holy convocation. You shall do no regular work.' "
⁹ Yahweh spoke to Moses, saying, ¹⁰ "Speak to the children of Israel, and tell them, 'When you have come into the land which I give to you, and shall reap its harvest, then you shall bring the sheaf of the first fruits of your harvest to the priest. ¹¹ He shall wave the sheaf before Yahweh, to be accepted for you. On the next day after the Sabbath the priest shall wave it.
¹⁵ " 'You shall count from the next day after the Sabbath, from the day that you brought the sheaf of the wave offering: seven Sabbaths shall be completed. ¹⁶ The next day after the seventh Sabbath you shall count fifty days; and you shall offer a new meal offering to Yahweh.
²⁷ "However on the tenth day of this seventh month is the day of atonement. It shall be a holy convocation to you. You shall afflict yourselves and you shall offer an offering made by fire to Yahweh.
³⁴ "Speak to the children of Israel, and say, 'On the fifteenth day of this seventh month is the feast of booths‡ for seven days to Yahweh. ³⁵ On the first day shall be a holy convocation. You shall do no regular work. ³⁶ Seven days you shall offer an offering made by fire to

Yahweh. On the eighth day shall be a holy convocation to you. You shall offer an offering made by fire to Yahweh. It is a solemn assembly; you shall do no regular work.

37 "These are the appointed feasts of Yahweh which you shall proclaim to be holy convocations, to offer an offering made by fire to Yahweh, a burnt offering, a meal offering, a sacrifice, and drink offerings, each on its own day

Responsorial Psalm: Psalms 81: 3-4, 5-6, 10-11ab

3 Blow the trumpet at the New Moon,
at the full moon, on our feast day.
4 For it is a statute for Israel,
an ordinance of the God of Jacob.
5 He appointed it in Joseph for a covenant,
when he went out over the land of Egypt,
I heard a language that I didn't know.
6 "I removed his shoulder from the burden.
His hands were freed from the basket.
10 I am Yahweh, your God,
who brought you up out of the land of Egypt.
Open your mouth wide, and I will fill it.
11 But my people didn't listen to my voice.
Israel desired none of me.

Gospel: Matthew 13: 54-58

54 Coming into his own country, he taught them in their synagogue, so that they were astonished and said, "Where did this man get this wisdom and these mighty works? 55 Isn't this the carpenter's son? Isn't his mother called Mary, and his brothers James, Joses, Simon, and Judas? 56 Aren't all of his sisters with us? Where then did this man get all of these things?" 57 They were offended by him.
But Jesus said to them, "A prophet is not without honor, except in his own country and in his own house." 58 He didn't do many mighty works there because of their unbelief.

1. Invite the Holy Spirit into this reading, asking the Author of Scripture to speak to you through His Word
2. Read today's passage as many times as you need, take your time
3. Write down (below) what the Lord is saying to you today
4. Live with this Word in your heart through the day

Saturday, August 2, 2025
Saint Eusebius of Vercelli, Bishop; Saint Peter Julian Eymard, Priest

First Reading: Leviticus 25: 1, 8-17

[1] Yahweh said to Moses on Mount Sinai,
[8] " 'You shall count off seven Sabbaths of years, seven times seven years; and there shall be to you the days of seven Sabbaths of years, even forty-nine years. [9] Then you shall sound the loud trumpet on the tenth day of the seventh month. On the Day of Atonement you shall sound the trumpet throughout all your land. [10] You shall make the fiftieth year holy, and proclaim liberty throughout the land to all its inhabitants. It shall be a jubilee to you; and each of you shall return to his own property, and each of you shall return to his family. [11] That fiftieth year shall be a jubilee to you. In it you shall not sow, neither reap that which grows of itself, nor gather from the undressed vines. [12] For it is a jubilee; it shall be holy to you. You shall eat of its increase out of the field.
[13] " 'In this Year of Jubilee each of you shall return to his property.
[14] " 'If you sell anything to your neighbor, or buy from your neighbor, you shall not wrong one another. [15] According to the number of years after the Jubilee you shall buy from your neighbor. According to the number of years of the crops he shall sell to you. [16] According to the length of the years you shall increase its price, and according to the shortness of the years you shall diminish its price; for he is selling the number of the crops to you. [17] You shall not wrong one another, but you shall fear your God; for I am Yahweh your God.

Responsorial Psalm: Psalms 67: 2-3, 5, 7

[2] That your way may be known on earth,
and your salvation among all nations,
[3] let the peoples praise you, God.
Let all the peoples praise you.
[5] Let the peoples praise you, God.
Let all the peoples praise you.
[7] God will bless us.
All the ends of the earth shall fear him.

Gospel: Matthew 14: 1-12

¹ At that time, Herod the tetrarch heard the report concerning Jesus, ² and said to his servants, "This is John the Baptizer. He is risen from the dead. That is why these powers work in him." ³ For Herod had arrested John, bound him, and put him in prison for the sake of Herodias, his brother Philip's wife. ⁴ For John said to him, "It is not lawful for you to have her." ⁵ When he would have put him to death, he feared the multitude, because they counted him as a prophet. ⁶ But when Herod's birthday came, the daughter of Herodias danced among them and pleased Herod. ⁷ Therefore he promised with an oath to give her whatever she should ask. ⁸ She, being prompted by her mother, said, "Give me here on a platter the head of John the Baptizer."

⁹ The king was grieved, but for the sake of his oaths and of those who sat at the table with him, he commanded it to be given, ¹⁰ and he sent and beheaded John in the prison. ¹¹ His head was brought on a platter and given to the young lady; and she brought it to her mother. ¹² His disciples came, took the body, and buried it. Then they went and told Jesus.

1. Invite the Holy Spirit into this reading, asking the Author of Scripture to speak to you through His Word
2. Read today's passage as many times as you need, take your time
3. Write down (below) what the Lord is saying to you today
4. Live with this Word in your heart through the day

_____

_____

Sunday, August 3, 2025
EIGHTEENTH SUNDAY IN ORDINARY TIME

First Reading: Ecclesiastes 1: 2; 2: 21-23

² "Vanity of vanities," says the Preacher; "Vanity of vanities, all is vanity."
²¹ For there is a man whose labor is with wisdom, with knowledge, and with skillfulness; yet he shall leave it for his portion to a man who has not labored for it. This also is vanity and a great evil. ²² For what does a man have of all his labor and of the striving of his heart, in which he labors under the sun? ²³ For all his days are sorrows, and his travail is grief; yes, even in the night his heart takes no rest. This also is vanity.

Responsorial Psalm: Psalms 90: 3-6, 12-14 and 17

³ You turn man to destruction, saying,
"Return, you children of men."
⁴ For a thousand years in your sight are just like yesterday when it is past,
like a watch in the night.
⁵ You sweep them away as they sleep.
In the morning they sprout like new grass.
⁶ In the morning it sprouts and springs up.
By evening, it is withered and dry.
¹² So teach us to count our days,
that we may gain a heart of wisdom.
¹³ Relent, Yahweh!§
How long?
Have compassion on your servants!
¹⁴ Satisfy us in the morning with your loving kindness,
that we may rejoice and be glad all our days.
¹⁷ Let the favor of the Lord our God be on us.
Establish the work of our hands for us.
Yes, establish the work of our hands.

Second Reading: Colossians 3: 1-5, 9-11

¹ If then you were raised together with Christ, seek the things that are above, where Christ is, seated on the right hand of God. ² Set your mind on the things that are above, not on the things that are on the earth. ³ For you died, and your life is hidden with Christ in God. ⁴ When Christ, our life, is revealed, then you will also be revealed with him in glory.
⁵ Put to death therefore your members which are on the earth: sexual immorality, uncleanness, depraved passion, evil desire, and covetousness, which is idolatry.
⁹ Don't lie to one another, seeing that you have put off the old man with his doings, ¹⁰ and have put on the new man, who is being renewed in knowledge after the image of his Creator, ¹¹ where there can't be Greek and Jew, circumcision and uncircumcision, barbarian, Scythian, bondservant, or free person; but Christ is all, and in all.

Gospel: Luke 12: 13-21

¹³ One of the multitude said to him, "Teacher, tell my brother to divide the inheritance with me."
¹⁴ But he said to him, "Man, who made me a judge or an arbitrator over you?" ¹⁵ He said to them, "Beware! Keep yourselves from covetousness, for a man's life doesn't consist of the abundance of the things which he possesses."

16 He spoke a parable to them, saying, "The ground of a certain rich man produced abundantly. 17 He reasoned within himself, saying, 'What will I do, because I don't have room to store my crops?' 18 He said, 'This is what I will do. I will pull down my barns, build bigger ones, and there I will store all my grain and my goods. 19 I will tell my soul, "Soul, you have many goods laid up for many years. Take your ease, eat, drink, and be merry." '
20 "But God said to him, 'You foolish one, tonight your soul is required of you. The things which you have prepared—whose will they be?' 21 So is he who lays up treasure for himself, and is not rich toward God."

1. Invite the Holy Spirit into this reading, asking the Author of Scripture to speak to you through His Word
2. Read today's passage as many times as you need, take your time
3. Write down (below) what the Lord is saying to you today
4. Live with this Word in your heart through the day

Monday, August 4, 2025
Saint John Vianney, Priest

First Reading: Numbers 11: 4b-15

4b and the children of Israel also wept again, and said, "Who will give us meat to eat? 5 We remember the fish, which we ate in Egypt for nothing; the cucumbers, and the melons, and the leeks, and the onions, and the garlic; 6 but now we have lost our appetite. There is nothing at all except this manna to look at." 7 The manna was like coriander seed, and it looked like bdellium.± 8 The people went around, gathered it, and ground it in mills, or beat it in mortars, and boiled it in pots, and made cakes of it. Its taste was like the taste of fresh oil. 9 When the dew fell on the camp in the night, the manna fell on it.
10 Moses heard the people weeping throughout their families, every man at the door of his tent; and Yahweh's anger burned greatly; and Moses was displeased. 11 Moses said to Yahweh, "Why have you treated your servant so badly? Why haven't I found favor in your sight, that you lay the burden of all this people on me? 12 Have I conceived all this people? Have I brought them out, that you should tell me, 'Carry them in your bosom, as a nurse carries a nursing infant, to the land which you swore to their fathers'? 13 Where could I get meat to give all these people? For they weep before me, saying, 'Give us meat, that we may eat.' 14 I am not able to bear all this people alone, because it is too heavy for me. 15 If you

treat me this way, please kill me right now, if I have found favor in your sight; and don't let me see my wretchedness."

Responsorial Psalm: Psalms 81: 12-16

¹² So I let them go after the stubbornness of their hearts,
that they might walk in their own counsels.
¹³ Oh that my people would listen to me,
that Israel would walk in my ways!
¹⁴ I would soon subdue their enemies,
and turn my hand against their adversaries.
¹⁵ The haters of Yahweh would cringe before him,
and their punishment would last forever.
¹⁶ But he would have also fed them with the finest of the wheat.
I will satisfy you with honey out of the rock."

Gospel: Matthew 14: 13-21

¹³ Now when Jesus heard this, he withdrew from there in a boat to a deserted place apart. When the multitudes heard it, they followed him on foot from the cities.
¹⁴ Jesus went out, and he saw a great multitude. He had compassion on them and healed their sick. ¹⁵ When evening had come, his disciples came to him, saying, "This place is deserted, and the hour is already late. Send the multitudes away, that they may go into the villages, and buy themselves food."
¹⁶ But Jesus said to them, "They don't need to go away. You give them something to eat."
¹⁷ They told him, "We only have here five loaves and two fish."
¹⁸ He said, "Bring them here to me." ¹⁹ He commanded the multitudes to sit down on the grass; and he took the five loaves and the two fish, and looking up to heaven, he blessed, broke and gave the loaves to the disciples; and the disciples gave to the multitudes. ²⁰ They all ate and were filled. They took up twelve baskets full of that which remained left over from the broken pieces. ²¹ Those who ate were about five thousand men, in addition to women and children.

1. Invite the Holy Spirit into this reading, asking the Author of Scripture to speak to you through His Word
2. Read today's passage as many times as you need, take your time
3. Write down (below) what the Lord is saying to you today
4. Live with this Word in your heart through the day

Tuesday, August 5, 2025
The Dedication of the Basilica of Saint Mary Major

First Reading: Numbers 12: 1-13

¹ Miriam and Aaron spoke against Moses because of the Cushite woman whom he had married; for he had married a Cushite woman. ² They said, "Has Yahweh indeed spoken only with Moses? Hasn't he spoken also with us?" And Yahweh heard it.
³ Now the man Moses was very humble, more than all the men who were on the surface of the earth. ⁴ Yahweh spoke suddenly to Moses, to Aaron, and to Miriam, "You three come out to the Tent of Meeting!"
The three of them came out. ⁵ Yahweh came down in a pillar of cloud, and stood at the door of the Tent, and called Aaron and Miriam; and they both came forward. ⁶ He said, "Now hear my words. If there is a prophet among you, I, Yahweh, will make myself known to him in a vision. I will speak with him in a dream. ⁷ My servant Moses is not so. He is faithful in all my house. ⁸ With him, I will speak mouth to mouth, even plainly, and not in riddles; and he shall see Yahweh's form. Why then were you not afraid to speak against my servant, against Moses?" ⁹ Yahweh's anger burned against them; and he departed.
¹⁰ The cloud departed from over the Tent; and behold, Miriam was leprous, as white as snow. Aaron looked at Miriam, and behold, she was leprous.
¹¹ Aaron said to Moses, "Oh, my lord, please don't count this sin against us, in which we have done foolishly, and in which we have sinned. ¹² Let her not, I pray, be as one dead, of whom the flesh is half consumed when he comes out of his mother's womb."
¹³ Moses cried to Yahweh, saying, "Heal her, God, I beg you!"

Responsorial Psalm: Psalms 51: 3-7, 12-13

³ For I know my transgressions.
My sin is constantly before me.
⁴ Against you, and you only, I have sinned,
and done that which is evil in your sight,
so you may be proved right when you speak,
and justified when you judge.
⁵ Behold, I was born in iniquity.
My mother conceived me in sin.

⁶ Behold, you desire truth in the inward parts.
You teach me wisdom in the inmost place.
⁷ Purify me with hyssop, and I will be clean.
Wash me, and I will be whiter than snow.
¹² Restore to me the joy of your salvation.
Uphold me with a willing spirit.
¹³ Then I will teach transgressors your ways.
Sinners will be converted to you.

Gospel: Matthew 15: 1-2, 10-14

¹ Then Pharisees and scribes came to Jesus from Jerusalem, saying, ² "Why do your disciples disobey the tradition of the elders? For they don't wash their hands when they eat bread."
¹⁰ He summoned the multitude, and said to them, "Hear, and understand. ¹¹ That which enters into the mouth doesn't defile the man; but that which proceeds out of the mouth, this defiles the man."
¹² Then the disciples came and said to him, "Do you know that the Pharisees were offended when they heard this saying?"
¹³ But he answered, "Every plant which my heavenly Father didn't plant will be uprooted. ¹⁴ Leave them alone. They are blind guides of the blind. If the blind guide the blind, both will fall into a pit."

1. Invite the Holy Spirit into this reading, asking the Author of Scripture to speak to you through His Word
2. Read today's passage as many times as you need, take your time
3. Write down (below) what the Lord is saying to you today
4. Live with this Word in your heart through the day

Wednesday, August 6, 2025
The Transfiguration of the Lord

First Reading: Daniel 7: 9-10, 13-14

⁹ "I watched until thrones were placed,

and one who was Ancient of Days sat.
His clothing was white as snow,
and the hair of his head like pure wool.
His throne was fiery flames,
and its wheels burning fire.
¹⁰ A fiery stream issued and came out from before him.
Thousands of thousands ministered to him.
Ten thousand times ten thousand stood before him.
The judgment was set.
The books were opened.
¹³ "I saw in the night visions, and behold, one like a son of man came with the clouds, and he came to the Ancient of Days, and they brought him near before him. ¹⁴ Dominion was given him, with glory and a kingdom, that all the peoples, nations, and languages should serve him. His dominion is an everlasting dominion, which will not pass away, and his kingdom will not be destroyed.

Responsorial Psalm: Psalms 97: 1-2, 5-6, 9

¹ Yahweh reigns!
Let the earth rejoice!
Let the multitude of islands be glad!
² Clouds and darkness are around him.
Righteousness and justice are the foundation of his throne.
⁵ The mountains melt like wax at the presence of Yahweh,
at the presence of the Lord of the whole earth.
⁶ The heavens declare his righteousness.
All the peoples have seen his glory.
⁹ For you, Yahweh, are most high above all the earth.
You are exalted far above all gods.

Second Reading: Second Peter 1: 16-19

¹⁶ For we didn't follow cunningly devised fables when we made known to you the power and coming of our Lord Jesus Christ, but we were eyewitnesses of his majesty. ¹⁷ For he received from God the Father honor and glory when the voice came to him from the Majestic Glory, "This is my beloved Son, in whom I am well pleased." ¹⁸ We heard this voice come out of heaven when we were with him on the holy mountain.
¹⁹ We have the more sure word of prophecy; and you do well that you heed it as to a lamp shining in a dark place, until the day dawns and the morning star arises in your hearts,

Gospel: Luke 9: 28b-36

28b he took with him Peter, John, and James, and went up onto the mountain to pray. 29 As he was praying, the appearance of his face was altered, and his clothing became white and dazzling. 30 Behold, two men were talking with him, who were Moses and Elijah, 31 who appeared in glory and spoke of his departure, which he was about to accomplish at Jerusalem.

32 Now Peter and those who were with him were heavy with sleep, but when they were fully awake, they saw his glory, and the two men who stood with him. 33 As they were parting from him, Peter said to Jesus, "Master, it is good for us to be here. Let's make three tents: one for you, one for Moses, and one for Elijah," not knowing what he said.

34 While he said these things, a cloud came and overshadowed them, and they were afraid as they entered into the cloud. 35 A voice came out of the cloud, saying, "This is my beloved Son. Listen to him!" 36 When the voice came, Jesus was found alone. They were silent, and told no one in those days any of the things which they had seen.

1. Invite the Holy Spirit into this reading, asking the Author of Scripture to speak to you through His Word
2. Read today's passage as many times as you need, take your time
3. Write down (below) what the Lord is saying to you today
4. Live with this Word in your heart through the day

___

___

Thursday, August 7, 2025
Saint Sixtus II, Pope, and Companions, Martyrs; Saint Cajetan, Priest

First Reading: Numbers 20: 1-13

1 The children of Israel, even the whole congregation, came into the wilderness of Zin in the first month. The people stayed in Kadesh. Miriam died there, and was buried there. 2 There was no water for the congregation; and they assembled themselves together against Moses and against Aaron. 3 The people quarreled with Moses, and spoke, saying, "We wish that we had died when our brothers died before Yahweh! 4 Why have you brought Yahweh's assembly into this wilderness, that we should die there, we and our animals? 5 Why have you made us to come up out of Egypt, to bring us in to this evil place? It is no place of seed, or of figs, or of vines, or of pomegranates; neither is there any water to drink."

⁶ Moses and Aaron went from the presence of the assembly to the door of the Tent of Meeting, and fell on their faces. Yahweh's glory appeared to them. ⁷ Yahweh spoke to Moses, saying, ⁸ "Take the rod, and assemble the congregation, you, and Aaron your brother, and speak to the rock before their eyes, that it pour out its water. You shall bring water to them out of the rock; so you shall give the congregation and their livestock drink."
⁹ Moses took the rod from before Yahweh, as he commanded him. ¹⁰ Moses and Aaron gathered the assembly together before the rock, and he said to them, "Hear now, you rebels! Shall we bring water out of this rock for you?" ¹¹ Moses lifted up his hand, and struck the rock with his rod twice, and water came out abundantly. The congregation and their livestock drank.
¹² Yahweh said to Moses and Aaron, "Because you didn't believe in me, to sanctify me in the eyes of the children of Israel, therefore you shall not bring this assembly into the land which I have given them."

Responsorial Psalm: Psalms 95: 1-2, 6-9

¹ Oh come, let's sing to Yahweh.
Let's shout aloud to the rock of our salvation!
² Let's come before his presence with thanksgiving.
Let's extol him with songs!
⁶ Oh come, let's worship and bow down.
Let's kneel before Yahweh, our Maker,
⁷ for he is our God.
We are the people of his pasture,
and the sheep in his care.
Today, oh that you would hear his voice!
⁸ Don't harden your heart, as at Meribah,
as in the day of Massah in the wilderness,
⁹ when your fathers tempted me,
tested me, and saw my work.

Gospel: Matthew 16: 13-23

¹³ Now when Jesus came into the parts of Caesarea Philippi, he asked his disciples, saying, "Who do men say that I, the Son of Man, am?"
¹⁴ They said, "Some say John the Baptizer, some, Elijah, and others, Jeremiah or one of the prophets."
¹⁵ He said to them, "But who do you say that I am?"
¹⁶ Simon Peter answered, "You are the Christ, the Son of the living God."

17 Jesus answered him, "Blessed are you, Simon Bar Jonah, for flesh and blood has not revealed this to you, but my Father who is in heaven. 18 I also tell you that you are Peter,‡ and on this rock ‡ I will build my assembly, and the gates of Hades§ will not prevail against it. 19 I will give to you the keys of the Kingdom of Heaven, and whatever you bind on earth will have been bound in heaven; and whatever you release on earth will have been released in heaven." 20 Then he commanded the disciples that they should tell no one that he was Jesus the Christ.

21 From that time, Jesus began to show his disciples that he must go to Jerusalem and suffer many things from the elders, chief priests, and scribes, and be killed, and the third day be raised up.

22 Peter took him aside and began to rebuke him, saying, "Far be it from you, Lord! This will never be done to you."

23 But he turned and said to Peter, "Get behind me, Satan! You are a stumbling block to me, for you are not setting your mind on the things of God, but on the things of men."

1. Invite the Holy Spirit into this reading, asking the Author of Scripture to speak to you through His Word
2. Read today's passage as many times as you need, take your time
3. Write down (below) what the Lord is saying to you today
4. Live with this Word in your heart through the day

Friday, August 8, 2025
Saint Dominic, Priest

First Reading: Deuteronomy 4: 32-40

32 For ask now of the days that are past, which were before you, since the day that God created man on the earth, and from the one end of the sky to the other, whether there has been anything as great as this thing is, or has been heard like it? 33 Did a people ever hear the voice of God speaking out of the middle of the fire, as you have heard, and live? 34 Or has God tried to go and take a nation for himself from among another nation, by trials, by signs, by wonders, by war, by a mighty hand, by an outstretched arm, and by great terrors, according to all that Yahweh your God did for you in Egypt before your eyes? 35 It was shown to you so that you might know that Yahweh is God. There is no one else besides him. 36 Out of heaven he made you to hear his voice, that he might instruct you. On earth

he made you to see his great fire; and you heard his words out of the middle of the fire. 37 Because he loved your fathers, therefore he chose their offspring after them, and brought you out with his presence, with his great power, out of Egypt; 38 to drive out nations from before you greater and mightier than you, to bring you in, to give you their land for an inheritance, as it is today. 39 Know therefore today, and take it to heart, that Yahweh himself is God in heaven above and on the earth beneath. There is no one else. 40 You shall keep his statutes and his commandments which I command you today, that it may go well with you and with your children after you, and that you may prolong your days in the land which Yahweh your God gives you for all time.

Responsorial Psalm: Psalms 77: 12-16

12 I will also meditate on all your work,
and consider your doings.
13 Your way, God, is in the sanctuary.
What god is great like God?
14 You are the God who does wonders.
You have made your strength known among the peoples.
15 You have redeemed your people with your arm,
the sons of Jacob and Joseph.
Selah.
16 The waters saw you, God.
The waters saw you, and they writhed.
The depths also convulsed.

Gospel: Matthew 16: 24-28

24 Then Jesus said to his disciples, "If anyone desires to come after me, let him deny himself, take up his cross, and follow me. 25 For whoever desires to save his life will lose it, and whoever will lose his life for my sake will find it. 26 For what will it profit a man if he gains the whole world and forfeits his life? Or what will a man give in exchange for his life? 27 For the Son of Man will come in the glory of his Father with his angels, and then he will render to everyone according to his deeds. 28 Most certainly I tell you, there are some standing here who will in no way taste of death until they see the Son of Man coming in his Kingdom."

1. Invite the Holy Spirit into this reading, asking the Author of Scripture to speak to you through His Word
2. Read today's passage as many times as you need, take your time
3. Write down (below) what the Lord is saying to you today

4. Live with this Word in your heart through the day

Saturday, August 9, 2025
Saint Teresa Benedicta of the Cross, Virgin and Martyr

First Reading: Deuteronomy 6: 4-13

⁴ Hear, Israel: Yahweh is our God. Yahweh is one. ⁵ You shall love Yahweh your God with all your heart, with all your soul, and with all your might. ⁶ These words, which I command you today, shall be on your heart; ⁷ and you shall teach them diligently to your children, and shall talk of them when you sit in your house, and when you walk by the way, and when you lie down, and when you rise up. ⁸ You shall bind them for a sign on your hand, and they shall be for frontlets between your eyes. ⁹ You shall write them on the door posts of your house and on your gates.
¹⁰ It shall be, when Yahweh your God brings you into the land which he swore to your fathers, to Abraham, to Isaac, and to Jacob, to give you, great and goodly cities which you didn't build, ¹¹ and houses full of all good things which you didn't fill, and cisterns dug out which you didn't dig, vineyards and olive trees which you didn't plant, and you shall eat and be full; ¹² then beware lest you forget Yahweh, who brought you out of the land of Egypt, out of the house of bondage. ¹³ You shall fear Yahweh your God; and you shall serve him, and shall swear by his name.

Responsorial Psalm: Psalms 18: 2-4, 47

² Yahweh is my rock, my fortress, and my deliverer;
my God, my rock, in whom I take refuge;
my shield, and the horn of my salvation, my high tower.
³ I call on Yahweh, who is worthy to be praised;
and I am saved from my enemies.
⁴ The cords of death surrounded me.
The floods of ungodliness made me afraid.
⁴⁷ even the God who executes vengeance for me,
and subdues peoples under me.

Gospel: Matthew 17: 14-20

¹⁴ When they came to the multitude, a man came to him, kneeling down to him and saying, ¹⁵ "Lord, have mercy on my son, for he is epileptic and suffers grievously; for he often falls into the fire, and often into the water. ¹⁶ So I brought him to your disciples, and they could not cure him."
¹⁷ Jesus answered, "Faithless and perverse generation! How long will I be with you? How long will I bear with you? Bring him here to me." ¹⁸ Jesus rebuked the demon, and it went out of him, and the boy was cured from that hour.
¹⁹ Then the disciples came to Jesus privately, and said, "Why weren't we able to cast it out?" ²⁰ He said to them, "Because of your unbelief. For most certainly I tell you, if you have faith as a grain of mustard seed, you will tell this mountain, 'Move from here to there,' and it will move; and nothing will be impossible for you.

1. Invite the Holy Spirit into this reading, asking the Author of Scripture to speak to you through His Word
2. Read today's passage as many times as you need, take your time
3. Write down (below) what the Lord is saying to you today
4. Live with this Word in your heart through the day

Sunday, August 10, 2025
NINETEENTH SUNDAY IN ORDINARY TIME

First Reading: Wisdom 18: 6-9

⁶ Our fathers were made aware of that night beforehand,
that, having sure knowledge, they might be cheered by the oaths which they had trusted.
⁷ Salvation of the righteous and destruction of the enemies was expected by your people.
⁸ For as you took vengeance on the adversaries,
by the same means, calling us to yourself, you glorified us.
⁹ For holy children of good men offered sacrifice in secret,
and with one consent they agreed to the covenant of the divine law,
that they would partake alike in the same good things and the same perils,
the fathers already leading the sacred songs of praise.

Responsorial Psalm: Psalms 33: 1, 12, 18-22

¹ Rejoice in Yahweh, you righteous!
Praise is fitting for the upright.
¹² Blessed is the nation whose God is Yahweh,
the people whom he has chosen for his own inheritance.
¹⁸ Behold, Yahweh's eye is on those who fear him,
on those who hope in his loving kindness,
¹⁹ to deliver their soul from death,
to keep them alive in famine.
²⁰ Our soul has waited for Yahweh.
He is our help and our shield.
²¹ For our heart rejoices in him,
because we have trusted in his holy name.
²² Let your loving kindness be on us, Yahweh,
since we have hoped in you.

Second Reading: Hebrews 11: 1-2, 8-12

¹ Now faith is assurance of things hoped for, proof of things not seen. ² For by this, the elders obtained approval.
⁸ By faith Abraham, when he was called, obeyed to go out to the place which he was to receive for an inheritance. He went out, not knowing where he went. ⁹ By faith he lived as an alien in the land of promise, as in a land not his own, dwelling in tents with Isaac and Jacob, the heirs with him of the same promise. ¹⁰ For he was looking for the city which has foundations, whose builder and maker is God.
¹¹ By faith even Sarah herself received power to conceive, and she bore a child when she was past age, since she counted him faithful who had promised. ¹² Therefore as many as the stars of the sky in multitude, and as innumerable as the sand which is by the sea shore, were fathered by one man, and him as good as dead.

Gospel: Luke 12: 32-48

³² "Don't be afraid, little flock, for it is your Father's good pleasure to give you the Kingdom. ³³ Sell what you have and give gifts to the needy. Make for yourselves purses which don't grow old, a treasure in the heavens that doesn't fail, where no thief approaches and no moth destroys. ³⁴ For where your treasure is, there will your heart be also.
³⁵ "Let your waist be dressed and your lamps burning. ³⁶ Be like men watching for their lord when he returns from the wedding feast, that when he comes and knocks, they may immediately open to him. ³⁷ Blessed are those servants whom the lord will find watching when he comes. Most certainly I tell you that he will dress himself, make them recline, and

will come and serve them. ³⁸ They will be blessed if he comes in the second or third watch and finds them so. ³⁹ But know this, that if the master of the house had known in what hour the thief was coming, he would have watched and not allowed his house to be broken into. ⁴⁰ Therefore be ready also, for the Son of Man is coming in an hour that you don't expect him."

⁴¹ Peter said to him, "Lord, are you telling this parable to us, or to everybody?"

⁴² The Lord said, "Who then is the faithful and wise steward, whom his lord will set over his household, to give them their portion of food at the right times? ⁴³ Blessed is that servant whom his lord will find doing so when he comes. ⁴⁴ Truly I tell you that he will set him over all that he has. ⁴⁵ But if that servant says in his heart, 'My lord delays his coming,' and begins to beat the menservants and the maidservants, and to eat and drink and to be drunken, ⁴⁶ then the lord of that servant will come in a day when he isn't expecting him and in an hour that he doesn't know, and will cut him in two, and place his portion with the unfaithful. ⁴⁷ That servant who knew his lord's will, and didn't prepare nor do what he wanted, will be beaten with many stripes, ⁴⁸ but he who didn't know, and did things worthy of stripes, will be beaten with few stripes. To whomever much is given, of him will much be required; and to whom much was entrusted, of him more will be asked.

1. Invite the Holy Spirit into this reading, asking the Author of Scripture to speak to you through His Word
2. Read today's passage as many times as you need, take your time
3. Write down (below) what the Lord is saying to you today
4. Live with this Word in your heart through the day

Monday, August 11, 2025
Saint Clare, Virgin

First Reading: Deuteronomy 10: 12-22

¹² Now, Israel, what does Yahweh your God require of you, but to fear Yahweh your God, to walk in all his ways, to love him, and to serve Yahweh your God with all your heart and with all your soul, ¹³ to keep Yahweh's commandments and statutes, which I command you today for your good? ¹⁴ Behold, to Yahweh your God belongs heaven, the heaven of heavens, and the earth, with all that is therein. ¹⁵ Only Yahweh had a delight in your fathers to love them, and he chose their offspring after them, even you above all peoples, as it is

today. ¹⁶ Circumcise therefore the foreskin of your heart, and be no more stiff-necked. ¹⁷ For Yahweh your God, he is God of gods and Lord of lords, the great God, the mighty, and the awesome, who doesn't respect persons or take bribes. ¹⁸ He executes justice for the fatherless and widow and loves the foreigner in giving him food and clothing. ¹⁹ Therefore love the foreigner, for you were foreigners in the land of Egypt. ²⁰ You shall fear Yahweh your God. You shall serve him. You shall cling to him, and you shall swear by his name. ²¹ He is your praise, and he is your God, who has done for you these great and awesome things which your eyes have seen. ²² Your fathers went down into Egypt with seventy persons; and now Yahweh your God has made you as the stars of the sky for multitude.

Responsorial Psalm: Psalms 147: 12-15, 19-20

¹² Praise Yahweh, Jerusalem!
Praise your God, Zion!
¹³ For he has strengthened the bars of your gates.
He has blessed your children within you.
¹⁴ He makes peace in your borders.
He fills you with the finest of the wheat.
¹⁵ He sends out his commandment to the earth.
His word runs very swiftly.
¹⁹ He shows his word to Jacob,
his statutes and his ordinances to Israel.
²⁰ He has not done this for just any nation.
They don't know his ordinances.
Praise Yah!

Gospel: Matthew 17: 22-27

²² While they were staying in Galilee, Jesus said to them, "The Son of Man is about to be delivered up into the hands of men, ²³ and they will kill him, and the third day he will be raised up."
They were exceedingly sorry.
²⁴ When they had come to Capernaum, those who collected the didrachma coins§ came to Peter, and said, "Doesn't your teacher pay the didrachma?" ²⁵ He said, "Yes."
When he came into the house, Jesus anticipated him, saying, "What do you think, Simon? From whom do the kings of the earth receive toll or tribute? From their children, or from strangers?"
²⁶ Peter said to him, "From strangers."

Jesus said to him, "Therefore the children are exempt. ²⁷ But, lest we cause them to stumble, go to the sea, cast a hook, and take up the first fish that comes up. When you have opened its mouth, you will find a stater coin. Take that, and give it to them for me and you."

1. Invite the Holy Spirit into this reading, asking the Author of Scripture to speak to you through His Word
2. Read today's passage as many times as you need, take your time
3. Write down (below) what the Lord is saying to you today
4. Live with this Word in your heart through the day

Tuesday, August 12, 2025
Saint Jane Frances de Chantal, Religious

First Reading: Deuteronomy 31: 1-8

¹ Moses went and spoke these words to all Israel. ² He said to them, "I am one hundred twenty years old today. I can no more go out and come in. Yahweh has said to me, 'You shall not go over this Jordan.' ³ Yahweh your God himself will go over before you. He will destroy these nations from before you, and you shall dispossess them. Joshua will go over before you, as Yahweh has spoken. ⁴ Yahweh will do to them as he did to Sihon and to Og, the kings of the Amorites, and to their land, when he destroyed them. ⁵ Yahweh will deliver them up before you, and you shall do to them according to all the commandment which I have commanded you. ⁶ Be strong and courageous. Don't be afraid or scared of them, for Yahweh your God himself is who goes with you. He will not fail you nor forsake you."
⁷ Moses called to Joshua, and said to him in the sight of all Israel, "Be strong and courageous, for you shall go with this people into the land which Yahweh has sworn to their fathers to give them; and you shall cause them to inherit it. ⁸ Yahweh himself is who goes before you. He will be with you. He will not fail you nor forsake you. Don't be afraid. Don't be discouraged."

Responsorial Psalm: Deuteronomy 32: 3-4ab, 7, 8, 9 and 12

³ For I will proclaim Yahweh's name.
Ascribe greatness to our God!

4ab The Rock: his work is perfect,
for all his ways are just.
7 Remember the days of old.
Consider the years of many generations.
Ask your father, and he will show you;
your elders, and they will tell you.
8 When the Most High gave to the nations their inheritance,
when he separated the children of men,
he set the bounds of the peoples
according to the number of the children of Israel.
9 For Yahweh's portion is his people.
Jacob is the lot of his inheritance.
12 Yahweh alone led him.
There was no foreign god with him.

Gospel: Matthew 18: 1-5, 10, 12-14

1 In that hour the disciples came to Jesus, saying, "Who then is greatest in the Kingdom of Heaven?"
2 Jesus called a little child to himself, and set him in the middle of them 3 and said, "Most certainly I tell you, unless you turn and become as little children, you will in no way enter into the Kingdom of Heaven. 4 Whoever therefore humbles himself as this little child is the greatest in the Kingdom of Heaven. 5 Whoever receives one such little child in my name receives me,
10 See that you don't despise one of these little ones, for I tell you that in heaven their angels always see the face of my Father who is in heaven.
12 "What do you think? If a man has one hundred sheep, and one of them goes astray, doesn't he leave the ninety-nine, go to the mountains, and seek that which has gone astray? 13 If he finds it, most certainly I tell you, he rejoices over it more than over the ninety-nine which have not gone astray. 14 Even so it is not the will of your Father who is in heaven that one of these little ones should perish.

1. Invite the Holy Spirit into this reading, asking the Author of Scripture to speak to you through His Word
2. Read today's passage as many times as you need, take your time
3. Write down (below) what the Lord is saying to you today
4. Live with this Word in your heart through the day

Wednesday, August 13, 2025
Saints Pontian, Pope, and Hippolytus, Priest, Martyrs

First Reading: Deuteronomy 34: 1-12

¹ Moses went up from the plains of Moab to Mount Nebo, to the top of Pisgah, that is opposite Jericho. Yahweh showed him all the land of Gilead to Dan, ² and all Naphtali, and the land of Ephraim and Manasseh, and all the land of Judah, to the Western Sea, ³ and the south, and the Plain of the valley of Jericho the city of palm trees, to Zoar. ⁴ Yahweh said to him, "This is the land which I swore to Abraham, to Isaac, and to Jacob, saying, 'I will give it to your offspring.' I have caused you to see it with your eyes, but you shall not go over there."
⁵ So Moses the servant of Yahweh died there in the land of Moab, according to Yahweh's word. ⁶ He buried him in the valley in the land of Moab opposite Beth Peor, but no man knows where his tomb is to this day. ⁷ Moses was one hundred twenty years old when he died. His eye was not dim, nor his strength gone. ⁸ The children of Israel wept for Moses in the plains of Moab thirty days, until the days of weeping in the mourning for Moses were ended. ⁹ Joshua the son of Nun was full of the spirit of wisdom, for Moses had laid his hands on him. The children of Israel listened to him, and did as Yahweh commanded Moses. ¹⁰ Since then, there has not arisen a prophet in Israel like Moses, whom Yahweh knew face to face, ¹¹ in all the signs and the wonders which Yahweh sent him to do in the land of Egypt, to Pharaoh, and to all his servants, and to all his land, ¹² and in all the mighty hand, and in all the awesome deeds, which Moses did in the sight of all Israel.

Responsorial Psalm: Psalms 66: 1-3a, 5 and 8, 16-17

¹ Make a joyful shout to God, all the earth!
² Sing to the glory of his name!
Offer glory and praise!
³ᵃ Tell God, "How awesome are your deeds!
⁵ Come, and see God's deeds—
awesome work on behalf of the children of men.
⁸ Praise our God, you peoples!
Make the sound of his praise heard,
¹⁶ Come and hear, all you who fear God.
I will declare what he has done for my soul.
¹⁷ I cried to him with my mouth.
He was extolled with my tongue.

Gospel: Matthew 18: 15-20

¹⁵ "If your brother sins against you, go, show him his fault between you and him alone. If he listens to you, you have gained back your brother. ¹⁶ But if he doesn't listen, take one or two more with you, that at the mouth of two or three witnesses every word may be established. ¹⁷ If he refuses to listen to them, tell it to the assembly. If he refuses to hear the assembly also, let him be to you as a Gentile or a tax collector. ¹⁸ Most certainly I tell you, whatever things you bind on earth will have been bound in heaven, and whatever things you release on earth will have been released in heaven. ¹⁹ Again, assuredly I tell you, that if two of you will agree on earth concerning anything that they will ask, it will be done for them by my Father who is in heaven. ²⁰ For where two or three are gathered together in my name, there I am in the middle of them."

1. Invite the Holy Spirit into this reading, asking the Author of Scripture to speak to you through His Word
2. Read today's passage as many times as you need, take your time
3. Write down (below) what the Lord is saying to you today
4. Live with this Word in your heart through the day

Thursday, August 14, 2025
Saint Maximilian Kolbe, Priest and Martyr

First Reading: Joshua 3: 7-10a, 11, 13-17

⁷ Yahweh said to Joshua, "Today I will begin to magnify you in the sight of all Israel, that they may know that as I was with Moses, so I will be with you. ⁸ You shall command the priests who bear the ark of the covenant, saying, 'When you come to the brink of the waters of the Jordan, you shall stand still in the Jordan.'"
⁹ Joshua said to the children of Israel, "Come here, and hear the words of Yahweh your God." ¹⁰ᵃ Joshua said, "By this you shall know that the living God is among you, and that he will without fail drive the Canaanite
¹¹ Behold, the ark of the covenant of the Lord of all the earth passes over before you into the Jordan.
¹³ It shall be that when the soles of the feet of the priests who bear the ark of Yahweh, the Lord of all the earth, rest in the waters of the Jordan, that the waters of the Jordan will be cut off. The waters that come down from above shall stand in one heap."

¹⁴ When the people moved from their tents to pass over the Jordan, the priests who bore the ark of the covenant being before the people, ¹⁵ and when those who bore the ark had come to the Jordan, and the feet of the priests who bore the ark had dipped in the edge of the water (for the Jordan overflows all its banks all the time of harvest), ¹⁶ the waters which came down from above stood, and rose up in one heap a great way off, at Adam, the city that is beside Zarethan; and those that went down toward the sea of the Arabah, even the Salt Sea, were wholly cut off. Then the people passed over near Jericho. ¹⁷ The priests who bore the ark of Yahweh's covenant stood firm on dry ground in the middle of the Jordan; and all Israel crossed over on dry ground, until all the nation had passed completely over the Jordan.

Responsorial Psalm: Psalms 114: 1-6

¹ When Israel went out of Egypt,
the house of Jacob from a people of foreign language,
² Judah became his sanctuary,
Israel his dominion.
³ The sea saw it, and fled.
The Jordan was driven back.
⁴ The mountains skipped like rams,
the little hills like lambs.
⁵ What was it, you sea, that you fled?
You Jordan, that you turned back?
⁶ You mountains, that you skipped like rams?
You little hills, like lambs?

Gospel: Matthew 18: 21 – 19: 1

²¹ Then Peter came and said to him, "Lord, how often shall my brother sin against me, and I forgive him? Until seven times?"
²² Jesus said to him, "I don't tell you until seven times, but, until seventy times seven. ²³ Therefore the Kingdom of Heaven is like a certain king who wanted to settle accounts with his servants. ²⁴ When he had begun to settle, one was brought to him who owed him ten thousand talents.§ ²⁵ But because he couldn't pay, his lord commanded him to be sold, with his wife, his children, and all that he had, and payment to be made. ²⁶ The servant therefore fell down and knelt before him, saying, 'Lord, have patience with me, and I will repay you all!' ²⁷ The lord of that servant, being moved with compassion, released him and forgave him the debt.

28 "But that servant went out and found one of his fellow servants who owed him one hundred denarii, and he grabbed him and took him by the throat, saying, 'Pay me what you owe!'

29 "So his fellow servant fell down at his feet and begged him, saying, 'Have patience with me, and I will repay you!' 30 He would not, but went and cast him into prison until he should pay back that which was due. 31 So when his fellow servants saw what was done, they were exceedingly sorry, and came and told their lord all that was done. 32 Then his lord called him in and said to him, 'You wicked servant! I forgave you all that debt because you begged me. 33 Shouldn't you also have had mercy on your fellow servant, even as I had mercy on you?' 34 His lord was angry, and delivered him to the tormentors until he should pay all that was due to him. 35 So my heavenly Father will also do to you, if you don't each forgive your brother from your hearts for his misdeeds."

1 When Jesus had finished these words, he departed from Galilee and came into the borders of Judea beyond the Jordan.

1. Invite the Holy Spirit into this reading, asking the Author of Scripture to speak to you through His Word
2. Read today's passage as many times as you need, take your time
3. Write down (below) what the Lord is saying to you today
4. Live with this Word in your heart through the day

Friday, August 15, 2025
THE ASSUMPTION OF THE BLESSED VIRGIN MARY

First Reading: Revelation 11: 19a; 12: 1-6a, 10ab

19 God's temple that is in heaven was opened, and the ark of the Lord's covenant was seen in his temple. Lightnings, sounds, thunders, an earthquake, and great hail followed.
1 A great sign was seen in heaven: a woman clothed with the sun, and the moon under her feet, and on her head a crown of twelve stars. 2 She was with child. She cried out in pain, laboring to give birth.
3 Another sign was seen in heaven. Behold, a great red dragon, having seven heads and ten horns, and on his heads seven crowns. 4 His tail drew one third of the stars of the sky, and threw them to the earth. The dragon stood before the woman who was about to give birth, so that when she gave birth he might devour her child. 5 She gave birth to a son, a male

child, who is to rule all the nations with a rod of iron. Her child was caught up to God and to his throne. ⁶ᵃ The woman fled into the wilderness, where she has a place prepared by God,
¹⁰ I heard a loud voice in heaven, saying, "Now the salvation, the power, and the Kingdom of our God, and the authority of his Christ has come

Responsorial Psalm: Psalms 45: 10, 11, 12, 16

¹⁰ Listen, daughter, consider, and turn your ear.
Forget your own people, and also your father's house.
¹¹ So the king will desire your beauty,
honor him, for he is your lord.
¹² The daughter of Tyre comes with a gift.
The rich among the people entreat your favor.
¹⁶ Your sons will take the place of your fathers.
You shall make them princes in all the earth.

Second Reading: First Corinthians 15: 20-27

²⁰ But now Christ has been raised from the dead. He became the first fruit of those who are asleep. ²¹ For since death came by man, the resurrection of the dead also came by man. ²² For as in Adam all die, so also in Christ all will be made alive. ²³ But each in his own order: Christ the first fruits, then those who are Christ's at his coming. ²⁴ Then the end comes, when he will deliver up the Kingdom to God the Father, when he will have abolished all rule and all authority and power. ²⁵ For he must reign until he has put all his enemies under his feet. ²⁶ The last enemy that will be abolished is death. ²⁷ For, "He put all things in subjection under his feet."* But when he says, "All things are put in subjection", it is evident that he is excepted who subjected all things to him.

Gospel: Luke 1: 39-56

³⁹ Mary arose in those days and went into the hill country with haste, into a city of Judah, ⁴⁰ and entered into the house of Zacharias and greeted Elizabeth. ⁴¹ When Elizabeth heard Mary's greeting, the baby leaped in her womb; and Elizabeth was filled with the Holy Spirit. ⁴² She called out with a loud voice and said, "Blessed are you among women, and blessed is the fruit of your womb! ⁴³ Why am I so favored, that the mother of my Lord should come to me? ⁴⁴ For behold, when the voice of your greeting came into my ears, the baby leaped in my womb for joy! ⁴⁵ Blessed is she who believed, for there will be a fulfillment of the things which have been spoken to her from the Lord!"
⁴⁶ Mary said,

"My soul magnifies the Lord.
47 My spirit has rejoiced in God my Savior,
48 for he has looked at the humble state of his servant.
For behold, from now on, all generations will call me blessed.
49 For he who is mighty has done great things for me.
Holy is his name.
50 His mercy is for generations and generations on those who fear him.
51 He has shown strength with his arm.
He has scattered the proud in the imagination of their hearts.
52 He has put down princes from their thrones,
and has exalted the lowly.
53 He has filled the hungry with good things.
He has sent the rich away empty.
54 He has given help to Israel, his servant, that he might remember mercy,
55 as he spoke to our fathers,
to Abraham and his offspring§ forever."
56 Mary stayed with her about three months, and then returned to her house.

1. Invite the Holy Spirit into this reading, asking the Author of Scripture to speak to you through His Word
2. Read today's passage as many times as you need, take your time
3. Write down (below) what the Lord is saying to you today
4. Live with this Word in your heart through the day

Saturday, August 16, 2025
Saint Stephen of Hungary

First Reading: Joshua 24: 14-29

14 "Now therefore fear Yahweh, and serve him in sincerity and in truth. Put away the gods which your fathers served beyond the River, in Egypt; and serve Yahweh. 15 If it seems evil to you to serve Yahweh, choose today whom you will serve; whether the gods which your fathers served that were beyond the River, or the gods of the Amorites, in whose land you dwell; but as for me and my house, we will serve Yahweh."

¹⁶ The people answered, "Far be it from us that we should forsake Yahweh, to serve other gods; ¹⁷ for it is Yahweh our God who brought us and our fathers up out of the land of Egypt, from the house of bondage, and who did those great signs in our sight, and preserved us in all the way in which we went, and among all the peoples through the middle of whom we passed. ¹⁸ Yahweh drove out from before us all the peoples, even the Amorites who lived in the land. Therefore we also will serve Yahweh; for he is our God."

¹⁹ Joshua said to the people, "You can't serve Yahweh, for he is a holy God. He is a jealous God. He will not forgive your disobedience nor your sins. ²⁰ If you forsake Yahweh, and serve foreign gods, then he will turn and do you evil, and consume you, after he has done you good."

²¹ The people said to Joshua, "No, but we will serve Yahweh." ²² Joshua said to the people, "You are witnesses against yourselves that you have chosen Yahweh yourselves, to serve him."

They said, "We are witnesses."

²³ "Now therefore put away the foreign gods which are among you, and incline your heart to Yahweh, the God of Israel."

²⁴ The people said to Joshua, "We will serve Yahweh our God, and we will listen to his voice."

²⁵ So Joshua made a covenant with the people that day, and made for them a statute and an ordinance in Shechem. ²⁶ Joshua wrote these words in the book of the law of God; and he took a great stone, and set it up there under the oak that was by the sanctuary of Yahweh. ²⁷ Joshua said to all the people, "Behold, this stone shall be a witness against us, for it has heard all Yahweh's words which he spoke to us. It shall be therefore a witness against you, lest you deny your God." ²⁸ So Joshua sent the people away, each to his own inheritance.

²⁹ After these things, Joshua the son of Nun, the servant of Yahweh, died, being one hundred ten years old.

Responsorial Psalm: Psalms 16: 1-2a and 5, 7-8, 11

¹ Preserve me, God, for I take refuge in you.
²ᵃ My soul, you have said to Yahweh, "You are my Lord.
⁵ Yahweh assigned my portion and my cup.
You made my lot secure.
⁷ I will bless Yahweh, who has given me counsel.
Yes, my heart instructs me in the night seasons.
⁸ I have set Yahweh always before me.
Because he is at my right hand, I shall not be moved.
¹¹ You will show me the path of life.
In your presence is fullness of joy.

In your right hand there are pleasures forever more.

Gospel: Matthew 19: 13-15

¹³ Then little children were brought to him that he should lay his hands on them and pray; and the disciples rebuked them. ¹⁴ But Jesus said, "Allow the little children, and don't forbid them to come to me; for the Kingdom of Heaven belongs to ones like these." ¹⁵ He laid his hands on them, and departed from there.

1. Invite the Holy Spirit into this reading, asking the Author of Scripture to speak to you through His Word
2. Read today's passage as many times as you need, take your time
3. Write down (below) what the Lord is saying to you today
4. Live with this Word in your heart through the day

Sunday, August 17, 2025
TWENTIETH SUNDAY IN ORDINARY TIME

First Reading: Jeremiah 38: 4-6, 8-10

⁴ Then the princes said to the king, "Please let this man be put to death, because he weakens the hands of the men of war who remain in this city, and the hands of all the people, in speaking such words to them; for this man doesn't seek the welfare of this people, but harm."
⁵ Zedekiah the king said, "Behold, he is in your hand; for the king can't do anything to oppose you."
⁶ Then they took Jeremiah and threw him into the dungeon of Malchijah the king's son, that was in the court of the guard. They let down Jeremiah with cords. In the dungeon there was no water, but mire; and Jeremiah sank in the mire.
⁸ Ebedmelech went out of the king's house, and spoke to the king, saying, ⁹ "My lord the king, these men have done evil in all that they have done to Jeremiah the prophet, whom they have cast into the dungeon. He is likely to die in the place where he is, because of the famine; for there is no more bread in the city."
¹⁰ Then the king commanded Ebedmelech the Ethiopian, saying, "Take from here thirty men with you, and take up Jeremiah the prophet out of the dungeon, before he dies."

Responsorial Psalm: Psalms 40: 2, 3, 4

2 He brought me up also out of a horrible pit,
out of the miry clay.
He set my feet on a rock,
and gave me a firm place to stand.
3 He has put a new song in my mouth, even praise to our God.
Many shall see it, and fear, and shall trust in Yahweh.
4 Blessed is the man who makes Yahweh his trust,
and doesn't respect the proud, nor such as turn away to lies.

Second Reading: Hebrews 12: 1-4

1 Therefore let's also, seeing we are surrounded by so great a cloud of witnesses, lay aside every weight and the sin which so easily entangles us, and let's run with perseverance the race that is set before us, 2 looking to Jesus, the author and perfecter of faith, who for the joy that was set before him endured the cross, despising its shame, and has sat down at the right hand of the throne of God.
3 For consider him who has endured such contradiction of sinners against himself, that you don't grow weary, fainting in your souls. 4 You have not yet resisted to blood, striving against sin.

Gospel: Luke 12: 49-53

49 "I came to throw fire on the earth. I wish it were already kindled. 50 But I have a baptism to be baptized with, and how distressed I am until it is accomplished! 51 Do you think that I have come to give peace in the earth? I tell you, no, but rather division. 52 For from now on, there will be five in one house divided, three against two, and two against three. 53 They will be divided, father against son, and son against father; mother against daughter, and daughter against her mother; mother-in-law against her daughter-in-law, and daughter-in-law against her mother-in-law."

1. Invite the Holy Spirit into this reading, asking the Author of Scripture to speak to you through His Word
2. Read today's passage as many times as you need, take your time
3. Write down (below) what the Lord is saying to you today
4. Live with this Word in your heart through the day

Monday, August 18, 2025

First Reading: Judges 2: 11-19

¹¹ The children of Israel did that which was evil in Yahweh's sight, and served the Baals. ¹² They abandoned Yahweh, the God of their fathers, who brought them out of the land of Egypt, and followed other gods, of the gods of the peoples who were around them, and bowed themselves down to them; and they provoked Yahweh to anger. ¹³ They abandoned Yahweh, and served Baal and the Ashtaroth. ¹⁴ Yahweh's anger burned against Israel, and he delivered them into the hands of raiders who plundered them. He sold them into the hands of their enemies all around, so that they could no longer stand before their enemies. ¹⁵ Wherever they went out, Yahweh's hand was against them for evil, as Yahweh had spoken, and as Yahweh had sworn to them; and they were very distressed. ¹⁶ Yahweh raised up judges, who saved them out of the hand of those who plundered them. ¹⁷ Yet they didn't listen to their judges; for they prostituted themselves to other gods, and bowed themselves down to them. They quickly turned away from the way in which their fathers walked, obeying Yahweh's commandments. They didn't do so. ¹⁸ When Yahweh raised up judges for them, then Yahweh was with the judge, and saved them out of the hand of their enemies all the days of the judge; for it grieved Yahweh because of their groaning by reason of those who oppressed them and troubled them. ¹⁹ But when the judge was dead, they turned back, and dealt more corruptly than their fathers in following other gods to serve them and to bow down to them. They didn't cease what they were doing, or give up their stubborn ways.

Responsorial Psalm: Psalms 106: 34-37, 39-40, 43ab and 44

³⁴ They didn't destroy the peoples,
as Yahweh commanded them,
³⁵ but mixed themselves with the nations,
and learned their works.
³⁶ They served their idols,
which became a snare to them.
³⁷ Yes, they sacrificed their sons and their daughters to demons.
³⁹ Thus they were defiled with their works,
and prostituted themselves in their deeds.

⁴⁰ Therefore Yahweh burned with anger against his people.
He abhorred his inheritance.
⁴³ᵃᵇ He rescued them many times,
but they were rebellious in their counsel,
⁴⁴ Nevertheless he regarded their distress,
when he heard their cry.

Gospel: Matthew 19: 16-22

¹⁶ Behold, one came to him and said, "Good teacher, what good thing shall I do, that I may have eternal life?"
¹⁷ He said to him, "Why do you call me good? No one is good but one, that is, God. But if you want to enter into life, keep the commandments."
¹⁸ He said to him, "Which ones?"
Jesus said, " 'You shall not murder.' 'You shall not commit adultery.' 'You shall not steal.' 'You shall not offer false testimony.' ¹⁹ 'Honor your father and your mother.' And, 'You shall love your neighbor as yourself.' "
²⁰ The young man said to him, "All these things I have observed from my youth. What do I still lack?"
²¹ Jesus said to him, "If you want to be perfect, go, sell what you have, and give to the poor, and you will have treasure in heaven; and come, follow me." ²² But when the young man heard this, he went away sad, for he was one who had great possessions.

1. Invite the Holy Spirit into this reading, asking the Author of Scripture to speak to you through His Word
2. Read today's passage as many times as you need, take your time
3. Write down (below) what the Lord is saying to you today
4. Live with this Word in your heart through the day

Tuesday, August 19, 2025
Saint John Eudes, Priest

First Reading: Judges 6: 11-24a

¹¹ Yahweh's angel came and sat under the oak which was in Ophrah, that belonged to Joash the Abiezrite. His son Gideon was beating out wheat in the wine press, to hide it from the Midianites. ¹² Yahweh's angel appeared to him, and said to him, "Yahweh is with you, you mighty man of valor!"

¹³ Gideon said to him, "Oh, my lord, if Yahweh is with us, why then has all this happened to us? Where are all his wondrous works which our fathers told us of, saying, 'Didn't Yahweh bring us up from Egypt?' But now Yahweh has cast us off, and delivered us into the hand of Midian."

¹⁴ Yahweh looked at him, and said, "Go in this your might, and save Israel from the hand of Midian. Haven't I sent you?"

¹⁵ He said to him, "O Lord,⸸ how shall I save Israel? Behold, my family is the poorest in Manasseh, and I am the least in my father's house."

¹⁶ Yahweh said to him, "Surely I will be with you, and you shall strike the Midianites as one man."

¹⁷ He said to him, "If now I have found favor in your sight, then show me a sign that it is you who talk with me. ¹⁸ Please don't go away until I come to you, and bring out my present, and lay it before you."

He said, "I will wait until you come back."

¹⁹ Gideon went in and prepared a young goat and unleavened cakes of an ephah⸸ of meal. He put the meat in a basket and he put the broth in a pot, and brought it out to him under the oak, and presented it.

²⁰ The angel of God said to him, "Take the meat and the unleavened cakes, and lay them on this rock, and pour out the broth."

He did so. ²¹ Then Yahweh's angel stretched out the end of the staff that was in his hand, and touched the meat and the unleavened cakes; and fire went up out of the rock and consumed the meat and the unleavened cakes. Then Yahweh's angel departed out of his sight.

²² Gideon saw that he was Yahweh's angel; and Gideon said, "Alas, Lord Yahweh! Because I have seen Yahweh's angel face to face!"

²³ Yahweh said to him, "Peace be to you! Don't be afraid. You shall not die."

²⁴ᵃ Then Gideon built an altar there to Yahweh, and called it "Yahweh is Peace."

Responsorial Psalm: Psalms 85: 9, 11-13

⁹ Surely his salvation is near those who fear him,
that glory may dwell in our land.
¹⁰ Mercy and truth meet together.
Righteousness and peace have kissed each other.
¹¹ Truth springs out of the earth.
Righteousness has looked down from heaven.

¹² Yes, Yahweh will give that which is good.
Our land will yield its increase.
¹³ Righteousness goes before him,
and prepares the way for his steps.

Gospel: Matthew 19: 23-30

²³ Jesus said to his disciples, "Most certainly I say to you, a rich man will enter into the Kingdom of Heaven with difficulty. ²⁴ Again I tell you, it is easier for a camel to go through a needle's eye than for a rich man to enter into God's Kingdom."
²⁵ When the disciples heard it, they were exceedingly astonished, saying, "Who then can be saved?"
²⁶ Looking at them, Jesus said, "With men this is impossible, but with God all things are possible."
²⁷ Then Peter answered, "Behold, we have left everything and followed you. What then will we have?"
²⁸ Jesus said to them, "Most certainly I tell you that you who have followed me, in the regeneration when the Son of Man will sit on the throne of his glory, you also will sit on twelve thrones, judging the twelve tribes of Israel. ²⁹ Everyone who has left houses, or brothers, or sisters, or father, or mother, or wife, or children, or lands, for my name's sake, will receive one hundred times, and will inherit eternal life. ³⁰ But many will be last who are first, and first who are last.

1. Invite the Holy Spirit into this reading, asking the Author of Scripture to speak to you through His Word
2. Read today's passage as many times as you need, take your time
3. Write down (below) what the Lord is saying to you today
4. Live with this Word in your heart through the day

Wednesday, August 20, 2025
Saint Bernard, Abbot and Doctor of the Church

First Reading: Judges 9: 6-15

⁶ All the men of Shechem assembled themselves together with all the house of Millo, and went and made Abimelech king by the oak of the pillar that was in Shechem. ⁷ When they told it to Jotham, he went and stood on the top of Mount Gerizim and lifted up his voice, cried out, and said to them, "Listen to me, you men of Shechem, that God may listen to you. ⁸ The trees set out to anoint a king over themselves. They said to the olive tree, 'Reign over us.'

⁹ "But the olive tree said to them, 'Should I stop producing my oil, with which they honor God and man by me, and go to wave back and forth over the trees?'

¹⁰ "The trees said to the fig tree, 'Come and reign over us.'

¹¹ "But the fig tree said to them, 'Should I leave my sweetness, and my good fruit, and go to wave back and forth over the trees?'

¹² "The trees said to the vine, 'Come and reign over us.'

¹³ "The vine said to them, 'Should I leave my new wine, which cheers God and man, and go to wave back and forth over the trees?'

¹⁴ "Then all the trees said to the bramble, 'Come and reign over us.'

¹⁵ "The bramble said to the trees, 'If in truth you anoint me king over you, then come and take refuge in my shade; and if not, let fire come out of the bramble, and devour the cedars of Lebanon.'

Responsorial Psalm: Psalms 21: 2-7

² You have given him his heart's desire,
and have not withheld the request of his lips.
³ For you meet him with the blessings of goodness.
You set a crown of fine gold on his head.
⁴ He asked life of you and you gave it to him,
even length of days forever and ever.
⁵ His glory is great in your salvation.
You lay honor and majesty on him.
⁶ For you make him most blessed forever.
You make him glad with joy in your presence.
⁷ For the king trusts in Yahweh.
Through the loving kindness of the Most High, he shall not be moved.

Gospel: Matthew 20: 1-16

¹ "For the Kingdom of Heaven is like a man who was the master of a household, who went out early in the morning to hire laborers for his vineyard. ² When he had agreed with the laborers for a denarius⸸ a day, he sent them into his vineyard. ³ He went out about the third hour,⸸ and saw others standing idle in the marketplace. ⁴ He said to them, 'You also go into

the vineyard, and whatever is right I will give you.' So they went their way. 5 Again he went out about the sixth and the ninth hour,§ and did likewise. 6 About the eleventh hour‡ he went out and found others standing idle. He said to them, 'Why do you stand here all day idle?'

7 "They said to him, 'Because no one has hired us.'
"He said to them, 'You also go into the vineyard, and you will receive whatever is right.'
8 "When evening had come, the lord of the vineyard said to his manager, 'Call the laborers and pay them their wages, beginning from the last to the first.' 9 "When those who were hired at about the eleventh hour came, they each received a denarius. 10 When the first came, they supposed that they would receive more; and they likewise each received a denarius. 11 When they received it, they murmured against the master of the household, 12 saying, 'These last have spent one hour, and you have made them equal to us who have borne the burden of the day and the scorching heat!'
13 "But he answered one of them, 'Friend, I am doing you no wrong. Didn't you agree with me for a denarius? 14 Take that which is yours, and go your way. It is my desire to give to this last just as much as to you. 15 Isn't it lawful for me to do what I want to with what I own? Or is your eye evil, because I am good?' 16 So the last will be first, and the first last. For many are called, but few are chosen."

1. Invite the Holy Spirit into this reading, asking the Author of Scripture to speak to you through His Word
2. Read today's passage as many times as you need, take your time
3. Write down (below) what the Lord is saying to you today
4. Live with this Word in your heart through the day

Thursday, August 21, 2025
Saint Pius X, Pope

First Reading: Judges 11: 29-39a

29 Then Yahweh's Spirit came on Jephthah, and he passed over Gilead and Manasseh, and passed over Mizpah of Gilead, and from Mizpah of Gilead he passed over to the children of Ammon.
30 Jephthah vowed a vow to Yahweh, and said, "If you will indeed deliver the children of Ammon into my hand, 31 then it shall be, that whatever comes out of the doors of my house

to meet me when I return in peace from the children of Ammon, it shall be Yahweh's, and I will offer it up for a burnt offering."

32 So Jephthah passed over to the children of Ammon to fight against them; and Yahweh delivered them into his hand. 33 He struck them from Aroer until you come to Minnith, even twenty cities, and to Abelcheramim, with a very great slaughter. So the children of Ammon were subdued before the children of Israel.

34 Jephthah came to Mizpah to his house; and behold, his daughter came out to meet him with tambourines and with dances. She was his only child. Besides her he had neither son nor daughter. 35 When he saw her, he tore his clothes, and said, "Alas, my daughter! You have brought me very low, and you are one of those who trouble me; for I have opened my mouth to Yahweh, and I can't go back."

36 She said to him, "My father, you have opened your mouth to Yahweh; do to me according to that which has proceeded out of your mouth, because Yahweh has taken vengeance for you on your enemies, even on the children of Ammon." 37 Then she said to her father, "Let this thing be done for me. Leave me alone two months, that I may depart and go down on the mountains, and bewail my virginity, I and my companions."

38 He said, "Go." He sent her away for two months; and she departed, she and her companions, and mourned her virginity on the mountains. 39a At the end of two months, she returned to her father, who did with her according to his vow which he had vowed.

Responsorial Psalm: Psalms 40: 5, 7-10

5 Many, Yahweh, my God, are the wonderful works which you have done,
and your thoughts which are toward us.
They can't be declared back to you.
If I would declare and speak of them, they are more than can be counted.
7 Then I said, "Behold, I have come.
It is written about me in the book in the scroll.
8 I delight to do your will, my God.
Yes, your law is within my heart."
9 I have proclaimed glad news of righteousness in the great assembly.
Behold, I will not seal my lips, Yahweh, you know.
10 I have not hidden your righteousness within my heart.
I have declared your faithfulness and your salvation.
I have not concealed your loving kindness and your truth from the great assembly.

Gospel: Matthew 22: 1-14

1 Jesus answered and spoke to them again in parables, saying, 2 "The Kingdom of Heaven is like a certain king, who made a wedding feast for his son, 3 and sent out his servants to

call those who were invited to the wedding feast, but they would not come. ⁴ Again he sent out other servants, saying, 'Tell those who are invited, "Behold, I have prepared my dinner. My cattle and my fatlings are killed, and all things are ready. Come to the wedding feast!" ' ⁵ But they made light of it, and went their ways, one to his own farm, another to his merchandise; ⁶ and the rest grabbed his servants, treated them shamefully, and killed them. ⁷ When the king heard that, he was angry, and sent his armies, destroyed those murderers, and burned their city.

⁸ "Then he said to his servants, 'The wedding is ready, but those who were invited weren't worthy. ⁹ Go therefore to the intersections of the highways, and as many as you may find, invite to the wedding feast.' ¹⁰ Those servants went out into the highways and gathered together as many as they found, both bad and good. The wedding was filled with guests.

¹¹ "But when the king came in to see the guests, he saw there a man who didn't have on wedding clothing, ¹² and he said to him, 'Friend, how did you come in here not wearing wedding clothing?' He was speechless. ¹³ Then the king said to the servants, 'Bind him hand and foot, take him away, and throw him into the outer darkness. That is where the weeping and grinding of teeth will be.' ¹⁴ For many are called, but few chosen."

1. Invite the Holy Spirit into this reading, asking the Author of Scripture to speak to you through His Word
2. Read today's passage as many times as you need, take your time
3. Write down (below) what the Lord is saying to you today
4. Live with this Word in your heart through the day

_____

_____

Friday, August 22, 2025
The Queenship of the Blessed Virgin Mary

First Reading: Ruth 1: 1, 3-6, 14b-16, 22

¹ In the days when the judges judged, there was a famine in the land. A certain man of Bethlehem Judah went to live in the country of Moab with his wife and his two sons. \ ³ Elimelech, Naomi's husband, died; and she was left with her two sons. ⁴ They took for themselves wives of the women of Moab. The name of the one was Orpah, and the name of the other was Ruth. They lived there about ten years. ⁵ Mahlon and Chilion both died, and the woman was bereaved of her two children and of her husband. ⁶ Then she arose with her

daughters-in-law, that she might return from the country of Moab; for she had heard in the country of Moab how Yahweh[‡] had visited his people in giving them bread.

¹⁴ᵇ then Orpah kissed her mother-in-law, but Ruth stayed with her. ¹⁵ She said, "Behold,[‡] your sister-in-law has gone back to her people and to her god. Follow your sister-in-law."

¹⁶ Ruth said, "Don't urge me to leave you, and to return from following you, for where you go, I will go; and where you stay, I will stay. Your people will be my people, and your God[§] my God.

²² So Naomi returned, and Ruth the Moabitess, her daughter-in-law, with her, who returned out of the country of Moab. They came to Bethlehem in the beginning of barley harvest.

Responsorial Psalm: Psalms 146: 5-10

⁵ Happy is he who has the God of Jacob for his help,
whose hope is in Yahweh, his God,
⁶ who made heaven and earth,
the sea, and all that is in them;
who keeps truth forever;
⁷ who executes justice for the oppressed;
who gives food to the hungry.
Yahweh frees the prisoners.
⁸ Yahweh opens the eyes of the blind.
Yahweh raises up those who are bowed down.
Yahweh loves the righteous.
⁹ Yahweh preserves the foreigners.
He upholds the fatherless and widow,
but he turns the way of the wicked upside down.
¹⁰ Yahweh will reign forever;
your God, O Zion, to all generations.
Praise Yah!

Gospel: Matthew 22: 34-40

³⁴ But the Pharisees, when they heard that he had silenced the Sadducees, gathered themselves together. ³⁵ One of them, a lawyer, asked him a question, testing him. ³⁶ "Teacher, which is the greatest commandment in the law?"
³⁷ Jesus said to him, " 'You shall love the Lord your God with all your heart, with all your soul, and with all your mind.'[*] ³⁸ This is the first and great commandment. ³⁹ A second

likewise is this, 'You shall love your neighbor as yourself.' * 40 The whole law and the prophets depend on these two commandments."

1. Invite the Holy Spirit into this reading, asking the Author of Scripture to speak to you through His Word
2. Read today's passage as many times as you need, take your time
3. Write down (below) what the Lord is saying to you today
4. Live with this Word in your heart through the day

Saturday, August 23, 2025
Saint Rose of Lima, Virgin

First Reading: Ruth 2: 1-3, 8-11; 4: 13-17

¹ Naomi had a relative of her husband's, a mighty man of wealth, of the family of Elimelech, and his name was Boaz. ² Ruth the Moabitess said to Naomi, "Let me now go to the field, and glean among the ears of grain after him in whose sight I find favor."
She said to her, "Go, my daughter." ³ She went, and came and gleaned in the field after the reapers; and she happened to come to the portion of the field belonging to Boaz, who was of the family of Elimelech.
⁸ Then Boaz said to Ruth, "Listen, my daughter. Don't go to glean in another field, and don't go from here, but stay here close to my maidens. ⁹ Let your eyes be on the field that they reap, and go after them. Haven't I commanded the young men not to touch you? When you are thirsty, go to the vessels, and drink from that which the young men have drawn."
¹⁰ Then she fell on her face and bowed herself to the ground, and said to him, "Why have I found favor in your sight, that you should take knowledge of me, since I am a foreigner?"
¹¹ Boaz answered her, "I have been told all about what you have done for your mother-in-law since the death of your husband, and how you have left your father, your mother, and the land of your birth, and have come to a people that you didn't know before.
¹³ So Boaz took Ruth and she became his wife; and he went in to her, and Yahweh enabled her to conceive, and she bore a son. ¹⁴ The women said to Naomi, "Blessed be Yahweh, who has not left you today without a near kinsman. Let his name be famous in Israel. ¹⁵ He shall be to you a restorer of life and sustain you in your old age; for your daughter-in-law, who loves you, who is better to you than seven sons, has given birth to him." ¹⁶ Naomi took the child, laid him in her bosom, and became nurse to him. ¹⁷ The women, her neighbors, gave

him a name, saying, "A son is born to Naomi". They named him Obed. He is the father of Jesse, the father of David.

Responsorial Psalm: Psalms 128: 1b-2, 3, 4, 5

1b who walks in his ways.
2 For you will eat the labor of your hands.
You will be happy, and it will be well with you.
3 Your wife will be as a fruitful vine in the innermost parts of your house,
your children like olive shoots around your table.
4 Behold, this is how the man who fears Yahweh is blessed.
5 May Yahweh bless you out of Zion,
and may you see the good of Jerusalem all the days of your life.

Gospel: Matthew 23: 1-12

1 Then Jesus spoke to the multitudes and to his disciples, 2 saying, "The scribes and the Pharisees sit on Moses' seat. 3 All things therefore whatever they tell you to observe, observe and do, but don't do their works; for they say, and don't do. 4 For they bind heavy burdens that are grievous to be borne, and lay them on men's shoulders; but they themselves will not lift a finger to help them. 5 But they do all their works to be seen by men. They make their phylacteries‡ broad and enlarge the fringes‡ of their garments, 6 and love the place of honor at feasts, the best seats in the synagogues, 7 the salutations in the marketplaces, and to be called 'Rabbi, Rabbi'§ by men. 8 But you are not to be called 'Rabbi', for one is your teacher, the Christ, and all of you are brothers. 9 Call no man on the earth your father, for one is your Father, he who is in heaven. 10 Neither be called masters, for one is your master, the Christ. 11 But he who is greatest among you will be your servant. 12 Whoever exalts himself will be humbled, and whoever humbles himself will be exalted.

1. Invite the Holy Spirit into this reading, asking the Author of Scripture to speak to you through His Word
2. Read today's passage as many times as you need, take your time
3. Write down (below) what the Lord is saying to you today
4. Live with this Word in your heart through the day

_____

_____

Sunday, August 24, 2025
TWENTY-FIRST SUNDAY IN ORDINARY TIME

First Reading: Isaiah 66: 18-21

[18] "For I know their works and their thoughts. The time comes that I will gather all nations and languages, and they will come, and will see my glory.
[19] "I will set a sign among them, and I will send those who escape of them to the nations, to Tarshish, Pul, and Lud, who draw the bow, to Tubal and Javan, to far-away islands, who have not heard my fame, nor have seen my glory; and they shall declare my glory among the nations. [20] They shall bring all your brothers out of all the nations for an offering to Yahweh, on horses, in chariots, in litters, on mules, and on camels, to my holy mountain Jerusalem, says Yahweh, as the children of Israel bring their offering in a clean vessel into Yahweh's house. [21] Of them I will also select priests and Levites," says Yahweh.

Responsorial Psalm: Psalms 117: 1, 2

[1] Praise Yahweh, all you nations!
Extol him, all you peoples!
[2] For his loving kindness is great toward us.
Yahweh's faithfulness endures forever.
Praise Yah!

Second Reading: Hebrews 12: 5-7, 11-13

[5] You have forgotten the exhortation which reasons with you as with children,
"My son, don't take lightly the chastening of the Lord,
nor faint when you are reproved by him;
[6] for whom the Lord loves, he disciplines,
and chastises every son whom he receives."*
[7] It is for discipline that you endure. God deals with you as with children, for what son is there whom his father doesn't discipline?
[11] All chastening seems for the present to be not joyous but grievous; yet afterward it yields the peaceful fruit of righteousness to those who have been trained by it. [12] Therefore lift up the hands that hang down and the feeble knees,* [13] and make straight paths for your feet,* so what is lame may not be dislocated, but rather be healed.

Gospel: Luke 13: 22-30

22 He went on his way through cities and villages, teaching, and traveling on to Jerusalem. 23 One said to him, "Lord, are they few who are saved?"
He said to them, 24 "Strive to enter in by the narrow door, for many, I tell you, will seek to enter in and will not be able. 25 When once the master of the house has risen up and has shut the door, and you begin to stand outside and to knock at the door, saying, 'Lord, Lord, open to us!' then he will answer and tell you, 'I don't know you or where you come from.' 26 Then you will begin to say, 'We ate and drank in your presence, and you taught in our streets.' 27 He will say, 'I tell you, I don't know where you come from. Depart from me, all you workers of iniquity.' 28 There will be weeping and gnashing of teeth when you see Abraham, Isaac, Jacob, and all the prophets in God's Kingdom, and yourselves being thrown outside. 29 They will come from the east, west, north, and south, and will sit down in God's Kingdom. 30 Behold, there are some who are last who will be first, and there are some who are first who will be last."

1. Invite the Holy Spirit into this reading, asking the Author of Scripture to speak to you through His Word
2. Read today's passage as many times as you need, take your time
3. Write down (below) what the Lord is saying to you today
4. Live with this Word in your heart through the day

_____

_____

Monday, August 25, 2025
Saint Louis; Saint Joseph Calasanz, Priest

First Reading: First Thessalonians 1: 1-5, 8b-10

¹ Paul, Silvanus, and Timothy, to the assembly of the Thessalonians in God the Father and the Lord Jesus Christ: Grace to you and peace from God our Father and the Lord Jesus Christ.
² We always give thanks to God for all of you, mentioning you in our prayers, ³ remembering without ceasing your work of faith and labor of love and perseverance of hope in our Lord Jesus Christ, before our God and Father. ⁴ We know, brothers loved by God, that you are chosen, ⁵ and that our Good News came to you not in word only, but also in power, and in the Holy Spirit and with much assurance. You know what kind of men we showed ourselves to be among you for your sake.

⁸ᵇ but also in every place your faith toward God has gone out, so that we need not to say anything. ⁹ For they themselves report concerning us what kind of a reception we had from you, and how you turned to God from idols to serve a living and true God, ¹⁰ and to wait for his Son from heaven, whom he raised from the dead: Jesus, who delivers us from the wrath to come.

Responsorial Psalm: Psalms 149: 1b-2, 3-4, 5-6a and 9b

¹ᵇ Sing to Yahweh a new song,
his praise in the assembly of the saints.
² Let Israel rejoice in him who made them.
Let the children of Zion be joyful in their King.
³ Let them praise his name in the dance!
Let them sing praises to him with tambourine and harp!
⁴ For Yahweh takes pleasure in his people.
He crowns the humble with salvation.
⁵ Let the saints rejoice in honor.
Let them sing for joy on their beds.
⁶ᵃ May the high praises of God be in their mouths,
⁹ᵇ All his saints have this honor.
Praise Yah!

Gospel: Matthew 23: 13-22

¹³ "Woe to you, scribes and Pharisees, hypocrites! For you devour widows' houses, and as a pretense you make long prayers. Therefore you will receive greater condemnation.
¹⁴ "But woe to you, scribes and Pharisees, hypocrites! Because you shut up the Kingdom of Heaven against men; for you don't enter in yourselves, neither do you allow those who are entering in to enter.‡ ¹⁵ Woe to you, scribes and Pharisees, hypocrites! For you travel around by sea and land to make one proselyte; and when he becomes one, you make him twice as much a son of Gehenna‡ as yourselves.
¹⁶ "Woe to you, you blind guides, who say, 'Whoever swears by the temple, it is nothing; but whoever swears by the gold of the temple, he is obligated.' ¹⁷ You blind fools! For which is greater, the gold or the temple that sanctifies the gold? ¹⁸ And, 'Whoever swears by the altar, it is nothing; but whoever swears by the gift that is on it, he is obligated.' ¹⁹ You blind fools! For which is greater, the gift, or the altar that sanctifies the gift? ²⁰ He therefore who swears by the altar, swears by it and by everything on it. ²¹ He who swears by the temple, swears by it and by him who has been living§ in it. ²² He who swears by heaven, swears by the throne of God and by him who sits on it.

1. Invite the Holy Spirit into this reading, asking the Author of Scripture to speak to you through His Word
2. Read today's passage as many times as you need, take your time
3. Write down (below) what the Lord is saying to you today
4. Live with this Word in your heart through the day

Tuesday, August 26, 2025

First Reading: First Thessalonians 2: 1-8

¹ For you yourselves know, brothers, our visit to you wasn't in vain, ² but having suffered before and been shamefully treated, as you know, at Philippi, we grew bold in our God to tell you the Good News of God in much conflict. ³ For our exhortation is not of error, nor of uncleanness, nor in deception. ⁴ But even as we have been approved by God to be entrusted with the Good News, so we speak—not as pleasing men, but God, who tests our hearts. ⁵ For neither were we at any time found using words of flattery, as you know, nor a cloak of covetousness (God is witness), ⁶ nor seeking glory from men (neither from you nor from others), when we might have claimed authority as apostles of Christ. ⁷ But we were gentle among you, like a nursing mother cherishes her own children.
⁸ Even so, affectionately longing for you, we were well pleased to impart to you not the Good News of God only, but also our own souls, because you had become very dear to us.

Responsorial Psalm: Psalms 139: 1-6

¹ Yahweh, you have searched me,
and you know me.
² You know my sitting down and my rising up.
You perceive my thoughts from afar.
³ You search out my path and my lying down,
and are acquainted with all my ways.
⁴ For there is not a word on my tongue,
but behold, Yahweh, you know it altogether.
⁵ You hem me in behind and before.
You laid your hand on me.
⁶ This knowledge is beyond me.

It's lofty.
I can't attain it.

Gospel: Matthew 23: 23-26

23 "Woe to you, scribes and Pharisees, hypocrites! For you tithe mint, dill, and cumin,‡ and have left undone the weightier matters of the law: justice, mercy, and faith. But you ought to have done these, and not to have left the other undone. 24 You blind guides, who strain out a gnat, and swallow a camel!
25 "Woe to you, scribes and Pharisees, hypocrites! For you clean the outside of the cup and of the platter, but within they are full of extortion and unrighteousness.‡ 26 You blind Pharisee, first clean the inside of the cup and of the platter, that its outside may become clean also.

1. Invite the Holy Spirit into this reading, asking the Author of Scripture to speak to you through His Word
2. Read today's passage as many times as you need, take your time
3. Write down (below) what the Lord is saying to you today
4. Live with this Word in your heart through the day

Wednesday, August 27, 2025
Saint Monica

First Reading: First Thessalonians 2: 9-13

9 For you remember, brothers, our labor and travail; for working night and day, that we might not burden any of you, we preached to you the Good News of God. 10 You are witnesses with God how holy, righteously, and blamelessly we behaved ourselves toward you who believe. 11 As you know, we exhorted, comforted, and implored every one of you, as a father does his own children, 12 to the end that you should walk worthily of God, who calls you into his own Kingdom and glory.
13 For this cause we also thank God without ceasing that when you received from us the word of the message of God, you accepted it not as the word of men, but as it is in truth, God's word, which also works in you who believe.

Responsorial Psalm: Psalms 139: 7-12ab

⁷ Where could I go from your Spirit?
Or where could I flee from your presence?
⁸ If I ascend up into heaven, you are there.
If I make my bed in Sheol, behold, you are there!
⁹ If I take the wings of the dawn,
and settle in the uttermost parts of the sea,
¹⁰ even there your hand will lead me,
and your right hand will hold me.
¹¹ If I say, "Surely the darkness will overwhelm me.
The light around me will be night,"
¹²ᵃᵇ even the darkness doesn't hide from you,
but the night shines as the day.

Gospel: Matthew 23: 27-32

²⁷ "Woe to you, scribes and Pharisees, hypocrites! For you are like whitened tombs, which outwardly appear beautiful, but inwardly are full of dead men's bones and of all uncleanness. ²⁸ Even so you also outwardly appear righteous to men, but inwardly you are full of hypocrisy and iniquity.

²⁹ "Woe to you, scribes and Pharisees, hypocrites! For you build the tombs of the prophets and decorate the tombs of the righteous, ³⁰ and say, 'If we had lived in the days of our fathers, we wouldn't have been partakers with them in the blood of the prophets.' ³¹ Therefore you testify to yourselves that you are children of those who killed the prophets. ³² Fill up, then, the measure of your fathers.

1. Invite the Holy Spirit into this reading, asking the Author of Scripture to speak to you through His Word
2. Read today's passage as many times as you need, take your time
3. Write down (below) what the Lord is saying to you today
4. Live with this Word in your heart through the day

Thursday, August 28, 2025
Saint Augustine, Bishop and Doctor of the Church

First Reading: First Thessalonians 3: 7-13

⁷ For this cause, brothers, we were comforted over you in all our distress and affliction through your faith. ⁸ For now we live, if you stand fast in the Lord. ⁹ For what thanksgiving can we render again to God for you, for all the joy with which we rejoice for your sakes before our God, ¹⁰ night and day praying exceedingly that we may see your face and may perfect that which is lacking in your faith?
¹¹ Now may our God and Father himself, and our Lord Jesus Christ, direct our way to you. ¹² May the Lord make you to increase and abound in love toward one another and toward all men, even as we also do toward you, ¹³ to the end he may establish your hearts blameless in holiness before our God and Father at the coming of our Lord Jesus with all his saints.

Responsorial Psalm: Psalms 90: 3-5a, 12-13, 14 and 17

³ You turn man to destruction, saying,
"Return, you children of men."
⁴ For a thousand years in your sight are just like yesterday when it is past,
like a watch in the night.
⁵ᵃ You sweep them away as they sleep.
¹² So teach us to count our days,
that we may gain a heart of wisdom.
¹³ Relent, Yahweh!§
How long?
Have compassion on your servants!
¹⁴ Satisfy us in the morning with your loving kindness,
that we may rejoice and be glad all our days.
¹⁷ Let the favor of the Lord our God be on us.
Establish the work of our hands for us.
Yes, establish the work of our hands.

Gospel: Matthew 24: 42-51

⁴² Watch therefore, for you don't know in what hour your Lord comes. ⁴³ But know this, that if the master of the house had known in what watch of the night the thief was coming, he would have watched, and would not have allowed his house to be broken into. ⁴⁴ Therefore also be ready, for in an hour that you don't expect, the Son of Man will come.

⁴⁵ "Who then is the faithful and wise servant, whom his lord has set over his household, to give them their food in due season? ⁴⁶ Blessed is that servant whom his lord finds doing so when he comes. ⁴⁷ Most certainly I tell you that he will set him over all that he has. ⁴⁸ But if that evil servant should say in his heart, 'My lord is delaying his coming,' ⁴⁹ and begins to beat his fellow servants, and eat and drink with the drunkards, ⁵⁰ the lord of that servant will come in a day when he doesn't expect it and in an hour when he doesn't know it, ⁵¹ and will cut him in pieces and appoint his portion with the hypocrites. That is where the weeping and grinding of teeth will be.

1. Invite the Holy Spirit into this reading, asking the Author of Scripture to speak to you through His Word
2. Read today's passage as many times as you need, take your time
3. Write down (below) what the Lord is saying to you today
4. Live with this Word in your heart through the day

Friday, August 29, 2025
The Passion of Saint John the Baptist

First Reading: First Thessalonians 4: 1-8

¹ Finally then, brothers, we beg and exhort you in the Lord Jesus, that as you received from us how you ought to walk and to please God, that you abound more and more. ² For you know what instructions we gave you through the Lord Jesus. ³ For this is the will of God: your sanctification, that you abstain from sexual immorality, ⁴ that each one of you know how to control his own body in sanctification and honor, ⁵ not in the passion of lust, even as the Gentiles who don't know God, ⁶ that no one should take advantage of and wrong a brother or sister in this matter; because the Lord is an avenger in all these things, as also we forewarned you and testified. ⁷ For God called us not for uncleanness, but in sanctification. ⁸ Therefore he who rejects this doesn't reject man, but God, who has also given his Holy Spirit to you.

Responsorial Psalm: Psalms 97: 1 and 2b, 5-6, 10, 11-12

¹ Yahweh reigns!
Let the earth rejoice!

Let the multitude of islands be glad!
² ᵇ Righteousness and justice are the foundation of his throne.
⁵ The mountains melt like wax at the presence of Yahweh,
at the presence of the Lord of the whole earth.
⁶ The heavens declare his righteousness.
All the peoples have seen his glory.
¹⁰ You who love Yahweh, hate evil!
He preserves the souls of his saints.
He delivers them out of the hand of the wicked.
¹¹ Light is sown for the righteous,
and gladness for the upright in heart.
¹² Be glad in Yahweh, you righteous people!
Give thanks to his holy Name.

Gospel: Mark 6: 17-29

¹⁷ For Herod himself had sent out and arrested John and bound him in prison for the sake of Herodias, his brother Philip's wife, for he had married her. ¹⁸ For John had said to Herod, "It is not lawful for you to have your brother's wife." ¹⁹ Herodias set herself against him and desired to kill him, but she couldn't, ²⁰ for Herod feared John, knowing that he was a righteous and holy man, and kept him safe. When he heard him, he did many things, and he heard him gladly.
²¹ Then a convenient day came when Herod on his birthday made a supper for his nobles, the high officers, and the chief men of Galilee. ²² When the daughter of Herodias herself came in and danced, she pleased Herod and those sitting with him. The king said to the young lady, "Ask me whatever you want, and I will give it to you." ²³ He swore to her, "Whatever you ask of me, I will give you, up to half of my kingdom."
²⁴ She went out and said to her mother, "What shall I ask?"
She said, "The head of John the Baptizer."
²⁵ She came in immediately with haste to the king and requested, "I want you to give me right now the head of John the Baptizer on a platter."
²⁶ The king was exceedingly sorry, but for the sake of his oaths and of his dinner guests, he didn't wish to refuse her. ²⁷ Immediately the king sent out a soldier of his guard and commanded to bring John's head; and he went and beheaded him in the prison, ²⁸ and brought his head on a platter, and gave it to the young lady; and the young lady gave it to her mother.
²⁹ When his disciples heard this, they came and took up his corpse and laid it in a tomb.

1. Invite the Holy Spirit into this reading, asking the Author of Scripture to speak to you through His Word

2. Read today's passage as many times as you need, take your time
3. Write down (below) what the Lord is saying to you today
4. Live with this Word in your heart through the day

_____

_____

Saturday, August 30, 2025

First Reading: First Thessalonians 4: 9-11

⁹ But concerning brotherly love, you have no need that one write to you. For you yourselves are taught by God to love one another, ¹⁰ for indeed you do it toward all the brothers who are in all Macedonia. But we exhort you, brothers, that you abound more and more; ¹¹ and that you make it your ambition to lead a quiet life, and to do your own business, and to work with your own hands, even as we instructed you,

Responsorial Psalm: Psalms 98: 1, 7-9

¹ Sing to Yahweh a new song,
for he has done marvelous things!
His right hand and his holy arm have worked salvation for him.
⁷ Let the sea roar with its fullness;
the world, and those who dwell therein.
⁸ Let the rivers clap their hands.
Let the mountains sing for joy together.
⁹ Let them sing before Yahweh,
for he comes to judge the earth.
He will judge the world with righteousness,
and the peoples with equity.

Gospel: Matthew 25: 14-30

¹⁴ "For it is like a man going into another country, who called his own servants and entrusted his goods to them. ¹⁵ To one he gave five talents, to another two, to another one, to each according to his own ability. Then he went on his journey. ¹⁶ Immediately he who received the five talents went and traded with them, and made another five talents. ¹⁷ In

the same way, he also who got the two gained another two. ¹⁸ But he who received the one talent went away and dug in the earth and hid his lord's money.

¹⁹ "Now after a long time the lord of those servants came, and settled accounts with them. ²⁰ He who received the five talents came and brought another five talents, saying, 'Lord, you delivered to me five talents. Behold, I have gained another five talents in addition to them.'

²¹ "His lord said to him, 'Well done, good and faithful servant. You have been faithful over a few things, I will set you over many things. Enter into the joy of your lord.'

²² "He also who got the two talents came and said, 'Lord, you delivered to me two talents. Behold, I have gained another two talents in addition to them.'

²³ "His lord said to him, 'Well done, good and faithful servant. You have been faithful over a few things. I will set you over many things. Enter into the joy of your lord.'

²⁴ "He also who had received the one talent came and said, 'Lord, I knew you that you are a hard man, reaping where you didn't sow, and gathering where you didn't scatter. ²⁵ I was afraid, and went away and hid your talent in the earth. Behold, you have what is yours.'

²⁶ "But his lord answered him, 'You wicked and slothful servant. You knew that I reap where I didn't sow, and gather where I didn't scatter. ²⁷ You ought therefore to have deposited my money with the bankers, and at my coming I should have received back my own with interest. ²⁸ Take away therefore the talent from him and give it to him who has the ten talents. ²⁹ For to everyone who has will be given, and he will have abundance, but from him who doesn't have, even that which he has will be taken away. ³⁰ Throw out the unprofitable servant into the outer darkness, where there will be weeping and gnashing of teeth.'

1. Invite the Holy Spirit into this reading, asking the Author of Scripture to speak to you through His Word
2. Read today's passage as many times as you need, take your time
3. Write down (below) what the Lord is saying to you today
4. Live with this Word in your heart through the day

Sunday, August 31, 2025
TWENTY-SECOND SUNDAY IN ORDINARY TIME

First Reading: Sirach 3: 17-18, 20, 28-29

¹⁷ My son, go on with your business in humility;
so you will be loved by an acceptable man.
¹⁸ The greater you are, humble yourself the more,
and you will find favor before the Lord.
²⁰ For the power of the Lord is great,
and he is glorified by those who are lowly.
²⁸ The calamity of the proud has no healing,
for a weed of wickedness has taken root in him.
²⁹ The heart of the prudent will understand a proverb.
A wise man desires the ear of a listener.

Responsorial Psalm: Psalms 68: 4-7, 10-11

⁴ Sing to God! Sing praises to his name!
Extol him who rides on the clouds:
to Yah, his name!
Rejoice before him!
⁵ A father of the fatherless, and a defender of the widows,
is God in his holy habitation.
⁶ God sets the lonely in families.
He brings out the prisoners with singing,
but the rebellious dwell in a sun-scorched land.
⁷ God, when you went out before your people,
when you marched through the wilderness...
Selah.
¹⁰ Your congregation lived therein.
You, God, prepared your goodness for the poor.
¹¹ The Lord announced the word.
The ones who proclaim it are a great company.

Second Reading: Hebrews 12: 18-19, 22-24

¹⁸ For you have not come to a mountain that might be touched and that burned with fire, and to blackness, darkness, storm, ¹⁹ the sound of a trumpet, and the voice of words; which those who heard it begged that not one more word should be spoken to them,
²² But you have come to Mount Zion and to the city of the living God, the heavenly Jerusalem, and to innumerable multitudes of angels, ²³ to the festal gathering and assembly of the firstborn who are enrolled in heaven, to God the Judge of all, to the spirits of just men made perfect, ²⁴ to Jesus, the mediator of a new covenant, and to the blood of sprinkling that speaks better than that of Abel.

Gospel: Luke 14: 1, 7-14

¹ When he went into the house of one of the rulers of the Pharisees on a Sabbath to eat bread, they were watching him.

⁷ He spoke a parable to those who were invited, when he noticed how they chose the best seats, and said to them, ⁸ "When you are invited by anyone to a wedding feast, don't sit in the best seat, since perhaps someone more honorable than you might be invited by him, ⁹ and he who invited both of you would come and tell you, 'Make room for this person.' Then you would begin, with shame, to take the lowest place. ¹⁰ But when you are invited, go and sit in the lowest place, so that when he who invited you comes, he may tell you, 'Friend, move up higher.' Then you will be honored in the presence of all who sit at the table with you. ¹¹ For everyone who exalts himself will be humbled, and whoever humbles himself will be exalted."

¹² He also said to the one who had invited him, "When you make a dinner or a supper, don't call your friends, nor your brothers, nor your kinsmen, nor rich neighbors, or perhaps they might also return the favor, and pay you back. ¹³ But when you make a feast, ask the poor, the maimed, the lame, or the blind; ¹⁴ and you will be blessed, because they don't have the resources to repay you. For you will be repaid in the resurrection of the righteous."

1. Invite the Holy Spirit into this reading, asking the Author of Scripture to speak to you through His Word
2. Read today's passage as many times as you need, take your time
3. Write down (below) what the Lord is saying to you today
4. Live with this Word in your heart through the day

_____

_____

Monday, September 1, 2025

First Reading: First Thessalonians 4: 13-18

¹³ But we don't want you to be ignorant, brothers, concerning those who have fallen asleep, so that you don't grieve like the rest, who have no hope. ¹⁴ For if we believe that Jesus died and rose again, even so God will bring with him those who have fallen asleep in Jesus. ¹⁵ For this we tell you by the word of the Lord, that we who are alive, who are left until the coming of the Lord, will in no way precede those who have fallen asleep. ¹⁶ For the Lord himself

will descend from heaven with a shout, with the voice of the archangel and with God's trumpet. The dead in Christ will rise first, ¹⁷ then we who are alive, who are left, will be caught up together with them in the clouds to meet the Lord in the air. So we will be with the Lord forever. ¹⁸ Therefore comfort one another with these words.

Responsorial Psalm: Psalms 96: 1 and 3, 4-5, 11-12, 13

¹ Sing to Yahweh a new song!
Sing to Yahweh, all the earth.
³ Declare his glory among the nations,
his marvelous works among all the peoples.
⁴ For Yahweh is great, and greatly to be praised!
He is to be feared above all gods.
⁵ For all the gods of the peoples are idols,
but Yahweh made the heavens.
¹¹ Let the heavens be glad, and let the earth rejoice.
Let the sea roar, and its fullness!
¹² Let the field and all that is in it exult!
Then all the trees of the woods shall sing for joy
¹³ before Yahweh; for he comes,
for he comes to judge the earth.
He will judge the world with righteousness,
the peoples with his truth.

Gospel: Luke 4: 16-30

¹⁶ He came to Nazareth, where he had been brought up. He entered, as was his custom, into the synagogue on the Sabbath day, and stood up to read. ¹⁷ The book of the prophet Isaiah was handed to him. He opened the book, and found the place where it was written,
¹⁸ "The Spirit of the Lord is on me,
because he has anointed me to preach good news to the poor.
He has sent me to heal the broken hearted,‡
to proclaim release to the captives,
recovering of sight to the blind,
to deliver those who are crushed,
¹⁹ and to proclaim the acceptable year of the Lord."∗
²⁰ He closed the book, gave it back to the attendant, and sat down. The eyes of all in the synagogue were fastened on him. ²¹ He began to tell them, "Today, this Scripture has been fulfilled in your hearing."

²² All testified about him and wondered at the gracious words which proceeded out of his mouth; and they said, "Isn't this Joseph's son?"
²³ He said to them, "Doubtless you will tell me this proverb, 'Physician, heal yourself! Whatever we have heard done at Capernaum, do also here in your hometown.' " ²⁴ He said, "Most certainly I tell you, no prophet is acceptable in his hometown. ²⁵ But truly I tell you, there were many widows in Israel in the days of Elijah, when the sky was shut up three years and six months, when a great famine came over all the land. ²⁶ Elijah was sent to none of them, except to Zarephath, in the land of Sidon, to a woman who was a widow. ²⁷ There were many lepers in Israel in the time of Elisha the prophet, yet not one of them was cleansed, except Naaman, the Syrian."
²⁸ They were all filled with wrath in the synagogue as they heard these things. ²⁹ They rose up, threw him out of the city, and led him to the brow of the hill that their city was built on, that they might throw him off the cliff. ³⁰ But he, passing through the middle of them, went his way.

1. Invite the Holy Spirit into this reading, asking the Author of Scripture to speak to you through His Word
2. Read today's passage as many times as you need, take your time
3. Write down (below) what the Lord is saying to you today
4. Live with this Word in your heart through the day

_____

_____

Tuesday, September 2, 2025

First Reading: First Thessalonians 5: 1-6, 9-11

¹ But concerning the times and the seasons, brothers, you have no need that anything be written to you. ² For you yourselves know well that the day of the Lord comes like a thief in the night. ³ For when they are saying, "Peace and safety," then sudden destruction will come on them, like birth pains on a pregnant woman. Then they will in no way escape. ⁴ But you, brothers, aren't in darkness, that the day should overtake you like a thief. ⁵ You are all children of light and children of the day. We don't belong to the night, nor to darkness, ⁶ so then let's not sleep, as the rest do, but let's watch and be sober.
⁹ For God didn't appoint us to wrath, but to the obtaining of salvation through our Lord Jesus Christ, ¹⁰ who died for us, that, whether we wake or sleep, we should live together with him. ¹¹ Therefore exhort one another, and build each other up, even as you also do.

Responsorial Psalm: Psalms 27: 1, 4, 13-14

¹ Yahweh is my light and my salvation.
Whom shall I fear?
Yahweh is the strength of my life.
Of whom shall I be afraid?
⁴ One thing I have asked of Yahweh, that I will seek after:
that I may dwell in Yahweh's house all the days of my life,
to see Yahweh's beauty,
and to inquire in his temple.
¹³ I am still confident of this:
I will see the goodness of Yahweh in the land of the living.
¹⁴ Wait for Yahweh.
Be strong, and let your heart take courage.
Yes, wait for Yahweh.

Gospel: Luke 4: 31-37

³¹ He came down to Capernaum, a city of Galilee. He was teaching them on the Sabbath day, ³² and they were astonished at his teaching, for his word was with authority. ³³ In the synagogue there was a man who had a spirit of an unclean demon; and he cried out with a loud voice, ³⁴ saying, "Ah! what have we to do with you, Jesus of Nazareth? Have you come to destroy us? I know who you are: the Holy One of God!"
³⁵ Jesus rebuked him, saying, "Be silent and come out of him!" When the demon had thrown him down in the middle of them, he came out of him, having done him no harm.
³⁶ Amazement came on all and they spoke together, one with another, saying, "What is this word? For with authority and power he commands the unclean spirits, and they come out!" ³⁷ News about him went out into every place of the surrounding region.

1. Invite the Holy Spirit into this reading, asking the Author of Scripture to speak to you through His Word
2. Read today's passage as many times as you need, take your time
3. Write down (below) what the Lord is saying to you today
4. Live with this Word in your heart through the day

_____

_____

Wednesday, September 3, 2025
Saint Gregory the Great, Pope and Doctor of the Church

First Reading: Colossians 1: 1-8

¹ Paul, an apostle of Christ Jesus through the will of God, and Timothy our brother, ² to the saints and faithful brothers in Christ at Colossae: Grace to you and peace from God our Father and the Lord Jesus Christ.
³ We give thanks to God the Father of our Lord Jesus Christ, praying always for you, ⁴ having heard of your faith in Christ Jesus and of the love which you have toward all the saints, ⁵ because of the hope which is laid up for you in the heavens, of which you heard before in the word of the truth of the Good News ⁶ which has come to you, even as it is in all the world and is bearing fruit and growing, as it does in you also, since the day you heard and knew the grace of God in truth, ⁷ even as you learned from Epaphras our beloved fellow servant, who is a faithful servant of Christ on your behalf, ⁸ who also declared to us your love in the Spirit.

Responsorial Psalm: Psalms 52: 8, 9

⁸ But as for me, I am like a green olive tree in God's house.
I trust in God's loving kindness forever and ever.
⁹ I will give you thanks forever, because you have done it.
I will hope in your name, for it is good,
in the presence of your saints.

Gospel: Luke 4: 38-44

³⁸ He rose up from the synagogue and entered into Simon's house. Simon's mother-in-law was afflicted with a great fever, and they begged him to help her. ³⁹ He stood over her and rebuked the fever, and it left her. Immediately she rose up and served them. ⁴⁰ When the sun was setting, all those who had any sick with various diseases brought them to him; and he laid his hands on every one of them, and healed them. ⁴¹ Demons also came out of many, crying out and saying, "You are the Christ, the Son of God!" Rebuking them, he didn't allow them to speak, because they knew that he was the Christ.
⁴² When it was day, he departed and went into an uninhabited place and the multitudes looked for him, and came to him, and held on to him, so that he wouldn't go away from them. ⁴³ But he said to them, "I must preach the good news of God's Kingdom to the other cities also. For this reason I have been sent." ⁴⁴ He was preaching in the synagogues of Galilee.

1. Invite the Holy Spirit into this reading, asking the Author of Scripture to speak to you through His Word
2. Read today's passage as many times as you need, take your time
3. Write down (below) what the Lord is saying to you today
4. Live with this Word in your heart through the day

_____

_____

Thursday, September 4, 2025

First Reading: Colossians 1: 9-14

⁹ For this cause, we also, since the day we heard this, don't cease praying and making requests for you, that you may be filled with the knowledge of his will in all spiritual wisdom and understanding, ¹⁰ that you may walk worthily of the Lord, to please him in all respects, bearing fruit in every good work and increasing in the knowledge of God, ¹¹ strengthened with all power, according to the might of his glory, for all endurance and perseverance with joy, ¹² giving thanks to the Father, who made us fit to be partakers of the inheritance of the saints in light, ¹³ who delivered us out of the power of darkness, and translated us into the Kingdom of the Son of his love, ¹⁴ in whom we have our redemption, the forgiveness of our sins.

Responsorial Psalm: Psalms 98: 2-6

² Yahweh has made known his salvation.
He has openly shown his righteousness in the sight of the nations.
³ He has remembered his loving kindness and his faithfulness toward the house of Israel.
All the ends of the earth have seen the salvation of our God.
⁴ Make a joyful noise to Yahweh, all the earth!
Burst out and sing for joy, yes, sing praises!
⁵ Sing praises to Yahweh with the harp,
with the harp and the voice of melody.
⁶ With trumpets and sound of the ram's horn,
make a joyful noise before the King, Yahweh.

Gospel: Luke 5: 1-11

¹ Now while the multitude pressed on him and heard the word of God, he was standing by the lake of Gennesaret. ² He saw two boats standing by the lake, but the fishermen had gone out of them and were washing their nets. ³ He entered into one of the boats, which was Simon's, and asked him to put out a little from the land. He sat down and taught the multitudes from the boat.
⁴ When he had finished speaking, he said to Simon, "Put out into the deep and let down your nets for a catch."
⁵ Simon answered him, "Master, we worked all night and caught nothing; but at your word I will let down the net." ⁶ When they had done this, they caught a great multitude of fish, and their net was breaking. ⁷ They beckoned to their partners in the other boat, that they should come and help them. They came and filled both boats, so that they began to sink. ⁸ But Simon Peter, when he saw it, fell down at Jesus' knees, saying, "Depart from me, for I am a sinful man, Lord." ⁹ For he was amazed, and all who were with him, at the catch of fish which they had caught; ¹⁰ and so also were James and John, sons of Zebedee, who were partners with Simon.
Jesus said to Simon, "Don't be afraid. From now on you will be catching people alive."
¹¹ When they had brought their boats to land, they left everything, and followed him.

1. Invite the Holy Spirit into this reading, asking the Author of Scripture to speak to you through His Word
2. Read today's passage as many times as you need, take your time
3. Write down (below) what the Lord is saying to you today
4. Live with this Word in your heart through the day

_____

_____

Friday, September 5, 2025

First Reading: Colossians 1: 15-20

¹⁵ He is the image of the invisible God, the firstborn of all creation. ¹⁶ For by him all things were created in the heavens and on the earth, visible things and invisible things, whether thrones or dominions or principalities or powers. All things have been created through him and for him. ¹⁷ He is before all things, and in him all things are held together. ¹⁸ He is the head of the body, the assembly, who is the beginning, the firstborn from the dead, that in all things he might have the preeminence. ¹⁹ For all the fullness was pleased to dwell in

him, ²⁰ and through him to reconcile all things to himself by him, whether things on the earth or things in the heavens, having made peace through the blood of his cross.

Responsorial Psalm: Psalms 100: 1-5

¹ Shout for joy to Yahweh, all you lands!
² Serve Yahweh with gladness.
Come before his presence with singing.
³ Know that Yahweh, he is God.
It is he who has made us, and we are his.
We are his people, and the sheep of his pasture.
⁴ Enter into his gates with thanksgiving,
and into his courts with praise.
Give thanks to him, and bless his name.
⁵ For Yahweh is good.
His loving kindness endures forever,
his faithfulness to all generations.

Gospel: Luke 5: 33-39

³³ They said to him, "Why do John's disciples often fast and pray, likewise also the disciples of the Pharisees, but yours eat and drink?"
³⁴ He said to them, "Can you make the friends of the bridegroom fast while the bridegroom is with them? ³⁵ But the days will come when the bridegroom will be taken away from them. Then they will fast in those days."
³⁶ He also told a parable to them. "No one puts a piece from a new garment on an old garment, or else he will tear the new, and also the piece from the new will not match the old. ³⁷ No one puts new wine into old wine skins, or else the new wine will burst the skins, and it will be spilled and the skins will be destroyed. ³⁸ But new wine must be put into fresh wine skins, and both are preserved. ³⁹ No man having drunk old wine immediately desires new, for he says, 'The old is better.' "

1. Invite the Holy Spirit into this reading, asking the Author of Scripture to speak to you through His Word
2. Read today's passage as many times as you need, take your time
3. Write down (below) what the Lord is saying to you today
4. Live with this Word in your heart through the day

Saturday, September 6, 2025

First Reading: Colossians 1: 21-23

²¹ You, being in past times alienated and enemies in your mind in your evil deeds, ²² yet now he has reconciled in the body of his flesh through death, to present you holy and without defect and blameless before him, ²³ if it is so that you continue in the faith, grounded and steadfast, and not moved away from the hope of the Good News which you heard, which is being proclaimed in all creation under heaven, of which I, Paul, was made a servant.

Responsorial Psalm: Psalms 54: 3-4, 6 and 8

³ For strangers have risen up against me.
Violent men have sought after my soul.
They haven't set God before them.
⁴ Behold, God is my helper.
The Lord is the one who sustains my soul.
⁶ With a free will offering, I will sacrifice to you.
I will give thanks to your name, Yahweh, for it is good.

Gospel: Luke 6: 1-5

¹ Now on the second Sabbath after the first, he was going through the grain fields. His disciples plucked the heads of grain and ate, rubbing them in their hands. ² But some of the Pharisees said to them, "Why do you do that which is not lawful to do on the Sabbath day?" ³ Jesus, answering them, said, "Haven't you read what David did when he was hungry, he and those who were with him, ⁴ how he entered into God's house, and took and ate the show bread, and gave also to those who were with him, which is not lawful to eat except for the priests alone?" ⁵ He said to them, "The Son of Man is lord of the Sabbath."

1. Invite the Holy Spirit into this reading, asking the Author of Scripture to speak to you through His Word
2. Read today's passage as many times as you need, take your time
3. Write down (below) what the Lord is saying to you today
4. Live with this Word in your heart through the day

Sunday, September 7, 2025
TWENTY-THIRD SUNDAY IN ORDINARY TIME

First Reading: Wisdom 9: 13-18b

[13] For what man will know the counsel of God?
Or who will conceive what the Lord wills?
[14] For the thoughts of mortals are unstable,
and our plans are prone to fail.
[15] For a corruptible body weighs down the soul.
The earthy tent burdens a mind that is full of cares.
[16] We can hardly guess the things that are on earth,
and we find the things that are close at hand with labor;
but who has traced out the things that are in the heavens?
[17] Who gained knowledge of your counsel, unless you gave wisdom,
and sent your holy spirit from on high?
[18] It was thus that the ways of those who are on earth were corrected,
and men were taught the things that are pleasing to you.

Responsorial Psalm: Psalms 90: 3-6, 12-14 and 17

[3] You turn man to destruction, saying,
"Return, you children of men."
[4] For a thousand years in your sight are just like yesterday when it is past,
like a watch in the night.
[5] You sweep them away as they sleep.
In the morning they sprout like new grass.
[6] In the morning it sprouts and springs up.
By evening, it is withered and dry.
[12] So teach us to count our days,
that we may gain a heart of wisdom.
[13] Relent, Yahweh!§
How long?
Have compassion on your servants!
[14] Satisfy us in the morning with your loving kindness,
that we may rejoice and be glad all our days.
[17] Let the favor of the Lord our God be on us.
Establish the work of our hands for us.
Yes, establish the work of our hands.

Second Reading: Philemon 1: 9-10, 12-17

9 yet for love's sake I rather appeal to you, being such a one as Paul, the aged, but also a prisoner of Jesus Christ. 10 I appeal to you for my child Onesimus, whom I have become the father of in my chains,‡
12 I am sending him back. Therefore receive him, that is, my own heart, 13 whom I desired to keep with me, that on your behalf he might serve me in my chains for the Good News. 14 But I was willing to do nothing without your consent, that your goodness would not be as of necessity, but of free will. 15 For perhaps he was therefore separated from you for a while that you would have him forever, 16 no longer as a slave, but more than a slave, a beloved brother—especially to me, but how much rather to you, both in the flesh and in the Lord.
17 If then you count me a partner, receive him as you would receive me.

Gospel: Luke 14: 25-33

25 Now great multitudes were going with him. He turned and said to them, 26 "If anyone comes to me, and doesn't disregard§ his own father, mother, wife, children, brothers, and sisters, yes, and his own life also, he can't be my disciple. 27 Whoever doesn't bear his own cross and come after me, can't be my disciple. 28 For which of you, desiring to build a tower, doesn't first sit down and count the cost, to see if he has enough to complete it? 29 Or perhaps, when he has laid a foundation and isn't able to finish, everyone who sees begins to mock him, 30 saying, 'This man began to build and wasn't able to finish.' 31 Or what king, as he goes to encounter another king in war, will not sit down first and consider whether he is able with ten thousand to meet him who comes against him with twenty thousand? 32 Or else, while the other is yet a great way off, he sends an envoy and asks for conditions of peace. 33 So therefore, whoever of you who doesn't renounce all that he has, he can't be my disciple.

1. Invite the Holy Spirit into this reading, asking the Author of Scripture to speak to you through His Word
2. Read today's passage as many times as you need, take your time
3. Write down (below) what the Lord is saying to you today
4. Live with this Word in your heart through the day

Monday, September 8, 2025
The Nativity of the Blessed Virgin Mary

First Reading: Micah 5: 1-4a

¹ Now you shall gather yourself in troops,
daughter of troops.
He has laid siege against us.
They will strike the judge of Israel with a rod on the cheek.
² But you, Bethlehem Ephrathah,
being small among the clans of Judah,
out of you one will come out to me who is to be ruler in Israel;
whose goings out are from of old, from ancient times.
³ Therefore he will abandon them until the time that she who is in labor gives birth.
Then the rest of his brothers will return to the children of Israel.
⁴ He shall stand, and shall shepherd in the strength of Yahweh,
in the majesty of the name of Yahweh his God.
They will live, for then he will be great to the ends of the earth.

Responsorial Psalm: Psalms 13: 6ab, 6c

⁶ I will sing to Yahweh,
because he has been good to me.

Gospel: Matthew 1: 1-16, 18-23

¹ The book of the genealogy of Jesus Christ,‡ the son of David, the son of Abraham. ² Abraham became the father of Isaac. Isaac became the father of Jacob. Jacob became the father of Judah and his brothers. ³ Judah became the father of Perez and Zerah by Tamar. Perez became the father of Hezron. Hezron became the father of Ram. ⁴ Ram became the father of Amminadab. Amminadab became the father of Nahshon. Nahshon became the father of Salmon. ⁵ Salmon became the father of Boaz by Rahab. Boaz became the father of Obed by Ruth. Obed became the father of Jesse. ⁶ Jesse became the father of King David. David the king‡ became the father of Solomon by her who had been Uriah's wife. ⁷ Solomon became the father of Rehoboam. Rehoboam became the father of Abijah. Abijah became the father of Asa. ⁸ Asa became the father of Jehoshaphat. Jehoshaphat became the father of Joram. Joram became the father of Uzziah. ⁹ Uzziah became the father of Jotham. Jotham became the father of Ahaz. Ahaz became the father of Hezekiah. ¹⁰ Hezekiah became the father of Manasseh. Manasseh became the father of Amon. Amon became the

father of Josiah. ¹¹ Josiah became the father of Jechoniah and his brothers at the time of the exile to Babylon.

¹² After the exile to Babylon, Jechoniah became the father of Shealtiel. Shealtiel became the father of Zerubbabel. ¹³ Zerubbabel became the father of Abiud. Abiud became the father of Eliakim. Eliakim became the father of Azor. ¹⁴ Azor became the father of Zadok. Zadok became the father of Achim. Achim became the father of Eliud. ¹⁵ Eliud became the father of Eleazar. Eleazar became the father of Matthan. Matthan became the father of Jacob. ¹⁶ Jacob became the father of Joseph, the husband of Mary, from whom was born Jesus,§ who is called Christ.

¹⁸ Now the birth of Jesus Christ was like this: After his mother, Mary, was engaged to Joseph, before they came together, she was found pregnant by the Holy Spirit. ¹⁹ Joseph, her husband, being a righteous man, and not willing to make her a public example, intended to put her away secretly. ²⁰ But when he thought about these things, behold,‡ an angel of the Lord appeared to him in a dream, saying, "Joseph, son of David, don't be afraid to take to yourself Mary as your wife, for that which is conceived in her is of the Holy Spirit. ²¹ She shall give birth to a son. You shall name him Jesus,‡ for it is he who shall save his people from their sins."

²² Now all this has happened that it might be fulfilled which was spoken by the Lord through the prophet, saying,
²³ "Behold, the virgin shall be with child,
and shall give birth to a son.
They shall call his name Immanuel,"
which is, being interpreted, "God with us."

1. Invite the Holy Spirit into this reading, asking the Author of Scripture to speak to you through His Word
2. Read today's passage as many times as you need, take your time
3. Write down (below) what the Lord is saying to you today
4. Live with this Word in your heart through the day

Tuesday, September 9, 2025
Saint Peter Claver, Priest

First Reading: Colossians 2: 6-15

⁶ As therefore you received Christ Jesus the Lord, walk in him, ⁷ rooted and built up in him and established in the faith, even as you were taught, abounding in it in thanksgiving.
⁸ Be careful that you don't let anyone rob you through his philosophy and vain deceit, after the tradition of men, after the elemental spirits of the world, and not after Christ. ⁹ For in him all the fullness of the Deity dwells bodily, ¹⁰ and in him you are made full, who is the head of all principality and power. ¹¹ In him you were also circumcised with a circumcision not made with hands, in the putting off of the body of the sins of the flesh, in the circumcision of Christ, ¹² having been buried with him in baptism, in which you were also raised with him through faith in the working of God, who raised him from the dead. ¹³ You were dead through your trespasses and the uncircumcision of your flesh. He made you alive together with him, having forgiven us all our trespasses, ¹⁴ wiping out the handwriting in ordinances which was against us. He has taken it out of the way, nailing it to the cross. ¹⁵ Having stripped the principalities and the powers, he made a show of them openly, triumphing over them in it.

Responsorial Psalm: Psalms 145: 1b-2, 8-11

¹ᵇ I will praise your name forever and ever.
² Every day I will praise you.
I will extol your name forever and ever.
⁸ Yahweh is gracious, merciful,
slow to anger, and of great loving kindness.
⁹ Yahweh is good to all.
His tender mercies are over all his works.
¹⁰ All your works will give thanks to you, Yahweh.
Your saints will extol you.
¹¹ They will speak of the glory of your kingdom,
and talk about your power,

Gospel: Luke 6: 12-19

¹² In these days, he went out to the mountain to pray, and he continued all night in prayer to God. ¹³ When it was day, he called his disciples, and from them he chose twelve, whom he also named apostles: ¹⁴ Simon, whom he also named Peter; Andrew, his brother; James; John; Philip; Bartholomew; ¹⁵ Matthew; Thomas; James the son of Alphaeus; Simon who was called the Zealot; ¹⁶ Judas the son of James; and Judas Iscariot, who also became a traitor.
¹⁷ He came down with them and stood on a level place, with a crowd of his disciples and a great number of the people from all Judea and Jerusalem and the sea coast of Tyre and Sidon, who came to hear him and to be healed of their diseases, ¹⁸ as well as those who were

troubled by unclean spirits; and they were being healed. ¹⁹ All the multitude sought to touch him, for power came out of him and healed them all.

1. Invite the Holy Spirit into this reading, asking the Author of Scripture to speak to you through His Word
2. Read today's passage as many times as you need, take your time
3. Write down (below) what the Lord is saying to you today
4. Live with this Word in your heart through the day

_____

_____

Wednesday, September 10, 2025

First Reading: Colossians 3: 1-11

¹ If then you were raised together with Christ, seek the things that are above, where Christ is, seated on the right hand of God. ² Set your mind on the things that are above, not on the things that are on the earth. ³ For you died, and your life is hidden with Christ in God. ⁴ When Christ, our life, is revealed, then you will also be revealed with him in glory. ⁵ Put to death therefore your members which are on the earth: sexual immorality, uncleanness, depraved passion, evil desire, and covetousness, which is idolatry. ⁶ For these things' sake the wrath of God comes on the children of disobedience. ⁷ You also once walked in those, when you lived in them, ⁸ but now you must put them all away: anger, wrath, malice, slander, and shameful speaking out of your mouth. ⁹ Don't lie to one another, seeing that you have put off the old man with his doings, ¹⁰ and have put on the new man, who is being renewed in knowledge after the image of his Creator, ¹¹ where there can't be Greek and Jew, circumcision and uncircumcision, barbarian, Scythian, bondservant, or free person; but Christ is all, and in all.

Responsorial Psalm: Psalms 145: 2-3, 10-11, 12-13ab

² Every day I will praise you.
I will extol your name forever and ever.
³ Great is Yahweh, and greatly to be praised!
His greatness is unsearchable.
¹⁰ All your works will give thanks to you, Yahweh.
Your saints will extol you.

¹¹ They will speak of the glory of your kingdom,
and talk about your power,
¹² to make known to the sons of men his mighty acts,
the glory of the majesty of his kingdom.
¹³ Your kingdom is an everlasting kingdom.
Your dominion endures throughout all generations.

Gospel: Luke 6: 20-26

²⁰ He lifted up his eyes to his disciples, and said:
"Blessed are you who are poor,
for God's Kingdom is yours.
²¹ Blessed are you who hunger now,
for you will be filled.
Blessed are you who weep now,
for you will laugh.
²² Blessed are you when men hate you, and when they exclude and mock you, and throw out your name as evil, for the Son of Man's sake.
²³ Rejoice in that day and leap for joy, for behold, your reward is great in heaven, for their fathers did the same thing to the prophets.
²⁴ "But woe to you who are rich!
For you have received your consolation.
²⁵ Woe to you, you who are full now,
for you will be hungry.
Woe to you who laugh now,
for you will mourn and weep.
²⁶ Woe,‡ when‡ men speak well of you,
for their fathers did the same thing to the false prophets.

1. Invite the Holy Spirit into this reading, asking the Author of Scripture to speak to you through His Word
2. Read today's passage as many times as you need, take your time
3. Write down (below) what the Lord is saying to you today
4. Live with this Word in your heart through the day

_____

_____

Thursday, September 11, 2025

First Reading: Colossians 3: 12-17

¹² Put on therefore, as God's chosen ones, holy and beloved, a heart of compassion, kindness, lowliness, humility, and perseverance; ¹³ bearing with one another, and forgiving each other, if any man has a complaint against any; even as Christ forgave you, so you also do.
¹⁴ Above all these things, walk in love, which is the bond of perfection. ¹⁵ And let the peace of God rule in your hearts, to which also you were called in one body, and be thankful. ¹⁶ Let the word of Christ dwell in you richly; in all wisdom teaching and admonishing one another with psalms, hymns, and spiritual songs, singing with grace in your heart to the Lord.
¹⁷ Whatever you do, in word or in deed, do all in the name of the Lord Jesus, giving thanks to God the Father through him.

Responsorial Psalm: Psalms 150: 1b-2, 3-4, 5-6

¹ᵇ Praise God in his sanctuary!
Praise him in his heavens for his acts of power!
² Praise him for his mighty acts!
Praise him according to his excellent greatness!
³ Praise him with the sounding of the trumpet!
Praise him with harp and lyre!
⁴ Praise him with tambourine and dancing!
Praise him with stringed instruments and flute!
⁵ Praise him with loud cymbals!
Praise him with resounding cymbals!
⁶ Let everything that has breath praise Yah!
Praise Yah!

Gospel: Luke 6: 27-38

²⁷ "But I tell you who hear: love your enemies, do good to those who hate you, ²⁸ bless those who curse you, and pray for those who mistreat you. ²⁹ To him who strikes you on the cheek, offer also the other; and from him who takes away your cloak, don't withhold your coat also. ³⁰ Give to everyone who asks you, and don't ask him who takes away your goods to give them back again.
³¹ "As you would like people to do to you, do exactly so to them.
³² "If you love those who love you, what credit is that to you? For even sinners love those who love them. ³³ If you do good to those who do good to you, what credit is that to you?

For even sinners do the same. ³⁴ If you lend to those from whom you hope to receive, what credit is that to you? Even sinners lend to sinners, to receive back as much. ³⁵ But love your enemies, and do good, and lend, expecting nothing back; and your reward will be great, and you will be children of the Most High; for he is kind toward the unthankful and evil. ³⁶ "Therefore be merciful,
even as your Father is also merciful.
³⁷ Don't judge,
and you won't be judged.
Don't condemn,
and you won't be condemned.
Set free,
and you will be set free.
³⁸ "Give, and it will be given to you: good measure, pressed down, shaken together, and running over, will be given to you.§ For with the same measure you measure it will be measured back to you."

1. Invite the Holy Spirit into this reading, asking the Author of Scripture to speak to you through His Word
2. Read today's passage as many times as you need, take your time
3. Write down (below) what the Lord is saying to you today
4. Live with this Word in your heart through the day

_____

_____

Friday, September 12, 2025
The Most Holy Name of Mary

First Reading: First Timothy 1: 1-2, 12-14

¹ Paul, an apostle of Jesus Christ according to the commandment of God our Savior and the Lord Jesus Christ‡ our hope, ² to Timothy, my true child in faith: Grace, mercy, and peace from God our Father and Christ Jesus our Lord.
¹² I thank him who enabled me, Christ Jesus our Lord, because he counted me faithful, appointing me to service, ¹³ although I used to be a blasphemer, a persecutor, and insolent. However, I obtained mercy because I did it ignorantly in unbelief. ¹⁴ The grace of our Lord abounded exceedingly with faith and love which is in Christ Jesus.

Responsorial Psalm: Psalms 16: 1-2a and 5, 7-8, 11

¹ Preserve me, God, for I take refuge in you.
²ᵃ My soul, you have said to Yahweh, "You are my Lord.
⁵ Yahweh assigned my portion and my cup.
You made my lot secure.
⁷ I will bless Yahweh, who has given me counsel.
Yes, my heart instructs me in the night seasons.
⁸ I have set Yahweh always before me.
Because he is at my right hand, I shall not be moved.
¹¹ You will show me the path of life.
In your presence is fullness of joy.
In your right hand there are pleasures forever more.

Gospel: Luke 6: 39-42

³⁹ He spoke a parable to them. "Can the blind guide the blind? Won't they both fall into a pit? ⁴⁰ A disciple is not above his teacher, but everyone when he is fully trained will be like his teacher. ⁴¹ Why do you see the speck of chaff that is in your brother's eye, but don't consider the beam that is in your own eye? ⁴² Or how can you tell your brother, 'Brother, let me remove the speck of chaff that is in your eye,' when you yourself don't see the beam that is in your own eye? You hypocrite! First remove the beam from your own eye, and then you can see clearly to remove the speck of chaff that is in your brother's eye.

1. Invite the Holy Spirit into this reading, asking the Author of Scripture to speak to you through His Word
2. Read today's passage as many times as you need, take your time
3. Write down (below) what the Lord is saying to you today
4. Live with this Word in your heart through the day

Saturday, September 13, 2025
Saint John Chrysostom, Bishop and Doctor of the Church

First Reading: First Timothy 1: 15-17

¹⁵ The saying is faithful and worthy of all acceptance, that Christ Jesus came into the world to save sinners, of whom I am chief. ¹⁶ However, for this cause I obtained mercy, that in me first, Jesus Christ might display all his patience for an example of those who were going to believe in him for eternal life. ¹⁷ Now to the King eternal, immortal, invisible, to God who alone is wise, be honor and glory forever and ever. Amen.

Responsorial Psalm: Psalms 113: 1b-2, 3-4, 5a and 6-7

¹ᵇ Praise, you servants of Yahweh,
praise Yahweh's name.
² Blessed be Yahweh's name,
from this time forward and forever more.
³ From the rising of the sun to its going down,
Yahweh's name is to be praised.
⁴ Yahweh is high above all nations,
his glory above the heavens.
⁵ᵃ Who is like Yahweh, our God,
⁶ who stoops down to see in heaven and in the earth?
⁷ He raises up the poor out of the dust,
and lifts up the needy from the ash heap,

Gospel: Luke 6: 43-49

⁴³ "For there is no good tree that produces rotten fruit, nor again a rotten tree that produces good fruit. ⁴⁴ For each tree is known by its own fruit. For people don't gather figs from thorns, nor do they gather grapes from a bramble bush. ⁴⁵ The good man out of the good treasure of his heart brings out that which is good, and the evil man out of the evil treasure of his heart brings out that which is evil, for out of the abundance of the heart, his mouth speaks.
⁴⁶ "Why do you call me, 'Lord, Lord,' and don't do the things which I say? ⁴⁷ Everyone who comes to me, and hears my words and does them, I will show you who he is like. ⁴⁸ He is like a man building a house, who dug and went deep and laid a foundation on the rock. When a flood arose, the stream broke against that house, and could not shake it, because it was founded on the rock. ⁴⁹ But he who hears and doesn't do, is like a man who built a house on the earth without a foundation, against which the stream broke, and immediately it fell; and the ruin of that house was great."

1. Invite the Holy Spirit into this reading, asking the Author of Scripture to speak to you through His Word
2. Read today's passage as many times as you need, take your time

3. Write down (below) what the Lord is saying to you today
4. Live with this Word in your heart through the day

Sunday, September 14, 2025
THE EXALTATION OF THE HOLY CROSS

First Reading: Numbers 21: 4b-9

4b The soul of the people was very discouraged because of the journey. 5 The people spoke against God and against Moses: "Why have you brought us up out of Egypt to die in the wilderness? For there is no bread, there is no water, and our soul loathes this disgusting food!"
6 Yahweh sent venomous snakes among the people, and they bit the people. Many people of Israel died. 7 The people came to Moses, and said, "We have sinned, because we have spoken against Yahweh and against you. Pray to Yahweh, that he take away the serpents from us." Moses prayed for the people.
8 Yahweh said to Moses, "Make a venomous snake, and set it on a pole. It shall happen that everyone who is bitten, when he sees it, shall live." 9 Moses made a serpent of bronze, and set it on the pole. If a serpent had bitten any man, when he looked at the serpent of bronze, he lived.

Responsorial Psalm: Psalms 78: 1bc-2, 34-38

1 Hear my teaching, my people.
Turn your ears to the words of my mouth.
2 I will open my mouth in a parable.
I will utter dark sayings of old,
34 When he killed them, then they inquired after him.
They returned and sought God earnestly.
35 They remembered that God was their rock,
the Most High God, their redeemer.
36 But they flattered him with their mouth,
and lied to him with their tongue.
37 For their heart was not right with him,
neither were they faithful in his covenant.

38 But he, being merciful, forgave iniquity, and didn't destroy them.
Yes, many times he turned his anger away,
and didn't stir up all his wrath.

Second Reading: Philippians 2: 6-11

6 who, existing in the form of God, didn't consider equality with God a thing to be grasped, 7 but emptied himself, taking the form of a servant, being made in the likeness of men. 8 And being found in human form, he humbled himself, becoming obedient to the point of death, yes, the death of the cross. 9 Therefore God also highly exalted him, and gave to him the name which is above every name, 10 that at the name of Jesus every knee should bow, of those in heaven, those on earth, and those under the earth, 11 and that every tongue should confess that Jesus Christ is Lord, to the glory of God the Father.

Gospel: John 3: 13-17

13 No one has ascended into heaven but he who descended out of heaven, the Son of Man, who is in heaven. 14 As Moses lifted up the serpent in the wilderness, even so must the Son of Man be lifted up, 15 that whoever believes in him should not perish, but have eternal life. 16 For God so loved the world, that he gave his only born§ Son, that whoever believes in him should not perish, but have eternal life. 17 For God didn't send his Son into the world to judge the world, but that the world should be saved through him.

1. Invite the Holy Spirit into this reading, asking the Author of Scripture to speak to you through His Word
2. Read today's passage as many times as you need, take your time
3. Write down (below) what the Lord is saying to you today
4. Live with this Word in your heart through the day

_____

_____

Monday, September 15, 2025
Our Lady of Sorrows

First Reading: First Timothy 2: 1-8

¹ I exhort therefore, first of all, that petitions, prayers, intercessions, and givings of thanks be made for all men, ² for kings and all who are in high places, that we may lead a tranquil and quiet life in all godliness and reverence. ³ For this is good and acceptable in the sight of God our Savior, ⁴ who desires all people to be saved and come to full knowledge of the truth. ⁵ For there is one God and one mediator between God and men, the man Christ Jesus, ⁶ who gave himself as a ransom for all, the testimony at the proper time, ⁷ to which I was appointed a preacher and an apostle—I am telling the truth in Christ, not lying—a teacher of the Gentiles in faith and truth.

⁸ I desire therefore that the men in every place pray, lifting up holy hands without anger and doubting.

Responsorial Psalm: Psalms 28: 2, 7, 8-9

² Hear the voice of my petitions, when I cry to you,
when I lift up my hands toward your Most Holy Place.
⁷ Yahweh is my strength and my shield.
My heart has trusted in him, and I am helped.
Therefore my heart greatly rejoices.
With my song I will thank him.
⁸ Yahweh is their strength.
He is a stronghold of salvation to his anointed.
⁹ Save your people,
and bless your inheritance.
Be their shepherd also,
and bear them up forever.

Gospel: John 19: 25-27

²⁵ But standing by Jesus' cross were his mother, his mother's sister, Mary the wife of Clopas, and Mary Magdalene. ²⁶ Therefore when Jesus saw his mother, and the disciple whom he loved standing there, he said to his mother, "Woman, behold, your son!" ²⁷ Then he said to the disciple, "Behold, your mother!" From that hour, the disciple took her to his own home.

1. Invite the Holy Spirit into this reading, asking the Author of Scripture to speak to you through His Word
2. Read today's passage as many times as you need, take your time
3. Write down (below) what the Lord is saying to you today
4. Live with this Word in your heart through the day

Tuesday, September 16, 2025
Saints Cornelius, Pope, and Cyprian, Bishop, Martyrs

First Reading: First Timothy 3: 1-13

¹ This is a faithful saying: someone who seeks to be an overseer⁺ desires a good work. ² The overseer therefore must be without reproach, the husband of one wife, temperate, sensible, modest, hospitable, good at teaching; ³ not a drinker, not violent, not greedy for money, but gentle, not quarrelsome, not covetous; ⁴ one who rules his own house well, having children in subjection with all reverence; ⁵ (for how could someone who doesn't know how to rule his own house take care of God's assembly?) ⁶ not a new convert, lest being puffed up he fall into the same condemnation as the devil. ⁷ Moreover he must have good testimony from those who are outside, to avoid falling into reproach and the snare of the devil.
⁸ Servants,⁺ in the same way, must be reverent, not double-tongued, not addicted to much wine, not greedy for money, ⁹ holding the mystery of the faith in a pure conscience. ¹⁰ Let them also first be tested; then let them serve§ if they are blameless. ¹¹ Their wives in the same way must be reverent, not slanderers, temperate, and faithful in all things. ¹² Let servants⁺ be husbands of one wife, ruling their children and their own houses well. ¹³ For those who have served well⁺ gain for themselves a good standing and great boldness in the faith which is in Christ Jesus.

Responsorial Psalm: Psalms 101: 1b-6

¹ I will sing of loving kindness and justice.
To you, Yahweh, I will sing praises.
² I will be careful to live a blameless life.
When will you come to me?
I will walk within my house with a blameless heart.
³ I will set no vile thing before my eyes.
I hate the deeds of faithless men.
They will not cling to me.
⁴ A perverse heart will be far from me.
I will have nothing to do with evil.
⁵ I will silence whoever secretly slanders his neighbor.

I won't tolerate one who is arrogant and conceited.
⁶ My eyes will be on the faithful of the land,
that they may dwell with me.
He who walks in a perfect way,
he will serve me.

Gospel: Luke 7: 11-17

¹¹ Soon afterwards, he went to a city called Nain. Many of his disciples, along with a great multitude, went with him. ¹² Now when he came near to the gate of the city, behold, one who was dead was carried out, the only born⁺ son of his mother, and she was a widow. Many people of the city were with her. ¹³ When the Lord saw her, he had compassion on her and said to her, "Don't cry." ¹⁴ He came near and touched the coffin, and the bearers stood still. He said, "Young man, I tell you, arise!" ¹⁵ He who was dead sat up and began to speak. Then he gave him to his mother.
¹⁶ Fear took hold of all, and they glorified God, saying, "A great prophet has arisen among us!" and, "God has visited his people!" ¹⁷ This report went out concerning him in the whole of Judea and in all the surrounding region.

1. Invite the Holy Spirit into this reading, asking the Author of Scripture to speak to you through His Word
2. Read today's passage as many times as you need, take your time
3. Write down (below) what the Lord is saying to you today
4. Live with this Word in your heart through the day

Wednesday, September 17, 2025
Saint Robert Bellarmine, Bishop and Doctor of the Church;
Saint Hildegard of Bingen, Virgin and Doctor of the Church

First Reading: First Timothy 3: 14-16

¹⁴ These things I write to you, hoping to come to you shortly, ¹⁵ but if I wait long, that you may know how men ought to behave themselves in God's house, which is the assembly of the living God, the pillar and ground of the truth. ¹⁶ Without controversy, the mystery of godliness is great:

God[§] was revealed in the flesh,
justified in the spirit,
seen by angels,
preached among the nations,
believed on in the world,
and received up in glory.

Responsorial Psalm: Psalms 111: 1-2, 3-4, 5-6

¹ Praise Yah![£]
I will give thanks to Yahweh with my whole heart,
in the council of the upright, and in the congregation.
² Yahweh's works are great,
pondered by all those who delight in them.
³ His work is honor and majesty.
His righteousness endures forever.
⁴ He has caused his wonderful works to be remembered.
Yahweh is gracious and merciful.
⁵ He has given food to those who fear him.
He always remembers his covenant.
⁶ He has shown his people the power of his works,
in giving them the heritage of the nations.

Gospel: Luke 7: 31-35

31 [±] "To what then should I compare the people of this generation? What are they like? 32 They are like children who sit in the marketplace and call to one another, saying, 'We piped to you, and you didn't dance. We mourned, and you didn't weep.' 33 For John the Baptizer came neither eating bread nor drinking wine, and you say, 'He has a demon.' 34 The Son of Man has come eating and drinking, and you say, 'Behold, a glutton and a drunkard, a friend of tax collectors and sinners!' 35 Wisdom is justified by all her children."

1. Invite the Holy Spirit into this reading, asking the Author of Scripture to speak to you through His Word
2. Read today's passage as many times as you need, take your time
3. Write down (below) what the Lord is saying to you today
4. Live with this Word in your heart through the day

Thursday, September 18, 2025

First Reading: First Timothy 4: 12-16

¹² Let no man despise your youth; but be an example to those who believe, in word, in your way of life, in love, in spirit, in faith, and in purity. ¹³ Until I come, pay attention to reading, to exhortation, and to teaching. ¹⁴ Don't neglect the gift that is in you, which was given to you by prophecy with the laying on of the hands of the elders. ¹⁵ Be diligent in these things. Give yourself wholly to them, that your progress may be revealed to all. ¹⁶ Pay attention to yourself and to your teaching. Continue in these things, for in doing this you will save both yourself and those who hear you.

Responsorial Psalm: Psalms 111: 7-8, 9, 10

⁷ The works of his hands are truth and justice.
All his precepts are sure.
⁸ They are established forever and ever.
They are done in truth and uprightness.
⁹ He has sent redemption to his people.
He has ordained his covenant forever.
His name is holy and awesome!
¹⁰ The fear of Yahweh is the beginning of wisdom.
All those who do his work have a good understanding.
His praise endures forever!

Gospel: Luke 7: 36-50

³⁶ One of the Pharisees invited him to eat with him. He entered into the Pharisee's house and sat at the table. ³⁷ Behold, a woman in the city who was a sinner, when she knew that he was reclining in the Pharisee's house, brought an alabaster jar of ointment. ³⁸ Standing behind at his feet weeping, she began to wet his feet with her tears, and she wiped them with the hair of her head, kissed his feet, and anointed them with the ointment. ³⁹ Now when the Pharisee who had invited him saw it, he said to himself, "This man, if he were a prophet, would have perceived who and what kind of woman this is who touches him, that she is a sinner."

⁴⁰ Jesus answered him, "Simon, I have something to tell you."

He said, "Teacher, say on."

⁴¹ "A certain lender had two debtors. The one owed five hundred denarii, and the other fifty. ⁴² When they couldn't pay, he forgave them both. Which of them therefore will love him most?"

⁴³ Simon answered, "He, I suppose, to whom he forgave the most."

He said to him, "You have judged correctly." ⁴⁴ Turning to the woman, he said to Simon, "Do you see this woman? I entered into your house, and you gave me no water for my feet, but she has wet my feet with her tears, and wiped them with the hair of her head. ⁴⁵ You gave me no kiss, but she, since the time I came in, has not ceased to kiss my feet. ⁴⁶ You didn't anoint my head with oil, but she has anointed my feet with ointment. ⁴⁷ Therefore I tell you, her sins, which are many, are forgiven, for she loved much. But one to whom little is forgiven, loves little." ⁴⁸ He said to her, "Your sins are forgiven."

⁴⁹ Those who sat at the table with him began to say to themselves, "Who is this who even forgives sins?"

⁵⁰ He said to the woman, "Your faith has saved you. Go in peace."

1. Invite the Holy Spirit into this reading, asking the Author of Scripture to speak to you through His Word
2. Read today's passage as many times as you need, take your time
3. Write down (below) what the Lord is saying to you today
4. Live with this Word in your heart through the day

Friday, September 19, 2025
Saint Januarius, Bishop and Martyr

First Reading: First Timothy 6: 2c-12

²ᶜ Teach and exhort these things.

³ If anyone teaches a different doctrine and doesn't consent to sound words, the words of our Lord Jesus Christ, and to the doctrine which is according to godliness, ⁴ he is conceited, knowing nothing, but obsessed with arguments, disputes, and word battles, from which come envy, strife, insulting, evil suspicions, ⁵ constant friction of people of corrupt minds

and destitute of the truth, who suppose that godliness is a means of gain. Withdraw yourself from such.‡

⁶ But godliness with contentment is great gain. ⁷ For we brought nothing into the world, and we certainly can't carry anything out. ⁸ But having food and clothing, we will be content with that. ⁹ But those who are determined to be rich fall into a temptation, a snare, and many foolish and harmful lusts, such as drown men in ruin and destruction. ¹⁰ For the love of money is a root of all kinds of evil. Some have been led astray from the faith in their greed, and have pierced themselves through with many sorrows.

¹¹ But you, man of God, flee these things, and follow after righteousness, godliness, faith, love, perseverance, and gentleness. ¹² Fight the good fight of faith. Take hold of the eternal life to which you were called, and you confessed the good confession in the sight of many witnesses.

Responsorial Psalm: Psalms 49: 6-7, 8-10, 17-18, 19-20

⁶ Those who trust in their wealth,
and boast in the multitude of their riches—
⁷ none of them can by any means redeem his brother,
nor give God a ransom for him.
⁸ For the redemption of their life is costly,
no payment is ever enough,
⁹ that he should live on forever,
that he should not see corruption.
¹⁰ For he sees that wise men die;
likewise the fool and the senseless perish,
and leave their wealth to others.
¹⁷ for when he dies he will carry nothing away.
His glory won't descend after him.
¹⁸ Though while he lived he blessed his soul—
and men praise you when you do well for yourself—
¹⁹ he shall go to the generation of his fathers.
They shall never see the light.
²⁰ A man who has riches without understanding,
is like the animals that perish.

Gospel: Luke 8: 1-3

¹ Soon afterwards, he went about through cities and villages, preaching and bringing the good news of God's Kingdom. With him were the twelve, ² and certain women who had been healed of evil spirits and infirmities: Mary who was called Magdalene, from whom

seven demons had gone out; ³ and Joanna, the wife of Chuzas, Herod's steward; Susanna; and many others who served them⁺ from their possessions.

1. Invite the Holy Spirit into this reading, asking the Author of Scripture to speak to you through His Word
2. Read today's passage as many times as you need, take your time
3. Write down (below) what the Lord is saying to you today
4. Live with this Word in your heart through the day

Saturday, September 20, 2025
Saints Andrew Kim Tae-gŏn, Priest, and Paul Chŏng Ha-sang, red and Companions, Martyrs

First Reading: First Timothy 6: 13-16

¹³ I command you before God who gives life to all things, and before Christ Jesus who before Pontius Pilate testified the good confession, ¹⁴ that you keep the commandment without spot, blameless until the appearing of our Lord Jesus Christ, ¹⁵ which at the right time he will show, who is the blessed and only Ruler, the King of kings and Lord of lords. ¹⁶ He alone has immortality, dwelling in unapproachable light, whom no man has seen nor can see, to whom be honor and eternal power. Amen.

Responsorial Psalm: Psalms 100: 1b-2, 3, 4, 5

¹ Shout for joy to Yahweh, all you lands!
² Serve Yahweh with gladness.
Come before his presence with singing.
³ Know that Yahweh, he is God.
It is he who has made us, and we are his.
We are his people, and the sheep of his pasture.
⁴ Enter into his gates with thanksgiving,
and into his courts with praise.
Give thanks to him, and bless his name.
⁵ For Yahweh is good.
His loving kindness endures forever,

his faithfulness to all generations.

Gospel: Luke 8: 4-15

4 When a great multitude came together and people from every city were coming to him, he spoke by a parable: 5 "The farmer went out to sow his seed. As he sowed, some fell along the road, and it was trampled under foot, and the birds of the sky devoured it. 6 Other seed fell on the rock, and as soon as it grew, it withered away, because it had no moisture. 7 Other fell amid the thorns, and the thorns grew with it and choked it. 8 Other fell into the good ground and grew and produced one hundred times as much fruit." As he said these things, he called out, "He who has ears to hear, let him hear!"
9 Then his disciples asked him, "What does this parable mean?"
10 He said, "To you it is given to know the mysteries of God's Kingdom, but to the rest it is given in parables, that 'seeing they may not see, and hearing they may not understand.'
11 "Now the parable is this: The seed is the word of God. 12 Those along the road are those who hear; then the devil comes and takes away the word from their heart, that they may not believe and be saved. 13 Those on the rock are they who, when they hear, receive the word with joy; but these have no root. They believe for a while, then fall away in time of temptation. 14 What fell among the thorns, these are those who have heard, and as they go on their way they are choked with cares, riches, and pleasures of life; and they bring no fruit to maturity. 15 Those in the good ground, these are those who with an honest and good heart, having heard the word, hold it tightly, and produce fruit with perseverance.

1. Invite the Holy Spirit into this reading, asking the Author of Scripture to speak to you through His Word
2. Read today's passage as many times as you need, take your time
3. Write down (below) what the Lord is saying to you today
4. Live with this Word in your heart through the day

Sunday, September 21, 2025
TWENTY-FIFTH SUNDAY IN OPRDINARY TIME

First Reading: Amos 8: 4-7

4 Hear this, you who desire to swallow up the needy,

and cause the poor of the land to fail,
⁵ saying, 'When will the new moon be gone, that we may sell grain?
And the Sabbath, that we may market wheat,
making the ephah⸸ small, and the shekel⸸ large,
and dealing falsely with balances of deceit;
⁶ that we may buy the poor for silver,
and the needy for a pair of sandals,
and sell the sweepings with the wheat?' "
⁷ Yahweh has sworn by the pride of Jacob,
"Surely I will never forget any of their works.

Responsorial Psalm: Psalms 113: 1-2, 4-6, 7-8

¹ Praise Yah!
Praise, you servants of Yahweh,
praise Yahweh's name.
² Blessed be Yahweh's name,
from this time forward and forever more.
⁴ Yahweh is high above all nations,
his glory above the heavens.
⁵ Who is like Yahweh, our God,
who has his seat on high,
⁶ who stoops down to see in heaven and in the earth?
⁷ He raises up the poor out of the dust,
and lifts up the needy from the ash heap,
⁸ that he may set him with princes,
even with the princes of his people.

Second Reading: First Timothy 2: 1-8

¹ I exhort therefore, first of all, that petitions, prayers, intercessions, and givings of thanks be made for all men, ² for kings and all who are in high places, that we may lead a tranquil and quiet life in all godliness and reverence. ³ For this is good and acceptable in the sight of God our Savior, ⁴ who desires all people to be saved and come to full knowledge of the truth. ⁵ For there is one God and one mediator between God and men, the man Christ Jesus, ⁶ who gave himself as a ransom for all, the testimony at the proper time, ⁷ to which I was appointed a preacher and an apostle—I am telling the truth in Christ, not lying—a teacher of the Gentiles in faith and truth.
⁸ I desire therefore that the men in every place pray, lifting up holy hands without anger and doubting.

Gospel: Luke 16: 1-13

¹ He also said to his disciples, "There was a certain rich man who had a manager. An accusation was made to him that this man was wasting his possessions. ² He called him, and said to him, 'What is this that I hear about you? Give an accounting of your management, for you can no longer be manager.'

³ "The manager said within himself, 'What will I do, seeing that my lord is taking away the management position from me? I don't have strength to dig. I am ashamed to beg. ⁴ I know what I will do, so that when I am removed from management, they may receive me into their houses.' ⁵ Calling each one of his lord's debtors to him, he said to the first, 'How much do you owe to my lord?' ⁶ He said, 'A hundred batos‡ of oil.' He said to him, 'Take your bill, and sit down quickly and write fifty.' ⁷ Then he said to another, 'How much do you owe?' He said, 'A hundred cors‡ of wheat.' He said to him, 'Take your bill, and write eighty.'

⁸ "His lord commended the dishonest manager because he had done wisely, for the children of this world are, in their own generation, wiser than the children of the light. ⁹ I tell you, make for yourselves friends by means of unrighteous mammon, so that when you fail, they may receive you into the eternal tents. ¹⁰ He who is faithful in a very little is faithful also in much. He who is dishonest in a very little is also dishonest in much. ¹¹ If therefore you have not been faithful in the unrighteous mammon, who will commit to your trust the true riches? ¹² If you have not been faithful in that which is another's, who will give you that which is your own? ¹³ No servant can serve two masters, for either he will hate the one and love the other; or else he will hold to one and despise the other. You aren't able to serve God and Mammon."

1. Invite the Holy Spirit into this reading, asking the Author of Scripture to speak to you through His Word
2. Read today's passage as many times as you need, take your time
3. Write down (below) what the Lord is saying to you today
4. Live with this Word in your heart through the day

Monday, September 22, 2025

First Reading: Ezra 1: 1-6

¹ Now in the first year of Cyrus king of Persia, that Yahweh's word by Jeremiah's mouth might be accomplished, Yahweh stirred up the spirit of Cyrus king of Persia, so that he made a proclamation throughout all his kingdom, and put it also in writing, saying,
² "Cyrus king of Persia says, 'Yahweh, the God of heaven, has given me all the kingdoms of the earth; and he has commanded me to build him a house in Jerusalem, which is in Judah. ³ Whoever there is among you of all his people, may his God be with him, and let him go up to Jerusalem, which is in Judah, and build the house of Yahweh, the God of Israel (he is God), which is in Jerusalem. ⁴ Whoever is left, in any place where he lives, let the men of his place help him with silver, with gold, with goods, and with animals, in addition to the free will offering for God's house which is in Jerusalem.' "
⁵ Then the heads of fathers' households of Judah and Benjamin, the priests and the Levites, all whose spirit God had stirred to go up, rose up to build Yahweh's house which is in Jerusalem. ⁶ All those who were around them strengthened their hands with vessels of silver, with gold, with goods, with animals, and with precious things, in addition to all that was willingly offered.

Responsorial Psalm: Psalms 126: 1b-2ab, 2cd-3, 4-5, 6

¹ When Yahweh brought back those who returned to Zion,
we were like those who dream.
² Then our mouth was filled with laughter,
and our tongue with singing.
Then they said among the nations,
"Yahweh has done great things for them."
³ Yahweh has done great things for us,
and we are glad.
⁴ Restore our fortunes again, Yahweh,
like the streams in the Negev.
⁵ Those who sow in tears will reap in joy.
⁶ He who goes out weeping, carrying seed for sowing,
will certainly come again with joy, carrying his sheaves.

Gospel: Luke 8: 16-18

¹⁶ "No one, when he has lit a lamp, covers it with a container or puts it under a bed; but puts it on a stand, that those who enter in may see the light. ¹⁷ For nothing is hidden that will not be revealed, nor anything secret that will not be known and come to light. ¹⁸ Be careful therefore how you hear. For whoever has, to him will be given; and whoever doesn't have, from him will be taken away even that which he thinks he has."

1. Invite the Holy Spirit into this reading, asking the Author of Scripture to speak to you through His Word
2. Read today's passage as many times as you need, take your time
3. Write down (below) what the Lord is saying to you today
4. Live with this Word in your heart through the day

_____

_____

Tuesday, September 23, 2025
Saint Pius of Pietrelcina, Priest

First Reading: Ezra 6: 7-8, 12b, 14-20

⁷ Leave the work of this house of God alone; let the governor of the Jews and the elders of the Jews build this house of God in its place. ⁸ Moreover I make a decree regarding what you shall do for these elders of the Jews for the building of this house of God: that of the king's goods, even of the tribute beyond the River, expenses must be given with all diligence to these men, that they not be hindered.
¹²ᵇ I Darius have made a decree. Let it be done with all diligence.
¹⁴ The elders of the Jews built and prospered, through the prophesying of Haggai the prophet and Zechariah the son of Iddo. They built and finished it, according to the commandment of the God of Israel, and according to the decree of Cyrus, Darius, and Artaxerxes king of Persia. ¹⁵ This house was finished on the third day of the month Adar, which was in the sixth year of the reign of Darius the king.
¹⁶ The children of Israel, the priests, the Levites, and the rest of the children of the captivity, kept the dedication of this house of God with joy. ¹⁷ They offered at the dedication of this house of God one hundred bulls, two hundred rams, four hundred lambs; and for a sin offering for all Israel, twelve male goats, according to the number of the tribes of Israel. ¹⁸ They set the priests in their divisions and the Levites in their courses, for the service of God which is at Jerusalem, as it is written in the book of Moses.
¹⁹ The children of the captivity kept the Passover on the fourteenth day of the first month. ²⁰ Because the priests and the Levites had purified themselves together, all of them were pure. They killed the Passover for all the children of the captivity, for their brothers the priests, and for themselves.

Responsorial Psalm: Psalms 122: 1-2, 3-4ab, 4cd-5

¹ I was glad when they said to me,
"Let's go to Yahweh's house!"
² Our feet are standing within your gates, Jerusalem!
³ Jerusalem is built as a city that is compact together,
⁴ where the tribes go up, even Yah's tribes,
according to an ordinance for Israel,
to give thanks to Yahweh's name.
⁵ For there are set thrones for judgment,
the thrones of David's house.

Gospel: Luke 8: 19-21

¹⁹ His mother and brothers came to him, and they could not come near him for the crowd. ²⁰ Some people told him, "Your mother and your brothers stand outside, desiring to see you." ²¹ But he answered them, "My mother and my brothers are these who hear the word of God and do it."

1. Invite the Holy Spirit into this reading, asking the Author of Scripture to speak to you through His Word
2. Read today's passage as many times as you need, take your time
3. Write down (below) what the Lord is saying to you today
4. Live with this Word in your heart through the day

Wednesday, September 24, 2025

First Reading: Ezra 9: 5-9

⁵ At the evening offering I rose up from my humiliation, even with my garment and my robe torn; and I fell on my knees, and spread out my hands to Yahweh my God; ⁶ and I said, "My God, I am ashamed and blush to lift up my face to you, my God, for our iniquities have increased over our head, and our guiltiness has grown up to the heavens. ⁷ Since the days of our fathers we have been exceedingly guilty to this day; and for our iniquities we, our kings, and our priests have been delivered into the hand of the kings of the lands, to the sword, to captivity, to plunder, and to confusion of face, as it is this day. ⁸ Now for a little

moment grace has been shown from Yahweh our God, to leave us a remnant to escape, and to give us a stake in his holy place, that our God may lighten our eyes, and revive us a little in our bondage. ⁹ For we are bondservants; yet our God has not forsaken us in our bondage, but has extended loving kindness to us in the sight of the kings of Persia, to revive us, to set up the house of our God, and to repair its ruins, and to give us a wall in Judah and in Jerusalem.

Responsorial Psalm: Tobit 13: 2, 3-4a, 6, 8

² For he scourges, and shows mercy.
He leads down to the grave,‡ and brings up again.
There is no one who will escape his hand.
³ Give thanks to him before the Gentiles, all you children of Israel!
For he has scattered us among them.
⁴ᵃ Declare his greatness, there.
⁶ If you turn to him with your whole heart and with your whole soul,
to do truth before him,
then he will turn to you,
and won't hide his face from you.
See what he will do with you.
Give him thanks with your whole mouth.
Bless the Lord of righteousness.
Exalt the everlasting King.
I give him thanks in the land of my captivity,
and show his strength and majesty to a nation of sinners.
Turn, you sinners, and do righteousness before him.
Who can tell if he will accept you and have mercy on you?
⁸ Let all men speak,
and let them give him thanks in Jerusalem.

Gospel: Luke 9: 1-6

¹ He called the twelve‡ together and gave them power and authority over all demons, and to cure diseases. ² He sent them out to preach God's Kingdom and to heal the sick. ³ He said to them, "Take nothing for your journey—no staffs, nor wallet, nor bread, nor money. Don't have two tunics each. ⁴ Into whatever house you enter, stay there, and depart from there. ⁵ As many as don't receive you, when you depart from that city, shake off even the dust from your feet for a testimony against them."
⁶ They departed and went throughout the villages, preaching the Good News and healing everywhere.

1. Invite the Holy Spirit into this reading, asking the Author of Scripture to speak to you through His Word
2. Read today's passage as many times as you need, take your time
3. Write down (below) what the Lord is saying to you today
4. Live with this Word in your heart through the day

___

___

Thursday, September 25, 2025

First Reading: Haggai 1: 1-8

¹ In the second year of Darius the king, in the sixth month, in the first day of the month, Yahweh's word came by Haggai the prophet, to Zerubbabel the son of Shealtiel, governor of Judah, and to Joshua the son of Jehozadak, the high priest, saying, ² "This is what Yahweh of Armies says: These people say, 'The time hasn't yet come, the time for Yahweh's house to be built.' "
³ Then Yahweh's word came by Haggai the prophet, saying, ⁴ "Is it a time for you yourselves to dwell in your paneled houses, while this house lies waste? ⁵ Now therefore this is what Yahweh of Armies says: 'Consider your ways. ⁶ You have sown much, and bring in little. You eat, but you don't have enough. You drink, but you aren't filled with drink. You clothe yourselves, but no one is warm; and he who earns wages earns wages to put them into a bag with holes in it.'
⁷ "This is what Yahweh of Armies says: 'Consider your ways. ⁸ Go up to the mountain, bring wood, and build the house. I will take pleasure in it, and I will be glorified," says Yahweh.

Responsorial Psalm: Psalms 149: 1b-2, 3-4, 5-6a and 9b

¹ᵇ Sing to Yahweh a new song,
his praise in the assembly of the saints.
² Let Israel rejoice in him who made them.
Let the children of Zion be joyful in their King.
³ Let them praise his name in the dance!
Let them sing praises to him with tambourine and harp!
⁴ For Yahweh takes pleasure in his people.
He crowns the humble with salvation.

⁵ Let the saints rejoice in honor.
Let them sing for joy on their beds.
⁶ᵃ May the high praises of God be in their mouths,
⁹ᵇ All his saints have this honor.
Praise Yah!

Gospel: Luke 9: 7-9

⁷ Now Herod the tetrarch heard of all that was done by him; and he was very perplexed, because it was said by some that John had risen from the dead, ⁸ and by some that Elijah had appeared, and by others that one of the old prophets had risen again. ⁹ Herod said, "I beheaded John, but who is this about whom I hear such things?" He sought to see him.

1. Invite the Holy Spirit into this reading, asking the Author of Scripture to speak to you through His Word
2. Read today's passage as many times as you need, take your time
3. Write down (below) what the Lord is saying to you today
4. Live with this Word in your heart through the day

Friday, September 26, 2025
Saints Cosmas and Damian, Martyrs

First Reading: Haggai 2: 1-9

¹ In the seventh month, in the twenty-first day of the month, Yahweh's word came by Haggai the prophet, saying, ² "Speak now to Zerubbabel the son of Shealtiel, governor of Judah, and to Joshua the son of Jehozadak, the high priest, and to the remnant of the people, saying, ³ 'Who is left among you who saw this house in its former glory? How do you see it now? Isn't it in your eyes as nothing? ⁴ Yet now be strong, Zerubbabel,' says Yahweh. 'Be strong, Joshua son of Jehozadak, the high priest. Be strong, all you people of the land,' says Yahweh, 'and work, for I am with you,' says Yahweh of Armies. ⁵ This is the word that I covenanted with you when you came out of Egypt, and my Spirit lived among you. 'Don't be afraid.' ⁶ For this is what Yahweh of Armies says: 'Yet once more, it is a little while, and I will shake the heavens, the earth, the sea, and the dry land; ⁷ and I will shake all nations. The treasure of all nations will come, and I will fill this house with glory, says

Yahweh of Armies. ⁸ The silver is mine, and the gold is mine,' says Yahweh of Armies. ⁹ 'The latter glory of this house will be greater than the former,' says Yahweh of Armies; 'and in this place I will give peace,' says Yahweh of Armies."

Responsorial Psalm: Psalms 43: 1, 2, 3, 4

¹ Vindicate me, God, and plead my cause against an ungodly nation.
Oh, deliver me from deceitful and wicked men.
² For you are the God of my strength. Why have you rejected me?
Why do I go mourning because of the oppression of the enemy?
³ Oh, send out your light and your truth.
Let them lead me.
Let them bring me to your holy hill,
to your tents.
⁴ Then I will go to the altar of God,
to God, my exceeding joy.
I will praise you on the harp, God, my God.

Gospel: Luke 9: 18-22

¹⁸ As he was praying alone, the disciples were near him, and he asked them, "Who do the multitudes say that I am?"
¹⁹ They answered, " 'John the Baptizer,' but others say, 'Elijah,' and others, that one of the old prophets has risen again."
²⁰ He said to them, "But who do you say that I am?"
Peter answered, "The Christ of God."
²¹ But he warned them and commanded them to tell this to no one, ²² saying, "The Son of Man must suffer many things, and be rejected by the elders, chief priests, and scribes, and be killed, and the third day be raised up."

1. Invite the Holy Spirit into this reading, asking the Author of Scripture to speak to you through His Word
2. Read today's passage as many times as you need, take your time
3. Write down (below) what the Lord is saying to you today
4. Live with this Word in your heart through the day

_____

_____

Saturday, September 27, 2025
Saint Vincent de Paul, Priest

First Reading: Zechariah 2: 5-11

5 For I,' says Yahweh, 'will be to her a wall of fire around it, and I will be the glory in the middle of her. 6 Come! Come! Flee from the land of the north,' says Yahweh; 'for I have spread you abroad as the four winds of the sky,' says Yahweh. 7 'Come, Zion! Escape, you who dwell with the daughter of Babylon.' 8 For Yahweh of Armies says: 'For honor he has sent me to the nations which plundered you; for he who touches you touches the apple of his eye. 9 For, behold, I will shake my hand over them, and they will be a plunder to those who served them; and you will know that Yahweh of Armies has sent me. 10 Sing and rejoice, daughter of Zion! For behold, I come and I will dwell within you,' says Yahweh. 11 Many nations shall join themselves to Yahweh in that day, and shall be my people; and I will dwell among you, and you shall know that Yahweh of Armies has sent me to you.

Responsorial Psalm: Jeremiah 31: 10, 11-12ab, 13

10 "Hear Yahweh's word, you nations,
and declare it in the distant islands. Say,
'He who scattered Israel will gather him,
and keep him, as a shepherd does his flock.'
11 For Yahweh has ransomed Jacob,
and redeemed him from the hand of him who was stronger than he.
12 They will come and sing in the height of Zion,
and will flow to the goodness of Yahweh,
to the grain, to the new wine, to the oil,
and to the young of the flock and of the herd.
Their soul will be as a watered garden.
13 Then the virgin will rejoice in the dance,
the young men and the old together;
for I will turn their mourning into joy,
and will comfort them, and make them rejoice from their sorrow.

Gospel: Luke 9: 43b-45

43 They were all astonished at the majesty of God.
But while all were marveling at all the things which Jesus did, he said to his disciples, 44 "Let these words sink into your ears, for the Son of Man will be delivered up

into the hands of men." ⁴⁵ But they didn't understand this saying. It was concealed from them, that they should not perceive it, and they were afraid to ask him about this saying.

1. Invite the Holy Spirit into this reading, asking the Author of Scripture to speak to you through His Word
2. Read today's passage as many times as you need, take your time
3. Write down (below) what the Lord is saying to you today
4. Live with this Word in your heart through the day

_____

_____

Sunday, September 28, 2025
TWENTY-SIXTH SUNDAY IN ORDINARY TIME

First Reading: Amos 6: 1a, 4-7

¹ᵃ Woe to those who are at ease in Zion,
⁴ who lie on beds of ivory,
and stretch themselves on their couches,
and eat the lambs out of the flock,
and the calves out of the middle of the stall,
⁵ who strum on the strings of a harp,
who invent for themselves instruments of music, like David;
⁶ who drink wine in bowls,
and anoint themselves with the best oils,
but they are not grieved for the affliction of Joseph.
⁷ Therefore they will now go captive with the first who go captive.
The feasting and lounging will end.

Responsorial Psalm: Psalms 146: 7, 8-9, 9-10

⁷ who executes justice for the oppressed;
who gives food to the hungry.
Yahweh frees the prisoners.
⁸ Yahweh opens the eyes of the blind.
Yahweh raises up those who are bowed down.
Yahweh loves the righteous.

⁹ Yahweh preserves the foreigners.
He upholds the fatherless and widow,
but he turns the way of the wicked upside down.
¹⁰ Yahweh will reign forever;
your God, O Zion, to all generations.
Praise Yah!

Second Reading: First Timothy 6: 11-16

¹¹ But you, man of God, flee these things, and follow after righteousness, godliness, faith, love, perseverance, and gentleness. ¹² Fight the good fight of faith. Take hold of the eternal life to which you were called, and you confessed the good confession in the sight of many witnesses. ¹³ I command you before God who gives life to all things, and before Christ Jesus who before Pontius Pilate testified the good confession, ¹⁴ that you keep the commandment without spot, blameless until the appearing of our Lord Jesus Christ, ¹⁵ which at the right time he will show, who is the blessed and only Ruler, the King of kings and Lord of lords. ¹⁶ He alone has immortality, dwelling in unapproachable light, whom no man has seen nor can see, to whom be honor and eternal power. Amen.

Gospel: Luke 16: 19-31

¹⁹ "Now there was a certain rich man, and he was clothed in purple and fine linen, living in luxury every day. ²⁰ A certain beggar, named Lazarus, was taken to his gate, full of sores, ²¹ and desiring to be fed with the crumbs that fell from the rich man's table. Yes, even the dogs came and licked his sores. ²² The beggar died, and he was carried away by the angels to Abraham's bosom. The rich man also died and was buried. ²³ In Hades, he lifted up his eyes, being in torment, and saw Abraham far off, and Lazarus at his bosom. ²⁴ He cried and said, 'Father Abraham, have mercy on me, and send Lazarus, that he may dip the tip of his finger in water and cool my tongue! For I am in anguish in this flame.'
²⁵ "But Abraham said, 'Son, remember that you, in your lifetime, received your good things, and Lazarus, in the same way, bad things. But here he is now comforted and you are in anguish. ²⁶ Besides all this, between us and you there is a great gulf fixed, that those who want to pass from here to you are not able, and that no one may cross over from there to us.'
²⁷ "He said, 'I ask you therefore, father, that you would send him to my father's house— ²⁸ for I have five brothers—that he may testify to them, so they won't also come into this place of torment.'
²⁹ "But Abraham said to him, 'They have Moses and the prophets. Let them listen to them.'
³⁰ "He said, 'No, father Abraham, but if one goes to them from the dead, they will repent.'

³¹ "He said to him, 'If they don't listen to Moses and the prophets, neither will they be persuaded if one rises from the dead.' "

1. Invite the Holy Spirit into this reading, asking the Author of Scripture to speak to you through His Word
2. Read today's passage as many times as you need, take your time
3. Write down (below) what the Lord is saying to you today
4. Live with this Word in your heart through the day

_____

_____

Monday, September 29, 2025
Saints Michael, Gabriel and Raphael, Archangels

First Reading: Revelation 12: 7-12ab

⁷ There was war in the sky. Michael and his angels made war on the dragon. The dragon and his angels made war. ⁸ They didn't prevail. No place was found for them any more in heaven. ⁹ The great dragon was thrown down, the old serpent, he who is called the devil and Satan, the deceiver of the whole world. He was thrown down to the earth, and his angels were thrown down with him.
¹⁰ I heard a loud voice in heaven, saying, "Now the salvation, the power, and the Kingdom of our God, and the authority of his Christ has come; for the accuser of our brothers has been thrown down, who accuses them before our God day and night. ¹¹ They overcame him because of the Lamb's blood, and because of the word of their testimony. They didn't love their life, even to death. ¹² Therefore rejoice, heavens, and you who dwell in them. Woe to the earth and to the sea, because the devil has gone down to you, having great wrath, knowing that he has but a short time."

Responsorial Psalm: Psalms 138: 1-2ab, 2cde-3, 4-5

¹ I will give you thanks with my whole heart.
Before the gods,‡ I will sing praises to you.
² I will bow down toward your holy temple,
and give thanks to your Name for your loving kindness and for your truth;
for you have exalted your Name and your Word above all.
³ In the day that I called, you answered me.

You encouraged me with strength in my soul.
⁴ All the kings of the earth will give you thanks, Yahweh,
for they have heard the words of your mouth.
⁵ Yes, they will sing of the ways of Yahweh,
for Yahweh's glory is great!

Gospel: John 1: 47-51

⁴⁷ Jesus saw Nathanael coming to him, and said about him, "Behold, an Israelite indeed, in whom is no deceit!"
⁴⁸ Nathanael said to him, "How do you know me?"
Jesus answered him, "Before Philip called you, when you were under the fig tree, I saw you."
⁴⁹ Nathanael answered him, "Rabbi, you are the Son of God! You are King of Israel!"
⁵⁰ Jesus answered him, "Because I told you, 'I saw you underneath the fig tree,' do you believe? You will see greater things than these!" ⁵¹ He said to him, "Most certainly, I tell you all, hereafter you will see heaven opened, and the angels of God ascending and descending on the Son of Man."

1. Invite the Holy Spirit into this reading, asking the Author of Scripture to speak to you through His Word
2. Read today's passage as many times as you need, take your time
3. Write down (below) what the Lord is saying to you today
4. Live with this Word in your heart through the day

Tuesday, September 30, 2025
Saint Jerome, Priest and Doctor of the Church

First Reading: Zechariah 8: 20-23

²⁰ Yahweh of Armies says: "Many peoples and the inhabitants of many cities will yet come. ²¹ The inhabitants of one will go to another, saying, 'Let's go speedily to entreat the favor of Yahweh, and to seek Yahweh of Armies. I will go also.' ²² Yes, many peoples and strong nations will come to seek Yahweh of Armies in Jerusalem and to entreat the favor of Yahweh." ²³ Yahweh of Armies says: "In those days, ten men out of all the languages of

the nations will take hold of the skirt of him who is a Jew, saying, 'We will go with you, for we have heard that God is with you.' "

Responsorial Psalm: Psalms 87: 1b-3, 4-5, 6-7

¹ His foundation is in the holy mountains.
² Yahweh loves the gates of Zion more than all the dwellings of Jacob.
³ Glorious things are spoken about you, city of God.
⁴ I will record Rahab⁺ and Babylon among those who acknowledge me.
Behold, Philistia, Tyre, and also Ethiopia:
"This one was born there."
⁵ Yes, of Zion it will be said, "This one and that one was born in her;"
the Most High himself will establish her.
⁶ Yahweh will count, when he writes up the peoples,
"This one was born there."
⁷ Those who sing as well as those who dance say,
"All my springs are in you."

Gospel: Luke 9: 51-56

⁵¹ It came to pass, when the days were near that he should be taken up, he intently set his face to go to Jerusalem ⁵² and sent messengers before his face. They went and entered into a village of the Samaritans, so as to prepare for him. ⁵³ They didn't receive him, because he was traveling with his face set toward Jerusalem. ⁵⁴ When his disciples, James and John, saw this, they said, "Lord, do you want us to command fire to come down from the sky and destroy them, just as Elijah did?"
⁵⁵ But he turned and rebuked them, "You don't know of what kind of spirit you are. ⁵⁶ For the Son of Man didn't come to destroy men's lives, but to save them."
They went to another village.

1. Invite the Holy Spirit into this reading, asking the Author of Scripture to speak to you through His Word
2. Read today's passage as many times as you need, take your time
3. Write down (below) what the Lord is saying to you today
4. Live with this Word in your heart through the day

Wednesday, October 1, 2025
Saint Thérèse of the Child Jesus, Virgin and Doctor of the Church

First Reading: Nehemiah 2: 1-8

¹ In the month Nisan, in the twentieth year of Artaxerxes the king, when wine was before him, I picked up the wine, and gave it to the king. Now I had not been sad before in his presence. ² The king said to me, "Why is your face sad, since you are not sick? This is nothing else but sorrow of heart."
Then I was very much afraid. ³ I said to the king, "Let the king live forever! Why shouldn't my face be sad, when the city, the place of my fathers' tombs, lies waste, and its gates have been consumed with fire?"
⁴ Then the king said to me, "What is your request?"
So I prayed to the God of heaven. ⁵ I said to the king, "If it pleases the king, and if your servant has found favor in your sight, I ask that you would send me to Judah, to the city of my fathers' tombs, that I may build it."
⁶ The king said to me (the queen was also sitting by him), "How long will your journey be? When will you return?"
So it pleased the king to send me, and I set a time for him. ⁷ Moreover I said to the king, "If it pleases the king, let letters be given me to the governors beyond the River, that they may let me pass through until I come to Judah; ⁸ and a letter to Asaph the keeper of the king's forest, that he may give me timber to make beams for the gates of the citadel by the temple, for the wall of the city, and for the house that I will occupy."
The king granted my requests, because of the good hand of my God on me.

Responsorial Psalm: Psalms 137: 1-2, 3, 4-5, 6

¹ By the rivers of Babylon, there we sat down.
Yes, we wept, when we remembered Zion.
² On the willows in that land,
we hung up our harps.
³ For there, those who led us captive asked us for songs.
Those who tormented us demanded songs of joy:
"Sing us one of the songs of Zion!"
⁴ How can we sing Yahweh's song in a foreign land?
⁵ If I forget you, Jerusalem,
let my right hand forget its skill.
⁶ Let my tongue stick to the roof of my mouth if I don't remember you,
if I don't prefer Jerusalem above my chief joy.

Gospel: Luke 9: 57-62

⁵⁷ As they went on the way, a certain man said to him, "I want to follow you wherever you go, Lord."
⁵⁸ Jesus said to him, "The foxes have holes and the birds of the sky have nests, but the Son of Man has no place to lay his head."
⁵⁹ He said to another, "Follow me!"
But he said, "Lord, allow me first to go and bury my father."
⁶⁰ But Jesus said to him, "Leave the dead to bury their own dead, but you go and announce God's Kingdom."
⁶¹ Another also said, "I want to follow you, Lord, but first allow me to say good-bye to those who are at my house."
⁶² But Jesus said to him, "No one, having put his hand to the plow and looking back, is fit for God's Kingdom."

1. Invite the Holy Spirit into this reading, asking the Author of Scripture to speak to you through His Word
2. Read today's passage as many times as you need, take your time
3. Write down (below) what the Lord is saying to you today
4. Live with this Word in your heart through the day

_____

_____

Thursday, October 2, 2025
The Holy Guardian Angels

First Reading: Nehemiah 8: 1-4a, 5-6, 7b-12

¹ All the people gathered themselves together as one man into the wide place that was in front of the water gate; and they spoke to Ezra the scribe to bring the book of the law of Moses, which Yahweh had commanded to Israel. ² Ezra the priest brought the law before the assembly, both men and women, and all who could hear with understanding, on the first day of the seventh month. ³ He read from it before the wide place that was in front of the water gate from early morning until midday, in the presence of the men and the women, and of those who could understand. The ears of all the people were attentive to the book of the law. ⁴ᵃ Ezra the scribe stood on a pulpit of wood, which they had made for the purpose;

⁵ Ezra opened the book in the sight of all the people (for he was above all the people), and when he opened it, all the people stood up. ⁶ Then Ezra blessed Yahweh, the great God. All the people answered, "Amen, Amen," with the lifting up of their hands. They bowed their heads, and worshiped Yahweh with their faces to the ground. ⁷ᵇ and the people stayed in their place. ⁸ They read in the book, in the law of God, distinctly; and they gave the sense, so that they understood the reading.

⁹ Nehemiah, who was the governor, Ezra the priest and scribe, and the Levites who taught the people said to all the people, "Today is holy to Yahweh your God. Don't mourn, nor weep." For all the people wept when they heard the words of the law. ¹⁰ Then he said to them, "Go your way. Eat the fat, drink the sweet, and send portions to him for whom nothing is prepared, for today is holy to our Lord. Don't be grieved, for the joy of Yahweh is your strength."

¹¹ So the Levites calmed all the people, saying, "Hold your peace, for the day is holy. Don't be grieved."

¹² All the people went their way to eat, to drink, to send portions, and to celebrate, because they had understood the words that were declared to them.

Responsorial Psalm: Psalms 19: 8, 9, 10, 11

⁸ Yahweh's precepts are right, rejoicing the heart.
Yahweh's commandment is pure, enlightening the eyes.
⁹ The fear of Yahweh is clean, enduring forever.
Yahweh's ordinances are true, and righteous altogether.
¹⁰ They are more to be desired than gold, yes, than much fine gold,
sweeter also than honey and the extract of the honeycomb.
¹¹ Moreover your servant is warned by them.
In keeping them there is great reward.

Gospel: Matthew 18: 1-5, 10

¹ In that hour the disciples came to Jesus, saying, "Who then is greatest in the Kingdom of Heaven?"

² Jesus called a little child to himself, and set him in the middle of them ³ and said, "Most certainly I tell you, unless you turn and become as little children, you will in no way enter into the Kingdom of Heaven. ⁴ Whoever therefore humbles himself as this little child is the greatest in the Kingdom of Heaven. ⁵ Whoever receives one such little child in my name receives me,

¹⁰ See that you don't despise one of these little ones, for I tell you that in heaven their angels always see the face of my Father who is in heaven.

1. Invite the Holy Spirit into this reading, asking the Author of Scripture to speak to you through His Word
2. Read today's passage as many times as you need, take your time
3. Write down (below) what the Lord is saying to you today
4. Live with this Word in your heart through the day

___

___

Friday, October 3, 2025

First Reading: Baruch 1: 15-22

¹⁵ You shall say: To the Lord our God belongs righteousness, but to us confusion of face, as at this day—to the men of Judah, to the inhabitants of Jerusalem, ¹⁶ to our kings, to our princes, to our priests, to our prophets, and to our fathers, ¹⁷ because we have sinned before the Lord. ¹⁸ We have disobeyed him and have not listened to the voice of the Lord our God, to walk in the commandments of the Lord that he has set before us. ¹⁹ Since the day that the Lord brought our fathers out of the land of Egypt to this present day, we have been disobedient to the Lord our God, and we have been negligent in not listening to his voice. ²⁰ Therefore the plagues have clung to us, along with the curse which the Lord declared through Moses his servant in the day that he brought our fathers out of the land of Egypt to give us a land that flows with milk and honey, as at this day. ²¹ Nevertheless we didn't listen to the voice of the Lord our God, according to all the words of the prophets whom he sent to us, ²² but we each walked in the imagination of his own wicked heart, to serve strange gods and to do what is evil in the sight of the Lord our God.

Responsorial Psalm: Psalms 79: 1b-2, 3-5, 8, 9

¹ God, the nations have come into your inheritance.
They have defiled your holy temple.
They have laid Jerusalem in heaps.
² They have given the dead bodies of your servants to be food for the birds of the sky,
the flesh of your saints to the animals of the earth.
³ They have shed their blood like water around Jerusalem.
There was no one to bury them.
⁴ We have become a reproach to our neighbors,
a scoffing and derision to those who are around us.

⁵ How long, Yahweh?
Will you be angry forever?
Will your jealousy burn like fire?
⁸ Don't hold the iniquities of our forefathers against us.
Let your tender mercies speedily meet us,
for we are in desperate need.
⁹ Help us, God of our salvation, for the glory of your name.
Deliver us, and forgive our sins, for your name's sake.

Gospel: Luke 10: 13-16

¹³ "Woe to you, Chorazin! Woe to you, Bethsaida! For if the mighty works had been done in Tyre and Sidon which were done in you, they would have repented long ago, sitting in sackcloth and ashes. ¹⁴ But it will be more tolerable for Tyre and Sidon in the judgment than for you. ¹⁵ You, Capernaum, who are exalted to heaven, will be brought down to Hades. ¹⁶ Whoever listens to you listens to me, and whoever rejects you rejects me. Whoever rejects me rejects him who sent me."

1. Invite the Holy Spirit into this reading, asking the Author of Scripture to speak to you through His Word
2. Read today's passage as many times as you need, take your time
3. Write down (below) what the Lord is saying to you today
4. Live with this Word in your heart through the day

Saturday, October 4, 2025
Saint Francis of Assisi

First Reading: Baruch 4: 5-12, 27-29

⁵ Be of good cheer, my people, the memorial of Israel. ⁶ You were not sold to the nations for destruction, but because you moved God to wrath, you were delivered to your adversaries. ⁷ For you provoked him who made you by sacrificing to demons and not to God. ⁸ You forgot the everlasting God who brought you up. You also grieved Jerusalem, who nursed you. ⁹ For she saw the wrath that came upon you from God, and said, "Listen, you who dwell near Zion; for God has brought upon me great mourning. ¹⁰ For I have seen

the captivity of my sons and daughters, which the Everlasting has brought upon them. ¹¹ For with joy I nourished them, but sent them away with weeping and mourning. ¹² Let no man rejoice over me, a widow and forsaken by many. For the sins of my children, I am left desolate, because they turned away from the law of God

²⁷ Take courage, my children, and cry to God; for you will be remembered by him who has brought this upon you. ²⁸ For as it was your decision to go astray from God, return and seek him ten times more. ²⁹ For he who brought these calamities upon you will bring you everlasting joy again with your salvation.

Responsorial Psalm: Psalms 69: 33-35, 36

³³ For Yahweh hears the needy,
and doesn't despise his captive people.
³⁴ Let heaven and earth praise him;
the seas, and everything that moves therein!
³⁵ For God will save Zion, and build the cities of Judah.
They shall settle there, and own it.
³⁶ The children also of his servants shall inherit it.
Those who love his name shall dwell therein.

Gospel: Luke 10: 17-24

¹⁷ The seventy returned with joy, saying, "Lord, even the demons are subject to us in your name!"
¹⁸ He said to them, "I saw Satan having fallen like lightning from heaven. ¹⁹ Behold, I give you authority to tread on serpents and scorpions, and over all the power of the enemy. Nothing will in any way hurt you. ²⁰ Nevertheless, don't rejoice in this, that the spirits are subject to you, but rejoice that your names are written in heaven."
²¹ In that same hour, Jesus rejoiced in the Holy Spirit, and said, "I thank you, O Father, Lord of heaven and earth, that you have hidden these things from the wise and understanding, and revealed them to little children. Yes, Father, for so it was well-pleasing in your sight."
²² Turning to the disciples, he said, "All things have been delivered to me by my Father. No one knows who the Son is, except the Father, and who the Father is, except the Son, and he to whomever the Son desires to reveal him."
²³ Turning to the disciples, he said privately, "Blessed are the eyes which see the things that you see, ²⁴ for I tell you that many prophets and kings desired to see the things which you see, and didn't see them, and to hear the things which you hear, and didn't hear them."

1. Invite the Holy Spirit into this reading, asking the Author of Scripture to speak to you through His Word
2. Read today's passage as many times as you need, take your time
3. Write down (below) what the Lord is saying to you today
4. Live with this Word in your heart through the day

_____

_____

Sunday, October 5, 2025
TWENTY-SEVENTH SUNDAY IN ORDINARY TIME

First Reading: Habakkuk 1: 2-3; 2: 2-4

² Yahweh, how long will I cry, and you will not hear? I cry out to you "Violence!" and will you not save? ³ Why do you show me iniquity, and look at perversity? For destruction and violence are before me. There is strife, and contention rises up.
² Yahweh answered me, "Write the vision, and make it plain on tablets, that he who runs may read it. ³ For the vision is yet for the appointed time, and it hurries toward the end, and won't prove false. Though it takes time, wait for it, because it will surely come. It won't delay. ⁴ Behold, his soul is puffed up. It is not upright in him, but the righteous will live by his faith.

Responsorial Psalm: Psalms 95: 1-2, 6-7, 8-9

¹ Oh come, let's sing to Yahweh.
Let's shout aloud to the rock of our salvation!
² Let's come before his presence with thanksgiving.
Let's extol him with songs!
⁶ Oh come, let's worship and bow down.
Let's kneel before Yahweh, our Maker,
⁷ for he is our God.
We are the people of his pasture,
and the sheep in his care.
Today, oh that you would hear his voice!
⁸ Don't harden your heart, as at Meribah,
as in the day of Massah in the wilderness,
⁹ when your fathers tempted me,

tested me, and saw my work.

Second Reading: Second Timothy 1: 6-8, 13-14

⁶ For this cause, I remind you that you should stir up the gift of God which is in you through the laying on of my hands. ⁷ For God didn't give us a spirit of fear, but of power, love, and self-control. ⁸ Therefore don't be ashamed of the testimony of our Lord, nor of me his prisoner; but endure hardship for the Good News according to the power of God,
¹³ Hold the pattern of sound words which you have heard from me, in faith and love which is in Christ Jesus. ¹⁴ That good thing which was committed to you, guard through the Holy Spirit who dwells in us.

Gospel: Luke 17: 5-10

⁵ The apostles said to the Lord, "Increase our faith."
⁶ The Lord said, "If you had faith like a grain of mustard seed, you would tell this sycamore tree, 'Be uprooted and be planted in the sea,' and it would obey you. ⁷ But who is there among you, having a servant plowing or keeping sheep, that will say when he comes in from the field, 'Come immediately and sit down at the table'? ⁸ Wouldn't he rather tell him, 'Prepare my supper, clothe yourself properly, and serve me while I eat and drink. Afterward you shall eat and drink'? ⁹ Does he thank that servant because he did the things that were commanded? I think not. ¹⁰ Even so you also, when you have done all the things that are commanded you, say, 'We are unworthy servants. We have done our duty.' "

1. Invite the Holy Spirit into this reading, asking the Author of Scripture to speak to you through His Word
2. Read today's passage as many times as you need, take your time
3. Write down (below) what the Lord is saying to you today
4. Live with this Word in your heart through the day

Monday, October 6, 2025
Saint Bruno, Priest; Blessed Marie Rose Durocher, Virgin

First Reading: Jonah 1: 1 – 2: 1-2, 10

¹ Now Yahweh's word came to Jonah the son of Amittai, saying, ² "Arise, go to Nineveh, that great city, and preach against it, for their wickedness has come up before me."
³ But Jonah rose up to flee to Tarshish from the presence of Yahweh. He went down to Joppa, and found a ship going to Tarshish; so he paid its fare, and went down into it, to go with them to Tarshish from the presence of Yahweh.
⁴ But Yahweh sent out a great wind on the sea, and there was a mighty storm on the sea, so that the ship was likely to break up. ⁵ Then the mariners were afraid, and every man cried to his god. They threw the cargo that was in the ship into the sea to lighten the ship. But Jonah had gone down into the innermost parts of the ship and he was laying down, and was fast asleep. ⁶ So the ship master came to him, and said to him, "What do you mean, sleeper? Arise, call on your God! Maybe your God will notice us, so that we won't perish."
⁷ They all said to each other, "Come! Let's cast lots, that we may know who is responsible for this evil that is on us." So they cast lots, and the lot fell on Jonah. ⁸ Then they asked him, "Tell us, please, for whose cause this evil is on us. What is your occupation? Where do you come from? What is your country? Of what people are you?"
⁹ He said to them, "I am a Hebrew, and I fear Yahweh, the God of heaven, who has made the sea and the dry land."
¹⁰ Then the men were exceedingly afraid, and said to him, "What have you done?" For the men knew that he was fleeing from the presence of Yahweh, because he had told them. ¹¹ Then they said to him, "What shall we do to you, that the sea may be calm to us?" For the sea grew more and more stormy.
¹² He said to them, "Take me up, and throw me into the sea. Then the sea will be calm for you; for I know that because of me this great storm is on you."
¹³ Nevertheless the men rowed hard to get them back to the land; but they could not, for the sea grew more and more stormy against them. ¹⁴ Therefore they cried to Yahweh, and said, "We beg you, Yahweh, we beg you, don't let us die for this man's life, and don't lay on us innocent blood; for you, Yahweh, have done as it pleased you." ¹⁵ So they took up Jonah and threw him into the sea; and the sea ceased its raging. ¹⁶ Then the men feared Yahweh exceedingly; and they offered a sacrifice to Yahweh and made vows.
¹⁷ Yahweh prepared a huge fish to swallow up Jonah, and Jonah was in the belly of the fish three days and three nights.
¹ Then Jonah prayed to Yahweh, his God, out of the fish's belly. ² He said,
"I called because of my affliction to Yahweh.
He answered me.
Out of the belly of Sheol I cried.
You heard my voice.
¹⁰ Then Yahweh spoke to the fish, and it vomited out Jonah on the dry land.

Responsorial Psalm: Jonah 2: 3, 4, 5, 8

³ For you threw me into the depths,
in the heart of the seas.
The flood was all around me.
All your waves and your billows passed over me.
⁴ I said, 'I have been banished from your sight;
yet I will look again toward your holy temple.'
⁵ The waters surrounded me,
even to the soul.
The deep was around me.
The weeds were wrapped around my head.
⁸ Those who regard vain idols forsake their own mercy.

Gospel: Luke 10: 25-37

²⁵ Behold, a certain lawyer stood up and tested him, saying, "Teacher, what shall I do to inherit eternal life?"
²⁶ He said to him, "What is written in the law? How do you read it?"
²⁷ He answered, "You shall love the Lord your God with all your heart, with all your soul, with all your strength, and with all your mind; and your neighbor as yourself."
²⁸ He said to him, "You have answered correctly. Do this, and you will live."
²⁹ But he, desiring to justify himself, asked Jesus, "Who is my neighbor?"
³⁰ Jesus answered, "A certain man was going down from Jerusalem to Jericho, and he fell among robbers, who both stripped him and beat him, and departed, leaving him half dead. ³¹ By chance a certain priest was going down that way. When he saw him, he passed by on the other side. ³² In the same way a Levite also, when he came to the place and saw him, passed by on the other side. ³³ But a certain Samaritan, as he traveled, came where he was. When he saw him, he was moved with compassion, ³⁴ came to him, and bound up his wounds, pouring on oil and wine. He set him on his own animal, brought him to an inn, and took care of him. ³⁵ On the next day, when he departed, he took out two denarii, gave them to the host, and said to him, 'Take care of him. Whatever you spend beyond that, I will repay you when I return.' ³⁶ Now which of these three do you think seemed to be a neighbor to him who fell among the robbers?"
³⁷ He said, "He who showed mercy on him."
Then Jesus said to him, "Go and do likewise."

1. Invite the Holy Spirit into this reading, asking the Author of Scripture to speak to you through His Word
2. Read today's passage as many times as you need, take your time
3. Write down (below) what the Lord is saying to you today
4. Live with this Word in your heart through the day

Tuesday, October 7, 2025
Our Lady of the Rosary

First Reading: Jonah 3: 1-10

¹ Yahweh's word came to Jonah the second time, saying, ² "Arise, go to Nineveh, that great city, and preach to it the message that I give you."
³ So Jonah arose, and went to Nineveh, according to Yahweh's word. Now Nineveh was an exceedingly great city, three days' journey across. ⁴ Jonah began to enter into the city a day's journey, and he cried out, and said, "In forty days, Nineveh will be overthrown!"
⁵ The people of Nineveh believed God; and they proclaimed a fast and put on sackcloth, from their greatest even to their least. ⁶ The news reached the king of Nineveh, and he arose from his throne, took off his royal robe, covered himself with sackcloth, and sat in ashes. ⁷ He made a proclamation and published through Nineveh by the decree of the king and his nobles, saying, "Let neither man nor animal, herd nor flock, taste anything; let them not feed, nor drink water; ⁸ but let them be covered with sackcloth, both man and animal, and let them cry mightily to God. Yes, let them turn everyone from his evil way and from the violence that is in his hands. ⁹ Who knows whether God will not turn and relent, and turn away from his fierce anger, so that we might not perish?"
¹⁰ God saw their works, that they turned from their evil way. God relented of the disaster which he said he would do to them, and he didn't do it.

Responsorial Psalm: Psalms 130: 1b-2, 3-4ab, 7-8

¹ Out of the depths I have cried to you, Yahweh.
² Lord, hear my voice.
Let your ears be attentive to the voice of my petitions.
³ If you, Yah, kept a record of sins,
Lord, who could stand?
⁴ But there is forgiveness with you,
therefore you are feared.
⁷ Israel, hope in Yahweh,
for there is loving kindness with Yahweh.
Abundant redemption is with him.

⁸ He will redeem Israel from all their sins.

Gospel: Luke 10: 38-42

³⁸ As they went on their way, he entered into a certain village, and a certain woman named Martha received him into her house. ³⁹ She had a sister called Mary, who also sat at Jesus' feet and heard his word. ⁴⁰ But Martha was distracted with much serving, and she came up to him, and said, "Lord, don't you care that my sister left me to serve alone? Ask her therefore to help me."
⁴¹ Jesus answered her, "Martha, Martha, you are anxious and troubled about many things, ⁴² but one thing is needed. Mary has chosen the good part, which will not be taken away from her."

1. Invite the Holy Spirit into this reading, asking the Author of Scripture to speak to you through His Word
2. Read today's passage as many times as you need, take your time
3. Write down (below) what the Lord is saying to you today
4. Live with this Word in your heart through the day

Wednesday, October 8, 2025

First Reading: Jonah 4: 1-11

¹ But it displeased Jonah exceedingly, and he was angry. ² He prayed to Yahweh, and said, "Please, Yahweh, wasn't this what I said when I was still in my own country? Therefore I hurried to flee to Tarshish, for I knew that you are a gracious God and merciful, slow to anger, and abundant in loving kindness, and you relent of doing harm. ³ Therefore now, Yahweh, take, I beg you, my life from me, for it is better for me to die than to live."
⁴ Yahweh said, "Is it right for you to be angry?"
⁵ Then Jonah went out of the city and sat on the east side of the city, and there made himself a booth and sat under it in the shade, until he might see what would become of the city. ⁶ Yahweh God prepared a vine and made it to come up over Jonah, that it might be a shade over his head to deliver him from his discomfort. So Jonah was exceedingly glad because of the vine. ⁷ But God prepared a worm at dawn the next day, and it chewed on the vine so that it withered. ⁸ When the sun arose, God prepared a sultry east wind; and the

sun beat on Jonah's head, so that he was faint and requested for himself that he might die. He said, "It is better for me to die than to live."

⁹ God said to Jonah, "Is it right for you to be angry about the vine?"

He said, "I am right to be angry, even to death."

¹⁰ Yahweh said, "You have been concerned for the vine, for which you have not labored, neither made it grow; which came up in a night and perished in a night. ¹¹ Shouldn't I be concerned for Nineveh, that great city, in which are more than one hundred twenty thousand persons who can't discern between their right hand and their left hand, and also many animals?"

Responsorial Psalm: Psalms 86: 3-4, 5-6, 9-10

³ Be merciful to me, Lord,
for I call to you all day long.
⁴ Bring joy to the soul of your servant,
for to you, Lord, do I lift up my soul.
⁵ For you, Lord, are good, and ready to forgive,
abundant in loving kindness to all those who call on you.
⁶ Hear, Yahweh, my prayer.
Listen to the voice of my petitions.
⁹ All nations you have made will come and worship before you, Lord.
They shall glorify your name.
¹⁰ For you are great, and do wondrous things.
You are God alone.

Gospel: Luke 11: 1-4

¹ When he finished praying in a certain place, one of his disciples said to him, "Lord, teach us to pray, just as John also taught his disciples."
² He said to them, "When you pray, say,
'Our Father in heaven,
may your name be kept holy.
May your Kingdom come.
May your will be done on earth, as it is in heaven.
³ Give us day by day our daily bread.
⁴ Forgive us our sins,
for we ourselves also forgive everyone who is indebted to us.
Bring us not into temptation,
but deliver us from the evil one.' "

1. Invite the Holy Spirit into this reading, asking the Author of Scripture to speak to you through His Word
2. Read today's passage as many times as you need, take your time
3. Write down (below) what the Lord is saying to you today
4. Live with this Word in your heart through the day

Thursday, October 9, 2025
Saint Denis, Bishop, and Companions, Martyrs; Saint John Leonardi, Priest

First Reading: Malachi 3: 13-18, 4: 1-2b

13 "Your words have been harsh against me," says Yahweh. "Yet you say, 'What have we spoken against you?' 14 You have said, 'It is vain to serve God,' and 'What profit is it that we have followed his instructions and that we have walked mournfully before Yahweh of Armies? 15 Now we call the proud happy; yes, those who work wickedness are built up; yes, they tempt God, and escape.'
16 Then those who feared Yahweh spoke one with another; and Yahweh listened and heard, and a book of memory was written before him for those who feared Yahweh and who honored his name. 17 They shall be mine," says Yahweh of Armies, "my own possession in the day that I make. I will spare them, as a man spares his own son who serves him. 18 Then you shall return and discern between the righteous and the wicked, between him who serves God and him who doesn't serve him.
1 "For behold, the day comes, burning like a furnace, when all the proud and all who work wickedness will be stubble. The day that comes will burn them up," says Yahweh of Armies, "so that it will leave them neither root nor branch. 2 But to you who fear my name shall the sun of righteousness arise with healing in its wings. You will go out and leap like calves of the stall.

Responsorial Psalm: Psalms 1: 1-2, 3, 4 and 6

1 Blessed is the man who doesn't walk in the counsel of the wicked,
nor stand on the path of sinners,
nor sit in the seat of scoffers;
2 but his delight is in Yahweh's law.
On his law he meditates day and night.

³ He will be like a tree planted by the streams of water,
that produces its fruit in its season,
whose leaf also does not wither.
Whatever he does shall prosper.
⁴ The wicked are not so,
but are like the chaff which the wind drives away.
⁶ For Yahweh knows the way of the righteous,
but the way of the wicked shall perish.

Gospel: Luke 11: 5-13

⁵ He said to them, "Which of you, if you go to a friend at midnight and tell him, 'Friend, lend me three loaves of bread, ⁶ for a friend of mine has come to me from a journey, and I have nothing to set before him,' ⁷ and he from within will answer and say, 'Don't bother me. The door is now shut, and my children are with me in bed. I can't get up and give it to you'? ⁸ I tell you, although he will not rise and give it to him because he is his friend, yet because of his persistence, he will get up and give him as many as he needs.
⁹ "I tell you, keep asking, and it will be given you. Keep seeking, and you will find. Keep knocking, and it will be opened to you. ¹⁰ For everyone who asks receives. He who seeks finds. To him who knocks it will be opened.
¹¹ "Which of you fathers, if your son asks for bread, will give him a stone? Or if he asks for a fish, he won't give him a snake instead of a fish, will he? ¹² Or if he asks for an egg, he won't give him a scorpion, will he? ¹³ If you then, being evil, know how to give good gifts to your children, how much more will your heavenly Father give the Holy Spirit to those who ask him?"

1. Invite the Holy Spirit into this reading, asking the Author of Scripture to speak to you through His Word
2. Read today's passage as many times as you need, take your time
3. Write down (below) what the Lord is saying to you today
4. Live with this Word in your heart through the day

Friday, October 10, 2025

First Reading: Joel 1: 13-15; 2: 1-2

¹³ Put on sackcloth and mourn, you priests!
Wail, you ministers of the altar.
Come, lie all night in sackcloth, you ministers of my God,‡
for the meal offering and the drink offering are withheld from your God's house.
¹⁴ Sanctify a fast.
Call a solemn assembly.
Gather the elders and all the inhabitants of the land to the house of Yahweh, your God,
and cry to Yahweh.
¹⁵ Alas for the day!
For the day of Yahweh is at hand,
and it will come as destruction from the Almighty.
¹ Blow the trumpet in Zion,
and sound an alarm in my holy mountain!
Let all the inhabitants of the land tremble,
for the day of Yahweh comes,
for it is close at hand:
² A day of darkness and gloominess,
a day of clouds and thick darkness.
As the dawn spreading on the mountains,
a great and strong people;
there has never been the like,
neither will there be any more after them,
even to the years of many generations.

Responsorial Psalm: Psalms 9: 2-3, 6 and 16, 8-9

² I will be glad and rejoice in you.
I will sing praise to your name, O Most High.
³ When my enemies turn back,
they stumble and perish in your presence.
⁶ The enemy is overtaken by endless ruin.
The very memory of the cities which you have overthrown has perished.
¹⁶ Yahweh has made himself known.
He has executed judgment.
The wicked is snared by the work of his own hands.
⁸ He will judge the world in righteousness.
He will administer judgment to the peoples in uprightness.
⁹ Yahweh will also be a high tower for the oppressed;
a high tower in times of trouble.

Gospel: Luke 11: 15-26

¹⁵ But some of them said, "He casts out demons by Beelzebul, the prince of the demons." ¹⁶ Others, testing him, sought from him a sign from heaven. ¹⁷ But he, knowing their thoughts, said to them, "Every kingdom divided against itself is brought to desolation. A house divided against itself falls. ¹⁸ If Satan also is divided against himself, how will his kingdom stand? For you say that I cast out demons by Beelzebul. ¹⁹ But if I cast out demons by Beelzebul, by whom do your children cast them out? Therefore they will be your judges. ²⁰ But if I by God's finger cast out demons, then God's Kingdom has come to you.
²¹ "When the strong man, fully armed, guards his own dwelling, his goods are safe. ²² But when someone stronger attacks him and overcomes him, he takes from him his whole armor in which he trusted, and divides his plunder.
²³ "He who is not with me is against me. He who doesn't gather with me scatters.
²⁴ The unclean spirit, when he has gone out of the man, passes through dry places, seeking rest; and finding none, he says, 'I will turn back to my house from which I came out.' ²⁵ When he returns, he finds it swept and put in order. ²⁶ Then he goes and takes seven other spirits more evil than himself, and they enter in and dwell there. The last state of that man becomes worse than the first."

1. Invite the Holy Spirit into this reading, asking the Author of Scripture to speak to you through His Word
2. Read today's passage as many times as you need, take your time
3. Write down (below) what the Lord is saying to you today
4. Live with this Word in your heart through the day

Saturday, October 11, 2025
Saint John XXIII, Pope

First Reading: Joel 4: 12-21

¹² "Let the nations arouse themselves,
and come up to the valley of Jehoshaphat;
for there I will sit to judge all the surrounding nations.
¹³ Put in the sickle;

for the harvest is ripe.
Come, tread, for the wine press is full,
the vats overflow, for their wickedness is great."
¹⁴ Multitudes, multitudes in the valley of decision!
For the day of Yahweh is near in the valley of decision.
¹⁵ The sun and the moon are darkened,
and the stars withdraw their shining.
¹⁶ Yahweh will roar from Zion,
and thunder from Jerusalem;
and the heavens and the earth will shake;
but Yahweh will be a refuge to his people,
and a stronghold to the children of Israel.
¹⁷ "So you will know that I am Yahweh, your God,
dwelling in Zion, my holy mountain.
Then Jerusalem will be holy,
and no strangers will pass through her any more.
¹⁸ It will happen in that day,
that the mountains will drop down sweet wine,
the hills will flow with milk,
all the brooks of Judah will flow with waters;
and a fountain will flow out from Yahweh's house,
and will water the valley of Shittim.
¹⁹ Egypt will be a desolation
and Edom will be a desolate wilderness,
for the violence done to the children of Judah,
because they have shed innocent blood in their land.
²⁰ But Judah will be inhabited forever,
and Jerusalem from generation to generation.
²¹ I will cleanse their blood
that I have not cleansed,
for Yahweh dwells in Zion."

Responsorial Psalm: Psalms 97: 1-2, 5-6, 11-12

¹ Yahweh reigns!
Let the earth rejoice!
Let the multitude of islands be glad!
² Clouds and darkness are around him.
Righteousness and justice are the foundation of his throne.
⁵ The mountains melt like wax at the presence of Yahweh,

at the presence of the Lord of the whole earth.
⁶ The heavens declare his righteousness.
All the peoples have seen his glory.
¹¹ Light is sown for the righteous,
and gladness for the upright in heart.
¹² Be glad in Yahweh, you righteous people!
Give thanks to his holy Name.

Gospel: Luke 11: 27-28

²⁷ It came to pass, as he said these things, a certain woman out of the multitude lifted up her voice and said to him, "Blessed is the womb that bore you, and the breasts which nursed you!"
²⁸ But he said, "On the contrary, blessed are those who hear the word of God, and keep it."

1. Invite the Holy Spirit into this reading, asking the Author of Scripture to speak to you through His Word
2. Read today's passage as many times as you need, take your time
3. Write down (below) what the Lord is saying to you today
4. Live with this Word in your heart through the day

Sunday, October 12, 2025
TWENTY-EIGHTH SUNDAY IN ORDINARY TIME

First Reading: Second Kings 5: 14-17

¹⁴ Then went he down and dipped himself seven times in the Jordan, according to the saying of the man of God; and his flesh was restored like the flesh of a little child, and he was clean. ¹⁵ He returned to the man of God, he and all his company, and came, and stood before him; and he said, "See now, I know that there is no God in all the earth, but in Israel. Now therefore, please take a gift from your servant."
¹⁶ But he said, "As Yahweh lives, before whom I stand, I will receive none."
He urged him to take it; but he refused. ¹⁷ Naaman said, "If not, then, please let two mules' load of earth be given to your servant; for your servant will from now on offer neither burnt offering nor sacrifice to other gods, but to Yahweh.

Responsorial Psalm: Psalms 98: 1, 2-3ab, 3c-4

¹ Sing to Yahweh a new song,
for he has done marvelous things!
His right hand and his holy arm have worked salvation for him.
² Yahweh has made known his salvation.
He has openly shown his righteousness in the sight of the nations.
³ He has remembered his loving kindness and his faithfulness toward the house of Israel.
All the ends of the earth have seen the salvation of our God.
⁴ Make a joyful noise to Yahweh, all the earth!
Burst out and sing for joy, yes, sing praises!

Second Reading: Second Timothy 2: 8-13

⁸ Remember Jesus Christ, risen from the dead, of the offspring⁺ of David, according to my Good News, ⁹ in which I suffer hardship to the point of chains as a criminal. But God's word isn't chained. ¹⁰ Therefore I endure all things for the chosen ones' sake, that they also may obtain the salvation which is in Christ Jesus with eternal glory. ¹¹ This saying is trustworthy:
"For if we died with him,
we will also live with him.
¹² If we endure,
we will also reign with him.
If we deny him,
he also will deny us.
¹³ If we are faithless,
he remains faithful;
for he can't deny himself."

Gospel: Luke 17: 11-19

¹¹ As he was on his way to Jerusalem, he was passing along the borders of Samaria and Galilee. ¹² As he entered into a certain village, ten men who were lepers met him, who stood at a distance. ¹³ They lifted up their voices, saying, "Jesus, Master, have mercy on us!"
¹⁴ When he saw them, he said to them, "Go and show yourselves to the priests." As they went, they were cleansed. ¹⁵ One of them, when he saw that he was healed, turned back, glorifying God with a loud voice. ¹⁶ He fell on his face at Jesus' feet, giving him thanks; and he was a Samaritan.

17 Jesus answered, "Weren't the ten cleansed? But where are the nine? 18 Were there none found who returned to give glory to God, except this foreigner?" 19 Then he said to him, "Get up, and go your way. Your faith has healed you."

1. Invite the Holy Spirit into this reading, asking the Author of Scripture to speak to you through His Word
2. Read today's passage as many times as you need, take your time
3. Write down (below) what the Lord is saying to you today
4. Live with this Word in your heart through the day

___

___

Monday, October 13, 2025

First Reading: Romans 1: 1-7

1 Paul, a servant of Jesus Christ, called to be an apostle, set apart for the Good News of God, 2 which he promised before through his prophets in the holy Scriptures, 3 concerning his Son, who was born of the offspring of David according to the flesh, 4 who was declared to be the Son of God with power according to the Spirit of holiness, by the resurrection from the dead, Jesus Christ our Lord, 5 through whom we received grace and apostleship for obedience of faith among all the nations for his name's sake; 6 among whom you are also called to belong to Jesus Christ; 7 to all who are in Rome, beloved of God, called to be saints: Grace to you and peace from God our Father and the Lord Jesus Christ.

Responsorial Psalm: Psalms 98: 1, 2-3ab, 3cd-4

1 Sing to Yahweh a new song,
for he has done marvelous things!
His right hand and his holy arm have worked salvation for him.
2 Yahweh has made known his salvation.
He has openly shown his righteousness in the sight of the nations.
3 He has remembered his loving kindness and his faithfulness toward the house of Israel.
All the ends of the earth have seen the salvation of our God.
4 Make a joyful noise to Yahweh, all the earth!
Burst out and sing for joy, yes, sing praises!

Gospel: Luke 11: 29-32

²⁹ When the multitudes were gathering together to him, he began to say, "This is an evil generation. It seeks after a sign. No sign will be given to it but the sign of Jonah the prophet. ³⁰ For even as Jonah became a sign to the Ninevites, so the Son of Man will also be to this generation. ³¹ The Queen of the South will rise up in the judgment with the men of this generation and will condemn them, for she came from the ends of the earth to hear the wisdom of Solomon; and behold, one greater than Solomon is here. ³² The men of Nineveh will stand up in the judgment with this generation, and will condemn it, for they repented at the preaching of Jonah; and behold, one greater than Jonah is here.

1. Invite the Holy Spirit into this reading, asking the Author of Scripture to speak to you through His Word
2. Read today's passage as many times as you need, take your time
3. Write down (below) what the Lord is saying to you today
4. Live with this Word in your heart through the day

Tuesday, October 14, 2025
Saint Callistus I, Pope and Martyr

First Reading: Romans 1: 16-25

¹⁶ For I am not ashamed of the Good News of Christ, because it is the power of God for salvation for everyone who believes, for the Jew first, and also for the Greek. ¹⁷ For in it is revealed God's righteousness from faith to faith. As it is written, "But the righteous shall live by faith."˟
¹⁸ For the wrath of God is revealed from heaven against all ungodliness and unrighteousness of men who suppress the truth in unrighteousness, ¹⁹ because that which is known of God is revealed in them, for God revealed it to them. ²⁰ For the invisible things of him since the creation of the world are clearly seen, being perceived through the things that are made, even his everlasting power and divinity, that they may be without excuse. ²¹ Because knowing God, they didn't glorify him as God, and didn't give thanks, but became vain in their reasoning, and their senseless heart was darkened.
²² Professing themselves to be wise, they became fools, ²³ and traded the glory of the incorruptible God for the likeness of an image of corruptible man, and of birds, four-footed

animals, and creeping things. ²⁴ Therefore God also gave them up in the lusts of their hearts to uncleanness, that their bodies should be dishonored among themselves; ²⁵ who exchanged the truth of God for a lie, and worshiped and served the creature rather than the Creator, who is blessed forever. Amen.

Responsorial Psalm: Psalms 19: 2-3, 4-5

² Day after day they pour out speech,
and night after night they display knowledge.
³ There is no speech nor language
where their voice is not heard.
⁴ Their voice has gone out through all the earth,
their words to the end of the world.
In them he has set a tent for the sun,
⁵ which is as a bridegroom coming out of his room,
like a strong man rejoicing to run his course.

Gospel: Luke 11: 37-41

³⁷ Now as he spoke, a certain Pharisee asked him to dine with him. He went in and sat at the table. ³⁸ When the Pharisee saw it, he marveled that he had not first washed himself before dinner. ³⁹ The Lord said to him, "Now you Pharisees cleanse the outside of the cup and of the platter, but your inward part is full of extortion and wickedness. ⁴⁰ You foolish ones, didn't he who made the outside make the inside also? ⁴¹ But give for gifts to the needy those things which are within, and behold, all things will be clean to you.

1. Invite the Holy Spirit into this reading, asking the Author of Scripture to speak to you through His Word
2. Read today's passage as many times as you need, take your time
3. Write down (below) what the Lord is saying to you today
4. Live with this Word in your heart through the day

_____

_____

Wednesday, October 15, 2025
Saint Teresa of Jesus, Virgin and Doctor of the Church

First Reading: Romans 2: 1-11

¹ Therefore you are without excuse, O man, whoever you are who judge. For in that which you judge another, you condemn yourself. For you who judge practice the same things. ² We know that the judgment of God is according to truth against those who practice such things. ³ Do you think this, O man who judges those who practice such things, and do the same, that you will escape the judgment of God? ⁴ Or do you despise the riches of his goodness, forbearance, and patience, not knowing that the goodness of God leads you to repentance? ⁵ But according to your hardness and unrepentant heart you are treasuring up for yourself wrath in the day of wrath, revelation, and of the righteous judgment of God, ⁶ who "will pay back to everyone according to their works:" ⁷ to those who by perseverance in well-doing seek for glory, honor, and incorruptibility, eternal life; ⁸ but to those who are self-seeking and don't obey the truth, but obey unrighteousness, will be wrath, indignation, ⁹ oppression, and anguish on every soul of man who does evil, to the Jew first, and also to the Greek.
¹⁰ But glory, honor, and peace go to every man who does good, to the Jew first, and also to the Greek. ¹¹ For there is no partiality with God.

Responsorial Psalm: Psalms 62: 2-3, 6-7, 9

² He alone is my rock, my salvation, and my fortress.
I will never be greatly shaken.
³ How long will you assault a man?
Would all of you throw him down,
like a leaning wall, like a tottering fence?
⁶ He alone is my rock and my salvation, my fortress.
I will not be shaken.
⁷ My salvation and my honor is with God.
The rock of my strength, and my refuge, is in God.
⁹ Surely men of low degree are just a breath,
and men of high degree are a lie.
In the balances they will go up.
They are together lighter than a breath.

Gospel: Luke 11: 42-46

⁴² But woe to you Pharisees! For you tithe mint and rue and every herb, but you bypass justice and God's love. You ought to have done these, and not to have left the other undone. ⁴³ Woe to you Pharisees! For you love the best seats in the synagogues and the

greetings in the marketplaces. ⁴⁴ Woe to you, scribes and Pharisees, hypocrites! For you are like hidden graves, and the men who walk over them don't know it."
⁴⁵ One of the lawyers answered him, "Teacher, in saying this you insult us also."
⁴⁶ He said, "Woe to you lawyers also! For you load men with burdens that are difficult to carry, and you yourselves won't even lift one finger to help carry those burdens.

1. Invite the Holy Spirit into this reading, asking the Author of Scripture to speak to you through His Word
2. Read today's passage as many times as you need, take your time
3. Write down (below) what the Lord is saying to you today
4. Live with this Word in your heart through the day

___

___

Thursday, October 16, 2025
Saint Hedwig, Religious; Saint Margaret Mary Alacoque, Virgin

First Reading: Romans 3: 21-30

²¹ But now apart from the law, a righteousness of God has been revealed, being testified by the law and the prophets; ²² even the righteousness of God through faith in Jesus Christ to all and on all those who believe. For there is no distinction, ²³ for all have sinned, and fall short of the glory of God; ²⁴ being justified freely by his grace through the redemption that is in Christ Jesus, ²⁵ whom God sent to be an atoning sacrifice through faith in his blood, for a demonstration of his righteousness through the passing over of prior sins, in God's forbearance; ²⁶ to demonstrate his righteousness at this present time, that he might himself be just and the justifier of him who has faith in Jesus.
²⁷ Where then is the boasting? It is excluded. By what kind of law? Of works? No, but by a law of faith. ²⁸ We maintain therefore that a man is justified by faith apart from the works of the law. ²⁹ Or is God the God of Jews only? Isn't he the God of Gentiles also? Yes, of Gentiles also, ³⁰ since indeed there is one God who will justify the circumcised by faith and the uncircumcised through faith.

Responsorial Psalm: Psalms 130: 1b-2, 3-4, 5-6ab

¹ Out of the depths I have cried to you, Yahweh.
² Lord, hear my voice.

Let your ears be attentive to the voice of my petitions.
³ If you, Yah, kept a record of sins,
Lord, who could stand?
⁴ But there is forgiveness with you,
therefore you are feared.
⁵ I wait for Yahweh.
My soul waits.
I hope in his word.
⁶ My soul longs for the Lord more than watchmen long for the morning,
more than watchmen for the morning.

Gospel: Luke 11: 47-54

⁴⁷ Woe to you! For you build the tombs of the prophets, and your fathers killed them. ⁴⁸ So you testify and consent to the works of your fathers. For they killed them, and you build their tombs. ⁴⁹ Therefore also the wisdom of God said, 'I will send to them prophets and apostles; and some of them they will kill and persecute, ⁵⁰ that the blood of all the prophets, which was shed from the foundation of the world, may be required of this generation, ⁵¹ from the blood of Abel to the blood of Zachariah, who perished between the altar and the sanctuary.' Yes, I tell you, it will be required of this generation. ⁵² Woe to you lawyers! For you took away the key of knowledge. You didn't enter in yourselves, and those who were entering in, you hindered."
⁵³ As he said these things to them, the scribes and the Pharisees began to be terribly angry, and to draw many things out of him, ⁵⁴ lying in wait for him, and seeking to catch him in something he might say, that they might accuse him.

1. Invite the Holy Spirit into this reading, asking the Author of Scripture to speak to you through His Word
2. Read today's passage as many times as you need, take your time
3. Write down (below) what the Lord is saying to you today
4. Live with this Word in your heart through the day

_____

_____

Friday, October 17, 2025
Saint Ignatius of Antioch, Bishop and Martyr

First Reading: Romans 4: 1-8

1 What then will we say that Abraham, our forefather, has found according to the flesh? 2 For if Abraham was justified by works, he has something to boast about, but not toward God. 3 For what does the Scripture say? "Abraham believed God, and it was accounted to him for righteousness."* 4 Now to him who works, the reward is not counted as grace, but as something owed. 5 But to him who doesn't work, but believes in him who justifies the ungodly, his faith is accounted for righteousness. 6 Even as David also pronounces blessing on the man to whom God counts righteousness apart from works:
7 "Blessed are they whose iniquities are forgiven,
whose sins are covered.
8 Blessed is the man whom the Lord will by no means charge with sin."

Responsorial Psalm: Psalms 32: 1b-2, 5, 11

1 Blessed is he whose disobedience is forgiven,
whose sin is covered.
2 Blessed is the man to whom Yahweh doesn't impute iniquity,
in whose spirit there is no deceit.
5 I acknowledged my sin to you.
I didn't hide my iniquity.
I said, I will confess my transgressions to Yahweh,
and you forgave the iniquity of my sin.
11 Be glad in Yahweh, and rejoice, you righteous!
Shout for joy, all you who are upright in heart!

Gospel: Luke 12: 1-7

1 Meanwhile, when a multitude of many thousands had gathered together, so much so that they trampled on each other, he began to tell his disciples first of all, "Beware of the yeast of the Pharisees, which is hypocrisy. 2 But there is nothing covered up that will not be revealed, nor hidden that will not be known. 3 Therefore whatever you have said in the darkness will be heard in the light. What you have spoken in the ear in the inner rooms will be proclaimed on the housetops.
4 "I tell you, my friends, don't be afraid of those who kill the body, and after that have no more that they can do. 5 But I will warn you whom you should fear. Fear him who after he has killed, has power to cast into Gehenna.† Yes, I tell you, fear him.
6 "Aren't five sparrows sold for two assaria coins‡? Not one of them is forgotten by God. 7 But the very hairs of your head are all counted. Therefore don't be afraid. You are of more value than many sparrows.

1. Invite the Holy Spirit into this reading, asking the Author of Scripture to speak to you through His Word
2. Read today's passage as many times as you need, take your time
3. Write down (below) what the Lord is saying to you today
4. Live with this Word in your heart through the day

Saturday, October 18, 2025
Saint Luke, Evangelist

First Reading: Second Timothy 4: 10-17b

¹⁰ for Demas left me, having loved this present world, and went to Thessalonica; Crescens to Galatia; and Titus to Dalmatia. ¹¹ Only Luke is with me. Take Mark and bring him with you, for he is useful to me for service. ¹² But I sent Tychicus to Ephesus. ¹³ Bring the cloak that I left at Troas with Carpus when you come—and the books, especially the parchments. ¹⁴ Alexander the coppersmith did much evil to me. The Lord will repay him according to his deeds. ¹⁵ Beware of him, for he greatly opposed our words.

¹⁶ At my first defense, no one came to help me, but all left me. May it not be held against them. ¹⁷ But the Lord stood by me and strengthened me, that through me the message might be fully proclaimed, and that all the Gentiles might hear. So I was delivered out of the mouth of the lion.

Responsorial Psalm: Psalms 145: 10-11, 12-13, 17-18

¹⁰ All your works will give thanks to you, Yahweh.
Your saints will extol you.
¹¹ They will speak of the glory of your kingdom,
and talk about your power,
¹² to make known to the sons of men his mighty acts,
the glory of the majesty of his kingdom.
¹³ Your kingdom is an everlasting kingdom.
Your dominion endures throughout all generations.
Yahweh is faithful in all his words,
and loving in all his deeds.‡

¹⁴ Yahweh upholds all who fall,
and raises up all those who are bowed down.
¹⁵ The eyes of all wait for you.
You give them their food in due season.
¹⁶ You open your hand,
and satisfy the desire of every living thing.
¹⁷ Yahweh is righteous in all his ways,
and gracious in all his works.
¹⁸ Yahweh is near to all those who call on him,
to all who call on him in truth.

Gospel: Luke 10: 1-9

¹ Now after these things, the Lord also appointed seventy others, and sent them two by two ahead of him into every city and place where he was about to come. ² Then he said to them, "The harvest is indeed plentiful, but the laborers are few. Pray therefore to the Lord of the harvest, that he may send out laborers into his harvest. ³ Go your ways. Behold, I send you out as lambs among wolves. ⁴ Carry no purse, nor wallet, nor sandals. Greet no one on the way. ⁵ Into whatever house you enter, first say, 'Peace be to this house.' ⁶ If a son of peace is there, your peace will rest on him; but if not, it will return to you. ⁷ Remain in that same house, eating and drinking the things they give, for the laborer is worthy of his wages. Don't go from house to house. ⁸ Into whatever city you enter and they receive you, eat the things that are set before you. ⁹ Heal the sick who are there and tell them, 'God's Kingdom has come near to you.'

1. Invite the Holy Spirit into this reading, asking the Author of Scripture to speak to you through His Word
2. Read today's passage as many times as you need, take your time
3. Write down (below) what the Lord is saying to you today
4. Live with this Word in your heart through the day

Sunday, October 19, 2025
TWENTY-NINTH SUNDAY IN ORDINARY TIME

First Reading: Exodus 17: 8-13

⁸ Then Amalek came and fought with Israel in Rephidim. ⁹ Moses said to Joshua, "Choose men for us, and go out to fight with Amalek. Tomorrow I will stand on the top of the hill with God's rod in my hand." ¹⁰ So Joshua did as Moses had told him, and fought with Amalek; and Moses, Aaron, and Hur went up to the top of the hill. ¹¹ When Moses held up his hand, Israel prevailed. When he let down his hand, Amalek prevailed. ¹² But Moses' hands were heavy; so they took a stone, and put it under him, and he sat on it. Aaron and Hur held up his hands, the one on the one side, and the other on the other side. His hands were steady until sunset. ¹³ Joshua defeated Amalek and his people with the edge of the sword.

Responsorial Psalm: Psalms 121: 1-2, 3-4, 5-6, 7-8

¹ I will lift up my eyes to the hills.
Where does my help come from?
² My help comes from Yahweh,
who made heaven and earth.
³ He will not allow your foot to be moved.
He who keeps you will not slumber.
⁴ Behold, he who keeps Israel
will neither slumber nor sleep.
⁵ Yahweh is your keeper.
Yahweh is your shade on your right hand.
⁶ The sun will not harm you by day,
nor the moon by night.
⁷ Yahweh will keep you from all evil.
He will keep your soul.
⁸ Yahweh will keep your going out and your coming in,
from this time forward, and forever more.

Second Reading: Second Timothy 3: 14 – 4: 2

¹⁴ But you remain in the things which you have learned and have been assured of, knowing from whom you have learned them. ¹⁵ From infancy, you have known the holy Scriptures which are able to make you wise for salvation through faith which is in Christ Jesus. ¹⁶ Every Scripture is God-breathed and⸵ profitable for teaching, for reproof, for correction, and for instruction in righteousness, ¹⁷ that each person who belongs to God may be complete, thoroughly equipped for every good work.

¹ I command you therefore before God and the Lord Jesus Christ, who will judge the living and the dead at his appearing and his Kingdom: ² preach the word; be urgent in season and out of season; reprove, rebuke, and exhort with all patience and teaching.

Gospel: Luke 18: 1-8

¹ He also spoke a parable to them that they must always pray and not give up, ² saying, "There was a judge in a certain city who didn't fear God and didn't respect man. ³ A widow was in that city, and she often came to him, saying, 'Defend me from my adversary!' ⁴ He wouldn't for a while; but afterward he said to himself, 'Though I neither fear God nor respect man, ⁵ yet because this widow bothers me, I will defend her, or else she will wear me out by her continual coming.' "
⁶ The Lord said, "Listen to what the unrighteous judge says. ⁷ Won't God avenge his chosen ones who are crying out to him day and night, and yet he exercises patience with them? ⁸ I tell you that he will avenge them quickly. Nevertheless, when the Son of Man comes, will he find faith on the earth?"

1. Invite the Holy Spirit into this reading, asking the Author of Scripture to speak to you through His Word
2. Read today's passage as many times as you need, take your time
3. Write down (below) what the Lord is saying to you today
4. Live with this Word in your heart through the day

Monday, October 20, 2025
Saint Paul of the Cross, Priest

First Reading: Romans 4: 20-25

²⁰ Yet, looking to the promise of God, he didn't waver through unbelief, but grew strong through faith, giving glory to God, ²¹ and being fully assured that what he had promised, he was also able to perform. ²² Therefore it also was "credited to him for righteousness."* ²³ Now it was not written that it was accounted to him for his sake alone, ²⁴ but for our sake also, to whom it will be accounted, who believe in him who raised Jesus our Lord from the dead, ²⁵ who was delivered up for our trespasses, and was raised for our justification.

Responsorial Psalm: Luke 1: 69-70, 71-72, 73-75

⁶⁹ and has raised up a horn of salvation for us in the house of his servant David
⁷⁰ (as he spoke by the mouth of his holy prophets who have been from of old),
⁷¹ salvation from our enemies and from the hand of all who hate us;
⁷² to show mercy toward our fathers,
to remember his holy covenant,
⁷³ the oath which he swore to Abraham our father,
⁷⁴ to grant to us that we, being delivered out of the hand of our enemies,
should serve him without fear,
⁷⁵ in holiness and righteousness before him all the days of our life.

Gospel: Luke 12: 13-21

¹³ One of the multitude said to him, "Teacher, tell my brother to divide the inheritance with me."
¹⁴ But he said to him, "Man, who made me a judge or an arbitrator over you?" ¹⁵ He said to them, "Beware! Keep yourselves from covetousness, for a man's life doesn't consist of the abundance of the things which he possesses."
¹⁶ He spoke a parable to them, saying, "The ground of a certain rich man produced abundantly. ¹⁷ He reasoned within himself, saying, 'What will I do, because I don't have room to store my crops?' ¹⁸ He said, 'This is what I will do. I will pull down my barns, build bigger ones, and there I will store all my grain and my goods. ¹⁹ I will tell my soul, "Soul, you have many goods laid up for many years. Take your ease, eat, drink, and be merry." '
²⁰ "But God said to him, 'You foolish one, tonight your soul is required of you. The things which you have prepared—whose will they be?' ²¹ So is he who lays up treasure for himself, and is not rich toward God."

1. Invite the Holy Spirit into this reading, asking the Author of Scripture to speak to you through His Word
2. Read today's passage as many times as you need, take your time
3. Write down (below) what the Lord is saying to you today
4. Live with this Word in your heart through the day

_____

_____

Tuesday, October 21, 2025

First Reading: Romans 5: 12, 15b, 17-19, 20b-21

¹² Therefore, as sin entered into the world through one man, and death through sin, so death passed to all men because all sinned
¹⁵ᵇ For if by the trespass of the one the many died, much more did the grace of God and the gift by the grace of the one man, Jesus Christ, abound to the many.
¹⁷ For if by the trespass of the one, death reigned through the one; so much more will those who receive the abundance of grace and of the gift of righteousness reign in life through the one, Jesus Christ.
¹⁸ So then as through one trespass, all men were condemned; even so through one act of righteousness, all men were justified to life. ¹⁹ For as through the one man's disobedience many were made sinners, even so through the obedience of the one, many will be made righteous.
²⁰ᵇ but where sin abounded, grace abounded more exceedingly, ²¹ that as sin reigned in death, even so grace might reign through righteousness to eternal life through Jesus Christ our Lord.

Responsorial Psalm: Psalms 40: 7-8a, 8b-9, 10, 17

⁷ Then I said, "Behold, I have come.
It is written about me in the book in the scroll.
⁸ I delight to do your will, my God.
Yes, your law is within my heart."
⁹ I have proclaimed glad news of righteousness in the great assembly.
Behold, I will not seal my lips, Yahweh, you know.
¹⁰ I have not hidden your righteousness within my heart.
I have declared your faithfulness and your salvation.
I have not concealed your loving kindness and your truth from the great assembly.
¹⁷ But I am poor and needy.
May the Lord think about me.
You are my help and my deliverer.
Don't delay, my God.

Gospel: Luke 12: 35-38

³⁵ "Let your waist be dressed and your lamps burning. ³⁶ Be like men watching for their lord when he returns from the wedding feast, that when he comes and knocks, they may immediately open to him. ³⁷ Blessed are those servants whom the lord will find watching

when he comes. Most certainly I tell you that he will dress himself, make them recline, and will come and serve them. ³⁸ They will be blessed if he comes in the second or third watch and finds them so.

1. Invite the Holy Spirit into this reading, asking the Author of Scripture to speak to you through His Word
2. Read today's passage as many times as you need, take your time
3. Write down (below) what the Lord is saying to you today
4. Live with this Word in your heart through the day

Wednesday, October 22, 2025
Saint John Paul II, Pope

First Reading: Romans 6: 12-18

¹²Therefore don't let sin reign in your mortal body, that you should obey it in its lusts. ¹³Also, do not present your members to sin as instruments of unrighteousness, but present yourselves to God as alive from the dead, and your members as instruments of righteousness to God. ¹⁴ For sin will not have dominion over you, for you are not under law, but under grace.
¹⁵ What then? Shall we sin because we are not under law but under grace? May it never be! ¹⁶ Don't you know that when you present yourselves as servants and obey someone, you are the servants of whomever you obey, whether of sin to death, or of obedience to righteousness? ¹⁷ But thanks be to God that, whereas you were bondservants of sin, you became obedient from the heart to that form of teaching to which you were delivered. ¹⁸ Being made free from sin, you became bondservants of righteousness.

Responsorial Psalm: Psalms 124: 1b-3, 4-6, 7-8

¹ If it had not been Yahweh who was on our side,
let Israel now say,
² if it had not been Yahweh who was on our side,
when men rose up against us,
³ then they would have swallowed us up alive,
when their wrath was kindled against us,

4 then the waters would have overwhelmed us,
the stream would have gone over our soul.
5 Then the proud waters would have gone over our soul.
6 Blessed be Yahweh,
who has not given us as a prey to their teeth.
7 Our soul has escaped like a bird out of the fowler's snare.
The snare is broken, and we have escaped.
8 Our help is in Yahweh's name,
who made heaven and earth.

Gospel: Luke 12: 39-48

39 But know this, that if the master of the house had known in what hour the thief was coming, he would have watched and not allowed his house to be broken into. 40 Therefore be ready also, for the Son of Man is coming in an hour that you don't expect him."
41 Peter said to him, "Lord, are you telling this parable to us, or to everybody?"
42 The Lord said, "Who then is the faithful and wise steward, whom his lord will set over his household, to give them their portion of food at the right times? 43 Blessed is that servant whom his lord will find doing so when he comes. 44 Truly I tell you that he will set him over all that he has. 45 But if that servant says in his heart, 'My lord delays his coming,' and begins to beat the menservants and the maidservants, and to eat and drink and to be drunken, 46 then the lord of that servant will come in a day when he isn't expecting him and in an hour that he doesn't know, and will cut him in two, and place his portion with the unfaithful. 47 That servant who knew his lord's will, and didn't prepare nor do what he wanted, will be beaten with many stripes, 48 but he who didn't know, and did things worthy of stripes, will be beaten with few stripes. To whomever much is given, of him will much be required; and to whom much was entrusted, of him more will be asked.

1. Invite the Holy Spirit into this reading, asking the Author of Scripture to speak to you through His Word
2. Read today's passage as many times as you need, take your time
3. Write down (below) what the Lord is saying to you today
4. Live with this Word in your heart through the day

Thursday, October 23, 2025

Saint John of Capistrano, Priest

First Reading: Romans 6: 19-23

19 I speak in human terms because of the weakness of your flesh; for as you presented your members as servants to uncleanness and to wickedness upon wickedness, even so now present your members as servants to righteousness for sanctification. 20 For when you were servants of sin, you were free from righteousness. 21 What fruit then did you have at that time in the things of which you are now ashamed? For the end of those things is death. 22 But now, being made free from sin and having become servants of God, you have your fruit of sanctification and the result of eternal life. 23 For the wages of sin is death, but the free gift of God is eternal life in Christ Jesus our Lord.

Responsorial Psalm: Psalms 1: 1-2, 3, 4 and 6

1 Blessed is the man who doesn't walk in the counsel of the wicked,
nor stand on the path of sinners,
nor sit in the seat of scoffers;
2 but his delight is in Yahweh's⁺ law.
On his law he meditates day and night.
3 He will be like a tree planted by the streams of water,
that produces its fruit in its season,
whose leaf also does not wither.
Whatever he does shall prosper.
4 The wicked are not so,
but are like the chaff which the wind drives away.
6 For Yahweh knows the way of the righteous,
but the way of the wicked shall perish.

Gospel: Luke 12: 49-53

49 "I came to throw fire on the earth. I wish it were already kindled. 50 But I have a baptism to be baptized with, and how distressed I am until it is accomplished! 51 Do you think that I have come to give peace in the earth? I tell you, no, but rather division. 52 For from now on, there will be five in one house divided, three against two, and two against three. 53 They will be divided, father against son, and son against father; mother against daughter, and daughter against her mother; mother-in-law against her daughter-in-law, and daughter-in-law against her mother-in-law."

1. Invite the Holy Spirit into this reading, asking the Author of Scripture to speak to you through His Word
2. Read today's passage as many times as you need, take your time
3. Write down (below) what the Lord is saying to you today
4. Live with this Word in your heart through the day

Friday, October 24, 2025
Saint Anthony Mary Claret, Bishop

First Reading: Romans 7: 18-25a

18 For I know that in me, that is, in my flesh, dwells no good thing. For desire is present with me, but I don't find it doing that which is good. 19 For the good which I desire, I don't do; but the evil which I don't desire, that I practice. 20 But if what I don't desire, that I do, it is no more I that do it, but sin which dwells in me. 21 I find then the law that, while I desire to do good, evil is present. 22 For I delight in God's law after the inward person, 23 but I see a different law in my members, warring against the law of my mind, and bringing me into captivity under the law of sin which is in my members. 24 What a wretched man I am! Who will deliver me out of the body of this death? 25 I thank God through Jesus Christ, our Lord! So then with the mind, I myself serve God's law, but with the flesh, sin's law.

Responsorial Psalm: Psalms 119: 66, 68, 76, 77, 93, 94

66 Teach me good judgment and knowledge,
for I believe in your commandments.
67 Before I was afflicted, I went astray;
but now I observe your word.
68 You are good, and do good.
Teach me your statutes.
76 Please let your loving kindness be for my comfort,
according to your word to your servant.
77 Let your tender mercies come to me, that I may live;
for your law is my delight.
93 I will never forget your precepts,
for with them, you have revived me.

⁹⁴ I am yours.
Save me, for I have sought your precepts.

Gospel: Luke 12: 54-59

⁵⁴ He said to the multitudes also, "When you see a cloud rising from the west, immediately you say, 'A shower is coming,' and so it happens. ⁵⁵ When a south wind blows, you say, 'There will be a scorching heat,' and it happens. ⁵⁶ You hypocrites! You know how to interpret the appearance of the earth and the sky, but how is it that you don't interpret this time?

⁵⁷ "Why don't you judge for yourselves what is right? ⁵⁸ For when you are going with your adversary before the magistrate, try diligently on the way to be released from him, lest perhaps he drag you to the judge, and the judge deliver you to the officer, and the officer throw you into prison. ⁵⁹ I tell you, you will by no means get out of there until you have paid the very last penny.‡"

1. Invite the Holy Spirit into this reading, asking the Author of Scripture to speak to you through His Word
2. Read today's passage as many times as you need, take your time
3. Write down (below) what the Lord is saying to you today
4. Live with this Word in your heart through the day

_____

_____

Saturday, October 25, 2025

First Reading: Romans 8: 1-11

¹ There is therefore now no condemnation to those who are in Christ Jesus, who don't walk according to the flesh, but according to the Spirit.‡ ² For the law of the Spirit of life in Christ Jesus made me free from the law of sin and of death. ³ For what the law couldn't do, in that it was weak through the flesh, God did, sending his own Son in the likeness of sinful flesh and for sin, he condemned sin in the flesh, ⁴ that the ordinance of the law might be fulfilled in us who don't walk according to the flesh, but according to the Spirit. ⁵ For those who live according to the flesh set their minds on the things of the flesh, but those who live according to the Spirit, the things of the Spirit. ⁶ For the mind of the flesh is death, but the mind of the Spirit is life and peace; ⁷ because the mind of the flesh is hostile toward God,

for it is not subject to God's law, neither indeed can it be. ⁸ Those who are in the flesh can't please God.

Responsorial Psalm: Psalms 24: 1b-2, 3-4ab, 5-6

¹ The earth is Yahweh's, with its fullness;
the world, and those who dwell in it.
² For he has founded it on the seas,
and established it on the floods.
³ Who may ascend to Yahweh's hill?
Who may stand in his holy place?
⁴ He who has clean hands and a pure heart;
who has not lifted up his soul to falsehood,
and has not sworn deceitfully.
⁵ He shall receive a blessing from Yahweh,
righteousness from the God of his salvation.
⁶ This is the generation of those who seek Him,
who seek your face—even Jacob.

Gospel: Luke 13: 1-9

¹ Now there were some present at the same time who told him about the Galileans whose blood Pilate had mixed with their sacrifices. ² Jesus answered them, "Do you think that these Galileans were worse sinners than all the other Galileans, because they suffered such things? ³ I tell you, no, but unless you repent, you will all perish in the same way. ⁴ Or those eighteen on whom the tower in Siloam fell and killed them—do you think that they were worse offenders than all the men who dwell in Jerusalem? ⁵ I tell you, no, but, unless you repent, you will all perish in the same way."
⁶ He spoke this parable. "A certain man had a fig tree planted in his vineyard, and he came seeking fruit on it and found none. ⁷ He said to the vine dresser, 'Behold, these three years I have come looking for fruit on this fig tree, and found none. Cut it down! Why does it waste the soil?' ⁸ He answered, 'Lord, leave it alone this year also, until I dig around it and fertilize it. ⁹ If it bears fruit, fine; but if not, after that, you can cut it down.' "

1. Invite the Holy Spirit into this reading, asking the Author of Scripture to speak to you through His Word
2. Read today's passage as many times as you need, take your time
3. Write down (below) what the Lord is saying to you today
4. Live with this Word in your heart through the day

Sunday, October 26, 2025
THIRTIETH SUNDAY IN ORDINARY TIME

First Reading: Sirach 35: 12-14, 16-18

¹² Don't plan to bribe him with gifts, for he will not receive them.
Don't set your mind on an unrighteous sacrifice,
For the Lord is the judge,
and with him is no respect of persons.
¹³ He won't accept any person against a poor man.
He will listen to the prayer of him who is wronged.
¹⁴ He will in no way despise the supplication of the fatherless
or the widow, when she pours out her tale.
¹⁶ He who serves God according to his good pleasure will be accepted.
His supplication will reach to the clouds.
¹⁷ The prayer of the humble pierces the clouds.
until it comes near, he will not be comforted.
He won't depart until the Most High visits
and he judges righteously and executes judgment.
¹⁸ And the Lord will not be slack, neither will he be patient toward them,
until he has crushed the loins of the unmerciful.
He will repay vengeance to the heathen
until he has taken away the multitude of the arrogant
and broken in pieces the sceptres of the unrighteous,

Responsorial Psalm: Psalms 34: 2-3, 17-18, 19

² My soul shall boast in Yahweh.
The humble shall hear of it and be glad.
³ Oh magnify Yahweh with me.
Let's exalt his name together.
¹⁷ The righteous cry, and Yahweh hears,
and delivers them out of all their troubles.
¹⁸ Yahweh is near to those who have a broken heart,
and saves those who have a crushed spirit.
¹⁹ Many are the afflictions of the righteous,

but Yahweh delivers him out of them all.

Second Reading: Second Timothy 4: 6-8, 16-18

⁶ For I am already being offered, and the time of my departure has come. ⁷ I have fought the good fight. I have finished the course. I have kept the faith. ⁸ From now on, the crown of righteousness is stored up for me, which the Lord, the righteous judge, will give to me on that day; and not to me only, but also to all those who have loved his appearing.
¹⁶ At my first defense, no one came to help me, but all left me. May it not be held against them. ¹⁷ But the Lord stood by me and strengthened me, that through me the message might be fully proclaimed, and that all the Gentiles might hear. So I was delivered out of the mouth of the lion. ¹⁸ And the Lord will deliver me from every evil work and will preserve me for his heavenly Kingdom. To him be the glory forever and ever. Amen.

Gospel: Luke 18: 9-14

⁹ He also spoke this parable to certain people who were convinced of their own righteousness, and who despised all others: ¹⁰ "Two men went up into the temple to pray; one was a Pharisee, and the other was a tax collector. ¹¹ The Pharisee stood and prayed by himself like this: 'God, I thank you that I am not like the rest of men: extortionists, unrighteous, adulterers, or even like this tax collector. ¹² I fast twice a week. I give tithes of all that I get.' ¹³ But the tax collector, standing far away, wouldn't even lift up his eyes to heaven, but beat his chest, saying, 'God, be merciful to me, a sinner!' ¹⁴ I tell you, this man went down to his house justified rather than the other; for everyone who exalts himself will be humbled, but he who humbles himself will be exalted."

1. Invite the Holy Spirit into this reading, asking the Author of Scripture to speak to you through His Word
2. Read today's passage as many times as you need, take your time
3. Write down (below) what the Lord is saying to you today
4. Live with this Word in your heart through the day

_____

_____

Monday, October 27, 2025

First Reading: Romans 8: 12-17

¹² So then, brothers, we are debtors, not to the flesh, to live after the flesh. ¹³ For if you live after the flesh, you must die; but if by the Spirit you put to death the deeds of the body, you will live. ¹⁴ For as many as are led by the Spirit of God, these are children of God. ¹⁵ For you didn't receive the spirit of bondage again to fear, but you received the Spirit of adoption, by whom we cry, "Abba!⁺ Father!"

¹⁶ The Spirit himself testifies with our spirit that we are children of God; ¹⁷ and if children, then heirs—heirs of God and joint heirs with Christ, if indeed we suffer with him, that we may also be glorified with him.

Responsorial Psalm: Psalms 68: 2 and 4, 6-7ab, 20-21

² As smoke is driven away,
so drive them away.
As wax melts before the fire,
so let the wicked perish at the presence of God.
⁴ Sing to God! Sing praises to his name!
Extol him who rides on the clouds:
to Yah, his name!
Rejoice before him!
⁶ God sets the lonely in families.
He brings out the prisoners with singing,
but the rebellious dwell in a sun-scorched land.
⁷ God, when you went out before your people,
when you marched through the wilderness...
²⁰ God is to us a God of deliverance.
To Yahweh, the Lord, belongs escape from death.
²¹ But God will strike through the head of his enemies,
the hairy scalp of such a one as still continues in his guiltiness.

Gospel: Luke 13: 10-17

¹⁰ He was teaching in one of the synagogues on the Sabbath day. ¹¹ Behold, there was a woman who had a spirit of infirmity eighteen years. She was bent over and could in no way straighten herself up. ¹² When Jesus saw her, he called her and said to her, "Woman, you are freed from your infirmity." ¹³ He laid his hands on her, and immediately she stood up straight and glorified God.
¹⁴ The ruler of the synagogue, being indignant because Jesus had healed on the Sabbath, said to the multitude, "There are six days in which men ought to work. Therefore come on those days and be healed, and not on the Sabbath day!"

¹⁵ Therefore the Lord answered him, "You hypocrites! Doesn't each one of you free his ox or his donkey from the stall on the Sabbath and lead him away to water? ¹⁶ Ought not this woman, being a daughter of Abraham whom Satan had bound eighteen long years, be freed from this bondage on the Sabbath day?"

¹⁷ As he said these things, all his adversaries were disappointed; and all the multitude rejoiced for all the glorious things that were done by him.

1. Invite the Holy Spirit into this reading, asking the Author of Scripture to speak to you through His Word
2. Read today's passage as many times as you need, take your time
3. Write down (below) what the Lord is saying to you today
4. Live with this Word in your heart through the day

_____

_____

Tuesday, October 28, 2025
Saints Simon and Jude, Apostles

First Reading: Ephesians 2: 19-22

¹⁹ So then you are no longer strangers and foreigners, but you are fellow citizens with the saints and of the household of God, ²⁰ being built on the foundation of the apostles and prophets, Christ Jesus himself being the chief cornerstone; ²¹ in whom the whole building, fitted together, grows into a holy temple in the Lord; ²² in whom you also are built together for a habitation of God in the Spirit.

Responsorial Psalm: Psalms 19: 2-3, 4-5

² Day after day they pour out speech,
and night after night they display knowledge.
³ There is no speech nor language
where their voice is not heard.
⁴ Their voice has gone out through all the earth,
their words to the end of the world.
In them he has set a tent for the sun,
⁵ which is as a bridegroom coming out of his room,
like a strong man rejoicing to run his course.

Gospel: Luke 6: 12-16

¹² In these days, he went out to the mountain to pray, and he continued all night in prayer to God. ¹³ When it was day, he called his disciples, and from them he chose twelve, whom he also named apostles: ¹⁴ Simon, whom he also named Peter; Andrew, his brother; James; John; Philip; Bartholomew; ¹⁵ Matthew; Thomas; James the son of Alphaeus; Simon who was called the Zealot; ¹⁶ Judas the son of James; and Judas Iscariot, who also became a traitor.

1. Invite the Holy Spirit into this reading, asking the Author of Scripture to speak to you through His Word
2. Read today's passage as many times as you need, take your time
3. Write down (below) what the Lord is saying to you today
4. Live with this Word in your heart through the day

Wednesday, October 29, 2025

First Reading: Romans 8: 26-30

²⁶ In the same way, the Spirit also helps our weaknesses, for we don't know how to pray as we ought. But the Spirit himself makes intercession for us with groanings which can't be uttered. ²⁷ He who searches the hearts knows what is on the Spirit's mind, because he makes intercession for the saints according to God.
²⁸ We know that all things work together for good for those who love God, for those who are called according to his purpose. ²⁹ For whom he foreknew, he also predestined to be conformed to the image of his Son, that he might be the firstborn among many brothers.§ ³⁰ Whom he predestined, those he also called. Whom he called, those he also justified. Whom he justified, those he also glorified.

Responsorial Psalm: Psalms 13: 4-5, 6

⁴ lest my enemy say, "I have prevailed against him;"
lest my adversaries rejoice when I fall.
⁵ But I trust in your loving kindness.

My heart rejoices in your salvation.
⁶ I will sing to Yahweh,
because he has been good to me.

Gospel: Luke 13: 22-30

²² He went on his way through cities and villages, teaching, and traveling on to Jerusalem. ²³ One said to him, "Lord, are they few who are saved?"
He said to them, ²⁴ "Strive to enter in by the narrow door, for many, I tell you, will seek to enter in and will not be able. ²⁵ When once the master of the house has risen up and has shut the door, and you begin to stand outside and to knock at the door, saying, 'Lord, Lord, open to us!' then he will answer and tell you, 'I don't know you or where you come from.' ²⁶ Then you will begin to say, 'We ate and drank in your presence, and you taught in our streets.' ²⁷ He will say, 'I tell you, I don't know where you come from. Depart from me, all you workers of iniquity.' ²⁸ There will be weeping and gnashing of teeth when you see Abraham, Isaac, Jacob, and all the prophets in God's Kingdom, and yourselves being thrown outside. ²⁹ They will come from the east, west, north, and south, and will sit down in God's Kingdom. ³⁰ Behold, there are some who are last who will be first, and there are some who are first who will be last."

1. Invite the Holy Spirit into this reading, asking the Author of Scripture to speak to you through His Word
2. Read today's passage as many times as you need, take your time
3. Write down (below) what the Lord is saying to you today
4. Live with this Word in your heart through the day

_____

_____

Thursday, October 30, 2025

First Reading: Romans 8: 31b-39

³¹ᵇ If God is for us, who can be against us? ³² He who didn't spare his own Son, but delivered him up for us all, how would he not also with him freely give us all things? ³³ Who could bring a charge against God's chosen ones? It is God who justifies. ³⁴ Who is he who condemns? It is Christ who died, yes rather, who was raised from the dead, who is at the right hand of God, who also makes intercession for us.

³⁵ Who shall separate us from the love of Christ? Could oppression, or anguish, or persecution, or famine, or nakedness, or peril, or sword? ³⁶ Even as it is written,
"For your sake we are killed all day long.
We were accounted as sheep for the slaughter."
³⁷ No, in all these things we are more than conquerors through him who loved us. ³⁸ For I am persuaded that neither death, nor life, nor angels, nor principalities, nor things present, nor things to come, nor powers, ³⁹ nor height, nor depth, nor any other created thing will be able to separate us from God's love which is in Christ Jesus our Lord.

Responsorial Psalm: Psalms 109: 21-22, 26-27, 30-31

²¹ But deal with me, Yahweh the Lord, for your name's sake,
because your loving kindness is good, deliver me;
²² for I am poor and needy.
My heart is wounded within me.
²⁶ Help me, Yahweh, my God.
Save me according to your loving kindness;
²⁷ that they may know that this is your hand;
that you, Yahweh, have done it.
³⁰ I will give great thanks to Yahweh with my mouth.
Yes, I will praise him among the multitude.
³¹ For he will stand at the right hand of the needy,
to save him from those who judge his soul.

Gospel: Luke 13: 31-35

³¹ On that same day, some Pharisees came, saying to him, "Get out of here and go away, for Herod wants to kill you."
³² He said to them, "Go and tell that fox, 'Behold, I cast out demons and perform cures today and tomorrow, and the third day I complete my mission. ³³ Nevertheless I must go on my way today and tomorrow and the next day, for it can't be that a prophet would perish outside of Jerusalem.'
³⁴ "Jerusalem, Jerusalem, you who kills the prophets and stones those who are sent to her! How often I wanted to gather your children together, like a hen gathers her own brood under her wings, and you refused! ³⁵ Behold, your house is left to you desolate. I tell you, you will not see me until you say, 'Blessed is he who comes in the name of the Lord!' "

1. Invite the Holy Spirit into this reading, asking the Author of Scripture to speak to you through His Word
2. Read today's passage as many times as you need, take your time

3. Write down (below) what the Lord is saying to you today
4. Live with this Word in your heart through the day

Friday, October 31, 2025

First Reading: Romans 9: 1-5

¹ I tell the truth in Christ. I am not lying, my conscience testifying with me in the Holy Spirit ² that I have great sorrow and unceasing pain in my heart. ³ For I could wish that I myself were accursed from Christ for my brothers' sake, my relatives according to the flesh ⁴ who are Israelites; whose is the adoption, the glory, the covenants, the giving of the law, the service, and the promises; ⁵ of whom are the fathers, and from whom is Christ as concerning the flesh, who is over all, God, blessed forever. Amen.

Responsorial Psalm: Psalms 147: 12-13, 14-15, 19-20

¹² Praise Yahweh, Jerusalem!
Praise your God, Zion!
¹³ For he has strengthened the bars of your gates.
He has blessed your children within you.
¹⁴ He makes peace in your borders.
He fills you with the finest of the wheat.
¹⁵ He sends out his commandment to the earth.
His word runs very swiftly.
¹⁹ He shows his word to Jacob,
his statutes and his ordinances to Israel.
²⁰ He has not done this for just any nation.
They don't know his ordinances.
Praise Yah!

Gospel: Luke 14: 1-6

¹ When he went into the house of one of the rulers of the Pharisees on a Sabbath to eat bread, they were watching him. ² Behold, a certain man who had dropsy was in front of

him. ³ Jesus, answering, spoke to the lawyers and Pharisees, saying, "Is it lawful to heal on the Sabbath?"
⁴ But they were silent.
He took him, and healed him, and let him go. ⁵ He answered them, "Which of you, if your son or an ox fell into a well, wouldn't immediately pull him out on a Sabbath day?"
⁶ They couldn't answer him regarding these things.

1. Invite the Holy Spirit into this reading, asking the Author of Scripture to speak to you through His Word
2. Read today's passage as many times as you need, take your time
3. Write down (below) what the Lord is saying to you today
4. Live with this Word in your heart through the day

_____

_____

Saturday, November 1, 2025
ALL SAINTS

First Reading: Revelation 7: 2-4, 9-14

² I saw another angel ascend from the sunrise, having the seal of the living God. He cried with a loud voice to the four angels to whom it was given to harm the earth and the sea, ³ saying, "Don't harm the earth, the sea, or the trees, until we have sealed the bondservants of our God on their foreheads!" ⁴ I heard the number of those who were sealed, one hundred forty-four thousand, sealed out of every tribe of the children of Israel:
⁹ After these things I looked, and behold, a great multitude which no man could count, out of every nation and of all tribes, peoples, and languages, standing before the throne and before the Lamb, dressed in white robes, with palm branches in their hands. ¹⁰ They cried with a loud voice, saying, "Salvation be to our God, who sits on the throne, and to the Lamb!"
¹¹ All the angels were standing around the throne, the elders, and the four living creatures; and they fell on their faces before his throne, and worshiped God, ¹² saying, "Amen! Blessing, glory, wisdom, thanksgiving, honor, power, and might, be to our God forever and ever! Amen."
¹³ One of the elders answered, saying to me, "These who are arrayed in the white robes, who are they, and where did they come from?"
¹⁴ I told him, "My lord, you know."

He said to me, "These are those who came out of the great suffering. They washed their robes and made them white in the Lamb's blood.

Responsorial Psalm: Psalms 24: 1b-2, 3-4ab, 5-6

¹ The earth is Yahweh's, with its fullness;
the world, and those who dwell in it.
² For he has founded it on the seas,
and established it on the floods.
³ Who may ascend to Yahweh's hill?
Who may stand in his holy place?
⁴ He who has clean hands and a pure heart;
who has not lifted up his soul to falsehood,
and has not sworn deceitfully.
⁵ He shall receive a blessing from Yahweh,
righteousness from the God of his salvation.
⁶ This is the generation of those who seek Him,
who seek your face—even Jacob.

Second Reading: First John 3: 1-3

¹ See how great a love the Father has given to us, that we should be called children of God! For this cause the world doesn't know us, because it didn't know him. ² Beloved, now we are children of God. It is not yet revealed what we will be; but we know that when he is revealed, we will be like him, for we will see him just as he is. ³ Everyone who has this hope set on him purifies himself, even as he is pure.

Gospel: Matthew 5: 1-12a

¹ Seeing the multitudes, he went up onto the mountain. When he had sat down, his disciples came to him. ² He opened his mouth and taught them, saying,
³ "Blessed are the poor in spirit,
for theirs is the Kingdom of Heaven.
⁴ Blessed are those who mourn,
for they shall be comforted.
⁵ Blessed are the gentle,
for they shall inherit the earth.
⁶ Blessed are those who hunger and thirst for righteousness,
for they shall be filled.
⁷ Blessed are the merciful,

for they shall obtain mercy.
⁸ Blessed are the pure in heart,
for they shall see God.
⁹ Blessed are the peacemakers,
for they shall be called children of God.
¹⁰ Blessed are those who have been persecuted for righteousness' sake,
for theirs is the Kingdom of Heaven.
¹¹ "Blessed are you when people reproach you, persecute you, and say all kinds of evil against you falsely, for my sake. ¹²ᵃ Rejoice, and be exceedingly glad, for great is your reward in heaven.

1. Invite the Holy Spirit into this reading, asking the Author of Scripture to speak to you through His Word
2. Read today's passage as many times as you need, take your time
3. Write down (below) what the Lord is saying to you today
4. Live with this Word in your heart through the day

Sunday, November 2, 2025
THE COMMEMORATION OF ALL THE FAITHFUL DEPARTED (All Souls' Day)

First Reading: Wisdom 3: 1-9

¹ But the souls of the righteous are in the hand of God,
and no torment will touch them.
² In the eyes of the foolish they seemed to have died.
Their departure was considered a disaster,
³ and their travel away from us ruin,
but they are in peace.
⁴ For even if in the sight of men they are punished,
their hope is full of immortality.
⁵ Having borne a little chastening, they will receive great good;
because God tested them, and found them worthy of himself.
⁶ He tested them like gold in the furnace,
and he accepted them as a whole burnt offering.
⁷ In the time of their visitation they will shine.

They will run back and forth like sparks among stubble.
⁸ They will judge nations and have dominion over peoples.
The Lord will reign over them forever.
⁹ Those who trust him will understand truth.
The faithful will live with him in love,
because grace and mercy are with his chosen ones.

Responsorial Psalm: Psalms 23: 1-3a, 3b-4, 5, 6

¹ Yahweh is my shepherd;
I shall lack nothing.
² He makes me lie down in green pastures.
He leads me beside still waters.
³ He restores my soul.
He guides me in the paths of righteousness for his name's sake.
⁴ Even though I walk through the valley of the shadow of death,
I will fear no evil, for you are with me.
Your rod and your staff,
they comfort me.
⁵ You prepare a table before me
in the presence of my enemies.
You anoint my head with oil.
My cup runs over.
⁶ Surely goodness and loving kindness shall follow me all the days of my life,
and I will dwell in Yahweh's house forever.

Second Reading: Romans 6: 3-9

³ Or don't you know that all of us who were baptized into Christ Jesus were baptized into his death? ⁴ We were buried therefore with him through baptism into death, that just as Christ was raised from the dead through the glory of the Father, so we also might walk in newness of life.
⁵ For if we have become united with him in the likeness of his death, we will also be part of his resurrection; ⁶ knowing this, that our old man was crucified with him, that the body of sin might be done away with, so that we would no longer be in bondage to sin. ⁷ For he who has died has been freed from sin. ⁸ But if we died with Christ, we believe that we will also live with him, ⁹ knowing that Christ, being raised from the dead, dies no more. Death no longer has dominion over him!

Gospel: John 6: 37-40

37 All those whom the Father gives me will come to me. He who comes to me I will in no way throw out. 38 For I have come down from heaven, not to do my own will, but the will of him who sent me. 39 This is the will of my Father who sent me, that of all he has given to me I should lose nothing, but should raise him up at the last day. 40 This is the will of the one who sent me, that everyone who sees the Son and believes in him should have eternal life; and I will raise him up at the last day."

1. Invite the Holy Spirit into this reading, asking the Author of Scripture to speak to you through His Word
2. Read today's passage as many times as you need, take your time
3. Write down (below) what the Lord is saying to you today
4. Live with this Word in your heart through the day

Monday, November 3, 2025
Saint Martin de Porres, Religious

First Reading: Romans 11: 29-36

29 For the gifts and the calling of God are irrevocable. 30 For as you in time past were disobedient to God, but now have obtained mercy by their disobedience, 31 even so these also have now been disobedient, that by the mercy shown to you they may also obtain mercy. 32 For God has bound all to disobedience, that he might have mercy on all.
33 Oh the depth of the riches both of the wisdom and the knowledge of God! How unsearchable are his judgments, and his ways past tracing out!
34 "For who has known the mind of the Lord?
Or who has been his counselor?"*
35 "Or who has first given to him,
and it will be repaid to him again?"*
36 For of him and through him and to him are all things. To him be the glory for ever! Amen.

Responsorial Psalm: Psalms 69: 30-31, 33-34, 36

30 I will praise the name of God with a song,
and will magnify him with thanksgiving.

³¹ It will please Yahweh better than an ox,
or a bull that has horns and hoofs.
³³ For Yahweh hears the needy,
and doesn't despise his captive people.
³⁴ Let heaven and earth praise him;
the seas, and everything that moves therein!
³⁶ The children also of his servants shall inherit it.
Those who love his name shall dwell therein.

Gospel: Luke 14: 12-14

¹² He also said to the one who had invited him, "When you make a dinner or a supper, don't call your friends, nor your brothers, nor your kinsmen, nor rich neighbors, or perhaps they might also return the favor, and pay you back. ¹³ But when you make a feast, ask the poor, the maimed, the lame, or the blind; ¹⁴ and you will be blessed, because they don't have the resources to repay you. For you will be repaid in the resurrection of the righteous."

1. Invite the Holy Spirit into this reading, asking the Author of Scripture to speak to you through His Word
2. Read today's passage as many times as you need, take your time
3. Write down (below) what the Lord is saying to you today
4. Live with this Word in your heart through the day

Tuesday, November 4, 2025
Saint Charles Borromeo, Bishop

First Reading: Romans 12: 5-16ab

⁵ so we, who are many, are one body in Christ, and individually members of one another, ⁶ having gifts differing according to the grace that was given to us: if prophecy, let's prophesy according to the proportion of our faith; ⁷ or service, let's give ourselves to service; or he who teaches, to his teaching; ⁸ or he who exhorts, to his exhorting; he who gives, let him do it with generosity; he who rules, with diligence; he who shows mercy, with cheerfulness.

⁹ Let love be without hypocrisy. Abhor that which is evil. Cling to that which is good. ¹⁰ In love of the brothers be tenderly affectionate to one another; in honor prefer one another, ¹¹ not lagging in diligence, fervent in spirit, serving the Lord, ¹² rejoicing in hope, enduring in troubles, continuing steadfastly in prayer, ¹³ contributing to the needs of the saints, and given to hospitality.

¹⁴ Bless those who persecute you; bless, and don't curse. ¹⁵ Rejoice with those who rejoice. Weep with those who weep. ¹⁶ Be of the same mind one toward another. Don't set your mind on high things, but associate with the humble.

Responsorial Psalm: Psalms 131: 1bcde, 2, 3

¹ Yahweh, my heart isn't arrogant, nor my eyes lofty;
nor do I concern myself with great matters,
or things too wonderful for me.
² Surely I have stilled and quieted my soul,
like a weaned child with his mother,
like a weaned child is my soul within me.
³ Israel, hope in Yahweh,
from this time forward and forever more.

Gospel: Luke 14: 15-24

¹⁵ When one of those who sat at the table with him heard these things, he said to him, "Blessed is he who will feast in God's Kingdom!"
¹⁶ But he said to him, "A certain man made a great supper, and he invited many people. ¹⁷ He sent out his servant at supper time to tell those who were invited, 'Come, for everything is ready now.' ¹⁸ They all as one began to make excuses.
"The first said to him, 'I have bought a field, and I must go and see it. Please have me excused.'
¹⁹ "Another said, 'I have bought five yoke of oxen, and I must go try them out. Please have me excused.'
²⁰ "Another said, 'I have married a wife, and therefore I can't come.'
²¹ "That servant came, and told his lord these things. Then the master of the house, being angry, said to his servant, 'Go out quickly into the streets and lanes of the city, and bring in the poor, maimed, blind, and lame.'
²² "The servant said, 'Lord, it is done as you commanded, and there is still room.'
²³ "The lord said to the servant, 'Go out into the highways and hedges, and compel them to come in, that my house may be filled. ²⁴ For I tell you that none of those men who were invited will taste of my supper. For many are called, but few are chosen.'"

1. Invite the Holy Spirit into this reading, asking the Author of Scripture to speak to you through His Word
2. Read today's passage as many times as you need, take your time
3. Write down (below) what the Lord is saying to you today
4. Live with this Word in your heart through the day

_____

_____

Wednesday, November 5, 2025

First Reading: Romans 13: 8-10

⁸ Owe no one anything, except to love one another; for he who loves his neighbor has fulfilled the law. ⁹ For the commandments, "You shall not commit adultery," "You shall not murder," "You shall not steal," "You shall not covet," and whatever other commandments there are, are all summed up in this saying, namely, "You shall love your neighbor as yourself." ¹⁰ Love doesn't harm a neighbor. Love therefore is the fulfillment of the law.

Responsorial Psalm: Psalms 112: 1b-2, 4-5, 9

¹ᵇ Blessed is the man who fears Yahweh,
who delights greatly in his commandments.
² His offspring will be mighty in the land.
The generation of the upright will be blessed.
⁴ Light dawns in the darkness for the upright,
gracious, merciful, and righteous.
⁵ It is well with the man who deals graciously and lends.
He will maintain his cause in judgment.
⁹ He has dispersed, he has given to the poor.
His righteousness endures forever.
His horn will be exalted with honor.

Gospel: Luke 14: 25-33

²⁵ Now great multitudes were going with him. He turned and said to them, ²⁶ "If anyone comes to me, and doesn't disregard his own father, mother, wife, children, brothers, and

sisters, yes, and his own life also, he can't be my disciple. ²⁷ Whoever doesn't bear his own cross and come after me, can't be my disciple. ²⁸ For which of you, desiring to build a tower, doesn't first sit down and count the cost, to see if he has enough to complete it? ²⁹ Or perhaps, when he has laid a foundation and isn't able to finish, everyone who sees begins to mock him, ³⁰ saying, 'This man began to build and wasn't able to finish.' ³¹ Or what king, as he goes to encounter another king in war, will not sit down first and consider whether he is able with ten thousand to meet him who comes against him with twenty thousand? ³² Or else, while the other is yet a great way off, he sends an envoy and asks for conditions of peace. ³³ So therefore, whoever of you who doesn't renounce all that he has, he can't be my disciple.

1. Invite the Holy Spirit into this reading, asking the Author of Scripture to speak to you through His Word
2. Read today's passage as many times as you need, take your time
3. Write down (below) what the Lord is saying to you today
4. Live with this Word in your heart through the day

_____

_____

Thursday, November 6, 2025

First Reading: Romans 14: 7-12

⁷ For none of us lives to himself, and none dies to himself. ⁸ For if we live, we live to the Lord. Or if we die, we die to the Lord. If therefore we live or die, we are the Lord's. ⁹ For to this end Christ died, rose, and lived again, that he might be Lord of both the dead and the living.
¹⁰ But you, why do you judge your brother? Or you again, why do you despise your brother? For we will all stand before the judgment seat of Christ. ¹¹ For it is written,
" 'As I live,' says the Lord, 'to me every knee will bow.
Every tongue will confess to God.' "
¹² So then each one of us will give account of himself to God.

Responsorial Psalm: Psalms 27: 1bcde, 4, 13-14

¹ Yahweh is my light and my salvation.
Whom shall I fear?

Yahweh is the strength of my life.
Of whom shall I be afraid?
4 One thing I have asked of Yahweh, that I will seek after:
that I may dwell in Yahweh's house all the days of my life,
to see Yahweh's beauty,
and to inquire in his temple.
13 I am still confident of this:
I will see the goodness of Yahweh in the land of the living.
14 Wait for Yahweh.
Be strong, and let your heart take courage.
Yes, wait for Yahweh.

Gospel: Luke 15: 1-10

1 Now all the tax collectors and sinners were coming close to him to hear him. 2 The Pharisees and the scribes murmured, saying, "This man welcomes sinners, and eats with them."

3 He told them this parable: 4 "Which of you men, if you had one hundred sheep and lost one of them, wouldn't leave the ninety-nine in the wilderness and go after the one that was lost, until he found it? 5 When he has found it, he carries it on his shoulders, rejoicing. 6 When he comes home, he calls together his friends and his neighbors, saying to them, 'Rejoice with me, for I have found my sheep which was lost!' 7 I tell you that even so there will be more joy in heaven over one sinner who repents, than over ninety-nine righteous people who need no repentance.

8 "Or what woman, if she had ten drachma coins, if she lost one drachma coin, wouldn't light a lamp, sweep the house, and seek diligently until she found it? 9 When she has found it, she calls together her friends and neighbors, saying, 'Rejoice with me, for I have found the drachma which I had lost!' 10 Even so, I tell you, there is joy in the presence of the angels of God over one sinner repenting."

1. Invite the Holy Spirit into this reading, asking the Author of Scripture to speak to you through His Word
2. Read today's passage as many times as you need, take your time
3. Write down (below) what the Lord is saying to you today
4. Live with this Word in your heart through the day

Friday, November 7, 2025

First Reading: Romans 15: 14-21

¹⁴ I myself am also persuaded about you, my brothers, that you yourselves are full of goodness, filled with all knowledge, able also to admonish others. ¹⁵ But I write the more boldly to you in part as reminding you, because of the grace that was given to me by God, ¹⁶ that I should be a servant of Christ Jesus to the Gentiles, serving as a priest of the Good News of God, that the offering up of the Gentiles might be made acceptable, sanctified by the Holy Spirit. ¹⁷ I have therefore my boasting in Christ Jesus in things pertaining to God. ¹⁸ For I will not dare to speak of any things except those which Christ worked through me for the obedience of the Gentiles, by word and deed, ¹⁹ in the power of signs and wonders, in the power of God's Spirit; so that from Jerusalem and around as far as to Illyricum, I have fully preached the Good News of Christ; ²⁰ yes, making it my aim to preach the Good News, not where Christ was already named, that I might not build on another's foundation. ²¹ But, as it is written,
"They will see, to whom no news of him came.
They who haven't heard will understand."

Responsorial Psalm: Psalms 98: 1, 2-3ab, 3cd-4

¹ Sing to Yahweh a new song,
for he has done marvelous things!
His right hand and his holy arm have worked salvation for him.
² Yahweh has made known his salvation.
He has openly shown his righteousness in the sight of the nations.
³ He has remembered his loving kindness and his faithfulness toward the house of Israel.
All the ends of the earth have seen the salvation of our God.
⁴ Make a joyful noise to Yahweh, all the earth!
Burst out and sing for joy, yes, sing praises!

Gospel: Luke 16: 1-8

¹ He also said to his disciples, "There was a certain rich man who had a manager. An accusation was made to him that this man was wasting his possessions. ² He called him, and said to him, 'What is this that I hear about you? Give an accounting of your management, for you can no longer be manager.'
³ "The manager said within himself, 'What will I do, seeing that my lord is taking away the management position from me? I don't have strength to dig. I am ashamed to beg. ⁴ I know what I will do, so that when I am removed from management, they may receive me into

their houses.' ⁵ Calling each one of his lord's debtors to him, he said to the first, 'How much do you owe to my lord?' ⁶ He said, 'A hundred batos⸸ of oil.' He said to him, 'Take your bill, and sit down quickly and write fifty.' ⁷ Then he said to another, 'How much do you owe?' He said, 'A hundred cors⸸ of wheat.' He said to him, 'Take your bill, and write eighty.' ⁸ "His lord commended the dishonest manager because he had done wisely, for the children of this world are, in their own generation, wiser than the children of the light.

1. Invite the Holy Spirit into this reading, asking the Author of Scripture to speak to you through His Word
2. Read today's passage as many times as you need, take your time
3. Write down (below) what the Lord is saying to you today
4. Live with this Word in your heart through the day

Saturday, November 8, 2025

First Reading: Romans 16: 3-9, 16, 22-24

³ Greet Prisca and Aquila, my fellow workers in Christ Jesus, ⁴ who risked their own necks for my life, to whom not only I give thanks, but also all the assemblies of the Gentiles. ⁵ Greet the assembly that is in their house. Greet Epaenetus, my beloved, who is the first fruits of Achaia to Christ. ⁶ Greet Mary, who labored much for us. ⁷ Greet Andronicus and Junia, my relatives and my fellow prisoners, who are notable among the apostles, who were also in Christ before me. ⁸ Greet Amplias, my beloved in the Lord. ⁹ Greet Urbanus, our fellow worker in Christ, and Stachys, my beloved.
¹⁶ Greet one another with a holy kiss. The assemblies of Christ greet you.
²² I, Tertius, who write the letter, greet you in the Lord. ²³ Gaius, my host and host of the whole assembly, greets you. Erastus, the treasurer of the city, greets you, as does Quartus, the brother. ²⁴ The grace of our Lord Jesus Christ be with you all! Amen.

Responsorial Psalm: Psalms 145: 2-3, 4-5, 10-11

² Every day I will praise you.
I will extol your name forever and ever.
³ Great is Yahweh, and greatly to be praised!
His greatness is unsearchable.

⁴ One generation will commend your works to another,
and will declare your mighty acts.
⁵ I will meditate on the glorious majesty of your honor,
on your wondrous works.
¹⁰ All your works will give thanks to you, Yahweh.
Your saints will extol you.
¹¹ They will speak of the glory of your kingdom,
and talk about your power,

Gospel: Luke 16: 9-15

⁹ I tell you, make for yourselves friends by means of unrighteous mammon, so that when you fail, they may receive you into the eternal tents. ¹⁰ He who is faithful in a very little is faithful also in much. He who is dishonest in a very little is also dishonest in much. ¹¹ If therefore you have not been faithful in the unrighteous mammon, who will commit to your trust the true riches? ¹² If you have not been faithful in that which is another's, who will give you that which is your own? ¹³ No servant can serve two masters, for either he will hate the one and love the other; or else he will hold to one and despise the other. You aren't able to serve God and Mammon."§
¹⁴ The Pharisees, who were lovers of money, also heard all these things, and they scoffed at him. ¹⁵ He said to them, "You are those who justify yourselves in the sight of men, but God knows your hearts. For that which is exalted among men is an abomination in the sight of God.

1. Invite the Holy Spirit into this reading, asking the Author of Scripture to speak to you through His Word
2. Read today's passage as many times as you need, take your time
3. Write down (below) what the Lord is saying to you today
4. Live with this Word in your heart through the day

Sunday, November 9, 2025
THE DEDICATION OF THE LATERAN BASILICA

First Reading: Ezekiel 47: 1-2, 8-9, 12

¹ He brought me back to the door of the temple; and behold, waters flowed out from under the threshold of the temple eastward, for the front of the temple faced toward the east. The waters came down from underneath, from the right side of the temple, on the south of the altar. ² Then he brought me out by the way of the gate northward, and led me around by the way outside to the outer gate, by the way of the gate that looks toward the east. Behold, waters ran out on the right side.

⁸ Then he said to me, "These waters flow out toward the eastern region and will go down into the Arabah. Then they will go toward the sea and flow into the sea which will be made to flow out; and the waters will be healed. ⁹ It will happen that every living creature which swarms, in every place where the rivers come, will live. Then there will be a very great multitude of fish; for these waters have come there, and the waters of the sea will be healed, and everything will live wherever the river comes.

¹² By the river banks, on both sides, will grow every tree for food, whose leaf won't wither, neither will its fruit fail. It will produce new fruit every month, because its waters issue out of the sanctuary. Its fruit will be for food, and its leaf for healing."

Responsorial Psalm: Psalms 46: 2-3, 5-6, 8-9

² Therefore we won't be afraid, though the earth changes,
though the mountains are shaken into the heart of the seas;
³ though its waters roar and are troubled,
though the mountains tremble with their swelling.
⁵ God is within her. She shall not be moved.
God will help her at dawn.
⁶ The nations raged. The kingdoms were moved.
He lifted his voice and the earth melted.
⁸ Come, see Yahweh's works,
what desolations he has made in the earth.
⁹ He makes wars cease to the end of the earth.
He breaks the bow, and shatters the spear.
He burns the chariots in the fire.

Second Reading: First Corinthians 3: 9c-11, 16-17

⁹ᶜ You are God's farming, God's building.
¹⁰ According to the grace of God which was given to me, as a wise master builder I laid a foundation, and another builds on it. But let each man be careful how he builds on it. ¹¹ For no one can lay any other foundation than that which has been laid, which is Jesus Christ.
¹⁶ Don't you know that you are God's temple and that God's Spirit lives in you? ¹⁷ If anyone destroys God's temple, God will destroy him; for God's temple is holy, which you are.

Gospel: John 2: 13-22

13 The Passover of the Jews was at hand, and Jesus went up to Jerusalem. 14 He found in the temple those who sold oxen, sheep, and doves, and the changers of money sitting. 15 He made a whip of cords and drove all out of the temple, both the sheep and the oxen; and he poured out the changers' money and overthrew their tables. 16 To those who sold the doves, he said, "Take these things out of here! Don't make my Father's house a marketplace!" 17 His disciples remembered that it was written, "Zeal for your house will eat me up."

18 The Jews therefore answered him, "What sign do you show us, seeing that you do these things?"

19 Jesus answered them, "Destroy this temple, and in three days I will raise it up."

20 The Jews therefore said, "It took forty-six years to build this temple! Will you raise it up in three days?" 21 But he spoke of the temple of his body. 22 When therefore he was raised from the dead, his disciples remembered that he said this, and they believed the Scripture and the word which Jesus had said.

1. Invite the Holy Spirit into this reading, asking the Author of Scripture to speak to you through His Word
2. Read today's passage as many times as you need, take your time
3. Write down (below) what the Lord is saying to you today
4. Live with this Word in your heart through the day

_____

_____

Monday, November 10, 2025
Saint Leo the Great, Pope and Doctor of the Church

First Reading: Wisdom 1: 1-7

1 Love righteousness, all you who are judges of the earth.
Think of the Lord with a good mind.
Seek him in singleness of heart,
2 because he is found by those who don't put him to the test,
and is manifested to those who trust him.
3 for crooked thoughts separate from God.

His Power convicts when it is tested,
and exposes the foolish;
⁴ because wisdom will not enter into a soul that devises evil,
nor dwell in a body that is enslaved by sin.
⁵ For a holy spirit of discipline will flee deceit,
and will depart from thoughts that are without understanding,
and will be ashamed when unrighteousness has come in.
⁶ For⁺ wisdom is a spirit who loves man,
and she will not hold a§ blasphemer guiltless for his lips,
because God is witness of his inmost self,
and is a true overseer of his heart,
and a hearer of his tongue.
⁷ Because the spirit of the Lord has filled⁺ the world,
and that which holds all things together knows what is said.

Responsorial Psalm: Psalms 139: 1b-3, 4-6, 7-8, 9-10

¹ Yahweh, you have searched me,
and you know me.
² You know my sitting down and my rising up.
You perceive my thoughts from afar.
³ You search out my path and my lying down,
and are acquainted with all my ways.
⁴ For there is not a word on my tongue,
but behold, Yahweh, you know it altogether.
⁵ You hem me in behind and before.
You laid your hand on me.
⁶ This knowledge is beyond me.
It's lofty.
I can't attain it.
⁷ Where could I go from your Spirit?
Or where could I flee from your presence?
⁸ If I ascend up into heaven, you are there.
If I make my bed in Sheol,⁺ behold, you are there!
⁹ If I take the wings of the dawn,
and settle in the uttermost parts of the sea,
¹⁰ even there your hand will lead me,
and your right hand will hold me.

Gospel: Luke 17: 1-6

¹ He said to the disciples, "It is impossible that no occasions of stumbling should come, but woe to him through whom they come! ² It would be better for him if a millstone were hung around his neck, and he were thrown into the sea, rather than that he should cause one of these little ones to stumble. ³ Be careful. If your brother sins against you, rebuke him. If he repents, forgive him. ⁴ If he sins against you seven times in the day, and seven times returns, saying, 'I repent,' you shall forgive him."
⁵ The apostles said to the Lord, "Increase our faith."
⁶ The Lord said, "If you had faith like a grain of mustard seed, you would tell this sycamore tree, 'Be uprooted and be planted in the sea,' and it would obey you.

1. Invite the Holy Spirit into this reading, asking the Author of Scripture to speak to you through His Word
2. Read today's passage as many times as you need, take your time
3. Write down (below) what the Lord is saying to you today
4. Live with this Word in your heart through the day

Tuesday, November 11, 2025
Saint Martin of Tours, Bishop

First Reading: Wisdom 2: 23 – 3: 9

²³ Because God created man for incorruption,
and made him an image of his own everlastingness;
²⁴ but death entered into the world by the envy of the devil,
and those who belong to him experience it.
¹ But the souls of the righteous are in the hand of God,
and no torment will touch them.
² In the eyes of the foolish they seemed to have died.
Their departure was considered a disaster,
³ and their travel away from us ruin,
but they are in peace.
⁴ For even if in the sight of men they are punished,
their hope is full of immortality.
⁵ Having borne a little chastening, they will receive great good;

because God tested them, and found them worthy of himself.
⁶ He tested them like gold in the furnace,
and he accepted them as a whole burnt offering.
⁷ In the time of their visitation they will shine.
They will run back and forth like sparks among stubble.
⁸ They will judge nations and have dominion over peoples.
The Lord will reign over them forever.
⁹ Those who trust him will understand truth.
The faithful will live with him in love,
because grace and mercy are with his chosen ones.

Responsorial Psalm: Psalms 34: 2-3, 16-17, 18-19

² My soul shall boast in Yahweh.
The humble shall hear of it and be glad.
³ Oh magnify Yahweh with me.
Let's exalt his name together.
¹⁶ Yahweh's face is against those who do evil,
to cut off their memory from the earth.
¹⁷ The righteous cry, and Yahweh hears,
and delivers them out of all their troubles.
¹⁸ Yahweh is near to those who have a broken heart,
and saves those who have a crushed spirit.
¹⁹ Many are the afflictions of the righteous,
but Yahweh delivers him out of them all.

Gospel: Luke 17: 7-10

⁷ But who is there among you, having a servant plowing or keeping sheep, that will say when he comes in from the field, 'Come immediately and sit down at the table'? ⁸ Wouldn't he rather tell him, 'Prepare my supper, clothe yourself properly, and serve me while I eat and drink. Afterward you shall eat and drink'? ⁹ Does he thank that servant because he did the things that were commanded? I think not. ¹⁰ Even so you also, when you have done all the things that are commanded you, say, 'We are unworthy servants. We have done our duty.' "

1. Invite the Holy Spirit into this reading, asking the Author of Scripture to speak to you through His Word
2. Read today's passage as many times as you need, take your time
3. Write down (below) what the Lord is saying to you today

4. Live with this Word in your heart through the day

_____

_____

Wednesday, November 12, 2025
Saint Josaphat, Bishop and Martyr

First Reading: Wisdom 6: 1-11

¹ Hear therefore, you kings, and understand.
Learn, you judges of the ends of the earth.
² Give ear, you rulers who have dominion over many people,
and make your boast in multitudes of nations,
³ because your dominion was given to you from the Lord,
and your sovereignty from the Most High.
He will search out your works,
and will inquire about your plans,
⁴ because being officers of his kingdom, you didn't judge rightly,
nor did you keep the law,
nor did you walk according to God's counsel.
⁵ He will come upon you awfully and swiftly,
because a stern judgment comes on those who are in high places.
⁶ For the man of low estate may be pardoned in mercy,
but mighty men will be mightily tested.
⁷ For the Sovereign Lord of all will not be impressed with anyone,
neither will he show deference to greatness;
because it is he who made both small and great,
and cares about them all;
⁸ but the scrutiny that comes upon the powerful is strict.
⁹ Therefore, my words are to you, O princes,
that you may learn wisdom and not fall away.
¹⁰ For those who have kept the things that are holy in holiness will be made holy.
Those who have been taught them will find what to say in defense.
¹¹ Therefore set your desire on my words.
Long for them, and you princes will be instructed.

Responsorial Psalm: Psalms 82: 3-4, 6-7

³ "Defend the weak, the poor, and the fatherless.
Maintain the rights of the poor and oppressed.
⁴ Rescue the weak and needy.
Deliver them out of the hand of the wicked."
⁶ I said, "You are gods,
all of you are sons of the Most High.
⁷ Nevertheless you shall die like men,
and fall like one of the rulers."

Gospel: Luke 17: 11-19

¹¹ As he was on his way to Jerusalem, he was passing along the borders of Samaria and Galilee. ¹² As he entered into a certain village, ten men who were lepers met him, who stood at a distance. ¹³ They lifted up their voices, saying, "Jesus, Master, have mercy on us!" ¹⁴ When he saw them, he said to them, "Go and show yourselves to the priests." As they went, they were cleansed. ¹⁵ One of them, when he saw that he was healed, turned back, glorifying God with a loud voice. ¹⁶ He fell on his face at Jesus' feet, giving him thanks; and he was a Samaritan. ¹⁷ Jesus answered, "Weren't the ten cleansed? But where are the nine? ¹⁸ Were there none found who returned to give glory to God, except this foreigner?" ¹⁹ Then he said to him, "Get up, and go your way. Your faith has healed you."

1. Invite the Holy Spirit into this reading, asking the Author of Scripture to speak to you through His Word
2. Read today's passage as many times as you need, take your time
3. Write down (below) what the Lord is saying to you today
4. Live with this Word in your heart through the day

Thursday, November 13, 2025
Saint Frances Xavier Cabrini, Virgin

First Reading: Wisdom 7: 22b – 8: 1

²²ᵇ For there is in her a spirit that is quick to understand, holy,

unique, manifold, subtle, freely moving, clear in utterance, unpolluted,
distinct, invulnerable, loving what is good, keen, unhindered,
²³ beneficent, loving toward man, steadfast, sure, free from care, all-powerful, all-surveying,
and penetrating through all spirits that are quick to understand, pure, most subtle.
²⁴ For wisdom is more mobile than any motion.
Yes, she pervades and penetrates all things by reason of her purity.
²⁵ For she is a breath of the power of God,
and a pure emanation of the glory of the Almighty.
Therefore nothing defiled can find entrance into her.
²⁶ For she is a reflection of everlasting light,
an unspotted mirror of the working of God,
and an image of his goodness.
²⁷ Although she is one, she has power to do all things.
Remaining in herself, she renews all things.
From generation to generation passing into holy souls,
she makes friends of God and prophets.
²⁸ For God loves nothing as much as one who dwells with wisdom.
²⁹ For she is fairer than the sun,
and above all the constellations of the stars.
She is better than light.
³⁰ For daylight yields to night,
but evil does not prevail against wisdom.
¹ But she reaches from one end to the other with full strength,
and orders all things well.

Responsorial Psalm: Psalms 119: 89, 90, 91, 130, 135, 175

⁸⁹ Yahweh, your word is settled in heaven forever.
⁹⁰ Your faithfulness is to all generations.
You have established the earth, and it remains.
⁹¹ Your laws remain to this day,
for all things serve you.
¹³⁰ The entrance of your words gives light.
It gives understanding to the simple.
¹³⁵ Make your face shine on your servant.
Teach me your statutes.
¹⁷⁵ Let my soul live, that I may praise you.
Let your ordinances help me.

Gospel: Luke 17: 20-25

20 Being asked by the Pharisees when God's Kingdom would come, he answered them, "God's Kingdom doesn't come with observation; 21 neither will they say, 'Look, here!' or, 'Look, there!' for behold, God's Kingdom is within you."
22 He said to the disciples, "The days will come when you will desire to see one of the days of the Son of Man, and you will not see it. 23 They will tell you, 'Look, here!' or 'Look, there!' Don't go away or follow after them, 24 for as the lightning, when it flashes out of one part under the sky, shines to another part under the sky, so will the Son of Man be in his day. 25 But first, he must suffer many things and be rejected by this generation.

1. Invite the Holy Spirit into this reading, asking the Author of Scripture to speak to you through His Word
2. Read today's passage as many times as you need, take your time
3. Write down (below) what the Lord is saying to you today
4. Live with this Word in your heart through the day

_____

_____

Friday, November 14, 2025

First Reading: Wisdom 13: 1-9

1 For truly all men who had no perception of God were foolish by nature,
and didn't gain power to know him who exists from the good things that are seen.
They didn't recognize the architect from his works.
2 But they thought that either fire, or wind, or swift air,
or circling stars, or raging water, or luminaries of heaven
were gods that rule the world.
3 If it was through delight in their beauty that they took them to be gods,
let them know how much better their Sovereign Lord is than these,
for the first author of beauty created them.
4 But if it was through astonishment at their power and influence,
then let them understand from them how much more powerful he who formed them is.
5 For from the greatness of the beauty of created things,
mankind forms the corresponding perception of their Maker.‡
6 But yet for these men there is but small blame,

for they too perhaps go astray
while they are seeking God and desiring to find him.
7 For they diligently search while living among his works,
and they trust their sight that the things that they look at are beautiful.
8 But again even they are not to be excused.
9 For if they had power to know so much,
that they should be able to explore the world,
how is it that they didn't find the Sovereign Lord sooner?

Responsorial Psalm: Psalms 19: 2-3, 4-5ab

2 Day after day they pour out speech,
and night after night they display knowledge.
3 There is no speech nor language
where their voice is not heard.
4 Their voice has gone out through all the earth,
their words to the end of the world.
In them he has set a tent for the sun,
5 which is as a bridegroom coming out of his room,
like a strong man rejoicing to run his course.

Gospel: Luke 17: 26-37

26 As it was in the days of Noah, even so it will also be in the days of the Son of Man. 27 They ate, they drank, they married, and they were given in marriage until the day that Noah entered into the ship, and the flood came and destroyed them all. 28 Likewise, even as it was in the days of Lot: they ate, they drank, they bought, they sold, they planted, they built; 29 but in the day that Lot went out from Sodom, it rained fire and sulfur from the sky and destroyed them all. 30 It will be the same way in the day that the Son of Man is revealed. 31 In that day, he who will be on the housetop and his goods in the house, let him not go down to take them away. Let him who is in the field likewise not turn back. 32 Remember Lot's wife! 33 Whoever seeks to save his life loses it, but whoever loses his life preserves it. 34 I tell you, in that night there will be two people in one bed. One will be taken and the other will be left. 35 There will be two grinding grain together. One will be taken and the other will be left." 36 ‡
37 They, answering, asked him, "Where, Lord?"
He said to them, "Where the body is, there the vultures will also be gathered together."

1. Invite the Holy Spirit into this reading, asking the Author of Scripture to speak to you through His Word

2. Read today's passage as many times as you need, take your time
3. Write down (below) what the Lord is saying to you today
4. Live with this Word in your heart through the day

Saturday, November 15, 2025
Saint Albert the Great, Bishop and Doctor of the Church

First Reading: Wisdom 18: 14-16; 19: 6-9

¹⁴ For while peaceful silence wrapped all things,
and night in her own swiftness was half spent,
¹⁵ your all-powerful word leaped from heaven, from the royal throne,
a stern warrior, into the midst of the doomed land,
¹⁶ bearing as a sharp sword your authentic commandment,
and standing, it filled all things with death,
and while it touched the heaven it stood upon the earth.
⁶ For the whole creation, each part in its diverse kind, was made new again,
complying with your commandments,
that your servants might be kept unharmed.
⁷ Then the cloud that overshadowed the camp was seen,
and dry land rising up out of what had been water,
out of the Red sea an unhindered highway,
and a grassy plain out of the violent surge,
⁸ by which they passed over with all their army,
these who were covered with your hand,
having seen strange marvels.
⁹ For like horses they roamed at large,
and they skipped about like lambs,
praising you, O Lord, who was their deliverer.

Responsorial Psalm: Psalms 105: 2-3, 36-37, 42-43

² Sing to him, sing praises to him!
Tell of all his marvelous works.
³ Glory in his holy name.

Let the heart of those who seek Yahweh rejoice.
36 He struck also all the firstborn in their land,
the first fruits of all their manhood.
37 He brought them out with silver and gold.
There was not one feeble person among his tribes.
42 For he remembered his holy word,
and Abraham, his servant.
43 He brought his people out with joy,
his chosen with singing.

Gospel: Luke 18: 1-8

1 He also spoke a parable to them that they must always pray and not give up, 2 saying, "There was a judge in a certain city who didn't fear God and didn't respect man. 3 A widow was in that city, and she often came to him, saying, 'Defend me from my adversary!' 4 He wouldn't for a while; but afterward he said to himself, 'Though I neither fear God nor respect man, 5 yet because this widow bothers me, I will defend her, or else she will wear me out by her continual coming.' "
6 The Lord said, "Listen to what the unrighteous judge says. 7 Won't God avenge his chosen ones who are crying out to him day and night, and yet he exercises patience with them? 8 I tell you that he will avenge them quickly. Nevertheless, when the Son of Man comes, will he find faith on the earth?"

1. Invite the Holy Spirit into this reading, asking the Author of Scripture to speak to you through His Word
2. Read today's passage as many times as you need, take your time
3. Write down (below) what the Lord is saying to you today
4. Live with this Word in your heart through the day

Sunday, November 16, 2025
THIRTY-THIRD SUNDAY IN ORDINARY TIME

First Reading: Malachi 4: 1-2a

¹ "For behold, the day comes, burning like a furnace, when all the proud and all who work wickedness will be stubble. The day that comes will burn them up," says Yahweh of Armies, "so that it will leave them neither root nor branch. ² But to you who fear my name shall the sun of righteousness arise with healing in its wings.

Responsorial Psalm: Psalms 98: 5-6, 7-8, 9

⁵ Sing praises to Yahweh with the harp,
with the harp and the voice of melody.
⁶ With trumpets and sound of the ram's horn,
make a joyful noise before the King, Yahweh.
⁷ Let the sea roar with its fullness;
the world, and those who dwell therein.
⁸ Let the rivers clap their hands.
Let the mountains sing for joy together.
⁹ Let them sing before Yahweh,
for he comes to judge the earth.
He will judge the world with righteousness,
and the peoples with equity.

Second Reading: Second Thessalonians 3: 7-12

⁷ For you know how you ought to imitate us. For we didn't behave ourselves rebelliously among you, ⁸ neither did we eat bread from anyone's hand without paying for it, but in labor and travail worked night and day, that we might not burden any of you. ⁹ This was not because we don't have the right, but to make ourselves an example to you, that you should imitate us. ¹⁰ For even when we were with you, we commanded you this: "If anyone is not willing to work, don't let him eat." ¹¹ For we hear of some who walk among you in rebellion, who don't work at all, but are busybodies. ¹² Now those who are that way, we command and exhort in the Lord Jesus Christ, that they work with quietness and eat their own bread.

Gospel: Luke 21: 5-19

⁵ As some were talking about the temple and how it was decorated with beautiful stones and gifts, he said, ⁶ "As for these things which you see, the days will come in which there will not be left here one stone on another that will not be thrown down."
⁷ They asked him, "Teacher, so when will these things be? What is the sign that these things are about to happen?"

⁸ He said, "Watch out that you don't get led astray, for many will come in my name, saying, 'I am he‡,' and, 'The time is at hand.' Therefore don't follow them. ⁹ When you hear of wars and disturbances, don't be terrified, for these things must happen first, but the end won't come immediately."

¹⁰ Then he said to them, "Nation will rise against nation, and kingdom against kingdom. ¹¹ There will be great earthquakes, famines, and plagues in various places. There will be terrors and great signs from heaven. ¹² But before all these things, they will lay their hands on you and will persecute you, delivering you up to synagogues and prisons, bringing you before kings and governors for my name's sake. ¹³ It will turn out as a testimony for you. ¹⁴ Settle it therefore in your hearts not to meditate beforehand how to answer, ¹⁵ for I will give you a mouth and wisdom which all your adversaries will not be able to withstand or to contradict. ¹⁶ You will be handed over even by parents, brothers, relatives, and friends. They will cause some of you to be put to death. ¹⁷ You will be hated by all men for my name's sake. ¹⁸ And not a hair of your head will perish.

¹⁹ "By your endurance you will win your lives.

1. Invite the Holy Spirit into this reading, asking the Author of Scripture to speak to you through His Word
2. Read today's passage as many times as you need, take your time
3. Write down (below) what the Lord is saying to you today
4. Live with this Word in your heart through the day

_____

_____

Monday, November 17, 2025
Saint Elizabeth of Hungary, Religious

First Reading: First Maccabees 1: 10-15, 41-43, 54-57, 62-63

¹⁰ There came out of them a sinful root, Antiochus Epiphanes, son of Antiochus the king, who had been a hostage at Rome, and he reigned in‡ the one hundred thirty seventh year of the kingdom of the Greeks.

¹¹ In those days transgressors of the law came out of Israel and persuaded many, saying, "Let's go make a covenant with the§ Gentiles around us; for since we were separated from them many evils have befallen us." ¹² That proposal was good in their eyes. ¹³ Some of the people eagerly went to the king, and he authorized them to observe the ordinances of the‡ Gentiles. ¹⁴ So‡ they built a gymnasium in Jerusalem according to the laws of

the§ Gentiles. ¹⁵ They made themselves uncircumcised, forsook the holy covenant, joined themselves to the⁺ Gentiles, and sold themselves to do evil.
⁴¹ King Antiochus wrote to his whole kingdom that all should be one people, ⁴² and that each should forsake his own laws. All the nations agreed according to the word of the king. ⁴³ Many of Israel consented to his worship, sacrificed to the idols, and profaned the Sabbath.
⁵⁴ On the fifteenth day of Chislev, in§ the one hundred forty fifth year, they built an abomination of desolation upon the altar,⁺ and in the cities of Judah on every side they built idol altars.⁺ ⁵⁵ At the doors of the houses and in the streets they burned incense. ⁵⁶ They tore the books of the law which they found in pieces and set them on fire. ⁵⁷ Anyone who was found with any a book of the covenant, and if any consented to the law, the king's sentence delivered him to death.
⁶² Many in Israel were fully resolved and confirmed in themselves not to eat unclean things. ⁶³ ⁺They chose to die, that they might not be defiled with the food, and that they might not profane the holy covenant; and they died.

Responsorial Psalm: Psalms 119: 53, 61, 134, 150, 155, 158

⁵³ Indignation has taken hold on me,
because of the wicked who forsake your law.
⁶¹ The ropes of the wicked bind me,
but I won't forget your law.
¹³⁴ Redeem me from the oppression of man,
so I will observe your precepts.
¹⁵⁰ They draw near who follow after wickedness.
They are far from your law.
¹⁵⁵ Salvation is far from the wicked,
for they don't seek your statutes.
¹⁵⁸ I look at the faithless with loathing,
because they don't observe your word.

Gospel: Luke 18: 35-43

³⁵ As he came near Jericho, a certain blind man sat by the road, begging. ³⁶ Hearing a multitude going by, he asked what this meant. ³⁷ They told him that Jesus of Nazareth was passing by. ³⁸ He cried out, "Jesus, you son of David, have mercy on me!" ³⁹ Those who led the way rebuked him, that he should be quiet; but he cried out all the more, "You son of David, have mercy on me!"
⁴⁰ Standing still, Jesus commanded him to be brought to him. When he had come near, he asked him, ⁴¹ "What do you want me to do?"

He said, "Lord, that I may see again."
⁴² Jesus said to him, "Receive your sight. Your faith has healed you."
⁴³ Immediately he received his sight and followed him, glorifying God. All the people, when they saw it, praised God.

1. Invite the Holy Spirit into this reading, asking the Author of Scripture to speak to you through His Word
2. Read today's passage as many times as you need, take your time
3. Write down (below) what the Lord is saying to you today
4. Live with this Word in your heart through the day

Tuesday, November 18, 2025
The Dedication of the Basilicas of Saints Peter and Paul, Apostles;
Saint Rose Philippine Duchesne, Virgin

First Reading: Second Maccabees 6: 18-31

¹⁸ Eleazar, one of the principal scribes, a man already well advanced in years, and of a noble countenance, was compelled to open his mouth to eat swine's flesh. ¹⁹ But he, welcoming death with honor rather than life with defilement, advanced of his own accord to the instrument of torture, but first spat out the flesh, ²⁰ as men ought to come who are resolute to repel such things as not even for the natural love of life is it lawful to taste.
²¹ But those who had the charge of that forbidden sacrificial feast took the man aside, for the acquaintance which of old times they had with him, and privately implored him to bring flesh of his own providing, such as was proper for him to use, and to make as if he did eat of the flesh from the sacrifice, as had been commanded by the king; ²² that by so doing he might be delivered from death, and so his ancient friendship with them might be treated kindly. ²³ But he, having formed a high resolve, and one that became his years, the dignity of old age, and the gray hairs‡ which he had reached with honor, and his excellent§ education from a child, or rather the holy laws‡ of God's ordaining, declared his mind accordingly, bidding them to quickly send him to Hades.
²⁴ "For it doesn't become our years to dissemble," he said, "that many of the young should suppose that Eleazar, the man of ninety years, had gone over to an alien religion; ²⁵ and so they, by reason of my deception, and for the sake of this brief and momentary life, would be led astray because of me, and I defile and disgrace myself in my old age. ²⁶ For even if

for the present time I would remove from me the punishment of men, yet whether I live or die, I wouldn't escape the hands of the Almighty. ²⁷ Therefore, by bravely parting with my life now, I will show myself worthy of my old age, ²⁸ and ‡leave behind a noble example to the young to die willingly and nobly a glorious death for the revered and holy laws."
When he had said these words, he went immediately to the instrument of torture. ²⁹ § When they changed the good will they bore toward him a little before into ill will because these words of his were, as they thought, sheer madness, ³⁰ and when he was at the point to die with the‡ blows, he groaned aloud and said, "To the Lord, who has the holy knowledge, it is manifest that, while I might have been delivered from death, I endure severe pains in my body by being scourged; but in soul I gladly suffer these things because of my fear of him."
³¹ So this man also died like this, leaving his death for an example of nobleness and a memorial of virtue, not only to the young but also to the great body of his nation.

Responsorial Psalm: Psalms 3: 2-3, 4-5, 6-7

² Many there are who say of my soul,
"There is no help for him in God."‡
³ But you, Yahweh, are a shield around me,
my glory, and the one who lifts up my head.
⁴ I cry to Yahweh with my voice,
and he answers me out of his holy hill.
⁵ I laid myself down and slept.
I awakened, for Yahweh sustains me.
⁶ I will not be afraid of tens of thousands of people
who have set themselves against me on every side.
⁷ Arise, Yahweh!
Save me, my God!
For you have struck all of my enemies on the cheek bone.
You have broken the teeth of the wicked.

Gospel: Luke 19: 1-10

¹ He entered and was passing through Jericho. ² There was a man named Zacchaeus. He was a chief tax collector, and he was rich. ³ He was trying to see who Jesus was, and couldn't because of the crowd, because he was short. ⁴ He ran on ahead and climbed up into a sycamore tree to see him, for he was going to pass that way. ⁵ When Jesus came to the place, he looked up and saw him, and said to him, "Zacchaeus, hurry and come down, for today I must stay at your house." ⁶ He hurried, came down, and received him joyfully. ⁷ When they saw it, they all murmured, saying, "He has gone in to lodge with a man who is a sinner."

⁸ Zacchaeus stood and said to the Lord, "Behold, Lord, half of my goods I give to the poor. If I have wrongfully exacted anything of anyone, I restore four times as much."
⁹ Jesus said to him, "Today, salvation has come to this house, because he also is a son of Abraham. ¹⁰ For the Son of Man came to seek and to save that which was lost."

1. Invite the Holy Spirit into this reading, asking the Author of Scripture to speak to you through His Word
2. Read today's passage as many times as you need, take your time
3. Write down (below) what the Lord is saying to you today
4. Live with this Word in your heart through the day

Wednesday, November 19, 2025

First Reading: Second Maccabees 7: 1, 20-31

¹ It came to pass that seven brothers and their mother were at the king's command taken and shamefully handled with scourges and cords, to compel them to taste of the abominable swine's flesh.
²⁰ But above all, the mother was marvelous and worthy of honorable memory; for when she watched seven sons perishing within the space of one day, she bore the sight with a good courage because of her hope in the Lord. ²¹ She exhorted each one of them in the language of their fathers, filled with a noble spirit and stirring up her woman's thoughts with manly courage, saying to them, ²² "I don't know how you came into my womb. It wasn't I who gave you your ‡spirit and your life. It wasn't I who brought into order the first elements of each one of you. ²³ Therefore the Creator of the world, who shaped the first origin of man and devised the first origin of all things, in mercy gives back to you again both your §spirit and your life, as you now treat yourselves with contempt for his laws' sake."
²⁴ But Antiochus, thinking himself to be despised, and suspecting the reproachful voice, while the youngest was yet alive didn't only make his appeal to him by words, but also at the same time promised with oaths that he would enrich him and‡ raise him to high honor if he would turn from the ways of his ancestors, and that he would take him for his ‡friend and entrust him with public affairs. ²⁵ But when the young man would in no way listen, the king called to him his mother, and urged her to advise the youth to save himself. ²⁶ When he had urged her with many words, she undertook to persuade her son. ²⁷ But bending toward him, laughing the cruel tyrant to scorn, she spoke this in the language of her fathers:

"My son, have pity upon me who carried you nine months in my womb, and nursed you three years, and nourished and brought you up to this age, and sustained you. ²⁸ I beg you, my child, to lift your eyes to the sky and the earth, and to see all things that are in it, and thus to recognize that God made them not of things that were, and that the race of men in this way comes into being. ²⁹ Don't be afraid of this butcher, but, proving yourself worthy of your brothers, accept your death, that in God's mercy I may receive you again with your brothers."

³⁰ But before she had finished speaking, the young man said, "What are you all waiting for? I don't obey the commandment of the king, but I listen to the commandment of the law that was given to our fathers through Moses. ³¹ But you, who have devised all kinds of evil against the Hebrews, will in no way escape God's hands.

Responsorial Psalm: Psalms 17: 1bcd, 5-6, 8b and 15

¹ Hear, Yahweh, my righteous plea.
Give ear to my prayer that doesn't go out of deceitful lips.
⁵ My steps have held fast to your paths.
My feet have not slipped.
⁶ I have called on you, for you will answer me, God.
Turn your ear to me.
Hear my speech.
⁸ Keep me as the apple of your eye.
Hide me under the shadow of your wings,
¹⁵ As for me, I shall see your face in righteousness.
I shall be satisfied, when I awake, with seeing your form.

Gospel: Luke 19: 11-28

¹¹ As they heard these things, he went on and told a parable, because he was near Jerusalem, and they supposed that God's Kingdom would be revealed immediately. ¹² He said therefore, "A certain nobleman went into a far country to receive for himself a kingdom and to return. ¹³ He called ten servants of his and gave them ten mina coins, and told them, 'Conduct business until I come.' ¹⁴ But his citizens hated him, and sent an envoy after him, saying, 'We don't want this man to reign over us.'

¹⁵ "When he had come back again, having received the kingdom, he commanded these servants, to whom he had given the money, to be called to him, that he might know what they had gained by conducting business. ¹⁶ The first came before him, saying, 'Lord, your mina has made ten more minas.'

¹⁷ "He said to him, 'Well done, you good servant! Because you were found faithful with very little, you shall have authority over ten cities.'

¹⁸ "The second came, saying, 'Your mina, Lord, has made five minas.'
¹⁹ "So he said to him, 'And you are to be over five cities.'
²⁰ Another came, saying, 'Lord, behold, your mina, which I kept laid away in a handkerchief, ²¹ for I feared you, because you are an exacting man. You take up that which you didn't lay down, and reap that which you didn't sow.'
²² "He said to him, 'Out of your own mouth I will judge you, you wicked servant! You knew that I am an exacting man, taking up that which I didn't lay down and reaping that which I didn't sow. ²³ Then why didn't you deposit my money in the bank, and at my coming, I might have earned interest on it?' ²⁴ He said to those who stood by, 'Take the mina away from him and give it to him who has the ten minas.'
²⁵ "They said to him, 'Lord, he has ten minas!' ²⁶ 'For I tell you that to everyone who has, will more be given; but from him who doesn't have, even that which he has will be taken away from him. ²⁷ But bring those enemies of mine who didn't want me to reign over them here, and kill them before me.' " ²⁸ Having said these things, he went on ahead, going up to Jerusalem.

1. Invite the Holy Spirit into this reading, asking the Author of Scripture to speak to you through His Word
2. Read today's passage as many times as you need, take your time
3. Write down (below) what the Lord is saying to you today
4. Live with this Word in your heart through the day

Thursday, November 20, 2025

First Reading: First Maccabees 2: 15-29

¹⁵ And the king's officers who were enforcing the apostasy came into the city Modin to sacrifice. ¹⁶ Many of Israel came to them, and Mattathias and his sons were gathered together. ¹⁷ The king's officers answered and spoke to Mattathias, saying, "You are a ruler and an honorable and great man in this city, and strengthened with sons and kindred. ¹⁸ Now therefore come first and do the commandment of the king, as all the nations have done, including the men of Judah and those who remain in Jerusalem. You and your house will be numbered among the king's‡ friends, and you and your sons will be honored with silver and gold and many gifts."

¹⁹ And Mattathias answered and said with a loud voice, "If all the nations that are in the house of the king's dominion listen to him, to fall away each one from the worship of his fathers, and have made choice to follow his commandments, ²⁰ yet I and my sons and my kindred will walk in the covenant of our fathers. ²¹ Far be it from us that we should forsake the law and the ordinances. ²² We will not listen to the king's words, to turn aside from our worship, to the right hand, or to the left."

²³ When he had finished speaking these words, a Jew came in the sight of all to sacrifice on the altar which was at Modin, according to the king's commandment. ²⁴ Mattathias saw it, so his zeal was kindled, and his guts trembled, and he vented his wrath according to judgment, and ran and killed him upon the altar. ²⁵ He killed the king's officer, who compelled men to sacrifice, at the same time, and pulled down the altar. ²⁶ He was zealous for the law, even as Phinehas did to Zimri the son of Salu.

²⁷ Mattathias cried out in the city with a loud voice, saying, "Whoever is zealous for the law and maintains the covenant, let him follow me!" ²⁸ He and his sons fled into the mountains, and left all that they had in the city.

²⁹ Then many who sought justice and judgment went down into the wilderness to live there

Responsorial Psalm: Psalms 50: 1b-2, 5-6, 14-15

¹ The Mighty One, God, Yahweh, speaks,
and calls the earth from sunrise to sunset.
² Out of Zion, the perfection of beauty,
God shines out.
⁵ "Gather my saints together to me,
those who have made a covenant with me by sacrifice."
⁶ The heavens shall declare his righteousness,
for God himself is judge.
¹⁴ Offer to God the sacrifice of thanksgiving.
Pay your vows to the Most High.
¹⁵ Call on me in the day of trouble.
I will deliver you, and you will honor me."

Gospel: Luke 19: 41-44

⁴¹ When he came near, he saw the city and wept over it, ⁴² saying, "If you, even you, had known today the things which belong to your peace! But now, they are hidden from your eyes. ⁴³ For the days will come on you when your enemies will throw up a barricade against you, surround you, hem you in on every side, ⁴⁴ and will dash you and your children within you to the ground. They will not leave in you one stone on another, because you didn't know the time of your visitation."

1. Invite the Holy Spirit into this reading, asking the Author of Scripture to speak to you through His Word
2. Read today's passage as many times as you need, take your time
3. Write down (below) what the Lord is saying to you today
4. Live with this Word in your heart through the day

___

___

Friday, November 21, 2025
The Presentation of the Blessed Virgin Mary

First Reading: First Maccabees 4: 36-37, 52-59

36 But Judas and his kindred said, "Behold, our enemies are defeated. Let's go up to cleanse the holy place and to rededicate it." 37 All the army was gathered together, and they went up to mount Zion.
52 They rose up early in the morning, on the twenty-fifth day of the ninth month, which is the month Chislev, in§ the one hundred forty eighth year, 53 and offered sacrifice according to the law on the new altar of burnt offerings which they had made. 54 At the time and day the Gentiles had profaned it, even then it was dedicated with songs, harps, lutes, and with cymbals. 55 All the people fell on their faces, worshiped, and gave praise toward heaven, which had given them good success. 56 They celebrated the dedication of the altar eight days, and offered burnt offerings with gladness, and sacrificed a sacrifice of deliverance and praise. 57 They decorated the front of the temple with crowns of gold and small shields. They dedicated the gates and the priests' chambers, and made doors for them. 58 There was exceedingly great gladness among the people, and the reproach of the Gentiles was turned away.
59 Judas and his kindred and the whole congregation of Israel ordained that the days of the dedication of the altar should be kept in their seasons from year to year for eight days, from the twenty-fifth day of the month Chislev, with gladness and joy.

Responsorial Psalm: First Chronicles 29: 10bcd, 11abc, 11d-12a, 12bcd

10 Therefore David blessed Yahweh before all the assembly; and David said, "You are blessed, Yahweh, the God of Israel our father, forever and ever. 11 Yours, Yahweh, is the greatness, the power, the glory, the victory, and the majesty! For all that is in the heavens

and in the earth is yours. Yours is the kingdom, Yahweh, and you are exalted as head above all. ¹² Both riches and honor come from you, and you rule over all! In your hand is power and might! It is in your hand to make great, and to give strength to all!

Gospel: Luke 19: 45-48

⁴⁵ He entered into the temple and began to drive out those who bought and sold in it, ⁴⁶ saying to them, "It is written, 'My house is a house of prayer,' ⁎ but you have made it a 'den of robbers'!" ⁎

⁴⁷ He was teaching daily in the temple, but the chief priests, the scribes, and the leading men among the people sought to destroy him. ⁴⁸ They couldn't find what they might do, for all the people hung on to every word that he said.

1. Invite the Holy Spirit into this reading, asking the Author of Scripture to speak to you through His Word
2. Read today's passage as many times as you need, take your time
3. Write down (below) what the Lord is saying to you today
4. Live with this Word in your heart through the day

_____

_____

Saturday, November 22, 2025
Saint Cecilia, Virgin and Martyr

First Reading: First Maccabees 6: 1-13

¹ King Antiochus was traveling through the upper countries; and he heard that in Elymais in Persia there was a city renowned for riches, for silver and gold, ² and that the temple which was in it was exceedingly rich, and that in it were golden shields, breastplates, and weapons which Alexander, son of Philip, the Macedonian king, who reigned first among the Greeks, left behind there. ³ So he came and tried to take the city and to pillage it; and he was not able, because his plan was known to them of the city, ⁴ and they rose up against him in battle. He fled and returned to Babylon with great disappointment.
⁵ Then someone came into Persia bringing him news that the armies which went against the land of Judah had been put to flight, ⁶ and that Lysias went first with a strong army and was put to shame before them, and that they had grown strong because of weapons, power, and a supply of plunder which they took from the armies that they had cut off, ⁷ and that

they had pulled down the abomination which he had built upon the altar that was in Jerusalem, and that they had surrounded the sanctuary with high walls, as before, and also Bethsura, his city.

⁸ It came to pass, when the king heard these words, he was astonished and moved exceedingly. He laid himself down on his bed, and fell sick for grief, because it had not turned out for him as he had planned. ⁹ He was there many days, because great grief continually gripped him, and he realized that he would die. ¹⁰ He called for all his friends, and said to them, "Sleep departs from my eyes, and my heart fails because of worry. ¹¹ I said in my heart, 'To what suffering I have come! How great a flood it is that I'm in, now! For I was gracious and loved in my power.' ¹² But now I remember the evils which I did at Jerusalem, and that I took all the vessels of silver and gold that were in it, and sent out to destroy the inhabitants of Judah without a cause. ¹³ I perceive that it is because of this that these evils have come upon me. Behold, I am perishing through great grief in a strange land."

Responsorial Psalm: Psalms 9: 2-3, 4 and 6, 16 and 19

² I will be glad and rejoice in you.
I will sing praise to your name, O Most High.
³ When my enemies turn back,
they stumble and perish in your presence.
⁴ For you have maintained my just cause.
You sit on the throne judging righteously.
⁶ The enemy is overtaken by endless ruin.
The very memory of the cities which you have overthrown has perished.
¹⁶ Yahweh has made himself known.
He has executed judgment.
The wicked is snared by the work of his own hands.
¹⁹ Arise, Yahweh! Don't let man prevail.
Let the nations be judged in your sight.

Gospel: Luke 20: 27-40

²⁷ Some of the Sadducees came to him, those who deny that there is a resurrection. ²⁸ They asked him, "Teacher, Moses wrote to us that if a man's brother dies having a wife, and he is childless, his brother should take the wife and raise up children for his brother. ²⁹ There were therefore seven brothers. The first took a wife, and died childless. ³⁰ The second took her as wife, and he died childless. ³¹ The third took her, and likewise the seven all left no children, and died. ³² Afterward the woman also died. ³³ Therefore in the resurrection whose wife of them will she be? For the seven had her as a wife."

34 Jesus said to them, "The children of this age marry and are given in marriage. 35 But those who are considered worthy to attain to that age and the resurrection from the dead neither marry nor are given in marriage. 36 For they can't die any more, for they are like the angels and are children of God, being children of the resurrection. 37 But that the dead are raised, even Moses showed at the bush, when he called the Lord 'The God of Abraham, the God of Isaac, and the God of Jacob.' 38 Now he is not the God of the dead, but of the living, for all are alive to him."
39 Some of the scribes answered, "Teacher, you speak well." 40 They didn't dare to ask him any more questions.

1. Invite the Holy Spirit into this reading, asking the Author of Scripture to speak to you through His Word
2. Read today's passage as many times as you need, take your time
3. Write down (below) what the Lord is saying to you today
4. Live with this Word in your heart through the day

_____

_____

Sunday, November 23, 2025
OUR LORD JESUS CHRIST, KING OF THE UNIVERSE

First Reading: Second Samuel 5: 1-3

1 Then all the tribes of Israel came to David at Hebron and spoke, saying, "Behold, we are your bone and your flesh. 2 In times past, when Saul was king over us, it was you who led Israel out and in. Yahweh said to you, 'You will be shepherd of my people Israel, and you will be prince over Israel.' " 3 So all the elders of Israel came to the king to Hebron, and King David made a covenant with them in Hebron before Yahweh; and they anointed David king over Israel.

Responsorial Psalm: Psalms 122: 1-2, 3-4ab, 4cd-5

1 I was glad when they said to me,
"Let's go to Yahweh's house!"
2 Our feet are standing within your gates, Jerusalem!
3 Jerusalem is built as a city that is compact together,
4 where the tribes go up, even Yah's tribes,

according to an ordinance for Israel,
to give thanks to Yahweh's name.
⁵ For there are set thrones for judgment,
the thrones of David's house.

Second Reading: Colossians 1: 12-20

¹² giving thanks to the Father, who made us fit to be partakers of the inheritance of the saints in light, ¹³ who delivered us out of the power of darkness, and translated us into the Kingdom of the Son of his love, ¹⁴ in whom we have our redemption, the forgiveness of our sins.
¹⁵ He is the image of the invisible God, the firstborn of all creation. ¹⁶ For by him all things were created in the heavens and on the earth, visible things and invisible things, whether thrones or dominions or principalities or powers. All things have been created through him and for him. ¹⁷ He is before all things, and in him all things are held together. ¹⁸ He is the head of the body, the assembly, who is the beginning, the firstborn from the dead, that in all things he might have the preeminence. ¹⁹ For all the fullness was pleased to dwell in him, ²⁰ and through him to reconcile all things to himself by him, whether things on the earth or things in the heavens, having made peace through the blood of his cross.

Gospel: Luke 23: 35-43

³⁵ The people stood watching. The rulers with them also scoffed at him, saying, "He saved others. Let him save himself, if this is the Christ of God, his chosen one!"
³⁶ The soldiers also mocked him, coming to him and offering him vinegar, ³⁷ and saying, "If you are the King of the Jews, save yourself!"
³⁸ An inscription was also written over him in letters of Greek, Latin, and Hebrew: "THIS IS THE KING OF THE JEWS."
³⁹ One of the criminals who was hanged insulted him, saying, "If you are the Christ, save yourself and us!"
⁴⁰ But the other answered, and rebuking him said, "Don't you even fear God, seeing you are under the same condemnation? ⁴¹ And we indeed justly, for we receive the due reward for our deeds, but this man has done nothing wrong." ⁴² He said to Jesus, "Lord, remember me when you come into your Kingdom."
⁴³ Jesus said to him, "Assuredly I tell you, today you will be with me in Paradise."

1. Invite the Holy Spirit into this reading, asking the Author of Scripture to speak to you through His Word
2. Read today's passage as many times as you need, take your time
3. Write down (below) what the Lord is saying to you today

4. Live with this Word in your heart through the day

Monday, November 24, 2025
Saint Andrew Dũng-Lạc, Priest, and Companions, Martyrs

First Reading: Daniel 1: 1-6, 8-20

¹ In the third year of the reign of Jehoiakim king of Judah, Nebuchadnezzar king of Babylon came to Jerusalem and besieged it. ² The Lord‡ gave Jehoiakim king of Judah into his hand, with some of the vessels of the house of God;‡ and he carried them into the land of Shinar to the house of his god. He brought the vessels into the treasure house of his god.
³ The king spoke to Ashpenaz, the master of his eunuchs, that he should bring in some of the children of Israel, even of the royal offspring§ and of the nobles: ⁴ youths in whom was no defect, but well-favored, skillful in all wisdom, endowed with knowledge, understanding science, and who had the ability to stand in the king's palace; and that he should teach them the learning and the language of the Chaldeans. ⁵ The king appointed for them a daily portion of the king's delicacies and of the wine which he drank, and that they should be nourished three years, that at its end they should stand before the king.
⁶ Now among these of the children of Judah were Daniel, Hananiah, Mishael, and Azariah.
⁸ But Daniel purposed in his heart that he would not defile himself with the king's delicacies, nor with the wine which he drank. Therefore he requested of the prince of the eunuchs that he might not defile himself. ⁹ Now God made Daniel find kindness and compassion in the sight of the prince of the eunuchs. ¹⁰ The prince of the eunuchs said to Daniel, "I fear my lord the king, who has appointed your food and your drink. For why should he see your faces worse looking than the youths who are of your own age? Then you would endanger my head with the king."
¹¹ Then Daniel said to the steward whom the prince of the eunuchs had appointed over Daniel, Hananiah, Mishael, and Azariah: ¹² "Test your servants, I beg you, ten days; and let them give us vegetables to eat and water to drink. ¹³ Then let our faces be examined before you, and the face of the youths who eat of the king's delicacies; and as you see, deal with your servants." ¹⁴ So he listened to them in this matter, and tested them for ten days.
¹⁵ At the end of ten days, their faces appeared fairer and they were fatter in flesh than all the youths who ate of the king's delicacies. ¹⁶ So the steward took away their delicacies and the wine that they were given to drink, and gave them vegetables.

¹⁷ Now as for these four youths, God gave them knowledge and skill in all learning and wisdom; and Daniel had understanding in all visions and dreams.
¹⁸ At the end of the days which the king had appointed for bringing them in, the prince of the eunuchs brought them in before Nebuchadnezzar. ¹⁹ The king talked with them; and among them all was found no one like Daniel, Hananiah, Mishael, and Azariah. Therefore stood they before the king. ²⁰ In every matter of wisdom and understanding concerning which the king inquired of them, he found them ten times better than all the magicians and enchanters who were in all his realm.

Responsorial Psalm: Daniel 3: 52, 53, 54, 55, 56

⁵² "Blessed are you, O Lord, you God of our fathers, to be praised and exalted above all forever! ⁵³ Blessed is your glorious and holy name, to be praised and exalted above all forever! ⁵⁴ Blessed are you in the temple of your holy glory, to be praised and glorified above all forever! ⁵⁵ Blessed are you who see the depths and sit upon the cherubim, to be praised and exalted above all forever. ⁵⁶ Blessed are you on the throne of your kingdom, to be praised and extolled above all forever!

Gospel: Luke 21: 1-4

¹ He looked up and saw the rich people who were putting their gifts into the treasury. ² He saw a certain poor widow casting in two small brass coins. ³ He said, "Truly I tell you, this poor widow put in more than all of them, ⁴ for all these put in gifts for God from their abundance, but she, out of her poverty, put in all that she had to live on."

1. Invite the Holy Spirit into this reading, asking the Author of Scripture to speak to you through His Word
2. Read today's passage as many times as you need, take your time
3. Write down (below) what the Lord is saying to you today
4. Live with this Word in your heart through the day

Tuesday, November 25, 2025
Saint Catherine of Alexandria, Virgin and Martyr

First Reading: Daniel 2: 31-45

31 "You, O king, saw, and behold, a great image. This image, which was mighty, and whose brightness was excellent, stood before you; and its appearance was terrifying. 32 As for this image, its head was of fine gold, its chest and its arms of silver, its belly and its thighs of bronze, 33 its legs of iron, its feet part of iron, and part of clay. 34 You saw until a stone was cut out without hands, which struck the image on its feet that were of iron and clay, and broke them in pieces. 35 Then the iron, the clay, the bronze, the silver, and the gold were broken in pieces together, and became like the chaff of the summer threshing floors. The wind carried them away, so that no place was found for them. The stone that struck the image became a great mountain, and filled the whole earth.

36 "This is the dream; and we will tell its interpretation before the king. 37 You, O king, are king of kings, to whom the God of heaven has given the kingdom, the power, the strength, and the glory. 38 Wherever the children of men dwell, he has given the animals of the field and the birds of the sky into your hand, and has made you rule over them all. You are the head of gold.

39 "After you, another kingdom will arise that is inferior to you; and a third kingdom of bronze, which will rule over all the earth. 40 The fourth kingdom will be strong as iron, because iron breaks in pieces and subdues all things; and as iron that crushes all these, it will break in pieces and crush. 41 Whereas you saw the feet and toes, part of potters' clay, and part of iron, it will be a divided kingdom; but there will be in it of the strength of the iron, because you saw the iron mixed with miry clay. 42 As the toes of the feet were part of iron, and part of clay, so the kingdom will be partly strong, and partly brittle. 43 Whereas you saw the iron mixed with miry clay, they will mingle themselves with the seed of men; but they won't cling to one another, even as iron does not mix with clay.

44 "In the days of those kings the God of heaven will set up a kingdom which will never be destroyed, nor will its sovereignty be left to another people; but it will break in pieces and consume all these kingdoms, and it will stand forever. 45 Because you saw that a stone was cut out of the mountain without hands, and that it broke in pieces the iron, the bronze, the clay, the silver, and the gold. The great God has made known to the king what will happen hereafter. The dream is certain, and its interpretation sure."

Responsorial Psalm: Daniel 3: 57, 58, 59, 60, 61

57 Blessed are you in the firmament of heaven, to be praised and glorified forever!
58 O all you works of the Lord, bless the Lord! Praise and exalt him above all forever! 59 O you heavens, bless the Lord! Praise and exalt him above all for ever! 60 O you angels of the Lord, bless the Lord! Praise and exalt him above all forever! 61 O all you waters that are above the sky, bless the Lord! Praise and exalt him above all forever!

Gospel: Luke 21: 5-11

⁵ As some were talking about the temple and how it was decorated with beautiful stones and gifts, he said, ⁶ "As for these things which you see, the days will come in which there will not be left here one stone on another that will not be thrown down."
⁷ They asked him, "Teacher, so when will these things be? What is the sign that these things are about to happen?"
⁸ He said, "Watch out that you don't get led astray, for many will come in my name, saying, 'I am he,' and, 'The time is at hand.' Therefore don't follow them. ⁹ When you hear of wars and disturbances, don't be terrified, for these things must happen first, but the end won't come immediately."
¹⁰ Then he said to them, "Nation will rise against nation, and kingdom against kingdom. ¹¹ There will be great earthquakes, famines, and plagues in various places. There will be terrors and great signs from heaven.

1. Invite the Holy Spirit into this reading, asking the Author of Scripture to speak to you through His Word
2. Read today's passage as many times as you need, take your time
3. Write down (below) what the Lord is saying to you today
4. Live with this Word in your heart through the day

_____

_____

Wednesday, November 26, 2025

First Reading: Daniel 5: 1-6, 13-14, 16-17, 23-28

¹ Belshazzar the king made a great feast to a thousand of his lords, and drank wine before the thousand. ² Belshazzar, while he tasted the wine, commanded that the golden and silver vessels which Nebuchadnezzar his father had taken out of the temple which was in Jerusalem be brought to him, that the king and his lords, his wives and his concubines, might drink from them. ³ Then they brought the golden vessels that were taken out of the temple of God's house which was at Jerusalem; and the king and his lords, his wives and his concubines, drank from them. ⁴ They drank wine, and praised the gods of gold, and of silver, of bronze, of iron, of wood, and of stone.
⁵ In the same hour, the fingers of a man's hand came out and wrote near the lamp stand on the plaster of the wall of the king's palace. The king saw the part of the hand that

wrote. ⁶ Then the king's face was changed in him, and his thoughts troubled him; and the joints of his thighs were loosened, and his knees struck one against another.

¹³ Then Daniel was brought in before the king. The king spoke and said to Daniel, "Are you that Daniel of the children of the captivity of Judah, whom the king my father brought out of Judah? ¹⁴ I have heard of you, that the spirit of the gods is in you, and that light, understanding, and excellent wisdom are found in you.

¹⁶ But I have heard of you, that you can give interpretations and dissolve doubts. Now if you can read the writing, and make known to me its interpretation, you shall be clothed with purple, and have a chain of gold around your neck, and shall be the third ruler in the kingdom."

¹⁷ Then Daniel answered the king, "Let your gifts be to yourself, and give your rewards to another. Nevertheless, I will read the writing to the king, and make known to him the interpretation.

²² "You, his son, Belshazzar, have not humbled your heart, though you knew all this, ²³ but have lifted up yourself against the Lord of heaven; and they have brought the vessels of his house before you, and you and your lords, your wives, and your concubines, have drunk wine from them. You have praised the gods of silver, gold, bronze, iron, wood, and stone, which don't see, hear, or know; and you have not glorified the God in whose hand is your breath and whose are all your ways. ²⁴ Then the part of the hand was sent from before him, and this writing was inscribed.

²⁵ "This is the writing that was inscribed: 'MENE, MENE, TEKEL, UPHARSIN.'
²⁶ "This is the interpretation of the thing:
MENE: God has counted your kingdom, and brought it to an end.
²⁷ TEKEL: you are weighed in the balances, and are found wanting.
²⁸ PERES: your kingdom is divided, and given to the Medes and Persians."

Responsorial Psalm: Daniel 3: 62, 63, 64, 65, 66, 67

⁶² O all you powers of the Lord, bless the Lord! Praise and exalt him above all forever! ⁶³ O you sun and moon, bless the Lord! Praise and exalt him above all forever! ⁶⁴ O you stars of heaven, bless the Lord! Praise and exalt him above all forever! ⁶⁵ O every shower and dew, bless the Lord! Praise and exalt him above all forever! ⁶⁶ O all you winds, bless the Lord! Praise and exalt him above all forever! ⁶⁷ O you fire and heat, bless the Lord! Praise and exalt him above all forever!

Gospel: Luke 21: 12-19

¹² But before all these things, they will lay their hands on you and will persecute you, delivering you up to synagogues and prisons, bringing you before kings and governors for my name's sake. ¹³ It will turn out as a testimony for you. ¹⁴ Settle it therefore in your

hearts not to meditate beforehand how to answer, ¹⁵ for I will give you a mouth and wisdom which all your adversaries will not be able to withstand or to contradict. ¹⁶ You will be handed over even by parents, brothers, relatives, and friends. They will cause some of you to be put to death. ¹⁷ You will be hated by all men for my name's sake. ¹⁸ And not a hair of your head will perish.

¹⁹ "By your endurance you will win your lives.

1. Invite the Holy Spirit into this reading, asking the Author of Scripture to speak to you through His Word
2. Read today's passage as many times as you need, take your time
3. Write down (below) what the Lord is saying to you today
4. Live with this Word in your heart through the day

Thursday, November 27, 2025
Thanksgiving Day

First Reading: Daniel 6: 12-28

¹² Then they came near, and spoke before the king concerning the king's decree: "Haven't you signed a decree that every man who makes a petition to any god or man within thirty days, except to you, O king, shall be cast into the den of lions?"

The king answered, "This thing is true, according to the law of the Medes and Persians, which doesn't alter."

¹³ Then they answered and said before the king, "That Daniel, who is of the children of the captivity of Judah, doesn't respect you, O king, nor the decree that you have signed, but makes his petition three times a day." ¹⁴ Then the king, when he heard these words, was very displeased, and set his heart on Daniel to deliver him; and he labored until the going down of the sun to rescue him.

¹⁵ Then these men assembled together to the king, and said to the king, "Know, O king, that it is a law of the Medes and Persians, that no decree nor statute which the king establishes may be changed."

¹⁶ Then the king commanded, and they brought Daniel, and cast him into the den of lions. The king spoke and said to Daniel, "Your God whom you serve continually, he will deliver you."

¹⁷ A stone was brought, and laid on the mouth of the den; and the king sealed it with his own signet, and with the signet of his lords, that nothing might be changed concerning Daniel. ¹⁸ Then the king went to his palace, and passed the night fasting. No musical instruments were brought before him; and his sleep fled from him.

¹⁹ Then the king arose very early in the morning, and went in haste to the den of lions. ²⁰ When he came near to the den to Daniel, he cried with a troubled voice. The king spoke and said to Daniel, "Daniel, servant of the living God, is your God, whom you serve continually, able to deliver you from the lions?"

²¹ Then Daniel said to the king, "O king, live forever! ²² My God has sent his angel, and has shut the lions' mouths, and they have not hurt me; because I am innocent in his sight. Also before you, O king, I have done no harm."

²³ Then the king was exceedingly glad, and commanded that they should take Daniel up out of the den. So Daniel was taken up out of the den, and no kind of harm was found on him, because he had trusted in his God.

²⁴ The king commanded, and they brought those men who had accused Daniel, and they cast them into the den of lions—them, their children, and their wives; and the lions mauled them and broke all their bones in pieces before they came to the bottom of the den.

²⁵ Then King Darius wrote to all the peoples, nations, and languages, who dwell in all the earth:

"Peace be multiplied to you.

²⁶ "I make a decree that in all the dominion of my kingdom men tremble and fear before the God of Daniel;

"for he is the living God,
and steadfast forever.
His kingdom is that which will not be destroyed.
His dominion will be even to the end.
²⁷ He delivers and rescues.
He works signs and wonders in heaven and in earth,
who has delivered Daniel from the power of the lions."

²⁸ So this Daniel prospered in the reign of Darius, and in the reign of Cyrus the Persian.

Responsorial Psalm: Daniel 3: 68, 69, 70, 71, 72, 73, 74

⁶⁸ O you dews and storms of snow, bless the Lord! Praise and exalt him above all forever! ⁶⁹ O you nights and days, bless the Lord! Praise and exalt him above all forever! ⁷⁰ O you light and darkness, bless the Lord! Praise and exalt him above all forever! ⁷¹ O you cold and heat, bless the Lord! Praise and exalt him above all forever! ⁷² O you frost and snow, bless the Lord! Praise and exalt him above all forever! ⁷³ O you lightnings and clouds, bless the Lord! Praise and exalt him above all forever! ⁷⁴ O let the earth bless the Lord! Let it praise and exalt him above all forever!

Gospel: Luke 21: 20-28

20 "But when you see Jerusalem surrounded by armies, then know that its desolation is at hand. 21 Then let those who are in Judea flee to the mountains. Let those who are in the middle of her depart. Let those who are in the country not enter therein. 22 For these are days of vengeance, that all things which are written may be fulfilled. 23 Woe to those who are pregnant and to those who nurse infants in those days! For there will be great distress in the land and wrath to this people. 24 They will fall by the edge of the sword, and will be led captive into all the nations. Jerusalem will be trampled down by the Gentiles until the times of the Gentiles are fulfilled.
25 "There will be signs in the sun, moon, and stars; and on the earth anxiety of nations, in perplexity for the roaring of the sea and the waves; 26 men fainting for fear and for expectation of the things which are coming on the world, for the powers of the heavens will be shaken. 27 Then they will see the Son of Man coming in a cloud with power and great glory. 28 But when these things begin to happen, look up and lift up your heads, because your redemption is near."

1. Invite the Holy Spirit into this reading, asking the Author of Scripture to speak to you through His Word
2. Read today's passage as many times as you need, take your time
3. Write down (below) what the Lord is saying to you today
4. Live with this Word in your heart through the day

_____

_____

Friday, November 28, 2025

First Reading: Daniel 7: 2-14

2 Daniel spoke and said, "I saw in my vision by night and behold, the four winds of the sky broke out on the great sea. 3 Four great animals came up from the sea, different from one another.
4 "The first was like a lion, and had eagle's wings. I watched until its wings were plucked, and it was lifted up from the earth, and made to stand on two feet as a man. A man's heart was given to it.

⁵ "Behold, there was another animal, a second, like a bear. It was raised up on one side, and three ribs were in its mouth between its teeth. They said this to it: 'Arise! Devour much flesh!'

⁶ "After this I saw, and behold, another, like a leopard, which had on its back four wings of a bird. The animal also had four heads; and dominion was given to it.

⁷ "After this I saw in the night visions, and, behold, there was a fourth animal, awesome and powerful, and exceedingly strong. It had great iron teeth. It devoured and broke in pieces, and stamped the residue with its feet. It was different from all the animals that were before it. It had ten horns.

⁸ "I considered the horns, and behold, another horn came up among them, a little one, before which three of the first horns were plucked up by the roots: and behold, in this horn were eyes like the eyes of a man, and a mouth speaking great things.

⁹ "I watched until thrones were placed,
and one who was Ancient of Days sat.
His clothing was white as snow,
and the hair of his head like pure wool.
His throne was fiery flames,
and its wheels burning fire.
¹⁰ A fiery stream issued and came out from before him.
Thousands of thousands ministered to him.
Ten thousand times ten thousand stood before him.
The judgment was set.
The books were opened.

¹¹ "I watched at that time because of the voice of the great words which the horn spoke. I watched even until the animal was slain, its body destroyed, and it was given to be burned with fire. ¹² As for the rest of the animals, their dominion was taken away; yet their lives were prolonged for a season and a time.

¹³ "I saw in the night visions, and behold, one like a son of man came with the clouds, and he came to the Ancient of Days, and they brought him near before him. ¹⁴ Dominion was given him, with glory and a kingdom, that all the peoples, nations, and languages should serve him. His dominion is an everlasting dominion, which will not pass away, and his kingdom will not be destroyed.

Responsorial Psalm: Daniel 3: 75, 76, 77, 78, 79, 80, 81

⁷⁵ O you mountains and hills, bless the Lord! Praise and exalt him above all forever! ⁷⁶ O all you things that grow on the earth, bless the Lord! Praise and exalt him above all forever! ⁷⁷ §O sea and rivers, bless the Lord! Praise and exalt him above all forever! ⁷⁸ O you springs, bless the Lord! Praise and exalt him above all forever! ⁷⁹ O you whales and all that move in the waters, bless the Lord! Praise and exalt him above all forever! ⁸⁰ O all you birds

of the air, bless the Lord! Praise and exalt him above all forever! ⁸¹ O all you beasts and cattle, bless the Lord! Praise and exalt him above all forever!

Gospel: Luke 21: 29-33

²⁹ He told them a parable. "See the fig tree and all the trees. ³⁰ When they are already budding, you see it and know by your own selves that the summer is already near. ³¹ Even so you also, when you see these things happening, know that God's Kingdom is near. ³² Most certainly I tell you, this generation will not pass away until all things are accomplished. ³³ Heaven and earth will pass away, but my words will by no means pass away.

1. Invite the Holy Spirit into this reading, asking the Author of Scripture to speak to you through His Word
2. Read today's passage as many times as you need, take your time
3. Write down (below) what the Lord is saying to you today
4. Live with this Word in your heart through the day

_____

_____

Saturday, November 29, 2025

First Reading: Daniel 7: 15-27

¹⁵ "As for me, Daniel, my spirit was grieved within my body, and the visions of my head troubled me. ¹⁶ I came near to one of those who stood by, and asked him the truth concerning all this.
"So he told me, and made me know the interpretation of the things. ¹⁷ 'These great animals, which are four, are four kings, who will arise out of the earth. ¹⁸ But the saints of the Most High will receive the kingdom, and possess the kingdom forever, even forever and ever.'
¹⁹ "Then I desired to know the truth concerning the fourth animal, which was different from all of them, exceedingly terrible, whose teeth were of iron, and its nails of bronze; which devoured, broke in pieces, and stamped the residue with its feet; ²⁰ and concerning the ten horns that were on its head, and the other horn which came up, and before which three fell, even that horn that had eyes, and a mouth that spoke great things, whose look was more stout than its fellows. ²¹ I saw, and the same horn made war with the saints and

prevailed against them ²² until the Ancient of Days came, and judgment was given to the saints of the Most High, and the time came that the saints possessed the kingdom.
²³ "So he said, 'The fourth animal will be a fourth kingdom on earth, which will be different from all the kingdoms, and will devour the whole earth, and will tread it down, and break it in pieces. ²⁴ As for the ten horns, ten kings will arise out of this kingdom. Another will arise after them; and he will be different from the former, and he will put down three kings. ²⁵ He will speak words against the Most High, and will wear out the saints of the Most High. He will plan to change the times and the law; and they will be given into his hand until a time and times and half a time.
²⁶ " 'But the judgment will be set, and they will take away his dominion, to consume and to destroy it to the end. ²⁷ The kingdom and the dominion, and the greatness of the kingdoms under the whole sky, will be given to the people of the saints of the Most High. His kingdom is an everlasting kingdom, and all dominions will serve and obey him.'

Responsorial Psalm: Daniel 3: 82, 83, 84, 85, 86, 87

⁸² O you children of men, bless the Lord! Praise and exalt him above all forever! ⁸³ O let Israel bless the Lord! Praise and exalt him above all forever. ⁸⁴ O you priests of the Lord, bless the Lord! Praise and exalt him above all forever! ⁸⁵ O you servants of the Lord, bless the Lord! Praise and exalt him above all forever! ⁸⁶ O you spirits and souls of the righteous, bless the Lord! Praise and exalt him above all forever! ⁸⁷ O you who are holy and humble of heart, bless the Lord! Praise and exalt him above all forever!

Gospel: Luke 21: 34-36

³⁴ "So be careful, or your hearts will be loaded down with carousing, drunkenness, and cares of this life, and that day will come on you suddenly. ³⁵ For it will come like a snare on all those who dwell on the surface of all the earth. ³⁶ Therefore be watchful all the time, praying that you may be counted worthy to escape all these things that will happen, and to stand before the Son of Man."

1. Invite the Holy Spirit into this reading, asking the Author of Scripture to speak to you through His Word
2. Read today's passage as many times as you need, take your time
3. Write down (below) what the Lord is saying to you today
4. Live with this Word in your heart through the day

Sunday, November 30, 2025
FIRST SUNDAY OF ADVENT

First Reading: Isaiah 2: 1-5

¹ This is what Isaiah the son of Amoz saw concerning Judah and Jerusalem.
² It shall happen in the latter days, that the mountain of Yahweh's house shall be established on the top of the mountains,
and shall be raised above the hills;
and all nations shall flow to it.
³ Many peoples shall go and say,
"Come, let's go up to the mountain of Yahweh,
to the house of the God of Jacob;
and he will teach us of his ways,
and we will walk in his paths."
For the law shall go out of Zion,
and Yahweh's word from Jerusalem.
⁴ He will judge between the nations,
and will decide concerning many peoples.
They shall beat their swords into plowshares,
and their spears into pruning hooks.
Nation shall not lift up sword against nation,
neither shall they learn war any more.
⁵ House of Jacob, come, and let's walk in the light of Yahweh.

Responsorial Psalm: Psalms 122: 1-2, 3-4ab, 4cd-5, 6-7, 8-9

¹ I was glad when they said to me,
"Let's go to Yahweh's house!"
² Our feet are standing within your gates, Jerusalem!
³ Jerusalem is built as a city that is compact together,
⁴ where the tribes go up, even Yah's tribes,
according to an ordinance for Israel,
to give thanks to Yahweh's name.
⁵ For there are set thrones for judgment,
the thrones of David's house.
⁶ Pray for the peace of Jerusalem.
Those who love you will prosper.
⁷ Peace be within your walls,
and prosperity within your palaces.

⁸ For my brothers' and companions' sakes,
I will now say, "Peace be within you."
⁹ For the sake of the house of Yahweh our God,
I will seek your good.

Second Reading: Romans 13: 11-14

¹¹ Do this, knowing the time, that it is already time for you to awaken out of sleep, for salvation is now nearer to us than when we first believed. ¹² The night is far gone, and the day is near. Let's therefore throw off the deeds of darkness, and let's put on the armor of light. ¹³ Let's walk properly, as in the day; not in reveling and drunkenness, not in sexual promiscuity and lustful acts, and not in strife and jealousy. ¹⁴ But put on the Lord Jesus Christ, and make no provision for the flesh, for its lusts.

Gospel: Matthew 24: 37-44

³⁷ As the days of Noah were, so will the coming of the Son of Man be. ³⁸ For as in those days which were before the flood they were eating and drinking, marrying and giving in marriage, until the day that Noah entered into the ship, ³⁹ and they didn't know until the flood came and took them all away, so will the coming of the Son of Man be. ⁴⁰ Then two men will be in the field: one will be taken and one will be left. ⁴¹ Two women will be grinding at the mill: one will be taken and one will be left. ⁴² Watch therefore, for you don't know in what hour your Lord comes. ⁴³ But know this, that if the master of the house had known in what watch of the night the thief was coming, he would have watched, and would not have allowed his house to be broken into. ⁴⁴ Therefore also be ready, for in an hour that you don't expect, the Son of Man will come.

1. Invite the Holy Spirit into this reading, asking the Author of Scripture to speak to you through His Word
2. Read today's passage as many times as you need, take your time
3. Write down (below) what the Lord is saying to you today
4. Live with this Word in your heart through the day

_____

_____

Monday, December 1, 2025

First Reading: Isaiah 4: 2-6

² In that day, Yahweh's branch will be beautiful and glorious, and the fruit of the land will be the beauty and glory of the survivors of Israel. ³ It will happen that he who is left in Zion and he who remains in Jerusalem shall be called holy, even everyone who is written among the living in Jerusalem, ⁴ when the Lord shall have washed away the filth of the daughters of Zion, and shall have purged the blood of Jerusalem from within it, by the spirit of justice and by the spirit of burning. ⁵ Yahweh will create over the whole habitation of Mount Zion and over her assemblies, a cloud and smoke by day, and the shining of a flaming fire by night, for over all the glory will be a canopy. ⁶ There will be a pavilion for a shade in the daytime from the heat, and for a refuge and for a shelter from storm and from rain.

Responsorial Psalm: Psalms 122: 1-2, 3-4b, 4cd-5, 6-7, 8-9

¹ I was glad when they said to me,
"Let's go to Yahweh's house!"
² Our feet are standing within your gates, Jerusalem!
³ Jerusalem is built as a city that is compact together,
⁴ where the tribes go up, even Yah's tribes,
according to an ordinance for Israel,
to give thanks to Yahweh's name.
⁵ For there are set thrones for judgment,
the thrones of David's house.
⁶ Pray for the peace of Jerusalem.
Those who love you will prosper.
⁷ Peace be within your walls,
and prosperity within your palaces.
⁸ For my brothers' and companions' sakes,
I will now say, "Peace be within you."
⁹ For the sake of the house of Yahweh our God,
I will seek your good.

Gospel: Matthew 8: 5-11

⁵ When he came into Capernaum, a centurion came to him, asking him for help, ⁶ saying, "Lord, my servant lies in the house paralyzed, grievously tormented."
⁷ Jesus said to him, "I will come and heal him."
⁸ The centurion answered, "Lord, I'm not worthy for you to come under my roof. Just say the word, and my servant will be healed. ⁹ For I am also a man under authority, having

under myself soldiers. I tell this one, 'Go,' and he goes; and tell another, 'Come,' and he comes; and tell my servant, 'Do this,' and he does it."
[10] When Jesus heard it, he marveled and said to those who followed, "Most certainly I tell you, I haven't found so great a faith, not even in Israel. [11] I tell you that many will come from the east and the west, and will sit down with Abraham, Isaac, and Jacob in the Kingdom of Heaven,

1. Invite the Holy Spirit into this reading, asking the Author of Scripture to speak to you through His Word
2. Read today's passage as many times as you need, take your time
3. Write down (below) what the Lord is saying to you today
4. Live with this Word in your heart through the day

Tuesday, December 2, 2025

First Reading: Isaiah 11: 1-10

[1] A shoot will come out of the stock of Jesse,
and a branch out of his roots will bear fruit.
[2] Yahweh's Spirit will rest on him:
the spirit of wisdom and understanding,
the spirit of counsel and might,
the spirit of knowledge and of the fear of Yahweh.
[3] His delight will be in the fear of Yahweh.
He will not judge by the sight of his eyes,
neither decide by the hearing of his ears;
[4] but he will judge the poor with righteousness,
and decide with equity for the humble of the earth.
He will strike the earth with the rod of his mouth;
and with the breath of his lips he will kill the wicked.
[5] Righteousness will be the belt around his waist,
and faithfulness the belt around his waist.
[6] The wolf will live with the lamb,
and the leopard will lie down with the young goat,
the calf, the young lion, and the fattened calf together;

and a little child will lead them.
⁷ The cow and the bear will graze.
Their young ones will lie down together.
The lion will eat straw like the ox.
⁸ The nursing child will play near a cobra's hole,
and the weaned child will put his hand on the viper's den.
⁹ They will not hurt nor destroy in all my holy mountain;
for the earth will be full of the knowledge of Yahweh,
as the waters cover the sea.
¹⁰ It will happen in that day that the nations will seek the root of Jesse, who stands as a banner of the peoples; and his resting place will be glorious.

Responsorial Psalm: Psalms 72: 1-2, 7-8, 12-13, 17

¹ God, give the king your justice;
your righteousness to the royal son.
² He will judge your people with righteousness,
and your poor with justice.
⁷ In his days, the righteous shall flourish,
and abundance of peace, until the moon is no more.
⁸ He shall have dominion also from sea to sea,
from the River to the ends of the earth.
¹² For he will deliver the needy when he cries;
the poor, who has no helper.
¹³ He will have pity on the poor and needy.
He will save the souls of the needy.
¹⁷ His name endures forever.
His name continues as long as the sun.
Men shall be blessed by him.
All nations will call him blessed.

Gospel: Luke 10: 21-24

²¹ In that same hour, Jesus rejoiced in the Holy Spirit, and said, "I thank you, O Father, Lord of heaven and earth, that you have hidden these things from the wise and understanding, and revealed them to little children. Yes, Father, for so it was well-pleasing in your sight."
²² Turning to the disciples, he said, "All things have been delivered to me by my Father. No one knows who the Son is, except the Father, and who the Father is, except the Son, and he to whomever the Son desires to reveal him."

²³ Turning to the disciples, he said privately, "Blessed are the eyes which see the things that you see, ²⁴ for I tell you that many prophets and kings desired to see the things which you see, and didn't see them, and to hear the things which you hear, and didn't hear them."

1. Invite the Holy Spirit into this reading, asking the Author of Scripture to speak to you through His Word
2. Read today's passage as many times as you need, take your time
3. Write down (below) what the Lord is saying to you today
4. Live with this Word in your heart through the day

___

___

Wednesday, December 3, 2025
Saint Francis Xavier, Priest

First Reading: Isaiah 25: 6-10a

⁶ In this mountain, Yahweh of Armies will make all peoples a feast of choice meat, a feast of choice wines, of choice meat full of marrow, of well refined choice wines. ⁷ He will destroy in this mountain the surface of the covering that covers all peoples, and the veil that is spread over all nations. ⁸ He has swallowed up death forever! The Lord Yahweh will wipe away tears from off all faces. He will take the reproach of his people away from off all the earth, for Yahweh has spoken it.
⁹ It shall be said in that day, "Behold, this is our God! We have waited for him, and he will save us! This is Yahweh! We have waited for him. We will be glad and rejoice in his salvation!" ¹⁰ For Yahweh's hand will rest in this mountain.
Moab will be trodden down in his place, even like straw is trodden down in the water of the dunghill.

Responsorial Psalm: Psalms 23: 1-3a, 3b-4, 5, 6

¹ Yahweh is my shepherd;
I shall lack nothing.
² He makes me lie down in green pastures.
He leads me beside still waters.
³ He restores my soul.
He guides me in the paths of righteousness for his name's sake.

⁴ Even though I walk through the valley of the shadow of death,
I will fear no evil, for you are with me.
Your rod and your staff,
they comfort me.
⁵ You prepare a table before me
in the presence of my enemies.
You anoint my head with oil.
My cup runs over.
⁶ Surely goodness and loving kindness shall follow me all the days of my life,
and I will dwell in Yahweh's house forever.

Gospel: Matthew 15: 29-37

²⁹ Jesus departed from there and came near to the sea of Galilee; and he went up on the mountain and sat there. ³⁰ Great multitudes came to him, having with them the lame, blind, mute, maimed, and many others, and they put them down at his feet. He healed them, ³¹ so that the multitude wondered when they saw the mute speaking, the injured healed, the lame walking, and the blind seeing—and they glorified the God of Israel.
³² Jesus summoned his disciples and said, "I have compassion on the multitude, because they have continued with me now three days and have nothing to eat. I don't want to send them away fasting, or they might faint on the way."
³³ The disciples said to him, "Where could we get so many loaves in a deserted place as to satisfy so great a multitude?"
³⁴ Jesus said to them, "How many loaves do you have?"
They said, "Seven, and a few small fish."
³⁵ He commanded the multitude to sit down on the ground; ³⁶ and he took the seven loaves and the fish. He gave thanks and broke them, and gave to the disciples, and the disciples to the multitudes. ³⁷ They all ate and were filled. They took up seven baskets full of the broken pieces that were left over.

1. Invite the Holy Spirit into this reading, asking the Author of Scripture to speak to you through His Word
2. Read today's passage as many times as you need, take your time
3. Write down (below) what the Lord is saying to you today
4. Live with this Word in your heart through the day

Thursday, December 4, 2025
Saint John Damascene, Priest and Doctor of the Church

First Reading: Isaiah 26: 1-6

¹ In that day, this song will be sung in the land of Judah:
"We have a strong city.
God appoints salvation for walls and bulwarks.
² Open the gates, that the righteous nation may enter:
the one which keeps faith.
³ You will keep whoever's mind is steadfast in perfect peace,
because he trusts in you.
⁴ Trust in Yahweh forever;
for in Yah, Yahweh, is an everlasting Rock.
⁵ For he has brought down those who dwell on high, the lofty city.
He lays it low.
He lays it low even to the ground.
He brings it even to the dust.
⁶ The foot shall tread it down,
even the feet of the poor
and the steps of the needy."

Responsorial Psalm: Psalms 118: 1 and 8-9, 19-21, 25-27a

¹ Give thanks to Yahweh, for he is good,
for his loving kindness endures forever.
⁸ It is better to take refuge in Yahweh,
than to put confidence in man.
⁹ It is better to take refuge in Yahweh,
than to put confidence in princes.
¹⁹ Open to me the gates of righteousness.
I will enter into them.
I will give thanks to Yah.
²⁰ This is the gate of Yahweh;
the righteous will enter into it.
²¹ I will give thanks to you, for you have answered me,
and have become my salvation.
²⁵ Save us now, we beg you, Yahweh!
Yahweh, we beg you, send prosperity now.
²⁶ Blessed is he who comes in Yahweh's name!

We have blessed you out of Yahweh's house.
²⁷ Yahweh is God, and he has given us light.
Bind the sacrifice with cords, even to the horns of the altar.

Gospel: Matthew 7: 21, 24-27

²¹ "Not everyone who says to me, 'Lord, Lord,' will enter into the Kingdom of Heaven, but he who does the will of my Father who is in heaven.
²⁴ "Everyone therefore who hears these words of mine and does them, I will liken him to a wise man who built his house on a rock. ²⁵ The rain came down, the floods came, and the winds blew and beat on that house; and it didn't fall, for it was founded on the rock. ²⁶ Everyone who hears these words of mine and doesn't do them will be like a foolish man who built his house on the sand. ²⁷ The rain came down, the floods came, and the winds blew and beat on that house; and it fell—and its fall was great."

1. Invite the Holy Spirit into this reading, asking the Author of Scripture to speak to you through His Word
2. Read today's passage as many times as you need, take your time
3. Write down (below) what the Lord is saying to you today
4. Live with this Word in your heart through the day

_____

_____

Friday, December 5, 2025

First Reading: Isaiah 29: 17-24

¹⁷ Isn't it yet a very little while, and Lebanon will be turned into a fruitful field, and the fruitful field will be regarded as a forest? ¹⁸ In that day, the deaf will hear the words of the book, and the eyes of the blind will see out of obscurity and out of darkness. ¹⁹ The humble also will increase their joy in Yahweh, and the poor among men will rejoice in the Holy One of Israel. ²⁰ For the ruthless is brought to nothing, and the scoffer ceases, and all those who are alert to do evil are cut off— ²¹ who cause a person to be indicted by a word, and lay a snare for one who reproves in the gate, and who deprive the innocent of justice with false testimony.
²² Therefore Yahweh, who redeemed Abraham, says concerning the house of Jacob: "Jacob shall no longer be ashamed, neither shall his face grow pale. ²³ But when he sees his

children, the work of my hands, in the middle of him, they will sanctify my name. Yes, they will sanctify the Holy One of Jacob, and will stand in awe of the God of Israel. 24 They also who err in spirit will come to understanding, and those who grumble will receive instruction."

Responsorial Psalm: Psalms 27: 1, 4, 13-14

1 Yahweh is my light and my salvation.
Whom shall I fear?
Yahweh is the strength of my life.
Of whom shall I be afraid?
4 One thing I have asked of Yahweh, that I will seek after:
that I may dwell in Yahweh's house all the days of my life,
to see Yahweh's beauty,
and to inquire in his temple.
13 I am still confident of this:
I will see the goodness of Yahweh in the land of the living.
14 Wait for Yahweh.
Be strong, and let your heart take courage.
Yes, wait for Yahweh.

Gospel: Matthew 9: 27-31

27 As Jesus passed by from there, two blind men followed him, calling out and saying, "Have mercy on us, son of David!" 28 When he had come into the house, the blind men came to him. Jesus said to them, "Do you believe that I am able to do this?"
They told him, "Yes, Lord."
29 Then he touched their eyes, saying, "According to your faith be it done to you." 30 Then their eyes were opened. Jesus strictly commanded them, saying, "See that no one knows about this." 31 But they went out and spread abroad his fame in all that land.

1. Invite the Holy Spirit into this reading, asking the Author of Scripture to speak to you through His Word
2. Read today's passage as many times as you need, take your time
3. Write down (below) what the Lord is saying to you today
4. Live with this Word in your heart through the day

Saturday, December 6, 2025
Saint Nicholas, Bishop

First Reading: Isaiah 30: 19-21, 23-26

19 For the people will dwell in Zion at Jerusalem. You will weep no more. He will surely be gracious to you at the voice of your cry. When he hears you, he will answer you. 20 Though the Lord may give you the bread of adversity and the water of affliction, yet your teachers won't be hidden any more, but your eyes will see your teachers; 21 and when you turn to the right hand, and when you turn to the left, your ears will hear a voice behind you, saying, "This is the way. Walk in it."
23 He will give the rain for your seed, with which you will sow the ground; and bread of the increase of the ground will be rich and plentiful. In that day, your livestock will feed in large pastures. 24 The oxen likewise and the young donkeys that till the ground will eat savory feed, which has been winnowed with the shovel and with the fork. 25 There will be brooks and streams of water on every lofty mountain and on every high hill in the day of the great slaughter, when the towers fall. 26 Moreover the light of the moon will be like the light of the sun, and the light of the sun will be seven times brighter, like the light of seven days, in the day that Yahweh binds up the fracture of his people, and heals the wound they were struck with.

Responsorial Psalm: Psalms 147: 1-2, 3-4, 5-6

1 Praise Yah,
for it is good to sing praises to our God;
for it is pleasant and fitting to praise him.
2 Yahweh builds up Jerusalem.
He gathers together the outcasts of Israel.
3 He heals the broken in heart,
and binds up their wounds.
4 He counts the number of the stars.
He calls them all by their names.
5 Great is our Lord, and mighty in power.
His understanding is infinite.
6 Yahweh upholds the humble.
He brings the wicked down to the ground.

Gospel: Matthew 9: 35 – 10: 1, 5a, 6-8

³⁵ Jesus went about all the cities and the villages, teaching in their synagogues and preaching the Good News of the Kingdom, and healing every disease and every sickness among the people. ³⁶ But when he saw the multitudes, he was moved with compassion for them because they were harassed§ and scattered, like sheep without a shepherd. ³⁷ Then he said to his disciples, "The harvest indeed is plentiful, but the laborers are few. ³⁸ Pray therefore that the Lord of the harvest will send out laborers into his harvest."

¹ He called to himself his twelve disciples, and gave them authority over unclean spirits, to cast them out, and to heal every disease and every sickness.

⁵ Jesus sent these twelve out and commanded them, saying, "Don't go among the Gentiles, and don't enter into any city of the Samaritans. ⁶ Rather, go to the lost sheep of the house of Israel. ⁷ As you go, preach, saying, 'The Kingdom of Heaven is at hand!' ⁸ Heal the sick, cleanse the lepers,‡ and cast out demons. Freely you received, so freely give.

1. Invite the Holy Spirit into this reading, asking the Author of Scripture to speak to you through His Word
2. Read today's passage as many times as you need, take your time
3. Write down (below) what the Lord is saying to you today
4. Live with this Word in your heart through the day

_____

_____

Sunday, December 7, 2025
SECOND SUNDAY OF ADVENT

First Reading: Isaiah 11: 1-10

¹ A shoot will come out of the stock of Jesse,
and a branch out of his roots will bear fruit.
² Yahweh's Spirit will rest on him:
the spirit of wisdom and understanding,
the spirit of counsel and might,
the spirit of knowledge and of the fear of Yahweh.
³ His delight will be in the fear of Yahweh.
He will not judge by the sight of his eyes,
neither decide by the hearing of his ears;
⁴ but he will judge the poor with righteousness,
and decide with equity for the humble of the earth.

He will strike the earth with the rod of his mouth;
and with the breath of his lips he will kill the wicked.
⁵ Righteousness will be the belt around his waist,
and faithfulness the belt around his waist.
⁶ The wolf will live with the lamb,
and the leopard will lie down with the young goat,
the calf, the young lion, and the fattened calf together;
and a little child will lead them.
⁷ The cow and the bear will graze.
Their young ones will lie down together.
The lion will eat straw like the ox.
⁸ The nursing child will play near a cobra's hole,
and the weaned child will put his hand on the viper's den.
⁹ They will not hurt nor destroy in all my holy mountain;
for the earth will be full of the knowledge of Yahweh,
as the waters cover the sea.
¹⁰ It will happen in that day that the nations will seek the root of Jesse, who stands as a banner of the peoples; and his resting place will be glorious.

Responsorial Psalm: Psalms 72: 1-2, 7-8, 12-13, 17

¹ God, give the king your justice;
your righteousness to the royal son.
² He will judge your people with righteousness,
and your poor with justice.
⁷ In his days, the righteous shall flourish,
and abundance of peace, until the moon is no more.
⁸ He shall have dominion also from sea to sea,
from the River to the ends of the earth.
¹² For he will deliver the needy when he cries;
the poor, who has no helper.
¹³ He will have pity on the poor and needy.
He will save the souls of the needy.
¹⁷ His name endures forever.
His name continues as long as the sun.
Men shall be blessed by him.
All nations will call him blessed.

Second Reading: Romans 15: 4-9

⁴ For whatever things were written before were written for our learning, that through perseverance and through encouragement of the Scriptures we might have hope. ⁵ Now the God of perseverance and of encouragement grant you to be of the same mind with one another according to Christ Jesus, ⁶ that with one accord you may with one mouth glorify the God and Father of our Lord Jesus Christ.

⁷ Therefore accept one another, even as Christ also accepted you,⁺ to the glory of God. ⁸ Now I say that Christ has been made a servant of the circumcision for the truth of God, that he might confirm the promises given to the fathers, ⁹ and that the Gentiles might glorify God for his mercy. As it is written,

"Therefore I will give praise to you among the Gentiles
and sing to your name."

Gospel: Matthew 3: 1-12

¹ In those days, John the Baptizer came, preaching in the wilderness of Judea, saying, ² "Repent, for the Kingdom of Heaven is at hand!" ³ For this is he who was spoken of by Isaiah the prophet, saying,
"The voice of one crying in the wilderness,
make the way of the Lord ready!
Make his paths straight!"⁺

⁴ Now John himself wore clothing made of camel's hair with a leather belt around his waist. His food was locusts and wild honey. ⁵ Then people from Jerusalem, all of Judea, and all the region around the Jordan went out to him. ⁶ They were baptized by him in the Jordan, confessing their sins.

⁷ But when he saw many of the Pharisees and Sadducees coming for his baptism, he said to them, "You offspring of vipers, who warned you to flee from the wrath to come? ⁸ Therefore produce fruit worthy of repentance! ⁹ Don't think to yourselves, 'We have Abraham for our father,' for I tell you that God is able to raise up children to Abraham from these stones. ¹⁰ Even now the ax lies at the root of the trees. Therefore every tree that doesn't produce good fruit is cut down, and cast into the fire.

¹¹ "I indeed baptize you in water for repentance, but he who comes after me is mightier than I, whose sandals I am not worthy to carry. He will baptize you in the Holy Spirit.⁺ ¹² His winnowing fork is in his hand, and he will thoroughly cleanse his threshing floor. He will gather his wheat into the barn, but the chaff he will burn up with unquenchable fire."

1. Invite the Holy Spirit into this reading, asking the Author of Scripture to speak to you through His Word
2. Read today's passage as many times as you need, take your time
3. Write down (below) what the Lord is saying to you today
4. Live with this Word in your heart through the day

Monday, December 8, 2025
THE IMMACULATE CONCEPTION OF THE BLESSED VIRGIN MARY

First Reading: Genesis 3: 9-15, 20

⁹ Yahweh God called to the man, and said to him, "Where are you?"
¹⁰ The man said, "I heard your voice in the garden, and I was afraid, because I was naked; so I hid myself."
¹¹ God said, "Who told you that you were naked? Have you eaten from the tree that I commanded you not to eat from?"
¹² The man said, "The woman whom you gave to be with me, she gave me fruit from the tree, and I ate it."
¹³ Yahweh God said to the woman, "What have you done?"
The woman said, "The serpent deceived me, and I ate."
¹⁴ Yahweh God said to the serpent,
"Because you have done this,
you are cursed above all livestock,
and above every animal of the field.
You shall go on your belly
and you shall eat dust all the days of your life.
¹⁵ I will put hostility between you and the woman,
and between your offspring and her offspring.
He will bruise your head,
and you will bruise his heel."
²⁰ The man called his wife Eve because she would be the mother of all the living.

Responsorial Psalm: Psalms 98: 1, 2-3ab, 3cd-4

¹ Sing to Yahweh a new song,
for he has done marvelous things!
His right hand and his holy arm have worked salvation for him.
² Yahweh has made known his salvation.
He has openly shown his righteousness in the sight of the nations.
³ He has remembered his loving kindness and his faithfulness toward the house of Israel.

All the ends of the earth have seen the salvation of our God.
⁴ Make a joyful noise to Yahweh, all the earth!
Burst out and sing for joy, yes, sing praises!

Second Reading: Ephesians 1: 3-6, 11-12

³ Blessed be the God and Father of our Lord Jesus Christ, who has blessed us with every spiritual blessing in the heavenly places in Christ, ⁴ even as he chose us in him before the foundation of the world, that we would be holy and without defect before him in love, ⁵ having predestined us for adoption as children through Jesus Christ to himself, according to the good pleasure of his desire, ⁶ to the praise of the glory of his grace, by which he freely gave us favor in the Beloved.
¹¹ We were also assigned an inheritance in him, having been foreordained according to the purpose of him who does all things after the counsel of his will, ¹² to the end that we should be to the praise of his glory, we who had before hoped in Christ.

Gospel: Luke 1: 26-38

²⁶ Now in the sixth month, the angel Gabriel was sent from God to a city of Galilee named Nazareth, ²⁷ to a virgin pledged to be married to a man whose name was Joseph, of David's house. The virgin's name was Mary. ²⁸ Having come in, the angel said to her, "Rejoice, you highly favored one! The Lord is with you. Blessed are you among women!"
²⁹ But when she saw him, she was greatly troubled at the saying, and considered what kind of salutation this might be. ³⁰ The angel said to her, "Don't be afraid, Mary, for you have found favor with God. ³¹ Behold, you will conceive in your womb and give birth to a son, and shall name him 'Jesus.' ³² He will be great and will be called the Son of the Most High. The Lord God will give him the throne of his father David, ³³ and he will reign over the house of Jacob forever. There will be no end to his Kingdom."
³⁴ Mary said to the angel, "How can this be, seeing I am a virgin?"
³⁵ The angel answered her, "The Holy Spirit will come on you, and the power of the Most High will overshadow you. Therefore also the holy one who is born from you will be called the Son of God. ³⁶ Behold, Elizabeth your relative also has conceived a son in her old age; and this is the sixth month with her who was called barren. ³⁷ For nothing spoken by God is impossible."
³⁸ Mary said, "Behold, the servant of the Lord; let it be done to me according to your word." Then the angel departed from her.

1. Invite the Holy Spirit into this reading, asking the Author of Scripture to speak to you through His Word
2. Read today's passage as many times as you need, take your time

3. Write down (below) what the Lord is saying to you today
4. Live with this Word in your heart through the day

_____

_____

Tuesday, December 9, 2025
Saint Juan Diego Cuauhtlatoatzin

First Reading: Isaiah 40: 1-11

¹ "Comfort, comfort my people," says your God. ² "Speak comfortably to Jerusalem, and call out to her that her warfare is accomplished, that her iniquity is pardoned, that she has received of Yahweh's hand double for all her sins."
³ The voice of one who calls out,
"Prepare the way of Yahweh in the wilderness!
Make a level highway in the desert for our God.
⁴ Every valley shall be exalted,
and every mountain and hill shall be made low.
The uneven shall be made level,
and the rough places a plain.
⁵ Yahweh's glory shall be revealed,
and all flesh shall see it together;
for the mouth of Yahweh has spoken it."
⁶ The voice of one saying, "Cry out!"
One said, "What shall I cry?"
"All flesh is like grass,
and all its glory is like the flower of the field.
⁷ The grass withers,
the flower fades,
because Yahweh's breath blows on it.
Surely the people are like grass.
⁸ The grass withers,
the flower fades;
but the word of our God stands forever."
⁹ You who tell good news to Zion, go up on a high mountain.
You who tell good news to Jerusalem, lift up your voice with strength!
Lift it up! Don't be afraid!

Say to the cities of Judah, "Behold, your God!"
¹⁰ Behold, the Lord Yahweh will come as a mighty one,
and his arm will rule for him.
Behold, his reward is with him,
and his recompense before him.
¹¹ He will feed his flock like a shepherd.
He will gather the lambs in his arm,
and carry them in his bosom.
He will gently lead those who have their young.

Responsorial Psalm: Psalms 96: 1-2, 3 and 10ac, 11-12, 13

¹ Sing to Yahweh a new song!
Sing to Yahweh, all the earth.
² Sing to Yahweh!
Bless his name!
Proclaim his salvation from day to day!
³ Declare his glory among the nations,
his marvelous works among all the peoples.
¹⁰ Say among the nations, "Yahweh reigns."
The world is also established.
It can't be moved.
He will judge the peoples with equity.
¹¹ Let the heavens be glad, and let the earth rejoice.
Let the sea roar, and its fullness!
¹² Let the field and all that is in it exult!
Then all the trees of the woods shall sing for joy
¹³ before Yahweh; for he comes,
for he comes to judge the earth.
He will judge the world with righteousness,
the peoples with his truth.

Gospel: Matthew 18: 12-14

¹² "What do you think? If a man has one hundred sheep, and one of them goes astray, doesn't he leave the ninety-nine, go to the mountains, and seek that which has gone astray? ¹³ If he finds it, most certainly I tell you, he rejoices over it more than over the ninety-nine which have not gone astray. ¹⁴ Even so it is not the will of your Father who is in heaven that one of these little ones should perish.

1. Invite the Holy Spirit into this reading, asking the Author of Scripture to speak to you through His Word
2. Read today's passage as many times as you need, take your time
3. Write down (below) what the Lord is saying to you today
4. Live with this Word in your heart through the day

Wednesday, December 10, 2025
Our Lady of Loreto

First Reading: Isaiah 40: 25-31

25 "To whom then will you liken me?
Who is my equal?" says the Holy One.
26 Lift up your eyes on high,
and see who has created these,
who brings out their army by number.
He calls them all by name.
By the greatness of his might,
and because he is strong in power,
not one is lacking.
27 Why do you say, Jacob,
and speak, Israel,
"My way is hidden from Yahweh,
and the justice due me is disregarded by my God"?
28 Haven't you known?
Haven't you heard?
The everlasting God, Yahweh,
the Creator of the ends of the earth, doesn't faint.
He isn't weary.
His understanding is unsearchable.
29 He gives power to the weak.
He increases the strength of him who has no might.
30 Even the youths faint and get weary,
and the young men utterly fall;
31 but those who wait for Yahweh will renew their strength.

They will mount up with wings like eagles.
They will run, and not be weary.
They will walk, and not faint.

Responsorial Psalm: Psalms 103: 1-2, 3-4, 8 and 10

¹ Praise Yahweh, my soul!
All that is within me, praise his holy name!
² Praise Yahweh, my soul,
and don't forget all his benefits,
³ who forgives all your sins,
who heals all your diseases,
⁴ who redeems your life from destruction,
who crowns you with loving kindness and tender mercies,
⁸ Yahweh is merciful and gracious,
slow to anger, and abundant in loving kindness.
¹⁰ He has not dealt with us according to our sins,
nor repaid us for our iniquities.

Gospel: Matthew 11: 28-30

²⁸ "Come to me, all you who labor and are heavily burdened, and I will give you rest. ²⁹ Take my yoke upon you and learn from me, for I am gentle and humble in heart; and you will find rest for your souls. ³⁰ For my yoke is easy, and my burden is light."

1. Invite the Holy Spirit into this reading, asking the Author of Scripture to speak to you through His Word
2. Read today's passage as many times as you need, take your time
3. Write down (below) what the Lord is saying to you today
4. Live with this Word in your heart through the day

Thursday, December 11, 2025
Saint Damasus I, Pope

First Reading: Isaiah 41: 13-20

¹³ For I, Yahweh your God, will hold your right hand,
saying to you, 'Don't be afraid.
I will help you.'
¹⁴ Don't be afraid, you worm Jacob,
and you men of Israel.
I will help you," says Yahweh.
"Your Redeemer is the Holy One of Israel.
¹⁵ Behold, I have made you into a new sharp threshing instrument with teeth.
You will thresh the mountains,
and beat them small,
and will make the hills like chaff.
¹⁶ You will winnow them,
and the wind will carry them away,
and the whirlwind will scatter them.
You will rejoice in Yahweh.
You will glory in the Holy One of Israel.
¹⁷ The poor and needy seek water, and there is none.
Their tongue fails for thirst.
I, Yahweh, will answer them.
I, the God of Israel, will not forsake them.
¹⁸ I will open rivers on the bare heights,
and springs in the middle of the valleys.
I will make the wilderness a pool of water,
and the dry land springs of water.
¹⁹ I will put cedar, acacia, myrtle, and oil trees in the wilderness.
I will set cypress trees, pine, and box trees together in the desert;
²⁰ that they may see, know, consider, and understand together,
that Yahweh's hand has done this,
and the Holy One of Israel has created it.

Responsorial Psalm: Psalms 145: 1 and 9, 10-11, 12-13ab

¹ I will exalt you, my God, the King.
I will praise your name forever and ever.
⁹ Yahweh is good to all.
His tender mercies are over all his works.
¹⁰ All your works will give thanks to you, Yahweh.
Your saints will extol you.

¹¹ They will speak of the glory of your kingdom,
and talk about your power,
¹² to make known to the sons of men his mighty acts,
the glory of the majesty of his kingdom.
¹³ Your kingdom is an everlasting kingdom.
Your dominion endures throughout all generations.
Yahweh is faithful in all his words,
and loving in all his deeds.

Gospel: Matthew 11: 11-15

¹¹ Most certainly I tell you, among those who are born of women there has not arisen anyone greater than John the Baptizer; yet he who is least in the Kingdom of Heaven is greater than he. ¹² From the days of John the Baptizer until now, the Kingdom of Heaven suffers violence, and the violent take it by force. ¹³ For all the prophets and the law prophesied until John. ¹⁴ If you are willing to receive it, this is Elijah, who is to come. ¹⁵ He who has ears to hear, let him hear.

1. Invite the Holy Spirit into this reading, asking the Author of Scripture to speak to you through His Word
2. Read today's passage as many times as you need, take your time
3. Write down (below) what the Lord is saying to you today
4. Live with this Word in your heart through the day

Friday, December 12, 2025
Our Lady of Guadalupe

First Reading: Revelation 11: 19a; 12: 1-6a, 10ab

¹⁹ God's temple that is in heaven was opened, and the ark of the Lord's covenant was seen in his temple. Lightnings, sounds, thunders, an earthquake, and great hail followed.
¹ A great sign was seen in heaven: a woman clothed with the sun, and the moon under her feet, and on her head a crown of twelve stars. ² She was with child. She cried out in pain, laboring to give birth.

³ Another sign was seen in heaven. Behold, a great red dragon, having seven heads and ten horns, and on his heads seven crowns. ⁴ His tail drew one third of the stars of the sky, and threw them to the earth. The dragon stood before the woman who was about to give birth, so that when she gave birth he might devour her child. ⁵ She gave birth to a son, a male child, who is to rule all the nations with a rod of iron. Her child was caught up to God and to his throne. ⁶ The woman fled into the wilderness, where she has a place prepared by God, that there they may nourish her one thousand two hundred sixty days.

¹⁰ I heard a loud voice in heaven, saying, "Now the salvation, the power, and the Kingdom of our God, and the authority of his Christ has come; for the accuser of our brothers has been thrown down, who accuses them before our God day and night.

Responsorial Psalm: Judith 13: 18bcde, 19

¹⁸ Ozias said to her, "Blessed are you, daughter, in the sight of the Most High God, above all the women upon the earth; and blessed is the Lord God, who created the heavens and the earth, who directed you to cut off the head of the prince of our enemies. ¹⁹ For your hope will not depart from the heart of men that remember the strength of God forever.

Gospel: Luke 1: 26-38

²⁶ Now in the sixth month, the angel Gabriel was sent from God to a city of Galilee named Nazareth, ²⁷ to a virgin pledged to be married to a man whose name was Joseph, of David's house. The virgin's name was Mary. ²⁸ Having come in, the angel said to her, "Rejoice, you highly favored one! The Lord is with you. Blessed are you among women!"
²⁹ But when she saw him, she was greatly troubled at the saying, and considered what kind of salutation this might be. ³⁰ The angel said to her, "Don't be afraid, Mary, for you have found favor with God. ³¹ Behold, you will conceive in your womb and give birth to a son, and shall name him 'Jesus.' ³² He will be great and will be called the Son of the Most High. The Lord God will give him the throne of his father David, ³³ and he will reign over the house of Jacob forever. There will be no end to his Kingdom."
³⁴ Mary said to the angel, "How can this be, seeing I am a virgin?"
³⁵ The angel answered her, "The Holy Spirit will come on you, and the power of the Most High will overshadow you. Therefore also the holy one who is born from you will be called the Son of God. ³⁶ Behold, Elizabeth your relative also has conceived a son in her old age; and this is the sixth month with her who was called barren. ³⁷ For nothing spoken by God is impossible."‡
³⁸ Mary said, "Behold, the servant of the Lord; let it be done to me according to your word." Then the angel departed from her.

1. Invite the Holy Spirit into this reading, asking the Author of Scripture to speak to you through His Word
2. Read today's passage as many times as you need, take your time
3. Write down (below) what the Lord is saying to you today
4. Live with this Word in your heart through the day

___

___

Saturday, December 13, 2025
Saint Lucy, Virgin and Martyr

First Reading: Sirach 48: 1-4, 9-11

¹ Then Elijah arose, the prophet like fire.
His word burned like a torch.
² He brought a famine upon them,
and by his zeal made them few in number.
³ By the word of the Lord he shut up the heavens.
He brought down fire three times.
⁴ How you were glorified, O Elijah, in your wondrous deeds!
Whose glory is like yours?
⁹ You were taken up in a tempest of fire,
in a chariot of fiery horses.
¹⁰ You were recorded for reproofs in their seasons,
to pacify anger, before it broke out into wrath,
to turn the heart of the father to the son,
and to restore the tribes of Jacob.
¹¹ Blessed are those who saw you,
and those who have been beautified with love;
for we also shall surely live.

Responsorial Psalm: Psalms 80: 2ac and 3b, 15-16, 18-19

² Before Ephraim, Benjamin, and Manasseh, stir up your might!
Come to save us!
³ Turn us again, God.
Cause your face to shine,

and we will be saved.
¹⁵ the stock which your right hand planted,
the branch that you made strong for yourself.
¹⁶ It's burned with fire.
It's cut down.
They perish at your rebuke.
¹⁸ So we will not turn away from you.
Revive us, and we will call on your name.
¹⁹ Turn us again, Yahweh God of Armies.
Cause your face to shine, and we will be saved.

Gospel: Matthew 17: 9a, 10-13

⁹ As they were coming down from the mountain, Jesus commanded them, saying, "Don't tell anyone what you saw, until the Son of Man has risen from the dead." ¹⁰ His disciples asked him, saying, "Then why do the scribes say that Elijah must come first?" ¹¹ Jesus answered them, "Elijah indeed comes first, and will restore all things; ¹² but I tell you that Elijah has come already, and they didn't recognize him, but did to him whatever they wanted to. Even so the Son of Man will also suffer by them." ¹³ Then the disciples understood that he spoke to them of John the Baptizer.

1. Invite the Holy Spirit into this reading, asking the Author of Scripture to speak to you through His Word
2. Read today's passage as many times as you need, take your time
3. Write down (below) what the Lord is saying to you today
4. Live with this Word in your heart through the day

Sunday, December 14, 2025
THIRD SUNDAY OF ADVENT

First Reading: Isaiah 35: 1-6a, 10

¹ The wilderness and the dry land will be glad.
The desert will rejoice and blossom like a rose.

² It will blossom abundantly,
and rejoice even with joy and singing.
Lebanon's glory will be given to it,
the excellence of Carmel and Sharon.
They will see Yahweh's glory,
the excellence of our God.
³ Strengthen the weak hands,
and make the feeble knees firm.
⁴ Tell those who have a fearful heart, "Be strong!
Don't be afraid!
Behold, your God will come with vengeance, God's retribution.
He will come and save you.
⁵ Then the eyes of the blind will be opened,
and the ears of the deaf will be unstopped.
⁶ Then the lame man will leap like a deer,
and the tongue of the mute will sing;
for waters will break out in the wilderness,
and streams in the desert.
¹⁰ Then Yahweh's ransomed ones will return,
and come with singing to Zion;
and everlasting joy will be on their heads.
They will obtain gladness and joy,
and sorrow and sighing will flee away."

Responsorial Psalm: Psalms 146: 6-7, 8-9a, 9bc-10

⁶ who made heaven and earth,
the sea, and all that is in them;
who keeps truth forever;
⁷ who executes justice for the oppressed;
who gives food to the hungry.
Yahweh frees the prisoners.
⁸ Yahweh opens the eyes of the blind.
Yahweh raises up those who are bowed down.
Yahweh loves the righteous.
⁹ Yahweh preserves the foreigners.
He upholds the fatherless and widow,
but he turns the way of the wicked upside down.
¹⁰ Yahweh will reign forever;
your God, O Zion, to all generations.

Praise Yah!

Second Reading: James 5: 7-10

⁷ Be patient therefore, brothers, until the coming of the Lord. Behold, the farmer waits for the precious fruit of the earth, being patient over it, until it receives the early and late rain. ⁸ You also be patient. Establish your hearts, for the coming of the Lord is at hand. ⁹ Don't grumble, brothers, against one another, so that you won't be judged. Behold, the judge stands at the door. ¹⁰ Take, brothers, for an example of suffering and of perseverance, the prophets who spoke in the name of the Lord.

Gospel: Matthew 11: 2-11

² Now when John heard in the prison the works of Christ, he sent two of his disciples ³ and said to him, "Are you he who comes, or should we look for another?"
⁴ Jesus answered them, "Go and tell John the things which you hear and see: ⁵ the blind receive their sight, the lame walk, the lepers are cleansed, the deaf hear, the dead are raised up, and the poor have good news preached to them. ⁶ Blessed is he who finds no occasion for stumbling in me."
⁷ As these went their way, Jesus began to say to the multitudes concerning John, "What did you go out into the wilderness to see? A reed shaken by the wind? ⁸ But what did you go out to see? A man in soft clothing? Behold, those who wear soft clothing are in kings' houses. ⁹ But why did you go out? To see a prophet? Yes, I tell you, and much more than a prophet. ¹⁰ For this is he, of whom it is written, 'Behold, I send my messenger before your face, who will prepare your way before you.' ¹¹ Most certainly I tell you, among those who are born of women there has not arisen anyone greater than John the Baptizer; yet he who is least in the Kingdom of Heaven is greater than he.

1. Invite the Holy Spirit into this reading, asking the Author of Scripture to speak to you through His Word
2. Read today's passage as many times as you need, take your time
3. Write down (below) what the Lord is saying to you today
4. Live with this Word in your heart through the day

_____

_____

Monday, December 15, 2025

First Reading: Numbers 24: 2-7, 15-17

² Balaam lifted up his eyes, and he saw Israel dwelling according to their tribes; and the Spirit of God came on him. ³ He took up his parable, and said,
"Balaam the son of Beor says,
the man whose eyes are open says;
⁴ he says, who hears the words of God,
who sees the vision of the Almighty,
falling down, and having his eyes open:
⁵ How goodly are your tents, Jacob,
and your dwellings, Israel!
⁶ As valleys they are spread out,
as gardens by the riverside,
as aloes which Yahweh has planted,
as cedar trees beside the waters.
⁷ Water shall flow from his buckets.
His seed shall be in many waters.
His king shall be higher than Agag.
His kingdom shall be exalted.
¹⁵ He took up his parable, and said,
"Balaam the son of Beor says,
the man whose eyes are open says;
¹⁶ he says, who hears the words of God,
knows the knowledge of the Most High,
and who sees the vision of the Almighty,
falling down, and having his eyes open:
¹⁷ I see him, but not now.
I see him, but not near.
A star will come out of Jacob.
A scepter will rise out of Israel,
and shall strike through the corners of Moab,
and crush all the sons of Sheth.

Responsorial Psalm: Psalms 25: 4-5ab, 6 and 7bc, 8-9

⁴ Show me your ways, Yahweh.
Teach me your paths.
⁵ Guide me in your truth, and teach me,
for you are the God of my salvation.

I wait for you all day long.
⁶ Yahweh, remember your tender mercies and your loving kindness,
for they are from old times.
⁷ᵇ Remember me according to your loving kindness,
for your goodness' sake, Yahweh.
⁸ Good and upright is Yahweh,
therefore he will instruct sinners in the way.
⁹ He will guide the humble in justice.
He will teach the humble his way.

Gospel: Matthew 21: 23-27

²³ When he had come into the temple, the chief priests and the elders of the people came to him as he was teaching, and said, "By what authority do you do these things? Who gave you this authority?"
²⁴ Jesus answered them, "I also will ask you one question, which if you tell me, I likewise will tell you by what authority I do these things. ²⁵ The baptism of John, where was it from? From heaven or from men?"
They reasoned with themselves, saying, "If we say, 'From heaven,' he will ask us, 'Why then did you not believe him?' ²⁶ But if we say, 'From men,' we fear the multitude, for all hold John as a prophet." ²⁷ They answered Jesus, and said, "We don't know."
He also said to them, "Neither will I tell you by what authority I do these things.

1. Invite the Holy Spirit into this reading, asking the Author of Scripture to speak to you through His Word
2. Read today's passage as many times as you need, take your time
3. Write down (below) what the Lord is saying to you today
4. Live with this Word in your heart through the day

Tuesday, December 16, 2025

First Reading: Zephaniah 3: 1-2, 9-13

¹ Woe to her who is rebellious and polluted, the oppressing city! ² She didn't obey the voice. She didn't receive correction. She didn't trust in Yahweh. She didn't draw near to her God.

⁹ For then I will purify the lips of the peoples, that they may all call on Yahweh's name, to serve him shoulder to shoulder. ¹⁰ From beyond the rivers of Cush, my worshipers, even the daughter of my dispersed people, will bring my offering. ¹¹ In that day you will not be disappointed for all your doings in which you have transgressed against me; for then I will take away out from among you your proudly exulting ones, and you will no more be arrogant in my holy mountain. ¹² But I will leave among you an afflicted and poor people, and they will take refuge in Yahweh's name. ¹³ The remnant of Israel will not do iniquity nor speak lies, neither will a deceitful tongue be found in their mouth, for they will feed and lie down, and no one will make them afraid."

Responsorial Psalm: Psalms 34: 2-3, 6-7, 17-18, 19

² My soul shall boast in Yahweh.
The humble shall hear of it and be glad.
³ Oh magnify Yahweh with me.
Let's exalt his name together.
⁶ This poor man cried, and Yahweh heard him,
and saved him out of all his troubles.
⁷ Yahweh's angel encamps around those who fear him,
and delivers them.
¹⁷ The righteous cry, and Yahweh hears,
and delivers them out of all their troubles.
¹⁸ Yahweh is near to those who have a broken heart,
and saves those who have a crushed spirit.
¹⁹ Many are the afflictions of the righteous,
but Yahweh delivers him out of them all.

Gospel: Matthew 21: 28-32

²⁸ But what do you think? A man had two sons, and he came to the first, and said, 'Son, go work today in my vineyard.' ²⁹ He answered, 'I will not,' but afterward he changed his mind, and went. ³⁰ He came to the second, and said the same thing. He answered, 'I'm going, sir,' but he didn't go. ³¹ Which of the two did the will of his father?"
They said to him, "The first."
Jesus said to them, "Most certainly I tell you that the tax collectors and the prostitutes are entering into God's Kingdom before you. ³² For John came to you in the way of righteousness, and you didn't believe him; but the tax collectors and the prostitutes believed him. When you saw it, you didn't even repent afterward, that you might believe him.

1. Invite the Holy Spirit into this reading, asking the Author of Scripture to speak to you through His Word
2. Read today's passage as many times as you need, take your time
3. Write down (below) what the Lord is saying to you today
4. Live with this Word in your heart through the day

Wednesday, December 17, 2025

First Reading: Genesis 49: 2, 8-10

² Assemble yourselves, and hear, you sons of Jacob.
Listen to Israel, your father.
⁸ "Judah, your brothers will praise you.
Your hand will be on the neck of your enemies.
Your father's sons will bow down before you.
⁹ Judah is a lion's cub.
From the prey, my son, you have gone up.
He stooped down, he crouched as a lion,
as a lioness.
Who will rouse him up?
¹⁰ The scepter will not depart from Judah,
nor the ruler's staff from between his feet,
until he comes to whom it belongs.
The obedience of the peoples will be to him.

Responsorial Psalm: Psalms 72: 1-2, 3-4ab, 7-8, 17

¹ God, give the king your justice;
your righteousness to the royal son.
² He will judge your people with righteousness,
and your poor with justice.
³ The mountains shall bring prosperity to the people.
The hills bring the fruit of righteousness.
⁴ He will judge the poor of the people.
He will save the children of the needy,

and will break the oppressor in pieces.
7 In his days, the righteous shall flourish,
and abundance of peace, until the moon is no more.
8 He shall have dominion also from sea to sea,
from the River to the ends of the earth.
17 His name endures forever.
His name continues as long as the sun.
Men shall be blessed by him.
All nations will call him blessed.

Gospel: Matthew 1: 1-17

1 The book of the genealogy of Jesus Christ,‡ the son of David, the son of Abraham.
2 Abraham became the father of Isaac. Isaac became the father of Jacob. Jacob became the father of Judah and his brothers. 3 Judah became the father of Perez and Zerah by Tamar. Perez became the father of Hezron. Hezron became the father of Ram. 4 Ram became the father of Amminadab. Amminadab became the father of Nahshon. Nahshon became the father of Salmon. 5 Salmon became the father of Boaz by Rahab. Boaz became the father of Obed by Ruth. Obed became the father of Jesse. 6 Jesse became the father of King David. David the king‡ became the father of Solomon by her who had been Uriah's wife. 7 Solomon became the father of Rehoboam. Rehoboam became the father of Abijah. Abijah became the father of Asa. 8 Asa became the father of Jehoshaphat. Jehoshaphat became the father of Joram. Joram became the father of Uzziah. 9 Uzziah became the father of Jotham. Jotham became the father of Ahaz. Ahaz became the father of Hezekiah. 10 Hezekiah became the father of Manasseh. Manasseh became the father of Amon. Amon became the father of Josiah. 11 Josiah became the father of Jechoniah and his brothers at the time of the exile to Babylon.
12 After the exile to Babylon, Jechoniah became the father of Shealtiel. Shealtiel became the father of Zerubbabel. 13 Zerubbabel became the father of Abiud. Abiud became the father of Eliakim. Eliakim became the father of Azor. 14 Azor became the father of Zadok. Zadok became the father of Achim. Achim became the father of Eliud. 15 Eliud became the father of Eleazar. Eleazar became the father of Matthan. Matthan became the father of Jacob. 16 Jacob became the father of Joseph, the husband of Mary, from whom was born Jesus,§ who is called Christ.
17 So all the generations from Abraham to David are fourteen generations; from David to the exile to Babylon fourteen generations; and from the carrying away to Babylon to the Christ, fourteen generations.

1. Invite the Holy Spirit into this reading, asking the Author of Scripture to speak to you through His Word

2. Read today's passage as many times as you need, take your time
3. Write down (below) what the Lord is saying to you today
4. Live with this Word in your heart through the day

_____

_____

Thursday, December 18, 2025

First Reading: Jeremiah 23: 5-8

⁵ "Behold, the days come," says Yahweh,
"that I will raise to David a righteous Branch;
and he will reign as king and deal wisely,
and will execute justice and righteousness in the land.
⁶ In his days Judah will be saved,
and Israel will dwell safely.
This is his name by which he will be called:
Yahweh our righteousness.
⁷ "Therefore, behold, the days come," says Yahweh, "that they will no more say, 'As Yahweh lives, who brought up the children of Israel out of the land of Egypt;' ⁸ but, 'As Yahweh lives, who brought up and who led the offspring of the house of Israel out of the north country, and from all the countries where I had driven them.' Then they will dwell in their own land."

Responsorial Psalm: Psalms 72: 1-2, 12-13, 18-19

¹ God, give the king your justice;
your righteousness to the royal son.
² He will judge your people with righteousness,
and your poor with justice.
¹² For he will deliver the needy when he cries;
the poor, who has no helper.
¹³ He will have pity on the poor and needy.
He will save the souls of the needy.
¹⁸ Praise be to Yahweh God, the God of Israel,
who alone does marvelous deeds.
¹⁹ Blessed be his glorious name forever!

Let the whole earth be filled with his glory!
Amen and amen.

Gospel: Matthew 1: 18-25

[18] Now the birth of Jesus Christ was like this: After his mother, Mary, was engaged to Joseph, before they came together, she was found pregnant by the Holy Spirit. [19] Joseph, her husband, being a righteous man, and not willing to make her a public example, intended to put her away secretly. [20] But when he thought about these things, behold, an angel of the Lord appeared to him in a dream, saying, "Joseph, son of David, don't be afraid to take to yourself Mary as your wife, for that which is conceived in her is of the Holy Spirit. [21] She shall give birth to a son. You shall name him Jesus, for it is he who shall save his people from their sins."
[22] Now all this has happened that it might be fulfilled which was spoken by the Lord through the prophet, saying,
[23] "Behold, the virgin shall be with child,
and shall give birth to a son.
They shall call his name Immanuel,"
which is, being interpreted, "God with us."
[24] Joseph arose from his sleep, and did as the angel of the Lord commanded him, and took his wife to himself; [25] and didn't know her sexually until she had given birth to her firstborn son. He named him Jesus.

1. Invite the Holy Spirit into this reading, asking the Author of Scripture to speak to you through His Word
2. Read today's passage as many times as you need, take your time
3. Write down (below) what the Lord is saying to you today
4. Live with this Word in your heart through the day

Friday, December 19, 2025

First Reading: Judges 13: 2-7, 24-25a

[2] There was a certain man of Zorah, of the family of the Danites, whose name was Manoah; and his wife was barren, and childless. [3] Yahweh's angel appeared to the woman, and said

to her, "See now, you are barren and childless; but you shall conceive and bear a son. ⁴ Now therefore please beware and drink no wine nor strong drink, and don't eat any unclean thing; ⁵ for, behold, you shall conceive and give birth to a son. No razor shall come on his head, for the child shall be a Nazirite to God from the womb. He shall begin to save Israel out of the hand of the Philistines."

⁶ Then the woman came and told her husband, saying, "A man of God came to me, and his face was like the face of the angel of God, very awesome. I didn't ask him where he was from, neither did he tell me his name; ⁷ but he said to me, 'Behold, you shall conceive and bear a son; and now drink no wine nor strong drink. Don't eat any unclean thing, for the child shall be a Nazirite to God from the womb to the day of his death.' "

²⁴ The woman bore a son and named him Samson. The child grew, and Yahweh blessed him. ²⁵ Yahweh's Spirit began to move him in Mahaneh Dan, between Zorah and Eshtaol.

Responsorial Psalm: Psalms 71: 3-4a, 5-6ab, 16-17

³ Be to me a rock of refuge to which I may always go.
Give the command to save me,
for you are my rock and my fortress.
⁴ Rescue me, my God, from the hand of the wicked,
from the hand of the unrighteous and cruel man.
⁵ For you are my hope, Lord Yahweh,
my confidence from my youth.
⁶ I have relied on you from the womb.
You are he who took me out of my mother's womb.
I will always praise you.
¹⁶ I will come with the mighty acts of the Lord Yahweh.
I will make mention of your righteousness, even of yours alone.
¹⁷ God, you have taught me from my youth.
Until now, I have declared your wondrous works.

Gospel: Luke 1: 5-25

⁵ There was in the days of Herod, the king of Judea, a certain priest named Zacharias, of the priestly division of Abijah. He had a wife of the daughters of Aaron, and her name was Elizabeth. ⁶ They were both righteous before God, walking blamelessly in all the commandments and ordinances of the Lord. ⁷ But they had no child, because Elizabeth was barren, and they both were well advanced in years.

⁸ Now while he executed the priest's office before God in the order of his division ⁹ according to the custom of the priest's office, his lot was to enter into the temple

of the Lord and burn incense. ¹⁰ The whole multitude of the people were praying outside at the hour of incense.

¹¹ An angel of the Lord appeared to him, standing on the right side of the altar of incense. ¹² Zacharias was troubled when he saw him, and fear fell upon him. ¹³ But the angel said to him, "Don't be afraid, Zacharias, because your request has been heard. Your wife, Elizabeth, will bear you a son, and you shall call his name John. ¹⁴ You will have joy and gladness, and many will rejoice at his birth. ¹⁵ For he will be great in the sight of the Lord, and he will drink no wine nor strong drink. He will be filled with the Holy Spirit, even from his mother's womb. ¹⁶ He will turn many of the children of Israel to the Lord their God. ¹⁷ He will go before him in the spirit and power of Elijah, 'to turn the hearts of the fathers to the children,' and the disobedient to the wisdom of the just; to prepare a people prepared for the Lord."

¹⁸ Zacharias said to the angel, "How can I be sure of this? For I am an old man, and my wife is well advanced in years."

¹⁹ The angel answered him, "I am Gabriel, who stands in the presence of God. I was sent to speak to you and to bring you this good news. ²⁰ Behold, you will be silent and not able to speak until the day that these things will happen, because you didn't believe my words, which will be fulfilled in their proper time."

²¹ The people were waiting for Zacharias, and they marveled that he delayed in the temple. ²² When he came out, he could not speak to them. They perceived that he had seen a vision in the temple. He continued making signs to them, and remained mute. ²³ When the days of his service were fulfilled, he departed to his house. ²⁴ After these days Elizabeth his wife conceived, and she hid herself five months, saying, ²⁵ "Thus has the Lord done to me in the days in which he looked at me, to take away my reproach among men."

1. Invite the Holy Spirit into this reading, asking the Author of Scripture to speak to you through His Word
2. Read today's passage as many times as you need, take your time
3. Write down (below) what the Lord is saying to you today
4. Live with this Word in your heart through the day

Saturday, December 20, 2025

First Reading: Isaiah 7: 10-14

¹⁰ Yahweh spoke again to Ahaz, saying, ¹¹ "Ask a sign of Yahweh your God; ask it either in the depth, or in the height above."

¹² But Ahaz said, "I won't ask. I won't tempt Yahweh."

¹³ He said, "Listen now, house of David. Is it not enough for you to try the patience of men, that you will try the patience of my God also? ¹⁴ Therefore the Lord himself will give you a sign. Behold, the virgin will conceive, and bear a son, and shall call his name Immanuel.

Responsorial Psalm: Psalms 24: 1-2, 3-4ab, 5-6

¹ The earth is Yahweh's, with its fullness;
the world, and those who dwell in it.
² For he has founded it on the seas,
and established it on the floods.
³ Who may ascend to Yahweh's hill?
Who may stand in his holy place?
⁴ He who has clean hands and a pure heart;
who has not lifted up his soul to falsehood,
and has not sworn deceitfully.
⁵ He shall receive a blessing from Yahweh,
righteousness from the God of his salvation.
⁶ This is the generation of those who seek Him,
who seek your face—even Jacob.

Gospel: Luke 1: 26-38

²⁶ Now in the sixth month, the angel Gabriel was sent from God to a city of Galilee named Nazareth, ²⁷ to a virgin pledged to be married to a man whose name was Joseph, of David's house. The virgin's name was Mary. ²⁸ Having come in, the angel said to her, "Rejoice, you highly favored one! The Lord is with you. Blessed are you among women!"

²⁹ But when she saw him, she was greatly troubled at the saying, and considered what kind of salutation this might be. ³⁰ The angel said to her, "Don't be afraid, Mary, for you have found favor with God. ³¹ Behold, you will conceive in your womb and give birth to a son, and shall name him 'Jesus.' ³² He will be great and will be called the Son of the Most High. The Lord God will give him the throne of his father David, ³³ and he will reign over the house of Jacob forever. There will be no end to his Kingdom."

³⁴ Mary said to the angel, "How can this be, seeing I am a virgin?"

³⁵ The angel answered her, "The Holy Spirit will come on you, and the power of the Most High will overshadow you. Therefore also the holy one who is born from you will be called the Son of God. ³⁶ Behold, Elizabeth your relative also has conceived a son in her old age;

and this is the sixth month with her who was called barren. ³⁷ For nothing spoken by God is impossible."±
³⁸ Mary said, "Behold, the servant of the Lord; let it be done to me according to your word." Then the angel departed from her.

1. Invite the Holy Spirit into this reading, asking the Author of Scripture to speak to you through His Word
2. Read today's passage as many times as you need, take your time
3. Write down (below) what the Lord is saying to you today
4. Live with this Word in your heart through the day

Sunday, December 21, 2025
FOURTH SUNDAY OF ADVENT

First Reading: Isaiah 7: 10-14

¹⁰ Yahweh spoke again to Ahaz, saying, ¹¹ "Ask a sign of Yahweh your God; ask it either in the depth, or in the height above."
¹² But Ahaz said, "I won't ask. I won't tempt Yahweh."
¹³ He said, "Listen now, house of David. Is it not enough for you to try the patience of men, that you will try the patience of my God also? ¹⁴ Therefore the Lord himself will give you a sign. Behold, the virgin will conceive, and bear a son, and shall call his name Immanuel.

Responsorial Psalm: Psalms 24: 1-2, 3-4, 5-6

¹ The earth is Yahweh's, with its fullness;
the world, and those who dwell in it.
² For he has founded it on the seas,
and established it on the floods.
³ Who may ascend to Yahweh's hill?
Who may stand in his holy place?
⁴ He who has clean hands and a pure heart;
who has not lifted up his soul to falsehood,
and has not sworn deceitfully.
⁵ He shall receive a blessing from Yahweh,

righteousness from the God of his salvation.
⁶ This is the generation of those who seek Him,
who seek your face—even Jacob.

Second Reading: Romans 1: 1-7

¹ Paul, a servant of Jesus Christ,⁺ called to be an apostle, set apart for the Good News of God, ² which he promised before through his prophets in the holy Scriptures, ³ concerning his Son, who was born of the offspring⁺ of David according to the flesh, ⁴ who was declared to be the Son of God with power according to the Spirit of holiness, by the resurrection from the dead, Jesus Christ our Lord, ⁵ through whom we received grace and apostleship for obedience of faith among all the nations for his name's sake; ⁶ among whom you are also called to belong to Jesus Christ; ⁷ to all who are in Rome, beloved of God, called to be saints: Grace to you and peace from God our Father and the Lord Jesus Christ.

Gospel: Matthew 1: 18-24

¹⁸ Now the birth of Jesus Christ was like this: After his mother, Mary, was engaged to Joseph, before they came together, she was found pregnant by the Holy Spirit. ¹⁹ Joseph, her husband, being a righteous man, and not willing to make her a public example, intended to put her away secretly. ²⁰ But when he thought about these things, behold,⁺ an angel of the Lord appeared to him in a dream, saying, "Joseph, son of David, don't be afraid to take to yourself Mary as your wife, for that which is conceived in her is of the Holy Spirit. ²¹ She shall give birth to a son. You shall name him Jesus,⁺ for it is he who shall save his people from their sins."
²² Now all this has happened that it might be fulfilled which was spoken by the Lord through the prophet, saying,
²³ "Behold, the virgin shall be with child,
and shall give birth to a son.
They shall call his name Immanuel,"
which is, being interpreted, "God with us."⁺
²⁴ Joseph arose from his sleep, and did as the angel of the Lord commanded him, and took his wife to himself;

1. Invite the Holy Spirit into this reading, asking the Author of Scripture to speak to you through His Word
2. Read today's passage as many times as you need, take your time
3. Write down (below) what the Lord is saying to you today
4. Live with this Word in your heart through the day

Monday, December 22, 2025

First Reading: First Samuel 1: 24-28

²⁴ When she had weaned him, she took him up with her, with three bulls, and one ephah⸸ of meal, and a container of wine, and brought him to Yahweh's house in Shiloh. The child was young. ²⁵ They killed the bull, and brought the child to Eli. ²⁶ She said, "Oh, my lord, as your soul lives, my lord, I am the woman who stood by you here, praying to Yahweh. ²⁷ I prayed for this child, and Yahweh has given me my petition which I asked of him. ²⁸ Therefore I have also given him to Yahweh. As long as he lives he is given to Yahweh." He worshiped Yahweh there.

Responsorial Psalm: First Samuel 2: 1, 4-5, 6-7, 8abcd

¹ Hannah prayed, and said,
"My heart exults in Yahweh!
My horn is exalted in Yahweh.
My mouth is enlarged over my enemies,
because I rejoice in your salvation.
⁴ "The bows of the mighty men are broken.
Those who stumbled are armed with strength.
⁵ Those who were full have hired themselves out for bread.
Those who were hungry are satisfied.
Yes, the barren has borne seven.
She who has many children languishes.
⁶ "Yahweh kills and makes alive.
He brings down to Sheol⸸ and brings up.
⁷ Yahweh makes poor and makes rich.
He brings low, he also lifts up.
⁸ He raises up the poor out of the dust.
He lifts up the needy from the dunghill
to make them sit with princes
and inherit the throne of glory.
For the pillars of the earth are Yahweh's.
He has set the world on them.

Gospel: Luke 1: 46-56

⁴⁶ Mary said,
"My soul magnifies the Lord.
⁴⁷ My spirit has rejoiced in God my Savior,
⁴⁸ for he has looked at the humble state of his servant.
For behold, from now on, all generations will call me blessed.
⁴⁹ For he who is mighty has done great things for me.
Holy is his name.
⁵⁰ His mercy is for generations and generations on those who fear him.
⁵¹ He has shown strength with his arm.
He has scattered the proud in the imagination of their hearts.
⁵² He has put down princes from their thrones,
and has exalted the lowly.
⁵³ He has filled the hungry with good things.
He has sent the rich away empty.
⁵⁴ He has given help to Israel, his servant, that he might remember mercy,
⁵⁵ as he spoke to our fathers,
to Abraham and his offspring§ forever."
⁵⁶ Mary stayed with her about three months, and then returned to her house.

1. Invite the Holy Spirit into this reading, asking the Author of Scripture to speak to you through His Word
2. Read today's passage as many times as you need, take your time
3. Write down (below) what the Lord is saying to you today
4. Live with this Word in your heart through the day

___

___

Tuesday, December 23, 2025
Saint John of Kanty, Priest

First Reading: Malachi 3: 1-4, 4: 5-6

¹ "Behold, I send my messenger, and he will prepare the way before me! The Lord, whom you seek, will suddenly come to his temple. Behold, the messenger of the covenant, whom you desire, is coming!" says Yahweh of Armies. ² "But who can endure the day of his

coming? And who will stand when he appears? For he is like a refiner's fire, and like launderers' soap; 3 and he will sit as a refiner and purifier of silver, and he will purify the sons of Levi, and refine them as gold and silver; and they shall offer to Yahweh offerings in righteousness. 4 Then the offering of Judah and Jerusalem will be pleasant to Yahweh as in the days of old and as in ancient years.
5 Behold, I will send you Elijah the prophet before the great and terrible day of Yahweh comes. 6 He will turn the hearts of the fathers to the children and the hearts of the children to their fathers, lest I come and strike the earth with a curse."

Responsorial Psalm: Psalms 25: 4-5ab, 8-9, 10 and 14

4 Show me your ways, Yahweh.
Teach me your paths.
5 Guide me in your truth, and teach me,
for you are the God of my salvation.
I wait for you all day long.
8 Good and upright is Yahweh,
therefore he will instruct sinners in the way.
9 He will guide the humble in justice.
He will teach the humble his way.
10 All the paths of Yahweh are loving kindness and truth
to such as keep his covenant and his testimonies.
14 The friendship of Yahweh is with those who fear him.
He will show them his covenant.

Gospel: Luke 1: 57-66

57 Now the time that Elizabeth should give birth was fulfilled, and she gave birth to a son. 58 Her neighbors and her relatives heard that the Lord had magnified his mercy toward her, and they rejoiced with her. 59 On the eighth day, they came to circumcise the child; and they would have called him Zacharias, after the name of his father. 60 His mother answered, "Not so; but he will be called John."
61 They said to her, "There is no one among your relatives who is called by this name." 62 They made signs to his father, what he would have him called.
63 He asked for a writing tablet, and wrote, "His name is John."
They all marveled. 64 His mouth was opened immediately and his tongue freed, and he spoke, blessing God. 65 Fear came on all who lived around them, and all these sayings were talked about throughout all the hill country of Judea. 66 All who heard them laid them up in their heart, saying, "What then will this child be?" The hand of the Lord was with him.

1. Invite the Holy Spirit into this reading, asking the Author of Scripture to speak to you through His Word
2. Read today's passage as many times as you need, take your time
3. Write down (below) what the Lord is saying to you today
4. Live with this Word in your heart through the day

_____

_____

Wednesday, December 24, 2025

First Reading: Second Samuel 7: 1-5, 8b-12, 14a, 16

¹ When the king lived in his house, and Yahweh had given him rest from all his enemies all around, ² the king said to Nathan the prophet, "See now, I dwell in a house of cedar, but God's ark dwells within curtains."
³ Nathan said to the king, "Go, do all that is in your heart, for Yahweh is with you."
⁴ That same night, Yahweh's word came to Nathan, saying, ⁵ "Go and tell my servant David, 'Yahweh says, "Should you build me a house for me to dwell in?
⁸ Now therefore tell my servant David this: 'Yahweh of Armies says, "I took you from the sheep pen, from following the sheep, to be prince over my people, over Israel. ⁹ I have been with you wherever you went, and have cut off all your enemies from before you. I will make you a great name, like the name of the great ones who are in the earth. ¹⁰ I will appoint a place for my people Israel, and will plant them, that they may dwell in their own place and be moved no more. The children of wickedness will not afflict them any more, as at the first, ¹¹ and as from the day that I commanded judges to be over my people Israel. I will cause you to rest from all your enemies. Moreover Yahweh tells you that Yahweh will make you a house. ¹² When your days are fulfilled and you sleep with your fathers, I will set up your offspring after you, who will proceed out of your body, and I will establish his kingdom.
¹⁴ I will be his father, and he will be my son. If he commits iniquity, I will chasten him with the rod of men and with the stripes of the children of men;
¹⁶ Your house and your kingdom will be made sure forever before you. Your throne will be established forever."' "

Responsorial Psalm: Psalms 89: 2-3, 4-5, 27 and 29

² I indeed declare, "Love stands firm forever.

You established the heavens.
Your faithfulness is in them."
³ "I have made a covenant with my chosen one,
I have sworn to David, my servant,
⁴ 'I will establish your offspring forever,
and build up your throne to all generations.' "
Selah.
⁵ The heavens will praise your wonders, Yahweh,
your faithfulness also in the assembly of the holy ones.
²⁷ I will also appoint him my firstborn,
the highest of the kings of the earth.
²⁹ I will also make his offspring endure forever,
and his throne as the days of heaven.

Gospel: Luke 1: 67-79

⁶⁷ His father Zacharias was filled with the Holy Spirit, and prophesied, saying,
⁶⁸ "Blessed be the Lord, the God of Israel,
for he has visited and redeemed his people;
⁶⁹ and has raised up a horn of salvation for us in the house of his servant David
⁷⁰ (as he spoke by the mouth of his holy prophets who have been from of old),
⁷¹ salvation from our enemies and from the hand of all who hate us;
⁷² to show mercy toward our fathers,
to remember his holy covenant,
⁷³ the oath which he swore to Abraham our father,
⁷⁴ to grant to us that we, being delivered out of the hand of our enemies,
should serve him without fear,
⁷⁵ in holiness and righteousness before him all the days of our life.
⁷⁶ And you, child, will be called a prophet of the Most High;
for you will go before the face of the Lord to prepare his ways,
⁷⁷ to give knowledge of salvation to his people by the remission of their sins,
⁷⁸ because of the tender mercy of our God,
by which the dawn from on high will visit us,
⁷⁹ to shine on those who sit in darkness and the shadow of death;
to guide our feet into the way of peace."

1. Invite the Holy Spirit into this reading, asking the Author of Scripture to speak to you through His Word
2. Read today's passage as many times as you need, take your time
3. Write down (below) what the Lord is saying to you today

4. Live with this Word in your heart through the day

Thursday, December 25, 2025
THE NATIVITY OF THE LORD (Christmas)

First Reading: Isaiah 52: 7-10

⁷ How beautiful on the mountains are the feet of him who brings good news,
who publishes peace,
who brings good news,
who proclaims salvation,
who says to Zion, "Your God reigns!"
⁸ Your watchmen lift up their voice.
Together they sing;
for they shall see eye to eye when Yahweh returns to Zion.
⁹ Break out into joy!
Sing together, you waste places of Jerusalem;
for Yahweh has comforted his people.
He has redeemed Jerusalem.
¹⁰ Yahweh has made his holy arm bare in the eyes of all the nations.
All the ends of the earth have seen the salvation of our God.

Responsorial Psalm: Psalms 98: 1, 2-3, 3-4, 5-6

¹ Sing to Yahweh a new song,
for he has done marvelous things!
His right hand and his holy arm have worked salvation for him.
² Yahweh has made known his salvation.
He has openly shown his righteousness in the sight of the nations.
³ He has remembered his loving kindness and his faithfulness toward the house of Israel.
All the ends of the earth have seen the salvation of our God.
⁴ Make a joyful noise to Yahweh, all the earth!
Burst out and sing for joy, yes, sing praises!
⁵ Sing praises to Yahweh with the harp,
with the harp and the voice of melody.

⁶ With trumpets and sound of the ram's horn,
make a joyful noise before the King, Yahweh.

Second Reading: Hebrews 1: 1-6

¹ God, having in the past spoken to the fathers through the prophets at many times and in various ways, ² has at the end of these days spoken to us by his Son, whom he appointed heir of all things, through whom also he made the worlds. ³ His Son is the radiance of his glory, the very image of his substance, and upholding all things by the word of his power, who, when he had by himself purified us of our sins, sat down on the right hand of the Majesty on high, ⁴ having become as much better than the angels as the more excellent name he has inherited is better than theirs. ⁵ For to which of the angels did he say at any time,
"You are my Son.
Today I have become your father?"*
and again,
"I will be to him a Father,
and he will be to me a Son?"*
⁶ When he again brings in the firstborn into the world he says, "Let all the angels of God worship him."

Gospel: John 1: 1-18

¹ In the beginning was the Word, and the Word was with God, and the Word was God. ² The same was in the beginning with God. ³ All things were made through him. Without him, nothing was made that has been made. ⁴ In him was life, and the life was the light of men. ⁵ The light shines in the darkness, and the darkness hasn't overcome± it.
⁶ There came a man sent from God, whose name was John. ⁷ The same came as a witness, that he might testify about the light, that all might believe through him. ⁸ He was not the light, but was sent that he might testify about the light. ⁹ The true light that enlightens everyone was coming into the world.
¹⁰ He was in the world, and the world was made through him, and the world didn't recognize him. ¹¹ He came to his own, and those who were his own didn't receive him. ¹² But as many as received him, to them he gave the right to become God's children, to those who believe in his name: ¹³ who were born, not of blood, nor of the will of the flesh, nor of the will of man, but of God.
¹⁴ The Word became flesh and lived among us. We saw his glory, such glory as of the only born± Son of the Father, full of grace and truth. ¹⁵ John testified about him. He cried out, saying, "This was he of whom I said, 'He who comes after me has surpassed me, for he was before me.' " ¹⁶ From his fullness we all received grace upon grace. ¹⁷ For the law was given

through Moses. Grace and truth were realized through Jesus Christ.§ ¹⁸ No one has seen God at any time. The only born⁺ Son,⁺ who is in the bosom of the Father, has declared him.

1. Invite the Holy Spirit into this reading, asking the Author of Scripture to speak to you through His Word
2. Read today's passage as many times as you need, take your time
3. Write down (below) what the Lord is saying to you today
4. Live with this Word in your heart through the day

Friday, December 26, 2025
Saint Stephen, the First Martyr

First Reading: Acts 6: 8-10; 7: 54-59

⁸ Stephen, full of faith and power, performed great wonders and signs among the people. ⁹ But some of those who were of the synagogue called "The Libertines", and of the Cyrenians, of the Alexandrians, and of those of Cilicia and Asia arose, disputing with Stephen. ¹⁰ They weren't able to withstand the wisdom and the Spirit by which he spoke.
⁵⁴ Now when they heard these things, they were cut to the heart, and they gnashed at him with their teeth. ⁵⁵ But he, being full of the Holy Spirit, looked up steadfastly into heaven and saw the glory of God, and Jesus standing on the right hand of God, ⁵⁶ and said, "Behold, I see the heavens opened and the Son of Man standing at the right hand of God!"
⁵⁷ But they cried out with a loud voice and stopped their ears, then rushed at him with one accord. ⁵⁸ They threw him out of the city and stoned him. The witnesses placed their garments at the feet of a young man named Saul. ⁵⁹ They stoned Stephen as he called out, saying, "Lord Jesus, receive my spirit!"

Responsorial Psalm: Psalms 31: 3cd-4, 6 and 8ab, 16bc and 17

³ For you are my rock and my fortress,
therefore for your name's sake lead me and guide me.
⁴ Pluck me out of the net that they have laid secretly for me,
for you are my stronghold.
⁶ I hate those who regard lying vanities,
but I trust in Yahweh.

⁸ You have not shut me up into the hand of the enemy.
You have set my feet in a large place.
¹⁶ Make your face to shine on your servant.
Save me in your loving kindness.
¹⁷ Let me not be disappointed, Yahweh, for I have called on you.
Let the wicked be disappointed.
Let them be silent in Sheol.

Gospel: Matthew 10: 17-22

¹⁷ But beware of men, for they will deliver you up to councils, and in their synagogues they will scourge you. ¹⁸ Yes, and you will be brought before governors and kings for my sake, for a testimony to them and to the nations. ¹⁹ But when they deliver you up, don't be anxious how or what you will say, for it will be given you in that hour what you will say. ²⁰ For it is not you who speak, but the Spirit of your Father who speaks in you.
²¹ "Brother will deliver up brother to death, and the father his child. Children will rise up against parents and cause them to be put to death. ²² You will be hated by all men for my name's sake, but he who endures to the end will be saved.

1. Invite the Holy Spirit into this reading, asking the Author of Scripture to speak to you through His Word
2. Read today's passage as many times as you need, take your time
3. Write down (below) what the Lord is saying to you today
4. Live with this Word in your heart through the day

Saturday, December 27, 2025
Saint John, Apostle and Evangelist

First Reading: First John 1: 1-4

¹ That which was from the beginning, that which we have heard, that which we have seen with our eyes, that which we saw, and our hands touched, concerning the Word of life ² (and the life was revealed, and we have seen, and testify, and declare to you the life, the eternal life, which was with the Father, and was revealed to us); ³ that which we have seen and heard we declare to you, that you also may have fellowship with us. Yes, and our

fellowship is with the Father and with his Son, Jesus Christ. ⁱ ⁴ And we write these things to you, that our joy may be fulfilled.

Responsorial Psalm: Psalms 97: 1-2, 5-6, 11-12

¹ Yahweh reigns!
Let the earth rejoice!
Let the multitude of islands be glad!
² Clouds and darkness are around him.
Righteousness and justice are the foundation of his throne.
⁵ The mountains melt like wax at the presence of Yahweh,
at the presence of the Lord of the whole earth.
⁶ The heavens declare his righteousness.
All the peoples have seen his glory.
¹¹ Light is sown for the righteous,
and gladness for the upright in heart.
¹² Be glad in Yahweh, you righteous people!
Give thanks to his holy Name.

Gospel: John 20: 1a and 2-8

¹ Now on the first day of the week, Mary Magdalene went early, while it was still dark, to the tomb, and saw that the stone had been taken away from the tomb. ² Therefore she ran and came to Simon Peter and to the other disciple whom Jesus loved, and said to them, "They have taken away the Lord out of the tomb, and we don't know where they have laid him!"
³ Therefore Peter and the other disciple went out, and they went toward the tomb. ⁴ They both ran together. The other disciple outran Peter and came to the tomb first. ⁵ Stooping and looking in, he saw the linen cloths lying there; yet he didn't enter in. ⁶ Then Simon Peter came, following him, and entered into the tomb. He saw the linen cloths lying, ⁷ and the cloth that had been on his head, not lying with the linen cloths, but rolled up in a place by itself. ⁸ So then the other disciple who came first to the tomb also entered in, and he saw and believed.

1. Invite the Holy Spirit into this reading, asking the Author of Scripture to speak to you through His Word
2. Read today's passage as many times as you need, take your time
3. Write down (below) what the Lord is saying to you today
4. Live with this Word in your heart through the day

Sunday, December 28, 2025
THE HOLY FAMILY OF JESUS, MARY AND JOSEPH

First Reading: Sirach 3: 2-6, 12-14

² For the Lord honors the father over the children,
and has confirmed the judgment of the mother over her sons.
³ He who honors his father will make atonement for sins.
⁴ He who gives glory to his mother is as one who lays up treasure.
⁵ Whoever honors his father will have joy in his own children.
He will be heard in the day of his prayer.
⁶ He who gives glory to his father will have length of days.
He who listens to the Lord will bring rest to his mother,
¹² My son, help your father in his old age,
and don't grieve him as long as he lives.
¹³ If he fails in understanding, have patience with him.
Don't dishonor him in your full strength.
¹⁴ For the kindness to your father will not be forgotten.
Instead of sins it will be added to build you up.

Responsorial Psalm: Psalms 128: 1-2, 3, 4-5

¹ Blessed is everyone who fears Yahweh,
who walks in his ways.
² For you will eat the labor of your hands.
You will be happy, and it will be well with you.
³ Your wife will be as a fruitful vine in the innermost parts of your house,
your children like olive shoots around your table.
⁴ Behold, this is how the man who fears Yahweh is blessed.
⁵ May Yahweh bless you out of Zion,
and may you see the good of Jerusalem all the days of your life.

Second Reading: Colossians 3: 12-17

¹² Put on therefore, as God's chosen ones, holy and beloved, a heart of compassion, kindness, lowliness, humility, and perseverance; ¹³ bearing with one another, and forgiving

each other, if any man has a complaint against any; even as Christ forgave you, so you also do.

¹⁴ Above all these things, walk in love, which is the bond of perfection. ¹⁵ And let the peace of God rule in your hearts, to which also you were called in one body, and be thankful. ¹⁶ Let the word of Christ dwell in you richly; in all wisdom teaching and admonishing one another with psalms, hymns, and spiritual songs, singing with grace in your heart to the Lord.

¹⁷ Whatever you do, in word or in deed, do all in the name of the Lord Jesus, giving thanks to God the Father through him.

Gospel: Matthew 2: 13-15, 19-23

¹³ Now when they had departed, behold, an angel of the Lord appeared to Joseph in a dream, saying, "Arise and take the young child and his mother, and flee into Egypt, and stay there until I tell you, for Herod will seek the young child to destroy him."

¹⁴ He arose and took the young child and his mother by night and departed into Egypt, ¹⁵ and was there until the death of Herod, that it might be fulfilled which was spoken by the Lord through the prophet, saying, "Out of Egypt I called my son."

¹⁹ But when Herod was dead, behold, an angel of the Lord appeared in a dream to Joseph in Egypt, saying, ²⁰ "Arise and take the young child and his mother, and go into the land of Israel, for those who sought the young child's life are dead."

²¹ He arose and took the young child and his mother, and came into the land of Israel. ²² But when he heard that Archelaus was reigning over Judea in the place of his father, Herod, he was afraid to go there. Being warned in a dream, he withdrew into the region of Galilee, ²³ and came and lived in a city called Nazareth; that it might be fulfilled which was spoken through the prophets that he will be called a Nazarene.

1. Invite the Holy Spirit into this reading, asking the Author of Scripture to speak to you through His Word
2. Read today's passage as many times as you need, take your time
3. Write down (below) what the Lord is saying to you today
4. Live with this Word in your heart through the day

Monday, December 29, 2025
Saint Thomas Becket, Bishop and Martyr

First Reading: First John 2: 3-11

3 This is how we know that we know him: if we keep his commandments. 4 One who says, "I know him," and doesn't keep his commandments, is a liar, and the truth isn't in him. 5 But God's love has most certainly been perfected in whoever keeps his word. This is how we know that we are in him: 6 he who says he remains in him ought himself also to walk just like he walked.

7 Brothers, I write no new commandment to you, but an old commandment which you had from the beginning. The old commandment is the word which you heard from the beginning. 8 Again, I write a new commandment to you, which is true in him and in you, because the darkness is passing away and the true light already shines. 9 He who says he is in the light and hates his brother is in the darkness even until now. 10 He who loves his brother remains in the light, and there is no occasion for stumbling in him. 11 But he who hates his brother is in the darkness, and walks in the darkness, and doesn't know where he is going, because the darkness has blinded his eyes.

Responsorial Psalm: Psalms 96: 1-2a, 2b-3, 5b-6

1 Sing to Yahweh a new song!
Sing to Yahweh, all the earth.
2 Sing to Yahweh!
Bless his name!
Proclaim his salvation from day to day!
3 Declare his glory among the nations,
his marvelous works among all the peoples.
5 For all the gods of the peoples are idols,
but Yahweh made the heavens.
6 Honor and majesty are before him.
Strength and beauty are in his sanctuary.

Gospel: Luke 2: 22-35

22 When the days of their purification according to the law of Moses were fulfilled, they brought him up to Jerusalem to present him to the Lord 23 (as it is written in the law of the Lord, "Every male who opens the womb shall be called holy to the Lord"), 24 and to offer a sacrifice according to that which is said in the law of the Lord, "A pair of turtledoves, or two young pigeons."

25 Behold, there was a man in Jerusalem whose name was Simeon. This man was righteous and devout, looking for the consolation of Israel, and the Holy Spirit was on him. 26 It had been revealed to him by the Holy Spirit that he should not see death before he had seen the

Lord's Christ.± ²⁷ He came in the Spirit into the temple. When the parents brought in the child, Jesus, that they might do concerning him according to the custom of the law, ²⁸ then he received him into his arms and blessed God, and said,

²⁹ "Now you are releasing your servant, Master,

according to your word, in peace;

³⁰ for my eyes have seen your salvation,

³¹ which you have prepared before the face of all peoples;

³² a light for revelation to the nations,

and the glory of your people Israel."

³³ Joseph and his mother were marveling at the things which were spoken concerning him. ³⁴ Simeon blessed them, and said to Mary, his mother, "Behold, this child is appointed for the falling and the rising of many in Israel, and for a sign which is spoken against. ³⁵ Yes, a sword will pierce through your own soul, that the thoughts of many hearts may be revealed."

1. Invite the Holy Spirit into this reading, asking the Author of Scripture to speak to you through His Word
2. Read today's passage as many times as you need, take your time
3. Write down (below) what the Lord is saying to you today
4. Live with this Word in your heart through the day

_____

_____

Tuesday, December 30, 2025

First Reading: First John 2: 12-17

¹² I write to you, little children, because your sins are forgiven you for his name's sake.

¹³ I write to you, fathers, because you know him who is from the beginning.

I write to you, young men, because you have overcome the evil one.

I write to you, little children, because you know the Father.

¹⁴ I have written to you, fathers, because you know him who is from the beginning.

I have written to you, young men, because you are strong, and the word of God remains in you, and you have overcome the evil one.

¹⁵ Don't love the world or the things that are in the world. If anyone loves the world, the Father's love isn't in him. ¹⁶ For all that is in the world—the lust of the flesh, the lust of the

eyes, and the pride of life—isn't the Father's, but is the world's. ¹⁷ The world is passing away with its lusts, but he who does God's will remains forever.

Responsorial Psalm: Psalms 96: 7-8a, 8b-9, 10

⁷ Ascribe to Yahweh, you families of nations,
ascribe to Yahweh glory and strength.
⁸ Ascribe to Yahweh the glory due to his name.
Bring an offering, and come into his courts.
⁹ Worship Yahweh in holy array.
Tremble before him, all the earth.
¹⁰ Say among the nations, "Yahweh reigns."
The world is also established.
It can't be moved.
He will judge the peoples with equity.

Gospel: Luke 2: 36-40

³⁶ There was one Anna, a prophetess, the daughter of Phanuel, of the tribe of Asher (she was of a great age, having lived with a husband seven years from her virginity, ³⁷ and she had been a widow for about eighty-four years), who didn't depart from the temple, worshiping with fastings and petitions night and day. ³⁸ Coming up at that very hour, she gave thanks to the Lord, and spoke of him to all those who were looking for redemption in Jerusalem.
³⁹ When they had accomplished all things that were according to the law of the Lord, they returned into Galilee, to their own city, Nazareth. ⁴⁰ The child was growing, and was becoming strong in spirit, being filled with wisdom, and the grace of God was upon him.

1. Invite the Holy Spirit into this reading, asking the Author of Scripture to speak to you through His Word
2. Read today's passage as many times as you need, take your time
3. Write down (below) what the Lord is saying to you today
4. Live with this Word in your heart through the day

_____

_____

Wednesday, December 31, 2025

Saint Sylvester I, Pope

First Reading: First John 2: 18-21

¹⁸ Little children, these are the end times, and as you heard that the Antichrist is coming, even now many antichrists have arisen. By this we know that it is the final hour. ¹⁹ They went out from us, but they didn't belong to us; for if they had belonged to us, they would have continued with us. But they left, that they might be revealed that none of them belong to us. ²⁰ You have an anointing from the Holy One, and you all have knowledge.§ ²¹ I have not written to you because you don't know the truth, but because you know it, and because no lie is of the truth.

Responsorial Psalm: Psalms 96: 1-2, 11-12, 13

¹ Sing to Yahweh a new song!
Sing to Yahweh, all the earth.
² Sing to Yahweh!
Bless his name!
Proclaim his salvation from day to day!
¹¹ Let the heavens be glad, and let the earth rejoice.
Let the sea roar, and its fullness!
¹² Let the field and all that is in it exult!
Then all the trees of the woods shall sing for joy
¹³ before Yahweh; for he comes,
for he comes to judge the earth.
He will judge the world with righteousness,
the peoples with his truth.

Gospel: John 1: 1-18

¹ In the beginning was the Word, and the Word was with God, and the Word was God. ² The same was in the beginning with God. ³ All things were made through him. Without him, nothing was made that has been made. ⁴ In him was life, and the life was the light of men. ⁵ The light shines in the darkness, and the darkness hasn't overcome± it.
⁶ There came a man sent from God, whose name was John. ⁷ The same came as a witness, that he might testify about the light, that all might believe through him. ⁸ He was not the light, but was sent that he might testify about the light. ⁹ The true light that enlightens everyone was coming into the world.
¹⁰ He was in the world, and the world was made through him, and the world didn't recognize him. ¹¹ He came to his own, and those who were his own didn't receive him. ¹² But

as many as received him, to them he gave the right to become God's children, to those who believe in his name: ¹³ who were born, not of blood, nor of the will of the flesh, nor of the will of man, but of God.

¹⁴ The Word became flesh and lived among us. We saw his glory, such glory as of the only born‡ Son of the Father, full of grace and truth. ¹⁵ John testified about him. He cried out, saying, "This was he of whom I said, 'He who comes after me has surpassed me, for he was before me.' " ¹⁶ From his fullness we all received grace upon grace. ¹⁷ For the law was given through Moses. Grace and truth were realized through Jesus Christ.§ ¹⁸ No one has seen God at any time. The only born‡ Son,‡ who is in the bosom of the Father, has declared him.

1. Invite the Holy Spirit into this reading, asking the Author of Scripture to speak to you through His Word
2. Read today's passage as many times as you need, take your time
3. Write down (below) what the Lord is saying to you today
4. Live with this Word in your heart through the day

_____

_____

Made in United States
Troutdale, OR
03/05/2025